In this bicentennial year of ce ___ of Dr. Melville's biography of Elizabeth Ann ___ se for celebration. By her skillful editing, Betty Ann McNeil, D.C., has provided the necessary revisions while respecting the scholarship and storytelling skills of Dr. Melville. This new edition will introduce Elizabeth Ann Seton to yet another generation of readers. Her timeless story of faith and struggle, love and loss, action and contemplation will ignite the imagination of all who meet her for the first time. Those familiar with her story will discover new insights and inspiration in this edition. All will rejoice in the life of this American woman and those women who retell her story with precision and passion.

Mary Ann Daly, S.C.
Executive Director
Sisters of Charity Federation

It is an extraordinary event when a biography stands well the tests of time. Annabelle Melville's biography of *Elizabeth Bayley Seton* is one such volume. Its portrayal of the life and times of this quintessential American saint still provides the reader with important insights into the early history of Catholicism in the United States, the role of women of ministry in that era, as well as the introduction into this country of the Vincentian tradition. The thoughtful revisions and updates provided by this edition will enable this generation to continue to enjoy this powerful story told so well by the late Annabelle Melville. This volume is a very welcome addition to the bicentennial celebration of the 1809 landmark foundation by St. Elizabeth Ann Seton of the Sisters of Charity of St. Joseph's, and the arrival of the saint and her companions in Emmitsburg, Maryland, beginning the Seton Legacy of Charity.

Rev. Edward R. Udovic, C.M., Ph.D.
Vincentian Studies Institute of the United States
DePaul University
Chicago, Illinois

ALSO BY ANNABELLE MELVILLE

John Carroll of Baltimore, Founder of the American Catholic Hierarchy. (New York: Charles Scribner's Sons, 1955).

Rue the Reservoir. (Milwaukee: The Bruce Publishing Co., 1956).

Jean Lefebvre de Cheverus, 1768-1836. (Milwaukee: Bruce Publishing Company, 1958).

Louis William DuBourg: Bishop of Louisiana and the Floridas, Bishop of Montauban, and Archbishop of Besancon, 1766-1833. 2 vols. (Chicago: Loyola University Press, 1986).

Elizabeth Seton: Selected Writings, Edited By Ellin M. Kelly and Annabelle Melville. (Mahwah, New Jersey: Paulist Press, 1987).

৩৵৶

Elizabeth Bayley Seton

1774-1821

by

Annabelle M. Melville

Edited by

Betty Ann McNeil, D.C.

જી૦૯

I am a citizen of the world!

Elizabeth Bayley Seton, 1817

જી૦૯

The Sheridan Press

Hanover, Pennsylvania

2009

ৡৡ

Elizabeth Bayley Seton 1774-1821
ISBN 978-0-9824936-0-1

Cover design by Stephanie Mummert. Landscape of Saint Joseph's Valley, featuring the Stone House and St. Joseph's House (the White House) in 1810, is attributed to Edward Augustus Seton. The cameo of St. Elizabeth Ann Seton is from the official portrait commissioned for her cause for canonization. Oil on canvas. Artist unknown, 1947.

ৡৡ

ABOUT THE AUTHOR

Annabelle McConnell Melville (1910-1991)

A native of Minotola, New Jersey, the daughter of the late Norman R. and Janet (Cunningham) McConnell, Dr. Melville received her undergraduate and master's degree from Albany State College, Albany, New York, and her doctorate from The Catholic University of America, Washington, D.C. She was named Commonwealth Professor and awarded the honorary doctor of laws degree from Stonehill College, North Easton, Massachusetts.

Melville held the Catholic Daughters of America Chair in American Church History at The Catholic University of America in 1978 and 1979; at that time she was the only person to hold that Chair for two consecutive years. She also received the *Distinguished Alumni Award* from The Catholic University of America and the State University of New York at Albany. Dr. Melville retired from Bridgewater State College, Bridgewater, Massachusetts, in 1975.

Melville was the first woman president of the American Catholic Historical Association. She received the *John Gilmary Shea Prize* for excellence in American Catholic history from the American Catholic Historical Society, and also the *General L. William Kemper Prize* from the Louisiana Historical Society, the latter for her biography of Archbishop Dubourg.

The National Shrine of St. Elizabeth Ann Seton conferred the *Seton Founder's Medal* on Annabelle Melville in 1983. The Daughters of Charity and the Associate Board of the Seton Shrine cited Dr. Melville for her "outstanding works in keeping alive the memory and the spirit of Elizabeth Ann Seton, her community, and the founders of the Catholic Church in America." Msgr. John Tracey Ellis, dean of American Catholic historians, was mentor for Dr. Melville's doctoral dissertation on Elizabeth Bayley Seton. In addition to the definitive Seton biography, Dr. Melville is also the biographer of *John Carroll of Baltimore, Founder of the American Catholic Hierarchy* (1955); *Jean Lefebvre de Cheverus, 1768-1836* (1958); and *Louis William Dubourg*, 2 vols., (1986).

DEDICATION

In commemoration of the bicentennial of the establishment of the Sisters of Charity of St. Joseph's by Saint Elizabeth Ann Seton, this edition of *Elizabeth Bayley Seton 1774-1821* is dedicated with deep gratitude:

○ To Annabelle McConnell Melville, twentieth-century Seton scholar and author of this work which is recognized as the definitive Seton biography.

○ To all of Saint Elizabeth Ann Seton's spiritual daughters, associates, affiliates, devotees, collaborators, and colleagues of the Sisters of Charity Federation and the extended Vincentian family who seek to love God and serve those who are poor through compassionate care, quality education, and advocacy for justice by endeavoring to encircle the globe in a network of charity.

○ To all those who nurtured the growth of the "little mustard seed," planted 31 July 1809 at the Stone House in Saint Joseph's Valley near Emmitsburg, Maryland, and who have contributed to the growth, development, and expansion of the Sisters and Daughters of Charity to serve the people of God.

Together may we continue the legacy of Saint Elizabeth Ann Seton!

৽৹৻

꿍ꕔ

When one finds a worthy wife, her value is far beyond pearls.
Her husband, entrusting his heart to her, has an unfailing prize.
Her children rise up and praise her; her husband, too, extols her.

Charm is deceptive and beauty fleeting;
the woman who fears the Lord is to be praised.
Give her a reward of her labors,
and let her works praise her at the city gates.

Proverbs 31

꿍ꕔ

ILLUSTRATIONS

Illustrations are used with permission. The Bayley-Seton wedding miniatures and
Mother and Child by Joseph Dawley are courtesy of the Archives Sisters of Charity of New York,
Mount St. Vincent, Bronx, New York. All other illustrations are courtesy of the
Daughters of Charity Archives, Emmitsburg, Maryland.

CONTENTS

FOREWORD

Sixty years ago in 1949, Annabelle Melville completed a biography of Elizabeth Bayley Seton under Rev. John Tracy Ellis for her Ph.D. at Catholic University in Washington, D.C. Two years later in 1951, Charles Scribner's Sons published her manuscript as *Elizabeth Bayley Seton 1774-1821*.

Appointed to the faculty of St. Joseph College in Emmitsburg, Maryland, in 1947, Annabelle Melville had access to an extensive collection of Elizabeth Seton's letters and other writings gathered at the suggestion of Father Simon Gabriel Bruté after Mother Seton's death. Later that collection was augmented by the gift of 133 letters and notes written to Julia Scott from 1798 to 1820 and by the Seton-Jevons Collection from the Mother Seton Guild. With these documents and those in the archives of other Seton communities, Dr. Melville created a documented life of Elizabeth Bayley Seton that has stood the test of time as the definitive biography. Reissued on several occasions, it became the starting point for any significant work on Saint Elizabeth Ann Seton. That 1951 publication and its subsequent reissues created new interest in the life of this religious foundress.

Two new books appeared in the late 1950s: Alma Power-Walters's *Mother Seton and the Sisters of Charity* (1957) and Rose Marie Laverty's *Loom of Many Threads* (1958). In the 1960s, anticipation of the beatification produced a new biography by Joseph I. Dirvin, C.M., *Mrs. Seton, Foundress of the American Sisters of Charity* (1962). In Europe three new publications appeared: an Italian translation of Dirvin's text (1963), a reissue of Raffaele Ricciardelli's 1929 *Elizabetta Anna Seton*, updated for the beatification (1963), and Marie-Dominique Poinsenet's *Je ne cherche que Dieu et son Eglise* (1967).

The canonization in 1975 brought reissues with revisions of Melville's and Dirvin's biographies, and Leonard Feeney's *Elizabeth Seton, An American Woman* (1938) retitled *Mother Seton: Saint Elizabeth of New York*. Roberto Angeli's *La Donna della Speranza* was published in Rome. Publications in 1977 included Victor Landeras' Spanish translation, *Isabel Seton* of Poinsenet's 1967 book, and my edition of *Elizabeth Seton's Two Bibles*.

In 1980, the American Broadcasting Company produced and offered *A Time for Miracles*, a movie about Saint Elizabeth Ann's life with Kate Mulgrew, John Forsythe, Lorne Greene, and Rossano Brazzi. In the first volume of *Numerous Choirs* (1981), I linked the years of Elizabeth

Seton's life with the histories of America and its Catholic Church. The 1986 publication *Elizabeth Ann Seton: A Self Portrait* by Marie Celeste Cuzzolina, S.C. offered a new perspective on her life.

Dr. Melville continued her scholarly writing with three biographies essential for the early history of the Catholic Church in the United States: *John Carroll of Baltimore, Founder of the American Catholic Hierarchy* (1955), *Jean Lefebvre de Cheverus, 1768-1836* (1958), and *Louis William Dubourg*, in two volumes (1986). But her interest in St. Elizabeth Ann Seton never wavered. I had the privilege of working with her for the Paulist Press edition, *Elizabeth Seton: Selected Writings* (1987). Her descriptive introduction displays her sensitive insights and deep appreciation for the spiritual aspects of the Elizabeth's religious faith. Two years later, Dr. Melville was a distinguished scholar during the first triennial History of Women Religious Conference held in June 1989, at the College of St. Catherine in Minnesota. During the session "Telling the Story through Biography" Dr. Melville spoke on "Writing the Life of a Future Saint: Elizabeth Ann Seton, History, Hagiography."

Three new books appeared in the 1990s: *The Soul of Elizabeth Seton* by Joseph I. Dirvin, C.M. (1990), *Praying with Elizabeth Seton* by Margaret Alderman and Josephine Burns, D.C, (1992), *A Retreat with Elizabeth Seton* by Judith Metz, S.C. (1999), plus a revised edition of the play *Elizabeth of New York* by Francis Maria Cassidy, S.C. (1992). In 1995, ABC issued a video cassette of *A Time for Miracles*.

Dr. Melville died on May 17, 1991. One year after her death, her writings on St. Elizabeth Ann Seton played a vital role in the Seton Legacy 1992 Symposium, "Elizabeth Seton in Dialogue with her Times and Ours" at two locations: Dayton, Ohio, October 22-25, and Convent Station, New Jersey, November 12-15, sponsored by the Sisters of Charity Federation. Papers from the symposium were published in *Vincentian Heritage*, Vol. 14 (1993).

As a result of that symposium, the Sisters of Charity Federation proposed a complete edition of Saint Elizabeth Ann's writings. The project involved all known archival holdings and became the principle publication of the new century's first decade: *Elizabeth Bayley Seton, Collected Writings*, edited by Regina Bechtle, S.C. and Judith Metz, S.C., Volume I, "Correspondence and Journals 1793-1808" in 2000, Volume II "Correspondence and Journals 1808-1820" in 2002, and Volume IIIa & IIIb "Spiritual Writings, Notebooks, and Other Documents" in 2004. Two other books were published in 2002: *Elizabeth Ann Seton, a Saint for a New Nation* by Julie Walters and *15 Days of Prayer with Saint Elizabeth*

Seton by Betty Ann McNeil, D.C. Editasca-Liverno in Italy published two new translations for the bicentennial celebration of Elizabeth Seton's Italian Journey. *Il Viaggio in Italia: Lettere e Diari* (2003) presents Pietro Bindelli's translations of the letters and diaries from her journey and visit, October 1803 to June 1804. *Cari Ricordi: Diario* in 2004 provides photo copies from the original pages of "Dear Remembrances" on the even numbered pages with Lara Bellagotti's Italian translation on the opposing pages.

Annabelle Melville has had a vital role in Seton publications and activities from 1951 to "The Seton Legacy of Charity" bicentennial celebration commemorating the foundation of the Sisters of Charity of St. Joseph's, Emmitsburg, Maryland. This reissue of her definitive biography, updated where possible with references to specific volumes of *Elizabeth Bayley Seton: Collected Writings*, is a fitting tribute to St. Elizabeth Ann and her biographer.

Ellin M. Kelly, Ph.D.
Evanston, Illinois
2009

ↂↄ

FOREWORD (1951)

With a view to meeting the demands of scholarship as well as of justice to a name that is held in reverence, the author of this biography has spared herself no inconvenience in collecting and arranging the material pertaining to the life and career of Elizabeth Ann Seton. Happily, the result of her painstaking and exhaustive research is a storehouse of helpful and reliable information which no future historian of Mother Seton can afford to by-pass in a quest for knowledge of the Foundress of the Sisters of Charity in the United States.

While engaged in writing this biography, the author, Mrs. Melville, who is a convert to the Faith, resided at Saint Joseph College, Emmitsburg, where, amid scenes that recall the most fruitful years of Elizabeth Seton's life, she pursued her laborious and inspiring task. From her place of residence she could see in the distance Mount Saint Mary's College where Mother Seton and her companions, following their arrival in Emmitsburg, found lodgment in a log cabin with a dirt floor. The cabin has long since rotted into dust, but the little stone house in Saint Joseph's Valley to which she came when it was ready for occupancy still stands as a witness to the hardships which she and her associates endured for the cause they had come to serve. The mountains which Elizabeth Seton loved remain as of old. At their base is the cemetery where well-worn stones record the names of her young companions who went down to their graves in the springtime of life. Close by the cemetery are gnarled and knotted oaks that may have been planted by Elizabeth Seton's hand and paths that knew the tread of her feet. With these and other mementoes of the past the author is quite familiar but, despite their appeal to sentiment, she has refused to depart from her purpose of writing a factual biography. In truth, her volume is intended for the critical as well as for the casual reader. Hence, her approach to her subject is not that of one who would write a eulogy but of an earnest and discriminating scholar who would share with her readers the fruits of her study and research. The evidence of her purpose and not less of her industry is quite apparent in the facts which she has brought to light from hitherto unpublished manuscripts and in the numerous annotations, the delight of the historian, and at the same time a witness to the author's resolve to produce a biography notable for its accuracy and reliability.

Some readers may feel that the early chapters which relate the facts pertaining to the trying ordeal that preceded the reception of Mother Seton into the Church do not convey the poignancy of her suffering or stress the spiritual intensity of her life. They will find, however, in these chapters a vivid description of the social and religious background against which they must see Elizabeth Seton if they would appreciate her true spiritual stature. What is more, in the picture that emerges from the concluding chapters of the biography they will see a person of Christ-like charity and courage who might well be regarded as a model for Catholic womanhood.

In the religious life of New York City before and after the American Revolution, the Protestant Episcopal Church, because of the wealth and distinction of its members, enjoyed especial prominence. On the other hand, the Catholic Church, which was represented by one lone parish consisting for the most part of recently arrived immigrants, had little of wealth and less of prestige. Elizabeth Ann Seton was a devout member of the Episcopal Church and was never more happy than when in attendance at its services. Her co-religionists were leaders not only in society, but in the professional and business life of the city. Small wonder, then, that they stood aghast when they saw her detach herself from the ranks of those who were on their way to Trinity or Saint Paul's Episcopal Church and fall in line with the motley crowd that was on its way to Mass in Saint Peter's Church, Barclay Street. It was a daring thing for Elizabeth Seton to do, but what made it especially daring was not so much the physical detachment from a particular group of persons as the spirit of detachment with which she regarded the loss sustained by the change in her religious affiliation. Socially and financially it was a great loss and by the same token an eloquent witness to the greatness of a soul that could speak of it only in the words of Saint Paul: "I even consider everything as a loss because of the supreme good of knowing Christ Jesus my Lord. For his sake I have accepted the loss of all things and I consider them so much rubbish, that I may gain Christ." [Philippians 3:8]

Because she was resolved to make her will one with the Will of God, Elizabeth Seton was unusually sensitive to the challenge of the Cross. There was no hedging on her part in accepting the terms laid down by Christ for one who would be His disciple: "Whoever wishes to come after me must deny himself, take up his cross, and follow me." [Matthew 16:24] In choosing a course of action it was not her way to ask, "Is it easy?" She asked only, "Is it right?" Once convinced of its rightness, she made her decision, not counting the cost. Except for the Holy Bible, there was no book that spoke to her soul with greater eloquence than the image of Christ on the Cross. It was not a thing of metal or wood she saw when looking at her crucifix but the Face of the Crucified and her response to the challenge which she read in that Face was a life of heroic sacrifice. An apt pupil in the school of the Cross, Elizabeth Seton had learned to say with the saints: "In Thy will is my peace." [Cf. Luke 22:42]

Nearly one hundred and thirty years [1821-1951] have passed since Mother Seton breathed forth her soul to God in the White House at Emmitsburg. Today, pilgrims from her native land and visitors from overseas are beating a pathway to her tomb. Those who ridiculed her sacrifice are dead; their names are as though they had been written in water. But she lives on not only in the pages of history but in the hearts and lives of nearly nine thousand spiritual daughters who, in schools, in orphanages, and hospitals, bear witness to the power and beauty of the ideal that dominated her life: "to serve the Church in its purpose of reflecting the image of Christ to all mankind."

In concluding an article on Mother Seton in his volume, *Sanctity in America,* the Most Reverend Amleto Giovanni Cicognani, Apostolic Delegate to the United States, has written these welcome words: "Certainly the beatification of a distinguished woman born and reared in America will bring to the United States particular joy, prestige, and protection." In response to the sentiments expressed by His Excellency, the many thousand admirers of Elizabeth Ann Seton will cry out from the fullness of their hearts a fervent "Amen."

May this timely and scholarly volume serve to hasten Mother Seton's hour of triumph. It is the fruit of much study and labor, and merits the recognition which undoubtedly this publication will receive from the historian and reading public alike as an outstanding biography of a great servant of God.

John Michael McNamara
Auxiliary Bishop of Washington, D.C.
1951

PREFACE (1976)

On a warm, sunny Sunday morning in mid-September 1975, some sixteen thousand Americans crowding St. Peter's Square in Rome heard Pope Paul VI pronounce the words:

> For the honor of the Most Holy Trinity, for the exaltation of the Catholic Faith and the increase of the Christian life, by the authority of Our Lord Jesus Christ, of the holy Apostles Peter and Paul and by our authority, after mature deliberation and most frequent prayer for divine assistance, having obtained the counsel of many of our brother bishops, we declare and we define that Blessed Elizabeth Ann Bayley Seton is a saint, and we inscribe her name in the calendar of saints, and mandate that she should be devoutly honored among the saints in the universal Church.

It was the culmination of the Cause first conceived in 1882, and it elicited in the weeks that followed commentary, both oral and written, of many sorts. The Apostolic Delegate to the United States, the Most Reverend Jean Jadot, remarked on more than one occasion that he found it very interesting that the first native-born American saint [of the United States] was a woman.[a] In the same vein others found the new saint's canonization to be most appropriately timed to take place in a year commemorating a worldwide rise in women's influence. The National Catholic Bishops' Committee for the Bicentennial [of the United States] rejoiced that their support for canonization had come to fruition amid the nation's two hundredth anniversary celebration. [The United Nations had declared 1975 as The International Year of the Woman and the following ten years as the Decade of the Woman (1976-1985).] The *Wall Street Journal* was sure the timing was "a political decision;" and one Catholic journalist commented sardonically that the event was simply an attempt on the part of the sovereign pontiff to bolster the sagging morale of the Church in the United States.

Whether intended to impute motives or to find in the ceremonies of September 14th some relevance to the larger contemporary scene, these speculations are less important to the sober biographer than the demonstrable sequence of events, particularly those of the decade and a half between the last printing of this work and the canonization in 1975. In order to bring up

---

[a] St. Rose of Lima (1586-1617), who was canonized in 1671, is the first native-born saint of the Americas. Saint Elizabeth Ann Seton is the first native-born saint of the United States of America although in 1938 Saint Frances Xavier Cabrini (1850-1917) became the first United States citizen to be canonized.

to date the outline of the Process or Cause of Elizabeth Bayley Seton a new preface seems advisable.

Following the declaration of the Sacred Congregation of Rites on December 18, 1959, that Mother Seton's virtues were heroic and that she should be called "Venerable," the work of authenticating miracles accelerated. One case alleging the cure in Louisiana of a Daughter of Charity, Sister Gertrude Korzendorfer (1872-1942), whose cancer of the pancreas had vanished in January 1935, had been under investigation since November 23, 1945. A second investigation began in Baltimore, Maryland, on February 14, 1961, when evidence was presented to support the cure nine years earlier of a four-year-old girl, Ann Theresa O'Neill (1948-), suffering from acute leukemia. The results of these two investigations were forwarded to Rome and on December 14, 1961, the Sacred Congregation of Rites issued a Decree of Validity subsequently confirmed by Pope John XXIII in his Decree *De Tuto*.

With two valid miracles attested, Beatification was certain to follow, and with this in mind on October 26, 1962, an official exhumation of Mother Seton's remains was made. From their resting place under a small Gothic chapel in the original graveyard of the Sisters of Charity, St. Joseph's Cemetery, Emmitsburg, Maryland, they were enshrined in the Sisters Chapel at Saint Joseph College and placed above the main altar April 18, 1963. On Saint Patrick's Day, 1963, the actual Beatification took place inside St. Peter's Basilica in the presence of two thousand Americans who had arrived by what the *New York Herald Tribune* called "the largest air-lift pilgrimage in history."

Ordinarily two more miracles are required to complete the Process. One was claimed almost immediately. In the fall of 1963, a Protestant workingman, Carl Eric Kalin (1902-1976), was admitted to St. Joseph's Hospital in Yonkers, New York, dying of a rare disease termed "fulminating meningo-encephalitis complicated by primary rubeola." Only five such cases had previously been recorded in medical history, and in each case the disease had proved fatal. Kalin was not expected to live through the night. Instead, on October 16 he awakened with temperature and other signs back to normal and by November 2 could be discharged as fully recovered. On December 13, 1973, the medical investigators were unanimous in pronouncing Kalin's recovery miraculous, and a year later—lacking a day—Pope Paul VI concurred. On December 12, 1974, he announced that a second post-Beatification miracle could be dispensed with in Mother Seton's case and that she would be proclaimed a saint amid the special ceremonies of the Holy Year of 1975. The Process was thus completed.

In the light of the more extensive interest in her career generated by her elevation it is more than ever proper to have available a straightforward, carefully documented, historical life of this famous American.

Annabelle McConnell Melville
Bridgewater, Massachusetts
1976

PREFACE (1960)

In a sermon delivered on the occasion of a pilgrimage from the Archdiocese of Washington to the tomb of Elizabeth Seton on June 14, 1959, the Right Reverend John Tracy Ellis remarked, "The Church in the American Republic has indeed made giant strides in both spiritual and material development, but there still remains something unfulfilled in the Catholic life of this land. No native-born American has as yet been declared blessed or been canonized as a saint." His listeners were in no wise downcast, however, by this statement; nor need they have been. Only six months earlier, on December 18, 1958, the new pontiff, John XXIII, in his very first consistory had delighted the four new American cardinals present by including on that historic occasion the pleading of Mother Seton's Cause by Advocate Consistorale Francesco Saverio Parisi. And a year later, to the very month and day, in the Consistorial Hall of the Vatican, was publicly read the decree by which the Sacred Congregation of Rites declared, the virtues of Elizabeth Seton heroic and that Mother Seton could henceforth be called, "Venerable." Thus, in the sesquicentennial year of her foundation of the Sisters of Charity at Emmitsburg, Maryland, Elizabeth Seton's Cause had successfully passed the first of three major stages in the process of canonization.

It is perhaps only natural that a biographer of Elizabeth Seton should muse over the events which intervened between the death of the American foundress and the happy portent of 1959; to the uninitiated, or those who recall that in the earlier Church canonization could result almost immediately by acclamation, the lapse in time may be equally perplexing. Some summary in retrospect is almost inevitable with the re-issue of a major historical study of Elizabeth Seton's career.

There is little doubt that those contemporaries who knew Mother Seton best believed her to be of extraordinary sanctity. Archbishop John Carroll used the word "saint" when writing of her to a mutual friend; Bishop John Cheverus exclaimed, "What an impression must she not make on the young students with the miracles of grace and the sanctity to which she witnesses!" Her confessor, Simon Bruté, later Bishop of Vincennes, wrote in the summer following her death, "I will say that, as a result of my long and intimate acquaintance with Mother Seton, I believe her to have been one of those truly chosen souls who, if placed in circumstances similar to those of Saint Teresa [of Avila] or Saint Jane Frances de Chantal, would be equally remarkable in the scale of sanctity." It was Bruté who admonished the Sisters of Charity that they should treasure everything Mother Seton left behind. "Preserve all carefully and gather up the fragments lest any be lost," he insisted, "for some day how precious they will be."

Nevertheless, almost a century elapsed before the Cause was formally begun. Only two tangible efforts were made in the interim to preserve the heroic memory of the American foundress: the erection in 1845 of a marble monument over her remains, and the publication in 1853 of the full-length biography by Charles Ignatius White. True, James Cardinal Gibbons did, on August 3, 1882, propose to the Emmitsburg Community the introduction of the Cause for Canonization; but it was not until another quarter of a century had passed that the proposal materialized.

Then, in 1907, the first session of an ecclesiastical court created for that purpose began an investigation of the merits of the Cause, with the Very Reverend Edward R. Dyer, S.S., acting as Judex Delegatus. Thus was undertaken the first active promotion of the "Fama sanctitatis." By 1914 the process, "De Scripturis" was accomplished and twelve volumes of Mother Seton's writings were presented to Rome by the Very Reverend Charles L. Souvay, C.M. But 1914 was the year that World War I erupted; once again the Cause languished.

It was not until 1931 that effective steps were taken to reactivate the process. That year, however, witnessed four influential events. On July 9, 1931, a pilgrimage of American women representing the Federation of Catholic Alumnae and the Committee on Mother Seton left for Rome to petition Pope Pius XI on Mother Seton's behalf; in 1931 a plaque was installed at St. Peter's Church in New York commemorating the conversion of Mrs. Seton; in November of that year the American hierarchy at their annual meeting voted unanimously to approve the Cause. Most important of all, 1931 was the year in which Pius XI took action to remove the impediment stemming from the former requirement in the Informative Process of living witnesses. An Historical Section of the Sacred Congregation of Rites was created; new life was given to the Cause. By January 15, 1936, the formal examination of Mother Seton's own writings was completed; two years later, to facilitate research into the other aspects of the historical background, the Reverend Salvator M. Burgio, C.M., was named American Vice-Postulator of the Cause of Mother Seton. The Mother Seton Guild came into being. In spite of the outbreak of another war, World War II, on February 28, 1940, a decree of the Congregation of Rites at last introduced the cause of beatification and canonization at Rome.

Before the war was over the six different communities of Sisters of Charity who trace their roots directly to the Sisters of Charity of St. Joseph's at Emmitsburg and constitute "Mother Seton's Daughters" were holding the first of an annual series of conferences to stimulate the progress of the Cause; and in February, 1947, the superior of the Daughters of Charity whose Provincial House is at Emmitsburg, Maryland, gave the impulse to a modern historical study of Mother Seton, a study which was destined to become the definitive biography of the Emmitsburg foundress.

One could not foresee, of course, in 1947 that the work authorized by Sister Isabel Toohey, D.C., Provincial Superior of the Eastern Province, would return from Rome stamped with the approval of the Sacred Congregation of Rites on January 5, 1950. Nor could it have been expected that when the author visited that Congregation in July 1951, the official in charge of documenting Mother Seton's Cause should comment, "We wish we might have had your manuscript sooner. It is of great assistance." Even less could one have anticipated the jubilant, if slightly tinged with Latin hyperbole, words of the Vice-Postulator of the Cause when he wrote from Emmitsburg on June 7, 1957, "When in Rome I was able to procure the Documentation of the Cause. Your heart will exalt in the fact that you are enshrined in this book for all times. Your historical efforts have been highly appraised in Rome and you have contributed much in the process."

The subsequent action taken in Rome in 1958 and 1959 was certain to gladden the heart of any biographer of Elizabeth Seton. For the first time since the Informative Process was introduced a substantial hope flourishes that the beatification of Mother Seton may soon follow, and that in due time the third and last step, canonization, will be a reality. With this renewed interest in the woman who well may be the first American-born saint in the Church in the United States, the need for a definitive evaluation of her life is perhaps even greater than it was in 1951 when this biography was first made available to the general reader.

Indeed, it is to be hoped that Elizabeth Seton never loses her attraction for the biographer, editor, novelist, playwright, or poet. A great woman is a public legacy and should be enjoyed by all ages and in many guises. Nevertheless, a very real, particular person helped to shape our history between the years 1774 and 1821. And with the modest hope of presenting again the actual Elizabeth Bayley Seton, this new printing goes forth.

Annabelle McConnell Melville
Bridgewater Teachers College
Bridgewater, Massachusetts, 1960

PREFACE (1951)

When Tennyson's Ulysses said, "I am a part of all that I have met," he unwittingly pronounced the primary principle of much of modern biography. In this genre of historical writing the author no longer writes of his hero as the protagonist of a Greek play, in which plot predominates and background remains inchoate. Rather, the task of contemporary biography is to destroy the vacuum which time has placed around the event, and to revivify the scene through which the hero actually strode. In this rhetorical resurrection the author arbitrarily assumes the functions of qualification and limitation. Those events which delimit the course of his hero's life must be included; but those which, however significant in other aspects, do not cross the pattern of the narrative may be, and often must be, discarded.

The biographer is, in some cases, further constrained to dispel a cloud of sentiment, illusion, and positive error which legend, deliberate fiction, careless research, and wishful thinking have created and which obscure the exact proportions of the hero as he or she was. It was with these dual purposes in mind that a new biography of Elizabeth Bayley Seton was undertaken. The numerous existing biographies have hitherto been concerned primarily with Mrs. Seton as a woman in religion; this present work seeks to present her as an American woman of the early Republic, a woman whose career was immediately influenced by the exigencies of its infancy. Her material fortunes, and those of her family, rose and fell with the fortunes of the new nation. The development of her character and the expansion of her work illustrate the operation of forces and powers which were the yeast of the fermentation of the United States in the early nineteenth century. Elizabeth Seton was in every sense a woman of America, though she was to become a "citizen of the world."

The second justification for a new biography lies in the necessity for establishing, as accurately as present sources allow, the exact details of Mrs. Seton's life. Although there exists a good-sized shelf of printed works pertaining to her life, not since 1853, when Charles Ignatius White (1807-1878) published his first edition, has there been a careful attempt made to write the whole story of Mrs. Seton. The White biography was translated, with some additions, into French by Madame Hélène Roederer Bailly de Barberey (1823-1898) and appeared in 1868 in two volumes under the title, *Elizabeth Seton et les commencements de l'eglise catholique aux Etats-Unis*. After this French work went through six editions, Joseph Bernard Code (1899-1980) in 1927 translated the de Barberey work back into English, used some letters which had come to light in the meantime to correct many errors in dates, and printed Simon Bruté's account of Mrs. Seton's last days, not included in the French edition. Needless to say, some deviations from the White account and the original documents it cited crept in during these two translations. These two English works of White and Code have become the basis for most subsequent biographical sketches, plays, novels, and poetry.

In 1917, Sister Mary Agnes McCann, Sister of Charity of Cincinnati, (1851-1931), in the first volume of her ambitious *History of Mother Seton's Daughters* brought to the public eye many letters from the Baltimore Cathedral Archives pertaining to Mrs. Seton's affairs, and some material preserved at the Sisters of Charity of Cincinnati Archives at Mount Saint Joseph's in Ohio. *The Life of Mother Elizabeth Boyle of New York,* by Sister Maria Dodge, (1832-1893), Sister of Charity of New York, published in 1893, added some letters, especially one of Mrs. Seton written in 1820 and excerpts from those of John Moranvillé to Elizabeth Boyle. No single work, however, since White's in 1853, has made use of all the materials now available to the biographer. A mere revision of White's book is not the answer to the demand for a definitive biography. A new biography is not only warranted but indispensable in the face of an increasing interest in this great American woman.

The writer acknowledges with warm appreciation the valuable assistance and unfailing courtesy of the custodians of the archival treasures, particularly the Right Reverend Joseph M. Nelligan, then Chancellor of the Archdiocese of Baltimore, the Reverends Thomas T. McAvoy, C.S.C., of the University of Notre Dame; William J. O'Shea, S.S., St. Mary's Seminary, Roland Park, Baltimore; William C. Repetti, S.J., Georgetown University; Hugh J. Philips, Mount Saint Mary's College, Emmitsburg; Salvator M. Burgio, C.M., Mother Seton Guild, Emmitsburg. To the Sisters of Charity, especially at Mount Saint Joseph's, Ohio, Mount Saint Vincent's, New York, and Saint Joseph's Central House, Emmitsburg, the writer owes an immeasurable debt of gratitude for the cheerful assistance given in searching out the truth, even when cherished tradition sometimes fell by the way. To the Reverend John Tracy Ellis, professor of American Church history in the Catholic University of America, who directed this study, the writer is immeasurably indebted for his unfailing encouragement, exacting criticisms, and seasoned judgments. The writer can be no less appreciative of the reading and criticisms of John T. Farrell, associate professor of American history, and Sister Marie Carolyn Klinkhamer, O.P., assistant professor of American history in the Catholic University of America. To the

Reverend Henry J. Browne, archivist of the Catholic University of America, who brought the writer and her subject together and offered innumerable helpful suggestions along the way, the writer is warmly grateful. To the librarians of the New York Public Library, the New York Historical Society, the Library of Congress, the Enoch Pratt Library of Baltimore, the New York State Library of Albany, and to all those who helped bring this work to a conclusion, the writer is sincerely grateful. The work was originally published on microcards by the Catholic University of America Press.

Annabelle McConnell Melville
Saint Joseph College
Emmitsburg, Maryland
1951

 споси

ACKNOWLEDGEMENTS

Many persons have contributed to the publication of this edition of *Elizabeth Bayley Seton 1774-1821.* While the responsibility for the accuracy of updates and revisions of Annabelle M. Melville's work rests solely with me, I would like to thank the following individuals and institutions.

I would like to first express my appreciation to Sister Mary Clare Hughes, D.C., who envisioned the possibility of this revision years ago and whose interest and prayerful support helped transform this idea into reality.

I am grateful for the generous enthusiasm and meticulous research and technical assistance rendered by the staff of the Daughters of Charity Archives at St. Joseph's Provincial House, Emmitsburg, Maryland. No request was too demanding nor were time constraints too daunting for them whom I count among my friends and colleagues, Bonnie Weatherly, Selin James, and Mary Anne Weatherly. Sister Eleanor Casey, D.C., was also very helpful by doing preliminary research regarding publication and copyright history. Her findings elucidated the tasks ahead.

I wish to express my heartfelt appreciation to Katherine M. Marshall for her wholehearted and generous legal consultation; to Simon & Schuster, successor to the original publisher Charles Scribner's Sons, for their amicable cooperation; to Ellin M. Kelly, Ph. D., for her kind assistance; and to Elizabeth J. Barth and Paul M. Callahan, whose gracious collaboration made this publication possible.

I am indebted to V. Rev. Mark T. Cregan, C.S.C., President, Stonehill College; Thomas P. Looney, C.S.C., Vice President for Mission, Stonehill College and V. Rev. David O'Connell, C.M., President, The Catholic University of America, for clearing the way for acquisition of rights to this work and for its publication by the Daughters of Charity. I appreciate the invaluable assistance of V. Rev. Michael J. Carroll, C.M., Provincial Superior, Congregation of the Mission, Eastern Province, and Rev. Paul Doyle, C.S.C., University of Notre Dame, and Sister Joan Keating, D.C., who greatly facilitated the process. We appreciate the Sisters of Charity of New York permitting the publication of the Bayley-Seton wedding miniatures and the painting by Joseph Dawley from the Archives of Mount St. Vincent for illustrations in this work.

Many individuals lent their time, talent, and research skills to locate missing data and clarify historical issues. I would especially like to thank the following individuals for their helpfulness: Sheridan Harvey, Reference Specialist/Women's Studies, Humanities and Social Sciences Division,

Library of Congress; William Kevin Cawley, Archivist, University of Notre Dame Archives; Tricia Pyne and Alison M. Foley, Archivists, Associated Archives, St. Mary's University, Baltimore; Shawn Weldon, Assistant Archivist, Philadelphia Archdiocesan Historical Research Center; Regina Seigfried, A.S.C, and the History of Women Religious network; Rev. Albert H. Ledoux; Sister Kathleen Flanagan, S.C., Professor, Director of Graduate Program in Theology, College of St. Elizabeth, Morristown, New Jersey; and Dolores Liptak, R.S.M.

The Daughters of Charity Communications Department has rendered timely and high-quality service in the production and design of this edition. I am grateful to Lori L. Stewart, Director, for her creative insights, and to Stephanie Mummert, Graphic Designer, for her expertise and willing spirit. No request has been too minute for their consideration. This revision represents a team effort which utilized the diverse experience of numerous persons dedicated to Vincentian studies, Setonian scholarship, and devotion to St. Elizabeth Ann Seton. I wish to commend the following individuals who untiringly and astutely reviewed and corrected several versions of this manuscript and provided constructive input: Sister Joan Angermaier, D.C., Sister Regina Bechtle, S.C., Sister Francine Brown, D.C., Sister Vincentia Goeb, D.C., Sister Judith Metz, S.C., Mary Ann Osborne, Rev. John E. Rybolt, C.M., and Rev. Edward R. Udovic, C.M. The advice and suggestions of Nathaniel Michaud, Publications Editor, Vincentian Studies Institute of the United States, DePaul University, has resolved many an editorial dilemma, for which I am most grateful.

I thank Sister Mary Ann Daly, S.C., Executive Director, Sisters of Charity Federation, and Rev. Edward R. Udovic, C.M., Ph.D., Vincentian Studies Institute of the United States, DePaul University, Chicago, Illinois, for their kind words of endorsement.

Sister Claire Debes, D.C., and her Provincial Council, and Sister Vincentia Goeb, D.C., Director of Heritage Ministries, made my involvement in this initiative possible and supported the hard work of transforming an idea into reality. I would like to thank the Daughters of Charity at Mother Seton House in Emmitsburg, Maryland, who provided me with a listening ear along with sisterly support and encouragement during this project.

In the words of Saint Elizabeth Ann Seton, "God only can measure my joy and gratitude."[b]

Betty Ann McNeil, D.C.

---

[b] 7.19, Elizabeth Seton to Antonio Filicchi, 22 April 1816, Regina Bechtle, S.C., and Judith Metz, S.C., eds., Ellin M. Kelly, mss. ed., *Elizabeth Bayley Seton Collected Writings*, 3 vols. (New City Press: New York, 2000-2006), 2:390.

EDITORIAL INTRODUCTION

Public interest in St. Elizabeth Ann Seton as a wife, mother, and saint has grown since her canonization. Simultaneously the classic publication, *Elizabeth Bayley Seton* by Annabelle M. Melville, became less available in bookstores. It was last reprinted in 1985. Yet this biography remains the definitive historical study of the first canonized saint native to the United States.

Two hundred years ago a tiny, faith-filled woman from New York came to Maryland and founded the Sisters of Charity of St. Joseph's in an old, stone farm house in St. Joseph's Valley near Emmitsburg, Maryland. In order to honor the Seton legacy of charity which her spiritual daughters, associates and affiliates share, it is fitting that *Elizabeth Bayley Seton* be updated and published anew.

Annabelle M. Melville remains the Seton scholar par excellence of the 20th century. Her friend and colleague Ellin M. Kelly, who has also contributed her time, talent, and expertise to Seton scholarship kindly accepted the invitation to write the 2009 Foreword. The 2009 edition would be incomplete without also including Dr. Melville's own prefaces and the 1951 contribution of John M. McNamara, auxiliary bishop of Washington, D.C., and staunch advocate for the Seton cause for canonization. This front material offers a wealth of information about Saint Elizabeth Ann Seton and her path to canonization by Pope Paul VI, 14 September 1975.

The 2009 edition reflects appropriate updating and revisions, particularly to annotations but still retains the meticulous research, organization, and insights originally presented by Dr. Melville in 1951. Significant changes appear in brackets in this edition. In a few instances, recent research has elucidated some new facts and nuances of the Seton story as Melville understood it from the resources she used. The 2009 edition has benefited from technological advances, archival developments, increased access to information, recent research, and the publication by the Sisters of Charity Federation of *Elizabeth Bayley Seton Collected Writings*, which contains the corpus of the Seton papers. Such progress has made it possible to enhance the historical context presented in this work. Time constraints did not permit the pursuit of some illusive facts and intriguing questions. We leave that and other lacunae for a future generation to address.

The 2009 edition contains the corrected text of quotations based on a review of the original Seton documents and/or authenticated transcriptions, whereas in many instances Dr. Melville only had typescripts rather than original documents for her use. Discrepancies of Seton quotations have been resolved in this edition using the definitive texts published in *Elizabeth Bayley Seton Collected Writings*. Although Elizabeth Seton was a highly literate woman for her time, the written word in the early nineteenth century was not yet governed by the literary conventions of our day. For the convenience of modern readers the majority of nineteenth-century quotations have been edited to conform to current standards of spelling, punctuation, and grammar except for capitalization. In order for readers to gain insight into the intensity and range of feelings which Elizabeth Seton expressed in her writings, words which she emphasized through capitalization has been retained.

Another significant change in this edition appears in the numbering of chapters. The original chapter 6 was lengthy and appears as two chapters in the 2009 edition: Chapter 6, No Resting Place and Chapter 7, God's Blessed Time.

The organization and type of annotations has also changed. Melville's original annotations have been updated and relocated in some instances for greater clarity and convenience of readers. The number of explanatory footnotes has increased. These appear below at the bottom of the page with the related text. Endnotes, which usually refer to the source document and repository, appear at the conclusion of each chapter. The documentation for the majority of the notes appears in the endnotes unless given in a footnote. Two lengthy annotations on complex issues of Elizabeth Seton's first communion in the Protestant Episcopal Church and the citizenship of William Magee Seton have been moved to the Appendix in this edition.

When Dr. Melville was doing her original research in the late 1940's, the Seton papers were scattered and held by different repositories than at present. Some original documents were in the Filicchi family archives in Italy, some with the various branches of Sisters and Daughters of Charity in the United States and Canada. As a result of the preliminary work required to prepare *Elizabeth Bayley Seton Collected Writings* for publication, a comprehensive inventory of all extant Seton documents was developed. The annotations in this biography reflect the current repository for each citation and also are in accord with the identification and location of documents in *Elizabeth Bayley Seton Collected Writings*. The 2009 edition is also the fruit of modern scholarship since Dr. Melville first published this classic biography in 1951. It is my sincere hope that this edition will provide enjoyable reading and reflection on Elizabeth Bayley Seton. It is my sincere hope that this edition will provide enjoyable reading and reflection on *Elizabeth Bayley Seton*.

May readers gain an understanding of the life, mission, and legacy of Saint Elizabeth Ann Seton and enhance their appreciation of her as a real person and role model for today and a woman of faith for all ages. May the bicentennial celebration commemorating the foundation of the Sisters of Charity of St. Joseph's in St. Joseph's Valley be an inspiration for others to join in continuing the Seton Legacy of Charity.

Betty Ann McNeil, D.C., Editor
Archivist
Daughters of Charity of St. Vincent de Paul
Emmitsburg, Maryland
25 March 2009

৶৻৶

๙๛

THE BAYLEYS AND SETONS OF NEW YORK

The August heat hung over the city as the delegates from Massachusetts toured New York City, where they had stopped off on their way to Philadelphia, Pennsylvania. It was the summer of 1774. Only a few weeks earlier New York City had chosen Philip Livingston, Isaac Low, James Duane, John Jay, and John Alsop, Esquires, to represent the province at the Continental Congress. Now their colleagues from Boston, Massachusetts, after a brief respite at Hull's sign of The Bunch of Grapes, were casting their critical eyes about the thriving island. They visited Trinity Church and the new St. Paul's, which had cost a good eighteen thousand pounds in York money. It is to be hoped that these proper Bostonians did not discover that close by the consecrated grounds of St. Paul's some 500 "ladies of pleasure" kept lodgings and offered distractions to the students approaching King's College. The college was only now considering a report on a royal constitution "constituting the Seminary and University."

The city offered some impressive sights with its three hundred sail of shipping showing in the harbor and slips and the public buildings spreading out like a fan from the Battery.[a] Between twenty-five and thirty thousand inhabitants thronged the busy streets, and even though one-fifth of the population was African-American, the white majority was augmented regularly by the fresh adventurers from Britain and Ireland who were disgorged almost daily from the wooden bellies of the ships. The city had already drawn the boundaries for seven wards, and the more refined families were pushing out into the country in their search for exclusive dwelling places. The Massachusetts delegates rode three miles from the city to breakfast with John Morin Scott at his excellent country seat. Scott would one day be the father-in-law of Julianna Sitgreaves (1765–1842), but Julia was still a girl and her dearest future friend was born this very month.[b] They would all make history, and Boston, Philadelphia, and New York would all be part of the pattern.

---

[a] The southern shoreline of Manhattan Island has been called the Battery for generations and has long been a popular public area. Its name is derived from gun batteries that once protected the city.

[b] Julia Sitgreaves Scott, daughter of William and Susanna Deshon Sitgreaves, was born in Philadelphia. She married Lewis Allaire Scott, who succeeded his father as Secretary of State of New York. After being widowed in March 1798, Julia returned to live in Philadelphia and was a lifelong confidante and benefactor of Elizabeth Seton.

Elizabeth Ann Bayley was born on 28 August 1774. Aside from her parentage, little is known about her birth.[1] It is not possible to identify where Elizabeth Bayley was born in New York.[c] There are no records of the event, no baptismal records extant, not even a city directory to indicate her parents' residence. Trinity Church, where she may have been baptized, lost its records in the fire of 1776. The first directory of New York City was published in 1787. Even the records of St. Andrew's Church on Staten Island, New York, reveal no clue.[2] She was the second daughter of Dr. Richard Bayley (1744–1801) and his first wife, Catherine Charlton Bayley (?–1777). The mother, who died when Elizabeth was only three years old, was a daughter of Mary Bayeux Charlton and the Reverend Richard Charlton,[d] for many years the rector of St. Andrew's Church on Staten Island.[3] The father, Richard Bayley, was the elder son of William Bayley of Hoddeston, Hertfordshire, in England, who had come to New York in 1726.[4] William Bayley married Susanne Le Compte of New Rochelle, New York,[e] and of this union two sons were born. Richard was born in Fairfield, Connecticut, about 1744;[5] William Le Compte was born on 8 August 1745.[6]

Richard Bayley came to New York City from New Rochelle at the age of twenty to study under the society physician, Dr. John Charlton. Charlton, who had studied in England and had been rather prominent at the court of George III, had married Mary de Peyster, the daughter of Abraham de Peyster and Margaret van Courtlandt de Peyster. Everyone in New York knew by sight the stocky, ruddy-faced little man who "seemed quite ready to parade himself and horse for the benefit of inquisitive folk."[7] Dr. Charlton lived at 100 Broadway within easy call of the Jays, where he and his lady dined on occasion at small "en famille" repasts. His family connections alone kept Dr. Charlton with a thriving practice.[8] But this kind of professional experience did not satisfy the eager young Bayley, and after marrying his mentor's sister in 1767, he went to London where for two years he studied under the famous William Hunter.[9] On his return to New York, Dr. Bayley practiced medicine with Dr. Charlton, and together they shared the honor of being the first physicians to ride to visit their patients.[10] By 1774, the Bayleys had two

---

[c] In 1817 Elizabeth Seton refers to New York as "my native city." 7.103, Elizabeth Seton to Rev. Simon Bruté, S.S., 1 August 1817, Regina Bechtle, S.C., and Judith Metz, S.C., eds., Ellin M. Kelly, mss. ed., *Elizabeth Bayley Seton Collected Writings*, 3 vols. (New City Press: New York, 2000–2006), 2:494. Hereafter cited as *CW*.

[d] The Reverend Richard Charlton (1706–1777) was rector of St. Andrew's (1747–1777). The son of John Charlton of Longford, Ireland, Richard had graduated from Trinity College in Dublin and was sent as a missionary to New Windsor, New York, in 1730. In 1733 he was made catechist of the African-Americans of New York City and served in that capacity until he was appointed rector of St. Andrew's Church, 24 November 1747. He married Mary Bayeux. Dr. Charlton died of dysentery on 7 October 1777. His eldest daughter married John Dongan; his son was physician, Dr. John Charlton of New York City.

[e] Le Compte also appears as LeConte.

daughters, and Dr. Bayley had an avid interest in the causes of croup. In 1775 he left the former to pursue the latter, and again went to London to study with Hunter. When the war for independence broke out in America, Bayley returned on board a British man-of-war, a surgeon in the army of Major General William Howe. Bayley was sent to Newport, Rhode Island, in the first year of the war, and it was there he met the Hessian military surgeon, Dr. Christian Friedrich Michaelis, whose interest in croup rivaled Bayley's own.[11] It was at Newport that Bayley became increasingly interested in the pathology of disease and anatomy, and wild rumors eventually reached New York that he was performing cruel experiments on the soldiers to satisfy his scientific curiosity.[12]

Richard Bayley's career as an army surgeon was cut short by an urgent summons to Newtown, Long Island, where his wife lay dying, probably as a result of childbirth, in the spring of 1777. Left a widower in his early thirties, he found himself with the responsibility of three little girls,[f] and his thirst for medical experiment still unquenched. It is not surprising to find him remarrying scarcely more than a year later. Again Richard Bayley allied himself to good families of New York society, this time the Barclays and Roosevelts, by his marriage on 16 June 1778, to Charlotte Amelia Barclay (1759–1805), the daughter of Andrew and Helena Roosevelt Barclay.[13] With his children now given a second mother, Dr. Bayley turned again to his professional interests,[g] and the *Royal Gazette* for 5 July 1780, carried this advertisement:

> Mr. Bayley presents his compliments to the gentlemen who did him the honor of attending the operation in surgery last winter and will be happy to see them at his house on Friday the 7th at 5 o'clock P.M.[14]

Two years later he performed the first successful amputation of an arm at the shoulder joint. His fame was growing.

Richard Bayley, like the elder William Seton (1746-1798), was a consistent loyalist throughout the course of the revolutionary war.[15] New York City was the only port to remain continuously in British hands from

---

[f] These daughters were Mary Magdalen, Elizabeth Ann, and infant Catherine Charlton Bayley.

[g] Most biographers of Elizabeth Bayley Seton have stated that Dr. Bayley was closely connected with Sir Guy Carleton during the American Revolution. They probably based their statements on a claim made by Robert Seton in *An Old Family* that Dr. Bayley "began life as staff-surgeon to General Sir Guy Carleton in New York." Robert Seton, *An Old Family,* (Bretano's: New York, 1899), 275. The earliest biographer of Bayley, Thacher, states that Bayley resigned from the army in 1777. Sir Guy Carleton did not take command in New York City until May 1782. A search of the *Report on American Manuscripts* which contains the Carleton or Dorchester papers shows not a single mention of Richard Bayley in any capacity. It may be that Robert Seton drew erroneous conclusions from the name of Dr. Bayley's youngest son, Guy Carlton Bayley, born in 1786. Yet the boy's own mother spelled his name "Guy Charlton" in her will.

October 1776 to November 1783 and it thus became the natural Mecca for loyalists craving the protection of the British crown. The evacuation of Philadelphia alone directed some 3,000 pilgrims to New York. Among the regular residents of the city certainly many who were neutral in sentiment became Tory in public practice for reasons of expediency.[16] A third portion of the loyalist population comprised the merchants and professional classes, to whom politics will ever remain secondary to private economic or social motivation. Commerce, justice, and humanitarianism tended, rightly, to cut across the national or imperial boundaries of the time. The loyalism of a merchant Seton or a surgeon Bayley requires no ponderous polemic.

From its varied sources the loyalist population grew by leaps and bounds. At the time of the abortive American occupation scarcely a king's man existed within the city; yet immediately following the British entrance in October 1776, well over a thousand male inhabitants assembled at the city hall in Wall Street to take an oath of allegiance to the crown. By February of the following year this number had swelled to 3,000, and it is estimated that of the 27,000 people in New York City in 1781, practically all were classed as loyal to His Majesty's rule.[17]

Richard Bayley's loyalism was on occasion at odds with his humanitarianism. After General James Pattison became commandant of the city the corruption and cruelty of British rule horrified many of the citizens by the excesses which were tolerated. Pattison himself rarely let a day pass without offending someone. One day when Bayley happened to be passing through the streets he saw a drunken soldier thrown from a cart and run over by a careless African-American driver. Bayley got down from his chaise, administered first aid, and notified the hospital. For his pains Bayley received a call from the Provost Marshal the following day, was thrown in jail, denied access to Pattison, and did not get released until ten o'clock that evening. Such treatment so enraged Bayley that he threatened to quit the city rather than live under such military rule. Pattison, fortunately, was succeeded the following year and Bayley remained to practice his experiments in surgery.[18]

None of the problems of allegiance concerned the four-year-old daughter of Dr. Bayley, however, as she sat in the doorway of their house one day in October 1778. Inside the house lay the still form of little Catherine Charlton Bayley, dead at the age of two. The serious little girl on the doorstep looked at the clouds scudding greyly overhead and tried to work out the puzzle of the death and heaven, as she longed for a mother she scarcely remembered.[19] While Dr. Bayley performed his surgical experiments in 1780

4

his daughter Elizabeth was intrigued by other more abstract considerations, and climbed the garret stairs with Emma, her baby half-sister. Peering out the attic window, showing her the setting sun, Elizabeth told her, "God lived up in heaven and good children would go up there."[20]

Elizabeth Bayley's step-mother was busy during these years rearing a family of her own. In the first eight years of her marriage she had six children and was often in "great affliction."[h] Yet she found time to teach Elizabeth the 23rd psalm, "the Lord is my Shepherd" which all through her life was Elizabeth's favorite psalm.[21] Sometimes, perhaps to relieve the burdened woman, the daughters of the first Mrs. Bayley were sent to New Rochelle to stay with the Bayley relatives there.[i] At New Rochelle Elizabeth loved to play alone, or wander about the countryside. It is quite possible she was thus occupied when the British evacuated New York City.[22]

Two months after Elizabeth Ann Bayley's ninth birthday the New York journals and gazettes carried vivid descriptions of the elaborate ceremonies and noisy dinners with which the revolutionary patriots celebrated the evacuation of New York by the British. Besides General Washington, Governor George Clinton, and Major General Knox, a changing culture was ushered in 25 November 1783, which was to exert a tremendous influence on Elizabeth Bayley's life. The retiring British left behind them more problems to be solved than the irritating greased flagpole at Fort George.[23] The city was a shambles. The devastating fires of 1776 and 1778 had laid waste one-quarter of the city proper. Roads were nearly impassable, while water traffic was decreased by the deteriorated conditions into which docks and wharves had fallen from disuse. As if to add her sneering comment, nature visited southern Manhattan that fall with an earthquake severe enough to throw gentlemen from their seats and send china and glassware crashing to the floor. There was no clairvoyance to predict that from these ashes the Phoenix of the nineteenth-century metropolis would rise.

War takes a partial toll in deferred payment, and the Revolution left its own residue of disintegration in a weakened moral fiber accompanied by overt modifications of organized religion. Nowhere was the decline in public and private morality more in evidence than in the larger cities. One surface indication was the increased popularity of dueling. John Paul Jones' refusal to meet Pierre Landais after a disgraceful encounter in New York in

---

[h] Although the births of all these children are not definitely dated, the children were Charlotte Amelia (called Emma), Richard, Guy Carlton, Mary Fitch, William Augustus, and Andrew Barclay. A seventh child, Helen, was born 10 June 1790.

[i] Elizabeth Seton says in "Dear Remembrances": "New Rochelle at 8 years" then "12 years old...home again at my Fathers." If she were continuously at New Rochelle from eight to twelve years of age, she was not present for the evacuation of the city in 1783.

October 1787 was an exception to the general humor. More typical was the attack made by James Jones on Brockholst Livingston in 1798, in full view of the promenaders of the Battery. That Jones was killed in the resulting duel seems not to have materially affected the popularity of this method of establishing honor, so lately borrowed from the French officers of the Revolution.[24] Dr. Richard Bayley was himself a party to a long and acrid controversy which ensued when Wright Post (1766–1828) and Monsieur P. Micheau quarreled in 1788. Micheau challenged Dr. Post, who declined to meet his opponent, but friends of both parties took the affair to press, and "a number of affidavits relating to it appeared in the public prints of the city."[25] The matter was only ended by the departure of Micheau for England, which left the young doctor free to turn to thoughts of marriage and Mary Magdalen Bayley (1768–1856).[j]

At a lower level of society vice and crime emanated from the unsavory nooks and crannies of "Canvas Town," the area encompassed by Broad and Whitehall Streets, the legacy left by the great fires. Respectable citizens were attacked and robbed; and some, like Isaac Willetts, took the law into their own hands and fired upon suspicious characters.[26] Public as well as private morality gave evidence of the inroads made by the Revolution, and Chancellor Livingston wrote to Washington in 1783, lamenting the depravity pervading the mass of people who seemed to consider national faith and honor of little moment.[27] In this same decade the wave of financial speculation in the reputation of the new republic reached its peak; and in March 1788, the agents of William Seton, and that master gambler, William Duer, were found as far south as North Carolina where they were buying up all the certificates they could command.[28] Back in New York City resolutions were being passed to penalize the public tax collectors for their delinquencies, and the governor warned the citizenry to be on guard against counterfeited federal notes.[29]

Organized religion was also undergoing change. Before the Revolution religious affiliation and political power had frequently gone hand in hand. Four major groups had vied for power, with the Anglicans usually monopolizing civil offices. Their only serious rival had been the more numerous Presbyterians. The Dutch Reformed group was still strong, but its energies were being dissipated. The Lutherans were in fourth place, while the remaining denominations exerted no perceptible political influence.[30]

---

[j] Dr. Wright Post (1768–1856) married Bayley's oldest daughter 10 June 1790. New York *Journal and Weekly Register,* 19 June 1790. The couple had the following children: Edward, Lionel (Leo), Catherine Charlton, Richard Bayley, Eugene, Mary Elizabeth, and Emily.

During the Revolution, Anglicanism was rather generally a synonym for loyalism. Before the advent of the British occupation the Anglicans had suffered briefly at the hands of the Whigs, and their churches had been closed in August 1776. For a month no services were held at Trinity, St. Paul's or St. George's; but the arrival of the British reversed the situation and St. Paul's resumed services on 22 September 1776. Both St. Paul's and St. George's remained open for the duration of the British occupation, but Trinity, razed in the conflagration which accompanied the patriot retreat, was not rebuilt for another decade. By 1782 the two Anglican chapels were so overcrowded that worshipers had to make use of the city hall.[31] British occupation saw the rise of discrimination against the other sects, and it is not particularly surprising to find the Presbyterians suffering most severely. Churches were seized and converted into barracks, hospitals, and prisons. That much of this appropriation was military necessity may be assumed from the fact that even St. George's Chapel was considered as a possible Hessian hospital in 1779, and only the spirited protests of Dr. Charles Inglis prevented the event.[32] Certainly the churches so used were unfit for divine worship at the war's end. It was not until the closing decade of the century that any serious architectural retort was made to the Anglican threat of monopoly, and a French traveler could remark that the city seemed to contain as many churches as shops.[33]

The peace ushered in by the Treaty of Paris in 1783 found the Anglicans, or Episcopalians, still leading the political parade. "If the Tories of 1776 could be called Episcopalians, the same title could be used with far better right for the Federalists of 1788."[34] But changes within the framework of the church must be noted. A series of laws in 1784 provided disestablishment in New York and legalized the incorporation of all religious bodies. Under this latter provision Trinity Church was incorporated on 17 April 1784. Within the body ecclesiastic a Whig junta succeeded in substituting the Reverend Samuel Provoost for the ardent Tory, Benjamin Moore, as rector of Trinity Parish. The Protestant Episcopal Church in the United States separated itself from the Anglican Church in 1785. Provoost, formerly assistant of Trinity Church, became its pastor and the first bishop of the city in 1787.[35] Under his episcopal eye the cornerstone for the new Trinity Church was laid on 21 August 1788, and the dedication solemnized in 1790. It was Bishop Provoost who presided at St. Paul's in the service following Washington's inauguration in 1789,[36] and it was Provoost, too, who witnessed the marriage of Elizabeth Ann Bayley to William Magee Seton[k] (1768–1803) on 25 January 1794.[37] Although the politics of the

[k] The middle name "Magee" is from a merchant of London, his baptismal sponsor, who left him a legacy of 1000 British pounds and 1500 British pounds to his father.

Bayleys and Setons are less certain, there is no doubt that these two families and their connections belonged to the Episcopalian majority of the postwar era.

The evacuation of New York City in 1783, led to other changes which would affect the lives of the Bayleys and Setons. The position of the former loyalists was for a time precarious. Large numbers of them fled, and New York lost such dignitaries as Governor William Tryon, Sir Andrew Elliott, Judge Thomas Jones, Thomas Barclay, William Bayard, and some of the de Lanceys, not to mention such churchmen as Dr. Inglis and Myles Cooper. "Not only did the city suffer a deprivation of men and talent, but the fleeing Tories carried with them a not inconsiderable amount of wealth, despite their heavy financial losses."[38] The loyalists who chose to leave the city had been ordered by the Sons of Liberty to be gone by 1 May 1784; but "loyalism was of so many shades, and ties of blood were so numerous, that the great majority remained to make the best of the new situation."[39]

This new situation, at the outset, was not characterized by lenience, as the legislation of the day bears testimony. Restrictions were placed upon collections of debts due to Tories; suits for damages to patriot property were instituted; doctors were boycotted, and lawyers disbarred. An act of 27 March 1778, had excluded Tories from public office elsewhere in the state; this discrimination reached the city after 1783. In May, the following year, loyalists who had borne arms were disenfranchised forever; but the effects of this last enactment were not long lived, since the law was repealed in 1786.[40]

If Richard Bayley suffered from boycotting after 1783, there is no evidence of it; but his wartime sympathies may account for the lack of data concerning his activities from 1782–1787. By 1787, however, he was lecturing on anatomy in the virtually abandoned city hospital to such eager listeners as Wright Post and David Hosack. There is even a record of his having operated on patients there.[41] This building was the scene, in 1788, of the worst riot the city had yet witnessed.

In 1771, George III, through royal letters patent, had permitted the formation of the "Society of the Hospital in the City of New York."[42] This group erected a costly building on the west side of Broadway between Duane and Worth Streets, only to have the building razed by fire in 1775. Although it was rebuilt the following year, the war circumvented the plans of the founders, and the building served successively as a barracks for patriots or Hessians, a haven for immigrants, and a meeting place for the state legislature. Jacques Pierre Brissot de Warville noticed in 1788 that it was in bad condition, not fit for the lodging of sick people; but he added, "The building is vast; it is of brick and perfectly well-situated on the bank of the North River."[43] Dr. Bayley found it an excellent place to house his specimens and perform his experiments.

It was from this building, one April Sunday afternoon in 1788, that a brash young medical student displayed an arm from a cadaver to some young boys hanging about and taunted them with the words, "See, here is your mother's hand that has cuffed your ears many a time!" It was a grim coincidence that one of the boys had recently lost his mother and when a report of the remark reached his father the affair very quickly assumed alarming proportions. A mob of outraged citizens assembled to attack the hospital and Bayley with his students was barely rescued in time. The doctor was placed in protective custody with other medical men who were rescued during the same riot.[44]

The mob, after nursing their wrath overnight, on Monday attacked the jail. John Jay and Baron von Steuben, the revolutionary hero, tried to quell the rioters; and, in the melee, Steuben was knocked down. The irate veteran cried out to the mayor, "Fire, Duane, fire!" The militia took this as an official command and fired into the crowd, causing several fatalities. This temporary setback only served to deflect the attention of the mob and they turned their attention to the homes of the doctors. Private dwellings were wrecked and valuable collections of medical specimens were destroyed. Elizabeth Bayley, who was home again at her father's house,[1] passed the night "in a sweat of terror saying all the while OUR FATHER."[45] At the last, the city called out General Malcolm's brigade and Colonel Bauman's regiment of artillery before peace was finally restored.[46]

The "Doctors' Riot" was not unique, but rather the first of its kind in New York. It was a powerful protest against the practice so ghoulishly described in Robert Louis Stevenson's *The Body Snatcher* (1884). Medical students had for some time been secretly removing corpses from the potter's field and the African-American burying ground; and the suspicion was growing that supposedly more respectable graves were not inviolate. In the affidavit which Dr. Bayley published on Tuesday, 15 April, in the New York *Journal and Patriotic Register,* he denied that there had been any surreptitious acquisition of bodies from churchyards or places of high social character; yet the denial was so phrased as to leave unanswered the argument as regarding the potter's field. The riot produced two immediate

---

[1] The Bayleys lived at 15 Smith Street in 1787 and at 49 Smith Street from 1791–94. There was no directory for 1788; but in 1789 Dr. Bayley was listed at 60 King Street, and in 1790 at 51 Wall Street. It is thus quite impossible to determine where the Bayleys lived in April 1788.

results in this connection. On 6 January 1789, a state law was passed giving the corpses of criminals to surgeons for the purpose of advancing medical science; a federal law of 30 April 1790, gave judges discretionary power to add to sentences for convicted murder the post-mortem dissection. That Bayley's pioneering was not universally deplored is evidenced in the editorial comment of the New York *Packet* of 15 April 1788, which said dryly:

> It is sincerely wished that our fellow citizens would manifest their zeal against vice and wickedness (as it abounds in the city) which kill men's souls, and be less zealous for the preservation of the duller part.[47]

The governing board of the hospital was less philosophical and promptly disclaimed any responsibility in the affair. They presented the unfortunate doctors with a bill for £22:7:10, and forthwith ousted them from the premises.[48]

Dr. Bayley seemed to feel that another trip abroad could be made conveniently while heated passions were allowed to cool, and so he proceeded to put his affairs in order before leaving for England. He made a will leaving his farm in Westchester County to his mother, and the rest of his "estate both real and personal of what nature or kind soever" to his wife.[49] The older Bayley girls, Elizabeth and Mary, who had been educated at "Mama Pompelion's" where they learned to play the piano, speak French, and admire stories about "men with girlish modesty & reserve combined with manly strength & fortitude,"[50] now returned once more to New Rochelle.[51] Here they visited "Uncle Bayley," the doctor's brother William and his wife, Sarah Pell Bayley, while they awaited their father's return.[52] By 1790 the energetic Dr. Bayley was back in New York eagerly attacking the public health problems of the rapidly growing city.[m]

Although New York City's streets were superior to those of many other crowded areas and, according to John Adams, "vastly more regular and elegant than those in Boston," the attending problems of surface water and sewage presented an odious as well as odorous conundrum.[53] The nightly parade of African-Americans, bearing offal tubs to the waterfront, soon proved inadequate to the growing city's requirements.[54] The open wooden chutes which carried surface water from Fly Market to the East River had to be reinforced with stone and bridged with heavy arches. Stately Wall Street demanded stone sewers of its own.[55] But the streets around the sheds of the

---

[m] In 1790 Bayley was one of the promoters of the New York Dispensary established in that year to give medical care to the poor.

soap makers and candlemakers continued to plague the sensitivities of the more refined population.

More pressing were the threats of epidemics[n] which periodically invaded the city. Diseases which were most commonly feared in the eighteenth century were tuberculosis, sore throat "which when putrid is mortal," malaria (which could be combated by a liberal use of Peruvian bark, but yielded most readily to the remedy of a trip to the mountains), influenza, and the awe-inspiring yellow fever.[56] Little headway was made against consumption,[o] since the doctors of that day attributed its cause to such habits as the excessive use of hot tea and coffee, lying too long in bed, eating too much, or sleeping in feather ticks. Women were believed to be more subject to the ailment because "they take but little exercise, which is the only powerful remedy against the stagnation of the humors." Quaker women were thus doomed to consumption because of their "habit of gravity and immobility which they developed in early life."[57] In spite of all her activity, Elizabeth Bayley may have succumbed to the disease at last in 1821.

Malaria was prevalent in the eighteenth-century metropolis, although in recent years it would seem an oddity to find it so far north. In Bayley's time New York City was surrounded by sizable areas of swampland, and the region between the present Eighteenth and Twentieth Streets on Broadway was all swamp when it was granted to Sir Peter Warren in 1745. Jacob Roosevelt's leather industry centered in Beekman's Swamp, and it was from this fetid location that he extracted the fortune, part of which was left to Amelia Barclay, Bayley's second wife.[58] The Collect or "Fresh Water Pond" in the heart of the spreading city became more and more of a nuisance, when it was not an outright menace. The city purchased it in 1791, but it was not until after 1800 that it was filled in.[59] In addition, many of the low coastal areas remained partially submerged and furnished excellent breeding places for mosquitoes.

By far the most dreaded of all epidemics were those of yellow fever, and many of New York's most famous institutions related to public health trace their origins to the frantic efforts made to combat the fever. In 1791, for the first time since the Revolution, a virulent form appeared. In 1793 it recurred, and by the time the second visitation was felt the city had already begun to make plans to isolate fever patients at Governors Island. This feeble action on the part of the city officials was not sufficient to prevent

---

[n] Small pox was declining in severity as a result of inoculation. Elizabeth Bayley Seton makes frequent references to the inoculation of her children in her correspondence.

[o] Tuberculosis was referred to as consumption in the 19th century.

general hysteria, and the pace of preparation had to be accelerated. A law of 1794 made Governors Island the regular place of quarantine instead of Bedloe's Islands, which had been used intermittently for that purpose ever since 1738 when a temporary quarantine had been necessary to combat smallpox coming from South Carolina and the Indies.[60] In the same year, 1794, the Bellevue property was purchased for the purpose of establishing a hospital. Scarcely had these plans gotten under way when the scourge of 1795 swept over New York.

Those who could, fled the city. Those who could not, and the public-spirited citizens who would not, remained to fight. Among these last was, quite naturally, Dr. Bayley. Bayley had returned to New York after a brief stay in England, had helped promote the New York Dispensary in 1790 to give medical aid to the poor, and had taken a house at 51 Wall Street. In 1792 he joined the faculty of Columbia College as a lecturer in anatomy, while his son-in-law, Dr. Wright Post, held the chair in surgery. During Post's absence in Europe during 1792–1793 Bayley gave lectures in both fields, but upon Post's return the two doctors exchanged positions and Bayley returned to surgery. Although his residence changed frequently during the following years, Dr. Bayley's interest in public health remained constant. In 1794 he was one of the group which reorganized the Medical Society under the leadership of Dr. John Charlton, the president of that society since 1792. Bayley held office as censor until 1798, and the minutes of the society show that he served time and again on committees charged with investigating the causes of epidemics and their relation to immigration.[61] His committee had petitioned early in 1795 that the mayor and aldermen provide more adequate protection against the visitations of yellow fever.

The summer of 1795 was a dreadful one. The epidemic began in the middle of July, and by November more than 700 people were dead of the disease. Bellevue was used for the first time, but the drinking and quarreling of the nurses was a scandal, and undoubtedly contributed little to the welfare of the patients, two-thirds of whom died.[62] The day of thanksgiving proclaimed by Governor Jay on 26 November must have bewildered the Irish immigrants whose decimated ranks bore mournful testimony to the pestilential force. In February Bayley was appointed to a committee to investigate the full implications of the epidemic, and his findings were published in a report. *An Account of the Epidemic Fever Which Prevailed in the City of New York During Part of the Summer and Fall of 1795.*[63] The Reverend Richard Channing Moore of Staten Island wrote Dr. Bayley for his further opinions on yellow fever during the summer of 1796, and

Bayley's reply so impressed him that, with the doctor's consent, Moore forwarded the letter to the editor[p] of *Minerva*.[64]

Meanwhile Governor Jay sought the advice of the Medical Society in regard to establishing a lazaretto and quarantine in New York Harbor.[q] On 28 November 1796, Bayley wrote to Jay a "Report on the Subject of Yellow Fever" in which he summarized his findings in the earlier report, cited the opinions of ship's captains he had consulted, and described the horrible conditions in the region of Whitehall and the new docks which prevented people from opening their windows unless they had strong stomachs.[65] By this time Bayley's opinions carried weight because he was now the health officer of the newly created Board of Health Commissioners. When the board was later reduced from seven to three members there was a simultaneous enlargement of its powers, and among these was the health officer's right to clean up the city. Since Bayley believed that the causes for epidemics lay within the city itself he welcomed the opportunity to prove his theories.

The vigorous action taken by the health officer to improve the streets, fill in the swamps, and guard the slips and docks from contagion was not welcomed by the entire population. Elizabeth Bayley Seton, writing to Dr. Bayley at Albany in February 1797, warned him that "the soap boilers and tallow chandlers talk of petitioning the legislature for the removal of the Health Officer."[66] This opposition to the clean-up campaign was to continue, and Bayley himself in 1800 wrote humorously to his friend, the lieutenant-governor at Albany:

> Permit me to tell you that numerous tinkers tailors, coopers, shoemakers and soothsayers have forwarded a petition to Albany (I know not to whom directed) to remove the health officer, etc., etc. The applicants are the most violent of the Democratic Junta—*Sic Res Zeritur*. It would be very flattering to your very humble servant if he would be made acquainted as speedily as possible with the date of the petition. Much is necessary to be done to forward the view of the Health establishment, but nothing effective can take place until final arrangements are determined for the operations of the ensuing year.[67]

---

[p] Probably Daniel Webster who began New York's first daily newspaper, *American Minerva* (later known as *The Commercial Advertiser*), and edited it for four years. One of the ironies of history is that this same Reverend Moore officiated at Dr. Bayley's funeral after the physician died of the disease he had so eagerly studied.

[q] A lazaretto refers to an institution or place to quarantine persons with contagious diseases.

Regardless of the opposition from some quarters, Richard Bayley continued to hold public office until his death. When Jay's proposal of a lazaretto began to take substantial form, Bayley was the man who was considered the logical doctor to be made the quarantine officer. Temporary arrangements were first used at Bellevue, then at Bedloe's Island.ʳ In February 1797, the state appropriated $4,500 toward a new lazaretto, and added another appropriation in 1798. The question of site caused the most considerable controversy, but Dr. Bayley was finally able to write from Albany, "Staten Island—yes, it's more than probable. What then? Why, private considerations must be made to yield to the more interesting ones, the public welfare." The state capital had moved to Albany in January 1798. Dr. Bayley usually stayed in Watervliet when he made his annual trips to the legislature, 1798–1801. He received his mail in care of Lieutenant-Governor Steven van Rensselaer.[68] A year later his daughter Elizabeth wrote a friend:

> My father has obtained permission from the Legislature to
> perform all the plans he has contemplated on Staten Island—
> He is building a *hospital* and *dwelling house*, but I fear not
> to receive his family.[69]

While Dr. Bayley's public life was progressing satisfactorily, leaving a record fairly easy to follow, his private life during this period seems to have been more confusing; certainly its course is shrouded in mystery. Some family disagreements appear to have reached a crisis about the time of his last trip to England. The daughters of Catherine Charlton Bayley went to New Rochelle in 1789 because of this trouble. Twenty years later, when Mary Magdalen Bayley (1768–1856) revisited New Rochelle, she wrote her sister Elizabeth:

> I can scarcely describe to you the state of mind I was thrown
> into by recalling scenes and persons that every year of my
> life seems to have been somehow connected with. Beginning
> with the unhappy situation of our Mother—our taking refuge
> in the same place on our Father's going to England—the very
> very painful events that succeeded our leaving there until
> we married. Even that eventful step scarcely enabled us to
> shake off all that was disagreeably attached to our situation
> before.[70]

Mary Bayley did not have a very long period of "painful events," however, for in June of the year her father returned, she married Dr.

ʳ Bedloe's Island had been ceded by the common council to the state and was used after September 1796.

Wright Post and soon after went to live in John Street.ˢ Her younger sister, Elizabeth, had a longer period of confusion and unhappiness. She was only fourteen when her father went to England and although she loved the countryside of Westchester County, her lonely heart suffered at his absence. Her journal records a typical spring day of the year 1789 in these words:

> The air still a clear blue vault above, the numberless sounds
> of spring melody and joy—the sweet clovers and wild
> flowers I had got by the way...Still I can feel every sensation
> that passed thro' my soul...I thought at that time my Father
> did not care for me—well, God was my Father—my all. I
> prayed—sang hymns—cried—laughed in talking to myself
> of how far He could place me above all sorrow—then laid
> still to enjoy the Heavenly Peace that came over my soul.[71]

Elizabeth Bayley was beginning to be aware of that conflict between the sensual and the spiritual so disquieting to all ages, but especially disturbing to youth. She took "pleasure in everything: coarse, rough, smooth or easy."[72] She read the Bible and Milton, and yearned to become a Quaker "because they wore such pretty *plain* hats."[73] Sometimes she was filled with "transports of first pure enthusiasm" at the sight of the stars and felt that she was forever exuberant. At other times the cruelty of the young people about her caused her pain, and family disagreements cast her down. But always her heart was "as innocent as a human heart could be," filled as it was with youthful "enthusiastic love to [sic] God and admiration of his works."[74]

But she could not stay in New Rochelle forever, and soon Elizabeth was back in New York City facing an uncertain future. The two years before her marriage were trying. She seems to have had no place where she could stay, and spent part of the time on Staten Island with her mother's relatives, the Dongans, and much of her time with her sister, Mary Bayley Post. She dreamed of a little home in the country where she could gather little children around her and "teach them their prayers and keep them clean and teach them to be good." When she read stories of European convents she wished passionately that there were such places in America, "where people could be shut up from the world and pray, and be good always."[75] Sometimes this longing for escape brought her to the verge of despair and she reasoned, in her wretchedness, that God was too good to condemn her to such a life. Her terse wording reads: "This wretched

---

ˢ The New York City directories show Wright Post's residence as 180 Water Street in 1791, but John Street from 1792–98.

15

reasoning—Laudanum—the praise and thanks of excessive joy not to have done the horrid deed[t]—the thousand promises of Eternal gratitude."[76]

The melancholy moods did not persist. Elizabeth was too young, and New York too engaging, to allow a permanent gloom. New York society in the last decade of the eighteenth century was made up of three fairly distinct classes. The first was composed of "the constituted authorities, government officers, divines, lawyers, and physicians of eminence, with the principal merchants and people of independent property." The second was made up of the lesser merchants, retail dealers, and subordinate government clerks; the third consisted of "the inferior orders of people."[77] The Bayleys and Posts belonged to the first group, although not at its very top level, and were welcomed at tea, an evening of music, or dancing at the houses of the Sadlers, the Wilkeses, the Charltons, and other prosperous homes. The lively Elizabeth enjoyed music and dancing. Many years afterward, when she was advising her own daughter on the subject of social behavior, Elizabeth Seton said of dancing:

> When I was young I never found any effect from it but the most innocent cheerfulness both in public and private—I remember remorse of conscience about so much, much time lost in it, and my trouble at being so unable to say my prayers—seeing always my partners, instead of my God... also my vexation at the time it took to prepare dresses for balls.[78]

Although Richard Bayley was unable to provide a serene home for his daughter, he was most concerned about her happiness and her adjustment to life. The doctor, whom Brissot de Warville once characterized as a man of good abilities but perhaps, too inflammable and too caustic,[79] knew only too well the disadvantages of possessing a reckless nature. He tried to show Elizabeth the virtue in moderation, and advised:

> Calm that glowing of your soul, that warm emanation of your chest, for a more temperate climate, impressions on that case will be less readily admitted but their effects will last longer... Objects present strokes [sic] our mind more forcibly than I hope more at a distance. Thus we intend one thing to day, we are diverted from it tomorrow, the next day new Ideas occur and our former intentions are forgotten—This cursed

---

[t] Some biographers interpret this passage to indicate that Elizabeth Bayley contemplated suicide. Melville finds "the horrid deed" an insufficient description to serve as conclusive evidence of such an intention. [It is possible that an adolescent depression prompted thoughts of suicide but the fact is that Elizabeth said "No" to taking a drug overdose of laudanum, an opium derivative used to calm colicky babies, Ed.]

dysentery of the mind has been entailed on both sexes with a remarkable constancy from the time of Adam and Eve.[80]

Bayley had seen enough of the extremes of his daughter's emotions and moods to make him fear her sensibilities. Even after her marriage he continued to advocate prudence in preference to exaggerated expressions of feeling. "Guard against the sudden change of weather," he wrote. "Never dwell on triffle, be mistress of yourself, then I am convinced you will always have the credit of acting well."[81] On another occasion he asked her to learn to laugh at imaginary evils lest they cheapen her path of life.[82]

In addition to her unevenness of disposition, Bayley noticed in his second daughter a tendency toward introversion. At the age of fifteen Elizabeth had begun keeping her thoughts in writing, along with selections copied from authors she was currently reading. Her thought was to please her father, and she kept the journal "with great delight."[83] But the doctor saw some danger in this preoccupation with journaling and he called to her attention that "most of us are tinctured with a little of the selfish," and hers might be this habit of corresponding chiefly with herself. He approved of such a mode of correspondence, he said, only if "a new stock of information and useful knowledge were added from time to time."[84] Dr. Bayley soon found his worries in this respect at an end. In 1793 William Magee Seton became the object of Elizabeth Bayley's interest and the recipient of her correspondence.

Young Seton was the son of William Seton of the Parbroath branch of the famous Anglo-Scottish family. The elder William was born on 24 April 1746, while his mother was on a visit to Scotland. His boyhood was spent in Kirkbridge in Yorkshire, and with relatives in Sanlucar, Spain. Following a common eighteenth-century pattern this descendant of a long, illustrious line was impelled by the double force of economic circumstances at home and lure of the New World overseas to follow his relatives abroad. A brother-in-law, Andrew Seton, was already settled on Long Island, New York, and may have encouraged William to come over. At any rate, by 1763, he had crossed the Atlantic and found his way to New Jersey. In less than four years he had removed to New York City, acquired the "Mohawk Lands" in the interior of New York province, and had met the Curson[u] daughters, two of whom he was to marry.[85]

---

[u] The Curson sisters were members of the family of the Curson-Gouverneur firm. During the Revolution this firm was located at St. Eustatius, the Dutch Colony, which was notoriously open to American commerce until its capture by Rodney in 1781. After the Revolution the Curson family centered chiefly at Baltimore. The name also appears as Curzon.

William Seton married Rebecca Curson on 2 March 1767, and after her death espoused her sister, Anna-Maria in 1776.[86] By the first alliance five children were born; the eldest, William Magee, like his father before him, interrupted a family jaunt off the coast of Cape Henry, Virginia. The Seton family Bible records:

> Born 20th April 1768, 35 minutes after 4 P.M., on board the ship *Edward*, Captain Thomas Miller (long. 68. 30, lat. 36.) Baptized, 8th of May, at New York.[87]

Although the second marriage had to be made outside the Church of England and the Province of New York,[v] it was even more productive of progeny. At least eight children reached maturity and others died in infancy. Those were, indeed, "days when people in New York took wives unto themselves with the praiseworthy intention of increasing the native population of the city."[88]

The firm of Seton & Curson was already a thriving concern when the New York *Gazette* of 15 April 1771, had notified the public of its removal from Dock Street "to Hunter's Quay, opposite Mr. Gouverneur's." During the American Revolution, Seton, like Bayley, remained loyal to the British crown, and was rewarded for his sentiments by being made successively assistant warehouse keeper on 27 July 1777, a notary public in 1779, and assistant in 1782 to Andrew Elliott, who held the dual position of chief of police and superintendent of the port of New York.[89] That Seton performed the work relating to the port is obvious from even a cursory glance at the records. The vessel entries are all executed under Seton's hands; while for conclusive proof there remains the letter of Elliott to Sir Guy Carleton, of 15 November 1783, relating to the disposal of certain port records in the event of British evacuation. Elliott wrote, "I would propose lodging them [records] with Mr. Seton, who remains here, and has always transacted the business of this office and to whom such a reference would naturally be made."[90]

The experience Seton acquired during his incumbency was to serve him well in later years. Under his shrewd gaze the port of New York sustained many changes. When the British took over in 1776 there were about 500 vessels in New York harbor, four-fifths of which were merchant ships. Almost immediately thereafter trading was actively resumed. In spite of the restrictive decrees of 1777 commerce spread out in "its normally complicated fashion."[91] New York supplied not only its own citizens, but

---

[v] The ceremony was performed by a Presbyterian minister at Brunswick, New Jersey on 29 November 1776. The marriage to a deceased wife's sister was frowned upon.

became the entrepot for the illicit trade engaging so many patriots. Upstate New York was rapidly drained of gold by purchases of British manufactures; New Jersey openly set up shots to facilitate the exchange of produce for British goods; while on Long Island and Connecticut shores, merchants stole through the darkness of night to an appointed rendezvous where enemy enticements waited in whale boats whose ultimate destination was far-off Hartford or Wethersfield.

Luxurious tastes developed rather generally throughout the colonial cities during the Revolution, but nowhere more so than in New York City, where in 1777 Queen Charlotte's birthday was marked by an elegant exhibition of fireworks at Whitehall Slip,[w] and Lord Howe's super-ball in honor of his investiture as Knight of the Bath. Here such notables as Prince William Henry, Sir Henry Clinton, and Lord Cornwallis were wined and dined in the governor's spacious dining room overlooking the Battery; and if the young prince on occasion had to be carried aboard his ship, the *Prince George,* it cannot be considered a reflection upon his host's prodigality.[92]

Lesser lights burned proportionately bright and Captain Ralph Dundas, R.N., wrote home to England in March 1782, that his relative William Seton was "liked and esteemed by everyone and not spending less than six guineas a day." Charles Wilkes, who with his brother John was sponsored by Seton on his arrival from England, wrote back gratefully to Miss Berry "for having introduced him to the most agreeable house in New York."[93]

The end of the war brought to the merchant class sweeping changes not the least of which involved the confiscation of loyalist properties, with the city of New York probably contributing one-sixth of the total income the state derived from the sale of these lands. Yet notable exceptions were made, and Theophylact Bache, Thomas Buchanan, John Vanderbilt, and William Seton were among those who retained the bulk of their holdings. Robert East suggests that "probably the nepotism of relatives and friends, a prime factor in worldly affairs, protected the fortunate ones."[94] Alexander Flick argues that a thoroughgoing persecution to the point of decimation of merchant class was not feasible. "The majority of persons in southern New York had been loyalists and they simply could not be eliminated outright; though they were made to endure vindictive taxes."[95] The fine lines of nationalism or even patriotism were not yet distinctly drawn, and loyalism

---

[w] [Although Melville gave the occasion as the birthday of Queen Mary citing Rodman Gilder, a contemporary account of "Her Majesty's Birth Day" published in the *New-York Gazette and Weekly Mercury*, 20 January 1777, does not mention Queen Mary. "Her Majesty" in 1777 was Queen Charlotte, wife of George III. There were benefit birthday balls held in Queen Charlotte's honor during January every year. Ed.]

could be less condemned on the ground of treason than tolerated for the sake of expediency. A final explanation may lie in the American custom, in postwar periods, of attacking the famous fortunes, the spectacular swindlers, the notorious profiteers, while the little man goes serenely about his minor affairs. The token toll in the 1780's was taken of the Crugers, the Barclays, the Bayards, and de Lanceys; then the city turned her face to the future. Thus the representatives of the former colonial firms: the Gouverneur-Curson-Seton, and Ludlow-Crommelin-Verplancks continued, and commercial newcomers like Craigie, Duer, and Sands entered the partially cleared arena.[96]

The removal of the British in 1783 presented New York merchants with the harsh fact of a now hostile English mercantilism. Not only was their port the scene of the heaviest British "dumping" in the first three years of peace; but the Hessian fly[x] ruined the grain earmarked for export.[97] The British West Indies were closed to American trade, and the special trading privileges formerly accorded by the French and Spanish were revoked. The gravity of the situation may be gauged by the fact that at least one-third of New York's prewar tonnage had been involved in this West Indian trade.

Meanwhile the French, in what was, perhaps, an attempt to palliate the political rebuff of the separate treaty, tried to capture part of the American Atlantic trade. "Hector" St. John de Crèvecoeur, in spite of having supported the loyalists cause in the early years of the Revolution, was sent by France in 1783 as first consul to New York. Fortunately, for the Frenchman, a former friend, William Seton, was at the dock to greet him on his arrival. Upon inquiring for his wife and children whom he had left in America, Crèvecoeur learned that his home had been burned, his wife was dead, and his children vanished. Afterwards he wrote, "I should have fallen to the ground but for the support, at this instant, of my friend Mr. Seton, who had come to conduct me from the French vessel to his house."[98]

Whether from friendship, or a desire to capitalize upon Seton's wartime shipping experience, Crèvecoeur included William Seton in his scheme to operate a packet service[y] under French auspices between Lorient[z] and New York. Seton was to be in charge of the New York terminus of the run, and the *Royal Gazette* of 10 December 1783, ran his advertisement as

---

[x] The Hessian fly or barley midge, (*Mayetiola destructor*), is a significant pest of cereal crops and was transported from Asia into Europe and later into North America, possibly by Hessian troops who used bedding during the American Revolution (1775–83).

[y] A packet was a boat which carried mail and cargo along with passengers.

[z] Lorient, or L'Orient, is a commune and a seaport in the Morbihan department in Brittany in northwestern France. The French East India Company, founded in 1664 and chartered by King Louis XIV, established shipyards which gave an impetus to the development of the city.

deputy agent of the French Packet, with an office at 215 Water Street. The first vessel to reach New York under such auspices was the *Sylphe,* which arrived in March 1784. The career of "this meritorious enterprise" was short-lived, however; and it remained for the Seton-Crèvecoeur friendship to be perpetuated in another form: the dedication of the *Letters of an American Farmer.*[99]

However the failure of the packet project may have disappointed the French, William Seton was at no loss for business interests during the critical period. He seems not to have joined the revived Chamber of Commerce,[aa] but he became in 1784 the cashier of the newly organized Bank of New York.[100] This institution was the culmination of several separate movements toward the establishment of a state bank. Although its critics accused it of being Tory, it is fairly safe to assert that no single faction dominated the bank in 1784. Such notables as Alexander Hamilton, Isaac Roosevelt, Joshua Waddington, and John Vanderbilt were on the board of directors chosen on 15 March 1784. Hamilton wrote the bank's constitution.[101] Seton was sent to Philadelphia to get what banking information he could from the Bank of North America, since few of the newly-elected officers knew much about banking practices. On Wednesday, 9 June 1784, the bank formally began to do business at its first location in the Walton House[bb] at 67 St. George's Square.

Of Seton's appointment as cashier Henry Domett wrote:

He was especially fitted for the office...by his sterling business qualifications, his diligent, precise, and methodical habits, and by an amiability and courtesy which made him very popular. His appointment as an officer of the bank with General (Alexander) McDougal, the early leader of the Sons of Liberty, shows the esteem in which Mr. Seton was held by the liberal party at the close of the war.[102]

Brissot de Warville, in his *New Travels Performed in 1788,* commented:

The Bank of New York enjoys a good reputation; it is well-administered. Its cashier is Mr. William Seton, to whom M. de Crèvecoeur has addressed his letters; and what will give

---

[aa] The Chamber of Commerce was organized in 1768 at Fraunces Tavern. William Seton was an active member from 1768-1781. When the Chamber was rechartered in 1784 only four members and the President were Tories. Soon after this six other loyalists were admitted; but it was not until 1787 that old grudges were sufficiently forgotten to allow the passage of a motion to readmit all old members who were citizens of the state. This may partially explain Seton's failure to belong after 1784.

[bb] The Walton House in lower Manhattan at 828 Pearl (formerly 68 Queens) Street was built by William Walton in 1757. A Walton daughter married into the Roosevelt family. Isaac Roosevelt was the president of the Bank of New York in 1784.

you a good idea of his integrity is that he was chosen to an important place notwithstanding his known attachment to the English cause.[103]

Although the bank was kept without a charter until 1791, because of the public fear of monied institutions, it loaned money to the state and federal governments, as well as to private enterprise. It furnished the funds for the remodeling of the city hall according to Major Pierre L'Enfant's plan, when the city became the nation's capital, and in 1790 it became the agent for the United States for the sale of 200,000 guilders.[104] William Seton remained as cashier for the first ten years of the bank's history, and was undoubtedly instrumental in securing the appointments of Charles Wilkes as teller and William Magee Seton as clerk of discount.[105] After Alexander Hamilton was made Secretary of the Treasury, the elder Seton became involved in Hamilton's financial plans for the federal government.[106] When the capital removed to Philadelphia Seton was one of Hamilton's chief informants on money conditions in New York. Because of his connections with the state institution, Hamilton opposed the establishment of a branch of the Bank of the United States. When, over his protest, such a branch was opened in 1792, Hamilton encouraged co-operation between the two financial agencies, and Mr. Seton and his directors were "far from backward" in calling upon the Secretary of the Treasury for aid or leniency when they found the competition of the Bank of the United States hard to meet, or treasury drafts coming at inconvenient times.[107]

It was through Hamilton that Seton became interested in S.U.M., or the Society for Establishing Useful Manufactures, which was New Jersey's first corporation. When William Pearce came from England to work with Thomas Marshall on the project of erecting mills on the Arkwright plan,[cc] Pearce bore letters to the President, to Jefferson, and to Seton. It was Seton who, on Jefferson's reassurance of repayment, furnished the passage money and sent Pearce on his way to Hamilton. Once more the designing major, Charles Pierre L'Enfant, was called into service, and at Passaic, New Jersey, laid out plans for the most pretentious business scheme of the decade.[108]

In 1794 William Seton resigned as cashier of the bank at the annual June meeting, and he saw his good friend Charles Wilkes replace him. The reason for this resignation probably had its roots in the appearance for the first time, in that same year, of the firm, Seton, Maitland, & Company of

---

[cc] Richard Arkwright developed the first successful water powered cotton spinning mill at Cromford in Derbyshire, England, in 1771. His system pioneered the dominance of machinery, factory, and mill as a work ethic over skill-based, family-driven, common work. This achievement provided the true blueprint for factory production which was replicated in the United States and elsewhere.

61 Stone Street.[109] The elder Seton was a man with a great sense of family solidarity. Although his family trait became in later generations something of an obsession, with William Seton it expressed itself in concern for the economic welfare of his children. He used to say, "Let all come to my strong box while I am alive, and when I am gone you will take care of each other."[110] Years after the elder Seton's death, Elizabeth Bayley Seton recounted his generosity and told her son, another William Seton, of his grandfather, "who was incessantly employing himself to procure ease and convenience for others, never in his bed after day light or in it till night, and so indifferent to every ease or indulgence for himself."[111] The marriages of his two eldest sons may have influenced Seton's resignation from the bank, and his subsequent concentration on the mercantile pursuits of the family. James Seton, the second son, married Mary Gillon Hoffman in March 1792, and brought his bride to his father's house; William Magee followed this pattern in January 1794. The reorganized firm and enlarged family, was found at 61 Stone Street although the Seton property ran through to Mill Street and the counting house of Seton, Maitland & Company was listed at 38 Mill Street after 1795.[112] It was at Mill Street that the firm offered for sale such luxury items as: "marble chimney pieces superby (sic) wrought," fine wines from France and Italy, damasks from the East, "Florence oil," and raisins.[113]

The young man in whom Elizabeth Bayley became interested after her return from New Rochelle had been thoroughly prepared to share in his father's business affairs. William Magee Seton had been educated in England for six years,[114] and he had served briefly in the Bank of New York. In 1788 his father had sent him abroad to visit the various counting houses and ports of importance on the continent. From Barcelona and Madrid he went to Genoa, Leghorn, and Rome. At Leghorn he "received much attention" because of his friendship with Philip Filicchi. He went frequently to the opera and met many "handsome" ladies, but none who appealed to American taste. He wrote home that marriages abroad were always made for fortune and never for love.[115] At Cremona, young Seton purchased a violin and brought home to New York what was probably the first genuine Stradivarius in the city.[116] Love for music was one of the things he found in common with Elizabeth Bayley when he met her.

Some time in 1791 young Seton met Elizabeth Bayley. It was not a case of love at first sight; instead, Seton told his brother:

It is currently reported and generally believed that I am to be married to Miss Bayley[dd] but I shall think twice before I commit myself in any direction. Though I must confess I admire her mental accomplishments very much, and were I inclined to matrimony [it is] not at all impossible but what I might fall in love with her; and I have no doubt she will make an excellent wife and happy the man who gets her.[117]

But as time went on Seton's passionate appraisal of women became something warmer, and Elizabeth Bayley was courted in the approved eighteenth-century style. Her billets-doux to young Seton were concerned with meetings at the homes of mutual friends. About her evening visit to Mrs. Wilkes, Elizabeth wrote that William Magee "may have the honor of seeing me."[118] Likewise the evening that Mrs. Sadler did not attend a concert Elizabeth informed him that she "wishes very much to see *us* there this Evening" but warned him "do not be too late."[119] Once when "an unavoidable something" obliged Mrs. Sadler to cancel a tea party, plans were hastily rearranged and Miss Bayley wrote archly, "If you are *anxious* to see your Eliza, you will find her at Mrs. Atkinsons, at the piano."[120] Again, when a stye might have deterred a more reluctant beauty, she wrote with all the imperiousness of certainty:

Your Eliza's eye is very ugly but not very painful, but it will prevent the possibility of my going out—therefore you must devote a great deal of your time to me—Come as early as possible. We shall dine at one today as Post is going out of town.[121]

Elizabeth Ann Bayley, Miniature exchanged on Wedding Day.

It was not long before William Seton tried to seek out Dr. Bayley to ask the important question. He was not at first successful in catching the busy doctor, and Elizabeth wrote:

My Father dined with us and has gone I don't know where—I do not think you will meet him until evening. Your apology is already made by one who is most earnestly interested in his

William Magee Seton, Miniature exchanged on Wedding Day.

[dd] [It is not known why the 1976 edition of this work substituted Mary Hoffman instead of Elizabeth Bayley whose name clearly appears in the source Melville cited in the first edition (1951) of this work. The change is inexplicable. Although the original letter from which Robert Seton quoted is no longer available for consultation, in this edition the paragraph names Elizabeth Bayley as did Robert Seton. Ed.]

good opinion of you—*Your E.* will be on Wall Street by five o'clock and you shall then know more on the subject.[122]

But love will be served, and the New York *Weekly Museum* of 1 February 1794, announced that on Sunday evening last were married "by the Rev. Bishop Provoost, Mr. William M. Seton to Miss Eliza Anne Bailey[sic]—both of this city."[ee] The Seton family Bible was a trifle more detailed and recorded:

> William Magee Seton, on 25th Jan. 1794, by Rev. Bishop [Samuel] Provoost, in John Street, to E. A. Bayley aged 19 years and five months, daughter of Richard Bayley, M.D. of New York.[123]

[ee] It would appear that the ceremony was performed at the Post home, since Dr. Bayley in 1794 was listed at 46 Broadway. At no time did the Bayleys live on John Street. The name Bayley was frequently spelled "Bailey" during this period.

CHAPTER 1. THE BAYLEYS AND SETONS OF NEW YORK
Notes

[1] [See Appendix A. Bayley-Seton Genealogy. Ed.]

[2] A thorough search was made by the late Charles L. Souvay, C.M. *Catholic Historical Review,* V (July–October, 1919), 231.

[3] J. J. Clute, *The Annals of Staten Island from its Discovery to the Present Time* (New York, 1877), 264; *The Correspondence of John Henry Hobart* (New York, 1912), III, 515-7.

[4] For further identification of William Bayley, see Sister M. Hildegarde Yeager, C.S.C, *The Life of James Roosevelt Bayley, First Bishop of Newark and Eighth Archbishop of Baltimore, 1814–1877* (Washington, 1947), 1-2.

[5] Robert Seton, *An Old Family* (New York: Bretano's, 1899), 277. Seton states "The church records and registers were burnt during the Revolution, hence the uncertainty of the date."

[6] "Record of the Bayley Family in America," Archives of the University of Notre Dame, Notre Dame, Indiana. Hereinafter cited as UNDA. This typed manuscript was prepared by Robert Seton, the grandson of Elizabeth Bayley Seton.

[7] James J. Walsh, *History of Medicine in New York* (New York, 1919), I, 56.

[8] James Grant Wilson, *Memorial History of the City of New York* (New York, 1893), III, 101.

[9] Catherine Charlton Bayley did not accompany her husband to England. James Thacher, *American Medical Biography* (Boston, 1828), I, 157.

[10] Walsh, I, 54.

[11] Henry R. Viets, "Richard Bayley," *Dictionary of American Biography* (New York, 1929), II, 74-5. Bayley's views on croup were expressed in a letter to Hunter in 1781, and were published in Richter's *Surgical Repository.* Michaelis gave way to Bayley's ideas. Howard A. Kelly and Walter Burrage, *Dictionary of American Medicine, Biography* (New York, 1920), 51.

[12] Ibid.

[13] *Names of Persons for whom Marriage Licenses were Issued by the Secretary of the Province of New York Previous to 1784* (Albany, 1860), 21. This record shows no license taken by Bayley for his previous marriage in 1767, although William Seton's license to marry Rebecca Curson that same year appears in good order on p. 346.

[14] Walsh, I, 53, reprints this advertisement. See Arthur Burns, "New Light on Mother Seton," *Historical Records and Studies* of the United States Catholic Historical Society, XXII (1932), 98. If there was

any connection between Dorchester and Bayley, it was probably unofficial.

[15] Lorenzo Sabine, *The American Loyalists* (Boston, 1847), devotes one half page to Bayley and gives Seton two lines.

[16] Oscar Barck, "The Occupation of New York City by the British," *History of the State of New York* (New York, 1933), IV, 39-43.

[17] Ibid., 43.

[18] New York Historical Society, William Smith Papers, VI, Diary, 4 October 1779.

[19] 10.4, "Dear Remembrances," Regina Bechtle, S.C., and Judith Metz, S.C., eds., Ellin M. Kelly, mss. ed., *Elizabeth Bayley Seton Collected Writings*, 3 vols. (New City Press: New York, 2000-2006). Hereafter cited as *CW*, 3a:510. This notebook was compiled in later life by Elizabeth Seton to record the outstanding events of her life as she recalled them.

[20] Ibid.

[21] 10.4, "Dear Remembrances," *CW*, 3a:510.

[22] Ibid.

[23] The incident of John Jacob Van Arsdale's climb up the flag pole to substitute the Stars and Stripes for the British colors is told in the New York *Times,* 26 November 1934, and Rodman Gilder, *The Battery* (Boston, 1936), 102-3. For a list of sources for the evacuation of the city, see Irving Pomerantz, *New York, an American City, 1783–1803* (New York, 1938), 16, n. 4.

[24] T.E.V. Smith, *The City of New York in the Year of Washington's Inauguration, 1789* (New York, 1889), 69 ff.; Evarts B. Greene, *The Revolutionary Generation, 1763–1790* (New York, 1943), 286. Pomerantz, 299-300.

[25] W. W. Pasko, *Old New York* (New York, 1889), I, 373.

[26] Gilder, 121-2. Willet was robbed of over £500. He fired upon some suspects, but his aim was poor and the ruffians seized him, beat him, and made off.

[27] Livingston to Washington, 9 April 1783. Livingston Papers, Bancroft Transcripts, II, in the New York Public Library.

[28] New York Historical Society, Duer Correspondence, William Steele to William Duer, 6 March 1788.

[29] E. Wilder Spaulding, *New York in the Critical Period, 1783–1789* (New York, 1932), 13.

[30] George W. Edwards, *New York as an Eighteenth Century Municipality, 1731—1776* (New York, 1917), 57-8.

[31] Barck, 156-7. Fine old prints depicting these two chapels are reproduced in Henry C. Brown, *Old New York* (New York, 1917), 139, 183.

[32] Ibid., 162.

[33] Frank Monaghan, "The Results of the Revolution," *The History of the State of New York* (New York, 1933), IV, 346.

[34] Spaulding, 33.

[35] Pomerantz, 374. Benjamin Moore succeeded Provoost in 1801 and served actively until incapacitated by paralysis in 1811.

[36] Wilson, III, 19, 54.

[37] New York *Weekly Museum,* 1 February 1794. The wedding took place on Sunday evening.

[38] Pomerantz, 77.

[39] Alexander C. Flick, "The Loyalists," *History of the State of New York,* III, 356-7. Probably one-third of the city's population in 1784 was composed of former Tories.

[40] Pomerantz, 81.

[41] Francis R. Packard, *History of Medicine in the United States* (New York, 1931), I, 236.

[42] Edwards, 101. The name "The Society of the New York Hospital," was adopted in 1810, but the institution has always been popularly called the New York Hospital.

[43] J. P. Brissot de Warville, *New Travels in the United States of America Performed in 1788* (Dublin, 1792), 161.

[44] *New York, a Metropolitan City of America* (New York, 1853), 157-160. The author of this book signs himself simply, "A New Yorker." W.J. Bell, Jr., "Doctors' Riot, New York 1788," *Bulletin New York Academy of Medicine, December 1971,* 47 (12):1501-03.

[45] 10.4, "Dear Remembrances," *CW,* 3a:511.

[46] Joel T. Headly, *Great Riots of New York* (New York, 1873), 56-65; Walsh, II, 378-84; Pomerantz, 401-2. Some of the best press accounts on the riot are to be found in the New York letters to Philadelphia and Boston. See also, *CW,* 3a:511, n.7 for a discussion of the Doctors' Riot of 1788 and ibid., 1:425, n.7, regarding the Highbinders' Riot of 1806.

[47] Cited in Walsh, II, 382.

[48] Packard, I, 236.

[49] Surrogate's Court, New York City, Liber 43, 490. This will may be found in the *Historical Records and Studies,* XXII, (1932), 97.

[50] Mary Bayley Post to Elizabeth Seton, New York, 12 June 1815, Daughters of Charity Archives, Saint Joseph's Provincial House, Emmitsburg, Maryland, ASJPH 1-3-3-11:21. Hereafter cited as ASJPH.

[51] 2.7 Journal to Rebecca Seton, entry of 1 December 1803, *CW,* 1:264. The context indicates New Rochelle. Elizabeth mentions being in New Rochelle in 1788. She and her sister remained there with Bayley relatives until 1790. 10.4 "Dear Remembrances," *CW,* 3a:511.

[52] Mary Bayley Post to Elizabeth Seton, New York, 1 August [1808], ASJPH 1-3-3-11:3.

[53] The best study of New York City during this period is that of Sidney I. Pomerantz, *New York, An American City, 1783-1803*, 338-355; 395-416 are devoted to health problems.

[54] Smith, 9.

[55] Edwards, 169-170.

[56] Brissot de Warville, 346-7.

[57] Ibid., 347.

[58] The will of Jacobus Roosevelt, probated 5 June 1776, is reprinted in Pasko, I, 365.

[59] Wilson, III, 141.

[60] Pomerantz, 340-342; Edwards, 100.

[61] Walsh, I, 59-60.

[62] "Dr. Anderson's Diary" gives an account of Bellevue in the plague of 1795. Pasko, II, 217-226; 284-301.

[63] This report was published in 1796 by T. J. Swords, printers to the Faculty of Physic of Columbia University.

[64] *Medical Repository and Review* (New York, 1801), I, 119.

[65] New York Historical Society, John Jay Papers, II, 9, Bayley to Jay, New York, 28 November 1796. Bayley did not believe yellow fever was brought in from outside but was fostered by conditions within the city.

[66] 1.10, Elizabeth Seton to Dr. Richard Bayley, New York, 13 February 1797, *CW*, 1:14.

[67] Dr. Richard Bayley to Van Rensselaer, Esqr., New York, 19 March 1800, ASJPH 1-3-3-9:101.

[68] Dr. Richard Bayley to Elizabeth Seton, New York, [1798], ASJPH 1-3-3-9:100.

[69] 1.41, Elizabeth Seton to Julia Scott, New York, 15 March 1799, *CW*, 1:65. The lazaretto was located at Tompkinsville on the island. In 1800 two smaller buildings were added to receive yellow fever patients.

[70] Mary Bayley Post to Elizabeth Seton, New York, 1 August [1808], ASJPH 1-3-3-11:3.

[71] 2.7, Elizabeth Seton to Rebecca Seton, entry of 1 December 1803, *CW*, 1:264.

[72] 10.4, "Dear Remembrances," *CW*, 3a:511.

[73] Ibid., *CW*, 3a:512.

[74] 2.7, Elizabeth Seton to Rebecca Seton, entry of 1 December 1803, *CW*, 1:264.

[75] 10.4, "Dear Remembrances," *CW*, 3a:512.

[76] 10.4, "Dear Remembrances," *CW*, 3a:513. There is no doubt that Elizabeth Bayley suffered deeply at this time. 6.71, Writing to Henry Seton on 19 February 1811, in reply to his question whether it was a crime

to lament that his life was saved from shipwreck, Elizabeth Bayley Seton recalled "the moment twenty years ago in which I asked myself the same question, dictated by that anguish of soul which can find no relief," *CW*, 2:175. Emotions recollected after twenty years were probably extremely vivid when originally felt.

[77] Martha J. Lamb, *History of the City of New York* (New York, 1877), II, 440.

[78] 10.3, "Catherine Seton's Little Red Book," *CW*, 3a:492.

[79] Brissot de Warville, 352.

[80] Dr. Richard Bayley to Elizabeth Seton, n.p., Tuesday morning in June, ASJPH 1-3-3-9:105.

[81] Dr. Richard Bayley to Elizabeth Seton, n.p., n.d., ASJPH 1-3-3-9:97.

[82] Dr. Richard Bayley to Elizabeth Seton, n.p., n.d., ASJPH 1-3-3-9:107.

[83] 1.171, Elizabeth Seton to Anna Maria Seton, [1803], *CW*, 1:219.

[84] Dr. Richard Bayley to Elizabeth Seton, New York, 29 May 1793, ASJPH 1-3-3-9:92.

[85] Robert Seton, *An Old Family,* 255. Another Seton genealogy, George Seton's *A History of the Family of Seton during Eight Centuries* (Edinburgh, 1896), has a very faulty account of the American branch of the family and is of little use in this connection. E. B. O'Callaghan, *Calendar of Historical Manuscripts in the Office of the Secretary of State* (Albany, 1866), LXXXVIII, 5 March 1760, shows that a William Seton, merchant of New York, owner of a sloop *Orleans* petitioned for a commission for one, Joseph Dagget, to command the vessel. This would suggest that Seton came to America earlier than 1763.

[86] See J. Franklin Jameson, "St. Eustatius and the American Revolution," *American Historical Review,* VIII (July, 1903), 683-708.

[87] Robert Seton, *Memoir, Letters and Journal*, I, 32. The other children were James, John Curson, Henry and Anna Maria. See Genealogy, The Seton Line, *CW*, 2:*xxvii*.

[88] Ibid.

[89] Elliott replaced Robertson as governor in 1783. See Barck in the *History of the State of New York,* IV, 45.

[90] *Report on American Manuscripts in the Royal Institution of Great Britain* (Hereford, 1907), IV, 457-58. John A. Stevens, *Colonial Records of the New York Chamber of Commerce, 1768-1784* (New York, 1867), 161-163. The biography of Seton contained in these pages was based on facts furnished by his son, Samuel Waddington Seton. The letter of Elliott to Carleton is cited in Barck, 252.

[91] Robert E. East, *Business Enterprise in the American Revolutionary Era* (New York, 1939), 184.

[92] James Robertson replaced Tryon as civilian governor in 1780. Andrew Elliott succeeded Robertson in 1783. Gilder, 94-100.

[93] Robert Seton, *An Old Family,* 261. The Archives of the University of Notre Dame, Indiana, possess transcripts made by Robert Seton of excerpts of letters from William Seton's mother in England, to William Seton in New York, from 2 September 1779 to May 1797. These excerpts prove that both John and Charles Wilkes were given assistance by Seton. A letter of 4 December 1780 contains the reference to the gratitude of Charles Wilkes. An original letter of Elizabeth Seton of Chiswick to William Seton of New York, dated October 1780 is preserved in the Archives of the Sisters of Charity of New York, Mount St. Vincent. Hereafter cited as AMSV.

[94] East, 222.

[95] Flick, *Loyalism in New York During the American Revolution* (New York, 1901), 165-166.

[96] East, 223, 230.

[97] Robert G. Albion, "The Port of New York," *The History of the State of New York,* VIII, 170.

[98] St. John de Crèvecoeur, *Sketches of Eighteenth Century America,* edited by Henri L. Bourdin, Ralph Gabriel, and Stanley Williams (New Haven, 1925), 11.

[99] Ludwig Lewisohn, in the introduction to Crèvecoeur's *Letters from an American Farmer* (New York, 1925), x-xiv, clarifies the subject of Crèvecoeur's dedications. The first edition of the *Letters,* printed in London in 1782, was dedicated to Abbé Raynal. A second English edition was printed in Philadelphia in 1793 by Matthew Carey. In the interim, Crèvecoeur had "translated" the letters into French in 1784 and dedicated this edition to William Seton, Esquire. This French edition was republished again in 1787.

[100] See J. A. Stevens, *Colonial Records of the New York Chamber of Commerce* (New York, 1867), 303, 161-3.

[101] Henry Williams Domett, *A History of the Bank of New York, 1784-1884* (Cambridge, 1884), 1-11.

[102] Ibid., 17.

[103] Brissot de Warville, 171.

[104] Domett, 39; Pomerantz, 234-5.

[105] *Directory of the City of New York, 1786.*

[106] During the crisis of 1791-1792 the Bank of New York made purchases on Hamilton's orders of small lots of 6% issues to provide the temporary relief the market desperately needed. See Joseph S. Davis, *Essays in the Earlier History of American Corporations* (Cambridge, 1917), 297-311.

[107] Ibid., 421.

[108] Ibid., 401.

[109] *New York City Directory and Register, 1791.*

[110] 7.69, Elizabeth Seton to William Seton, *CW,* 2:459. Copy. The original is at AMSV.

[111] 6.194, Elizabeth Seton to William Seton, 17 June 1815, *CW,* 2:314.

[112] "Seton and Company, Merchants" was located at Number 12, Hanover Square prior to the enlargement of the firm. See *New York City Directories, 1787-1793.*

[113] *Commercial Advertiser,* 1 October 1797.

[114] Robert Seton, *An Old Family,* 274-5.

[115] William Magee Seton to William Seton, Leghorn, 28 December 1788, Daughters of Charity Archives Marillac Provincialate, St. Louis, Missouri, #446-451. Hereafter cited as AMP.

[116] Robert Seton, *An Old Family,* 275.

[117] Robert Seton, *Memoir, Letters and Journal,* I, 13.

[118] 1.1, Elizabeth Ann Bayley to William Magee Seton, n.d., *CW,* 1:2.

[119] 1.3, Elizabeth Ann Bayley to William Magee Seton, n.d., *CW,* 1:3.

[120] 1.5, Elizabeth Ann Bayley to William Magee Seton, n.d., *CW,* 1:4.

[121] 1.4, Elizabeth Ann Bayley to William Magee Seton, *CW,* 1:3. "Post" was Dr. Wright Post. Eliza Bayley was living with her sister, Mary Bayley Post, at 18 John Street.

[122] 1.6, Elizabeth Ann Bayley to William Magee Seton, n.p., n.d., *CW,* 1:4.

[123] Robert Seton, *Memoir, Letters and Journal,* I, 14. See *Directories of City of New York, 1786-1801.*

☙

CHAPTER 2

৩৯৯

MANHATTAN MATRON

William Magee Seton brought his young bride to his father's house on Stone Street that January 1794. He was very proud of the ease with which she charmed his father, brothers, and sisters. The elder Seton quickly came to admire and respect his first son's wife. To her he confided many of the details of his own career. He showed her family letters which he treasured, with the words:

The Shrine of St. Elizabeth Ann Seton on site of former Seton residence, New York City.

You are the first of my children to whom I have submitted a perusal of them, and I request you will return them to me unsullied by the eye of impertinent curiosity. Let no one look at them. The parental affection I ever felt for my dear William, your husband, you will find strongly marked in every letter. This will give you pleasure, but when I add that this affection has increased ever since, I think every page where I mention him will be doubly dear to you. That you may long, very long enjoy every blessing together is the sincere prayer of your affectionate and fond father.[1]

When the young couple moved to a home of their own the bond was in no way weakened. The spring of 1796 which took them to Philadelphia, on a trip combining business and pleasure, left the older Seton impatient for their return; and he wrote Elizabeth the news of the city, but demanded to know the exact hour of their expected return. "No heart," he said, "will rejoice to see you both more."[2] Elizabeth, for her part, was equally fond of her father-in-law. Often in later years she used his example to inspire her sons, and she once wrote to a younger William:[a]

---

[a] William M. Seton (25 November 1796–14 January 1868) is believed to have been named after his father, William Magee. Extant documents bear the younger Seton's signature as "William M. Seton." William took Vincent for his confirmation name and later sailed with the United States Navy. Married to Emily Prime (1832), the couple had nine children. William died in his seventy-second year and is buried in the original cemetery at Mount Saint Mary's University near Emmitsburg.

33

It is necessary to have seen him in the several situations of Husband, Father, Friend, Protector, to form any just idea of the perfections of his character; which bright example impress indelibly on your mind. You bear his name—and I pray to Heaven with all the fervor of a Mother's hopes that you will preserve it unblemished and yield it to the author of your being as spotless as he did.[3]

The first years of marriage were for Elizabeth Seton blessed in many ways. Her husband had married for love, and not for fortune, and he cherished his lively little wife with all the devotion at his command. When he had to leave her, to go on the firm's business to Newark, Trenton, and Philadelphia, he wrote daily letters home, urging her to spend whatever she liked, but pleading, "Be as much at my Father's as you can."[4] He was delighted to find a picture of her tucked away in his shaving case, and he proudly displayed it to his friends. His "darling theme" on all occasions was his beautiful little wife at home in New York.[5] One year he took Elizabeth and their infant daughter, Anna Maria,[b] with him as far as Philadelphia, where his wife preferred to remain with friends while William went on to Delaware. From the capital city of Delaware now located at Dover, he wrote her of his sister's[c] disappointment that Elizabeth and the baby had not come all the way.[6]

Elizabeth's love matched his own, and she took to the pen with even greater ease during their brief separations by addressing many an ardent missive to "my dearest treasure." She confessed, however, to William, "your picture is so melancholy that I don't love to look at it in your absence." Some nights she could not fall asleep until three o'clock, and would take her Bible and read until sleep came.[7] Her love from the very beginning was tinctured with sadness, for her husband's health was uncertain. William Magee Seton must have contracted tuberculosis as a very young man. His letters from Europe in 1788 and 1789 contain frequent references to "pain in the breast," and Elizabeth was aware from the start that her husband was subject to these pains. The worry had a sobering effect on her enthusiastic disposition, and

---

[b] Anna Maria Seton (3 May 1795–12 March 1812) was named after her paternal aunt and step-grandmother. Her mother usually referred to her as Anna but after their return from Italy in 1804, she was often called by the affectionate name of Annina (Little Anna). On her deathbed Sister Annina made vows as a Sister of Charity and died at age sixteen. She is buried in St. Joseph's Cemetery, original graveyard of the Sisters of Charity at Emmitsburg.

[c] The sister was Anna Maria Seton Vining, wife of Senator John Vining, who lived at "The Oakes," near Dover, Delaware.

she matured very rapidly in those early months of marriage. She wrote to Eliza Sadler[d] in Paris:

> I have learned to commune with my own Heart, and I try to govern it by reflection, and yet that Heart grows every day more tender and softened, which in great measure I attribute to the state of my William's health. That health on which my every Hope of Happiness depends, and which continues me either [in] the most perfect *Human* felicity, or sinks me in the lowest depths of sorrow.[8]

Marriage was for Elizabeth Seton a continual growth as well as a constant lesson in self-denial. As her husband's responsibilities grew heavier, she tried to put aside her own wishes. She told Julia Scott,[e] her friend from girlhood, that all considerations must "yield to Affection for my Will, and when I consider his vexations and cares I bless my God who allows me to share and lessen them."[9] When yellow fever threatened the city in 1798 Elizabeth refused to leave because "Poor Seton is chained," as she explained it to Julia, "and where he is, there am I also."[10] The neighborhood was deserted, only three doors away death had come to one victim in the streets. Her father, Dr. Bayley, was spending every hour in the hospital and lazaretto. But while her loved ones were "so much exposed" Elizabeth Seton infinitely preferred remaining near them.[11]

Next to the deep love which existed between the two young Setons, the greatest joy Elizabeth found in the early months of marriage was derived from having a home of her own. After the bitter years of insecurity immediately preceding her wedding, the young bride found the prospect of the house on Wall Street too good to be true. Years later, looking back at that fall in 1794, Elizabeth Seton recorded in her "Dear Remembrances:"[f]

> My own home at 20—the world—that and heaven too, quite impossible! Every moment clouded with that fear, "My God, if I enjoy this I lose you"—yet no true thought of Whom

---

[d] Eliza Sadler was the wife of Henry Sadler, merchant, and was one of Elizabeth Seton's closest friends throughout her life. Mrs. Sadler was in Paris in 1796 but after her return, the Sadler residence was at Courtlandt Street. The name is sometimes spelled "Saidler."

[e] Julia Sitgreaves had been Julia Sitgreaves before her marriage. Her brother, Samuel Sitgreaves, was a member of the House of Representatives from Pennsylvania in the fourth and fifth sessions of Congress. As Mrs. Lewis A. Scott, Julia had lived several years in New York City. Lewis Allaire Scott, son of John Morin Scott, was Secretary of State of New York in 1791. Elizabeth Bayley had known her. At the time this letter was written Mrs. Scott was a widow and lived in Philadelphia with her sister, Mrs. James Cox.

[f] This retrospective memoir is found in a little volume which was a note book started for Anna Maria Seton, but after her daughter's death Mrs. Seton used the pages to record the highlights of her own life. These last pages are commonly called "Dear Remembrances."

I would lose, rather fear of hell and [being] shut out from heaven.[12]

The Wall Street of the 1790's was a far cry from the Wall Street of today. Just prior to the Revolution the street had begun to give way to splendid private residences; the Verplanck mansion replaced the old Bayard sugar refinery, to cite one instance. The revival of Wall Street was considered one of the wonders of the postwar period. The trees which had been cut down for fuel during the cruel winter of 1788 were being replaced. The walls of the new Trinity Church rose after 1790 to grace the upper end of the street. The beauty of the remodeled city hall made the center of Wall Street the focal point of all civic and official life; while Tontine Coffee House, near Coffee Slip, made a faint prediction of the street's future.

Although she lived there only four years, 27 Wall Street was the scene of many happy events in the life of Elizabeth Seton.[g] It was here that her first daughter, Anna Maria, was born on 3 May 1795; and news of the event quickly reached Philadelphia where Julia and her sister, Charlotte, enjoyed every word of William Seton's proud announcement, "even the parent's impartial account" of the little girl's attractions.[13] The little world contained within its walls quite subdued the former "reigning passion" Elizabeth had had "to see the world and Europeans in particular." The sight of William playing "Rosy Dimpled Boy," "Pauvre Madelon," "Return Enraptured Hours," and "Carmignol," all as fast as the violin could sound them in succession, coupled with the knowledge that a certain pair of eyes, "much nearer black than any other color," were shut fast in sleep, in a room near by, brought deep contentment to her heart. Elizabeth concluded a letter to Eliza Sadler with the homely words, "My husband begins to gap, the clock strikes ten, and my fingers are cold."[14]

Three children were born in the house on Wall Street. After Anna Maria came William Seton, who was born on 25 November 1796. This first son held a place in Elizabeth's heart that could never be usurped. His every illness filled her with terror and after one such crisis in his first year, she wrote to "Sad," her friend Eliza Sadler:

My Father thought he could not recover. Could I speak
to you in the language of my feelings? Should I attempt
to express what passed in my Heart in any moment of
that time while his recovery was uncertain, you would

[g] *The New York City Directory, 1795*, gives the address as "17 Wall," but this was the same house as that listed as 27 Wall Street in the directories of 1796, 1797, and 1798. After the Setons returned to Stone Street in 1798 the Wall Street house was occupied for a few years by the Wright Posts. There is no evidence to show whether the Setons ever owned this house or not.

lament that Heaven had allowed me the privilege of being a Mother. For what is there in the uncertainty of human happiness to repay the agonizing convulsion of those twenty-four hours in which I witnessed his sufferings?[15]

About the same time little Anna was beginning to show signs of the Bayley disposition and Elizabeth said ruefully that Anna Maria "possesses from her Mother a most ungovernable temper." William Magee, her husband, left all discipline to the child's mother; Dr. Bayley recommended conquest through gentleness, while Dr. Post and Mary suggested whipping. This last seemed to Elizabeth "an unnatural resource" and the last she would resort to.[16] Fortunately Mrs. Seton could share her worries with her sister Mary. The summer of 1797 found them escaping from the city's heat to a house on the East River, opposite the Battery and facing Governors Island. The pleasure the wives took in receiving their husbands together in the evening, and the companionship and protection they shared during the day while the men were away, counterbalanced any inconvenience that "a union of families always occasions."[17] The crises of the summer passed and the proud mother sat down to practice writing a letter to her husband's grandmother in England, asserting that "never were there two sweeter children" than little William and Anna Maria, "our heart's delight and already our companion."[18]

The third child born at Wall Street was Richard Bayley Seton,[h] whose arrival on 20 July 1798 nearly cost his mother her life. The young Setons had undergone a severe blow earlier that summer in the death of their beloved father, the elder William Seton. Mr. Seton had suffered a bad fall on the ice while escorting a guest to his carriage the previous winter. By June it was quite obvious that the older man was seriously ill, and all thoughts of leaving the city must be abandoned. The news of Seton's illness even reached Germany, and Eliza Sadler wrote from Hamburg of her concern, adding, "His life is so interesting to all who know or have heard of him that his health is a subject of anxious inquiry whenever Americans meet."[19]

[h] Richard Bayley Seton (20 July 1798–26 June 1823) was named after his paternal grandfather. While sailing with the Navy off the coast of Liberia, Richard contracted a contagious fever from the United States consul whom he had nursed back to health there. The fever was fatal and Richard died at age twenty-five. He is buried at sea. Jehudi Ashmun was the United States representative to Liberia in 1822. Ashmun had been an agent of the American Colonization Society which promoted the settlement of blacks at Monrovia, Liberia.

Thomas Greenleaf's *New Daily Advertiser,* although erring in regard to Seton's age,[i] generally represented public opinion when it noted that "he was ranked among the most respectable citizens of the community, and has left thirteen children to lament this sad bereftment of a tender parent. The loss of this valuable citizen is universally regretted."[20] The death of this parent was a great shock to the whole family, but especially so to the eldest son, William Magee Seton, and to his wife. Of the seven youngest children only Rebecca, who was eighteen, was old enough to accept responsibility. For Elizabeth, who so dearly loved quiet and her small family, to become all at once the mother of six more children, and the head of an even larger family, was a frightening prospect. But her own dismay was overshadowed by her husband's, who found he had not only lost his closest friend, but was now faced with the responsibility of adjusting and managing the business affairs of the firm, Seton, Maitland & Company. His wife was his chief support, and for four weeks the pen was scarcely out of her hand, William Magee kept her so busy with the arrangements of family papers and business letters. As her pregnancy progressed the approach of her confinement found Elizabeth Seton "woefully fatigued, and so unwell."[21]

It was physically impossible for Elizabeth to move to the family home on Stone Street before August. Temporary arrangements were made for the bereaved Seton children in Connecticut, and at Cragdon.[j] Eliza Maitland, William Magee's sister, was spending the summer at the latter place, and took charge in the emergency. The combined burdens of work and worry resulted in the near death of Elizabeth Seton in July. Her condition was so grave that both mother and child were for some hours in a very doubtful state; and in order to save the mother the child was nearly lost. Elizabeth saw from under heavy eyelids her father, Dr. Bayley, on his knees blowing breath into the baby's inert lungs. The little boy was very appropriately named after his grandfather, who literally gave him the breath of life that day.[22] The baby's father received news of his birth at Philadelphia where he had gone on business. William Magee Seton had fully expected to be home before the event and wrote fearfully that he suspected Elizabeth was not "as well as usual." He asked her to have his sister Rebecca write at once to

---

[i] William Seton, senior, was fifty-two when he died on 9 June 1798. He was buried in Trinity churchyard, "attended by a procession, which, from its numbers and respectability spoke an eulogium as strong and sympathetic as words can easily convey." *Commercial Advertiser.* [His burial record at Trinity Church is no longer extant. *Ed.*] [The Argus, or Greenleaf's *New Daily Advertiser*, was established in 1766. John Holt was succeeded as publisher by Thomas Greenleaf in 1790 until 1810 when the paper was discontinued. *Ed.*]

[j] Cragdon was a country home which the elder William Seton had leased and furnished. The name is reminiscent of Seton roots in Scotland and is derived from the Celtic word *carraig*, a rock, and the Anglo-Saxon *Dun* or *Don*, a hill.

Brunswick[k] so that he might have news on his way home.[23] Elizabeth was, indeed, greatly weakened for the remainder of the summer, and her eyes in particular troubled her. But her spirits refused to be kept down, and she wrote happily to Julia Scott on 20 August:

> Since I last wrote to you my Julia—my Pains and Aches are all over and I have one of the loveliest Boys to repay me that my fond imagination could have formed. [He is] not a little additionally dear to me for bearing the name of Richard Bayley which softened by Seton at the end are sounds which very much delight me and are the promise of much future Hope and Comfort.[24]

After a brief trip to Bloomingdale[l]—in the last week of August, Elizabeth expected to settle down to face the problems of her enlarged family.[25]

The Seton girls,[m] William's younger sisters, were all with Elizabeth Seton during September. Elizabeth found them very little trouble and told Julia, "It is impossible to meet with more amiable dispositions."[26] Wall Street was practically deserted at this time, for the yellow fever epidemic of 1798 was spreading. Moving to Stone Street before November was out of the question, since it was in the very center of the infected area. Dr. Bayley was spending all his time caring for victims, and for a week at a time his daughter did not catch a glimpse of the busy man. Both Mary and Wright Post suffered mild attacks of fever and went to Long Island to recover. But until William succumbed Elizabeth remained courageously in the city. Her husband's illness, noticed on a week end at Cragdon, caused all her old fears to revive, and Elizabeth determined not to go back to Wall Street until cold weather removed all danger.[27]

Life at Cragdon was far from restful. There were "eighteen in the family, in a house containing only five small rooms." Wherever she turned, Elizabeth heard some small voice calling "Sister" or "Mother." She seldom had a minute to herself, what with being constant nurse to little Dick; and when he was not in her arms, the "two paddlers" were always close on her heels begging to go to the garden, the woods, or "the bread and butter closet." William was very weak, even though convalescing; while the older

---

[k] New Brunswick, New Jersey.

[l] Cragdon was located in Bloomingdale, which was then about where 78th Street, New York City, is located today. Elizabeth Seton went there in August 1798, summoned by the illness of her two older children, who had been sent there during her confinement prior to the birth of her third child. The infant Richard did not flourish under the changed conditions at Cragdon and the Setons returned to the city about 29 August.

[m] These girls were Rebecca, Mary, Charlotte, Henrietta (Harriet), and Cecilia. The boys, Samuel and Edward, attended the Cheshire Academy in Cheshire, Connecticut, where Dr. John Bowden was principal (1796-1802) of this episcopal school for boys.

girls began to catch colds as October progressed.[28] By November she was only too glad to return to New York, in spite of the trials which awaited her there.

The sight of her own home again, the cheerfulness of the blazing fire, her treasured piano answering her touch with its sweet tone, were more than she could bear with equanimity, and Elizabeth sank to her knees, crying briefly and bitterly for the past joys the room had shared. "Who," she wondered, "can help looking back on Innocent and past pleasure without sorrow, I can more forceably say without *anguish*?"[29] But it was not her way to look backward long, and she turned to the more immediate problem of preparing the house on Stone Street for fall occupancy. The house was practically empty. William Magee Seton, on the advice of his friends, and with the consent of the family, had sold most of his father's furnishings.[n] The greater part had been in use since the elder Seton's first marriage, and further, family disputes might have arisen if one son had kept the furniture.[30] Elizabeth and William had an abundance of their own at Wall Street which would be moved to the family house, after papering, painting, and whitewashing had removed all danger of fever. The energetic little Mrs. Seton attacked pantries, closets, store-rooms, and cellar like a commanding general. Soon the place was ready to receive the family from Cragdon, and life at Stone Street settled down into its winter pattern. Charlotte and Mary Seton went off to boarding school at Brunswick, New Jersey;[o] while Rebecca Seton and Elizabeth took charge of the younger children, Harriet, Cecilia, Anna Marie, and the little boys. It was Elizabeth Seton's first experiment at teaching and she enjoyed it. These three young pupils who came early under her influence were indelibly marked with her stamp. They followed her physically and spiritually, throughout their lives. All three lie buried near her grave in Maryland. But that story will be told in another chapter.

Rebecca Seton, William Seton's sister, proved a great blessing to her sister-in-law during the hectic days of readjustment in family life. Before Elizabeth knew her well, she had believed Bec to be a rather uninformed girl, possessing some good qualities, but these much neglected.[31] Now she discovered Bec to be a charming young woman of exceptional virtues. From this period on the two women, who were six years apart in age, became the closest of friends. Elizabeth Seton was irresistibly drawn to virtue and

[n] The articles, such as silver, which were not sold were valued by competent judges and divided among the children. William Seton, senior, left no will.

[o] Miss Sophia Hay, an Englishwoman, opened this school in 1798, probably in a house on Burnet Street in present day New Brunswick. The school continued until at least 1815 and was well known in its day as a "fashionable institution of learning," and drew students from prominent families in the Northeast. See Mary Demarest, "Some Early New Brunswick Schools for Girls," *New Jersey Historical Society Proceedings*," 53 (1935), 163-185.

later said of Rebecca that while she lived she taught people how to live, and at her death showed them how to die. Elizabeth in her turn exerted an enormous influence over the life of her sister-in-law. The two women were kindred spirits who shared deep spiritual bonds.

Rebecca, like William, suffered from the Seton complaint, tuberculosis, and although the disease was not understood, the frequent attacks of fever and weakness were a real source of anxiety to the family. When Bec was forced to take to her bed in the spring of 1799 Elizabeth was sorely tried. Calamities seem never to come singly in large households, and Bec's illness was accompanied by that of baby Richard's, the arrival home of Sam and Edward for the spring vacation, to be followed by the girls from New Jersey. By the middle of May every one of the thirteen children had had the "intermittent fever" except little Will.[32] But the end of May brought relief. The boys and their sisters returned to their respective schools, and this time Harriet Seton accompanied Mary and Charlotte. It was hoped that a trip southward would benefit Bec, and so in the company of young Cecilia and escorted by Jack Seton, their brother, the invalid left New York on 3 June 1799 for Delaware.[33]

Elizabeth and Rebecca missed each other during the months they were separated, and after the young mother went again to Cragdon for a change she wrote longingly to her "soul's sister":

> I never sweep the hall, or dress the flower pots, or walk around the pear tree walk, but you are as much my companion as if you were actually near me, and last evening finding myself accidentally by the garden fence at the head of the lane where we once stood at sunset last Fall anticipating what we would do this summer if Willy hired Cragdon, I was so struck with the recollection and the uncertainty of when I should see you again, that I had a hearty crying spell, which is not a very common thing for me.[34]

It was, perhaps, one of the penalties of her ardent nature that caused Elizabeth Seton, surrounded by so many, to reach out in longing for the others who were gone. She once wrote to Julia Scott, "Surely the next blessing in our future existence to that of being near the Source of Perfection will be the enjoyment of each other's Society without dread of interruption from evil."[35] Rebecca, for her part, was as eager to be with Elizabeth, and she wrote in July, "The idea of my spending the winter away from you makes me miserable."[36]

Nevertheless, the winter months found Bec still away and the mails between New York and Dover were kept busy. Elizabeth reported all the happenings, the progress of the children, her husband's attacks of "fever," and vacation problems of the older children. She described Bec's rosy "Ricksy" who shut his little eyes when the wind blew in his face and "laughs as he used to when you blew at him."[37] She related the details of the sewing session in which bolts of dimity, flannel, and calico were transformed into wardrobes for Mary and her sisters. She reported the rebellion of the young ladies when Elizabeth insisted on head coverings for evening, and the compromise for "muslin of finer quality" in the place of the objectionable jackonet kerchiefs. She added wryly:

> I mention this particularly to you as you may also have another account of it from those who thought it "foolish to muffle girls like old women." Well, I think we are all muffled now and shall not be puzzled to follow the fashion![38]

When Bec got these amusing accounts, and heard from her sisters in Brunswick who wrote "in ecstasy of the happy hours at home," she longed the more to return. But winter weather was too severe for traveling and she contented herself with such queries as "What are your plans for New Year's Day? Do you all dine together as usual?"[39] Not until the following May did the two friends meet again.

Although her family's demands upon her time were unusually heavy, Elizabeth Seton had many other interests as well. The Seton household was never without servants and conveyances, so that the young matron could indulge in civic and social affairs while the Seton fortunes flourished. Although in later life she wrote[p] that she turned "with abhorrence only at a remembrance of the effect the frequentation of the theatre had on my passions, and the extravagant ideas I imbibed in it." Elizabeth Seton as a young married woman "shared the pleasures of her associates in attending the performances of the day."[40] The old John Street Theatre had been the only theatre until the Park Theatre opened in 1798. After this time theatre going became increasingly popular.[41] Elizabeth sometimes went with her sister, Mary Post, and once a violent April thunderstorm came up as the sisters emerged from the theatre. They found themselves in the center of a traffic snarl, with coachmen quarreling and driving their hacks against each other's wheels. Elizabeth, when recounting the incident to Julia Scott said whimsically that she now had full proof of the doctrine of the angels, for

---

[p] *Catherine Seton's Little Red Book,* was written by Elizabeth Seton for her daughter, Catherine Charlton, also called Catherine Josephine (after March of 1810) or simply Josephine, contains advice written by a mother to her adolescent sometime after 1816.

her own guardian had landed her safe in Wall Street "without one single Hysterick."[42] In later years, it was the danger within the theatre which frightened her more, and Elizabeth wrote:

> The *Passions* represented on a theatre [stage] are represented in quite a different form from their reality. We know that they are the secret springs of the human heart and the source of all our evils, yet on the stage it would appear that the spirit of dominion, pride, resentment, vengeance, etc., proceed from greatness of soul and the elevation of a noble mind, while a veil is thrown over the corruption of the heart, and the horrid consequences they draw us in—[43]

Elizabeth Seton had other diversions than thoughtless pleasures, however. In 1797 a group of public-spirited women met at the home of Mrs. Isabella Marshall Graham to form a society to aid destitute widows with children. Mrs. Graham, a Scotswoman, had been in New York City since 1789 and was already the directress of a school for girls.[44] Elizabeth Seton and many of her friends:[q] Sarah Hoffman, Catherine Mann Dupleix, Eliza Livingston, Rebecca Seton, Sarah Clarke Startin, and Eliza Craig Sadler, took an active part in this benevolent enterprise which included many Quakers.[45] Elizabeth became treasurer of the society[r] and spent much time and energy to assist the widows.[46] The "continual contrast" she saw between their lot and hers made her feel very grateful, and she tried to resign her own blessings to God in order not to offend Him.[47] Even when her own fortunes began to wane, Elizabeth Seton wrote Rebecca:

> I have cut out my two *suits* today and partly made one, [then] heard all the lessons, too, and had a two hours visit from my Poor Widow, [Mrs.] Veley—[who has] no work—no wood—child sick, etc...Should I complain with a bright fire within—bright, bright *Moon* over my shoulder and the Darlings all well, hallooing, and dancing?[48]

Meanwhile the society grew. In 1812 it received a charter, and in March 1803 the officers and managers petitioned the New York State legislature for permission to conduct a lottery to raise $15,000 for low-rent housing for the widows and a school for their children.[49] Elizabeth Seton

---

[q] Elizabeth called her closest friends by nick-names: "Dué" was the former Catherine Mann, now Mrs. George Dupleix, and "Sad " was formerly Eliza Craig, now Mrs. Henry Sadler. They stood by Elizabeth after her conversion and their friendship continued throughout her life.

[r] Mrs. Seton's name does not appear as an officer of the society after 1804. She became a widow herself in 1803, and was sorely in need of assistance for her own children. [There is no extant record that she received assistance. *Ed.*]

busied herself collecting money and visiting the unfortunate. She reported happily to Bec:

> Who shall dare to distrust *His* mercy? This morning's Sun found me without a *Penny*. It is now setting and *We* are worth 20 Dollars in possession and the Ladies have to refund me *10* tomorrow, then we shall have 30—delightful. *The cruse[s] does not fail* [Cf. 1 Kings17:14-16].[50]

The charitable work she engaged in during this period had a far-reaching influence upon Elizabeth's life; and although her connection with the New York widows' society was brief, she never lost her interest in the progress of such work in her native city.[51]

At the same time that Elizabeth engaged in an active life of good works and family duties, she was also interested in the intellectual currents which ebbed and flowed through New York at the close of the eighteenth century. The great era of American Deism, which extended from 1789 to around 1805, was at its peak. Organized religion after the Revolution faced not only changes within its administrative framework, but had to cope with the challenge to its tenets which Deism was insidiously asserting. The French philosophers had, of course, been known in America prior to the war. Voltaire was read rather widely after 1763, but Rousseau's "prudent skepticism" was even more in harmony with the milder Deism of America.[52] In 1794, New Yorkers had founded a society devoted to the spread of French revolutionary principles, and in the winter of 1796–1797 a deistical society was organized.[53] The attacks on Christianity were led by Thomas Paine, and were not confined to any one class of society. The *Age of Reason* could be found in nearly every village. From 1797 to 1800, "the skeptical current swept forward so rapidly that Christianity itself seemed about to be engulfed in a sea of deistic oblivion."[54] It is not surprising that the receding wave caught the attention of Elizabeth Bayley Seton, whose close friend Eliza Sadler had returned from France in January 1799, filled with enthusiasm for French culture and Rousseau's *Emile*. Rev. Simon Gabriel Bruté[t] in later years wrote in distress, "Never let go that poor Mother [Seton was] perverted to Rousseau and Emilius by her unhappy friend Mrs. Sadler."[55]

During the summer of 1799 William Magee Seton traveled to Baltimore and his wife retired to Cragdon, at Bloomingdale, for the hottest weather. Elizabeth took with her a copy of Rousseau, and invited Sad to visit her with the words:

---

[s] A cruse is a small container for liquid, such as water or oil.

[t] Rev. Simon Gabriel Bruté de Remur, (1779-1839), a Sulpician priest from France and later first bishop of Vincennes, Indiana, was Mrs. Seton's confessor and spiritual director in the last two years of her life.

My William continues his determination of going to Baltimore, I cannot be left alone, and if dear *J. Jacques* I find it—Rousseau!!! *and you* are my company I shall have a reproach to make myself [which] I never felt before, that of being satisfied in his absence.[56]

Elizabeth explained her uneasy interest to Eliza Sadler by saying:

Your J. J. [Jean Jacques] has awakened many ideas which had long since been at rest. Indeed he is the writer I shall always refer to in a season of sorrow, for he makes me forget myself while reading, but leaves the most consoling impression on every thought—I hope we shall enjoy his society together.[57]

There was real danger in this reading which elicited the rapturous praise:

Every half hour I can catch goes to *Emilius*— three volumes I have read with delight and were I to express half my thoughts about it—particularly his Religious Ideas—I should lose that circumspection I have so long limited myself to and be E.A.B. instead of E.A.S. Dear J. J. I am yours.[58]

Years after the first flush of elation produced by this intellectual expedition had cooled, Elizabeth Seton was informed of the last hours of a friend who died in despair, denouncing the influence of these same writings. Recalling her own danger in 1799, Elizabeth Seton said sorrowfully:

I, too, have felt their fatal Influence and once they composed my *Sunday* devotion—dazzled by the glare of seductive eloquences how many nights of repose and days of deceitful pleasure have I passed in the charm of their deceptions—Mrs. W. is gone—hopeless and convinced there is no mercy for her—I remain, the daily subject of that boundless Mercy— the mists of night and darkness dispersed, and if even at the eleventh hour, Yet permitted to share in the vineyard and gather the fruits of Eternal Life—glory, glory, glory, forever, forever, and forever—[59]

But Elizabeth Seton's delusion in 1799 was only part of the general trend in which more sober Christians saw a just cause for the visitations of yellow fever which, oddly enough, grew proportionately with infidelity. It remained for the nineteenth century to usher in a revival of religious fervor; and this same ardent advocate of Rousseau became the apologist for purest orthodoxy. In the serene security of a religious community in Maryland, Elizabeth Seton received the following account of Thomas Paine's death written by a Jesuit priest:

> I wish it were in my power to rejoice your pious and compassionate heart with a consoling account of Tom Payne's [sic] death but it seems that unfortunate wretch had vomited too horried blasphemies against the most High and his only Son, as to deserve the most signal of all graces, that of the death of the just. He died as he had lived, an unbeliever, an impious, and according to all appearances, a reprobate; in calling to your mind the tragic end of Voltaire, you may form some idea of that of Payne. We were indeed called upon to visit him, but, helas [alas], he could not bear hearing [us] speak of God and Futurity. Why? He said, are you come to disturb me? Worried in his mind, afflicted in his body, and unwilling to suffer, in fine given up to all the horrors of despair he requested us repeatedly to retire and to let him alone. No persuasion would receive his corpse into its churchyard. There was not one single person, I am told, to attend his funeral.[60]

The Setons had more practical problems to face in 1799. Elizabeth's first reaction as the New Year was ushered in, was one of relief "that the terrible ninety-eight" was past.[61] Accompanied by the death of the elder William Seton, it had been a year of reversal of the family's highest hopes. The heavy burden resting upon her husband, as head of the Setons, was to press even more painfully if Elizabeth had but known it. The Seton financial situation was definitely critical in 1799, owing to a variety of causes. The progress of the "undeclared war" with France, the rapidly declining health of William Magee Seton, and his failure as head of the firm to exert the same forceful pressures that the elder Seton had known how to apply, all conspired against the firm. Failures among their connections in Hamburg and London dismayed William, and Elizabeth had to use every exertion she could summon to keep his spirits up and prevent him from retreating "to the *back woods* where we shall not calculate the dollars per load."[62] In December 1799 Elizabeth wrote to Rebecca that Maitlands in London had stopped payments of the Seton-Maitland obligations in England. James Seton was nearly crazy with worry, but after consultation with their friends, and the directors of the banks, the brothers were advised that stoppage of payments would be a necessity on this side of the Atlantic as well.[63] William

Seton was frantic, partly from the shock he had received and "partly from the necessity of immediate payments of accounts, etc. which is necessary for his personal honor and the satisfaction of his friends."[64] What was to become of his father's family Heaven only knew, for as principal partner the estate of the Setons would bear the brunt of the claims against the company. Nevertheless, William decided to let matters stand until the partnership expired in June; he refused three different offers of money which confidence in the integrity of the firm elicited.[65] Neither Elizabeth nor her husband quite realized yet the full extent of the disaster.

The New Year, 1800, was ushered in at Stone Street in rather somber fashion. Only George Busch, a friend of William's augmented the family group. The Setons tried to act toward each other as if each did not make silent comparisons with happier days. With William, this was only a temporary attitude, since his moods varied from those when he believed all would work out, to those when he envisioned only state prison and direst poverty.[66] With Elizabeth the little sham was more nearly sincere; she really believed that where hope and affection existed nothing was quite irreparable. To her it was not the most unpleasant New Year's Day she had ever passed.[67] Disasters produced in tubercular Seton a patient apathy alternating with despair. His wife, on the contrary, was roused to energetic attack. As she explained to Sad, "Trouble always creates great exertions of my mind, and give it a force to which at other times it is incapable."[68] She was more inclined to the view Rebecca took of their misfortunes when she wrote from Alexandria, "The blessings of life are only lent us and we ought not to repine when they are taken from us."[69] Although at times her courage threatened to desert her in the face of William's "constant reflections on what is to become of *us*, and that us such a number," Elizabeth was more often inclined to exclaim, "What avails melancholy forebodings, and an indulgence of feelings which can never alter the Event of things!"[70]

The firm of Seton & Maitland dispatched two men abroad to seek some solution of the confusion of their affairs. Stone went to Leghorn, Ogden sailed for London. Mr. Stone was an eccentric old bachelor who worked for the firm but little is known about him, not even his first name. Abraham Ogden, Jr., was a member of the prolific Ogden clan. Charlotte Seton later married his brother, Gouverneur Ogden.[71] Elizabeth took over the correspondence of the firm and wrote far into the night. She apologized for neglecting her father with the explanation:

> I have of late been so much engaged in copying mercantile correspondence and assisting my friend in making statements

to his Partner in London that your letter was absolutely necessary to restore my thoughts in their usual channel.[72]

Although she was expecting another child in June,[u] Elizabeth welcomed the onerous letter writing as a distraction from her own discomfort, and she told Julia the task helped her to know "the whys and wherefores" of the business, and made her a better companion for her husband in his trials.

With Ogden and Stone away, she was his only confidant.[73] James Seton seemed interested in his own affairs exclusively, and had just purchased a handsome three-story house in Greenwich Street. Elizabeth added, pointedly, "Thank heaven we are not all sinking" when she related the news to Bec.[74] Besides the evening correspondence there was the daytime sewing. The children had reached that periodic stage where everything seemed to demand replacing at once. A dozen shirts needed ruffling, and there was always the June event to be remembered, and Elizabeth not "half ready." Dr. Bayley was already trying to find a place on Long Island for the summer confinement of his daughter.[75]

As March went by the firm's affairs grew steadily more grave. When the full truth seemed no longer repressible, Elizabeth wrote to the Seton girls in school at Brunswick, and explained more fully to Bec:

> How I wish I could write you a long letter without saying one word of *affairs* for in their present state they are too melancholy to think about, and that not from any impression I have received from my William for never did a mortal bear misfortune and all the aggravated distress of it with so much firmness and patience as he does. I say aggravated for vessel after vessel arrives and correspondents in London and Hamburg notify him that his bills are refused and his property detained there, and not one line of explanation from Maitland—either good or bad—and here we are with funds detained on one side the water, and *transferred* the other, for he is obliged to make over everything in trust to his friends, nothing coming in, and one [legal] suit already against him gives [us] but too much reason to expect more—[76]

Elizabeth was relieved to receive from Mary Seton, at Miss Sophia Hay's school, "such an answer as would do your heart good," but her greater joy was felt over Bec's decision to return home to New York in May. Bec

---

[u] Elizabeth Seton delivered her fourth child, Catherine Charlton Seton 28 June 1800 while on Staten Island at the home of her father in what became Tompkinsville.

was someone to whom Elizabeth could open her heart freely, someone to whom she could turn to discuss the problems of the family which she hated to add to her husband's heavy load. It was decided that the Setons at school should return again after their spring vacations, although Mary Seton was anxious to come home, now that the family finances were so strained. Elizabeth understood Mary's feeling and told Bec:

> Mary wishes very much to be with you and it is right she should be...It is necessary for her future comfort in life that her mind should be strengthened...Try to teach her to look at the events of life as they are, guided by a just and Merciful Protector who orders every occurrence in its time and place, and often by his trials, and disappointments, strives to turn the soul to Him who is the Resource and Comforter of the afflicted.[77]

Mother and Child,
Joseph Dawley, (1975).

Bec also kept the house on Stone Street running smoothly while Elizabeth went away for the summer months to await childbirth. The return to Stone Street that fall revived all the old anxieties, and in December Mr. Garret Killett arrived to make an inventory which presaged the bankruptcy action. Christmas that year was a sad time for the Setons. All their possessions, even to the children's clothing, had been listed and the lists were in the hands of the bankruptcy commissioners. Elizabeth had to watch the door to forestall any premature seizures of their property by the sheriff's officers. William Magee had been forced to hand over the key to the counting house which fronted on Mill Street. With the key the last vestige of control passed from Seton hands. The end of the year marked the end of a business venture which had made the Seton name widely known. The abdication of the son had followed only two years and a half after the death of the father.[78] It was the last Christmas in Stone Street, for in May the Setons were to move to the Battery, next door to Carey Ludlow's property, which was then a lodging house.[79]

During these first years of marriage Elizabeth Seton had changed from an emotional, untried girl in her teens to a mature, courageous woman. It is not difficult to understand the increasing incapacity of William Magee Seton as circumstances of health and business beyond his control became aggravated. It is much more interesting to account for the equanimity with which his wife faced the future and accepted each trial as "one more lesson on the uselessness of perplexing the mind with anxieties about fortune's favors."[80] A clue is contained, perhaps, in the wide diversity of her interests. In its simplest reduction the answer may be that she was too busy to become morbid. She told Julia that "it sometimes lessens personal sorrow to compare our condition with the case of others,"[81] and projecting herself into the lives of those about her seemed to increase Elizabeth's fortitude. The problems of her children, father, husband, other relatives, and friends all received Elizabeth Seton's attention. The more she did, the more she seemed able to do.

Elizabeth was a mother whose very nature made her enjoy every aspect of motherhood. She delighted in the infancy of her children and watched their first steps with fond gaze, writing to Sad of Richard Seton:

Imagine Dick running over the grass and garden, [he] tumbles down and turns to see the countenance that is watching him to know if he should cry, then off again as merry as a bird.[82]

The children were never neglected nor left to Mammy Huler, their nanny, entirely. If Elizabeth were away for any length of time, on her return she laughingly complained,

My precious children stick to me like little burrs; they are so fearful of losing me again. The moment I shake one off one side, another clings in the opposite, nor can I write one word without some sweet interruption.[83]

Although Elizabeth admitted that "a mother sees thro' a veil which renders the object as she wishes it,"[84] she was troubled by the appearance of any unusual traits of behavior in her offspring, and worried about her daughter Anna Maria's disposition. She began very early to make a companion of the moody little girl and while Anna was not yet four years old the mother wrote this for her on the last day of 1798:

The last, the first, and every day of the year my thoughts and time are yours, my Anna, but I enjoy a peculiar pleasure in devoting an hour generally appropriated to amusements, to you my precious Child, in whom my greatest delight and amusements are centered. May the Giver of all good, grant His Protection to you and assist me in my endeavors to promote your future good and advantage. The blessing and attentions of the tenderest parents and most affectionate friends are constantly yours, and by your conduct you will confer the gratification of our fondest wishes, or will inflict the most bitter disappointment. In you I view the friend, the companion, and consolation of my future years—delightful reflection.[85]

It was more of a prayer and a prophecy than either mother or daughter could foresee. Meanwhile, during the summer which followed, Elizabeth Seton welcomed Julia Scott and her daughter, Maria, whose example, Elizabeth confided to Sad, "answers all the good I had anticipated for my Anna who comes down every Morning after breakfast with the clean hands and Frock and gets on her ribbon bracers then sits down with her needle."[86] After the Scotts departed Elizabeth reported happily:

Anna is a perfect Angel. I am almost persuaded her fancies are somehow governed by the moon, for she is as different from what she was as the present darkness is from the beautiful light of that period when she perplexed [us] the most.[87]

In addition to her own children, there were always Elizabeth's Seton relatives to require attention as well. Holidays from school in the eighteenth century did not take place at Christmas and New Year's Day, so numerous New Year's cakes, honeycakes, raisins, keg biscuits, and almonds had to be shipped to Connecticut and New Jersey. As if Elizabeth were not busy enough, Dr. Bayley delegated to her the task of sending food to Helen Bayley, one of her younger-half sisters, who was also at Miss Hay's school. On the occasions when the girls forgot to take their stays with them, a trunk was required to carry the assorted goods.[88] When the spring and fall vacations arrived the Setons were often accompanied home by guests, and Stone Street became full to overflowing.

Nor was Elizabeth too busy to come to the aid of her friends in trouble. During the sad March of 1798, when Julia Scott's husband died, and the widow had to make plans for her two children, John and Maria, Elizabeth Seton never "left her night or day during the excess of her Sorrows."[89] She helped Julia pack and close her house in preparation for the move to Philadelphia. Later, when Julia successively lost her brother and father, Elizabeth Seton wrote letters which brought new courage to the older woman.[90] John Wilkes, too, had reason to be grateful to Elizabeth Seton for her kindness to his wife. Mary Seton Wilkes, a distant cousin of William Seton, was taken seriously ill in January 1800, at her home at 27 William Street and Elizabeth sat up two nights at the stricken woman's bedside until the crisis was past.[91] But Mary Wilkes was never completely well again, and a year later, in spite of Mrs. Seton's care, Mary grew worse. On 1 March 1801, Elizabeth wrote her father that Mary's last sigh was breathed on Friday morning,—and to Rebecca Seton she said:

The groans and anguish of her poor Wilkes is easily conceived. He has shed tears all over me which I hope will relieve him... Oh, Rebecca, if I dared to wish how gladly would I drink the cup—but My God knows best.[92]

In addition to the numerous affections and sympathies which crowded her heart, Elizabeth Seton was also attracted by the beauties of nature. She never outgrew the close communion with the earth and sky that had comforted her in those cruel days of adolescence. The summers at Cragdon offered solitary walks, while the others slept, and Elizabeth discovered many beauties that quite escaped the other noisier explorers. One Sunday morning, she told Eliza Sadler:

I retraced the honey-suckle walk and to my great astonishment found that those bushes with buds on them which grew near the honey suckle, and in great quantities in other places, bear the sweetest flower you can imagine with the greatest profusion. Its fragrance [is] beyond any flower I ever saw. I brought home a load of it on my back...O how it would delight me to send you a branch of it, for like other sweets, its season is passing.[93]

After Staten Island replaced Bloomingdale as the Seton summer residence Elizabeth became more interested in the sea and sights of the harbor. One evening in October she described what she saw while she waited for her father.

The most beautiful mild Evening my eyes ever beheld, the moon perfectly unclouded—a large cloud like a Bank of pure snow arises behind the fort and gradually spreads towards New York, retaining its whiteness from its center, but very dark beneath. Now and then [it was] lit up with lightening while the sky over our establishment and Long Island is clearest blue spangled with bright stars—this continued about a quarter of an hour the most perfect scene imagination could form—a light wind rises, the thunder is heard—the clouds approach and by degrees cover the bright moon, pass to Long Island and the fort is covered with a blue and spangled sky as before, while the rain beats over *us*.

Father visiting a vessel with a lantern in her shrouds. The clouds overspread the moon as he went on board, the storm vanished and the sky was perfectly bright again before he left her and the whole time of his being aboard was not more than 5 minutes.[94]

The third influence which kept Elizabeth Seton persevering in the face of adversity was her recurring interest in spiritual reading and serious thought. In later life she recalled those "evenings alone, writing, bible, psalms, in burning desires of heaven."[95] When the sudden, violent attacks of childhood disease beset her children Elizabeth said, "tho' time and chance and sorrow comes to all and I must take my share, they all united will only draw me nearer to that friend to whom I look for comfort..."[96] When death removed a friend she would ruminate:

> At this time when pain and a thousand nameless anxieties remind me continually of that hour in which the soul wavers between its future and its present Home, *mine* is transported at even the probability, for the bonds that hold it have scarcely strength to restrain it...and if reason and the best affections of this world did not withhold and draw back with more than common force its flying propensities, I should have renounced every other desire and aim long ago.[97]

Whether her sober reflections were aroused by the sermons of Dr. Benjamin Moore at Trinity Church, or the never quite suppressed worry over her husband's health, Elizabeth Seton as a young wife of twenty-four told Julia that nothing in this world, "were all its pleasures combined," would tempt her to be more than a passenger through life.[98] These sentiments did not imply a desire to escape. On the contrary, Elizabeth asserted "this life is worth possessing if it were only because while we have it we are candidates for a better,"[99] and while she lived she would "intend the best and be thankful for the present."[100]

Elizabeth was very human, for all her fine sentiments. Leaving her beloved home on Wall Street cost her bitter tears. "I turn over the Page with rapidity," she told Julia, "and looking towards Heaven *there* fix my *aim—there is no change*."[101] Sometimes the crowded conditions at Cragdon almost taxed her beyond the limits of endurance and she said wearily to Sad, "Patience—Resignation—heavenly virtues exercised in little things that keep the Soul in a sense of its dependent State, for I assure you I do not possess them on this occasion without a struggle."[102] Many times when the worry over financial matters harassed her, Elizabeth would turn her thoughts to the little daily blessings. In the dark November of 1800 she wrote to Julia Scott that in spite of all the heartaches the bankruptcy proceedings entailed "how much reason I have had [this twelve month past] to Bless my Maker for his goodness to my children, none of whom have been ill."[103] She seized the occasional moment of quiet, after the children were settled down for the night, to indulge her favorite pastime, sitting and reading of "the High and Lofty One who inhabits Eternity."[104] It was particularly her habit to spend the last evening of the year, sitting before the fire, "contemplating and tracing the boundless mercy of God." Her reverie would run:

> How pure the enjoyment and sweet the transition of every thought—the soul expands all earthly interests recede—and Heavenly Hopes become anxious wishes —Might not these mortal bonds be gently severed, loosed more easily than untying the fastening of a fine thread, at this moment without any perceptible changes, to find the soul at liberty—Heavenly Mercy—in Thy Presence and would it not tremble—or rather is it not forever under thy inspection can it be concealed from Thee—No, thou now perceivest it, oppressed, weighed and sinking under its mortal burden and also thou seest it can patiently, submissively submit to Thy Will, adoring in sweet confidence of Thy Mercy—preserve me but this Heavenly Peace, continue to me this privilege beyond all mortal computation, of resting in Thee, and adoring Thee my Father—Friend— and never failing Support. For this alone I implore, let all other concerns with their consequences be entirely and wholly submitted to *Thee*.[105]

Attention to the needs of others, love of nature, spiritual reverie, all served to produce in Elizabeth Seton a calm acceptance of the first great crisis which financial failure produced. She was quite sincere when she wrote Julia:

> Seton is quietly writing by my side, in as perfect health as he has ever enjoyed—my chicks quiet in bed, and [my] Father smiling over a list of books he had just made of those he chooses to retain as *one* of our creditors. For myself, I think the greatest happiness of this life is to be released from the cares and formalities of what is called the world—My World

is *my family*, and all the change to me will be that I can devote myself unmolested to my Treasure.[106]

CHAPTER 2. MANHATTAN MATRON

Notes

[1] William Seton to Elizabeth Seton, 28 February 1796, ASJPH 1-3-3-18:53.

[2] William Magee Seton to Elizabeth Seton, Oakes, near Dover, 15 May 1796, ASJPH 26-0-2, (6). Copy. The original is in the Archives of the Sisters of Charity of Seton Hill, Greensburg, Pennsylvania. Hereinafter cited as ASCSH.

[3] Eulogy of William Seton, Sr., ASJPH 1-3-3-18:1; see 1.22, Elizabeth Seton to Julia Scott, *CW,* 1:35, n.1.

[4] William Magee Seton to Elizabeth Seton, New Ark [Newark], Wednesday morning, 1794, ASJPH 26-0-1, (2). Copy. The original is in Archives Sisters of Charity of Cincinnati, Mount St. Joseph, Ohio. Hereinafter cited as AMSJ.

[5] William Magee Seton to Elizabeth Seton, Philadelphia, 27 July 1794, ASJPH 26-0-1, (2). Copy. The original is in AMSJ.

[6] William Magee Seton to Elizabeth Seton, 15 May 1796, ASJPH 26-0-2, (6). Copy. The original is in AMSJ.

[7] 1.7, Elizabeth Seton to William Magee Seton, 23 July 1794, *CW*, 1:7. This and all other letters of Mrs. Seton cited in this chapter were written from New York.

[8] 1.9, Elizabeth Seton to Eliza Sadler, 11 August 1796, *CW*, 1:10.

[9] 1.22, Elizabeth Seton to Julia Scott, 5 July 1798, *CW*, 1:36. See I. N. Stokes, *Iconography of Manhattan Island* (New York, 1915-1928), VI, 102.

[10] 1.26, Elizabeth Seton to Julia Scott, 8 September 1798, *CW*, 1:44.

[11] Ibid.

[12] 10.4, "Dear Remembrances," *CW*, 3a:513.

[13] Julia Scott to Elizabeth Seton, Philadelphia, 9 May 1795, ASJPH 1-3-3-11:B22.

[14] 1.8, Elizabeth Seton to Eliza Sadler, 8 February 1796, *CW*, 1:9.

[15] 1.12, Elizabeth Seton to Eliza Sadler, 1 August 1797, entry of 15 August, *CW*, 1:18.

[16] Ibid.

[17] 1.11, Elizabeth Seton to Eliza Sadler, 18 June 1797, *CW*, 1:15. The house the Setons and Posts shared was owned by a Mrs. Livingston but the sources do not identify her.

[18] 1.13, Elizabeth Seton to Mrs. John Seton, *CW*, 1:19. Elizabeth Seton usually wrote her formal letters in a rough draft before copying

them. Many times this rough draft is the only remaining evidence. Only a fragment of this draft survives.

[19] Eliza Sadler to Elizabeth Seton, 13 July [1798], ASJPH 1-3-3-11:B7.

[20] Greenleaf's *New Daily Advertiser,* 11 June 1798. Other obituaries appeared in the *Commercial Advertiser,* 11 June 1798; *The Spectator,* 9 June 1798, the *Weekly Museum,* 6 June 1798.

[21] 1.22, Elizabeth Seton to Julia Scott, 5 July 1798, *CW,* 1:36.

[22] 1.25, Elizabeth Seton to Julia Scott, 20 August 1798, *CW,* 1:42.

[23] William Magee Seton to Elizabeth Seton, 23 July 1798, ASJPH 1-3-3-18:54.

[24] 1.24, Elizabeth Seton to Julia Scott, 20 August 1798, *CW,* 1:40-41.

[25] 1.25, Elizabeth Seton to Julia Scott, 30 August 1798, *CW,* 1:42.

[26] Ibid.

[27] 1.27, Elizabeth Seton to Julia Scott, 28 September 1798, *CW,* 1:45.

[28] 1.28, Elizabeth Seton to Julia Scott, 14 October 1798, *CW,* 1:46; 1.30, Ibid., 28 October 1798, *CW,* 1:49.

[29] 1.32, Elizabeth Seton to Julia Scott, 3 November 1798, *CW,* 1:52.

[30] Elizabeth Seton to _____, n.d., ASJPH 26-0-1, (2). Copy. The original is in AMSJ.

[31] 1.33, Elizabeth Seton to Julia Scott, 25 November 1798, *CW,* 1:54.

[32] 1.43, Elizabeth Seton to Julia Scott, 20 April and 26 April 1799, *CW,* 1:67; 1.44, Ibid., 14 May 1799, *CW,* 1:70.

[33] 1.45, Elizabeth Seton to Julia Scott, 2 June 1799, *CW,* 1:71. Jack was John Curson Seton. He remained in Virginia at this time and married Miss Mary Wise of Alexandria.

[34] 1.61, Elizabeth Seton to Rebecca Seton, 3 August 1799, *CW,* 1:91.

[35] 1.30, Elizabeth Seton to Julia Scott, 28 October 1798, *CW,* 1:49.

[36] Rebecca Seton to Elizabeth Seton, 18 July 1799, ASJPH 1-3-3-18:49.

[37] 1.46, Elizabeth Seton to Rebecca Seton, 8 June 1799, *CW,* 1:73.

[38] 1.73, Elizabeth Seton to Rebecca Seton, 23 December 1799, *CW,* 1:107; 1.69, Elizabeth Seton to Julia Scott, 20 November 1799, *CW,* 1:102.

[39] Rebecca Seton to Elizabeth Seton, New York, 27 December 1799, ASJPH 1-3-3-18:50.

[40] 10.3, "Catherine Seton's Little Red Book," *CW,* 3a:491.

[41] James Grant Wilson, *Memorial History of the City of New York* (New York, 1893), III, 146. The Park Theatre was operated by William Dunlap and John Hodgkinson for a time. See William Dunlap, *Diary, 1766-1839* (New York, 1930) for interesting details of Dunlap's career.

[42] Elizabeth Seton to Julia Scott, 23 April 1798, ASJPH 1-3-3-6:2.

[43] 10.3, "Catherine Seton's Little Red Book," *CW,* 3a:498. Elizabeth Seton wrote in this connection, "Poor, poor Betsy B[ayley] had no mother

nor even principles to keep her from folly,"

[44] Harris E. Starr, "Isabella Marshall Graham," *Dictionary of American Biography* (New York, 1929), VII, 474-475.

[45] Sidney I. Pomerantz, *New York an American City, 1783-1803* (New York, 1938), 338; John Cox, *Quakerism in the City of New York, 1757-1930* (New York, 1930), 43. Pomerantz states that this society was started by Quakers but Cox simply calls it "a charitable Organization of Quaker Membership."

[46] *New York City Directory,* 1803-1804, p. 6.

[47] 10.4, "Dear Remembrances," *CW*, 3a:513.

[48] 1.150, Elizabeth Seton to Rebecca Seton, n.d., *CW*, 1:198.

[49] Petition of 4 March 1803, to the New York legislature, copy of the original in The American Catholic History Research Center and University Archives, The University Museum Collection of The Catholic University of America, Washington, D.C., 3120.

[50] 1.196, Elizabeth Seton to Rebecca Seton, n.d., *CW*, 1:235.

[51] Eliza Sadler to Elizabeth Seton, 4 May 1816, ASJPH 1-3-3-11:B18. Eliza Sadler wrote Mrs. Seton of the beginning in November 1814, of an institution to aid poor old women. Mrs. Sadler also sent to Emmitsburg a copy of Mrs. Graham's meditations, published that year by her daughter, Mrs. Bethune, under the title: *The Power of Faith: Exemplified in the Life and Writings of the Late Mrs. Isabella Graham of New York*. [The publication is no longer available at ASJPH. See *CW,* 1:27, n.3. Ed.]

[52] Herbert M. Morais, *Deism in Eighteenth-Century America* (New York, 1934), 50.

[53] Ibid., 131.

[54] Ibid., 154.

[55] 1.37, Elizabeth Seton to Julia Scott, 20 January 1799, *CW*, 1:58.

[56] 1.48, Elizabeth Seton to Eliza Sadler, 23 June 1799, *CW*, 1:76.

[57] 1.67, Elizabeth Seton to Eliza Sadler, n.d., *CW*, 1:99.

[58] 1.64, Elizabeth Seton to Eliza Sadler, n.d., *CW*, 1:95.

[59] 4.55, "Spiritual Journal to Cecilia Seton," *CW*, 1:475. This entry is undated and appears between entries for the 16th and 18th of September 1807.

[60] Rev. Anthony Kohlmann, S.J. to Elizabeth Seton, New York, 19 July 1813, ASJPH 1-3-3-2:32. Kohlmann was pastor of St. Peter's church on Barclay Street when he wrote this letter. Mrs. Seton was by then the foundress of the Sisters of Charity of St. Joseph's, Emmitsburg, Maryland.

[61] 1.36, Elizabeth Seton to Julia Scott, 3 January 1799, *CW*, 1:57.

[62] 1.69, Elizabeth Seton to Julia Scott, 20 November 1799, *CW*, 1:102.

[63] 1.73, Elizabeth Seton to Rebecca Seton, 23 December 1799, *CW*, 1:106.

[64] 1.74, Elizabeth Seton to Julia Scott, 3 January 1800, *CW*, 1:108.

[65] Ibid.

[66] 1.75, Elizabeth Seton to Rebecca Seton, 3 January 1800, *CW*, 1:109.

[67] Ibid.

[68] 1.67, Elizabeth Seton to Eliza Sadler, n.d., [October 1799], *CW*, 1:99.

[69] Rebecca Seton to Elizabeth Seton, New York, 29 December 1799, ASJPH 26-0-2, (6). Copy. The original is in ASCSH.

[70] 1.77, Elizabeth Seton to Rebecca Seton, 5 February 1800, *CW*, 1:112.

[71] 1.76, Elizabeth Seton to Julia Scott, 16 January 1800, *CW*, 1:111.

[72] 1.78, Elizabeth Seton to Dr. Richard Bayley, 12 February 1800, *CW*, 1:114. Dr. Bayley was in Albany on business for the health department.

[74] 1.77, Elizabeth Seton to Rebecca Seton, 5 February 1800, *CW*, 1:113.

[75] 1.82, Elizabeth Seton to Julia Scott, 18 March 1800, *CW*, 1:119.

[76] 1.83, Elizabeth Seton to Rebecca Seton, 20 March 1800, *CW*, 1:122.

[77] 1.95, Elizabeth Seton to Rebecca Seton, 14 August 1800, *CW*, 1:136.

[78] 1.100, Elizabeth Seton to Julia Scott, 7 December 1800, *CW*, 1:141; 1.101, Ibid., 26 December 1800, *CW*, 1:143.

[79] 1.108, Elizabeth Seton to Julia Scott, 10 March 1801, *CW*, 1:151.

[80] 1.91, Elizabeth Seton to Julia Scott, 26 July 1800, *CW*, 1:130.

[81] 1.100, Elizabeth Seton to Julia Scott, 7 December 1800, *CW*, 1:141.

[82] 1.66, Elizabeth Seton to Eliza Sadler, 2 October 1799, *CW*, 1:99.

[83] 1.14, Elizabeth Seton to Eliza Sadler, 27 March 1798, *CW*, 1:21.

[84] 1.11, Elizabeth Seton to Eliza Sadler, 29 June 1797, *CW*, 1:16.

[85] 1.35, Elizabeth Seton to Anna Maria Seton, 31 December 1798, *CW*, 1:56.

[86] 1.60, Elizabeth Seton to Eliza Sadler, n.d., *CW*, 1:90. A letter to Rebecca Seton dated 3 August 1799 says Julia Scott "came last Saturday with her daughter about Harriet's age."

[87] 1.58, Elizabeth Seton to Eliza Sadler, n.d., [July 1799], *CW*, 1:88.

[88] 1.75, Elizabeth Seton to Rebecca Seton, 3 January 1800, *CW*, 1:109.

[89] 1.14, Elizabeth Seton to Eliza Sadler, 27 March 1798, *CW*, 1:21.

[90] 1.26, Elizabeth Seton to Julia Scott, 8 September 1798, *CW*, 1:43; 1.101, Ibid., 26 December 1800, *CW*, 1:142.

[91] 1.76, Elizabeth Seton to Julia Scott, 16 January 1800, *CW*, 1:112.

[92] 1.106, Elizabeth Seton to Rebecca Seton, [27 February 1801], *CW*, 1:147; 1.107, Elizabeth Seton to Dr. Richard Bayley, 1 March 1801, *CW*, 1:148.

[93] 1.57, Elizabeth Seton to Eliza Sadler, [July or August 1799], *CW*, 1:86.

[94] 8.6, "The Most Beautiful Mild Evening," 2 October 1800, *CW*, 3a:19.

[95] 10.4, "Dear Remembrances," *CW*, 3a:513.

[96] 1.12, Elizabeth Seton to Eliza Sadler, 15 August 1797, *CW*, 1:19.

[97] 1.19, Elizabeth Seton to Julia Scott, 16 May 1798, *CW*, 1:30.

[98] 1.18, Elizabeth Seton to Julia Scott, 9 May 1798, *CW*, 1:29.

[99] 1.28, Elizabeth Seton to Julia Scott, 14 October 1798, *CW*, 1:47.

[100] 1.29, Elizabeth Seton to Julia Scott, 21 October 1798, *CW*, 1:48.

[101] 1.32, Elizabeth Seton to Julia Scott, 3 November 1798, *CW*, 1:52.

[102] 1.58, Elizabeth Seton to Eliza Sadler, n.d., [July 1799], *CW*, 1:88.

[103] 1.99, Elizabeth Seton to Julia Scott, 19 November 1800, *CW*, 1:140.

[104] 1.38, Elizabeth Seton to Dr. Richard Bayley, 2 February 1799, *CW*, 1:60.

[105] 8.4, "Sitting on a Little Bench," 31 December 1799, *CW*, 3a:18. Neither spelling nor grammatical construction were standardized in her day. For the convenience of modern readers, editorial corrections have been made.

[106] 1.100, Elizabeth Seton to Julia Scott, 7 December 1800, *CW*, 1:141.

ॐ

CHAPTER 3

♋

FATHER AND DAUGHTER

After Elizabeth Bayley married into the Seton mercantile family, her relations with her public-spirited father continued as close as before. When Dr. Bayley traveled away from New York, he corresponded with his daughter and complained on occasion, "Never was I more vexed or disappointed than this evening. Why did you not write by the post?"[1] He confided in her his fatigue and ennui in Newark. "Work, ache, cards, loss of money, sick of Pandora's box," were phrases he used to voice his dissatisfaction with his own life.[2] But the summers Elizabeth spent on Long Island found him cheerfully running out in his boat to see her and receive "the most cheerful welcome in the world."[3]

There is no way of conclusively defining the dislocation of family relations which seemed to have existed between Dr. Richard Bayley and his second wife, but the veiled references to these relations suggest that the quick-tempered surgeon at this period had forbidden Elizabeth to effect any reconciliation. This rift was pointed up by the return of Eliza Craig Sadler from Europe and the subsequent marriage of William Craig[a] to Emma Bayley, Elizabeth's half-sister.[4] Elizabeth found the joy in Sad's return diluted by the difficulty the family feud presented. She explained to Julia Scott:

> My Intercourse[b] with Mrs. Sadler—will be so much mixed with vexation, and our difference will be a source of so much mortification to her, that I can never visit her without expecting to meet those I do not wish to meet, and would rather now wish to avoid what was once so great a pleasure.[5]

Dr. Bayley commented on his own situation with the light remark:

> I love to think on the oddity of my life. What words afford the most inconsolable affliction to another person, that which would afford aching heart to most people, seem to me as a matter of amusement. Dear heady temper go on. Hail to the period when I shall be at rest.[6]

---

[a] It is possible that both William and Samuel Craig were brothers of Eliza Sadler, but final proof is lacking. "Emma" was Charlotte Amelia Bayley, oldest daughter of Charlotte Amelia Barclay Bayley and Dr. Richard Bayley. The marriage took place on 19 June 1799 and the bridal couple spent their honeymoon at the Sadler summer home on Long Island.

[b] Intercourse was the term commonly used in during the nineteenth century for social or business interactions between persons or groups.

But Elizabeth knew her father better than to be deceived by his flippancy and she confided her concern to Julia:

> My Father, in addition to his former uneasiness, has new sources of distress which make me tremble. Two of my brothers[c] have already shown the most unquestionable marks of unsteady dispositions—*We* cannot Wonder—but this is a sacred subject, and appears to have affected him above all other Evils.[7]

Elizabeth was determined to ease her father's burden in some way or other. "You are a philosopher," she consoled him. "Treasure up the blessed spirit."[8] She sent him inspirational poems, and praised his work. When the lack of appreciation for his efforts depressed the health officer, Elizabeth wrote:

> If the prayers of a good quiet little Female are supposed to be of any avail, it [your health] will be long continued to you, with the hope that the visual rays of our fellow citizens will in time be brightened by your labors, and their attention awakened by the voice of truth and *conscience*.[9]

She relayed to Dr. Bayley the compliment of a French physician who found her father's article on yellow fever in the *Monitor* "the best thing written on the subject."[10] She tried to arrange the family Christmas so that Dr. Bayley could spend it with his two oldest daughters and their children, and 25 December 1799, found the Posts and Setons together, and the doughty doctor entangled amid the sticky hands of his little grandchildren.[11]

After 1797, the state capital was removed to Albany, New York, and Dr. Bayley journeyed northward each winter to present the business of the health department to the legislature. Here he mingled with Alexander Hamilton, Gouverneur Morris, and other men of "superior sense" and "great brilliancy of wit." He told Elizabeth, "I esteem it a high good fortune to be on a footing of communication, of feeling, and sentiment with them."[12] He enjoyed lodging with them at the lieutenant-governor's at Watervliet.[13]

---

[c] The "brothers" were probably Elizabeth Seton's half-brothers, Richard and Andrew Barclay Bayley. Neither man lived long nor achieved any success while alive. Richard Bayley, Jr. was born on 7 August 1781. Sometime between 1799 and 1803 he was briefly associated with the Filicchi counting house in Leghorn, probably through William Seton's intercession. By 1805 he had lost $10,000 of his mother's money in abortive mercantile pursuits. He married Catherine White on 26 October 1812, and was killed three years later in a horse and carriage accident on 29 May 1815. Very little is known of Andrew Barclay Bayley except that he was once engaged to Harriet Seton, pursued a mercantile career in Jamaica and the West Indies, and died there prior to 8 December 1811, on which date Mary Bayley Post announced his death to Elizabeth Seton.

He wrote satirical descriptions of the flirtations at the capital, told whose portrait was receiving the most attention, and commented on the current theatrical offerings. But more often his thoughts were in New York, and he begged his "Lady Bet" not to miss a post for Albany.[14] He wanted news of his grandchildren, and he admonished Elizabeth "that a sound mind in a sound body ought to be your motto for educating your children."[15] His opinion was much more colored by his age than by any vein of prophecy, for he added, "Look up and urge forward your claims to preeminence; your children are to give you immortality. This is neither the world nor the age for you to enjoy it in."[16]

Dr. Bayley felt closer to his second daughter than to any other person living. It was to Elizabeth that he opened his heart fully and tried to explain himself. He wrote:

> Shall we be compelled to assign or connect motives to every action of our lives? To every impulse of mind? To every expression of a heart that feels? I hope not, for surely in such a case, I should be deprived of many little pleasures that a more cautious temper never feels. Calculations, intentions, cautions are all entitled to their place [but] to be always calculating, always cautious, to be always influenced by intentions are motives never to be applied to me.[17]

In trying to form some estimate of Elizabeth Seton's personality it is well to recall now and then this side of her father's character. There is a kind of personality which tolerates no opposition to what it deems the natural expression of its own impulses. Often this temperament views it pyrotechnics as rather amazing, even unfortunate, but certainly never unjustified. When the same tendency toward temper in a child is reinforced by the example of a beloved parent, the force of this personality trait can be considerable. It is not at all surprising, then, to find that in the mature Elizabeth Seton a deep-rooted tendency to imprudent self-expression sometimes won the battle over her will to self-control. She herself never lost consciousness of the fact that a hot temper was one of her sources of temptation. The serenity she displayed in later life was no gauge of the battles she had to fight. Her meekness and humility were hard-won.

As the Seton fortunes declined, Dr. Bayley became more concerned about the welfare of his favorite household. In March 1799, Elizabeth had told Julia "My Father has obtained permission from the Legislature to perform all the plans he has contemplated on Staten Island. He is building a hospital and dwelling house."[18] By the following spring the house was sufficiently completed to suggest to Bayley that he could offer it as a summer haven to his harassed daughter. Elizabeth in 1800 was expecting her fourth child and the doctor wanted no repetition of the crisis Richard's arrival had created. Late in May, Dr. Bayley went on ahead to Staten Island, taking with him young Anna Maria, Will, and Dick. Elizabeth was to follow in June, accompanied by Rebecca Seton, who had recently returned from the south.[19] And so it was that on 1 July 1800, William Magee Seton announced to Julia Scott:

> I have the pleasure to inform you that on Saturday last at dawn of day your little friend presented us with another daughter, if possible more lovely than the first, but as you are acquainted with my sentiments with respect to what is mine, I will forbear all description at present and let you judge for yourself—I left her and her mother yesterday at the *Health Establishment* where they cannot but thrive and indeed Eliza was never better.[20]

Although it was originally intended that the Setons would be on the island only a month, Dr. Bayley was so delighted with his new family life that he confessed "the habit of being a Christian and in some degree domesticated was not to be dispensed with after four weeks' enjoyment."[21] The decision was, then, that the Setons should remain all summer. For her part, Elizabeth asked no more. William Magee could get over at least four days a week; and Dr. Bayley seldom left the house except to visit the vessels in quarantine. The house itself was very comfortable and had an upper balcony which commanded "a view fifty miles beyond the hook."[22]

The new baby was one of those contented infants who slept serenely, and Elizabeth's recovery was amazingly rapid. In no time at all the house rang with the merriment of supper parties when Emma Bayley Craig and Eliza Sadler brought their husbands to view the new arrival.[23] When the Seton ship, the *Liberties,* put into port, so great was the rejoicing that for three days running Elizabeth poured bowls of tea for the arrivals, until, as she confessed to Rebecca, her arm ached.[24] She shrugged off the rumored criticism of other branches of the Bayley family at her presence on Staten Island and wrote spiritedly to Eliza Sadler:

> My Father cannot do more than he does to prove his regret for the past...

> Father is more than busy, and has many vexations, but he says he "can never rest in this world and it may as well be one thing as another" [is] the melancholy truth, and all that

can be done is to soothe—cruel would be the person who ever wished to deprive me of that power—but we must hope there is no such being.[25]

Elizabeth stayed on until October was nearly over. It was a reluctant family that returned to Stone Street on 25 October 1800. Dr. Bayley wrote the following day:

> I learned from Bayley[d] last night at 8 o'clock all the little iotas of your passage to New York, that Miss Cate[e] [sic] became torpid on her leaving Staten Island and continued in that state until she made her appearance at Stone Street. A smart sensible child exhibiting at so early an age such forebodings of future character. My friend Dick shall be received with open arms whenever he will pay grandpa a visit—all whining excepted.[26]

Less than a month later the fond grandfather was one of the five sponsors[f] at baby Catherine Charlton's[g] baptism, where the precocious child, mistaking the minister for her grandfather because of his spectacles, laughed "so drolly" at him when he threw the cold water on her that her mother could scarcely keep a straight face.[27]

The winter passed rather quickly. Dr. Bayley went once more to the capital, while a strong southerly wind at the end of February brought numerous arrivals to the Quarantine where the health officer's assistant was kept busy. Rebecca Seton went to help her sister, Eliza Seton Maitland, and Elizabeth's little circle lost "its key."[28] After Bec's departure, Elizabeth's daily routine became, perforce, rather inflexible. The "general tenor" was to rise early; by ten o'clock lessons were begun, and Cecilia Seton led the others in grammar, reading, and sewing. The boys learned to say their little pieces, name the states, and recite the commandments. Evenings found William Magee and Dr. Bayley, when the latter was in town, busy with their cribbage while Elizabeth took her turn at the piano. These were the last days at Stone Street, but life went on in the accustomed monotony

---

[d] "Bayley" was Joseph Bayley, a young doctor, who assisted Dr. Richard Bayley at the quarantine station. He was not directly related to the older man.

[e] Dr. Bayley spelled his granddaughter's name as Cate although Mrs. Seton initially called the child as Kate.

[f] The five sponsors were Julia Scott, Mary Bayley Post, Catherine Dupleix, who sent "an elegant christening suit" from Ireland, Dr. Richard Bayley, and one of the Curson family. The minister was Dr. Abraham Beach, an assistant at Trinity Church who became pastor in 1811 when Dr. Benjamin Moore was made inactive by paralysis.

[g] Catherine Charlton (Josephine) Seton (28 June 1800–3 April 1891) was named after her maternal grandmother. Her mother first refers to her as Josephine in a note dated March 1809. Josephine was probably her confirmation name although her mother also sometimes referred to her affectionately as Jos, Kit, Kitty. She entered the Sisters of Mercy in Manhattan at age forty-six and engaged in prison ministry until her death. She is buried in Section 4-2-D of Calvary Cemetery, Woodside, New York.

of minor events. The arrival of the *Minerva* in March brought, among other things, "four pineapples and a dolphin cheese" for Dr. Bayley. April was passed in hourly anticipation of Dué's[h] arrival from Ireland.[29] In no time at all the second departure for Staten Island was under way.[30]

The arrival on Staten Island that June was a joyous affair, and gave no warning of the tragic event which lay ahead. The welcome the Setons received was "such as dispelled all the gloom of my heart." Elizabeth was in such high elation that the simple gift of fine garden strawberries from a neighbor seemed more than she could bear. The house looked so neat; the birds, the garden, the sunshine were so cheerful. By six o'clock of the day they arrived all the bedsteads were up and the beds made. "How the heart did melt before Him the giver of all." Across the water Elizabeth could discern their new residence on the Battery, with the street doors and dining room windows tightly shut.[31] Meanwhile Anna Maria and the boys were knee deep in the clover beyond the yard, while baby Kate "tata'd" all over the house which the summer before had seen her birth.[32]

June went by in a succession of fine days. Company came and went; Emma Bayley Craig ferried over with friends and kept the house awake until twelve. Wright Post brought Dr. Miller to dine on black fish and chicken pie. Rebecca Seton spent several days on the island while William Magee Seton traveled to Baltimore. On clear days the household would breakfast in haste and board a well-provisioned schooner to go to Sandy Hook[i] for a picnic. Only two things marred the perfection of Elizabeth's June: that Julia Scott reached New York but not Staten Island, and that William Magee was only infrequently with his family.[33]

William Magee Seton had gone to Baltimore early in June for reasons of health and business combined. His grandfather, Richard Curson, was anxious to have the Setons settle in Baltimore, but William Magee refused to commit himself. The rumors of Seton-Maitland affairs in England caused him great uneasiness, particularly since aspersions were beginning to be made in regard to Seton's reliability. "I hope no blame can be attached to Filicchi or myself," he wrote Elizabeth.[34] While he was south William Magee went on to Alexandria, Virginia, to visit his brother, Jack,[j] and he reported of his trip through the capital, "We were all delighted with Washington and the buildings really excel anything I had an idea of. They are more numerous

[h] Dué was Catherine Dupleix, wife of a naval captain, George Dupleix. Mrs. Dupleix is also called "Doux" in some of the Seton correspondence.

[i] Sandy Hook, is a spit of land on the northern New Jersey shore at the outer reach of New York harbor. The lighthouse there, built in 1764, is the oldest in the United States.

[j] John (Jack) Curson Seton was by then married to Miss Mary Wise and lived in Alexandria, Virginia. Henry Seton, another brother who was in the Navy, was also one of the family party to visit Washington that June.

than could be expected but you see nothing in the streets but cows and pigs. It is a journey from one house to another."[35] He was quite content to return to New York in July.

Elizabeth enjoyed the long days spent with her children. They had discovered a beautiful rock out behind the cornfield, and Elizabeth found it a peaceful spot for reading.

They made a charming rustic scene, the dark-haired mother bending over her letters, the baby Kate sleeping in her lap, the others playing at "tea" with little shells gathered from along the shore. Elizabeth was unconsciously storing up strength for the ordeal to come. Mornings before her father rose, Elizabeth would take Kate to the porch where she paced slowly up and down, breathing deeply the mild morning air, soothed by the presence of the little child in her arms. "Precious companion," she mused; "here is at least one Peaceful spotless Soul, who never offends—how earnest is my prayer that it may continue so far as Human nature will allow."[36] One late afternoon she took Anna Maria to the attic of the little house "to experience the awe of a solemn thought greatly heightened by viewing the heavens in open space without an intervening object." Elizabeth wanted her daughter to sense the vastness yet closeness of her Creator, to understand that when she made promises to be good these promises were made before God Who knew all she said and did. When Elizabeth looked down into the serious little face, rosy in the sunset glow, her heart was filled with love and compassion, and she thought, "poor little Puss, she is very sensible [for her age] but she will have many hard struggles."[37]

Her own spiritual experiences were virtually undirected that summer. Sometimes the sight of St. Paul's steeple in the distance filled Elizabeth with longing to be back in New York at church with Rebecca, listening to the young assistant, Rev. John Henry Hobart,[k] whose fervor was beginning to attract her so much. One Sunday she wrote Rebecca:

> Dear Sister, I am a prisoner, too—with all this wide and beautiful creation before me the restless soul longs to enjoy its liberty and rest beyond its bound. When the Father calls His child how readily He will be obeyed.[38]

She sought relief for her yearning in her best-loved remedy, her Bible. Meditating over its phrases she turned to journaling by writing down her own reflections, as had been her custom in New York.

[k] Rev. John Henry Hobart, (1775-1830), came as curate to Trinity Church, New York, in December 1800 and was Elizabeth Seton's spiritual director until 1805. Hobart bitterly opposed her conversion to Roman Catholicism. Although he was an ordained minister in the Protestant Episcopal Church, usually he was referred to as "Mr." according to nineteenth-century custom until his appointment as assistant bishop in 1811.

"Blessed are they that mourn" elicited from Elizabeth the reflection:

> These divine assurances soothe and encourage the Christian's disturbed and dejected mind, and insensibly diffuse a holy composure. The tint may be solemn and even melancholy, but it is mild and grateful. The tumult of his soul has subsided, and he is possessed by complacency, hope and love. If a sense of this undeserved kindness fills his eyes with tears, they are tears of reconciliation and joy, while a generous ardour springing up within him sends him forth to his worldly labors "fervent in spirit" resolving through Divine Grace to be henceforth more diligent and exemplary in living to the Glory of God. And longing meanwhile for that blessed time when "being freed from the bondage of corruption" he shall be enabled to render to his Heavenly Benefactor more pure and acceptable service.[39]

Her ability to apply her theories was tested almost immediately.

The yellow fever came early that summer. By the middle of June young Joseph Bayley had a hundred patients on Staten Island to visit and provide for. The health establishment had to be hurriedly enlarged. There were already ten large tents in use and "other buildings filling up as fast as a half dozen carpenters, boatmen, and all hands" could work, spurred on as they were by Dr. Bayley. Bayley's house was re-enclosed by a fence which worried the children until they were promised a back gate to the hills, and then their spirits lifted. Immigrants were pouring in by boat loads and Elizabeth was intrigued by their practice of assembling on the grass to kneel and pray in thanksgiving.[40] By the middle of July the younger doctor was sick himself, and the burden on the elder Bayley pressed more heavily. The building went on night and day, but the migrants continued to arrive. On one day alone a small vessel disgorged between four and five hundred people, many of whom had never seen the light of day since they entered the vessel, and a hundred of whom were sick on arrival. Little infants died the moment they were brought into the fresh air, many of them dying of starvation even at their mother's breast.[41]

To all these sufferers Dr. Bayley was as a father. The rising sun found him already about his work some two or three hours. Except for an occasional moment of rest by the side of Elizabeth's piano, his labors were unceasing. Elizabeth wrote Sad a note asking her to try to find a cook for the quarantine and promised that if the cook liked Elizabeth for a mistress she could go home to State Street with her in the fall.[42] The horror of the scene pressed upon Elizabeth and nights found her unable to sleep. From her window, wherever she looked, she saw lights from the tents pitched in the yard of the convalescent house, from the large one made to adjoin the "Dead House." She was filled with a kind of guilt that her own child Kit was so amply nourished while those others lay dying.[43]

The weekly visits of her husband were often mixed with frustration. William Magee was tired from his work in the hot city, worried over his failure to solve the financial tangle of the Seton affairs, and weakened by consumption. At best, a weekend cannot repair the ravages of separation, and Elizabeth found "this strange way of living-meeting but once a week, and then wearied and out of spirits" as difficult as he. When he said she would have to stay on Staten Island until October she was not overjoyed but accepted his ultimatum. As she put it to Rebecca, "Father says I shall go as soon as I please [after] September 15th, but *Willy's* please must be *my* please."[44]

Fortunately, William Magee was not regularly so disgruntled, and often his visits offered a real relief to the misery of the scene. On the occasions when the expected arrival of a ship revived his hopes for business recovery, his elation spread through the family. The afternoon would pass with William Magee striding the sea wall, his spyglass in hand, followed by the small train of admirers, as happy a day for Elizabeth "as a mortal ought to have."[45]

In August the second great trial of Elizabeth's courage came. On the eleventh day of the month Dr. Bayley came in from his early morning rounds, quite sick. He had been out since daylight, and no one was surprised when he took his tea in silence. Elizabeth felt the first alarm when, a little later, she saw him sitting in the blazing sun on the wharf, his head in his hands. She hurriedly sent out an umbrella for shade, and when she saw his look of bewilderment and distress, she burst into tears. By the time the doctor was put to bed he was delirious. Plainly, he had the fever. Joseph Bayley, his friend and assistant, was sufficiently recovered to attend him, but neither opium nor any other remedy brought relief to the older man.[46]

The children, Anna Maria and Willy, were sent away to Mary Post's until Dr. Bayley should improve. Dr. Post sat up with his father-in-law, and brought Dr. Tillary[1] from town to stay until there should be a change.

---

[1] Probably Dr. James Tillary, a Scotsman, who came to New York at the time of the Revolution and was a colleague of Dr. Bayley.

Elizabeth, of course, was scarcely away from his side, except to nurse the baby. He seemed to gain some small relief from her presence, and held convulsively to her arm. The respected "blister" was tried again, but brought no relief. He could keep nothing on his stomach. The thoughts of his poor immigrants preyed upon his mind and he would call out in his delirium, "Cover me warm; I have covered many! Poor little children—I would cover you more, but it can't always be as you wish." He seemed to realize that his fever was fatal and gave his keys to Elizabeth; and on the third day he told her he felt the hand of God was in it all. Mary came over and sat with Elizabeth as the end drew near. Sunday, 16 August, it was obvious, would tell the story. As Elizabeth let her thoughts drift back to the previous Sunday it seemed as if a nightmare must have enveloped her, for just a week ago her father had been well and sitting at the dining room window engrossed in the activity of the ships and pilots in the harbor. Just a week ago he had played with little Kit, feeding her with a spoon from his glass of drink. Was it only last Sunday she had played while he sang with gusto his favorite German hymns and "The Soldier's Adieu"? The only way she could bear it at all was to repeat over and over, "Thy will be done." If such suffering could be, and not be God's will—but the thought was insupportable.[47]

On Monday Dr. Bayley suffered extreme pain; then toward the middle of the afternoon the pain seemed to leave him. He turned toward Elizabeth, put his hand in hers, and died. How Elizabeth got through the days which followed can only be imagined. It was planned to bury Dr. Bayley in the Richmond Town churchyard of St. Andrew's Episcopal Church on Staten Island, and for a while complications developed over the refusal of the parish to allow his body to be carried through the island. A grave was dug near the house of the health establishment; but suddenly the solution occurred; the body could be taken by a barge to Richmond Town. And so Dr. Bayley went to his final repose by boat, accompanied by Joseph Bayley and Darby, the faithful boatman. Two wagons full of friends and relatives went by land to witness the service which Dr. Richard Channing Moore performed. Elizabeth and the children left Staten Island as fast as they could the following week. Joseph Bayley, who regarded Dr. Bayley as a father whose fostering hand had laid the foundation of his career, took care of the things left undone, sent back the Setons' little bird, and arranged for the transfer of their other effects. Elizabeth wrote a letter of appreciation to Dr. Moore in which she concluded:

The only remaining wish I have is that a small space may be reserved on each side of him for his two eldest children.[m] This request is not the impulse of unrestrained sorrow but of a heart that knows where its home is to be, and feels the greatest consolation in the hope that it may be permitted to repose by its dear parent.[48]

The house Elizabeth was to inhabit from the time of her father's death until the voyage to Italy began, "Number 8 State Street," was on the Battery. It was next to a three story brick building occupied by Joseph Corré, who operated the famous Columbia Garden south of the corner lot at State and Pearl.[n] Corré had recently obtained permission to make a gate in the Battery fence just opposite Columbia Garden and here he offered concerts, as well as ice cream, to the public on their evening walks along the Battery.[49] For fifty cents his patrons received ice cream, punch or wine, cake, and vocalists besides. The younger Setons probably were not allowed these evening pleasures but they enjoyed their new location nevertheless. Elizabeth's note to Rebecca ran,

> My own Rebecca would rejoice to see our cheerful countenances at the Nor'wester...Kit is calling Mamma as loud as she can hallow and Anna, Will, and Dick [are] on the Battery, only inside the Gate.[50]

Soon the cares and interest of family and friends once more began to press upon Elizabeth. Mrs. Sadler was depressed by family illness and needed comfort. Eliza Seton Maitland had sent her infant and its wet nurse to Elizabeth for the winter; Cecilia Seton, who had been at school for the summer term, was returning to continue her lessons under Elizabeth's supervision. James Maitland, husband of Eliza Seton Maitland, was "put in limits" in January and this left Eliza and her five children to the worry of William Magee Seton, who was forced to supply them from his own storeroom "as no other part of the family [would] keep them from starving—

[m] It is interesting to speculate as to why only the children of the first marriage were to lie by his side when the will of Dr. Bayley, probated 26 August 1800, left all his property to his second wife, her heirs, "and assigns." There is no solution in the historical evidence. However, it is erroneous to conclude that Bayley "disinherited" Elizabeth Seton and Mary Post. The will was an old one drawn up in December 1788, just prior to a voyage to England. Elizabeth was at the time only fourteen, and Mary was a few years older. It was quite proper and logical for the will to read as it did, under those circumstances. The failure of Dr. Bayley to make a new will is probably due to many reasons, chief among which could have been his temperament. We know from his own words that caution was not a virtue he admired. He probably did not expect to die at the age of fifty-six. There can be no doubt, from archival evidence, of the children closest to him prior to his death; these were the daughters of his first wife, Catherine Charlton.

[n] No. 8 State Street in 1793 was sold under foreclosure to a James Watson. It was probably a single house. Nos. 9-11 were the property of Carey Ludlow [there was no No. 10] and from 1797 Corré occupied No. 9. On 14 May 1798, he had secured permission to open the gate in the Battery fence. It seems probable that the Setons never owned 8 State Street.

or even in fire wood."[51] The Widows' Society was to need much of her time, since Elizabeth was the treasurer of the group and encountered the traditional difficulties in getting money. As she told Julia, she rose early and retired late, but "everybody has their Pride of some sort, I cannot deny that this is mine."[52] Her constant inspiration that winter was a new-found friend.

In February 1802, Elizabeth sent a letter to Julia Scott by John Henry Hobart which contained the following introduction:

> There are various kinds of attachments in this world, some of affection, without the soothing confidence of trust and esteem united—some of esteem for virtues which we can neither approach nor assimilate to our own natures, and some—the unbounded veneration, affection, esteem and the tribute of "the Heart Sincere"—The bearer of this letter possesses *in full* the reality of the last description in *my heart*—and, in fact, I can give no stronger proof of the affection and esteem I bear you than in expressing to you what I believe another would pervert or ridicule—
>
> The soother and comforter of the troubled *soul* is a kind of friend not often met with—the convincing, pious, and singular turn of mind, and argument possessed by this most amiable being, has made him, without his even having the least consciousness that he is so, the friend most my friend in this world, and one of those who after my Adored Creator I expect to receive the largest share of happiness from in the next.[53]

At the time Hobart carried this letter to Philadelphia he was twenty-six years old and had been ordained scarcely a year in the ministry of the Protestant Episcopal Church. He had come to Trinity Parish as an assistant in December 1800, from Hempstead, Long Island. Trinity, at that time, had one rector and three assistants; Dr. Benjamin Moore was rector, and Abraham Beach and Cave Jones° acted as assistants with Hobart.[54] Elizabeth Seton's maternal uncle, Dr. John Charlton, was the senior warden of Trinity when Hobart was called to serve on 8 September 1800, at a salary of $500 a year. Hobart had received almost simultaneously an invitation from St. Mark's, the Bowery church, but he accepted Trinity's offer as more desirable. That his decision was a wise one is clear from his subsequent career. A decade

---

° Cave Jones came to Trinity four months after John Henry Hobart. It was under his leadership that opposition to Hobart's appointment as bishop in 1811 came to a head. Hobart was made assistant bishop in 1811, diocesan bishop and rector in 1816. He died 12 September 1830, while visiting Auburn, New York.

later he was made assistant bishop, and by the time of his death he had reached the height of power and prestige in the church of his profession.[55]

His appearance in the pulpits of Trinity, St. Paul's, and St. George's was the sensation of the day. Elizabeth Seton was only one of the many parishioners to fall under the spell of his oratory. Hobart's personal appearance was responsible for very little of his appeal, since in size he was rather short, his head seemed too large for his body, and his nearsighted eyes were perpetually behind his thick spectacles. But what he missed in "the glance of the eye" he more than atoned for in voice and delivery. In a day when deliberate and sepulchral tones were used to deliver speeches from sheets of notes, Hobart's rapid, flexible voice uttering sentiments which seemed to spring from strongest conviction and which were apparently extemporaneously expounded could only amaze his listeners. Although the less fiery ministers criticized his method on the grounds of good taste, many a bored pew holder was roused to new attention by this first introduction to the evangelical kind of preaching which was to sweep all the branches of Protestantism in the early nineteenth century. As one of his admirers said of him:

> He appeared in the pulpit as a father anxious for the eternal happiness of his children—a man of God preparing them for Christian warfare—a herald from the other world, standing between the living and the dead, between heaven and earth entreating perishing sinners in the most tender accents, not to reject the message of reconciliation which the Son of the living God so graciously offered for their acceptance.[56]

Certainly to the feminine part of the congregation the new young minister epitomized Christian manhood. His young bride of less than a year was the daughter of the famous cleric Dr. Thomas Bradbury Chandler who had been well known in New Jersey religious circles. Mary Goodin Chandler gave birth to a daughter, Jane, on 8 March 1801, and continued thereafter to mother the increasing Hobart family. When Hobart stopped at Julia Scott's in Philadelphia that February 1802, he was on a mission of love and consolation. His sister was seriously ill in Frankfort, Pennsylvania, and his mother was failing rapidly. In August when he called on Elizabeth Seton he told her "about his mother and sister, and that he had brought home her son to educate him as his own."[57] Mr. Hobart himself never was physically robust and it is from this nephew's account that Hobart's biographer learned that the young minister sometimes fainted at family prayers.[p]

---

[p] This was the eldest son of Rebecca Hobart Smith.

The great devotion between Mr. Hobart and his mother offered a fine example to his congregation.[58] The months of 1802-1803 found him increasingly concerned over her health. One Sunday when Elizabeth was disappointed to see Cave Jones in Henry Hobart's place. She asked him, after the service was over, if they "had lost Mr. Hobart—Poor man, was the reply, he has been attending *his Mother* whom Dr. [Benjamen] Rush has given over and suffers a great deal of fatigue and distress on her account." Reporting the incident to Rebecca, Elizabeth added, "He was summoned to her the Monday after *our Sunday* [Sacrament Sunday]—Well might I see him heated, wearied and covered with dust."[59]

When Hobart's mother died, the same year that his second daughter was born,[q] the two events only served to endear him more to his ardent admirers, and Wright Post, who attended the young Mrs. Hobart, refused to accept any remuneration from the harassed husband.[60] John Henry Hobart was surely a man to inspire admiration and arouse sympathy. It was not surprising that once Elizabeth Seton came under his influence her interest in religion should grow rapidly. Mr. Hobart, in turn, was deeply impressed with the piety of Elizabeth and her sister-in-law, Rebecca Seton.[61]

The absorption of Elizabeth in spiritual concerns was very noticeable during the spring of 1802. She kept a kind of journal of her meditations, parts of which have long been available to the public.[62] Here we find the entry of the fourth Sunday in May, which begins:

This blessed day—Sunday 23rd May 1802—my Soul was first sensibly convinced of the blessing and practicability of an entire surrender of itself and all its faculties to God. [63]

The entry for the following Wednesday contains this added passage:[r]

Is it nothing to sleep serene under his Guardian Wing—to awake to the brightness of the glorious sun with renewed strength and renewed blessings—to be blessed with the power of instant communion with the Father of our Spirits the sense of His Presence, the influences of His Love —to be assured of that love is enough to tie us faithfully to Him and while we have fidelity to Him all the surrounding cares and contradictions of this

[q] Rebecca Smith Hobart was born 6 February 1803. It was this child who grew up to marry Levi Silliman Ives, and became a Catholic in later life. Joseph B. Code, *Letters of Mother Seton to Julia Scott,* 151, gives the name as Rebecca Seton Hobart and adds that Elizabeth Seton was the child's godmother. The name *Rebecca Smith Hobart* is the way it appears in the *Correspondence of John Henry Hobart* list of children given in volume I.

[r] This passage was not in print until the corpus of the Seton papers was published as *Elizabeth Bayley Seton Collected Writings.*

Life are but cords of mercy to bind us faster to Him who will hereafter make even their remembrances to vanish in the reality of our external felicity.[64]

Thursday, Ascension Day, witnessed the following entry, which was incorrectly given in previously published versions:

> Oh that my soul might go up with my blessed Lord—that it might be *where He is also*—Thy Will be done—my time is in Thy Hands—but O my Savior, while the pilgrimage of this life must still go on to fulfill Thy Gracious Purpose, let the spirit of my mind follow Thee to Thy mansions of glory—to Thee alone it belongs, receive it in mercy, perfect it in truth, and preserve it unspotted from the world. "Heaven cannot separate Thee from thy children, nor can earth detain them from Thee." Raise us up by a life of faith with Thee.[65]

Elizabeth's preoccupation with her journal caused a temporary falling off in her letters to Julia Scott. When she finally sat down the evening of 19 August to renew the former exchange, she was destined not to finish the letter she began. William Magee's addition the following day explained the reason:

> Thus far, my very amiable little Friend, did our dear Eliza write last night at 11 o'clock & this morning. At twelve I have the satisfaction to tell you she was safely delivered of a girl.... The mother is as well as she usually is on such occasions, *better* than could be expected for we had neither *Doctor* nor *anything of the kind,* till a quarter of an hour after the young Lady made her appearance.[66]

The birth of Rebecca Mary Seton[s] came quite close to the anniversary of Dr. Bayley's death. Just three days before, in a note to Rebecca, Elizabeth had written in sorrowful recollection, "Dear, dear Rebecca, *the 17th August last year about this time* 3 *o'clock* in *the afternoon—never* mind someone will be thinking of us in a few years."[67]

The new baby helped to fill the void left by the death of Elizabeth's father. To a household accustomed to the presence of a small baby, the arrival of a new one is salutary as well as pleasure-giving. The former "baby" of the family becomes a person in her own right, while all the children softened, however imperceptibly, by the helplessness of the new arrival, in their respective degrees are made more mature and responsible. For Elizabeth

---

[s] Rebecca Mary Seton (20 August 1802–3 November 1816), was named after her paternal aunt who was Elizabeth Seton's "soul sister." She died at age fourteen and is buried in St. Joseph's Cemetery, the original graveyard at Emmitsburg.

the birth of Rebecca was an added incentive to increase personal sanctity. Her journal note for 12 September recorded:

> Three weeks and two days after the birth of *my Rebecca* [I] renewed my covenant that I would strive with myself and use every endeavor to serve my dear Redeemer and to give myself wholly unto Him.[68]

Even before Rebecca was born Elizabeth had made her plans for the "christening," and this event took place on Wednesday, St. Michael's Day, 1802. The entry made by the young mother that day was a long joyous tribute of praise to "Him who has obtained for His servant these inestimable privileges—to enter into a covenant with Him—to commune with his spirit—to receive the blessings of our reconciled Father."[69] The baptism of Rebecca served to increase Elizabeth's fears for the soul of her poor servant, Mammy Huler, who had now been ailing for more than a year. She arranged to have Mr. Linn[t] come at eleven o'clock one Sunday to perform the ceremony and she herself remained, the Saturday before, by Mammy's side saying the sick prayers and instructing her for the next day's baptism.[70]

On 16 November 1802, Elizabeth wrote to Julia, *"Our Mammy [Huler] is gone*—O if you could have witnessed in her the comforts and consolations of a humble soul seeking a refuge of a Redeemer, you would teach your children that to know and love Him is the ONLY GOOD—She was literally 'born anew'—and died without a struggle or groan—as a child composed to rest in the arms of its Parent—sure of an awakening secure."[71]

Elizabeth's capacity for love and solicitude for her friends now seemed to increase as her cares and responsibilities at home redoubled. In the same letter carrying news of Mammy Huler's death, Elizabeth tried to explain to Julia that her devotion to the life of the spirit in no way detracted from her attachment to her friends.

> No, dear Julia—religion does not limit the powers of the affections, for our Blessed Savior Sanctifies and approves in us all the endearing ties and connections of our existence, but Religion alone can bind that cord over which neither circumstances, time, or death, can have no power—Death on the contrary perfect[s] that union which the cares, chances or sorrows of life may have interrupted by opening the scene where all the promises, hopes, and consolations we

---

[t] Possibly Mr. Linn was Rev. William Linn (1752-1833), a Presbyterian minister who joined the Dutch Reformed Church in 1787.

have received from our Redeemer will have their triumphant accomplishment.[72]

If the birth of her fifth child brought Elizabeth happiness, how much more was the change in William Magee to increase that joy. From scattered clues found in notes to Rebecca it is evident that William Magee did not, in the beginning, share his wife's fervor for churchgoing or for Mr. Hobart. He liked to beg off with the excuse that because of business he was "too much troubled." He would drive her to the church door, but leave her to attend alone or with Rebecca. When the weather grew bad Elizabeth had to write Rebecca,

> My spirits are heavy—Willy says so much about my going tomorrow and that we shall not without a carriage—that it is madness, the streets almost impassable, etc...You must not lose if *I* must—You had better go to Mrs. Bogert's pew as she has since pressed me to come there.[73]

On 15 August shortly before baby Rebecca was born, Elizabeth had been alone at the evening service conducted by her favorite "H. H.," and her elation, which lasted well into the next day, had been marred only by her husband's attitude. Her note to Rebecca ran,

> Never could I have thought of such enjoyment in *this world*— last night was surely a *foretaste* of the next—nor *pain* nor *weight* either soul or body...*Our H.H.* was at *St. Mark's* instead of St. Paul's [this morning]...Willy regretted very much he did not hear him—*regrets are idle things.* Oh when every regret will be forgot—*and every hope perfected.*[74]

Just when William Magee began to change in his attitude of indifference cannot be accurately determined, except to place the event between the birth of the fifth child and the fall of 1803, when the Setons sailed for Europe. A succession of undated notes to Rebecca carry such expressions as these: "Willy says he will *dine at home* tomorrow—with a significant smile—I shall be too happy if he means to keep his promise *freely* and without persuasion from me"[75] or "I think our Willy will go—he has not left me five minutes since yesterday's dinner and has had *Nelson*[u] in his hands very often—if he does, what a dinner will *today's* be for me."[76]

When he finally did attend, William Magee did not immediately fall under the spell of Hobart's oratory, as this line to Rebecca Seton indicates.

---

[u] "Nelson" refers to Robert Nelson's *Companion for Festivals and Fasts of the Church of England* (London, 1736). This was a favorite collection of prayers of John Henry Hobart's choosing. Hobart published an edition of his own in 1805 using Nelson as the basis for his *The Companion for Festivals and Fasts.*

"Mr. Hobart this morning—language cannot express the comfort, the Peace, the Hope—but Willy did not understand, that happy hour is yet to come."[77] But come it did at last and Elizabeth was able to confide to Mr. Hobart, when he visited the Seton home the Monday following the joyful occasion, that, "The last 24 hours were the happiest I had ever seen or could expect as the most earnest wish of my heart was fulfilled." To Rebecca she added the following words, "Dear Rebecca, if you had known how sweet last evening was—Willy's heart seemed to be nearer to me for being nearer to his God."[78]

The newly strengthened conjugal affection was tested almost at once—for Seton's health, long known to be precarious, in 1803 declined so steadily and so fast that the friends of the family despaired of his recovery. As a last resort, the Setons determined to try the time-honored remedy of a sea voyage, and they made plans to sail for Italy in the fall of 1803. Elizabeth must have done much of the last-minute arranging of the family affairs and disposal of their furniture, for her husband and children were at Mary Bayley Post's in August,[v] according to a note addressed to Anna Maria Seton which read, "Do as Mary tells you, and be very kind to her... take good care of dear Papa while he is with you and do all you can to please Him."[79] Elizabeth had debated the best arrangements to make in regard to the children. She asked Sad's advice about taking Anna Maria along, and said she thought the child was so young the voyage would "have its use to her in many ways and probably will be strongly remembered by her through life."[80] The baby, Rebecca, was to stay with Mary and Wright Post. Phoebe, the household servant, went along with the baby to relieve Mrs. Post of the burden of a child so young. It must have wrenched Elizabeth's heart to leave the smallest of her "darlings," especially since little Rebecca was ill at Post's even before the ship sailed.[81] The other three children were left in the charge of William Magee's sister, Rebecca Seton, who was still at Maitland's. The elder Seton girls, Elizabeth's sisters-in-law, went to live with James Seton, their elder half-brother,[82] James was by this time pretty well established as an insurance broker, with offices at 67 Wall Street and his residence at 85 Greenwich Street. The Maitlands were probably then located at Jay Street.[83]

The valuable items of furniture were left with young Mr. Hobart and his wife. We find this passage in a letter from Hobart to the Setons, written after they had sailed:

---

[v] That summer the Posts were at Far Rockaway enjoying the seashore on the Rockaway Peninsula in the present New York City borough of Queens.

Your furniture we gladly preserve as memorials of you. I never cast my eye on the escritoire without thinking of its inestimable owner, nor on the piano forte without having my soul in imagination enlivened and soothed by the chants of praise and consolation which it was my delight to hear burst forth from it. The sacred portrait of the Redeemer[w] recalls to my mind the ardent piety of her who before this endeared memorial poured forth the emotions of holy love and gratitude.[84]

Just before leaving, Elizabeth paid a last visit to Staten Island and the Quarantine. She walked through the garden, over the wooden wharf, and down to the boat her father had so often sailed. His old friends, Darby and William, who had gone snipe hunting with Dr. Bayley in the old days, took Elizabeth for a last sail around the bay. Joseph Bayley, who was now in charge of the health establishment, welcomed her for an hour's visit and she went to her father's room to stand in "the very spot" where she had last seen him alive. Her thoughts were so vivid she felt convinced his spirit was with her.[85] It was as close as she could return to the roots from which she had sprung. Armed with recollection and a memorandum from Mr. Hobart in regard to reading the psalms she went aboard the *Shepherdess*. True, "the Pangs of Parting Nature would press"; but Elizabeth took courage from her conviction that God "over rules all."[86]

---

[w] *The Redeemer* is an engraving with an inscription printed beneath the image which reads "G. Festolini *Excudit*, W. Miller *Pinxil*, and T. Gaugain *Sculpsil*." This engraving is preserved in the Archives of the Daughters of Charity, Emmitsburg, Maryland. According to tradition the picture was a gift from William Magee Seton to his wife.

CHAPTER 3. FATHER AND DAUGHTER

Notes

[1] Dr. Richard Bayley to Elizabeth Seton, Newark, 23 January 1795, ASJPH 1-3-3-9:93.

[2] Ibid.

[3] 1.9, Elizabeth Seton to Eliza Sadler, n.p., 11 August 1796, *CW*, 1:12.

[4] 1.47, Elizabeth Seton to Julia Scott, 11 June 1799, *CW,* 1:75.

[5] 1.37, Elizabeth Seton to Julia Scott, New York, 20 January 1799, *CW*, 1:59. This letter contains the suggestive sentence, "My Father perseveres in his resolution that I shall never admit a reconciliation with Mrs. B." Ibid.

[6] Dr. Richard Bayley to Elizabeth Seton, Water Vliet, n.d., ASJPH 1-3-3-9:100.

[7] 1.41, Elizabeth Seton to Julia Scott, New York, 15 March 1799, *CW*, 1:65; Mary Bayley Post to Elizabeth Seton, New York, 8 December 1811, ASJPH 1-3-3-11:12.

[8] 1.40, Elizabeth Seton to Richard Bayley, New York, 24 February 1799, *CW*, 1:63.

[9] 1.65, Elizabeth Seton to Richard Bayley, New York, 10 September 1799, *CW*, 1:96.

[10] Ibid.

[11] 1.75, Elizabeth Seton to Rebecca Seton, New York, 3 January 1800, *CW*, 1:109.

[12] Dr. Richard Bayley to Elizabeth Seton, Water Vliet, 8 February 1800, ASJPH 1-3-3-9:98. The capital of New York was moved in January 1798.

[13] Dr. Richard Bayley to Elizabeth Seton, Water Vliet, n.d., ASJPH 1-3-3-9:100.

[14] Dr. Richard Bayley to Elizabeth Seton, Water Vliet, 8 February 1800, ASJPH 1-3-3-9:98; Ibid., n.d., ASJPH 1-3-3-9:100.

[15] Dr. Richard Bayley to Elizabeth Seton, Water Vliet, 4 February 1798, ASJPH 1-3-3-9:95.

[16] Ibid.

[17] Dr. Richard Bayley to Elizabeth Seton, Water Vliet, 8 February 1800, ASJPH 1-3-3-9:98.

[18] 1.41, Elizabeth Seton to Julia Scott, New York, 15 March 1799, *CW*, 1:65.

[19] Dr. Richard Bayley to Elizabeth Seton, Staten Island, 24 May 1800, ASJPH 1-3-3-9:102; Ibid., 5 June 1800, ASJPH 1-3-3-9:103.

[20] 1.87, Elizabeth Seton to Julia Scott, Staten Island, 1 July 1800, *CW*, 1:124. The daughter was Catherine Charlton Seton.

21 1.91, Elizabeth Seton to Julia Scott, Staten Island, 26 July 1800, *CW*, 1:136.

22 Ibid. "The hook" probably meant Sandy Hook.

23 1.89, Elizabeth Seton to Catherine Dupleix, Staten Island, 12 July 1800, *CW*, 1:127.

24 1.93, Elizabeth Seton to Rebecca Seton, Staten Island, 11 August 1800, *CW*, 1:133-134.

25 1.96, Elizabeth Seton to Eliza Sadler, Staten Island, 27 September 1800, *CW*, 1:137.

26 Dr. Richard Bayley to Elizabeth Seton, Staten Island, 26 October 1800, ASJPH 1-3-3-9:104.

27 1.99, Elizabeth Seton to Julia Scott, New York, 19 November 1800, *CW*, 1:139.

28 1.108, Elizabeth Seton to Julia Scott, New York, 10 March 1801, *CW*, 1:149; 1.107, Elizabeth Seton to Richard Bayley, New York, 1 March 1801, *CW*, 1:148.

29 1.182, Elizabeth Seton to Richard Bayley, New York, n.d., *CW*, 1:227; 1.112, Ibid., 2 April 1801, *CW*, 1:154; 1.188, Ibid., n.d., *CW*, 1:230.

30 1.119, Elizabeth Seton to Eliza Sadler, Staten Island, n.d. [June 1801], *CW*, 1:161.

31 1.84, Elizabeth Seton to Rebecca Seton, Staten Island, n.d. [1800], *CW*, 1:123.

32 1.119, Elizabeth Seton to Eliza Sadler, Staten Island, n.d. [June 1801], *CW*, 1:161.

33 1.116, Elizabeth Seton to Rebecca Seton, Staten Island, n.d., Thursday Morning [1801], *CW*, 1:157; 1.118, Elizabeth Seton to Julia Scott, Staten Island, 11 June 1801, *CW*, 1:159; 1.115, Elizabeth Seton to Rebecca Seton, Staten Island, 7 June 1801, *CW*, 1:156-157.

34 William Magee Seton to Elizabeth Seton, Baltimore, 10 June 1801, ASJPH 26-0-2, (12). Copy. The original is in Archives Sisters of Charity of St. Elizabeth, Convent Station, New Jersey. Hereinafter cited as ASCSE.

35 William Magee Seton to Elizabeth Seton, Alexandria, 18 June 1801, ASJPH 26-0-2, (13). Copy. The original is in AMSV.

36 1.92, Elizabeth Seton to Rebecca Seton, Staten Island, n.d. [1800], *CW*, 1:133.

37 1.136, Elizabeth Seton to Rebecca Seton, Staten Island, 29 July 1801, *CW*, 1:181.

38 1.115, Elizabeth Seton to Rebecca Seton, Staten Island, 7 June 1801, *CW*, 1:156.

[39] 8.7, "O tarry thou thy Lord's leisure," 26 July 1801, *CW,* 3a:20.

[40] 1.121, Elizabeth Seton to Rebecca Seton, Staten Island, 14 June 1801, *CW,* 1:162-163.

[41] 8.8, "No words can describe," undated, *CW,* 3a:21; 1.132, Elizabeth Seton to Rebecca Seton, Staten Island, 15 July 1801, *CW,* 1:175.

[42] 1.133, Elizabeth Seton to Eliza Sadler, Staten Island, 20 July 1801, *CW,* 1:175.

[43] 1.137, Elizabeth Seton to Rebecca Seton, Staten Island, n.d., *CW,* 1:181.

[44] 1.130, Elizabeth Seton to Rebecca Seton, Tuesday afternoon [1801], *CW,* 1:173.

[45] 1.134, Elizabeth Seton to Rebecca Seton, Staten Island, 20 July 1801, *CW,* 1:177.

[46] 1.139, Elizabeth Seton to Rebecca Seton, Staten Island, 16 August 1801, *CW,* 1:183; 1.141, Elizabeth Seton to Julia Scott, New York, 5 September 1801, *CW,* 1:185.

[47] Joseph Bayley to Elizabeth Seton, Staten Island, 23 August 1801, ASJPH 1-3-3-2:97; 1.141, Elizabeth Seton to Julia Scott, New York, 5 September 1801, *CW,* 1:185.

[48] 1.140, Elizabeth Seton draft to Rev. Richard Channing Moore, New York, n.d. [17 August 1801], *CW,* 1:184. See Arthur J. Burns, "New Light on Mother Seton," *Historical Records and Studies, XXII, (1932),* 85-98.

[49] Rodman Gilder, *The Battery* (Boston, 1936), 125. Cf. Isaac N. Phelps Stokes, *Iconography of Manhattan Island* (New York, 1915-1928), I: 425.

[50] 1.117, Elizabeth Seton to Rebecca Seton, n.p., n.d. [1801], *CW,* 1:159.

[51] 1.155, Elizabeth Seton to Julia Scott, 1 February 1802, *CW,* 1:202 and 1.147, Seton to Scott, 27 October 1801, *CW,* 193.

[52] 1.149, Elizabeth Seton to Julia Scott, New York, 7 January 1802, *CW,* 1:197; 1.150, Elizabeth Seton to Rebecca Seton, n.p., n.d., *CW,* 1:198.

[53] 1.155, Elizabeth Seton to Julia Scott, New York, 1 February 1802, *CW,* 1:201.

[54] Henry Anstice, *History of St. George's Church* (New York, 1911), 46-7.

[55] John McVickar, *The Early Years and Professional Life of Bishop Hobart* (Oxford, 1838), 178-85.

[56] Ibid., 190.

[57] 1.202, Elizabeth Seton to Rebecca Seton, New York, n.d., *CW,* 1:239. McVickar, 192.

[58] The strength of this affection is amply evidenced in *The Correspondence of John Henry Hobart* (New York, 1911). Much of the first three volumes is composed of letters from his mother.

[59] 1.193, Elizabeth Seton to Rebecca Seton, New York, n.d., *CW*, 1:233. Dr. Rush was Dr. Benjamin Rush of Philadelphia.

[60] *Correspondence of John Henry Hobart,* III, 266, Post to Hobart, New York, 8 August 1803.

[61] Robert Seton, *Memoir, Letters and Journal,* I, 83, unfortunately uses the word "infatuation" in describing Elizabeth Seton's attitude toward Mr. Hobart. Except in the most literal sense of extravagant admiration, the word is not justified. Mme. de Barberey also leaves an erroneous impression when she states, "Une amitié qui remontait aux jours de son enfance unissait Elizabeth á M. Hobart." See Mme. de Barberey, *Elizabeth Seton,* 243. Until he came to Trinity at the close of 1800, Elizabeth Seton did not know him. She was in her twenty-seventh year at that time.

[62] Robert Seton, *Memoir, Letters and Journal,* I, 84, 90; C. I. White, *Life of Mrs. Eliza A. Seton* (New York, 1853), 35-37; 56-57.

[63] 8.10, "My peace I leave with you," 1802, *CW*, 3a:23.

[64] Ibid., 24.

[65] Ibid., 25. Code, in editing *A Daily Thought from the Writings of Mother Seton* (1929), entry May 26, reprints from Robert Seton's *Memoir, Letters and Journal,* I, 85, an entry which telescopes two entirely different entries, and reverses the chronological order, as well. It is this type of editing that makes both Joseph Code and Robert Seton unreliable. See Chapter 12, endnote 103, for another example of a published version of a letter of William Seton to his mother for which the original is no longer available for verification.

[66] 1.164, Elizabeth Seton to Julia Scott, New York, 20 August 1802, *CW*, 1:210. Charles I. White gives the birth of Rebecca Seton correctly. See White, 37; but other biographers like Seton, Code, Sadlier erroneously state that Rebecca was born on 20 July. On the part of Code this is strange in view of the fact that in *Letters to Mrs. Scott* he reprints Elizabeth's part of the letter correctly dated 19 August.

[67] 1.163, Elizabeth Seton to Rebecca Seton, New York, n.d., *CW*, 1:209.

[68] 8.25, Notebook of Psalm 23 and Rev. John Henry Hobart's Sermons, entry dated 12 September, *CW*, 3a:171.

[69] 8.12, "This day my little Rebecca," Wednesday, St. Michael's day, 1802, *CW*, 3a:26.

[70] 1.152, Elizabeth Seton to Rebecca Seton, New York, n.d., *CW*, 1:199-200.

[71] 1.165, Elizabeth Seton to Julia Scott, New York, 16 November 1802, *CW*, 1:213.

[72] Ibid., 212.

[73] 1.148, Elizabeth Seton to Rebecca Seton, n.d, *CW*, 1:194. See 1.157, Seton to Seton, n.d., *CW,* 1:204; 1.156, Ibid., *CW*, 1:203.

[74] 1.162, Elizabeth Seton to Rebecca Seton, New York, 16 August 1802, *CW*, 1:208. [See Appendix B. First Communion of Elizabeth Ann Bayley. Ed.] See also 10.4, "Dear Remembrances," *CW*, 3a:514. These words suggest that Mrs. Seton was accustomed, herself, to a strict observance of "Sacrament Sunday."

[75] 1.160, Elizabeth Seton to Rebecca Seton, New York, n.d., *CW*, 1:207.

[76] 1.191, Elizabeth Seton to Rebecca Seton, n.d., *CW*, 1:232.

[77] 1.102, Elizabeth Seton to Rebecca Seton, New York, n.d., *CW*, 1:144.

[78] 1.202, Elizabeth Seton to Rebecca Seton, New York, n.d., *CW*, 1:239.

[79] 1.170, Elizabeth Seton to Anna Maria Seton, 23 August 1803, *CW*, 1:218.

[80] 1.172, Elizabeth Seton to Eliza Sadler, n.d., *CW*, 1:220. 1.175, Elizabeth Seton to William Seton, [October 1803], *CW*, 1:223; 1.176 Elizabeth Seton to Richard Seton, [October 1803], *CW*, 1:223.

[81] Wright Post to Elizabeth Seton, New York, 22 September 1803, ASJPH 1-3-3-11:1.

[82] John Henry Hobart to Elizabeth Seton, New York, 23 November 1803, ASJPH 1-3-3-11:B70; Rebecca Seton to Elizabeth Seton, New York, 5 October 1803, ASJPH 1-3-3-8:61.

[83] Longworth's *American Almanac, New York Register and City Directory, 1801-1802, 1803-1804.* James Maitland appears in only one directory, that of 1801-1802. No Street number is given.

[84] John Henry Hobart to Elizabeth Seton, New York, 23 November 1803, ASJPH 1-3-3-11:B70.

[85] 1.172, Elizabeth Seton to Eliza Sadler, New York, n.d., *CW*, 1:220.

[86] 2.2, Elizabeth Seton to Eliza Sadler, New York, 3 October 1803, *CW*, 1:245.

৯০৶

CHAPTER 4

༄༅

ITALIAN INTERLUDE

Travelers to Europe in the tumultuous first decade of the nineteenth century went well-armed with credentials and letters of introduction, and the Setons were no exceptions. Two of the papers carried by William Magee Seton in 1803 have been preserved and cast an interesting light upon the past. The first of these bore the signature of Thomas Barclay, the British consul-general of the Eastern States of America, and proclaimed William Magee Seton to be a British subject.[1] Seton's motives in claiming British citizenship were probably colored by considerations of security in a period when Mediterranean travel was endangered by Napoleonic wars and the ravages of Barbary pirates. The document raises a brief question in regard to Elizabeth Seton's citizenship, but even more than this, it suggests the cloudy uncertainty which characterized concepts of citizenship in the United States in the period between the American Revolution and the Civil War.[a] There is little doubt that Mother Seton, foundress, was an American citizen; but the culture in which she lived was much less provincial than that which came after her death. The narrower nationalism of the latter nineteenth century was not her milieu.

The second paper of interest was a letter of introduction to Joseph Jaudenes, the intendante of Mallorca,[b] written for the Setons by James Barry.[c] It was this same James Barry who was to befriend Mrs. Seton some years later, after her conversion to Catholicism; in 1803 Elizabeth knew him only as a business friend of her husband.[2] The letter is doubly interesting because it mentions Captain William Bainbridge of the United States frigate *Philadelphia*.[3] The name of Bainbridge conjures up at once the ghosts of the Barbary pirates and the dread they once inspired in Mediterranean travelers. The tenuous peace established between the Sultan of Morocco[d] and the United States on 12 October 1803, was heard of by the Setons' friends with some relief, and Henry Hobart wrote, "The papers of this day lead us to expect you have not been in danger from the Pirates of Barbary

---

[a] The issues presented by William Magee Seton's claim to British citizenship are not easily resolved. [See Appendix B. Citizenship of William Magee Seton. Ed.]

[b] Traditionally, an intendante was the holder of a public administrative office.

[c] James Barry was a merchant of Washington and Baltimore whose business carried him to New York and Canada. In 1803 he was in New York City or rather on Long Island with his wife and daughters. Bishop John Carroll invited Barry to accompany him to Boston that September but Barry was unable to go.

[d] [Mulay Slimane (1760–1822), of the Alaouite dynasty, was the Sultan of Morocco from 1792 to 1822. Captain Edward Preble, met with Slimane to resolve violations of the treaty of 1786. Ed.]

as they state the Emperor [sic, Sultan] has ceased hostilities and that our frigates there have adequate protection from the other powers."[4] The truce of early October was, unfortunately, counterbalanced by the capture on 31 October of the *Philadelphia* and Captain Bainbridge during the blockade of Tripoli. In the months that followed, the *Enterprise* captured the Moorish *Mastico*, quickly renamed her the *Intrepid* and on 31 January 1804, the Navy Department commissioned the ship. The following month witnessed the epic boarding party led by Stephen Decatur, and the burning of the *Philadelphia*.[5] It was amid such circumstances that the Seton voyage to Italy was made.

Elizabeth Seton's thoughts were far from the physical dangers to be faced on the high seas as she boarded the vessel that first day in October; her last days on shore had been too occupied with other concerns. The last-minute letters and farewells had to be completed. A note to Julia Scott, hastily penned just before the signal for going on board was sounded, admitted that "in the view of mortal hopes"[6] Elizabeth knew she could not expect William Magee's recovery yet, knowing Him Who held the scale, she persisted in her faith in the Leghorn [Livorno] voyage. To young Cecilia Seton, who was following so eagerly the pattern of Rebecca and Elizabeth, Mrs. Seton wrote a note of encouragement, asking the girl to persevere in her habitual observance of "that Heavenly Christian life you have so early begun."[7]

William Magee Seton's younger brother, Henry, who was in the navy, planned to accompany the little group as far as the harbor lighthouse, where the pilot would be dropped. Rebecca and Harriet Seton, on shore, brought the children down to the Battery to see the *Shepherdess* pass, and they waved delightedly until the full import of the ship's passage struck them, and then they burst into tears. On board, their father was so upset by grief and coughing that neither he nor Elizabeth could enjoy their last glimpse of the children. At ten o'clock on the third day, Henry Seton left them to return to New York, carrying with him the first notes written by Elizabeth on board ship. With Henry disappeared the last tie with shore; the ocean and the voyage lay ahead.[8]

The days at sea passed pleasantly and swiftly. William Magee, contrary to all prediction, seemed to improve with each day. Captain O'Brien[e] was kind, and the stewardess reminded the Setons of their servant back home, so willing was she to please.[9] After the hectic flurry of farewells and

---

[e] There is no positive identification of O'Brien available. An Edward O'Brien, midshipman, served on the U.S.S. *Chesapeake* and U.S.S. *Adams* until 1803 when he entered the merchant service, but neither the name of his ship, nor his rank is given in this latter service. He may or may not have been the captain of the *Shepherdess*.

the fatigue of preparations, Elizabeth was only too glad to surrender to the monotony and leisure of a life at sea. She had time to enjoy the sunsets and to write her impressions of the moonlight. By the time the vessel passed the Western Isles she was making almost daily entries in a journal for Rebecca.[10] Anna Maria was a comfort to both parents, partly because she distracted their thoughts from the morbid contemplation of William Magee's future, but even more because Elizabeth could share her reading with the interested child. Together they studied the Psalms and made earnest resolutions to lead better lives. So intense were Mrs. Seton's reflections that they carried over to her dreams. One night, just after the ship had sighted the Rock of Gibraltar, she dreamed she was climbing such a dark mountain. When she had nearly reached the summit, spent and shaken, she heard a voice saying, "Never mind, take courage—there is a beautiful green hill on the other side—and on it an angel waits for you."[11] On other occasions the storms which beset the ship filled her with terror and a sense of unworthiness, and she prayed on trembling knees, "a helpless child clinging to the Mercy of its tender Father." Once when a midnight storm came up suddenly, little Anna Maria Seton, upon whose gentle heart the daily readings of the psalmist had left their print, whispered softly, "Come hither all ye weary Souls," and her mother crept into bed with her and was lost in refreshing sleep.[12] Two days later the *Shepherdess* put into port, to the ringing of the church bells of Leghorn.

Early in the morning of 19 November 1803, the impatient Setons heard a boat alongside, and Elizabeth flew to the deck to greet her brother, Carleton, who had come out to meet them. Guy Carleton Bayley was Dr. Richard Bayley's son by his second wife, Amelia Barclay Bayley. Carleton, as he was more often called, was working in the counting house of the Filicchi brothers in Leghorn, the same Filicchis whom William Magee Seton had known from youth.[f] In her joy at seeing someone from home Elizabeth did not at first perceive Carleton's reluctance to approach her. It was only when a guard brusquely ordered, "Don't touch!" that she had a premonition of danger. Her dismay mounted rapidly when she was informed

---

[f] Filippo (Philip) Filicchi (1763–1816) and Antonio Filicchi (1764–1847). Philip Filicchi is said to have spent the years 1785-1786 in the United States, at which time he became familiar to George Washington who later made Filicchi the American consul at Leghorn. Filicchi was appointed consul on 10 December 1794, assumed charge at Leghorn on 20 March 1795, and retired from office in November 1798. It is fairly certain Philip Filicchi was in the United States early in 1788. When he returned to Italy later that year he was accompanied by young William Magee Seton. It was during this visit that Seton became friendly with the younger brother, Antonio Filicchi, who was studying law at Rome. In 1789 Philip went again to the United States, and it was probably at this time that he married Mary Cowper of Boston. Late in 1789 the Filicchi house of commerce with its connections in the United States was "publicly established" in Leghorn. Mary Cowper Filicchi came to Italy in 1790, and the following year William Magee Seton again visited Leghorn in October. Seton had every reason to regard both Filicchi brothers as good friends in 1803.

that the *Shepherdess* was from New York, where yellow fever was raging, and because the vessel lacked "a bill of health" it would have to go into quarantine. The welcoming strains of "Hail Columbia," a tune to which her children at home had so loved to march, proved too much for Elizabeth's equanimity, and she took refuge in her cabin, sobbing bitterly at the odd chance that made her, who had watched with such pity the arrivals at the Staten Island quarantine, now herself a victim of similar precautions.[13]

The Leghorn lazaretto, or quarantine, was several miles from the city on a canal. The Setons were rowed out to the dungeon-like building, taking with them only the barest necessities, for someone had assured them mistakenly that the lazaretto was "the very place for the comfort of the sick." Elizabeth took her books and the small writing "secretary," but only one change of clothes went because they were promised the rest would be brought on Monday. The curious stares of the boatmen and their loud shouting in a foreign tongue made little Anna Maria tremble. Poor Seton was so weak he could scarcely walk, yet no one offered to assist him for fear of contracting the dread disease. The only bright spot in the whole proceeding was the welcome of Mrs. Philip Filicchi, who had come to the quarantine. True, a fence separated them, but the sound of an American voice, speaking words of consolation and greeting, was a salve to their lacerated feelings. Mary Filicchi was the former Mary Cowper of Boston, and she had made the trip to the lazaretto while she herself was in poor health.[g] Her action was symbolic of the warm friendship Mrs. Seton was to receive from all the Filicchi family.[14]

After the brief exchange with Mrs. Filicchi, the Setons were shown the door to "enter, No. 6—up 20 stone steps, a room with high arched ceilings like St. Paul's—brick floor, naked walls and a jug of water."[15]

The desolation of this room has been described too often to warrant a repetition. The sojourn in the lazaretto is vividly described in the journal Elizabeth kept for Rebecca Seton and the feeling of gloomy, damp discomfort which accompanied their isolation is easily recaptured from its pages. Mrs. Seton quite naturally viewed the dreary succession of days as so many postponements of her husband's chance for recovery. The constant presence of his melancholy face, his shivering frame, the racking cough, and the despairing sobs could only color her impressions with a somber hue. Yet her account contains innumerable notes of attentions and kindnesses received—for example, the captain of the lazaretto who had the warm eggs and wine brought on the arrival of the Setons and the supper sent in by the Filicchis,

---

[g] Mary Cowper (1760–1821) married Philip Filicchi in Boston. The couple had no children. The name Cowper, pronounced Cooper, sometimes appears as Cooper.

"with other necessaries." Two days after their arrival in the quarantine station the captain and guards came in to put up a bed for William Magee, curtains to prevent a draft, and benches to be used by Elizabeth and her daughter. A servant, old Luigi, was sent to serve them during their confinement, and he raced up and down the twenty stairs countless times a day.[16]

Some days Luigi brought in stiff little bouquets of jasmine, geraniums, and pinks, and the heavy sweetness of the flowers mingled with the salty air which always pervaded the room. The sound of the pealing church bells from the shore alternated with the roaring of the sea and the counterpoint of that serene pealing and the ominous thunder of the waves seemed to voice the inner intensity of emotion in which spiritual serenity met and mixed with premonitions of on-rushing calamity. In such a mood Elizabeth "forgot prison bolts and sorrow, and would have rejoiced to have sung with Paul and Silas." On days like these the encouragement given by Dr. Tutilli made them all happy; Elizabeth could borrow Anna Maria's jumping rope with only half the reason to keep warm.[17]

The quick sympathy Elizabeth felt for all suffering caused her to enter actively into the moods of her husband and child. With William Magee she shared the sudden pains and shivered with his cold; with Anna Maria she could cry until her eyes smarted; with them both she was swept with homesickness and longing on the day when all remembered young Willy's birthday at home. The matins bells which awakened her filled her at first with "most painful regrets and an agony of sorrow, which could not at first find relieve even in prayer." But Elizabeth's excesses of emotion were followed by cooler reflections and, the second day in the lazaretto, she wrote, "I came to my senses and reflected that I was offending my only Friend and resource in my misery."[18] This practice of sublimating sensibility was to be developed to a heroic degree by Mrs. Seton in later life. The journal of the lazaretto shows unmistakable evidences that she was already practicing fortitude in the face of heavy odds. Invariably a passage in her journal which describes the misery of the quarantine is followed by one expressing reflections such as this:

> With God for our portion there is no prison in high walls and
> bolts—no sorrow in the soul that waits on him, tho' beset
> with present cares and gloomy prospects. For this freedom I
> can never be sufficiently thankful, as in my William's case,
> it keeps alive what in his weak state of body would naturally
> fail. Often when he hears me repeat the Psalms of Triumph in
> God, and read St. Paul's faith in Christ, with my whole soul,

it so enlivens his Spirit that he makes them his own—and all our sorrows are turned to joy. Oh well may I love God! Well may my whole soul strive to please Him, for what but the pen of an Angel can ever express what He has done and is constantly doing for me. While I live, while I have my being in time and thro' Eternity, let me sing praises to my God.[19]

The first week in December all her fine hopes for her husband came crashing to the ground. On 5 December, William Magee Seton woke in severe pain and the doctor was summoned immediately. Dr. Tutilli took one brief look at the sick man and told Elizabeth it was a doctor of souls who was needed here. Mrs. Seton spent the day by William Magee's side, kneeling on a mat by his bed. Carleton Bayley got word that his brother-in-law was dying and he came with the captain to persuade Elizabeth to have someone stay with her, with death so near. Her matter-of-fact "what have I to fear?" silenced them. Her chief sensation was one of gratitude that God was giving her—the strength to face the hour.

When Mr. Thomas Hall, the British chaplain, arrived the next morning he was amazed to find Mr. Seton alive and to all appearances improved. It was only a reprieve, but the weeks which followed were truly "days of grace" for William Magee Seton. From that crisis on, his thoughts turned almost constantly toward heaven. He often said that this was the period of his life, whether he lived or died, that he would consider blessed, "the only time which he has not lost."[20] He liked to dwell on the inspiring words he had heard from John Henry Hobart's lips; but he always returned to his wife as his greatest source of inspiration. His serene resignation roused in Elizabeth a fierce protective impulse, and when the "capitano" shrugged his shoulders and pointed toward the sky as if in silent reminder that all was in the hands of God, Elizabeth had the thought, "You need not always point your silent look and finger there—if I thought our condition the Providence of man, instead of the 'weeping Magdalene' as you so graciously call me, you would find me willing to tear down your Lazaretto about your ears, if it were possible to carry off my poor prisoner to breathe the air of Heaven in some more seasonable place."[21] As her anger mounted within her, her thoughts continued:

> To keep a poor soul who came to your country for his life, thirty days shut up in damp walls, smoke, and wind from all corners blowing even the curtain round his bed, which is only a mattress on boards, and his bones almost through— and now the shadow of death, trembling if he only stands a

few minutes. He is to go to Pisa for his health—this day his prospects are very far from Pisa. [22]

And then, ashamed of her spirit of rebellion, she prayed,

O my Heavenly Father, I know that these contradictory events are permitted and guided by Thy Wisdom, which only is *light*. We are in darkness, and must be thankful that our knowledge is not wanted to perfect Thy Work.[23]

William Magee Seton did go to Pisa in the end. For two damp days uncertainty prevailed at the lazaretto while the release of the Setons hung in the balance; but 19 December found the invalid being carried to the waiting coach of the Filicchis. Elizabeth held her breath during the trip downstairs, fearing that this exertion might prove fatal, but once in the carriage her fears were dispelled. The air seemed to revive William Magee and at the end of the fifteen-mile journey his spirits were higher than at any time since the day they first saw Leghorn's shores. The comfort of the lodgings the Setons found waiting was luxury in contrast to the drab lazaretto they had left behind. William Magee Seton felt, mistakenly, that health was returning; he insisted on daily rides in the carriage. Christmas Eve proved his hopes all vain.

This time there was no further doubt. The unmistakable last stages of the disease could not be misread. Seton sent for Captain O'Brien from the *Shepherdess,* and solemnly charged him to see that Elizabeth and Anna Maria got back safely to the United States. After that he refused to see anyone except his wife. He seemed anxious to be gone and refused the nourishment his wife pleadingly offered. In his weakness his mind began to wander. He imagined a ticket he had bought for Elizabeth in a London lottery had won the royal prize. He became convinced that a letter from James Seton had arrived, with news that the Setons no longer owed a penny in the world. Elizabeth's heart ached as she heard him, in tones of childlike gratitude, thank God that he was taken first, "he was not wanted for our support" he need not see his wife and children die.[24] Once he dreamed he saw little baby Rebecca in Heaven, beckoning to him.[h] At the last he reached out with wasted arms to Elizabeth and cried piteously "you promised me you would go, come, come, fly—" At a quarter past seven on the morning of Tuesday, 27 December 1803, he died.[25]

---

[h] Elizabeth Seton's belief in her husband's nearness to heaven was so firm that she interpreted this dream to mean their youngest child, Rebecca, had died in their absence. She had not received the letter of 23 November 1803 from her sister-in-law, telling of the baby's recovery. Her surprise at seeing the child alive when she returned to New York is noted in Mrs. Seton's journal for Rebecca Seton and "Dear Remembrances."

Scarcely knowing what she did, Mrs. Seton called Anna Maria and told her they must thank God that Papa's frightful sufferings were over. Together the mother and daughter prayed briefly. Then followed a nightmare of final arrangements. The mistress of the lodging house, fearing tuberculosis as greatly as she feared yellow fever, refused to go near the dead man. Elizabeth wrote Rebecca afterward,

> I was obliged with the assistance of a poor woman who had washed for him, to lay him out myself, which added to three nights not laying my head down and two days fasting seemed almost enough. Notwithstanding [I] was forced to ride the fifteen miles to Leghorn with Mrs. Filicchi without even lying down, as my dear William must be carried there to be buried; it is a law that it must be done within the 24 hours. However by putting him in the burying house in the church yard we were allowed to wait 'till eleven the next day.[26]

The trip Mrs. Filicchi made with Elizabeth was just one more example of her kindness; scarcely able to be up herself, she rode with the bereaved young widow to Leghorn that morning. Carleton Bayley and old Luigi brought William Magee Seton's remains to Leghorn on the afternoon of the same day.

Elizabeth was too dazed to notice the journey or arrival in Leghorn. Over and over the words kept repeating in her head, "My God, you are my God—and so I am alone in the world with you and my little ones, but you are my Father and doubly theirs." Mr. Hall came from the British "Factory" or consulate that night to arrange the next day's service, and said in his bluff British way, "As the tree falls, ma'm, there it lies"; and Mrs. Seton scarcely heard him. But when the old "capitano" of the lazaretto arrived, with black crepe on his hat and genuine sorrow on his wrinkled face, Elizabeth's heart was really touched.[27]

The Americans and English in Leghorn attended the services which were conducted by Mr. Hall. The death certificate was signed by this same Thomas Hall, the chaplain to the British Factory at Leghorn on 20 January 1804, and was witnessed by the American consul, Thomas Appleton. It stated simply that William Magee Seton "died at Pisa, 27th December 1803, aged 37 years" and was interred in the English burial ground at Leghorn on the day following.[28] Mrs. Seton now faced the trial of sending the news home to New York. She wrote first to Rebecca and asked her to tell the other Setons, since the pain of writing was such that she could not bear writing each one separately. By the *Salem,* bound for Boston, she also sent letters to Mary Bayley Post, Eliza Sadler, Uncle John Charlton, and John Wilkes. When it came to writing Mr. Hobart, her strength failed her, and she asked Rebecca to tell him the tragic story. Elizabeth had written Hobart while still on board the *Shepherdess,* but since the news it contained was quite overshadowed by the later events, she decided not to send it. She expected to be home herself as soon as letters would arrive; she would carry it with her.[i]

At this juncture there occurred a minor incident in Mrs. Seton's life which is little known but which adds something to appreciating her personality. The wife of Captain O'Brien had been indisposed for some time. New Year's night she was taken suddenly ill and sent to shore for Mrs. Seton. Elizabeth had only the most irritating memories of the woman who had brought on the voyage two children with whooping cough. Not only did the incessant coughing of the two distress William Magee Seton, but quite naturally Anna Maria Seton contracted the disease herself and added to her mother's problems. This sudden summons to the *Shepherdess,* coming so soon after William Magee's death was most unwelcome. But feeling was one thing with Mrs. Seton, action quite another. Without waiting for a carriage, she went through mud over her shoetops, was hoisted up to the ship's deck like a bundle of old clothes, and remained on board all night with the unfortunate woman. Elizabeth wrote Rebecca ruefully, "but these three months has been a hard lesson—pray for me that I may make a good use of it."[29]

The energy and courage of the small widow intrigued the Filicchis and their friends, and Mrs. Seton soon found herself "hard pushed by these charitable Romans who wish that so much goodness should be improved by a conversion."[30] Abbé Peter Plunkett, an Irish priest and considered the most able apologist in Leghorn, led the attack. Elizabeth was rather amused at first, having been too recently warned against such appeals by John Henry Hobart, who was confident the "sumptuous and splendid worship" of Italy would not "withdraw your affections from the simple but affecting worship at Trinity Church."[31] She wrote Rebecca in a light vein, "they find me so willing to hear their enlightened conversation, that consequently as learned people like to hear themselves best, I have but little to say, and as yet keep friends with all as the best comment on my Profession [of faith]—"[32] Her complaisance was soon to be ruffled.

The Filicchis persuaded Mrs. Seton that while the ship was being made ready to sail some time should be devoted to sightseeing. January

---

[i] Since the printed *Correspondence of Henry Hobart* includes no letters from Mrs. Seton written at any time, it is not possible to state what this letter contained or whether it was ever delivered to Mr. Hobart.

found her and Anna Maria in Florence with the Filicchi women, visiting museums, churches, and other places of interest. Mrs. Seton kept a journal of her impressions of Florence for Rebecca Seton, and it is from this journal that we derive some knowledge of Elizabeth's first reactions to Catholic worship.[33] The visitors stayed in what was once the famous palace of the Medici, facing the Arno River. From its windows the Setons looked out upon Monte Morelli in the distance. In their room at night the mother and daughter read their Thomas à Kempis, the Psalms, and prayed; but during the day they saw sights which were to arouse even keener interest in things religious. Tuscany in 1804 was styled the Kingdom of Etruria, and it was no longer the mildly contented duchy that Archduke Leopold had once governed. On 1 October 1800, Spain had promised Louisiana to France in exchange for the pledge that a Spanish Bourbon should rule at Florence as King of Etruria. Since 1801 the grand duchy of Tuscany was part and parcel of Napoleon's Northern Italian system. Louis Bourbon, Duke of Parma, reigned but briefly and at his death his widow, Maria Louisa, assumed the government. It was this daughter of Ferdinand VII who inhabited the palace in 1804.[34]

With Amabilia Filicchi,[j] Elizabeth Seton visited the Church of the Annunciation and there she saw hundreds of people kneeling in the half-gloom while "that kind of soft and distant musick which lifts the mind to a foretaste of heavenly pleasure called up in an instant every dear and tender idea of my Soul," resulting in such memories that the young widow cried unrestrainedly. It was so long since she had been in the house of her God. The Church of the Santissima Annunziata stood in the Piazza of the same name not far from the statue of Ferdinand di Medici whom Robert Browning was later to immortalize in "The Statue and the Bust." The church contained faultless frescoes by Andrea del Sarto, and bas-reliefs, and a magnificent crucifix by John of Bologna, of whose work Hawthorne once commented, "I think there has been no better sculptor since the days of Phidias."[35] But Elizabeth Seton was more concerned with her sorrow and she felt grateful to the preoccupation of those around her, so busy with "their prayers and Rosary that it is very immaterial what a stranger does." When Amabilia drew the Setons closer to the altar to see the beauty of the ornament and the pictures, Mrs. Seton was amazed at the old men, young men, old women and girls, "all sorts of people kneeling promiscuously about the altar as inattentive to us or any other passengers as if we were not there." When the women passed into the simple elegance of St. Firenze's chapel, Elizabeth was struck by the pious composure of the young priest.

---

[j] Amabilia Baragazzi (1773–1853) married Antonio Filicchi. They provided gracious hospitality to the Setons after the death of William Magee at Pisa. They had ten children.

When he unlocked "his little chapel with that composed and equal eye, as if his soul had entered before him," her heart would willingly have followed.[36] The Church of San Lorenzo's altar evoked in her soul the words of the "Magnificat." This church, which a half-century later impressed Hawthorne as rather somber and shabby, recalled to the earlier American traveler rather "the ideas of the offerings of David and Solomon to the Lord, when the rich and valuable productions of nature and art were devoted to His holy temple and sanctified to His service."[37]

The daily jaunts were not solely directed toward churches. The tourists visited the queen's country palace, and twice saw the royal lady herself. Little Anna Maria was disappointed to discover that queens looked like everyone else, except for the number of attendants.[38] The Boboli Gardens, adjacent to the queen's residence, were visited. Here Elizabeth wandered among the bowered walks of box and shrubbery, gazed on the weathered faces of the innumerable statues, avoiding when she could the noisy parties of Florentines whose children rolled happily on the slopes or threw crumbs to the minnows in the pond. She climbed on up to the esplanade and laughingly complained of being "well-exercised in running up the flights of steps in the style of the hanging gardens." The view from the top was worth the climb, however, and while she rested, and gazed out over the panorama of fir and pine, she reflected that "If the Tuscans are to be judged by their taste they are a happy people for every thing without is very shabby, and within elegant. The exterior of their best buildings are to appearance in a state of ruin."[39] She found it odd that even the best buildings gave the appearance of ruins on the outside; she found nothing to complain of in the wonders they contained.

The art galleries were not ignored. Elizabeth found the bronze statues "beautiful, but being only an American could not look very straight at them."[40] A painting of John the Baptist was much more to her liking. The splendor of the Pitti Palace was quite forgotten in her awe upon discovering the life-sized picture of "The Descent from the Cross" in the church of Sta. Maria Novella. It engaged her whole attention. She was reluctant to leave it, and in the hours that followed she had only to close her eyes to see again "Mary, at the foot of it, [who] expressed well that the iron had entered into her—and the shades of death over her agonized countenance so strongly contrasted the heavenly Peace of the dear Redeemer's [expression] that it seems as if His Pains had fallen on her."[41] She forgot her disappointment over discovering that the gallery was nowhere nearly so wonderful as William Magee had led her to believe.[42] Another morning was spent in the anatomical museum and cabinet of natural history. The Museum contained a fine collection of almost everything in nature: stones, shells, vegetables, insects, fishes, reptiles, animals, and man. The greatest wonders were the models in wax of all the parts of the human frame.[43] Mrs. Seton's delicacy made her shrink from some of the displays in the latter, but in the former she saw "the work of the Almighty Hand in every object." [44] How she wished Dr. Wright Post, her brother-in-law, could see these marvels.

The evenings, as a rule, were spent in seclusion, Elizabeth often thought gratefully of the inspiration which had prompted her to bring her daughter on the voyage. Anna Maria, who was on many occasions to present an enigma to her mother, was on this occasion her greatest confidant and comfort. Together they discussed the wonders of the day, reflected over the spiritual reading habitual to their evenings, and talked of home. Only once did the two leave their rooms at night, and this was occasioned by the urgent persuasion of their friends, that the Setons must hear the celebrated Giacomo Davide at the opera.[k] Elizabeth went heavily veiled, instead of masking as was the custom, and she entered only after the theatre was darkened. Anna Maria was open-mouthed in amazement at the grimaces and trilling of the singers, while poor Elizabeth found not "the least gratification in their quavers." Only her courtesy and the memory that William Magee had so wanted her to hear this particular man made her try to look pleased. After a half hour of this discomfort she was "relieved from the most unwilling exertion" she had been forced to make in Florence, and the Setons retired to the peace of their lodgings "redoubled delight", where the joys of Thomas à Kempis seemed "as the joys of heaven in comparison."[45]

When the Setons returned to Leghorn at the end of January they found Captain O'Brien still unprepared to sail,[l] and they were thus able to enjoy another week or two in Florence.[46] The Leghorn interval, however, provided several opportunities for Elizabeth to become further interested in Catholicism. It was at this time that Philip Filicchi gave her a copy of the spiritual classic *Introduction to the Devout Life* by St. Francis de Sales which sent her to her knees begging God for light. On Candlemas Day she went to Mass with Amabilia and when she was presented with the idea that God was really present on the altar, she covered her face with her hands, while the tears slipped through her fingers.[47] Leghorn was the place where Philip

---

[k] Giacomo Davide was the first tenor of his time and is better known as "Davide le Pere." He had a great vogue in London in 1791 and performed at one of the last Handel festivals there. He returned to Florence in 1802 where he delighted his audiences with his powerful, "well-toned" voice and perfection of execution.

[l] White, 100, states that the Setons embarked for America on 3 February 1804, but this seems contradicted by Mrs. Seton's entry of 2 February which states, "Now we go to Florence...Captain O'Brien is to be ready by our return." The false start White describes is clearly dated 18 February in the journal. White seems to have based his date on information given by Antonio Filicchi in October 1843.

Filicchi pointed out that there was only one true religion, and that without the right faith we are not acceptable to God. When Elizabeth asked the obvious question, "If there is but one Faith and nobody pleases God without it, where are all the good people who die out of it?" Philip told her gravely, "I don't know; that depends on what light of faith they had received. But I know where people go who can know the right faith, if they pray for it, and inquire for it, and yet do neither."[48] Elizabeth was still incredulous, and wrote Rebecca,

> So, dearest Bec, I am laughing with God when I try to be serious and say daily as the good gentleman told me in old Mr. Pope's[m] words "*if I am right, O teach my heart still in the right to stay, if I am wrong, Thy Grace impart to find the better way.*" Not that I can think there is a better way than I know—but everyone must be respected in their own."[49]

Joseph Forsyth's handbook for tourists visiting Leghorn in the nineteenth century carried a description of a famous church which had been erected "by the piety of sailors to an old picture of the Virgin which had flown from India [sic] through the air and perched on top of this hill for their especial protection."[50] The hill was Montenero, and the chapel was thought to be the scene of many miraculous cures. The walls, at any rate, were covered with cable ends, crutches, and chains of delivered slaves. No Italian ship sailed past Montenero without saluting the Lady of the hill, Mary of Montenero, Patron of Tuscany. The Filicchis had an added reason for wishing their guests to visit the place, for once, during a political revolution, Philip Filicchi had been sheltered by the monks of the church.[51]

The day Elizabeth Seton attended Mass at this famous chapel another non-Catholic visitor was present in the person of a young Englishman. Thinking he recognized a fellow curiosity-seeker, he turned at the elevation of the Host, and whispered loudly, "This is what they call their Real PRESENCE." The rude remark in the presence of the prostrate worshipers was in itself enough to offend the sensitive American widow, and deeply distressed she leaned as far away as possible. But the words started a train of thought which soon caused her to shiver with dread. The words of St. Paul came to her, "They discern not the Lord's Body" and her startled thoughts continued,

> How should they eat and drink their very damnation for not discerning it, if indeed it is not there. Yet how should it be there, and how did He breathe my Soul in me, and how and how a hundred other things I know nothing about. I am a Mother so the Mothers thought came also how was my GOD

---

[m] Alexander Pope, English essayist and poet (1688–1744).

a little babe in the first stage of his mortal existence in Mary, but I lost these thoughts in my babes at home, which I daily long for more and more, but they wait a fair wind—[52]

And if the wind had been fair, that day at Montenero might have been permanently lost in thoughts of home. But the Setons did not sail the third week in February, as they had planned. True, they said their good byes, they boarded the *Shepherdess,* they arranged their gifts and property. In the night a violent storm arose, and ramming the vessels against each other in the harbor, wreaked such havoc that the passengers were obliged to go ashore. The full implication of disaster was not realized by Elizabeth until she discovered Anna Maria had a high fever. The doctor summoned to examine the child pronounced it scarlet fever, and he told Mrs. Seton they must give up the voyage or risk Anna Maria's life. Elizabeth later confessed to Rebecca that she was by this time so anxious to get home that she would have gone anyway, trusting Anna Maria's life to God's mercy, but the simple fact was that Captain O'Brien refused to take them. With Anna Maria on board, he would have been refused a bill of health for Barcelona, and a delay in quarantine there would ruin his voyage. Mrs. Seton had to face another delay, with the reflection that "Well the hand of our God is all I must see in the whole—but it pinches to the Soul."[53] The first part of her remark was true; but her soul was to expand in the months to follow.

The three weeks of Anna Maria's illness were a severe trial for the girl's mother. It was not till the end of February that Elizabeth was sure she might not leave two graves behind instead of one. The care and attention of the Filicchis were enough to melt the heart. When Elizabeth herself came down with the fever, and the delay was prolonged another several weeks, she could only marvel at all the kindness she saw about her. The faith which motivated such Christian charity was bound to interest her as her strength returned. She was deeply touched by the rigorous Lenten fasting she saw Amabilia Filicchi practicing. She contrasted this mortification with the ludicrous inconsistency she had perceived in New York on an earlier Ash Wednesday, when after a hearty breakfast of buckwheat cakes she had gone to Trinity Church to pray, "I come to you in fasting, weeping and mourning." Mr. Hobart had explained her question with the remark that fasting was an "old custom." Here in Italy she saw people fasting until three o'clock, and offering their weakness as penance for their sins. She liked it very much. Even more, she liked the idea of being able to go to church every day. She wrote Rebecca:

How often you and I used to give the sigh and you would press your arm in mine of a Sunday evening and say no more till next Sunday as we turned from the church door which closed on us (unless a prayer day was given out in the week)—well here they go to church at 4 every morning, if they please—and you know how we were laughed at for running from one church to the other [on] Sacrament Sundays, that we might receive as often as we could, well here people that love God and live a good regular life can go (tho' many do not do it) yet they can go [to communion] every day.

O my—I don't know how any body can have any trouble in this world who believe all these dear Souls believe—if I don't believe it, it shall not be for want of praying—why they must be as happy as the angels almost.[54]

The procession which carried the Blessed Sacrament through the street, past Mrs. Seton's window, affected her visibly and she cried to herself, How happy I would be to find God "in the chapel, in the sacrament"; and she asked God to bless her if He were really there. In the heartbreaking loneliness of William Magee's absence, she found consolation in the *Memorare.* It seemed as if the mother she had missed all those years were at last a reality and Elizabeth cried herself "to sleep in her heart." [55] When she was taught by Antonio Filicchi to make the sign of the cross she grew cold with the thought of the Cross of Christ upon her and her eager heart was filled with earnest desires to be united to Him Who died upon it.[56]

Elizabeth Seton and Antonio Filicchi began in Italy a friendship which was to last for the rest of her life. Scarcely had Mrs. Seton left Leghorn for Florence in January 1804 when she received from Antonio a warm letter containing the words:

Your dear William was the early friend of my youth: you are now come in his room. Your soul is even dearer to Antonio, and will be so forever. May the good almighty God enlighten your mind and strengthen your heart to see and follow in religion the surest true way to eternal blessings. I shall call for you in Paradise if it is decreed that the vast plains of the ocean shall be betwixt us. Don't discontinue meanwhile to pray, to knock at the door. I am confident that our Redeemer will not be deaf to the humble prayers of so dear a creature.[57]

By April the younger Filicchi and the American widow were better acquainted with each other and the following exchange of notes took place. Antonio wrote his "Dearest Sister,"

> Afraid of some reproaches or of a like thing that I might have deserved for my too crazy manners, I have been most agreeably surprised in perusing all over ten times your favorite lines addressed to me in so delicate, so easy, so witty a style, and I hasten to give them my poor reply of acknowledgment and admiration. Believe me, my beloved Sister, that for the purpose of obtaining one of your letters in the week I could cheerfully scribble all the 24 hours of the day.[58]

Elizabeth wrote her "Most dear A.,"

> We often receive blessing from the hand of God and convert them into evils; this has been my fault in respect to the very sincere and uncommon affections I have for you, and I am determined with God's help no more to abuse the very great favor he bestows on me in giving me your friendship and in future will endeavor to show you how much I value it by doing all I can to contribute to your happiness. On your part, I entreat, you will behave to me with confidence and affection—the more you confide in me the more careful I shall be—trust me and the Angel—[59]

By this time Antonio Filicchi and his brother Philip had agreed that the Filicchi affairs in America warranted an investigation and that Antonio might combine business and charity by making the voyage at the same time that Mrs. Seton and her daughter returned to the United States. Elizabeth wrote to Rebecca on 5 April 1804 that passage had been taken for New York on the *Pyomingo* which would sail as soon as the equinox was past. The *Pyomingo*[n] was a fast vessel, she added, and the season could not be more favorable.[60] Antonio would accompany the Setons to New York, and then proceed to Boston, Philadelphia, Baltimore, and Canada, to transact the firm's business. Probably the elder Filicchi had this plan in mind when in answer to Mrs. Seton's fears for the future he said drily, "My little sister, God the Almighty is laughing at you. He takes care of little birds and makes the lilies grow, and you fear He will not take care of you—I tell you He will take care of you."[61]

---

[n] Filicchi called the ship *Vyomingo* in this letter. Elizabeth Seton spelled it "Piamingo" while contemporary newspaper accounts of the ship's arrival also used "Piamingo" and "Pyomento." John Blagge was the captain.

The last day in Leghorn began early and bright. The Filicchis rose at four o'clock and took Elizabeth to her last Mass there probably at the nearby church of Sta. Caterina on via Forte S. Pietro where the Filicchi family worshipped. The two-hour warning from the *Pyomingo* could be heard as they entered the chapel door. Seeing Antonio and Amabilia together at communion made Elizabeth pray that their gift of faith might be hers, and she promised "all in return for such a gift." The sun was bright upon the balcony of the Filicchi house as the little party set off for the ship. At the health office Carleton Bayley and Philip Filicchi made their farewells and handed over their letters for America. By eight o'clock the three travelers were seated on the quarter deck and the anchor was weighed.[62]

How firmly attached to Catholicism was Elizabeth Seton, when she left Italy? There are some strong indications that she was ready to become a Catholic before she left. There is the enigmatic entry in "Dear Remembrances" describing the day of departure:

> Last Mass at Leghorn at 4 in the morning—lost in the indescribable reverence and impressions kneeling in a little confessional perceived not [that] the *ear* was waiting for me till the Friar came out to ask Mrs. F. "why I did not begin."[63]

It seems hard to believe that Mrs. Seton could have entered the confessional by mistake, after having been more than three months in Italy, and having been so amply instructed by the Filicchis who were anxious that she understand all the aspects of Catholic worship. Her use of the word "confessional" was made in full knowledge of the word's significance since "Dear Remembrances" was written many years after she was a Catholic. Did she attempt to make a general confession at this time?[o] Is there any significance to her use of the words "this good" to limit the confession she made in New York in March 1805? She wrote Amabilia in regard to her first confession after her conversion, "so delighted now to prepare for this good confession, which bad as I am, I would be ready to make on the housetop, to insure the good absolution I hope for after it."[64]

Whatever the answer to the puzzle thus presented, it is rather clear that neither a formal retraction nor profession of faith was made in Italy, if Philip Filicchi is to be believed. After Elizabeth Seton returned to New York and entered the phase of vacillation, she received a letter from the elder

---

[o] [The confessional remains at an angle by the wall of a circular, side chapel. It is plausible that Mrs. Seton was overcome with emotion and sought privacy there in the obscurity of its shadow while she wept. Ed.]

Filicchi in which he quoted St. Luke in reference to putting the hand to the plough-share and then turning back. He continued:

> I fear that an imprudent confidence in your firmness may be placed to my account. Perhaps a secret pride made me trust in the power of my persuasions. The vanity of giving proof to your friends that your change of religion could not be imputed to surprise made me prefer your delaying your action of retraction. I consider myself guilty of all this and can only plead a sort of good intention.[65]

It is a fact that Elizabeth Seton's profession of faith in Roman Catholicism was not made until 14 March 1805. It also seems evident that she had given the Filicchis every reason to believe she was intellectually convinced of the validity of the Catholic faith. Was she guilty of deceit? If she was, she deceived herself as well. Here are her words upon setting sail from Leghorn:

> My Father and my God—and yet I must always love to retrospect thy wonderful dispensations—to be sent so many thousand miles on so hopeless an errand—to be constantly supported and accompanied by thy consoling mercy, through scenes of trial which nature alone must have sunk under—to be brought to the light of thy truth, notwithstanding every affection of my heart and power of my will was opposed to it—to be succored and cherished by the tenderest friendship, while separated and far from those that I loved—my Father and my God, while I live, let me praise—while I have my being let me serve and adore Thee.[66]

It was the old story of the immeasurable gulf which lies between an intellectual comprehension which eager apologists have fostered, and the gift of faith which only supernatural power may confer. It is not unusual for great souls to go through a prolonged period of torment between seeing and believing. Elizabeth's struggle was to begin almost as soon as the *Pyomingo* weighed anchor; it was to grow in violence after she reached New York; it was to end nearly a year later at St. Peter's on Barclay Street. The struggle was undoubtedly complicated by the circumstances under which she had been introduced to Catholicism, by the ardor of her temperament, and by the emotional crisis her widowhood induced. One of the most convincing explanations for the duration of Mrs. Seton's uncertainty lies in the observation John Carroll, (1735–1815), bishop of Baltimore,[p] made to

---

[p] [John Carroll was the first Catholic bishop in the United States (1789). Carroll was the first bishop (1789–1808) and first archbishop (1808–1815) of Baltimore, the premier see. Ed.]

Antonio Filicchi a short time before Elizabeth entered the Church. Carroll wrote,

> The ordinary course of Providence with respect to those who are tried by interior darkness and tribulation, is to subject them to it after their conversion is completed; and it often happens that those trials become highly useful and dispose those who are subjected to them, to disclose with utmost sincerity the entire state of their consciences, all their weaknesses, and even those imperfections of which formerly they made no account. Perhaps in the case of your most esteemed and respected friend, it pleases God to suffer her to experience now, before her union with His Church, those agitations of conscience which will induce her to perform with the greatest care and attention all previous duties, necessary for her adoption into it.[67]

Whatever the explanation for its duration, the period of "interior darkness and tribulation" which Mrs. Seton endured began on board the ship which carried her home. The voyage was long, lasting fifty-six days, and Elizabeth passed some of the time reading Alban Butler's *Lives of the Primitive Fathers, Martyrs and other Principal Saints*.[68] For days she could not summon the courage to write in her journal, and when at last she did she noted, "For four days past the trial has been hard—oh Lord, deal not with me in displeasure—let not my enemy triumph."[69] The nature of these preliminary trials and temptations can be guessed from her entry of 21 April which contained this revealing passage:

> When a soul whose only hope is in God, whose concern and desires are so limited that it would forsake all human beings, and account the dearest ties of life as foolishness compared with his love—when this soul sincerely desirous of serving and obeying him, is beset by the lowest passions of human nature, and from tears and prayers of earnest penitence can, by apparently the most trivial incitements, pass to the most humiliating compliances to sin—apparently, for until the effects are experienced it would be incredible that the commonest affections and unintentional actions should produce a confusion and disturbance in the mind that is exalted to the love of God, and destroy every impression but momentary gratification—this can only be the work of the enemy of our souls—our souls that have so often prayed to

Him for grace and mercy, and while lamenting our errors and trying to gain mutual strength, have solemnly declared that we would embrace our cross, follow our Leader, and valiantly oppose the enemy of our salvation. Most dear Antonio, a thousand times endeared to me by the struggles of your soul, our Lord is with us—once more the mark is— + to God.[70]

The entries which follow read like a rising crescendo of supplication. When the *Pyomingo* was becalmed off the coast of Valencia, and Horatio Nelson's fleet sent boarding parties from the *Belle Isle* and the *Excellent,*[q] Elizabeth recorded in terror, "Oh, my God, if I should die in the midst of so much sin and so little penitence. How terrible it will be to fall into thy hands!"[71] Yet her fear was mixed with love and she added, "my soul must still praise thee for so long sparing the punishment so justly due it, must still adore that infinite mercy that has given me so many means of grace, though my corrupt nature has made so bad a use of them. Oh, Lord Jesus Christ, still be merciful to a miserable sinner."[72]

The vehemence of the first trial seems to have subsided as the ship neared American shores. As Elizabeth's thoughts turned more and more to her children and her former attachments, her confidence returned. Recalling some coral she had watched rising from the ocean's seething foam, she found herself comparing it to the human soul and she wrote in her journal that when the soul is submerged in an ocean of worldly interests it is ready to yield to temptations.[r] As soon as the soul raises itself to God, like the coral, its pale green is transformed to a purer rosy hue by God's constant and Divine Love. The soul is then ready to view with confidence the overthrow of its baser impulses.[73] Her own soul welcomed the brief respite. On 4 June 1804, the *Pyomingo* released its passengers at New York. Very soon Mrs. Seton was to feel the onslaught of fresh attacks; but the voyage, at least, was safely past.

---

[q] Between 30 March and 1 June 1805, Napoleon had planned to have a naval maneuver led by Villeneuve lure Nelson from the Mediterranean, Cornwallis from Brest, and thus raise the blockade of Brest preparatory to Napoleon's "destruction" of England. The naval plans miscarried and Nelson was still cruising in the Mediterranean, where he had been for some time, when the *Pyomingo made* motionless by lack of wind 20 October of the same year, Nelson and Collingwood defeated Villeneuve off Cape Trafalgar. Nelson was killed, but Villeneuve was made prisoner and subsequently committed suicide.

[r] White does not reprint this part of the journal and, therefore, de Barberey is the closest to the original source. ["The coral in the ocean is a branch of pale green. Take it from its native bed, it becomes firm, bends no more, it is almost a rock. Its tender color is changed to a brilliant red: so, too, we, submerged in the ocean of this world, subjected to the succession of the waves, ready to give up under the stress of each wave and temptation. But as soon as our soul rises, and it breathes toward heaven, the pale green of our island hopes is changed into that pure bright red of divine and constant love. Then we regard the disruptions of nature and the fall of worlds with a constant and unshakeable confidence." See de Barberey, 97. Ed.]

Notes

1 William Magee Seton, Passport, British Consulate, New York City, 28 September 1803, ASJPH 1-3-3-9:64.

2 John Carroll to James Barry, 25 August and 8 September 1803, Archives of the Archdiocese of Baltimore 9-D-3, 9-D-4, located in Associated Archives at St. Mary's Seminary & University, Baltimore, Maryland. Carroll went to Boston to dedicate the Church of the Holy Cross on 29 September 1803. Hereinafter cited as AAB, AASMSU.

3 James Barry to Senor Don Joseph de Jaudenes, New York, 8 September 1803, ASJPH 1-3-3-2:45.

4 John Henry Hobart to Elizabeth Seton, New York, 23 November 1803, ASJPH 1-3-3-11:B70.

5 *Naval Documents Related to the United States Wars with the Barbary Pirates* (Washington, D.C., 1941), III, iii.

6 1.174, Elizabeth Seton to Julia Scott, New York, 1 October 1803, *CW*, 1:222; 10.4, "Dear Remembrances," *CW*, 3a:514.

7 1.177, Elizabeth Seton to Cecilia Seton, New York, 1 October 1803, *CW*, 1:224. Robert Seton, *Memoir, Letters and Journal,* I, 98, dates this letter 29 September, but the original at Emmitsburg bears the date 1 October.

8 2.1, Elizabeth Seton to Rebecca Seton, New York, 3 October 1803, *CW*, 1:243; 1.175, Elizabeth Seton to William Seton, *CW*, 1:223; 1.176, Elizabeth Seton to Richard Seton, *CW*, 1:223.

9 2.3, Elizabeth Seton to Julia Scott, 28 October 1803, *CW*, 1:245; 10.4, "Dear Remembrances," *CW*, 3a:514. See Naval Documents Related to Wars of the United States with the *Barbary Powers* (Washington, 1944), VI supplement, 41.

10 2.5, Journal to Rebecca Seton, Gibraltar Bay, 8 November, *CW*, 1:246. The complete journal Elizabeth Seton wrote to Rebecca Seton for the Setons appears in *CW*, 1:243-304. White, *Life of Mrs. Eliza A. Seton* (1853 ed.), 63-89 prints entries for 19 November 1803 to 28 December 1803. Robert Seton, *Memoir, Letters and Journal,* I, 108, 132, reprints the journal with one entry, 26 December 1803, and that considerably deleted.

11 Ibid.

12 Ibid., 16 November 1803, *CW*, 1:248.

13 2.6, Journal to Rebecca Seton, 19 November 1803, *CW*, 1:249-250. Elizabeth Seton used the spelling "Carlton," when referring to her

half-brother.

[14] The Seton-Jevons Collection contains one letter written by Filicchi from Philadelphia on 15 December 1785, to Samuel Curson in New York. Regarding Philip Filicchi's appointment as counselor, see Records of the Department of State in the National Archives, Washington, D.C. See John Carroll to William O'Brien, 10 May 1788, AAB, AASMSU, 9-S-1. See also John Thorpe to John Carroll, 24 February 1789, 13 May 1789, 22 January 1790, 5 October 1791, AAB, AASMSU, 8-J-3, 8-J-6, 8-K-3, 8-L-6.

[15] White, 64-73; de Barberey-Code, *Elizabeth Seton* (New York, 1923), 44-53; Robert Seton, *Memoir, Letters and Journal,* I, 109-120. [See 2.7, Journal to Rebecca Seton, *CW,* 1:252. Ed.]

[16] 2.7, Journal to Rebecca Seton, 19-20 November 1803, *CW,* 1:255.

[17] Ibid., 256. Dr. Tutilli was a friend of the Filicchis who was sent to attend William Seton. His first name does not appear.

[18] Ibid., 254.

[19] Ibid., 265.

[20] Ibid., 269.

[21] Ibid., 270.

[22] Ibid.

[23] Ibid., 271.

[24] Ibid., 278.

[25] 2.7, Journal to Rebecca Seton, Monday [26 December] entry, *CW,* 1:274. See 2.8, Elizabeth Seton to Rebecca Seton, Leghorn, 3 January 1804, *CW,* 1:276-280, contains a full account of Seton's last hours, See also 2.7, Journal to Rebecca Seton, Monday [26 December 1803], *CW,* 1:274-276.

[26] Ibid, 278. The journal disagrees as to the number of women who assisted, giving them as two.

[27] 2.11, Journal to Rebecca Seton, 28 January 1803, *CW,* 1:289.

[28] William Magee Seton's Death and Burial Certificate, Leghorn, 20 January 1804, ASJPH 1-3-3-9:65. William Magee was buried at Leghorn in the English cemetery on via degli Elisi until his remains were transferred to the parish garden of Sta. Elisabetta Seton parish in that city in 2004.

[29] 2.9, Elizabeth Seton to Rebecca Seton, Leghorn, 6 January 1804, *CW,* 1:282.

[30] 2.8, Elizabeth Seton to Rebecca Seton, Leghorn, 3 January 1804, *CW,* 1:279.

[31] John Henry Hobart to Elizabeth Seton, New York, 23 November 1803,

ASJPH 1-3-3-11:B70.

32 2.8, Elizabeth Seton to Rebecca Seton, Leghorn, 3 January 1804, *CW*, 1:276.

33 2.5-2.12, Journal to Rebecca Seton, *CW*, 1:246-95; Ibid., 296-304. Elizabeth Seton's journal was kept by Antonio Filicchi as a souvenir of her Italian stay. He made a copy in his own hand for Mrs. Seton. It is this latter copy which is found in ASJPH. See 2.5, Ibid., *CW*, 2:246, n.1.

34 *Geoffrey Bruun, Europe and the French Imperium, 1799-1814* (New York, 1938, 56, 85, 112.

35 Nathaniel Hawthorne, *Passages from the French and Italian Notebooks* (New York, 1871), 360. Entry, 8 July 1858.

36 2.10, Florence Journal to Rebecca Seton, 8 January 1804, *CW*, 1:284.

37 Ibid., 285.

38 Ibid., 284.

39 Ibid., 288.

40 Ibid., 285.

41 Ibid., 287.

42 Ibid. Part of the failure of the gallery to live up to Mrs. Seton's expectations was due to the depredations made by the French during the earlier Napoleonic campaigns.

43 Hawthorne, 303.

44 2.10, Florence Journal to Rebecca Seton, 10 January 1804, *CW*, 1:287.

45 Ibid., 286. For information about Davide, see *Grove's Dictionary of Music and Musicians* (New York, 1937), II, 19.

46 2.11, Elizabeth Seton to Rebecca Seton, 28 January 1804, *CW*, 1:290. See Antonio Filicchi to Charles I. White, 20 October 1846, ASJPH 26-0-1, (2). Copy. The original is in AMSJ.

47 Ibid.

48 Ibid.

49 2.11, Journal to Rebecca, 10 February 1804, *CW*, 1:290.

50 The name of this holy place at Montenero is the Shrine of Our Lady of Grace. Robert Seton, Diary for 1919, New York Historical Society, 77. Seton quotes the entire item from Joseph Forsyth and adds that he was "a prejudiced Scotchman." The painting mentioned, Seton believed [correctly], was of Greek origin and showed the Blessed Virgin seated on a cushion, holding the Infant Jesus on her left, while a bird on a string perched on her right arm. Robert Seton, *Memoir, Letters and Journal,* I, 143. Cf. Joseph Forsyth's Remarks *on Antiquities, Arts, and Letters during an Excursion in Italy in*

the Years 1802 and 1803, 2 vols. 3rd ed., (Geneva: P.G. Ledouble, 1824).

[51] The Congregation of Vallombroso, a branch of the Benedictines.

[52] 2.11, Elizabeth Seton to Rebecca Seton, 10 February 1804, *CW,* 1:291.

[53] Ibid., 292.

[54] 2.14, Journal to Rebecca Seton (continued), *CW,* 1:297.

[55] Ibid., 293.

[56] Ibid., 296.

[57] Antonio Filicchi to Elizabeth Seton, Leghorn, 9 January 1804, ASJPH 1-3-3-10:1.

[58] Antonio Filicchi to Elizabeth Seton, Leghorn, 6 April 1804, ASJPH 1-3-3-10:3.

[59] 2.13, Elizabeth Seton to Antonio Filicchi, 6 April 1804, *CW,* 1:295.

[60] Antonio Filicchi to Monsignor Joseph Pecci, Leghorn, 17 October 1821, ASJPH 26-0-1, (2). Copy. The original is in AMSJ.

[61] 2.14, Journal to Rebecca Seton (continued), 18 April 1804, *CW,* 1:298.

[62] White, 107. The original journal Mrs. Seton kept of the voyage home is not available. In the 1902 Diary of Robert Seton, now in the possession of the New York Historical Society, Seton states "I gave Madame de Barberey (Rome '66) a little book all written [sic] Mother Seton's hand... My aunt Catherine (Catherine Josephine Seton) gave me the book. Mme. de Barberey is dead and the book is, now, God knows where. I remember only that it had some notes of her return voyage from Leghorn to New York after her husband's death." (p.90). Since de Barberey gives the excerpts in French, and Code's English version is a translation of her French, it has been deemed wiser to use White's version as most probably the nearest to the original. [Some de Barberey papers are now archived at Parrocchia Madre Seton, Piazza Maria Lavagna, 15, Leghorn, Italy. Ed.]

[63] 10.4, "Dear Remembrances," *CW,* 3a:517.

[64] 3.31, Journal to Amabilia Filicchi, *CW,* 1:376.

[65] Philip Filicchi to Elizabeth Seton, Leghorn, 22 October 1804, ASJPH 1-3-3-10:14.

[66] 2.14, Journal to Rebecca Seton (continued), *CW,* 1:299. Cf. White, 107-108, quoting the lost journal, entry of 8 April 1804.

[67] John Carroll to Antonio Filicchi, Boston, 13 January 1805, ASJPH 1-3-3-1:38.

[68] Antonio Filicchi to Monsignor Joseph Pecci, Leghorn, 17 October 1821, ASJPH 26-0-1, (2). Copy. The original is in AMSJ.

[69] 2.14, Journal to Rebecca Seton (continued), 19 April 1804, *CW,* 1:300.

Cf. White, 108.

[70] Ibid., 301. Cf. White, 109, entry for 21 April 1804.

[71] Ibid., 302. See Louis Madelin, *The Consulate and Empire* (New York, 1934), 249-251.

[72] Ibid., 303.

[73] Ibid., 304. Melville quoted from Mme. de Barberey, *Elizabeth Seton* (Paris, 1906), 225-6.

෨෪

CHAPTER 5

శ్రీ

TO OLD SAINT PETER'S

The arrival in New York from Italy on 4 June 1804, was for Elizabeth Seton an occasion of mingled anticipation and dread. She experienced that indescribable poignancy produced by revisiting in sorrow the scenes of former joy. At no time had her husband's death been so keenly felt as in this moment when Mrs. Seton saw her fatherless children waiting to meet her. Her heart cried out within her, "My God well may I cling to thee for whom have I in Heaven but thee and who upon Earth beside thee, My heart and my flesh fail but thou art the Strength of my heart and my portion forever."[1] The joy of holding the children again in her arms was her consolation. Little Rebecca, whom she had feared dead, was her special delight.[2] It was not until the first flurry of greetings was over that Elizabeth noticed the absence of her sister-in-law Rebecca Seton.

Bec, the devoted sister-in-law, was scarcely alive. It seemed as if she had been only waiting for Elizabeth's return. Now all the things Elizabeth had wanted to discuss with her "soul's sister" must be told in haste or left unsaid. Bec's weakness and pain were constant interruptions to the returned traveler's attempts to point out "the few lines...of the true faith and service of our God," the eager readings of the Mass together, the urgent desire to share, before it was forever too late, her newly found beliefs. Rebecca in her exhaustion could only repeat, "Your people are my people; your God my God."[3]

Elizabeth Seton, faced with the prospect of Rebecca's death, was forcibly reminded of the death-bed consolations she had witnessed in Italy, when the priest "the one you call *Father* of your Soul attends and watches it in the weakness and trials of parting nature" with the same care a mother lavishes on her child when it first enters the world. It seemed to her that these last trials and temptations were the worst of all, and she endured a kind of inner agony of her own, even while trying to present an outward appearance of reassuring serenity to the dying woman. She was filled with a peculiarly vivid sense of participation in this "last passage" from time to Eternity.[4] Heaven seemed very near when she prayed with Rebecca that their "tender and faithful love" for each other might be perfected hereafter.[5]

Rebecca Seton's last moments were recounted by Mrs. Seton to John Wilkes in the words:

You will have heard before this of the departure of our dear Angel. She suffered extremely for about an hour, on Friday night so much, that we thought all was over, but [she] recovered her senses again and became perfectly composed and seemed free from pain. On Sunday she was delighted with the beauty of the morning, and pointed to the clouds that were brightening with the rising Sun and said—'Ah, my Sister, that this might be my day of rest—shut the windows and I will sleep.' I raised her head to make it easier, and immediately without the least strain she gave her last sigh.[6]

Elizabeth Seton thus lost the faithful sharer of many years of pleasure and pain.[7] Her heart was heavy as she reflected on her losses:

The home of plenty and comfort—the Society of Sisters united by prayer and divine affections—the evening hymns, the daily lectures [readings], the sunset contemplations, the Service of Holy Days together, the kiss of Peace, the widows' visits—all—all—gone—forever! And is Poverty and Sorrow the only exchange? Poverty and sorrow! Well, with God's blessing, you, too, shall be changed into dearest friends.[8]

The most immediate task Mrs. Seton faced after Rebecca's death was that of finding a small house for her family. Less than a week later she wrote to John Wilkes:

Your brother Charles...was quite pleased with my little house and my darlings whom he found eating their bread and milk with a very good appetite, but I observed that he was really so affected at the tolling of bells for the death of poor Hamilton that he could scarcely command himself— how much you will be distressed at this melancholy event—the circumstances of which are really too bad to think of.[9]

The "melancholy event" had shocked all New York. Only the fortnight previous Aaron Burr had challenged Alexander Hamilton to the now famous rendezvous. Shortly after dawn, on the Wednesday following Rebecca Seton's death, some boats crossed over to the opposite shore of Weehawken, New Jersey, carrying the principals and their retinues. Burr and Hamilton exchanged shots but Burr's was fatally accurate. Burr returned to New York to pretend to read in his library while Hamilton's inert form was carried back by horrified friends. All that day and the morning of the next the city waited for news. At 2 o'clock on Thursday afternoon Hamilton died. It was the tolling of the bells that day which so disturbed Charles Wilkes and Mrs. Seton.

Charles Wilkes, like the elder William Seton before him, had been closely associated with Alexander Hamilton as a result of Charles' position as cashier of the Bank of New York. With the officers of all the banks of the city, Wilkes marched the long funeral procession Saturday as it passed through Pearl Street, Whitehall, along Bowling Green, and up Broadway to Trinity Church. The obsequies were as elaborate as they had been for Washington in the procession of 31 December 1799. There were the riderless horse, the lawyers in deep mourning, the students and teachers from Columbia wearing cap and gown and paying tribute to a distinguished alumnus. James Seton's brother-in-law, Josiah Ogden Hoffman, was one of the pall-bearers. If Dr. Richard Bayley had been alive he might have marched with Wright Post as the cortege went solemnly past the doorways filled with weeping women, while above on the housetops curious spectators leaned over to watch Hamilton's last journey through New York.[10]

The small house which the Setons occupied the summer after Elizabeth's return from Italy was supported by John Wilkes, Wright Post, and Elizabeth's prosperous godmother, Sarah Clarke Startin[a]. These three agreed to maintain the household for at least a year because baby Rebecca was still too young to allow Mrs. Seton to undertake any enterprise herself.[11] John Wilkes felt an obligation to assist Mrs. Seton because she was the widow of his patron's son. He did not forget that the elder Seton had taken both John and Charles Wilkes into his home when they had first come to America from England. John's wife had been a Seton, and he had only the kindest memories of Elizabeth's aid and sympathy at the time of Mary Seton Wilkes' death. His generosity to the young widow was quite natural. Dr. Wright Post felt equally interested, in part because Elizabeth was his wife's only full sister, but perhaps even more because of his gratitude to the late Dr. Richard Bayley, their father. The friendship of Post was one of the things upon which Elizabeth Seton could rely throughout her life. Julia Scott in Philadelphia had invited Elizabeth to come there to live, but the latter preferred her own home, even though it be less luxurious. July found her quite content with the "neat house about half a mile from town where we occupy the upper story and will let the lower floor as soon as I can find a tenant."[b] When Julia came herself that summer to see how the small New

---

[a] [Sarah Clarke Startin (1750–1802) was the widow of Charles Clarke. Ed.]

[b] This may have been the house on North Moore Street listed as Widow Seton's residence in 1805. The directory for 1804 does not list Mrs. Seton at all. North Moore Street ran eastward from Greenwich Street in Manhattan and was north of Duane and Jay Streets.

York ménage was prospering she tried to persuade her friend to let Anna Maria return with her to Philadelphia. But Elizabeth proved adamant; she wanted her family all together and explained that she believed they would be better off without "the pretensions and indulgences" which ruined so many.[12]

Although Mrs. Seton was holding her ground in regard to a united family circle, she was in other ways succumbing to the pressure put upon her by relatives and friends despite the exposition of the Catholic faith which Philip Filicchi had given her.[c] Antonio Filicchi, who had hoped to see her safely in the Roman Catholic Church before he left for Boston, became increasingly uneasy as he watched her compromising the beliefs she seemed to have held when they left Leghorn. Instead of writing for advice from Bishop John Carroll as the Filicchi brothers had suggested, Elizabeth allowed her friends to dissuade her on the grounds that further inquiry was unnecessary. Antonio wrote bluntly that he failed to understand how her "priests who call loud for investigation, who do not acknowledge any authority above the private reason of any human being," should persuade her as her sacred duty to decline examination. If worldly considerations of security were influencing her, he added, she had his repeated assurances that both he and his brother would assist her. "It grieves me profoundly," he said, "to keep your anxiety so awakened, but according to my sacred principles and my most solid affection how can I spare you?"[13]

If Antonio Filicchi was concerned about Mrs. Seton's convictions, so was her pastor and friend of longer standing, John Henry Hobart. When Elizabeth was leaving Leghorn Philip Filicchi had given her a concise statement of the Catholic Church's claims based upon the profession of faith issued by Pope Pius IV in 1564.[14] Mrs. Seton had used this to justify to Hobart her interest in Catholicism. Hobart's remarks on the document caused uncertainty to modify Mrs. Seton's views since, as she confessed to Amabilia Filicchi, whatever her pastor said to her had the weight of her partiality for him as well as the respect she could scarcely accord anyone else.[15] Hobart told her:

> When I see a person whose sincere and ardent piety I have always thought worthy of imitation in danger of connecting herself with a communion which my sober judgment tells me is a corrupt and sinful communion, I cannot be otherwise than deeply affected...If it should appear that you have forsaken the religion of your forefathers, not from prejudices

---

[c] When Elizabeth was leaving Leghorn, Italy, in April 1804, Philip Filicchi gave her a manuscript to assist her in understanding the beliefs of the Catholic Church. It is based on the profession of faith issued by Pope Pius IV in 1564.

of education, not for want of better information, but in opposition to light and knowledge which few have enjoyed, my soul anxiously inquires, what answer will you make to your Almighty Judge?[16]

The argument of Hobart, made in the full sincerity of the young minister's concern for his parishioner, was insidious. To one of Elizabeth Seton's inclinations, who was vividly aware of God's blessings throughout her life, the implication that she might be guilty of willfulness and ingratitude was painful. The specious argument based upon the virtue of her friends who found their salvation within the Protestant Episcopal communion also served to confuse her. It is sometimes easier for the hardened sinner to leave his state of unbelief for the joys of faith than for the good Protestant who sees his friends, whom he judges more virtuous than himself, finding peace in the fold of their fathers. Elizabeth Seton, in her humility, could not doubt the goodness of Hobart, of Rebecca Seton, of Eliza Sadler, and of her other Anglican friends. Even though she felt it simplistic to claim that "wherever a child is born, and wherever its parents placed it, there it will find truth,"[17] she explained to Amabilia that she felt as if she were:

living all my days in the thought that all and everybody would be saved who meant well, it grieves my very soul to see that Protestants as well as your (as I thought, hard and severe principles) see the thing so differently.[18]

When Filicchi, on the recommendation of Rev. Matthew O'Brien, gave Elizabeth a book on *England's Conversion*,[19] it was offset by Hobart's recommendation of *Dissertations on the Prophecies* (1754-1758), by Thomas Newton, bishop of Bristol.[20] As his time in New York grew short and Antonio saw his friend's confusion increasing, he decided to appeal to Bishop Carroll himself. On 26 July 1804, he began a letter to the Bishop of Baltimore explaining his interest in Mrs. Seton, relating Hobart's observations on the Church's claims, and begging Carroll for "an invincible direct reply." He enclosed a letter from his brother introducing Antonio to the bishop,[21] and intended forwarding one from Mrs. Seton with Hobart's remarks on Catholicism. But before the letter could be sent, Filicchi received notes from both Elizabeth and the minister telling the Italian they had decided not to enter into further controversy. Filicchi had to add a postscript explaining this *volte face* and he concluded urgently:

Notwithstanding whatever I could be able to say to her she appears decided in maintaining her former communion and was but with great difficulty prevailed upon to wait the result of my present application to you. I must beg you with all my soul to hasten to come to my relief.[22]

When Filicchi failed to receive an immediate response from Baltimore he wrote again two weeks later, stressing the subject's vital importance involving as it did "the eternal salvation of six souls," the children's as well as the mother's. "From your instructions," he pleaded, "must depend the tranquillity of my conscience in regard to the conduct to pursue in such an important and delicate affair." He concluded that he was already due in Boston but he would wait one more week for a reply from Carroll.[23]

This second appeal was successful and on 20 August 1804, John Carroll penned his first letter relating to the career of Elizabeth Seton.[24] When Filicchi received the long-awaited advice he took it at once to Mrs. Seton and departed for Boston. The importance of Carroll's letter can be surmised from the young widow's comments to Antonio Filicchi:

> The Bishop's letter has been held to my heart on my knees beseeching God to enlighten me to see the truth, unmixed with doubts and hesitations—I read the promises given to St. Peter and the 6th Chap. [of] John every day and then ask God [if] can I offend him by believing those express words... God will not forsake me, Antonio, I know he will unite me to his flock.[25]

Antonio Filicchi kept Bishop Carroll informed of Elizabeth Seton's difficulties by letters of his own and enclosures of some written by her. He thanked Carroll for his first intervention, and said, "Sensible of my incapacity, particularly in a foreign language, I suggested to her to address you herself with her doubts and questions. Your wise and holy instructions in such a delicate and interesting case, direct or through me, are certainly the only adequate ones."[26] Once again, however, Elizabeth was reluctant to address the bishop herself and the brief encouragement she took from his advice in August was soon enough counteracted by the warnings of her friends that her interest in Catholicism was only temptation.[27] John Carroll did not write again for several months because he was ill that fall, and by the time he recovered he expected to see Antonio Filicchi in person.[28] The task of directing Elizabeth's faltering steps during that autumn remained solely Antonio's. It is from their correspondence that the story of Elizabeth Seton's struggle can be reconstructed.

Almost as soon as Antonio left for Boston, Elizabeth began her letters. Even before she knew his address she started jotting down her thoughts for him and watching for the arrival of James Seton's sedan chair, hoping for a letter from Boston.[d] "This you may think childish," she admitted to him, "but remember you have not a female heart, and mine is most truly and fondly attached to you, as you have [had] proved when I have been most contradictory and troublesome to you."[29] She laid bare her indecision with the words:

> Hideous objects will present themselves which disturb my soul and unsettle my faith, and tho' God is so gracious as to give me the fullest assurance that thro' the Name of Jesus my prayers shall finally be answered, yet there seems now a cloud before my way that keeps me always asking Him which is the right path—[30]

Antonio Filicchi refused to become discouraged. In his first letter after his arrival, he said,

> I want to know every thought, everything of you. Your worthy soul is mine; I shall call for it everywhere, from whomsoever. Help me with your prayers. I trust a good deal in them. God must bless you in this and in the other world, and I believe He blesses me for your sake.[31]

It is interesting to note the confidence Antonio had from the outset in the ultimate success of his efforts. It is equally worthy of note that he possessed from the beginning an unusual trust in the efficacy of Elizabeth's prayers. Throughout the sixteen years of their friendship, fourteen of which were spent with an ocean between them, the letters of Filicchi reiterated this refrain of gratitude for her intercession. One of his last letters to Elizabeth Seton declared:

> To your prayers, I doubt not, I owe the uninterrupted prosperity of all my concerns in this world, and I am confident that, when you will be in Heaven, you will not let the door be shut against your own true brother and friend, who so fortunately contributed to open it for you.

The warmth of his devotion had never cooled from its early ardor and the letter concluded:

> In spite of my stubborn silence, you are constantly in my mind, you have my warmest wishes. I love, I esteem, I

---

[d] Sedan chairs were a common method of conveyance in New York City. Mrs. Seton received mail sent through the public channels in care of James Seton. Most people preferred to send letters by travelers because of the element of safety and to avoid the excessive postage charges the recipient paid. See Souvay, pp. 230-7; *Mother Seton Guild Bulletin,* XXVII (November, 1948), 3.

venerate you. I boast of your benevolence towards me, and for you I shall always be ready to fight men and devils.[32]

Certainly that winter of 1804-1805 he seemed literally called upon to fight "men and devils" on behalf of his New York protégée. As the days grew shorter and the weather colder, Elizabeth Seton's uncertainty grew greater. When she stayed away from church services at Trinity or its chapels, as Antonio had advised, she was chided by Wright Post. Her brother-in-law, who was subsidizing part of her household, was less heated in his criticism than some of her other attackers, but his indirect approach through comments on the "errors and imperfections" of practicing Catholics in New York was not designed to produce peace of mind. Meanwhile, Mr. Hobart was losing patience with his recalcitrant member, and his call on 7 September was accompanied by charges against the Catholic Church of corrupting the "primitive doctrine." Elizabeth sensed the futility of bringing Bishop Carroll's letter into the discussion, and "the visit was short and painful on both sides."[33] Mrs. Seton was not unmoved by these calls, however, and she allowed herself to yield on the arguments of propriety and peace. Another Sunday found her at St. Paul's Chapel where, as she later wrote Amabilia Filicchi, "I got in a side pew which turned my face toward the Catholic Church in the next street, and found myself twenty times speaking to the Blessed Sacrament there instead of looking at the naked altar where I was, or minding the routine of prayers."[34] This kind of equivocation could only produce a multitude of other mazes. Mrs. Seton said she "smiled" at Hobart's question, "How can you believe there are as many gods as there are millions of altars and tens of millions of blessed hosts all over the world?" Yet she wrote Antonio Filicchi of her difficulty in believing that she should be "satisfied with his Bread and believe the cup, which he equally commanded unnecessary."[35] From bewilderment in regard to the Blessed Sacrament her mind darted to the subject of the Blessed Virgin. To Amabilia she wrote that if anyone were in heaven surely the Mother of God must be exalted there and that "I beg her with the confidence and tenderness of her child to pity us and guide us to the true faith if we are not in it."[36] To Antonio, on the other hand, she wondered how she could believe "that the Prayers and litanies addressed to the Blessed Lady were acceptable to God, though not commanded in Scripture."[37] In July Mrs. Seton had been chiefly concerned as to whether the Protestant Episcopal Church could be the "true church." By October she was enmeshed in numberless speculations which only confused her more.

Two very salutary letters from Philip Filicchi and one from Bishop Carroll were written that fall and winter. If they had arrived at this period in Mrs. Seton's struggle, they might have hastened the outcome. On 17 October the elder Filicchi brother wrote from Leghorn reprovingly:

> Your anxiety is unreasonable, your trouble a temptation. You pray to your Father...and you tremble. You do not know His Goodness. These were not the sentiments which accompany'd the prodigal son nor Mary Magdalen. St. Paul fallen from his horse[e] & called by Him whom he knew not did not trouble himself. He calmly said, "What will you have me do?"[38]

He said Hobart's arguments presented nothing new. The devil, Filicchi suggested, delights in trouble; it is his element. "He knows he cannot catch fish in clear water."[39] The letter closed with a stern admonition that she stop haggling over details and answer the question: what is the true Church established by Christ?

How much effect so strong a tone might have had can only be guessed. From his vantage point across the sea Philip Filicchi could speak more bluntly to Mrs. Seton in regard to her vacillation. A few days later he wrote:

> In a spiritual Concern you have followed only worldly prudence, that prudence which the Gospel calls folly. You have acted as if you had thought God was not to be obeyed without the consent & advice of your friends. You have met the predicament you deserve.[40]

In her defense it must be said that Elizabeth felt she was following Antonio's advice when, on her return to the United States, she entered into the unfortunate discussion with Hobart. But Philip Filicchi was not alone in condemning her subsequent conduct. John Carroll told Antonio his friend ought to consider whether the tears she sheds and the prayers she offers heaven are purely for God's sake and arise solely from compunction for him & are unmixed with any alloy of worldly respect or inordinate solicitude for the attainment of some worldly purpose.[41]

Continuing his speculation about Mrs. Seton's difficulties, the Bishop of Baltimore wrote:

---

[e] Sacred Scripture does not mention that Saul of Tarsus fell from a horse on his journey to Damascus. Acts of the Apostles 9:1-9. A medieval collection of hagiography by Jacopo da Varagine popularized this legend about St. Paul which has been perpetuated through art, especially the painting entitled *The Conversion on the Way to Damascus* by Caravaggio, 1601.

Indeed, when I read the words you copied from her letters, and her letters themselves, I remain convinced of the sincerity of her endeavors to make herself conformable in all things to the Divine Will; but afterwards a fear arises in my mind that God discovers in her some lurking imperfection and defers the final grace of her conversion 'till her soul be entirely purified of its irregular attachments.[42]

Like Philip Filicchi, the prelate advocated abandoning further controversy. He advised that Mrs. Seton ask God "to revive in her heart the grace of her baptism" and fortify her resolution to follow the voice of God without reservations. Unfortunately, the Leghorn letters were delayed by the winter weather, and the letter from Baltimore was not sent until the worst of Mrs. Seton's tormenting doubts were lifting. In the black period of her indecision Elizabeth turned more and more to Antonio at Boston. In September she had written:

Antonio, Antonio, why cannot my poor Soul be satisfied... how can it hesitate—why must it struggle...I am ashamed of my own letters, they are all egotism, but my soul is so entirely engrossed by one subject that it cannot speak with freedom on any other...You know my heart, you know my thoughts, my pains and sorrows, hopes and fears—Jonathan loved David as his own soul, and if I was your brother, Antonio, I would never leave you for one hour—but as it is I try rather to turn every affection to God, well knowing that there alone their utmost exercise cannot be misapplied.[43]

Antonio had replied consolingly that she should "be easy"; he knew her prayers would prove effective. Certainly he was benefited by them. "Never," he wrote in his stilted English, "I was so less bad in my life as I think I am now." He expressed the wish that she could be in Boston to derive the benefits of the Church there.

Oh, my good friend, with what worthy clergymen are here Catholics blessed! Their countenance, their conduct, their doctrine are acknowledged almost with enthusiasm by most Protestants themselves. Every Sunday our church is mostly crowded by them to hear the sermons of our learned & eloquent Cheverus, and some conversations from time to time take place without any murmuring at all.[44]

But Elizabeth was not in Boston and many months passed before this "learned and eloquent Cheverus" came to her aid. As the old year waned her spirits sank lower. The journal kept for Amabilia bore testimony to the inner turmoil which racked her soul. In November she recorded, "I do not get on, Amabilia, cannot cast the balance for the peace of this poor soul." She turned from the controversial reading and pored over the Psalms, reread the *Imitation of Christ* and the spiritual advice of St. Francis de Sales. Even when her suffering was the worst, Elizabeth never abandoned the hope that constant prayer would eventually bring surcease. While yet deprived of it, she perceived clearly the nature of faith.

> I see FAITH is a gift of God to be diligently sought and earnestly desired and groan to Him for it in silence, since our Saviour says I cannot come to Him unless the Father draw me—so it is. By and by I trust this storm will cease. How painful and often agonizing He only knows who can and will still it in His own good time.[45]

Meanwhile the Seton children came down with whooping cough and the simultaneous illness of the serving woman kept Elizabeth busy. She lived through November in hourly expectation of Antonio's return. "My heart," she explained to him, "has jumped almost out of me every time our street door opened, and trembled so much at the sight of Mr. [John] Wilkes, James Seton or anyone who might inform me of you that I have scarcely been able to speak."[46] But November passed and he did not arrive. When his note arrived on 3 December with news of even further delay Elizabeth's disappointment was so keen that her own reply was a trifle tart in tone. She hoped his new engagements in Boston would recompense him for the loss of her letters which he claimed he had missed. "The 2 or 3 weeks you purpose still to remain there," she wrote, "will lengthen to months as easily as those that are past." [47] Then, whether in pique or simple sincerity it is difficult to say, she told him of her decision to take the advice of John Wilkes in regard to her future economic plans. Having held off for two months in vain, hoping to discuss the matter with Antonio, she had finally yielded to circumstances, "pushed by necessity, and compelled by my unprovided condition, and another offering to take the situation unconditionally which I have so long hesitated to accept."[48]

The plan which John Wilkes had suggested to Mrs. Seton was one which had its origin in the problem of his motherless sons and the children of his brother Charles. The plan involved Mrs. Seton's taking as boarders the Wilkes boys and a dozen more from the school conducted by the curate of St. Mark's, [Rev. William Harris]. It was expected that the plan would take shape about the first of the year.[49] Whether Wilkes was premature in his suggestion, or whether Elizabeth exaggerated the urgency of the project to Antonio, the plan did not actually materialize for another year.

The letter Elizabeth received from Boston on 13 December explained that the initiation of a lawsuit in Philip Filicchi's interests was the cause for Antonio's delay, and Antonio's complaints of having received no word from her filled Elizabeth with mingled joy and shame at her impatience. She sat down at once to reply:

> Certainly I was obliged to make the dear sign [of the Cross] to
> help me keep my good resolution of trying to be indifferent—
> I should wish earnestly, my most dear Brother, never to think
> of you with tenderness but when calling on Almighty God to
> bless you, then often indeed my heart overflows.[50]

Then she poured out all the doubts and fears of the past months. It was not interest in temporal concerns which really distressed her, she admitted, but rather "the horror of neglecting to hear His voice, if indeed he has spoken to me through you."[51] She told how the Scriptures which had once brought her joy served now only to confuse her. The Sabbath, which a year ago had been her week's reward, had now become a torment of fear whether she went to the right church. How could she determine which friends were guides to truth or tempters? She wrote:

> You can easily conceive that as the view of my sins always
> rises against me as the veil between my soul and the truth,
> that I earnestly desire that God will keep me from all created
> beings that by a broken and contrite heart I may find Mercy
> through my Redeemer.[52]

In trying to remove this "veil" forcibly, Elizabeth had begun to fast rigorously and her small frame soon became little more than a skeleton. When Eliza Sadler saw her friend's ravaged figure she was distressed and she remarked to Elizabeth it seemed to her the Seton lot held enough penance without seeking more among the Catholics. Elizabeth explained that she hoped that the more she suffered here the more she might be spared in the next world. Sad rejoined dryly that it seemed a comfortable enough doctrine; she wished she could believe it.[53] But Elizabeth would not be dissuaded.

A heavy snow fell over the city and the roads became impassable. Not even Mary Bayley Post could get through to see her sister. The children had to be diverted and Elizabeth tried to devise special games to keep up their spirits. Together they lived over the Bible stories of David, Daniel, and Judith, and the white world of New York vanished in the re-created days of heroic valor. In the evening the mother played spirited tunes on the piano for the children's hilarious dancing before she gathered them close to the fire to say their prayers. Anna Maria, who still relived the trip to Italy, begged to have the "Ave Maria" included, and even little Bec tried to join in with her sweet high lisping voice. Sometimes the neighbor children pleaded to join in the play and prayers. It was after the children were all safe in bed that their mother's fears returned, and in the midnight hours the tears rolled down her cheeks while she stared through the darkness with such intensity she sometimes almost expected "to see His finger writing on the wall," for her relief.[54]

In January a kind of crisis was reached. New Year's Day passed with its traditional visits from friends. John Wilkes stopped in to announce that the plan for boarding the schoolboys would be delayed until at least May. Mrs. Seton's half-brother, Richard Bayley, in New York for a few weeks, called to pick up any messages for Italy, and to get Antonio's address in Boston, before returning to Leghorn. After the social exchanges were over, Elizabeth Seton, wishing to read something appropriate to the season, took down a volume of Bourdaloue and turned to the sermon on the Epiphany. When she came to the words of the wise man, "Where is He who is born king of the Jews," the whole painful question as to the one true church was immediately before her. "The inference that when we no longer discern the Star of Faith we must seek it where only it is to be found, with the depositors of His Word" seemed to her too plain to be ignored. In desperation she decided that once and for all the issue must be resolved. She tried to reach Rev. Matthew O'Brien, whom she mistakenly believed to be the only Catholic priest in New York City. Besides Matthew O'Brien there were Rev. William Vincent O'Brien, O.P., the pastor, Rev. John Byrne and a "Mr. Vrennay"[f] in New York in January 1805.[55] Failing in this attempt, she "looked straight up to God and told him, since I cannot see the way to please you, whom alone I wish to please, everything is indifferent to me and until you do show me the way you mean me to walk in I will trudge on the path you suffered me to be born in." Leaving the children home with the serving

---

[f] At this time the distinction between a layman and a clergyman was not as clearly delineated as it became later. Generally diocesan or secular priests were called "Rev." or simply "Mr." About the middle of the nineteenth-century, only priests belonging to a religious order would be addressed as "Father." Cf. Thomas W. Spalding, C.F.X., *The Premier See* (Baltimore: Johns Hopkins University Press, 1989), 58. Elizabeth Seton and the early Sisters of Charity usually followed the convention of their time but not always.

woman she went defiantly off to St. George's, one of Trinity's two chapels in 1805. It did not achieve a separate status until 1811.[56]

In keeping with her tendency never to do things halfheartedly, Elizabeth Seton had chosen a "Sacrament Sunday" for her return to the church of her family; the ordeal she experienced that day nearly turned her mind. When she bowed her head to receive the bishop's absolution, which was given "publickly & universally to all in the church," she found she had not the least faith in its efficacy. She remembered only too well that the books Mr. Hobart had recommended did not claim or even admit any apostolic loosening from sins. Nevertheless, trembling to communion she went, "half-dead with the inward struggle." When she heard the words, "The Body and blood of Christ," she was undone. Afterward the "bold excesses" of the morning could not be banished from her mind. On her arrival home she seized the daily exercise book Abbé Plunkett had provided in Italy, and she turned to the "Prayers after Communion." But finding each prayer "addressed to our dear Saviour as really present" she was filled with renewed horror at the morning's mockery, and became "half-crazy."[57] For the first time she could not bear the children near her, nor could she say the blessing for their dinner. Her record reads:

> Oh, my God, that day—but it finished calmly at last, abandoning all to God, and a renewed confidence in the Blessed Virgin...I WILL GO PEACEABLY & FIRMLY TO THE CATHOLIC CHURCH, for if Faith is so important to our Salvation, I will seek it where true Faith first began, seek it among those who received it from GOD HIMSELF—the controversies on it I am quite incapable of deciding, and as the strictest Protestant allows salvation to a good Catholic, to the Catholics I will go, and try to be a good one. May God accept my intention and pity me.[58]

This decision was made about 16 January 1805. Several years later Mrs. Seton recalled the moment: "Precisely this time that the Divine Light of Faith, which I so long resisted forced its way[in]to [my soul]—an overwhelming power which made me to see and taste its infinite sweetness."[59]

Elizabeth waited for Antonio's return in February before taking the final step toward Roman Catholicism. In that month temptation made its last feeble effort to dissuade her. Matthew O'Brien, the priest Mrs. Seton met through Filicchi, wrote to Bishop Carroll on 19 February 1805,

Mrs. Morris[g] has become a Catholic without any further solicitation and is performing the Stations of the Jubilee with astonishing edification. There are two more ladies converted. Mrs. Seaton [sic] is yet in the scale. Mr. Filicchi is here and has good hopes, and presents you his respects.[60]

Mr. Filicchi's "good hopes" were soon to be realized. A lesser man might have lost patience after a year of fruitless efforts on behalf of Mrs. Seton, but not Antonio Filicchi. Elizabeth had written him in January, "You speak so highly of the Catholic Priests in Boston perhaps it would be best you should give a short history of your dear Sister to the one you esteem most— as I may one day find the benefit of your doing so."[61] The day was now at hand. While O'Brien was writing to Carroll, Antonio and Elizabeth both addressed themselves to Jean Lefebvre de Cheverus (1768–1836) of Boston. Filicchi said:

> Mrs. [Seton] I am in full hopes, will be finally a good Roman Catholic with her 5 children. Considering Bishop Carroll too much occupied I have suggested her to have recourse to *you* in her scruples & anxieties, for instruction, comfort, advice, and she is actually writing to you. You will have [as] it becomes you, the merit of determining & perfecting the work.[62]

A few days after receiving Filicchi's petition, Cheverus replied and enclosed a lengthy letter for Mrs. Seton. The Boston priest told Mrs. Seton that she had heard enough argument on both sides, and that while she was "never for a moment a strong protestant," she was often, as she said, a good Catholic. Cheverus continued:

> I believe you are always a good Catholic. The doubts which arise in your mind do not destroy your faith, they only disturb your mind. Who in this life, my dear Madam, is perfectly free from such troubles? "We see as through a glass in an obscure manner," we stand like Israelites at the foot of the holy mountain, but in spite of dark clouds and the noise of thunder, we perceive some rays of the glory of the Lord and we hear His divine voice. I would therefore advise your joining the Catholic Church as soon as possible, and when doubts arise, say only: "I believe, O Lord, help Thou my unbelief."[63]

---

[g] Mrs. Morris may have been the wife of Andrew Morris, the first Catholic office-holder in New York City. There is no way of identifying the other converts to Catholicism in 1805.

When Antonio received the letters from Boston, he "ran immediately to deliver the enclosed" to Elizabeth. The advice of Cheverus was exactly what she required. "She accepted of it as a distinguished blessing from God; she prayed, she meditated on it."[h]

Since Ash Wednesday she had been going to Mass at St. Peter's Catholic Church, Barclay Street, and finally on 14 March 1805, in the presence of Antonio and Rev. Matthew O'Brien, she made "the requisite profession of faith in the Roman Catholic Church."[64]

If ever there were serious questions as to the chronology of this period of Elizabeth Seton's life none need now remain. It is quite clear that she began going to St. Peter's Church on Ash Wednesday, 27 February 1805. In regard to this visit Mrs. Seton wrote, "It was a day they received Ashes, the beginning of Lent and [a] drole but most venerable Irish priest... talked of Death so familiarly that he delighted and revived me."[65] In reply to her sister's question later, "Tell me candidly if you go to our church or not," Elizabeth Seton replied, "Since the first day of Lent I have been to St. Peter's."[66] There is no doubt at all that Mrs. Seton knew the liturgical calendar of the Church sufficiently to know when Lent began.[i] Filicchi's letter to Cheverus stated clearly that Mrs. Seton had been at St. Peter's "several days" previous to her formal abjuration, which took place on 14 March. In a grateful letter to Father Cheverus Mrs. Seton wrote, "My Soul has offered all its hesitations and reluctancies a Sacrifice with the blessed sacrifice on the Altar, on the 14th of March, and the next day was admitted to the true Church of Jesus Christ."[67] Antonio's letter to Boston on 16 March said, "She went the day before yesterday morning to make her profession of faith." A copy of the *Following of Christ* which Elizabeth gave Antonio bore the inscription, "to commemorate the happy day he presented her to the Church of God, the 14th March 1805."[68] In "Dear Remembrances," written years later, Mrs. Seton recorded, "14th March 1805 it [her soul] entered the Ark of St. Peter with its beloved ones."[69] In a letter to Antonio Filicchi written the year following the important step, Mrs. Seton referred to "the 14th (the day in which your idea must necessarily be connected with my very prayers and thankfulness to God)."[70] The actual event of the day was described in the journal for Amabilia Filicchi:

---

[h] Seton wrote on the reverse of the Cheverus letter, "Bishop Cheverus first answer to an earnest entreaty for his advice— Entered the church immediately afterward—14th March one year after returning from Leghorn."

[i] Long before she became a Catholic Mrs. Seton was accustomed to dating her journal entries, "Wednesday, St. Michael's," "Ascension Day," or "Nov. 1 All Saints." Her reading of the Bourdaloue sermon on the Epiphany "to enjoy a good sermon of the season" bears testimony to her interest in the liturgical cycle. Note has already been made of her observance of Ash Wednesday as an Episcopalian.

After all were gone I was called to the little room next [to] the Altar and there PROFESSED to believe what the Council of Trent believes and teaches, laughing with my heart to my Saviour, who saw that I knew not what the Church of God believed, only that it believed what the church of God declared to be its belief, and consequently is now my belief— for as to going a walking any more about what all the different people believe, I cannot, being quite tired out.[71]

The gift of Catholic faith which Elizabeth Seton received in 1805 was not accompanied by any profound theological insight or immediate comprehension. Not long before her death in the Maryland mountains, after years of practical Catholic living, she still felt her heart "tremble and faint before Him here in His little sacristy, close to His Tabernacle," while she asked, *"How am I here?"* She wrote to Rev. Simon Bruté, her friend and confessor, from the depths of her humility:

I tell you a secret hidden almost from my own soul it is so delicate, *that* my hatred of opposition, troublesome inquiries, etc. brought me in the Church more than conviction—how often I argued to my fearful uncertain heart at all events Catholics must be as safe as any other religion, they say none are safe but themselves—*perhaps it is true.* If not, at all events I shall be as safe with them as any other. It is the way of Suffering and the Cross for me that is another point of Security—I shall be rid, too, of all the endless salutations of Trinity Church and the dissipated dress and— among strangers unknown, and if indeed (as I have most reason to believe) the *Blessed Sacrament is my Jesus, the daily sacrifice,* the opening, the pained and suffering heart to a guide and friend—My God pity me—I was in the Church many times before I dared look at the Sacred Host at the elevation, so daunted by their cry of idolatry. There ...you read what I would have carried to the grave, only I wish you to know well. . .the impossibility for a poor Protestant to see *our Meaning* without being led step by step and the Veil lifted little by little.[72]

What Elizabeth Seton missed in intellectual comprehension she made up for in love. When the questions of her pupils in later life were beyond her, her solution was to "pour out the soul to God in answer, hoping He will put the right words in my mouth." Speaking of an occasion when a young lady came to her in confusion over the matter of salvation outside the Church, Mother Seton said:

> My vacant brains were never busy enough about that to mind even what I have read of it, except to *Adore* and skip up to the scene where all will be revealed—she stared when I told her gravely they were *mysteries of love,* as much as when I assured her I was only an *Adorer* too, of the Mystery of *the Church* the only Ark in *the world*, and all the heathens, savages, sects, etc. were only in my heart for prayer, but never in my brain for what became of them, or to trouble my Faith in His wisdom and mercy, the Father most tender, Father of *all,* my immense God, I His alone.[73]

The church in which Mrs. Seton made her profession of faith in 1805 was, at that time, the only Catholic church in New York City, St. Peter's of Barclay Street. It had only officially opened its doors on 4 November 1786, when Elizabeth Bayley was twelve years old. "Amidst a brilliant assemblage," assisted by the chaplains of the French and Spanish legations, Andrew Nugent, O.F.M.Cap., had celebrated the solemn high Mass.[74] The following year John Carroll, then prefect apostolic, had appointed Rev. William O'Brien, O.P., pastor.[75] In the early years of his incumbency O'Brien[j] had worked valiantly to promote the interests of his infant parish. For two years he traveled in Cuba and Mexico collecting money and religious objects for New York.[k] In the years following his return in November 1792, Father O'Brien had struggled against the attacks of yellow fever which threatened his immigrant congregation. Dr. Bayley, Elizabeth's father, had commended the priest as the only clergyman to remain in the city during the worst of the epidemics.[76] By the time, however, that Dr. Bayley's daughter was ready to begin her life as a member of St. Peter's parish William Vincent O'Brien was no longer active. The eminent Dr. John Charlton, Elizabeth's maternal uncle, had once warned O'Brien that he might become a martyr to rheumatism, and violent attacks of this malady seem to have discouraged the Dominican from active parish duties.[77]

The clerical duties by 1805 had devolved principally upon Rev. Matthew O'Brien, often referred to as "the young Dr.," who had come to New York from Albany sometime before 1802. The two O'Brien's were not

---

[j] Rev. William Vincent O'Brien, a Dominican priest, is believed to have come to the United States about 1786, and was a Preacher General in his order. Before coming to St. Peter's he served in and around Philadelphia.

[k] One of these objects was the painting of the Crucifixion by José Maria Vallejo, a Mexican artist. The first day Mrs. Seton visited St. Peter's she wrote, "How that heart died away, as it were, in silence before that little tabernacle and the great crucifixion above it." See 3.31, Journal for Amabilia Filicchi, *CW*, 1:375.

related.[78] The younger O'Brien was assisted by an old French priest and the Irish John Byrne.[79] "Mr. Vrennay," the Frenchman, was in New York during Mrs. Seton's first year in the Church; John Byrne was in New York until she left for Baltimore.[80] The latter priest lived with Matthew O'Brien on Elm Street but the two men were not always on the best of terms. Byrne was frequently away on trips to Georgetown, Baltimore, and Albany, and once threatened to go to Baltimore permanently.[81] The older O'Brien thought highly of Byrne, however, and at the time Bishop Carroll planned to replace William O'Brien by a more active pastor, the invalid wrote, "As for the Rev. good Mr. Byrne, he is very well calculated for this city...No clergyman you could send would answer so well."[82] After Rev. Louis Sibourd became pastor of St. Peter's in the summer of 1807, the pious Frenchman and Byrne became good friends and lived together.[83] When Sibourd became discouraged with conditions within his congregation in 1808, he too recommended that John Byrne be left with the pastoral charges.[84] Elizabeth Seton came to respect and admire Father Byrne and she was filled with "great delight" when "our dear Father Burns" appeared again on the altar after one of his periodic trips.[85]

Of all the factual details surrounding Elizabeth Seton's conversion the most interesting one must still remain in question. Final certainty in regard to her baptism is not possible. White believed that Mrs. Seton was baptized conditionally;[86] while Rev. Charles Souvay, C.M., after careful examination of existing evidence, concluded that "the probability of her being baptized is hardly more than a possibility."[87] There is no record of her baptism, conditional or otherwise at St. Peter's. This indicates that either her baptism in the Episcopalian church was regarded as valid, or that no records were kept of conditional baptisms. Bishop Carroll accepted the validity of Episcopalian baptisms as he indicated in his letter advising Mrs. Seton to "revive in her heart the grace of baptism" two months before her conversion.[88] Jean Cheverus of Boston held the same view in regard to the Episcopalian sacrament when he wrote to Mrs. Seton in regard to Cecilia Seton's baptism, six months before Cecilia became a convert to Catholicism:

> Your beloved sister has been made by baptism a member of the Church. Willful error, I have reason to think, has never separated her from that sacred body. Her singular innocence of mind and ardent piety have also, very likely, preserved her from offending God in any grievous manner, and I hope that in consequence even if she cannot receive the Sacraments

[of Penance and Holy Eucharist] she will be a member of the triumphant church in heaven.[89]

In addition to the weight of these opinions of Carroll and Cheverus, there is the complete lack of reference to any baptism ceremony in the accounts kept by Mrs. Seton of this momentous period in her life. She describes with high emotion and vivid detail her first visit of Ash Wednesday, her profession of faith of the 14th of March, her first general confession, and her first communion; yet no phrase or sentence suggests anything resembling baptism.[1] Mrs. Seton herself wrote on a page of a *Following of Christ,* "Was I not signed with the cross of salvation in Baptism?"[90] The weight of evidence bears out the Souvay contention that the possibility of a Catholic baptism in 1805 is very slight.[91]

The culmination of Elizabeth Seton's step that March of 1805 was the reception of the sacraments. Contrary to the usual trepidation which accompanies an adult convert's first confession, Elizabeth's joy at the resolution of her conflict was so great that she was "ready to make [it] on the house top to insure the GOOD ABOSOLUTION." She found Matthew O'Brien most kind and she felt nothing but incredible relief at "the words of unloosing" after her thirty years of bondage. From that day until the feast of the Annunciation, she counted the hours. Mornings as she trudged through the deep snow, or picked her way warily over the ice formed from yesterday's thaw, she seemed to hear only the words, "Unless you eat My Flesh and drink My Blood you can have no part with ME"— she saw only the bright cross on St. Peter's steeple.[92]

Elizabeth never forgot the night before that first communion. She could describe it as vividly in "Dear Remembrances" as she did in the contemporary journal for Amabilia. As she waited through the darkness for dawn to appear she was torn between the fear and humility of wondering if she were properly prepared, and "transports of confidence and hope" that flooded her when she contemplated God's goodness and love. The long walk to town, counting the steps as she neared Barclay Street, the overwhelming conviction of utter unworthiness as she entered the door, all culminated in that "moment when He would enter the poor, poor little dwelling so all His own."

---

[1] Although there is no record of her baptism in the Protestant Episcopal Church, there is no question that Elizabeth Bayley was baptized. A list of regular communicants at Trinity Church from 1800 to 1816 contains her name, and a "Communicant" was a validly baptized person who received communion at least three times a year. The absence of any records before 1776 at Trinity Church is due to the fire which destroyed the church in that year. Search made at Staten Island, and other places which might have revealed proof of infant baptism, has proved fruitless.

And when He did—the first thought, I remember, was let God arise, let His enemies be scattered, for it seemed to me my King had come to take His throne, and instead of the humble tender welcome I had expected to give Him, it was but a triumph of joy and gladness.[93]

The two miles of the return home were scarcely noted as she sped back to carry to her children "the first kiss and blessing," wrapt up as she was in the joy of bringing *such a Master* to our little dwelling." [94]

Bishop Carroll received the happy news of Mrs. Seton's conversion from Antonio Filicchi that May when the Italian merchant wrote:

Your learned remarks & advices have not been in vain. You will certainly thank God & rejoice in the happy intelligence that at last Mrs. W. M. Seton is numbered in your flock with her five children, and proves an edifying example of piety & zeal.[95]

The gratitude Elizabeth Seton felt toward Antonio Filicchi knew no bounds. "You have led me," she wrote him in Philadelphia, "to a happiness which admits of no description, and daily even hourly increases my soul's peace—and really supplies strength and resolution superior to anything I could have conceived possible in so frail a being."[96] Mrs. Seton was indebted to both the Filicchi brothers. Where Philip's lucid theology had pointed the way, Antonio's unfailing zeal had urged her lagging steps. But there are times in the soul's progress when logic falls short and love makes up the balance, and so it was to Antonio that Elizabeth wrote, "I shall not go to the Altar in spirit or in reality without remembering my most dear brother."[97]

CHAPTER 5. TO OLD SAINT PETER'S

Notes

[1] 3.1, Elizabeth Seton to Rebecca Seton, *CW*, 1:308.

[2] 10.4, "Dear Remembrances," 4 June 1804, *CW*, 3a:517. Mrs. Seton had not yet received John Hobart's letter telling of the child's recovery. John Henry Hobart to Elizabeth Seton, New York, 23 November 1803, ASJPH 1-3-3-11:B70.

[3] Ibid., 518. Ruth 1:16.

[4] 3.31, Journal to Amabilia Filicchi, July 1804, *CW*, 1:367. This journal was kept for Amabilia Baragazzi Filicchi, the wife of Antonio Filicchi, and covers the period from Mrs. Seton's return to New York until her first communion, 25 March 1805.

[5] 3.1, Journal to Rebecca Seton (continued), 8 July 1804, *CW*, 1:310.

[6] 3.4, Draft of Elizabeth Seton to John Wilkes, [July 1804], *CW*, 1:312. This fragmentary letter gives internal evidence of having been written from New York to John Wilkes on 13 July 1804.

[7] 3.5, Rebecca Seton, sister-in-law to Elizabeth Seton, died 8 July 1804, *CW*, 1:313; C. I. White gives the date as 18 July, based probably on the first entry of Mrs. Seton's journal for Amabilia Filicchi; 3.1, but Mrs. Seton wrote to Julia Scott on 15 July saying, "My soul's sister departed for the happier world this day [a] week [ago]," *CW*, 1:313. 3.5, Elizabeth Seton to Julia Scott, *CW*, 1:313. The last entry in the journal for Rebecca is dated 8 July, and begins, "This is my Rebecca's birthday in heaven."

[8] 3.1, Journal to Rebecca Seton (continued), 4 June 1804, *CW*, 1:308.

[9] 3.4, Draft of Elizabeth Seton to John Wilkes, New York, 13 July 1804, *CW*, 1:311. John Wilkes was in Albany, New York, at this time.

[10] James G. Wilson, *Memorial History of the City of New York* (New York, 5893), III, 160-164; Rodman Gilder, *The Battery* (Boston, 1936), pp. 127-8.

[11] 3.5, Elizabeth Seton to Julia Scott, New York, 15 July 1804, *CW*, 1:313.

[12] Ibid., 315; 3.13, New York, 24 November 1804, *CW*, 1:334.

[13] Antonio Filicchi to Elizabeth Seton, New York, 26 July 1804, ASJPH 1-3-3-10:4.

[14] A-8.27, Philip Filicchi's Exposition of the Catholic Faith for Elizabeth Seton, *CW*, 3b:585-616. Although Elizabeth's grandson Robert Seton questioned the authorship of the document, internal evidence indicates it was written by Philip Filicchi. In a note Bishop John Carroll wrote to Antonio Filicchi 9 September 1804, he said: "I now

return you the valuable manuscript of your highly respected brother, and entertain an humble reliance that so much zeal united with so much knowledge, will finally produce its desired effect." (White, 521.) In addition, an 20 October 1846, letter of Antonio Filicchi to Charles White states that Philip Filicchi provided a manuscript for Elizabeth which argued the claims of the Roman Catholic Church, AMSJ A 111 094. Apparently Annabelle Melville did not see the Filicchi letter to Charles White. Based on her research, Annabelle Melville had cited Robert Seton who said that this statement was drawn up by Joseph Pecci, later provost of the cathedral and bishop of his native place Gubbio. He believed that Filicchi simply turned it into English for Mrs. Seton. See Seton, *Memoirs, Letters and Journal,* I, 151-186. This may explain Antonio's letter to Pecci after Mrs. Seton's death in which Antonio Filicchi told Pecci that Mrs. Seton "non cessera mai di venerare e amare il Veneratissimo e Amatissimo suo Amico e Padrone Monsignor Proposto Gius^e Pecci *per omnia secula seculorum."* (Mrs. Seton "never stopped venerating and loving her Very Venerable and Most Loved friend and patron Monsignor Proposto Giuseppe Pecci forever and ever.") See Antonio Filicchi to Monsignor Pecci, Leghorn, 17 October 1821, and 23 October 1821, 26-0-1, (2). Copy. The original is in AMSJ. The document in question may also be found in Seton's *Memoir, Letters and Journal,* I, 151-186; C. I. White, *The Life of Mrs. Eliza A. Seton,* 521-51.

[15] 3.31, Journal to Amabilia Filicchi, 19 July 1804, *CW,* 1:367.

[16] Robert Seton, *Memoir, Letters and Journal,* I, 187-189. The original of Hobart's arguments has not been located.

[17] 3.31, Journal to Amabilia Filicchi, *CW,* 1:367.

[18] Ibid., 369.

[19] Antonio Filicchi to John Carroll, New York, 26 July 1804, ASJPH 26-0-2, (10). Copy. The original is in AAB, AASMSU. Reverend Robert Manning's *England's Conversion and Reformation Compared* first appeared in Antwerp in 1725. Wilfred Parsons, *Early Catholic Americana* (New York, 1939), 111.

[20] 3.31, Journal to Amabilia Filicchi, *CW,* 1:368. See S. Austin Alibone, *A Critical Dictionary of English Literature and British and American Authors* (Philadelphia, 1897), II, 1422.

[21] Philip Filicchi to John Carroll, Leghorn, 30 March 1804, AAB, AASMSU, 3-S-7.

[22] Antonio Filicchi to John Carroll, New York, 26 July 1804, ASJPH 26-

0-2, (10). Copy. The original is in AAB, AASMSU 3-S-2. Antonio Filicchi wrote that he intended showing Hobart's arguments to Matthew O'Brien that evening but there is no evidence of O'Brien's reply. Philip Filicchi, however, replied to Hobart's position in a letter to Mrs. Seton dated 17 October 1804. Mrs. Seton's letter to Carroll may be found in White, 125-126 and 3.6, *CW*, 1:315.

[23] Antonio Filicchi to John Carroll, New York, 13 August 1804, ASJPH 26-0-2, (10). Copy. The original is in AAB, AASMSU.

[24] John Carroll to Elizabeth Seton, 20 August 1804. This letter is not available. Charles I. White was unable to discover it in 1842-1843 after a careful search. Two hundred years later the letter is still missing. Its contents can only be approximated from the references made in Filicchi's letter to John Carroll, 4 October 1804, and Mrs. Seton's letter to Filicchi, 30 August 1804.

[25] 3.7, Elizabeth Seton to Antonio Filicchi, New York, 30 August 1804, *CW*, 1:317.

[26] Antonio Filicchi to John Carroll, Boston, 4 October 1804, ASJPH 26-0-2, (10). Copy. The original is in AAB, AASMSU.

[27] 3.9, Elizabeth Seton to Antonio Filicchi, New York, 27 September [1804], *CW*, 1:323.

[28] Antonio Filicchi to Elizabeth Seton, Boston, 7 November 1804, ASJPH 1-3-3-10:15. Carroll wrote to Mrs. Joanna Barry on 29 October, saying "To me it seems that my sickness was reported more serious than was justifiable by its symptoms, tho' Dr. Brown as I understand considered it as dangerous." Carroll to Barry, 29 October 1804, UNDA.

[29] 3.7, Elizabeth Seton to Antonio Filicchi, New York, 30 August 1804, *CW*, 1:318.

[30] Ibid.

[31] Antonio Filicchi to Elizabeth Seton, Boston, 7 September 1804, ASJPH 1-3-3-10:7.

[32] Antonio Filicchi to Elizabeth Seton, Leghorn, 8 March 1819, ASJPH 1-3-3-10:48.

[33] 3.7, Elizabeth Seton to Antonio Filicchi, New York, 8 September 1804, *CW*, 1:319.

[34] 3.31, Journal to Amabilia Filicchi, *CW*, 1:370. St. Paul's Chapel was at the corner Broadway Avenue and Vesey Street.

[35] Ibid. 3.8, Elizabeth Seton to Antonio Filicchi, New York, 19 September 1804, *CW*, 1:321.

[36] 3.31, Journal to Amabilia Filicchi, *CW*, 1:369.

37 3.8, Elizabeth Seton to Antonio Filicchi, New York, 19 September 1804, *CW*, 1:322.

38 Philip Filicchi to Elizabeth Seton, Leghorn, 17 October 1804, ASJPH 1-3-3-10:13.

39 Ibid.

40 Philip Filicchi to Elizabeth Seton, Leghorn, 22 October 1804, ASJPH 1-3-3-10:14.

41 John Carroll to Antonio Filicchi, Boston, 13 January 1805, ASJPH 1-3-3-1:38.

42 Ibid.

43 3.9, Elizabeth Seton to Antonio Filicchi, New York, 27 September [1804], *CW*, 1:325. This was probably one of the letters forwarded to Bishop Carroll since, with another dated 19 September 1804, it is to be found in the Emmitsburg archives rather than in the Filicchi family collection. The Archdiocese of Baltimore Archives list of Seton-Carroll Correspondence gives these two dates but the actual collection of Seton letters at Baltimore contains no letters of these dates.

44 Antonio Filicchi to Elizabeth Seton, Boston, 8 October 1804, ASJPH 1-3-3-10:11. Jean Cheverus became the first bishop of Boston six years later.

45 3.31, Journal for Amabilia Filicchi, *CW*, 1:371.

46 3.11, Elizabeth Seton to Antonio Filicchi, New York, 16 November 1804, *CW*, 1:329.

47 Ibid., 330.

48 Ibid.

49 3.12, Elizabeth Seton to an Unidentified Woman, New York, 20 November 1804, *CW*, 1:333. Annabelle Melville names the addressee as "Olive."

50 3.15, Elizabeth Seton to Antonio Filicchi, New York, 13 December 1804, *CW*, 1:338.

51 Ibid.

52 Ibid., 339.

53 3.31, Journal to Amabilia Filicchi, *CW*, 1:372.

54 Ibid., *CW*, 1:371.

55 Matthew O'Brien to John Carroll, New York, 7 January 1805 AAB, AASMSU, 5-V-2; 19 February 1805, AAB, AASMSU, 5-V-4.

56 3.31, Journal to Amabilia Filicchi, *CW*, 1:373. See Henry Anstice, *History of St. George's Church* (New York, 1911) for a history of the chapel.

[57] Ibid.

[58] Ibid., *CW*, 1:374.

[59] 5.14, Elizabeth Seton to Antonio Filicchi, Baltimore, 16 January 1809, *CW*, 2:46.

[60] Matthew O'Brien to John Carroll, New York, 19 February 1805, AAB, AASMSU, 5-V-4.

[61] 3.18, Elizabeth Seton to Antonio Filicchi, New York, 24 January 1805, *CW*, 1:342.

[62] Antonio Filicchi to Rev. Jean Cheverus , New York, 19 February 1805, ASJPH 26-0-2, (10). Copy. The original is in AAB, AASMSU. This copy was made from a letter (probably a duplicate) in the handwriting of Antonio Filicchi preserved in the family archives in Leghorn, Italy. Lord, Sexton, and Harrington, *The History of the Archdiocese of Boston,* I, 610, Note 55 states incorrectly that the original of this letter is in AMSJ. There is no record preserved of Mrs. Seton's letter to Jean Cheverus other than the indirect knowledge suggested in Cheverus' reply.

[63] Jean Cheverus to Elizabeth Seton, Boston, 4 March 1805, AMSV. The complete text of this letter is reproduced in Maria Dodge, S.C., *Mother Elizabeth Boyle first Superioress of the Sisters of Charity, Mount St. Vincent, New York* (New York, 1893), 26.

[64] Antonio Filicchi to Rev. Jean Cheverus , New York, 16 March 1805, ASJPH 26-0-2, (10). Copy. The original is in AAB, AASMSU.

[65] 3.31, Journal to Amabilia Filicchi, *CW*, 1:375.

[66] 3.23, Elizabeth Seton to Antonio Filicchi, New York, 15 April 1805, *CW*, 1:352.

[67] 3.20, Draft of Elizabeth Seton to Jean Cheverus, New York, [After 25 March 1805], *CW*, 1:346.

[68] Antonio Filicchi to Charles I. White, Leghorn, 20 October 1846, ASJPH 26-0-1 (2). Copy. The original is in ASCSE.

[69] 10.4, "Dear Remembrances," *CW*, 3a:519.

[70] 4.14, Elizabeth Seton to Antonio Filicchi, New York, 25 March 1806, *CW*, 1:401.

[71] 3.31, Journal to Amabilia Filicchi, *CW*, 1:375.

[72] 7.49, Elizabeth Seton to Simon Bruté, Emmitsburg, n.d., *CW*, 2:425.

[73] 7.66, Elizabeth Seton to Simon Bruté, Emmitsburg, 26 December 1817, *CW*, 2:454.

[74] Leo R. Ryan, *Old St. Peter's* (New York, 1935), 52.

[75] Ibid., 63.

[76] William O'Brien, O.P., to John Carroll, New York, 27 July 1807, AAB, AASMSU, 5-U-11. O'Brien believed that St. Peter's Church lost 344

members to yellow fever. See ibid., 31 May 1813, AAB, AASMSU, 5-U-12.

[77] William O'Brien, O.P., to John Carroll, New York, 27 July 1807, AAB, AASMSU, 5-U-11.

[78] Ryan, 76. Peter Guilday in his *Life and Times of John Carroll*, II, 631, stated that the two O'Briens were brothers and members of the same order. Ryan cites a letter from Victor F. O'Daniel, O.P., to prove Matthew O'Brien was not a Dominican. The Archdiocese of Baltimore Archives bear testimony to the fact that the men were not brothers. See William O'Brien to John Carroll, 9 June 1804, AAB, AASMSU, 5-U-10; Matthew O'Brien to John Carroll, 24 February 1806, 5-T-5.

[79] Matthew O'Brien to John Carroll, New York, 19 February 1804, AAB, AASMSU, 5-V-4. Matthew O'Brien wrote, "Rev. W. O'Brien continues still incapable of appearing abroad. ...Mr. Vrennay has resolved to remain here some time and officiates as usual." No identification of Vrennay is available.

[80] Vrennay seems to have gone from New York to St. Thomas Island. Matthew O'Brien to John Carroll, 24 February 1806, AAB, AASMSU, 5-T-6.

[81] Matthew O'Brien to John Carroll, New York, 7 January 1805, 8 January 1805, AAB, AASMSU, 5-V-2, 5-V-3.

[82] William O'Brien to John Carroll, New York, 27 July 1807, AAB, AASMSU, 5-U-11.

[83] Louis Sibourd to John Carroll, New York, 25 November 1807, AAB, AASMSU, 7-Q-7.

[84] Louis Sibourd to John Carroll, New York, 27 June 1808, AAB, AASMSU, 7-Q-16. John Byrne did not remain long in New York after Louis Sibourd left in August 1808. Ryan states that Byrne left New York after November 1808, and went to Philadelphia and Georgetown.

[85] 4.37, Elizabeth Seton to Cecilia Seton, New York, 31 May [1807], *CW*, 1:440. Mrs. Seton was never a good speller. Byrne's name was spelled in many ways by others as well. [For a woman of the late 18th and early 19th centuries, she was quite literate. Ed.] Noah Webster published his first dictionary, *A Compendious Dictionary of the English Language* in 1806. Later he compiled a more comprehensive dictionary, *An American Dictionary of the English Language* (1828) which contributed to the standardization of spelling in the United States.

[86] White, 169, note.

[87] Charles L. Souvay, C.M., "Questions About Mother Seton's Conversion,"

Catholic Historical Review, V (July-October, 1919), 237.

[88] John Carroll to Antonio Filicchi, Boston, 13 January 1805, ASJPH 1-3-3-1:38.

[89] Jean Cheverus to Elizabeth Seton, New York, 28 January 1806, ASJPH 1-3-3-1:4.

[90] This copy of the *Following of Christ* is preserved at ASCSH.

[91] Souvay, pp. 230-7; *Mother Seton Guild Bulletin,* XXVII (November, 1948), 3.

[92] 3.31, Journal for Amabilia Filicchi, entry of March 20th, *CW*, 1:376. The phrasing of the scriptural admonition is Mrs. Seton's own.

[93] Ibid., 377.

[94] 10.4, "Dear Remembrances," *CW*, 3a:519.

[95] Antonio Filicchi to John Carroll, Philadelphia, 27 May 1805, AAB, AASMSU, 3-S-5.

[96] 3.22, Elizabeth Seton to Antonio Filicchi, 6 April 1805, *CW,* 1:349.

[97] 3.21, Elizabeth Seton to Antonio Filicchi, 31 March 1805, *CW,* 1:348.

❦

CHAPTER 6

༷

NO RESTING PLACE

In the brief review of her life called "Dear Remembrances," Elizabeth Seton passes over the three years which lay between her conversion and her departure from New York, with the words, "Most painful remembrances now—yet grateful for *the order of our Grace,* so evident through *All*."[1] Those two threads of pain and grace run quite plainly through the period's pattern. If the year preceding her conversion was the severest test of Mrs. Seton's interior forces, the three years following extended into a period of exterior trial. Elizabeth Seton's profession of faith brought radical changes, not only in her spiritual life, but in the social changes of friendships and family relations, as well as in the economic aspects of her life.

Perhaps no Old Testament type so nearly foreshadows the convert to Catholicism as that of Ruth amid the alien corn.[a] The words of Rebecca Seton on her deathbed, repeating the pledge of Ruth, sound almost prophetic in their relation to Elizabeth Seton. Those whom blood and time have joined, faith seems to put asunder. Even in those cases where the widening of the breach is most imperceptibly accomplished, the convert is ultimately a citizen of a new state which precludes a return to his former soil. When, as in the case of Mrs. Seton, the change is made from the respectable majority to the disreputable minority, from a well-knit, prosperous, and literate citizenry to an impoverished assortment of alien immigrants, the expatriation is only rendered the more absolute.

The congregation of St. Peter's Church, New York City, in the first decade of the nineteenth century consisted chiefly of Irish, French, and German immigrants. The New York state constitution adopted at the close of the Revolution, although leaving intact the article on religious liberty, by including Jay's naturalization clause had "effectively deprived immigrant Catholics of every opportunity to rise in the social and political world of New York."[2] When Mrs. Seton became a Catholic, New York City had only one Catholic office-holder, Andrew Morris, who had been chosen Assistant-Alderman of the First Ward in 1802 and who held office until 1806.[3] The year following the beginning of Mrs. Seton's adherence to Catholicism,

---

[a] [John Keats uses the phrase "amid the alien corn" in his poem "Ode to a Nightingale," which refers to th biblical story of Ruth. The widowed Ruth loyally followed her mother-in-law Naomi to Bethlehem where Ruth became a gleaner in the fields. (Ruth 1:16)]

Francis Cooper made his momentous refusal to take the oath[b] required by the naturalization provisions, and the Catholics of New York presented their petition to the state legislature.[4] The opposition, led by William Van Ness, and Abraham Van Vechter, indulged in the lowest scurrility and bitterest invective.[5] But the Cooper forces won out, and Francis Cooper took his seat on 7 February in the New York State Assembly.

Catholics generally were regarded as a "public nuisance" and "the off-scourings of the people."[6] Mrs. Seton's friends had pointed to the shabbiness and squalor of the immigrant standard of living in their efforts to deter her. Before St. Peter's building was completed, it was inadequate to contain comfortably the rapidly increasing "dirty, filthy, red-faced" immigrant congregation, and the church was described by non-Catholics as "a horrid place of spits and pushing." Mrs. Seton, recalling her impressions of St. Peter's Church, in later years confessed, "Alas—*I* found it all that indeed..."[7]

Rev. Matthew O'Brien had written to his bishop in 1801 that an additional chapel was needed for the section of the city where the poor thronged.[8] The services were sometimes complicated by the heckling[c] of non-Catholics,[9] and Elizabeth Seton who had once held that "where *taste* is a natural quality of the disposition, nothing can eradicate it but sorrow and Indifference to the world,"[10] was to write Antonio Filicchi, "it requires indeed a superior mind to all externals to find real enjoyment here...I am forced to keep my eyes always on my Book, even when not using it."[11]

Within two years of the time of Mrs. Seton's first entrance to the Barclay Street church, she was writing to Antonio Filicchi that "a mob on Christmas Eve[d] assembled to pull down our Church or set fire to it—but were dispersed with only the death of a constable and the wounds of several others—they say it is high time the cross was pulled down, but the Mayor has issued a proclamation to check the evil."[12] Elizabeth Seton was referring to the Highbinders' riot which began the evening of Thursday, 24 December 1806, and continued until Christmas night. Some fifty men had gathered in front of the church on Christmas Eve, intending to disrupt the ceremonies.

[b] Andrew Morris and John Byrne signed as chairman and secretary respectively. The New York State Constitution of 1777 required applicants for naturalization to renounce their allegiance to all foreign rulers, "ecclesiastical" as well as civil. This oath obtained until it was superseded by federal regulations in 1790. A similar oath required of state officials prevailed, however, until the Cooper petition of 1806.

[c] Matthew O'Brien complained of a Jewish woman who came to St. Peter's in an outlandish costume and "insults our ceremonies by her irreverent conduct."

[d] The part of the letter mentioning the Highbinder's Riot was written at a later date. Mrs. Seton frequently adhered to the customary practice of the day that the writing of a letter often extend over a period of weeks since most people preferred to await the "occasion" of some traveler's carrying it in person to assure safe delivery.

Andrew Morris, a trustee of St. Peter's, as well as a member of the city council, persuaded the mob to disband once; but they returned and kept up a commotion well into the night. The indignant Irish met the next day to defend their church and the riot which ensued resulted in the death of the constable mentioned. Only the arrival of Mayor Dewitt Clinton terminated the imbroglio.[13] When the news of the riot reached Boston, Cheverus wrote Mrs. Seton. "I heard with concern of the disturbance which took place on Christmas Day. We had here the happiness to celebrate in peace."[14]

The immediate reactions of Elizabeth Seton's friends and relatives to her new affiliation varied in degree, but were, for the most part, rather moderate at first. John Henry Hobart was quite cool on the occasion of his last visit to her home the April after her conversion. From that time on, he felt it his duty to warn the widow's friends against "the falsity and danger of her principles."[15] Mrs. Seton told him that "if he thought it his duty he must act in conformity to it, as I on my part should do it to the full extent of my power."[16] It was a painful conversation and marked the end of any real understanding between the two; but Elizabeth wrote to Antonio, "We must keep the divine precept of doing as we would be done by, and consider how much reason Mr. H. has for being embittered on this occasion."[17]

Catherine Dupleix and Eliza Sadler showed no outward change in their warm friendship. When Mrs. Dupleix listened to the "kind ladies [who] shed tears for poor deluded Mrs. Seton," she told them bluntly that if there were anything in the world that could give any consolation to so distressed a creature, she for one was very happy.[18] Antonio Filicchi took Dué's support as a hopeful sign that some day she too might become a Catholic, saying, "I hope your good friend, Mrs. Dupleix will not reject the best reward you can offer her for her cordial friendship." Mrs. Dupleix did become a Catholic, but the conversion took place after Mrs. Seton was in Emmitsburg.[19] Antonio was pleased also that Mrs. John Livingstone was kind to Elizabeth. The interest of Mrs. Livingstone was perhaps more tinged with curiosity than sympathy. When she and a companion called on Mrs. Seton, she remarked that "generally a connection with a Deist was not feared, while a Roman Catholic was thought of with horror." The ladies were particularly eager to learn if it were true that repeating sixty or eighty prayers gained full forgiveness of sins. When Mrs. Seton appealed to their reason they retreated and begged that the subject of religion should not be mentioned among them, "as transient conversations seldom, seldom have good effects."[20]

Julia Scott, Mrs. Startin, and John Wilkes continued to befriend Elizabeth and to contribute to her support. Wilkes did make some "sharp yet gentle reproaches" for Elizabeth's imprudence in offending her wealthy, maternal uncle, John Charlton, and other friends upon whom she might later be forced to depend, but otherwise he remained interested in her welfare and was ready to advise her when she sought his opinion.[21] Elizabeth's godmother, Sarah Startin, was very kind during June and July when Elizabeth was ill and little Kate had inflammatory fever. She plied Elizabeth with "candle and old wine" daily, in an effort to restore her strength.[22] Julia Scott never changed; while Elizabeth lived, Julia never ceased to love her and to contribute generously to her welfare.

Elizabeth's own family acted very well. Guy Carleton Bayley wrote from Leghorn:

> I will say nothing to you about your change of faith, as you must know what you do. I can only assure you that it will not diminish in the least the sincere affection I have always had for you and yours: what troubles me most is that I fear it will serve for a cloak to those who could not otherwise have refused them to withdraw those little assistances which your own present situation necessarily requires...Rest assured however that if ever fickle fortune should place me in a situation to assist you,[e] nothing would afford me more pleasure.[23]

Mary Bayley Post, Elizabeth's own sister, came to the rescue in August 1805, when Mrs. Seton's financial affairs had reached a crisis by taking the whole family to live with the Posts. The addition of six extra people to any household is no small problem, and the Wright Posts must have suffered a serious disruption of their summer routine when the Setons moved in with them at Greenwich.[24]

Emma Bayley Craig did not live long enough to be concerned over her half-sister's new religion. She died on 22 July 1805, leaving a little son, Henry, who did not long survive her.[25] Mrs. Bayley, Elizabeth's stepmother, oddly enough seems to have lost her mysterious coldness toward the young widow. Elizabeth wrote Julia Scott that ever since her return from Italy, the older woman had shown her "every mark of Peace and reconciliation, which also gives me the double enjoyment of the confidence and affection of the girls, Helen and Mary."[26] When Mrs. Bayley became seriously ill in August

---

[e] Bayley was only nineteen years old at the time and was scarcely in a position to assist anyone financially. He later had a son, James Roosevelt Bayley, who became a Catholic convert.

1805, Mrs. Seton was called to attend her.[f] All misunderstandings of the past were forgotten and the new convert's only emotion was one of sorrow that "these poor souls die without Sacraments, without prayers, left in their last moments to the conflicts of parting Nature without the divine consolations which our Almighty God has so mercifully provided for us."[27]

The most pressing problem facing Mrs. Seton in the months following her conversion was the solution of her economic difficulties. Writing to Antonio Filicchi in April, she reported that the Wilkes plan, "so long agitated," was given up for the time, and as a result Mrs. Seton was "plagued for a House."[28] As an alternative she was considering the proposal of Mr. Patrick White, "an English gentleman of very respectable character and a compleat scholar," that Mrs. Seton join him and his wife in opening a school, an English Seminary.[g] White was in reduced circumstances, and had recently failed in a similar undertaking in Albany.[29] It was planned to take girls at first and, perhaps, boys later. Elizabeth was to assist the Whites in return for the education of her children and a small financial remuneration,[h] and even though the latter would be trifling, she felt that at least she would be doing something toward the support of her family.[30] Antonio advised her to consult O'Brien and Cheverus or even "your Mr. Wilkes" before committing herself to any long-term arrangement.[31]

Almost as soon as the White plan was contemplated, rumor had it that Mrs. Seton was working with two other Catholics to spread the principles of her new religion. John Henry Hobart reproached the men who had vouched for the Whites, and warned everyone of the dangerous consequences of such a school. Dué and Sad, out of patience with such foolishness, called upon Hobart to remonstrate. The Whites, they assured him, were Protestants, and Mrs. Seton was only interested in securing bread for her children. Hobart accepted the correction and tried to make amends by promising to use his influence for the school. But the damage was done.[32] Wright Post and John Wilkes gave only grudging consent to the plan, while others less reasonable indulged in wild speculations as to Mrs. Seton's intentions. Rev. Matthew O'Brien authorized Mrs. Seton to say "conscientiously that her principles and duties in this case were separate," and to the rude questions directed

[f] Charlotte Amelia Bayley died on 1 September 1805, at 48 Greenwich Street, two doors from John Henry Hobart's residence. Her will, proved on 21 November 1805, left all her property to her own seven children. Neither Elizabeth Bayley Seton nor Mary Bayley Post inherited from their step-mother. At the time the will was made, Emma Bayley Craig was still alive and her husband, William Craig, was named one of the executors, as well as guardian of the youngest girls, Mary and Helen Bayley. See Appendix A. Bayley-Seton Genealogy.

[g] [A private residential school for young ladies with an educational program comparable to a men's college or boarding school. Ed.]

[h] Mrs. Seton was to receive one-third of the profits which the school produced.

toward her, Elizabeth answered as calmly as she could that she did not consider herself a "teacher of Souls" and certainly would never subject herself to the charge of "returning ingratitude for the confidence reposed" in her.[33] In spite of the discouraging reception the plan received, Elizabeth went ahead with energy and the middle of May saw her moving to another house, one large enough to contain her family and serve as a school as well. To her delight the house was within one block of St. Peter's, "the greatest luxury this World can afford."[34] By the end of May, a few girls were already in her charge, and Mr. White went up the Hudson to bring his family from Albany.[i] The plan was doomed from the beginning. Religious prejudice, combined with a lack of business acumen on the part of the enterprisers, led to its early failure.[j] When Antonio Filicchi stopped in New York on his way from Philadelphia to Canada in July, he found his friend very comfortably situated, and the Whites very friendly. But only "three scholars" were added to the nine Seton and White Children.[35] Scarcely had Filicchi left New York when he received news from Mrs. Seton that the Whites were unable to pay their share of the next quarter's rent. To prevent the landlord from seizing the furniture, Dr. Post hurried his sister-in-law and her children out to the Post summer household in Greenwich.[36] The Setons left the city just as the yellow fever epidemic of 1805 was taking on alarming proportions.[k]

The failure of the White scheme brought a renewed interest of both Wilkes and Filicchi in Mrs. Seton's financial affairs. While in Montreal, Antonio conceived the plan of having the Seton boys enter the seminary there, with the possibility of Mrs. Seton working in some capacity as a teacher in the environs. The thought of going to Canada did not appeal to Elizabeth Seton when she first received the suggestion, and Antonio wrote, "do not be frightened about the idea of the Canada Seminary. I am not in any engagement. The idea you know was suggested by Mr. Tisserant."[l] Mrs. Seton was much more attracted by the revival of John Wilkes' old plan for the boardinghouse for boys. It was not at all certain that the Episcopalian Clergyman, Mr. William Harris, would be willing to be associated with a Catholic, nor that parents would consent to have their children live under

---

[i] [The acceptance of these pupils may be the source of the erroneous conclusion that Elizabeth herself operated a school in New York. Ed.]

[j] This short-lived project is the only historical basis for the numerous references to schools conducted by Mrs. Seton in New York City. At most it lasted two months, consisted of three pupils. [Mr. and Mrs. Patrick White employed Mrs. Seton as a teacher but the Whites who had initiated the enterprise were responsible for its management. Ed.]

[k] When Antonio Filicchi reached Albany in September 1805, he was "thunderstruck at the report of the prevailing fever at New York," and went directly from Albany to Boston to evade the epidemic. See Antonio Filicchi to Elizabeth Seton, Albany, 16 September 1805, ASJPH 1-3-3-10:24.

[l] Rev. Jean S. Tisserant was a French priest, a friend of Jean Cheverus in Boston; he subsequently became a friend of Mrs. Seton's. Antonio Filicchi to Elizabeth Seton, Boston, 22 October 1805, ASJPH 1-3-3-10:27.

Mrs. Seton's supervision; but John and Charles Wilkes were still inclined to place their own sons in her charge.[m] Elizabeth Seton was very anxious not to remain with the Posts any longer than was necessary, and she wished to put an end to the well-meant but sometimes ridiculous proposals for her future. As she told Antonio:

> Some proposals have been made me of keeping a Tea store—
> or China Shop—or small school for little children (too young,
> I suppose, to be taught the *Hail Mary*). In short, Tonino, they
> know not what to do with me, but God does—and when His
> blessed time is come, we shall know, and in the meantime
> He makes His poorest, feeblest creature strong.[37]

The temporary solution of the widow's difficulties was the execution of the Wilkes plan. Early in November the Setons left the Post home to move to "a pleasant dwelling two miles from the city," and Elizabeth wrote Julia Scott that she expected twelve or fourteen boys "to Board, Wash, and mend for" before the month was out. Elizabeth's happiness being under her own roof again was only exceeded by joy in being able to do something for her "darlings." She could now use the money Julia sent for Anna Maria Seton to provide the child with dancing lessons. Their home[38] was near enough to Aunt Farquhar's so that Anna Maria could take lessons along with her cousins.[n]

Meanwhile Elizabeth Seton was beginning to have serious worries over the education of her sons, Richard and William, who were eight and ten years old respectively. In the days when John Henry Hobart was her ideal of Christian manhood, Elizabeth had hoped that young William might follow in Hobart's steps and become a "preacher."[39] After she became a Catholic, she was eager to have her sons receive seminary training, if not to encourage a vocation to the priesthood at least to strengthen their faith. Since the girls could be kept close by her side, Mrs. Seton did not have such great fears for their spiritual welfare; but the boys were another matter. While they were staying at the Posts, Elizabeth had written Antonio urgently:

> Now, dearest Tonino, prove your true love to me by exerting
> your utmost power in getting my poor boys to Baltimore, if
> it is possible. If you could now see the situation they are in
> here, only your love for souls, independent of any personal

---

[m] One of the sons of John Wilkes was the Charles Wilkes who later gained fame for his part in the Trent Affair during the American Civil War.

[n] Rev. William Harris also lived in Stuyvesant Lane, the Bowery. "Aunt Farquhar" was Elizabeth Curson Farquhar, William Magee Seton's aunt, the sister of the elder Seton's two Curson wives. See Appendix A. Bayley-Seton Genealogy.

interest for me, would induce you to pity them in the ridicule they are forced to hear of our holy religion and the mockery at the Church and ministers, besides their minds being poisoned with bad principles of every kind which I cannot always check or control.[40]

Antonio Filicchi had already promised to pay for the boys' education, and he had said that when they were old enough they might replace Richard and Carleton Bayley in the Filicchi counting house at Leghorn.[41] After his Canadian trip, in the summer of 1805, Filicchi was anxious to see the Seton boys go to Montreal. On 8 October he had written:

At Montreal there is an eminent College and Seminary° which will prove preferable by far to that of Baltimore. I tried to obtain a place there and I have been promised a categorical answer...in a few weeks. Meanwhile let Mr. Tisserant write to Baltimore as he intended. It will not interfere in the choice of the best.[42]

The reply from Canada came by way of a letter from Jean Cheverus in Boston, who said, "Unhappily they give no hope of the immediate admission of your dear children. Mr. F. will try in Baltimore or in Georgetown and I think he will succeed. His recommendations alone will have great weight."[43]

Loath as he was to abandon the Montreal idea, Mr. Filicchi decided to investigate the rival excellence of the Georgetown and Baltimore schools on his trip south. By April 1806 he had visited Bishop Carroll in Baltimore and talked to him about Mrs. Seton and her children. Writing to his friend James Barry, in New York, the bishop said:

In concert with Bishop [Leonard] Neale, I provided means for the reception and education of her two sons at Georgetown for at least two years and trusted that in time Providence would open other resources. Mr. F. after expressing suitable acknowledgment seems rather disposed at present to advise

---

° The College of Montreal was founded by the Sulpician, M. Curatteau de la Blaiserie, in 1763. The Sisters of the Congregation were established two years later under the auspices of Saint Sulpice. It was probably this latter group which attracted Mrs. Seton's attention later when she made a request of Father Matignon to which Father Cheverus replied: "Dr. Matignon sends his best respects and desires me to tell you, he does not know how to procure the Rules of the Nunneries in Canada. Dr. Dubourg was to converse with you about another project which I should prefer, hoping it would do better for your family, and being sure it could be very conducive to the progress of Religion in this country [United States]. It has been no doubt a real satisfaction to you to get acquainted and converse with the worthy, pious and learned Dr. Dubourg" See Jean Cheverus to Elizabeth Seton, New York, 21 January 1807, ASJPH 1-3-3-1:7. See *The Catholic Encyclopedia* (New York, 1911), X, 548.

their mother to send them to Montreal, but nothing will be determined before his return to your city.[44]

Antonio himself wrote on 18 April 1806 that he had visited the schools and had all the information necessary to her decision, but he reiterated, "My preference is decidedly for Montreal both for the better education of your boys and your own dreams for your future old age."[45]

Meanwhile Georgetown made a bid for the Seton boys in the form of a letter written by a lay instructor, Mr. Thomas Kelly, to Mrs. Seton. Kelly was not reluctant to point out in full detail the disadvantages of the Sulpician school in Baltimore as contrasted with the superiority of Georgetown's claims. Baltimore, he wrote, was "divided into two houses, the Seminary for those intended for the Church, and the College, for those who are not." The seminary, composed as it was of adults, practiced a rule of life much too rigorous for the Seton boys to follow. The college was composed of 130 boys more than half of whom were Protestants who would be prone to laugh at and to ridicule any boys preparing for the Church. Mr. Kelly generously conceded that "Mr. Dubourg's intention in educating Protestants and other boys is undoubtedly very good," but Georgetown, he felt sure, was much more suited to Mrs. Seton's needs.

> This college [Georgetown] is intended for the use of the Society of Jesus, or Jesuits, founded by St. Ignatius, acknowledged, I believe, by the whole Catholic world, to be the best and most perfect order that has been established, yet those educated here are left at their own option, to choose the order, or to live [as] secular priests. There are no Protestant boys or boys of other denominations here...As for the Bishop [Neale] who is president and his Brother vice-president...the real piety of which they are possessed necessarily must, as it does, inspire those who are intrusted to their care.[46]

Mrs. Seton's choice was Georgetown in the end.[p] Her reasons, given in detail in a letter to Antonio Filicchi, again in Philadelphia, included the Kelly letter, Bishop Carroll's views which he had expressed to the Barrys, Mr. Tisserant's preference, and the fact that her new friends, the Barrys, had connections in Washington. After advancing all the arguments in favor of the Jesuit school,[q] she concluded, "You only can be the proper Judge of what

---

[p] It would appear that Mrs. Seton intended her sons to receive an education compatible with the priestly vocation since she sent her sons to Georgetown after receiving Kelly's letter.

[q] Filicchi's opinion of the Seton boys seems to reflect on their preparation for school. In October of the preceding year he had advised Mrs. Seton, "Your boys ought to prepare themselves to appear well-bred, to know how to read and write well at least. I know you will spare no pains for it." Antonio Filicchi to Elizabeth Seton, 8 October 1805, ASJPH 1-3-3-10:28.

is right."[47] On the receipt of this letter, Antonio replied immediately that the boys could certainly be safely placed in Georgetown for the time. He was perfectly content to act simply as cashier, leaving the details to Carroll, Tisserant, or Barry. Bishop Neale was willing to reduce all his demands to $250.00; Bishop Carroll would pay one hundred a year for two years. But, Antonio wrote, "The preference that we now conclude to give Georgetown does not exclude Montreal for the future, when I trust your boys will be more prepared and more susceptible of a more refined education."[48]

After receiving Filicchi's approval the mother lost no time in sending her boys to Georgetown. Within a week's time, William and Richard Seton, accompanied by Mr. Barry, appeared on Antonio's doorstep in Philadelphia, bearing notes for their patron and for Julia Scott. "I am in danger of becoming an idolater," their mother had written to Antonio, "and always shall consider you as my good angel." She had already written Mr. Kelly to procure for the boys what was "indispensably necessary," and had notified Bishops Carroll and Neale, "a task you may be sure performed with a trembling hand." She knew, she added, that Antonio would be "among the 'highest stars in glory'" for his unceasing efforts in her behalf.[49] Antonio Filicchi wrote back on 16 May 1806:

> My good sister, I admire your expediency and am only happy
> of your happiness. Your boys have proceeded this morning
> on their journey, and you may be sure that our Bishop Neale
> and Mr. Kelly will have for them all the requisite attention.
> It has certainly been very kind of Mr. Barry to accept the
> task of escorting them to Georgetown. His recommendations
> cannot fail to be useful.[50]

While these economic and maternal concerns were engaging Mrs. Seton's energies, her spiritual life was also progressing. Her earliest months within the Church were influenced by Rev. Matthew O'Brien, and Elizabeth wrote to Antonio that "the counsels and excellent directions of O.B....strengthen me and being sometimes enforced by commands give me a determination to my actions which is now indispensable."[51] Under the younger O'Brien, Mrs. Seton was learning to examine her conscience, to avoid the pitfalls of scruples, and to make good confessions. At first she hesitated about going when she had little or nothing to say. Although she was very conscious of "the cloud of imperfections surrounding every moment" of her life, she was so grateful to be free of "those things which have a name" that only her dread of temptation made her overcome her reluctance. Her own early difficulties with confession made Elizabeth Seton better able to guide the young people under her care in later life. Writing to Ellen Wiseman in 1820, when this former pupil was in the midst of the worldly life of Philadelphia, Mother Seton urged:

> Wake up your *Faith*. You know our Lord never meant us to mind who we go to, if they do but take us to Him, and the longer you stay back you will know the harder it is for you to go forward; and at last what does it end in dearest, to go through double, triple pain and examens, which will not be pains of grace and merit, but of your weakness and want of courage in *delaying*.[52]

Matthew O'Brien also advised Mrs. Seton to join the Society of the Holy Sacrament and told her he believed its rules would "aid in the Attainment of the much desired perfection." At this time, Mrs. Seton was "admitted" to Communion once a week.[53]

The hasty removal of the Setons to Greenwich in the summer of 1805 placed Elizabeth in a difficult situation. Living in a non-Catholic household is difficult enough for any new convert and Mrs. Seton's position was not ameliorated by her financial dependence at the time upon her sister's family. The desired Friday and Saturday abstinence was a source of embarrassment because Mary Post could secure fish only with great difficulty and expense, and Elizabeth's "bread and water spirit" was reluctant to necessitate Mary's rather obvious efforts. Friday and Saturday were both days of abstinence at the beginning of the nineteenth century. Prayerbooks of that day explained "The Church orders us to abstain from meat Fridays and Saturdays...Friday because our Saviour suffered death, Saturday to honor the memory of the Blessed Virgin."[54] Commenting on her difficulties at the Post's, Mrs. Seton wrote to Antonio Filicchi, "I am a poor creature. Before I was in the Blessed Ark I could fast *all* day on Friday; now can hardly wait from one meal to another without faintness!"[55] When Mrs. Seton consulted Father O'Brien, he reassured her, "In cases like yours the Bishop announces discretionary powers to the spirit of the Church which wills that neither strangers nor enemies shall have cause to criticize or blame her."[56] Even without the complications of menus, the Bayley sisters were by disposition prone to disagreement. When Elizabeth confided her grievances to her old friend, Eliza Sadler, Sad wrote reprovingly,[r]

---

[r] It is indicative of Mrs. Seton's character that she preserved this reproof and several years later referred to it in these words, "A little note of yours struck my eye the other day among papers of value and contains such advice, so worded and peculiarly expressed that reading it over in silence it seemed to me I was kneeling to our Rev. Friend, and actually listening to his voice of Peace and Reconciliation." 4.50, Elizabeth Seton to Eliza Sadler, New York, 28 August 1807, *CW*, 1:462.

Do your Sister and her husband really desire your remaining with them? Of this I think there can be little doubt, however some inequalities of temper may seem to contradict it. Were this not the case, I am inclined to rely upon the good judgment of [Mr.] Post that he would put an end to such domestic inquietudes.[57]

Mrs. Sadler went on to advise Elizabeth to accept her trials as her cross. She asked if Mary Post was ever any different or any happier, and concluded, "I am inclined to believe that you may be an instrument in God's hand to do her much good."

Mrs. Sadler's advice was similar to that of another of Mrs. Seton's friends, Rev. Jean S. Tisserant. He was one of those French emigré priests who briefly crossed the pages of American church history. A refugee from the Diocese of Bourges, he first fled to England in 1792, and appeared six years later in Wethersfield, Connecticut. He worked for a time in Connecticut, making frequent trips to Boston where he became friendly with both Matignon and Cheverus.[58] It was through Jean Cheverus that Mrs. Seton met Tisserant. Passing through New York City on his way to Elizabethtown, New Jersey, in June 1805 the priest carried a letter of introduction which recommended him to Mrs. Seton as "both learned and pious" and of pleasing conversation.[59] Mrs. Seton seems to have possessed an affinity for French clergy, and Tisserant became almost at once a close friend and spiritual adviser. From this first meeting until Tisserant sailed for Europe a year later, the French emigré and the American convert remained in constant communication with each other.[60] Until Rev. Michael Hurley, O.S.A. came to be admired so enthusiastically, Father Tisserant probably exerted the greatest influence upon Mrs. Seton's spiritual affairs. It was Tisserant whom Mrs. Seton asked to be her sponsor at confirmation in May 1806.[s]

When Tisserant heard of Mrs. Seton's worries over fasting and abstinence while she lived at the Posts, he told her that circumstances, "ties of sanguinity and friendship, dictates of charity," and economic considerations indicated that she should remain at her sister's for the time being; but her assumption that religious duty required her to perform the impossible was unjustified. The letter of the law required communing once a year; a dispensation could be secured in regard to the fast and abstinence regulations; even assisting at Mass could be omitted where grave reason existed. He could understand her zeal, her reluctance to abandon the practices

[s] When Tisserant was prevented by circumstances beyond his control from being present, Michael Hurley acted as proxy.

so beneficial to her spiritual life, but he believed she should consider these trials as sent by God.[61]

As time went by and the Setons moved once more to their own home, Mrs. Seton continued to receive the consolation of Tisserant's advice. In December he wrote of his happiness in her improved situation but he reminded her that piety continually requires sacrifices, and that her task was to learn to make these sacrifices in a spirit of resignation.[62] He took a deep interest in the progress of Cecilia Seton toward Catholicism.[63] When Elizabeth was distressed at being unable to begin Lent[t] with attendance at church, Tisserant wrote consolingly that even at home in the midst of her "little parish" of boys she could spend days of sacrifice and mortification. "Remember what you have to do as a mother, and in the employment you have undertaken," he admonished. He disapproved of her tendency to dwell on past faults and recommended concentrating on present performance, "particularly to perform the works of penance prescribed at this holy time."[64] As Lent progressed and Elizabeth's health declined, Tisserant reminded her that "a bodily suffering is an admonition to the Christian to indulge in these sentiments" which are related to her death. Nevertheless she must avoid indulging in her tendency toward melancholy, and avoid any excess of austerities which would prevent the fulfillment of her duties.[65]

In the brief year that Tisserant guided the eager convert's progress, he became sensible of her special charm as well as of her ardent piety. He shared her peculiar phrases, writing clumsily, "embracer les chers darlings" of her children; he became fond of her best friends, Mrs. Sadler and Mrs. Dupleix, and always sent regards to them in his letters. His hope of sailing to Europe in the company of her "brother," Antonio Filicchi, was not realized, but he left urgent appeals that Antonio meet him in London. April decided Tisserant's departure in the near future. He paid a last visit to Boston and to his dear friends, Cheverus and Matignon. He wrote enthusiastically of the 500 Communions at Easter there, and of the six adult converts who were baptized on Holy Thursday.[66] In the confusion of last minute traveling in Massachusetts, New York, and New Jersey, Tisserant failed to receive Elizabeth's letter in regard to her confirmation and he wrote in chagrin on 28 May 1806, "I have learned...that Monsignor the Bishop has been there [New York] several days and gave Confirmation on Monday. I leave you to judge what regret I feel." His disappointment was, he wrote, overshadowed by the joy he felt in her own pleasure.

---

[t] Lent began on 19 February 1806; Easter Sunday fell on April 6.

You have received graces which will confirm your faith, fortify your courage to sustain the martyrdom to which you have dedicated yourself, render fruitful the apostolate attached to your conversion and to your example. With these graces you have received those of consolation, indeed the Spirit of the Consoler himself, who I hope will make you more and more sensible of His Divine and Benign Influence. If only I could have been present when you received this precious sacrament which imprinted on you the character of a soldier of Jesus Christ; rendered you more and more capable of marching under His standards.[67]

Tisserant's departure for London, on 9 June 1806, deprived Elizabeth Seton of one of the most trusted friends of her first year in the Catholic Church. Although she continued to hope for his return to the United States for many years afterward, his letter from London, dated 27 August 1806, seems to have been her last direct contact with him.[68] From time to time Jean Cheverus of Boston relayed news of Tisserant and his hopes of returning,[69] but as the Napoleonic wars in Europe progressed these hopes dimmed. As late as 9 January 1810 Mrs. Seton wrote to Sad in New York:

Our Revd. Mr. Tisserant is not yet returned but still expected, the death of a sister in Germany has delayed him...we have reason to hope Mr. Tisserant will be our chaplain when he returns.[70]

Just what basis there was for Mrs. Seton's hope is not revealed, but that Cheverus knew of it is clear from his letter to her of the same month, which stated:

He [Tisserant] knew and rejoyced at your consecration to God. He speaks in stronger terms about his return to the U.S., than ever he did before. However I doubt still whether we shall have the happiness to see him. Should he return, you will, I am afraid, have the preference, and we shall lose him and be obliged to applaud his choice.[71]

But Tisserant never came to Emmitsburg as chaplain or in any other capacity. The last news of him was the letter from Cheverus telling that the French priest was well and in England in January 1816. In the spring he was to go to France, and "had given up every hope of visiting us again."[72]

While Tisserant was exerting an influence at closer range in 1805-1806, both John Carroll and Jean Cheverus were maintaining their interest in Mrs. Seton from their more remote locations in Baltimore and Boston. One of Elizabeth's first acts after her conversion was to write to Cheverus in gratitude for the part he had played, and to beg him to continue to advise her.[73] Cheverus quickly sent her a prayer book [u] with the wish, "May you, like the Blessed Virgin and the other holy women who were with the apostles, be filled with the Holy Ghost."[74] It was Cheverus who advised her to meet attacks on her religion with short, clear answers, and when discussion grew too heated to remain mute, since "silence is the best answer to scoffers."[75] When Mrs. Seton indulged in some flattering remarks to him Cheverus sternly reproved her, writing, "I must ask as a favor that you will never again write to me anything that has been said in my praise, but pray for me that I may be always sincerely humble."[76] This imagined rebuff produced a brief "tempest in a teapot." Mrs. Seton felt Cheverus was angry with her, and wrote an apology to Boston. Cheverus felt distressed that his humility had been misunderstood and he wrote Tisserant:

> She owes me no excuse, but unfortunately knowing very well that vanity is not dead in me, I begged her not to repeat to me praises made by those I love and respect. It is a temptation too delicate and to which I do not wish to be exposed. Thank you for having told her that I have no anger against her. If some words of mine made her believe it, I beg her pardon... My sentiments in her regard are not *anger* but *esteem* and *respectful friendship*.[77]

To the lady herself in New York Cheverus sent a peace offering of five volumes of Massillon's sermons for Advent and Lent,[v] and with them the apology:

> I am sorry if my letter made you suppose for a minute that I was angry with you. Never have I had any other sentiments towards you but those of the most sincere respect and friendship and with those I do and always shall remain.[78]

Although Cheverus was not destined to see his sensitive friend for several years to come,[w] Bishop Carroll was to see Mrs. Seton much

---

[u] Probably the prayer book was the *Roman Catholic Manual, or Collection of Prayers, Anthems, Hymns, etc.* (Boston, 1803) which Cheverus had printed. The University of Notre Dame Archives has this prayer book but the title page is missing.

[v] Jean Baptiste Massillon was classed with Bossuet and Bourdaloue as one of the great French writers of sermons. Many of Massillon's sermons were delivered during the reign of Louis XIV of France. The first printed edition of the sermons appeared posthumously in 1745 and was reprinted many times thereafter. It is impossible to determine which edition Cheverus sent Mrs. Seton.

[w] Cheverus wrote that to see Mrs. Seton and her children would be "a heartfelt pleasure to me, but I do not flatter myself of enjoying it very soon." After his consecration as Bishop of Boston, Jean Cheverus visited Emmitsburg in November 1810, and met Mrs. Seton for the first time.

sooner.[79] John Carroll was pleased when his friends James and Joanna Barry became acquainted with Elizabeth Seton and he wrote Mrs. Barry[x] of "Mrs. Seton whose situation and sacrifices have interested me so much in her favor."[80] When Elizabeth heard of Carroll's kind interest she told Antonio humbly, "Oh, if he knew what is known to you, how different would be his impressions!"[81] She studied the picture the Barrys had of the bishop and tried to imagine what it would be like to meet him. When Carroll arrived in New York in May and gave Mrs. Seton a week of instruction and direction, her joy knew no bounds. She was confirmed by him on 25 May 1806 taking the name of Mary,[y] which added to Ann and Elizabeth presented "the three most endearing ideas in the world."[82]

John Carroll, like others before him, was not impervious to the radiant charm which Mrs. Seton possessed and the elderly bishop and the convert became warm friends. He was delighted with her little girls and always inquired after them in his letters, requesting their prayers, and offering his services as a parent in God. After his return to Baltimore he intervened to untangle the financial transactions in regard to the Seton boys at Georgetown. When James Barry wrote him protesting an error made by Bishop Neale,[z] Carroll replied:

> My brother Bishop had brought the entire charge for the two boys against you as paymaster instead of deducting my contribution to their education, which he ought to have done, having received my instructions...When I go to Georgetown I shall examine this affair and if you have overpaid the sum

---

[x] In the fall of 1805 the Barrys had been at the Narrows, Long Island, when their daughter Mary was taken seriously ill. They took her to New York where she died on 17 November 1805. The Barrys remained in New York until James Barry's death in January 1808. They were relative strangers in New York society when Mrs. Seton met them.

[y] John Carroll thereafter addressed his letters to her as "Mrs. M. E. A. Seton."

[z] The difficulty over the financial arrangements also included a misunderstanding over the "requisite articles" the Seton boys were expected to provide. In lieu of bed linen, school books, etc., each student was to pay a $10 entrance fee. In addition, the Seton boys were charged $30 for "suits of uniform which they should have had along." The Georgetown ledger, 1803-1813, gives a full account of the Seton accounts from their entrance, 20 May 1806, to withdrawal, 22 June 1808. Carroll's payment of $200 is recorded on the first bill to James Barry, "Bishop Carroll has paid $200 to the college for his part of the sum which will arise & be due for the two amiable sons of Mrs. Seton in the course of two years." See bill to James Barry, 20 May 1806, UNDA. The Georgetown ledger lists a Carroll payment $150 under the date of 23 February 1807. AGU, Ledger 105. James Barry, who handled Mrs. Seton's negotiations at the entrance of her sons, was a hot-tempered man and he became highly incensed at what he believed injustice from Bishop Neale. He wrote to Carroll, "The letter I wrote you of the Setons and Mr. Neale would speak for itself, and its intent was so intended. Yes, I repeat what I once took the liberty to say to you, that if Mr. N. did not leave the College, the College must leave him." 1 August 1806, AAB, AASMSU, I-L-1. Carroll's letter to Barry on 19 September enclosed an answer "taken from the Bishop (Neale's) mouth," adding that Neale was no longer president of the College, Neale having resigned the week before to be replaced by Mr. Molyneux. If the resignation bore any relation to the Seton affairs, Bishop Carroll did not state it.

for which Mr. Filicchi became responsible it shall be returned to go to the credit of subsequent payments.[83]

While the Setons remained at Georgetown. Bishop Carroll continued his interest in the boys and wrote their mother encouraging reports of them.

Mrs. Seton's natural wit elicited from the dignified bishop a heavier humor and his letters contained such passages as the following apology for his style:

It [his letter] has been written amidst continued interruptions, one of which arose from a drunken woman finding access to my study and another from a drunken sailor, who was informed by inspiration or revelation, that all his excesses... have been forgiven ...without any penitential works on his side...The same spirit which assured him of his conversion and forgiveness has ordered him to write and publish a book highly important to the United States. When it comes from the press you will allow me to send you a copy.[84]

Part of Elizabeth Seton's charm lay in a happy combination of traits which, while bringing to the surface in others their latent capacity for lightheartedness, still reminded them of her steady desire to grow in virtue and humility. It can scarcely be coincidence that all of her friends felt that these reproofs, spoken or written, were the things she saved and treasured. Bishop Carroll could turn from his satire on the serenity of a bishop's study to a serious warning against pride in the same letter.

Whatever I learn of you, increases my solicitude, respect, and admiration. But attribute no merit to yourself on this account...it is beneath the dignity of a Christian, who has ever meditated on the folly, as well as the criminality of pride, to glory in that which belongs not to him. [85]

CHAPTER 6. NO RESTING PLACE

Notes

[1] 10.4, "Dear Remembrances," *CW*, 3a:519.

[2] Sister Mary Augustina Ray, B.V.M., *American Opinion of Roman Catholicism in the Eighteenth Century* (New York, 1936), 359.

[3] Thomas F. Meehan, "Tales of Old New York," *Historical Records and Studies, XVIII* (March 1928), 121 ff.

[4] Leo R. Ryan, *Old St. Peter's* (New York, 1935), 84-5. The full text of the petition is cited. See *History of the State of New York* (New York, 1933), IX, 169-170.

[5] Michael Hurley to John Carroll, New York, n.d., AAB, AASMSU, 4-G12.

[6] 3.31, Journal to Amabilia Filicchi, *CW*, 1:373.

[7] 7.49, Elizabeth Seton to Simon Bruté, Emmitsburg, n.d., *CW*, 2:424.

[8] Ryan, 77.

[9] Matthew O'Brien to John Carroll, New York, n.d., AAB, AASMSU, 5-T-12.

[10] 1.91, Elizabeth Seton to Julia Scott, Staten Island, 26 July 1800, *CW*, 1:132.

[11] 3.22, Elizabeth Seton to Antonio Filicchi, New York, 6 April 1805, *CW*, 1:350.

[12] 4.28, Elizabeth Seton to Antonio Filicchi, New York, 4 December 1806, *CW*, 1:425. See #20, "Riot at St. Peter's Church, New York, 24 December 1806," *American Catholic Historical Researches*, XVL, no. 1 (January 1899), 146-50.

[13] The *American Register*, 27 December 1806, reprinted in *Researches,* XVI (1899), 149-150.

[14] Jean Cheverus to Elizabeth Seton, New York, 21 January 1807, ASJPH 1-3-3-1:7.

[15] 3.26, Elizabeth Seton to Antonio Filicchi, New York, 30 April 1805, *CW*, 1: 358.

[16] Ibid.

[17] Ibid. See 3.23, Elizabeth Seton to Antonio Filicchi, New York, 15 April 1805, *CW*, 1:352.

[18] Ibid.

[19] Antonio Filicchi to Elizabeth Seton, Philadelphia, 21 May 1805, ASJPH 1-3-3-10:22.

[20] 3.30, Elizabeth Seton to Antonio Filicchi, New York, 1 June 1805, *CW*, 1:366.

[21] 3.23, Elizabeth Seton to Antonio Filicchi, New York, 15 April 1805, *CW*, 1:352.

[22] 4.3, Elizabeth Seton to Julia Scott, New York, 28 August 1805, *CW*, 1:383.

[23] Guy Carleton Bayley to Elizabeth Seton, New York, 12 September 1805, ASJPH 1-3-3-2:95. For a full account of Guy Carleton Bayley and his branch of the Bayley family, see Sister M. Hildegarde Yeager, C.S.C., *The Life of James Roosevelt Bayley, First Bishop of Newark and Eighth Archbishop of Baltimore, 1814-1877* (Washington, 1947). See also Appendix A. Bayley-Seton Genealogy.

[24] 4.2, Elizabeth Seton to Antonio Filicchi, New York, 28 August 1805, *CW*, 1:381; 4.3, Elizabeth Seton to Julia Scott, New York, 28 August 1805, *CW*, 1:383.

[25] "Record of the Bayley Family in America," UNDA. A typed, un-paginated manuscript compiled by Robert Seton; 4.13, Elizabeth Seton to Julia Scott, New York, 26 December 1805, *CW*, 1:399.

[26] 4.3, Elizabeth Seton to Julia Scott, New York, 28 August 1805, *CW*, 1:384.

[27] 4.4, Elizabeth Seton to Antonio Filicchi, New York, 9 September 1805, *CW*, 1:385. See *Historical Records and Studies,* XXII (1932), 97-98 for a copy of this will.

[28] 3.22, Elizabeth Seton to Antonio Filicchi, New York, 6 April 1805, *CW*, 1:349.

[29] 3.26, Elizabeth Seton to Antonio Filicchi, New York, 30 April 1805, *CW,* 1:359.

[30] 3.27, Elizabeth Seton to Julia Scott, New York, 6 May 1805, *CW*, 1:360.

[31] Antonio Filicchi to Elizabeth Seton, Philadelphia, 3 May 1805, ASJPH 1-3-3-10:21.

[32] 3.28, Elizabeth Seton to Antonio Filicchi, New York, 6 May 1805, *CW*, 1:362. Mme. de Barberey, *Elizabeth Seton,* 6th edition (Paris, 1906), 339, states, "M. et Mme. White étaient bons Catholiques tous les deux." Code's adaptation of de Barberey repeats this error. Mrs. Seton wrote Filicchi that it was rumored that the Whites were Catholics but that Mrs. Sadler and Mrs. Dupleix specifically corrected that impression "and explained that Mr. and Mrs. W. were Protestants."

[33] 3.30, Elizabeth Seton to Antonio Filicchi, New York, 1 June 1805, *CW*, 1:366.

[34] 3.29, Elizabeth Seton to Antonio Filicchi, New York, 17 May 1805, *CW*, 1:364.

[35] 4.1, Elizabeth Seton to Julia Scott, New York, 10 July 1805, *CW*, 1:380.

[36] 4.2, Elizabeth Seton to Antonio Filicchi, New York, 28 August 1805, *CW*, 1:382.

[37] 4.10, Elizabeth Seton to Antonio Filicchi, New York, 25 October 1805, *CW*, 1:394.

[38] This house was probably the one Mrs. Seton described as "Stuyvesant's Lane, Bowery, near St. Mark's Church, two white houses joined left hand." 4.11, Elizabeth Seton to Julia Scott, New York, 20 November 1805, *CW*, 1:395; 4.60, Seton to Scott, *CW*, 1:489. See *New York City Directory, 1806-1807.*

[39] 1.146, Elizabeth Seton to Rebecca Seton, New York, n.d., *CW*, 1:192.

[40] 4.5, Elizabeth Seton to Antonio Filicchi, New York, 2 October 1805, *CW*, 1:387.

[41] 4.13, Elizabeth Seton to Julia Scott, New York, 20 January 1806, *CW*, 1:401.

[42] Antonio Filicchi to Elizabeth Seton, Boston, 8 October 1805, ASJPH 1-3-3-10:28.

[43] Jean Cheverus to Elizabeth Seton, New York, 30 November 1805, ASJPH 1-3-3-1:3. Filicchi's high opinion of Montreal was shared by both Jean Cheverus and Francis A. Matignon, the pastor of Holy Cross, Boston. When differences arose between the American seminaries at Georgetown and Baltimore, Matignon sent his Boston candidates for the priesthood to Montreal. See Lord, Sexton, and Harrington, *History of the Archdiocese of Boston* (New York, 1944), I, 601.

[44] John Carroll to James Barry, Baltimore, 6 April 1806, AAB, AASMSU, 9-C-6; *Researches,* XXV (1908), 56.

[45] Antonio Filicchi to Elizabeth Seton, Baltimore, 18 April 1806, ASJPH 1-3-3-10:29.

[46] Thomas Kelly to Elizabeth Seton, Georgetown, 8 April 1806, ASJPH 1-3-3-2:54.

[47] 4.15, Elizabeth Seton to Antonio Filicchi, New York, 28 April 1806, *CW*, 1:404.

[48] Antonio Filicchi to Elizabeth Seton, Philadelphia, 2 May 1806, ASJPH 26-0-2, (6b), 24. Copy. The original is in AMSJ.

[49] 4.17, Elizabeth Seton to Antonio Filicchi, New York, 12 May 1806, *CW*, 1:406.

[50] Antonio Filicchi to Elizabeth Seton, Philadelphia, 16 May 1806, ASJPH 1-3-3-10:30.

[51] 3.25, Elizabeth Seton to Antonio Filicchi, New York, 22 April 1805, *CW*, 1:356.

[52] 7.250, Elizabeth Seton to Ellen Wiseman, Emmitsburg, 1 May 1820, *CW*, 2:656.

[53] 3.30, Elizabeth Seton to Antonio Filicchi, New York, 1 June 1805, *CW*, 1:365.

[54] 4.7, Elizabeth Seton to Antonio Filicchi, 11 October 1805, *CW*, 1:391. Cf. *Le Petit Paroissien Roman* (Paris, 1804), p. xv, "Six Commandments of the Church."

[55] Ibid., 390.

[56] Matthew O'Brien to Elizabeth Seton, New York, 11 October 1805, ASJPH 1-3-3-7:71.

[57] Eliza Sadler to Elizabeth Seton, New York, n.d., ASJPH 1-3-3-11:B1.

[58] Sexton-Lord-Harrington, I, 548.

[59] Jean Cheverus to Elizabeth Seton, Boston, 1 June 1805, ASJPH 1-3-3-1:2.

[60] Jean Tisserant's letters, written in French, though lengthy and difficult to read, are preserved in excellent condition at Emmitsburg. ASJPH 1-3-3-1, #20-29. Unfortunately none of Mrs. Seton's to him are available.

[61] Jean Tisserant to Elizabeth Seton, Elizabeth Town, 6 September 1805, ASJPH 1-3-3-1:20.

[62] Jean Tisserant to Elizabeth Seton, Elizabeth Town, 15 December 1805, ASJPH 1-3-3-1:21.

[63] Jean Tisserant to Elizabeth Seton, Elizabeth Town, 29 January 1806, UNDA.

[64] Jean Tisserant to Elizabeth Seton, Elizabeth Town, 9 March 1806, ASJPH 1-3-3-1:22.

[65] Jean Tisserant to Elizabeth Seton, Elizabeth Town, 15 March 1806, ASJPH 1-3-3-1:23; Ibid., 31 March 1806, ASJPH 1-3-3-1:24.

[66] Jean Tisserant to Elizabeth Seton, Elizabeth Town, 22 April 1806, ASJPH 1-3-3-1:25.

[67] Jean Tisserant to Elizabeth Seton, Elizabeth Town, 28 May 1806, ASJPH 1-3-3-1:26.

[68] Jean Tisserant to Elizabeth Seton, Elizabeth Town, 27 August 1806, ASJPH 1-3-3-1:29.

[69] Jean Cheverus to Elizabeth Seton, Boston, 8 June 1807, ASJPH 1-3-3-1:8; Ibid.,12 May 1808, ASJPH 1-3-3-1:9; Ibid., 13 April 1809, ASJPH 1-3-3-1:10; Ibid., 24 January 1810, ASJPH 1-3-3-1:11; Ibid., 20 January 1815, ASJPH 1-3-3-1:14; Ibid., 25 June 1816, ASJPH 1-3-3-1:15.

[70] 6.18, Elizabeth Seton to Eliza Sadler, Emmitsburg, 9 January 1810, *CW*, 2:99.

[71] Jean Cheverus to Elizabeth Seton, Baltimore, 24 January 1820, ASJPH 1-3-3-1:11.

[72] Jean Cheverus to Elizabeth Seton, Emmitsburg, 25 June 1816, ASJPH

1-3-3-1:15.

[73] 3.20, Elizabeth Seton to Jean Cheverus, *CW*, 1:347. The letter is a rough draft of the one sent to Cheverus, and bears no date. It may have been written on 2 April 1805.

[74] Jean Cheverus to Elizabeth Seton, 1 June 1805, ASJPH 1-3-3-1:2.

[75] Jean Cheverus to Elizabeth Seton, New York, 30 November 1805, ASJPH 1-3-3-1:3.

[76] Jean Cheverus to Elizabeth Seton, New York, 28 January 1806, ASJPH 1-3-3-1:4.

[77] Jean Tisserant to Elizabeth Seton, 9 March 1806, ASJPH 1-3-3-1:22.

[78] Jean Cheverus to Elizabeth Seton, New York, 3 April 1806, ASJPH 1-3-3-1:5. See *The Catholic Encyclopedia,* X, 34.

[79] Jean Cheverus to Elizabeth Seton, Boston, 3 February 1808, UNDA.

[80] *Researches,* IX (1893), 117. John Carroll to Joanna Barry, Baltimore, 19 March 1806. The original letter is in the possession of the American Catholic Historical Society in Philadelphia. See Barry to Carroll, 11 December 1805, AAB, AASMSU, 1-M-2.

[81] 4.14, Elizabeth Seton to Antonio Filicchi, New York, 25 March 1806, *CW*, 1:403.

[82] 4.19, Elizabeth Seton to Antonio Filicchi, New York, 28 May 1806, *CW*, 1:408.

[83] John Carroll to James Barry, Baltimore, 21 July 1806, AAB, AASMSU, 9-C-7. See 19 September 1806, AAB, AASMSU, 9-D-1.

[84] John Carroll to Elizabeth Seton, New York, 23 May 1807, ASJPH 1-3-3-1:39.

[85] Ibid.

ᔐᔑ

CHAPTER 7

୨ᢦᢣᡈ

GOD'S BLESSED TIME

The zeal which impressed her new Catholic friends was to cause a serious break in Mrs. Seton's relations with her older non-Catholic connections in the summer of 1806. It has been said that Elizabeth Seton was very fortunate in the number of men of exceptional virtue who crossed her path. If in proportionate degrees these men benefited from her friendship, how much more impressive is the evidence of Mrs. Seton's influence on women. Her encouragement to Rebecca Seton has already been noted. After her conversion, Mrs. Seton had an even greater influence on Cecilia Seton, Rebecca's youngest sister and Elizabeth's sister-in-law. Cecilia, together with her sister Harriet, and her cousin, Eliza Farquhar, had been tremendously aroused by the fervor of Elizabeth's formal inquiry on the Catholic faith. While Harriet, and "Zide's"[a] first enthusiasm cooled under parental frowns, Cecilia's only grew stronger. The girl became obstinate at James Seton's house where she lived, and many notes passed between her and the "sis" she adored. Elizabeth advised patience and told Cecilia to let the Lord be her first confidant in regard to the "secret" they shared. She must yield to those who had authority over her. "Of course you are a prisoner," she wrote, "but it is a Prisoner of the Lord."[1] As the girl's yearning to become a Catholic increased, her health grew worse. When Elizabeth began to fear that Cecilia might die outside the Church, she wrote to Father Cheverus in Boston, asking his advice. The solace Cheverus wrote in reply[2] allayed her fears but did not dissuade Cecilia. On 17 June 1806 Cecilia made the decision to become a Catholic,[b] and three days later she made her formal profession of faith to Rev. Michael Hurley, O.S.A.[3] The storm which now broke was violent. Up to the time of Cecilia's conversion, the Setons, Ogdens, Hoffmans, and other friends had disapproved of Mrs. Seton's course of action and family relations had been cool and restrained; but the general attitude had been more one of pity for the "poor fanatic" and her foreign friends. The conversion of one of their blood relations while she was living under their own roof was an entirely different matter. Even warmhearted Dué was alienated for a while.

---

[a] "Zide" was Eliza Farquhar, the third member of the trio of girls so interested in Catholicism after Mrs. Seton's conversion.

[b] Hurley in a letter to Cecilia used the words, "Remember the 17th of June; it stands recorded in Heaven." Cecilia herself said, "I was received and united to the Catholic Church on the 20th of June."

Cecilia had been staying at Charlotte Ogden's, at 44 Wall Street, when the Setons began to suspect her perfidy. Charlotte Seton Ogden, wife of Gouverneur Ogden, was Cecilia's older sister. She was the most bitter of all the Setons on the subject of Cecilia's conversion and it was the attitude of the Ogdens which remained most vividly in Mrs. Seton's memory in later years. Both Charlotte Ogden and Mary Hoffman Seton accused Cecilia of deception.[4] The family first tried to put pressure on Cecilia by confining her to her room. When she remained adamant, they told her that she would be responsible for depriving Elizabeth Seton of her livelihood. It is not clear what the Seton family believed the New York State Legislature could do but they spoke wildly of petitioning to remove Elizabeth from the state, but it is quite obvious that religious prejudice flamed wildly for a time as a result of Cecilia's conversion. They threatened to send Cecilia to the West Indies on a vessel then ready to sail. They even threatened to burn down Elizabeth's house over her head.[5] When they warned Cecilia that "if she persevered that they would consider themselves individually bound never to speak" to her or Elizabeth again, that she was no longer welcome in any of their homes, she quickly tied up her clothes in a bundle and went over to live with Elizabeth.[6] When Charlotte discovered Cecilia's absence, she wrote a peremptory demand that Cecilia answer the question, "Are you a Catholic?"[7] Cecilia replied that she had left Wall Street "in a firm resolution to adhere to the Catholic faith," and could only return when the family could receive her in that faith.[8] When she asked Charlotte about the rest of her clothes, Mrs. Ogden replied acidly, "You had best apply to those who have hitherto supplied you."[9] Later, when Charlotte had calmed enough to relent, she, wrote, "Fearful, you may want clothes, I send you those bundles which you left here. It is likewise your brother's wish that if you really intend to leave us all, you will let him know where the remainder are to be sent."[10]

Meanwhile back at James Seton's, Mary, his wife, was investigating Cecilia's bureau and when she found there Catholic literature she immediately blamed Elizabeth for proselytizing the girl. She wrote Cecilia coldly:

> In respect to your sister [Elizabeth Seton] I will be very explicit. If she had never been a Roman, neither would you. I decidedly say [that] I firmly believe that she has acted toward me both cruel and unjustifiable, and I candidly own to you so far from keeping your change of religion a secret, I openly shall confess it, that others may not trust Mrs. Seton's liberality of principle as I have done.[11]

In spite of Cecilia's assurances that she would not think of instilling Catholicism in Mary's children,[12] the James Setons told Cecilia she was no longer an example worthy of the children's emulation.[13]

When Elizabeth wrote an account of that July of violence and anger to Antonio Filicchi in London, she had high praise for Rev. Michael Hurley, who had "behaved like an angel" and was their one true friend through the crisis. She told Antonio that she wished "the so long desired refuge of a place in the order of St. Francis" could be obtained for his converts. Just what "a place in the order of St. Francis" implies is not clear. Mrs. Seton occasionally referred to a "secret" in her letters to Filicchi;[c] this may have been a secret fantasy to enter [or associate herself in some way with] a Franciscan order.[14] Antonio replied from London that the "new St. Cecilia" should remain with Elizabeth, and he enclosed a letter[d] for John Murray giving orders that Mrs. Seton be allowed to draw unlimited sums.[15] When Elizabeth showed her reluctance to accept such generosity, Filicchi spoke strongly, "I command you" to call upon Murray "for any and for as many pecuniary wants" as Cecilia and Elizabeth's family might have. Antonio Filicchi had just returned to Italy, having had a miraculous escape in the Alps Mountains which he attributed to Elizabeth Seton's prayers. He felt a better Christian, he said, through her good example, "Through you my mercantile interests are blessed by God with an uninterrupted success." It seemed simple justice to Antonio that Elizabeth accept in return a small part of the rewards he had through her prayers.[16]

Antonio was not the sole sympathizer. Francis Matignon[e] wrote from Boston, "A step so courageous of a person so tender in years and in spite of such obstacles, is without doubt, as you have expressed it, a visible miracle of grace...[assuring Elizabeth that] in spite of my silence I take a very lively interest in all which concerns you; I wish every day at Mass the action of God's grace in all your concerns and a continuation of His favors."[17] Harriet Seton and Eliza Farquhar hoped the storm would blow over and they wrote Cecilia, "How ardently we long and pray for that

---

[c] [Although Melville indicated that Mrs. Seton may have sought to "enter a Franciscan order," it is also possible that she wished to board and teach in a convent school since she had heard of the congregation of religious women established under the auspices of Saint Sulpice in Canada. She may have become acquainted with the Franciscans in Italy through the Filicchi family. Ed.]

[d] The enclosed letter to John Murray & Sons of New York was a scathing denunciation of Mrs. Seton's "Christian" friends. Mrs. Seton did not deliver it, but Filicchi himself sent a duplicate direct to Murray.

[e] Francis Anthony Matignon was the pastor of Holy Cross Church in Boston which Bishop Carroll had dedicated in 1803. At the time of this letter, 22 September 1806, Jean Cheverus was his assistant. When Cheverus became bishop in 1810 Matignon became his former assistant's subject and continued to serve at Holy Cross Cathedral, to complete twenty-six years of service in Boston's first church. Father Matignon wrote fewer letters to Mrs. Seton than some of her other friends.

hour which will bring us[f] to one fold, under one shepherd." And though they feared the consequences if they should be found in communication with the pariah, they added, "Tell the blessed H. [Hurley] to pray for us."[18]

The "angel," Mr. Hurley, so beloved by Cecilia, Elizabeth, and the others was a young Augustinian priest who had come to New York from St. Augustine's Church in Philadelphia in July 1805 to assist in the crisis caused by yellow fever that summer. At the time he arrived he was about twenty-five years old, of medium height, and possessing a clear, strong speaking voice.[19] He was never polished or elegant, and from a certain brusqueness of manner Cecilia and Elizabeth gave him a secret name, "Whyso." At the beginning of his stay in New York, he had not impressed Mrs. Seton, but later she wrote to Antonio Filicchi that Mr. Hurley was "very much improved in his official Character, and quite freed from those singularities we used to lament in him."[20] James Barry told Carroll that Hurley appeared proud without being so, that he kept only a "proper respectful distance" from the church dignitaries who were "non-lettered spalpeens" [rascals] who treated their priests like a tailor's or shoemaker's journeyman. "Mr. Hurley's moral character," wrote Barry, "I have invariably heard applauded. In his church duties he is solemn, dignified, and punctual. Without the least infringement of the truth, he is by far the first ornament of our church."[21] It was Michael Hurley who prepared young Anna Maria Seton for her first Communion, and Elizabeth told her daughter, "Remember that Mr. Hurley is now in the place of God to you, receive his instructions as from Heaven."[22]

Because of the distance of St. Peter's Church from her home, Mrs. Seton developed during this period the habit of spending Sunday at church. After her first Mass and Communion, she breakfasted with Mrs. Dupleix, the Barrys, or with Mr. Hurley or Mr. Byrne.[g] She sometimes assisted at three Masses in one morning. She would then take her dinner with nearby friends and conclude the day with vespers.[23] After the rift with Mrs. Dupleix following Cecilia's conversion, Elizabeth ate more frequently at Barclay Street. She spoke of dining on "beefsteak and claret" with Rev. John Byrne when he returned from a visit to Georgetown with news of her sons; and when Byrne was away at Norfolk she and Cecilia dined with

---

[f] Harriet Seton became a Catholic in 1809 at Emmitsburg. There is no evidence that Eliza Farquhar ever entered the Catholic Church.

[g] By the fall of 1806 St. Peter's Church had the services of Rev. Matthias Kelly, recently arrived from Dublin at Rev. John Byrne's invitation, and Rev. Michael Lacey who also served at Norfolk, Virginia, during this period. *A General History of the Christian Church* published by Bernard Dornin in 1807 contains an interesting list of Catholic subscribers, including "Dr. Matthew O'Brien, D.D.," Rev. L. Sibourd, Rector, Rev. John Byrne, Rev. Matthias Kelly, Rev. Michael Lacey of Norfolk, as well as a "Mrs. S." St. Peter's of Barclay Street gave evidence of the rapid turnover in priests, so characteristic of the American Church in the early days of the republic.

their "Whyso."[24] Needless to say, when Hurley was away from New York he was keenly missed. In May, 1807, when he was called to Philadelphia by his mother's illness, Mrs. Seton wrote, "I do not like your Philadelphia visits—Pitying Mercy, if you should not [return] ...surely the scourge would fall heavily."[25] And the scourge was all too soon to fall.

Michael Hurley was not at all happy about conditions at St. Peter's.[h] When he arrived he had noticed "many gross abuses" which he tried to reform.[26] The conduct of some of the clergy fell short of Hurley's expectations and he wrote his bishop:

> With regard to ourselves I can only say we are not as we should be. I fear some of us seek ourselves and not God— our own conveniences rather than the good of religion. The trustees are evidently discontented and inclined to interfere and adopt violent measures.[i] However as they generally consulted me I have uniformly opposed any step that might lead to scandal or to revolt. There is certainly a great field for exertion here.[27]

On his visit to Baltimore and Washington, in the early summer of 1807, Hurley discussed conditions in New York with Bishop Carroll, and learned of Carroll's intention of sending Rev. Louis Sibourd to New York as active pastor to Barclay Street. Sibourd had recently returned to the United States from Martinique.[28] When Hurley returned to New York and learned of his own recall to Philadelphia by his superior, Rev. Matthew Carr, O.S.A., he wrote to the bishop, "Rev. Sibourd's arrival at this [time] is singularly fortunate and seems to presage much good to this distracted congregation."[29]

Mrs. Seton received the news of Hurley's impending departure with dismay and she wrote to Cecilia:

> St. M. [Michael], our St. M. never known till lost, nor did we know our love and value for him until the blow is struck— He leaves us Monday to return NO MORE—the rector of St. Augustine Church has left it to Him and is going away in ill health...He wishes extremely to see you Sunday morning.[30]

---

[h] Bishop Carroll had condemned the practice of using the sanctuary as a thoroughfare when he visited New York, but the practice had continued. Hurley also complained that the Blessed Sacrament was carried by school boys from the church to the sexton's house.

[i] Some of the trustees opposed Hurley himself. James Barry wrote Carroll that Andrew Morris attributed politics to Hurley; Barry added, "The good old man got upon that hobby horse, party election, and saw everything as people do in an unsmooth state of mind." Matthew O'Brien's conduct was openly criticized in New York City and O'Brien was censured by Bishop Carroll in 1808, as was Matthias Kelly.

The two converts were sad, indeed, the last Sunday they heard Mr. Hurley offer Mass. Elizabeth never quite forgot his earnest admonition, "Sursum Corda," to them in the face of their grief.[j] Often in the days that followed, when her spirit seemed "deaf to every other remembrance," his last words sounded in her ears and she took fresh courage.[31] When Mrs. Morris teased Elizabeth and asked if she needed a bowl to catch the tears at Hurley's departure, Mrs. Seton answered simply, "They stream from my heart, tho' it rejoices in the happiness he has gained."[32]

Fortunately for Cecilia and Elizabeth Seton, by the time they lost their strong supporter and friend, the family quarrel was past its bitterest stage. Eliza Seton Maitland, Cecilia's older sister, had become seriously ill in March 1807 and had asked for Cecilia and Elizabeth. In the course of attending the dying woman, the two converts naturally saw many of their relatives and friends. The family was favorably impressed with Cecilia's "sweet submissive manner and prudent behavior" and asked her to come visit them.[33] In only a few weeks Mrs. James Seton asked for Cecilia's assistance with the children again. When Mary Seton died in June, Cecilia was kept on by James Seton to care for his motherless children. The reconciliation with Elizabeth was complete by fall, and she could write Sad who was again in Ireland:

> James walked in my room the other morning, took me in his arms like one of the children, asked some questions about a bundle at the Custom House, and seemed to have met me every day of the twelve months I have not seen him—I like that—so all the world should do.[34]

During the confusion caused by Cecilia's conversion, Elizabeth Seton's interior progress went steadily forward. She wrote happily to Antonio:

> Upon my word it is very pleasant to have the name of being persecuted and yet enjoy the sweetest favours, to be poor and wretched and yet to be happy, neglected, and forsaken, yet cherished and most tenderly indulged by God's most favored servants and friends. If now your sister did not wear her most cheerful and contented countenance she would indeed be a hypocrite.[35]

---

[j] It is interesting to note that the first Sisters of Charity of St. Joseph's to leave Mrs. Seton's foundation at Emmitsburg went to St. Joseph's Asylum for orphans in Philadelphia in 1814 at the trustees' request through Michael Hurley.

Her serenity overflowed and touched those around her and John Wilkes, who was now remarried and prospering, said wonderingly, "Providence does not do so much for me as for you, as it makes you happy and content in every situation."[k] These were her happiest days. Under particular trials of patience, she found her best consolation in the Litany of the Blessed Virgin. "How sweet," she told Cecilia, "to entreat her who bore Him in the Bosom of Peace to take our own case in hand—if she is not heard, who shall be?"[36] Once again Elizabeth turned to the practice of keeping a journal, and this series of meditations written from July to November 1807 while household cares pressed heavily, and the distance to St. Peter's was long, contains one of the most beautiful records of Elizabeth Seton's love. Here is found the moving meditation on the Blessed Sacrament, which a convert so truly understands.

> Which of us having once tasted how sweet the Lord is on his holy altar and in his true Sanctuary, who finding at that Altar our nourishment of soul and strength to labor, our propitiation, thanksgiving, hope, and refuge can think but with sorrow and anguish of heart of the naked, unsubstantial comfortless worship they partake who know not the treasure of our Faith—theirs founded on words of which they take the shadow, while we enjoy the adored Substance in the center of our Souls.[37]

Not that the path was straight upward. Many times during that summer of 1807 she became downcast at the failure of her good resolutions, "the constant presence of reproaches to the little ones," her darlings, whom she felt she herself deserved more than the trifles of their behavior did. Sometimes the paucity of the fruit that so many confessions and communions bore suggested the idea of abandoning them, "to fly from the fountain while in danger of dying of thirst."[38] But she raised her heart, as "St. Michael" had commanded, and wrote the lovely praise of Penance:

> Oh my soul, when our corrupted nature over-powers, when we are sick of ourselves, weakened on all sides, discouraged by repeated lapses, wearied with sin and sorrow, we, gently, sweetly lay the whole account at His feet, reconciled and encouraged by His appointed representative, yet trembling and conscious of our imperfect dispositions, we draw near

---

[k] Mrs. Seton had written Julia Scott on 10 November 1806, "J. W. is married as you probably know, and of course I am more interested not to trespass more on his benevolence." 4.56, Elizabeth Seton to Philip Filicchi, New York, 2 November 1807, *CW*, 1:480; 4.26, Elizabeth Seton to Julia Scott, 10 November 1806, *CW*, 1:418.

[to] the Sacred Fountain. Scarcely the expanded heart receives its longing desire than wrapt in His Love, covered with His Righteousness, we are no longer the same.[39]

As her spirit expanded, Elizabeth yearned more and more for retreat from the world. The Montreal scheme which Antonio Filicchi had never abandoned appealed increasingly to both Cecilia and Elizabeth. She wrote Philip Filicchi of her disappointment that the "long anticipated removal of my family to Canada" had not yet materialized.[40] She had already written Antonio that the Barrys approved the plan and that James Barry had taken steps to advance it.[41] When she began to have serious qualms in regard to the influence of her boarders on her daughters, she decided to consult Bishop Carroll. She wrote him a letter outlining the situation,[l] citing the ties which bound her to New York, giving the estimated cost of the Montreal project and asking his advice: She said she would rely on his decision.[42] Carroll replied at once, sympathizing with her concern for the girls and agreeing that they should not be exposed to improper company. But, he warned, before Mrs. Seton took any action, she should consider first: suppose the girls were unhappy in Canada—could, Mrs. Seton then return to New York; secondly, could Mrs. Seton get released from her present obligations to the boarders without being accused of unsteadiness?[43] Failing to receive a definite mandate to undertake the scheme, the young widow felt she should consider other possibilities.

Meanwhile Mrs. Seton was faced with the declining prosperity of her boardinghouse. The Wilkes brothers continued to pay the house rent, but Post had not contributed for some time, and Mrs. Startin had adopted an orphan[m] which rather absorbed her interest and charitable contributions.[44] More serious was the shrinking of her clientele. Some of the parents claimed to be dissatisfied with the treatment their sons received. By the end of November three out of a total ten had been withdrawn, and Mrs. Seton was "handsomely roasted for not keeping them in better order."[45] She was at first apprehensive lest she had failed in her duty to the boys, but Mr. Harris, who superintended the school they attended, assured her that only great injustice could tolerate such a view.[46] The simple fact was that the young boarders followed the attitude of a majority of their elders and began

---

[l] Mrs. Seton estimated the cost to be about $600 and she told Carroll she could count on more than that from a subscription Antonio Filicchi had arranged for her before he left America. This subscription consisted of annual pledges by friends to the following amounts: Julia Scott, $200; the Wilkes brothers, $200-$300; Dr. Wright Post, $200; Sarah Startin, $200; the Filicchi brothers, $400.

[m] The orphan was one of the Maitland children, child of Eliza Seton Maitland. Mrs. Startin had other reasons for discontinuing her support, chief of which was Cecilia Seton's conversion. It was after this event she changed her will to omit Elizabeth Seton and her children.

to grow ungovernable after Cecilia's conversion. As Elizabeth explained to Antonio, a year earlier:

> They have lost a portion of respect for me which it was impossible to avoid while we were the laughing stock of their dinner tables at home, and the talk of the neighborhood here—Mrs. Farquhar's children being forbidden [to] enter the house occasioned a great deal of amusement to them.[47]

Elizabeth would have abandoned her boarders then, if Cheverus and Matignon had not urged her to persevere.

Rev. Jean Cheverus and Rev. Francis Matignon in Boston were waiting for a different solution to evolve. The November following Cecilia's conversion, Rev. Louis William Valentine Dubourg, (1766–1833), the president of St. Mary's College in Baltimore, stopped in New York on his way to Boston. Accidentally meeting Mrs. Seton, Dubourg conversed with her about her boys and her intentions for them. Elizabeth told him of her hope of entering or residing in a convent in Montreal if the children could be arranged for there, and if she could make herself "useful as an assistant in teaching." Dubourg told her he felt that some such arrangement might be made within the United States.[n] As Elizabeth wrote Bishop Carroll, "This hope which had hitherto been but as a delightful dream...Mr. Dubourg brought to the nearest point of view and flattered me with the belief that it is not only possible, but may be accomplished without difficulty."[48]

In Boston, Dubourg discussed his hopes for Mrs. Seton with Cheverus and Matignon, who were equally impressed. Matignon wrote Elizabeth, "We are entirely agreed on what Mr. Dubourg has proposed for you," and he went on to say they felt Mrs. Seton was destined to take a great place in the United States where it was definitely preferable that she remain. There was no urgency for the moment, said Matignon; "God has His moments which we need not anticipate, and prudent slowness only ripens and brings to fruition the good desires which Grace inspires within us."[49]

While the Canadian dream still lingered, Elizabeth had been in no hurry to pursue Dubourg's proposal. She wrote Julia:

> A gentleman of very great respectability from Baltimore, the Superior of...[St. Mary's] college there, has endeavored to interest me in the establishment I have heard you mention

---

[n] Charles I. White tells a charming story of Dubourg's being struck by Mrs. Seton's fervor at the altar rail. Present researches indicate no archival sources for this account but since White has proved accurate in most other respects, the present writer [Melville] sees no reason to discount the probable truth of the incident. See White, 211-2.

with approbation in Philadelphia,° Madam (I do not know who), who keeps the celebrated boarding school—but the aim of my desires if I were to change the present situation is very different, tho certainly the idea of going to Philadelphia, or rather to you, would be delightful to me.[50]

When Jean Cheverus perceived Mrs. Seton's lack of interest in anything but Canada that winter, he wrote reprovingly,

> Dr. Matignon sends his respects and desires me to tell you he does not know how to procure the rules of the nunneries in Canada. Dr. Dubourg was to converse with you about another project which I should prefer, hoping it would be better for your family and being sure it would be very conducive to the progress of religion in this country [the United States].[51]

During the early spring of 1807, Mrs. Seton heard nothing from John Carroll, who was suffering from a painful inflammation of the eyes. He had begged Joanna Barry in April to "Make the best apology you can for me to Mrs. Seton whom I am ashamed of having neglected so long."[52] But in May Bishop Carroll gave a blanket approval to Dubourg's plan, writing, "Tho I am entirely ignorant of all particulars...it is enough for me to know that it has the concurrence of Dr. Matignon and Mr. Cheverus."[53] Dubourg, himself, reopened the whole question when he came to New York early in 1808.

Elizabeth had become very lonely for her two sons at Georgetown and she wrote Bishop Carroll at the end of February asking if the Seton boys might come to New York.[54] When Carroll learned that the president of St. Mary's College was going north he put the Seton boys in his care. Dubourg came to New York to assist with the Lenten services at St. Peter's Church; he lodged with Andrew Morris. Sibourd had been petitioning Carroll since early February for additional clergy. Sibourd's first choice had been Rev. Benedict Joseph Flaget (1763–1851), but Flaget demurred on the ground that he would be no good for preaching.[55]

Mrs. Seton's boarders had been reduced to five at this time, and the Setons had been forced to move to a house of lower rent. The house was so small that the Setons were living "five in a room and a closet."[56] This time

---

° There is no way of determining what school Mrs. Seton referred to, but it seems evident she believed Dubourg planned to establish her in Philadelphia. A Madame Grelaud had a French school on Mulberry Street in Philadelphia early in the 1800's. This school was very successful and many Maryland girls were sent there. Madame Grelaud was reputed to be a Huguenot and her pupils were chiefly Episcopalians, although some Jews and Roman Catholics attended. See *The Maryland Historical Magazine*, XXXIX (June 1944), 141-9. Dubourg may have hoped to establish a similar school for Catholic girls.

the Sulpician made Mrs. Seton a definite offer of "a formal grant of a lot of ground situated close to the college [St. Mary's in Baltimore] which is out of town and in a very healthy situation." Dubourg guaranteed the immediate charge of half a dozen girls and as many more as Elizabeth could manage. The Seton boys could enter St. Mary's at a nominal cost, thus leaving free part of the Filicchi funds for their education.[57] In May after his return to Baltimore, Dubourg wrote to Mrs. Seton:

> I have this moment written at large to our worthy Bostonian friends to submit to their consideration the scheme which now engrosses all my thoughts. Should they approve of it I would be for your coming in two or three months and taking the rent of a newly built house, which in every point of view would perfectly suit all our ideas at least during the first year, which, would give you sufficient time to reflect and consult on the propriety of building.

Dubourg believed it would be premature to buy a house. Renting for a year would give them time to consult the Filicchis in Italy, "and otherwise make a trial of our strength and prospects."[58]

The spring of 1808, seemed to demand a decision. The ties which bound Mrs. Seton to New York were being relaxed one by one. James Barry had died as the new year was ushered in, and Mrs. Barry with her daughter, Ann, had sailed for Madeira in the hope of improving Ann's health.[59] Mrs. Sadler and Mrs. Dupleix were both gone to Ireland and the Napoleonic wars in Europe made their return improbable.[60] Conditions within the church in New York were distressing. Rev. Louis Sibourd, who had replaced Rev. William O'Brien in July 1807 was very dissatisfied with the caliber of his assistants and he had written his bishop as early as 8 December 1807,[p] of his intention to resign.[61] It required only the approval of her friends to solidify Elizabeth Seton's resolution to depart.

The wholehearted approval of the Boston priests was not long in arriving. On 12 May Jean Cheverus wrote that he and Matignon were agreed with Dubourg and Sibourd on all points. "We infinitely prefer it to your project of retreat in Montreal," he said, and he urged that "prudence, but not extreme delicacy or timidity" should guide her reliance upon Filicchi's

---

[p] There may have been dissatisfaction on the part of some trustees in regard to Sibourd's diction but the real reason for his departure was not a recall by his bishop, but Sibourd's own determination to resign. As early as 7 December 1807, Sibourd regretted having accepted "the rectorship of this church." On 27 June 1808, he wrote his formal resignation giving reasons as conscience, poor eyesight, and lack of preaching ability. Even Dubourg's offer to go to New York "thrice a year" to help him did not deter Sibourd. In August the discouraged Frenchman who had "tried to bring back more regularity to the discipline of the church but found little support in the priesthood," left for Saratoga Springs, New York, for a rest.

unlimited resources. When Elizabeth consulted John Wilkes and Wright Post,[62] she received their approval as well. They told her she would have no trouble in renting the house she had just taken, for the season was a good one.[63] The only hesitation remaining in Elizabeth's mind centered around Cecilia. The girl wanted to be with her sister-in-law wherever she might go, but she was restrained by a sense of duty to James Seton's children and the precarious condition of her own health. Elizabeth was most eager to have Cecilia accompany her but Mr. Sibourd advised against the girl's going at this time. Dubourg felt Mrs. Seton would have enough on her hands without assuming any added responsibilities. He advised, however, that Cecilia disclose to her family at once her intentions of following Mrs. Seton to Baltimore as soon as circumstances permitted.[64]

Everything was now decided except the actual date of departure, and the route to be taken. Elizabeth wrote Julia Scott that she would come by way of Philadelphia if she could be of any assistance to Julia and her mother who were both ailing. "On your answer," she explained, "depends either my going round by Sea, or coming to you in two or three weeks by land. But be sincere in your statement as they tell me it will be much less expense to go by Water."[65] Whether Julia replied or not, the extant evidence does not indicate; but a week after writing this letter, Mrs. Seton was en route to Baltimore by boat. 9 June 1808, found Elizabeth and her three daughters on board the *Grand Sachem,* ready to leave New York never to return. The words of Dubourg probably matched Mrs. Seton's feelings as she started south; he had written, "I remain more and more satisfied that even were you to fail in the attempt you are going to make, it is the will of God you should make it."[66]

Notes

1. 4.78, Elizabeth Seton to Cecilia Seton, New York, n.d., *CW*, 1:514.
2. Jean Cheverus to Elizabeth Seton, New York, 3 April 1806, ASJPH 1-3-3-1:5. See 4.20, Elizabeth Seton to Cecilia Seton, *CW*, 1:409.
3. Michael Hurley to Cecilia Seton, 29 August 1807, ASJPH 1-3-3-4:197. 4.22, Elizabeth Seton to Cecilia Seton, 25 July 1806, *CW*, 1:411-412.
4. 6.180, Elizabeth Seton to Simon Bruté, 1 January 1815, *CW*, 2.294. 7.11, Elizabeth Seton to William Seton, Emmitsburg, 3 April 1816, *CW*, 2:381.
5. Ibid. 4.24, Elizabeth Seton to Antonio Filicchi, New York, 10 August 1806, *CW*, 1:414.
6. Ibid.
7. Mary Hoffman Seton to Cecilia Seton, New York, ASJPH 1-3-3-17:14.
8. Cecilia Seton to Charlotte Ogden Seton, New York, 1806, ASJPH 1-3-3-4:168.
9. C.O. [Charlotte Ogden] to Cecilia Seton, n.d., ASJPH 1-3-3-17, 12.
10. Charlotte Ogden Seton to Cecilia Seton, New York, ASJPH 1-3-3-17:13.
11. Mary Hoffman Seton to Cecilia Seton, New York, ASJPH 1-3-3-17:15.
12. Cecilia Seton to Mary Hoffman Seton, 1806, ASJPH 1-3-3-4:167; Cecilia Seton to Charlotte Ogden Seton, 25 July 1806, ASJPH 1-3-3-4:170.
13. Charlotte Ogden Seton to Cecilia Seton, New York, ASJPH 1-3-3-17:12, 13.
14. 4.24, Elizabeth Seton to Antonio Filicchi, New York, 10 August 1806, *CW*, 1:415.
15. Antonio Filicchi to Elizabeth Seton, 3 November 1806, ASJPH 1-3-3-10:33; Antonio Filicchi to John Murray & Sons, 3 November 1806, ASJPH 1-3-3-10:34.
16. Antonio Filicchi to Elizabeth Seton, Leghorn, ASJPH 1-3-3-10:26.
17. Francis Matignon to Elizabeth Seton, New York, 12 October 1806, ASJPH 1-3-3-1:35. For a summary of Matignon's career, see Richard J. Cushing, *Father Matignon, Boston's Pioneer Priest* (Boston, n.d.).
18. Harriet Seton and Eliza Farquhar to Elizabeth Seton, New York, 19 August 1806, ASJPH 1-3-3-8:67.
19. *Records* of the American Catholic Historical Society, I (1887), 173-199. The place and date of Hurley's birth are undetermined being given as either Ireland or Philadelphia and 1780 or 1781.
20. 4.31, Elizabeth Seton to Antonio Filicchi, New York, 30 March 1807, *CW*, 1:431.

[21] Barry to Carroll, New York, 10 June 1807, AAB, AASMSU, 1-K-5.

[22] 4.23, Elizabeth Seton to Anna Maria Seton, New York, 26 July 1806, *CW*, 1:413.

[23] Mrs. Seton referred to Matthias Kelly as "a very very great acquisition to our Church," and to Mr. Lacey as "an odd genius." (4.31, Elizabeth Seton to Antonio Filicchi, 14 March 1807, *CW*, 1:431; 4.86, Elizabeth Seton to Cecilia Seton, *CW*, 1:501.) Michael Hurley's letters to Carroll also testify to the presence of Kelly and Lacey in New York City. Hurley to Carroll, 7 October 1806 and 15 July 1807, AAB, AASMSU, 4-H-2, 4-H-3.

[24] 4.37, Elizabeth Seton to Cecilia Seton, New York, 31 May 1807, *CW*, 1:440.

[25] 4.35, Draft of Elizabeth Seton to Michael Hurley, New York, n.d., *CW*, 1:439; 4.36, Elizabeth Seton to Cecilia Seton, New York, 28 May 1807, *CW*, 1:439.

[26] Michael Hurley to John Carroll, New York, 10 March 1806, AAB, AASMSU, 4-G-9.

[27] Hurley to Carroll, New York, 2 January 1806, AAB, AASMSU, 4-H-1;1-K-5. See Carroll Letterbook I, p. 84, AAB, AASMSU.

[28] James Barry to John Carroll, New York, 10 June 1807, AAB, AASMSU, 1-K-5; Thomas Kelly to Elizabeth Seton, Georgetown, 10 June 1807, ASJPH 1-3-3-2:55. See Louis Sibourd to John Carroll, Martinique, 31 March 1807, AAB, AASMSU, 7-Q-S.

[29] Hurley to Carroll, New York, 15 July 1807, AAB, AASMSU, 4-H-2.

[30] 4.42, Elizabeth Seton to Cecilia Seton, New York, n.d., *CW*, 1:449.

[31] 4.45, Elizabeth Seton to Cecilia Seton, New York, n.d., *CW,* 1:455. See *Provincial Annals (1811-1821)*, ASJPH 7-8-2, 301.

[32] 4.44, Draft of Elizabeth Seton to Michael Hurley, New York, 28 July 1807, *CW*, 1:454.

[33] 4.31, Elizabeth Seton to Antonio Filicchi, New York, 14 March 1807, *CW*, 1:430; 4.33, Elizabeth Seton to Julia Scott, New York, 10 April 1807, *CW*, 1:434.

[34] 4.54, Elizabeth Seton to Eliza Sadler, New York, 6 October 1807, *CW*, 1:469.

[35] 4.31, Elizabeth Seton to Antonio Filicchi, New York, 30 March 1807, *CW*, 1:431. Mrs. Seton expresses the same sentiments in an undated draft of a letter to Mrs. Sarah Startin. See 4.119, Elizabeth Seton to Mrs. Sarah Startin, *CW*, 1:543.

[36] 4.38, Elizabeth Seton to Cecilia Seton, New York, 7 June 1807, *CW*, 1:442.

[37] 4.55, Spiritual Journal to Cecilia Seton, 16 October 1807, *CW*, 1:478.

[38] Ibid., 474.

[39] Ibid., 488.

[40] 4.56, Elizabeth Seton to Philip Filicchi, New York, 2 November 1807, *CW*, 1:479.

[41] 4.46, Elizabeth Seton to Antonio Filicchi, New York, 10 August 1807, *CW*, 1:456.

[42] 4.57, Elizabeth Seton to John Carroll, New York, 13 November 1807, *CW*, 1:482. See Barry to Carroll, 17 June 1806, AAB, AASMSU, 1-M-3. This subscription was not being fulfilled in 1807.

[43] John Carroll to Elizabeth Seton, New York, 2 December 1807, ASJPH 1-3-3-1:40.

[44] 4.46, Elizabeth Seton to Antonio Filicchi, New York, 10 August 1807, *CW*, 1:457. 6.180, Elizabeth Seton to Simon Bruté, *CW*, 2:295.

[45] 4.60, Elizabeth Seton to Julia Scott, New York, 29 November 1807, *CW*, 1:488.

[46] 4.58, Elizabeth Seton to Eliza Sadler, New York, 18 November 1807, *CW*, 1:484.

[47] 4.28, Elizabeth Seton to Antonio Filicchi, New York, 4 December 1806, *CW*, 1:423.

[48] 4.27, Elizabeth Seton to John Carroll, New York, 26 November 1806, *CW*, 1:420. Copy. The original is in AAB, AASMSU, 7-N-5. Dubourg lodged with Thomas A. Morris during his New York visit. See Thomas Morris to Louis Dubourg, New York, 16 December 1806, ASMSU.

[49] Francis Matignon to Elizabeth Seton, 25 November 1806, ASJPH 1-3-3-1:37.

[50] 4.26, Elizabeth Seton to Julia Scott, New York, 20 November 1806, *CW*, 1:419.

[51] Jean Cheverus to Elizabeth Seton, New York, 21 January 1807, ASJPH 1-3-3-1:39.

[52] John Carroll to James Barry, Baltimore, 2 April 1807, UNDA.

[53] John Carroll to Elizabeth Seton, New York, 23 May 1807, ASJPH 1-3-3-1:39.

[54] 4.66, Elizabeth Seton to John Carroll, New York, 28 February 1808, *CW*, 1:496.

[55] See Louis Sibourd to John Carroll, New York, 14 February, 12 and 19 March 1808, AAB, AASMSU, 7-Q-13, 7-Q-14, 7-Q-5.

[56] 4.73, Elizabeth Seton to Julia Scott, New York, 23 April 1808, *CW*, 1:506.

[57] Ibid.

[58] Louis Dubourg to Elizabeth Seton, Baltimore, 2 May 1808, UNDA; Dubourg to Seton, Baltimore, 27 May 1808, AMSV.

[59] 4.62, Elizabeth Seton to John Carroll, New York, 3 January, *CW*, 1:491; 4.72, Ibid., 28 March 1808, *CW*, 1:504-505; 4.66, Ibid., 28 February 1808, *CW*, 1:495-496.

[60] 4.43, Elizabeth Seton to Julia Scott, New York, 20 July 1807, *CW*, 1:451.

[61] Louis Sibourd to John Carroll, New York, 25 December 1807, AAB, AASMSU, 7-Q-10. Ryan, 89 and Peter Guilday, *The Life and Times of John Carroll,* II, 628, leave an erroneous impression as to Sibourd's reasons for leaving St. Peter's in 1808. The next day he wrote Carroll requesting permission to resign. AAB, AASMSU, 7-Q-8. On 25 December 1807, he suggested Jean Cheverus for New York, and added that he would do his best to complete his year but not to depend on him after July 1808. See Letters from January to June 1808 reiterate Sibourd's intention of resigning. AAB, AASMSU, 7-Q-10. See also AAB, AASMSU, 7-Q-16, 3-E-4. Theresa (Cecilia) Seton and Rev. Louis Sibourd to Elizabeth Seton, 3-4 August 1808, ASJPH 1-3-3-4:203. In October 1808, Anthony Kohlmann, S.J., came to St. Peter's as pastor and vicar-general of the newly created Diocese of New York. This whole chapter of the Church in New York deserves fresh treatment. Both Guilday and Ryan are not only inadequate, but in some instances in error.

[62] Jean Cheverus to Elizabeth Seton, 12 May 1808, ASJPH 1-3-3-1:9.

[63] 4.74, Elizabeth Seton to Julia Scott, New York, 1 June 1808, *CW*, 1:508.

[64] Louis Dubourg to Elizabeth Seton, 8 June 1808, ASJPH 1-3-3-2:1.

[65] 4.74, Elizabeth Seton to Julia Scott, New York, 1 June 1808, *CW*, 1:508.

[66] Louis Dubourg to Elizabeth Seton, 8 June 1808, ASJPH 1-3-3-2:1.

⹌∞⹌

CHAPTER 8

ৎৡৡ৶

A HOUSE ON PACA STREET

Thursday, 9 June 1808, Elizabeth Seton and her three daughters went to the wharf to board the *Grand Sachem* for Baltimore. Wright Post, who had secured their passage at a cost of fifty dollars, went with James Seton and William Craig to see the Setons safely on board. The eve of the

departure from New York had been spent in Eliza Sadler's former home on Courtlandt Street, now occupied by William Craig; it was the final glimpse Elizabeth ever had of Sad's rooms, and from the deck of the *Grand Sachem* she saw for the last time the windows of Number 8 State Street.[1] As the packet rounded the Battery, passing from the river to the ocean, and Staten Island loomed ahead, Elizabeth had a sudden overpowering urge to see once more her father's grave; but the pilot could not conveniently gratify her wish.[2] As the New York harbor faded in the

Mother Seton lived in this house on Paca Street, Baltimore.

distance Elizabeth wondered how her heart could "swell so high and not burst."[3] But she turned to settling the girls for the voyage, and soon they were all seated comfortably on a mattress, becoming acquainted with a Mrs. Smith and her daughter, and receiving kind attentions from the modest young mate, James Cork.[4]

The week passed rather swiftly and the two mothers relaxed under "the heaven so bright" while the children sang, "Oh where is my Highland Laddie gone?,"[5] ate raisins and almonds or sent paper ships overboard toward New York. At first the Seton girls wished to return to Cecilia in New York, but as the voyage continued their thoughts turned toward the south, and they became impatient to land and see "Willy and Dicksy." When storms came up in the night, Elizabeth kept Bec and Kit in her own narrow berth, holding her hand over the edge to comfort Anna Maria who slept below. Oddly enough, it was Anna Maria, the only seasoned traveler among the girls, who suffered most from seasickness. To Elizabeth, who was traveling for the first time without the protecting care of a male escort, death seemed closer than on previous voyages. She confessed to Cecilia that many times on the trip she resigned her three darlings to God's care, while striving to look straight upward "in firm and steadfast confidence."[6] In spite of these premonitions, Tuesday evening found the Setons sailing up Chesapeake Bay and Wednesday night, 15th June at eleven o'clock the *Grand Sachem* docked in the Baltimore basin. Thursday morning dawned almost imperceptibly through the grey mist and heavy rain. By the time all their goods were entered at the customs house,[a] it was after nine o'clock and Elizabeth's heart was pounding and her hands trembling as she waited for the first sight of their new home.

Baltimore in 1808 was the largest city in Maryland and the third largest in the United States, exceeding in commercial importance even the city of Boston. One of the most rapidly expanding urban areas on the continent, the population numbered between 35,000 and 46,555 inhabitants. Three-fourths of these were white; one-fourth were colored, either, "free persons or slaves."[7] The harbor was so excellent that ships came right up to the wharf; and as the non-intercourse regulations[b] of the Jefferson administration began to be felt, it was a common sight to find 100 vessels anchored close by with 200 more at the mouth of the harbor.[8] Fell's Point was a thriving shipbuilding center, and Baltimore merchants in 1800 had proudly given the federal government the sloop-of-war, the *Maryland,* made in their own city. The Baltimore clipper, which was the perfected adaptation of the topsail schooner, was to become the despair of the British in the years to follow. The most profitable merchant cargoes were of tobacco and wheat. The demand in Europe and in the West Indies for wheat and flour was so pressing that within a radius of eighteen miles the Baltimore area had half a hundred merchant mills, twelve of which were on Jones Falls alone.[9]

As the carriage bore the Setons rapidly from the waterfront, they looked out curiously at a metropolis not greatly changed from that visited by William Dunlap two years earlier. The actor-producer had found the city little to his liking, its manners "such as might be expected in a society formed of commercial adventurers from all nations, and in which slavery exists on the old colonial establishment." Counting houses were open on Sunday, gambling was popular, with "literature kept in due subordination to dancing and card-playing." Dunlap noted that Baltimore had more hackney coaches than any other city except Boston, but that the horses were much inferior to those of Philadelphia. Of the public buildings Dunlap wrote:

---

[a] [The portion of the Baltimore harbor known as the Basin was once more extensive than at present. The tides could reach almost to Baltimore and Gay Streets. The U.S. Congress established the U.S. Customs Service as the first federal agency in 1789 and named Baltimore as one of fifty-nine collection districts. The first Baltimore custom house was at the intersection of Gay and Water Streets. Apparently Mrs. Seton did not arrive at Fells Point as some have speculated. Ed.]

[b] The Non-Intercourse Act of March 1809.

I can say but little and I believe little is to be said. Places of worship are numerous for the size of the place, but none remarkable for size and structure. The Court House is a wretched old building standing in the center of the street with an arched gangway under it beautified by a pillory and whipping post.[10]

The brick court house, the New York visitor so deplored, stood where the Battle Monument now stands.[c] In 1808, it was situated on a cliff some sixty feet high, and the turbulent waters of Jones Falls had so undermined the bank that the court house had to be underpinned. The gangway below the court house was the result of Leonard Harbough's engineering, and on warm evenings it was a popular place for promenading. The year after Elizabeth Seton arrived in Baltimore the old brick court house was abandoned in favor of the new building erected at Lexington and Calvert Streets.[11]

In addition to the court house, Baltimore had a "new and handsome jail," a theatre, a public library, four "spacious market houses, and an elegant building nearly finished for the Union Bank."[12] The churches were numerous indeed, totaling twenty-five. John O'Neill's *Introduction to Universal Geography,* published in Baltimore that year, stated:

> Among the buildings of public worship now finished, the first Presbyterian church claims preference as a handsome specimen of recent architecture; but the Roman Catholic Cathedral now building must when finished excel. Among those buildings for public worship now erecting are a church for the use of the Seminary of St. Sulpice and the College of St. Mary; a Methodist meeting house, and an Episcopal church.[13]

The Sulpician chapel[d] was being dedicated the very day that Mrs. Seton arrived in Baltimore. It was the feast of Corpus Christi and as the tired travelers entered the little chapel inside the seminary grounds off the Hookstown Road they heard the organ's solemn tone, the "bursting of the choir," and then, was it possible, "St. Michael's"[e] voice resounding in the Kyrie Eleison.[14] "Human nature could scarcely bear it."[15] The little girls

---

[c] The Battle Monument commemorates the soldiers who died in the Battle of North Point during the War of 1812. It is located on Calvert Street, between Fayette Street and Lexington Street.

[d] [Today St. Mary's Spiritual Center and Historic Site on Paca Street includes the Chapel of the Presentation of the Virgin Mary in the Temple, the Mother Seton House, and a Visitor Center. Located at 600 North Paca Street, the site is open to the public and is listed on the *National Register of Historic Places*. Ed.]

[e] Michael Hurley, O.S.A., assisted at the consecration of St. Mary's Chapel. John Carroll celebrated the first Pontifical Mass. Hurley had come to Baltimore on 9 June with Samuel Sutherland Cooper, a fervent convert from Philadelphia. Cooper was considering entering the seminary that fall.

clung to their mother in astonishment, and all were filled with delight and wonder at the "awful [deeply reverential] ceremonies seen for the first time."[16]

Frances Trollope, whose comments on American manners in the nineteenth century were first published in 1832, has left this charming description of St. Mary's Chapel. Speaking of the great number of Baltimore churches, she wrote:

> The prettiest among them, a little bijou of a thing belonging to the Catholic College. This institution is dedicated to St. Mary, but this little chapel looks...as if it should have been sacred to St. John of the Wilderness. There is a sequestered little garden behind it, hardly large enough to plant cabbages in, which contains a Mount Calvary bearing a lofty Cross. The tiny path which leads up to this sacred spot is not much wider than a sheep track and its cedars are but shrubs, but all in proportion; and notwithstanding its fairy dimensions, there is something of holiness and quiet beauty about it that excites the imagination strangely. The little chapel itself has the same touching and imaginary character. A solitary lamp hangs before the altar; the light of day enters dimly yet richly through crimson curtains, and the silence...had something in it more calculated to generate holy thoughts than even the swelling anthems heard beneath the resounding dome of St. Peter's.[17]

Elizabeth wrote to Cecilia Seton of this same garden, "There is a little mount behind the Chapel called Calvary—olive trees and a Cross—at the foot of it are four Graves. 'There is your rest' said Mr. Dubourg as we passed it this morning."[18] If the garden was a spot designed to suit her meditative moments, the interior of the chapel was to become an integral part of Elizabeth's life in Baltimore. Here in the morning she went to Communion, and in the evening shared in Benediction of the Blessed Sacrament. Of the Easter week she spent in Baltimore, she said,

> Every night we have Benediction—imagine twenty priests all with the devotion of saints clothed in white, accompanied by the whole troop of young seminarians in surplices also, all in order surrounding the Blessed Sacrament exposed, singing the hymn of the Resurrection, when they came to the words "Peace be to all here" it seems as if our Lord is

again acting over the scene that passed with the assembled disciples.[19]

The chapel, designed by Maximilian Godefroy who was to design the Battle Monument and the Unitarian Church, contained a subterranean chapel of the Virgin, and it was in the solitude of its depths that First Communion was received by the children whom Mrs. Seton later prepared at Bishop Carroll's request.[20] It sometimes seemed as if Elizabeth's whole life were to be punctuated by the Angelus bells which rang from St. Mary's at five-thirty, one-forty-five, and a quarter before eight; [21] they were the melodious signal for the fervent prayers she said upon her knees, as Father Babade[f] recommended.

On the day of her arrival, however, Mrs. Seton was chiefly concerned with her pleasure in seeing Rev. Michael Hurley again, and her gratitude to Rev. Louis Dubourg and his sister, Madame Victoire Fournier, for the warmth of their welcome. The nieces of the college president greeted the Seton girls with a poem especially composed for the occasion by Rev. Pierre Babade (1763–1846).[22] Babade was a frail, white-haired Sulpician whose spiritual fervor attracted the Setons immediately. Babade became one of their best friends during the year they spent in Baltimore. Although he was only forty-eight when Elizabeth met him, she usually referred to him in her letters as "our venerable patriarch."[23] This same Father Babade was to play a very important role in shaping Mrs. Seton's future.

Babade was only one of the "most respectable of the French emigrant clergy,"[24] former friends of the beloved Mr. Tisserant, to whose society Mrs. Seton had access, and she wrote glowingly to Dué, "I find the difference of situation so great I can scarcely believe it is the same existence. All those little, dear attentions of human life which I was entirely weaned from are now my daily portion."[25] J. S. Buckingham, an English traveler to the United States in 1808, commented on this French influence on Baltimore society. "The influx of wealthy and accomplished colonists of San Domingo," he wrote, "who took refuge here at the time of the revolution in that island, and who brought with them the generosity of colonial hospitality and the ease and grace of French manners, served, no doubt, to give a new infusion of these qualities into the society of Baltimore."[26] Although Mrs. Seton did not attend the "gayer soirees, the most agreeable that can be enjoyed," the other aspects of this culture were appreciated by her, and she told Eliza

---

[f] Rev. Pierre Babade, a Sulpician priest, had come to Baltimore at the end of the eighteenth century by way of Spain and Cuba. He taught French and Spanish at the Sulpician College for boys. In later life he laid claim to being a founder of that college, writing Samuel Eccleston, "The college of which you are the president owes me its existence as I drew from Havana the numerous and wealthy pupils who raised the little house of St. Sulpice in Baltimore to the high degree of a university." His name is spelled "Babad" also.

Sadler of her happiness that Anna Maria was now to be molded "in the true style of the French system for young girls and a model for all who wish their daughters to be religious and discreet." Madame Fournier, the sister of Louis Dubourg, had come from Bordeaux to Baltimore in August 1805. Her hospitality was gratefully received by the Setons. In her capacity as manager of "the domestic part of the college," Madame Fournier was able also to give practical assistance to Mrs. Seton in the establishment of her school on Paca Street.[27]

Through her friendship with John Carroll, Elizabeth Seton also had access to the leading English Catholic families in Baltimore, the Pattersons, Catons, Harpers, and Barrys. Bishop Carroll had officiated at the marriage of Elizabeth Patterson and Jerome Bonaparte in Baltimore the same week William Magee Seton died in Italy.[28] The Eliza who lost her husband by death in Italy in 1803 was to befriend this younger Eliza who lost her husband to French imperial ambition; little Jerome Bonaparte was one of the lads Mrs. Seton encouraged later in Emmitsburg.[29] The bishop's grand-nieces, "The Three American Graces" as the Caton girls were called, were also to cross Mrs. Seton's path; one, Louisa, even briefly considered joining the religious community that was conceived during the Seton sojourn in Baltimore.[30] Robert Goodloe Harper,[g] Emily Carroll's husband, and one of Baltimore's leading citizens, offered the protection of his home to Mrs. Seton's daughter, Catherine Josephine, in later years. It was to the Harpers the bereaved girl went when her mother died in 1821.[31] But these events were all in the future; Elizabeth's present task was to settle her family in Baltimore and begin the work for which she had come to that city.

The Monday after her arrival in Baltimore Mrs. Seton went to Georgetown to get her boys.[32] She left the girls with the Robert Barrys, relatives of her former friends in New York. Robert, a nephew of the late James Barry, was at this time the Portuguese consul in Baltimore. He and his wife were unceasing in their kindness to the new arrivals.[33] Elizabeth was accompanied on the trip to Washington by Rev. Michael Hurley and a recent convert of the latter from Philadelphia, Mr. Samuel Cooper. Samuel Sutherland Cooper (1769–1843) had a most intriguing career and legends about him are numerous. Born in Norfolk, Virginia, he came to live in Philadelphia quite early in life. For a time he had pursued an active life at sea; but coming under the influence of Michael Hurley soon after the Augustinian's return to Philadelphia in 1807, Cooper had become a Catholic

---

[g] Robert Goodloe Harper was elected a member of the House of Representatives of the United States in 1794. He is credited with the toast "Millions for defense" given on 18 June 1798, at Philadelphia. In 1815 he was elected to the United States Senate and was reputed a fine orator. He was a legal and business advisor to Mrs. Seton. He died 15 January 1825.

and was confirmed by Bishop Carroll that October. News of the conversion had reached New York and Elizabeth Seton, having no premonition of the part Cooper was to play in her life, had written to Philip Filicchi in Leghorn on 21 November 1807,

> Mr. Hurley who acknowledges so many obligations to you is making brilliant conversions in Philadelphia. A Mr. Cooper of great intellectual attainments waited a few weeks ago on Bishop [William] White and other clergy of note inquiring their reasons of separation, and finding them as they are, was received [into the Catholic faith] on the Visitation[h] at St. Augustine's Church—he is of family and fortune and [it] therefore makes a great noise.[34]

The summer Mrs. Seton met him, Samuel Cooper was thirty-nine years old and was contemplating entering a seminary to prepare for the priesthood. Elizabeth confided to Cecilia:

> If we had not devoted ourselves to the Heavenly Spouse before we met I do not know how the attraction would have terminated; but as it is, I fear him not nor any other—but such a perfect character is a fit offering to the Fountain of All Perfection. He has my rosary and little red cross by way of memento of our Georgetown expedition.[35]

The attraction Elizabeth referred to she later described to Julia Scott as an "involuntary attraction of certain dispositions" resulting in an "interest and esteem understood." Mrs. Scott was assured that "the only result of this partiality had been the encouragement of each other to persevere in the path which each had chosen."[36] The understanding which seemed to exist from the first meeting led Mr. Cooper to take an interest in Mrs. Seton's friends as well. While he was in New York, in the weeks following the Georgetown trip, Cooper drank coffee with Cecilia and told her how Elizabeth longed for her sister-in-law's arrival. Cecilia discovered Cooper to be very different from the picture she had created of him, and she wrote Elizabeth that she found him "very silent and retired."[37] Elizabeth replied reprovingly that he was to enter St. Mary's Seminary [in September of 1808], and added, "I should not wish you to know him as I do."[38] Cooper also called upon Rev. Louis Sibourd, the pastor of St. Peter's, who was preparing to leave New York, and picked up a package the priest wished delivered to Mrs. Seton.[39]

---

[h] The "Visitation" mentioned here is the visitation of Bishop Carroll, not the Feast of the Visitation, as one might at first suppose. Cooper had been directed to Michael Hurley by Mrs. Rachel Montgomery, another of Hurley's converts. Mrs. Montgomery, who was also to meet Mrs. Seton in Baltimore, was a prominent Philadelphia matron whom Hurley had baptized conditionally, 2 February 1805.

By the end of the first week in August, the package was safely delivered, Samuel Cooper was preparing for his entrance into the seminary, and Mrs. Seton was preparing to receive the first young ladies at Paca Street.

The house which Elizabeth Seton occupied the year she remained in Baltimore was on Paca Street, adjoining the grounds of St. Mary's Seminary and College. When Rev. Charles François Nagot,[i] (1734–1816), selected *One-Mile Tavern* as the site of the Sulpician establishment in 1791, it was a quiet, secluded place almost in the forest; but by the time Mrs. Seton arrived, although it was still in the country, it was only a half-mile from town but possibly two miles from the waterfront and business section.[40] The Paca Street house, which sat between two orchards, was "entirely new" when Elizabeth entered it. She told Julia it was "a neat, delightful mansion...in the French style of folding windows and recesses."[41] Only a fence separated it from the chapel, "the most elegant in America," and Mrs. Seton could hear the altar

bells of St. Mary's from her dwelling.[42] One of her greatest joys in her new home was this proximity to a church, "from daylight till nine at Night."[43] The Seton financial affairs were greatly improved, too, since rent and prices were lower in Baltimore than they had been in New York,[j] and the boys were receiving free tuition at St. Mary's College.[44]

The school which Elizabeth had come south to operate was slow in getting underway. The two nieces of Mr. Dubourg were the only prospects when she arrived that June, but it was expected the outlook would improve "after the summer vacation when the inhabitants return."[45] Early in July Elizabeth wrote Julia,

Mother Seton Teaching Pupils,
Elizabeth Prongas, 1979.

I have one pensioner only but have two more engaged— several have offered [themselves] as day scholars which does not enter in my plan which I confine to 8 boarders for the first year or two. The best masters of music, drawing, etc., attend the seminary which enables me to procure their services, if necessary, at a very reasonable rate—[46]

[i] Rev. Charles François Nagot, superior of the first group of Sulpicians who were sent to the United States in 1791, is recognized as the founder of the Society of St. Sulpice in the United States. The Sulpicians opened the nation's first Roman Catholic seminary, St. Mary's in Baltimore, Maryland.
[j] Wood was $3 instead of $5; rent was $200 instead of $350; a very good servant did the washing, cleaning and cooking for $4.50 a month. Provisions were secured from the seminary at wholesale prices.

In August Cecilia Seton wrote from New York that she was astonished to hear that Elizabeth "had but two scholars" and thought it must be a mistake.[47] Dubourg, however, was not uneasy. Before Mrs. Seton left New York he had said plainly:

> I do not feel extremely anxious to see the number of your pupils increased with too great rapidity. The fewer you have in the beginning, the lighter your task, and the easier it will be to establish the spirit of regularity and piety, which must be the mainspring of your machine. There are in the country, and perhaps too many, mixed schools, in which ornamental accomplishments are the only objects of education; we have none that I know, where their acquisition is connected with, and made subservient to *pious* instructions; and such a one you certainly wish yours to be.[48]

The spirit of piety and regularity Dubourg desired was developing without difficulty. Elizabeth wrote Cecilia in September, "In the chapel at six until eight; school at nine—dine at one—school at three, chapel at six ½, examination of Conscience and Rosary, sometimes before that hour a Visit to someone in our limits or a walk, sometimes the chapel also at three—and so goes day after day without variation."[49] Although October brought only four boarders besides the three Seton girls, Elizabeth was satisfied. She admitted to Julia that the pain in her breast had weakened her enough to make the seven girls quite enough to manage.[50] In December, nevertheless, the number had increased to ten,[k] and Elizabeth found "from half past five in the morning until 9 at night every moment is full, no space even to be troubled." Several offers of assistance had come, but for the time being Elizabeth preferred to live "as a mother surrounded by her children." After school was over at five she could be found "with a Master of Arithmetic stuffing her brain with dollars cents and fractions, and actually going over the studies both in grammar and figures which are suited to the scholar better than the mistress."[51] In January she wrote to Antonio of Archbishop Carroll's request that she prepare five children for their First Communion.[52] As her days became busier Elizabeth wished more earnestly that Cecilia Seton might come from New York to assist in the Paca Street school.[53]

Back in New York, Mrs. Seton's concerns still occupied the thoughts of her friends. On hearing of her safe arrival, John Wilkes had asked to be

---

[k] Among these was a niece of Dubourg, Louise Elizabeth Aglae Dubourg, Celanire Delarue, who arrived in Baltimore with Aglae Dubourg in July of 1807 but who was not Dubourg's niece. The other pupils were Julia LeBreton, Isabella Editha O'Conway, and the three Seton girls. The roster of pupils is no longer extant. Julia LeBreton's name also appears as La Britton; earliest community records give LeBreton.

kept informed of further news "that I may fancy myself with you," he wrote, "overlooking your concerns which is the next pleasure to enjoying the Society of one's friends."[54] Whenever Dué's husband, Captain George Dupleix, put into New York he sent news to Baltimore, accompanied by gifts for the children. He teased Elizabeth about leaving her letters for Dué unsealed and promised to cure her stinginess by sending a box of Irish waxes. It was Dupleix who made the arrangements for sending on some articles of furniture which had never been recovered from Mr. Hobart's house after the Italian voyage.[55] Wright Post wrote his sister-in-law that he had no difficulty renting her former residence, and he forwarded a valued picture of Michael Hurley which Elizabeth had left to be framed.[1] He hoped her situation was going to continue as pleasing as it had at first proved. "You know," he added, "how much we are interested in your prosperity."[56] Joseph Bayley at the Quarantine was happy to hear that at last Providence had "mingled a little sweet to meliorate the bitter portion" that had been Elizabeth's lot for so many years.[57]

The two New Yorkers most interested in Mrs. Seton's new venture were her sisters-in-law, Harriet and Cecilia. Harriet was becoming unhappier as time passed and her marriage hopes failed to materialize. She and Elizabeth's half-brother, Andrew Barclay Bayley, who went by 'Barclay,' had for some time been expected to marry, but Barclay had gone to the West Indies and wrote only infrequently. By the time Elizabeth went to Baltimore, Barclay had already been gone two years and was still making only enough to support himself.[58] A letter received in August 1808, "destroyed every hope of his arrival in New York that fall," and when Harriet went to live with Charlotte Seton Ogden in October her unhappiness increased. She recalled with nostalgia the happier days at State Street with Elizabeth and wrote, "To you I owe more than I can express for instilling principles that will make the rugged paths of life smooth and easy."[59] Although she was still not a Catholic, she encouraged Elizabeth to pray for her conversion, and the hostile atmosphere at the Ogdens and Farquhars was very distressing to her. She delayed going to the Farquhars as long as she could, writing Elizabeth:

> Without Zide it would be insupportable...Whenever a
> discussion of religion takes place, which is very often, and,
> I believe, intentionally, too, she defends your dear faith with

---

[1] The picture of Hurley had been left behind to be framed and Mrs. Seton was most uneasy until she received it. Early in August she wrote urgently to Cecilia, "St. M's picture, I tremble lest something has happened to it...How unhappy I should be if St. M. knew that it is not in my possession." 5.5, Elizabeth Seton to Cecilia Seton, 8 July [1808], *CW*, 2:23. When September came and the picture was still missing Elizabeth Seton wrote again, "What am I to think about St. M's picture...do do see about it." 5.9, Seton to Seton, *CW*, 1:32. On 6 October, Mrs. Seton announced with relief that the profile was safe and "hung under the picture of our Lord." 5.10, Seton to Seton, *CW*, 1:33.

more than enthusiastic ardour for which she generally gets a set down from either Father or Mother.[60]

As Harriet's birthday approached she longed for the old days when Elizabeth had been accustomed to giving her a rule of conduct for the coming year, and she asked her sister-in-law to write a letter in the vein of admonition and encouragement. When the older woman complied, Harriet's gratitude was sincere.[61]

In March Harriet was temporarily elated by a letter from Barclay telling of his recovery from a serious illness. He had moved to a settlement called St. Mary's and was associating himself with a "medical gentleman." He promised Harriet that he would see her that summer. When Harriet Seton accompanied Cecilia to Baltimore she did not know that she would never return to New York, that in six months time she would lie in a grave in Emmitsburg.

While Harriet was suffering from pangs of unrequited love of one kind, her younger sister was enduring a frustration of a different nature. From the moment she had said good-bye to her sister-in-law, Cecilia Seton lived only for the day when she might be with Elizabeth and live a devout life.[m] With exceptional docility she had complied with the wishes of James Seton and the advice of Rev. Louis Sibourd that she remain behind. When James planned to operate a summer boardinghouse, depending on Cecilia to supervise the children, she felt she could not refuse.[62] James insisted on keeping Cecilia in spite of family opposition to her religion and the danger they saw in her influence over the children. This influence was no figment of the imagination, and Martin Hoffman and Gouverneur Ogden were so worried over the inclinations of James Seton's daughter, Catherine, that they paid the cost of sending the girl away to school, at Miss Brenton's in Harlem. Even then the child wrote her cousins in Baltimore, "The more they strive to set me against it the more I shall love it."[63]

As if Cecilia did not have enough trials to overcome before reaching Baltimore, others rose to vex her. A young man began calling upon her in the afternoon, ostensibly for the purpose of improving his Italian, but with other more romantic interests at heart. Cecilia wrote fearfully to Elizabeth that she hoped no rumor that she was in love had reached Baltimore; Cecilia was quite indifferent, if the young man was not.[64] When Elizabeth wrote of her disapproval, Cecilia replied, "I did not wait for your letter to

---

[m] [Although Melville uses the phrase "enter a religious life," extant documentation does not support this supposition beyond Cecilia's wish to be with her beloved aunt and practice her faith in a "house of peace and retirement." Cecilia Seton to Elizabeth Seton, 13 September 1808, ASJPH 1-3-3-4:210. Ed.]

be firm and resolute. Did you then think Cecil[n] would trifle with another's happiness?"[65]

A more serious complication arose with the determination of Cecilia's new pastor that she should not leave New York. On 6 October 1808, Elizabeth had written Cecilia, "you will find the best and most excellent assistants to our dear Mr. [Louis] Sibourd that could be obtained are on their way to our poor desolate congregation of New York—I cannot speak my joy, as it will so much glorify the Adored Name."[66]

These assistants were in reality the vicar-general, Rev. Anthony Kohlmann, S.J., Rev. Benedict Fenwick, S.J., and four Jesuit scholastics[o] including James Redmond.[67] New York had been created a See by a papal bull of 18 April 1808 at the same time as Philadelphia, Boston, and Bardstown. Rev. Richard Luke Concanen, O.P., had been named bishop and consecrated in Rome on 24 April 1808. Delays owing to the advance of the naval war in Europe, and the death of Concanen before he left Italy, conspired to keep Kohlmann the administrator of the new diocese until 1815, when Bishop John Connolly, O.P., arrived 14 November, to assume the duties of his office.[p]

Anthony Kohlmann had hopes of establishing a school for Catholic children in New York, and Cecilia reported to Mrs. Seton the January following his arrival,

> Mr. Kohlmann and Mr. Fenwick are contemplating a situation for me in an academy with a Miss Lacey (niece of the Mr. Lacey that was here) to teach Catholic children. They bid me study hard. I fear the undertaking as I tell the gentlemen they must judge and I will act in obedience to them. Mr. Coleman thinks I could do much more good in such a situation.[68]

The pastor and his fellow Jesuits became increasingly determined to keep Cecilia from Baltimore, and March found the confused girl writing to her sister-in-law:

> Mr. Kohlmann seems more and more averse than ever to my leaving New York. He has gone so far as to tell me I cannot go unless in opposition to his advice and the will of God & that in Baltimore I can do no good—but here I can do much for the glory of God. He is to write you a few lines about it.[69]

[n] Cecilia Seton was also called Cecil.

[o] The others were James Wallace, Michael White, and Adam Marshall.

[p] Bishop Concanen died in Naples, on 19 June 1810. The Filicchi brothers had done their best to arrange for the bishop's travel to America. See Peter Plunkett to John Carroll, Leghorn, 3 September 1810, AAB, AASMU 6-U-3.

When Mr. Redmond called on Cecilia he added his disapproval and told her it was foolish of her to even think of going; that moreover it would be a great indulgence.[70]

Mrs. Seton, knowing the tender heart of her young sister-in-law and the latter's docility under direction, wrote, "Stay courageously in your station and wait until he [God] makes it as clearly known in you."[71] While this letter was awaiting a carrier, Mrs. Seton showed Archbishop Carroll Cecilia's letter and asked his opinion of the matter. "Whatever he decided," she wrote Cecilia, "I shall conclude to be the will of God, and will never say one word more about your joining me until it pleases Him to show us it is right."[72] The intercession of Carroll had the desired effect, for on 20 March 1809, Cecilia reported that Kohlmann had heard from the bishop and had then told Cecilia if it was the will of God she should go. He, her pastor, still felt she should wait until fall in fairness to James Seton; but Cecilia was all "for being off the last of May."[73]

James Seton was giving up the "Wilderness" house at Clifton, selling the furniture, and moving back into town.[74] His daughter Ethelinda Agnes reported in a letter to Anna Maria Seton that her eldest sister, Emily (Emma), returned from Miss Brenton's school to assume charge of the younger children, and the plans for Cecilia's departure began to take shape.[75] Even her increasing illness did not deter the girl. When she received Elizabeth's happy note of anticipation, with its homely advice to bring only "a black gown (if you have it) and your flannels—" it was the best medicine she could have had.[76] Samuel Waddington Seton, Cecilia's "much-loved" older brother, wrote Elizabeth on 25 May 1809, that all the arrangements were complete. Harriet and Sam would "make all the party," he added, "since Brother Carlton cannot be permitted to leave."[77] Harriet was only going to see her sister safely in Elizabeth's arms; her own plans were more romantic. The most recent letter from Andrew Barclay Bayley spoke of settling in Jamaica and bringing "Hatch" [Harriet Seton] to the island for their first six or seven years.[78] The little group set out by sea on the first of June and by 12 June they had arrived at Paca Street, and were welcomed by another poem of Rev. Pierre Babade's, this time in honor of Cecilia.[79] Ten days later, Harriet and Cecilia were on their way from Baltimore to Emmitsburg.

The community, conceived in Baltimore but permanently established near Emmitsburg, developed gradually during the whole year that Elizabeth Seton spent in Baltimore. The desire for a religious routine was present from the very first, and Cecilia wrote whimsically, in September 1808, that she wished for a kiss from Elizabeth, but "I scarce expect it, for I fear your convent rules[q] would not permit you."[80] The next month Elizabeth replied in full seriousness:

> It is expected I shall be the Mother of many daughters. A letter received from Philadelphia where my blessed Father [Babade], our Patriarch, now is on a visit, tells me he has found two of the sweetest young women, who were going to Spain to seek a refuge from the world, tho they are both Americans, Cecilia and May, and now wait until my house is opened for them—Next Spring, we hope. He applies to me the Psalms in our Vespers "the Barren Woman shall be the joyful Mother of children."[81]

The girls Pierre Babade had met in Philadelphia were Cecilia Maria O'Conway and Anna Maria Murphy Burke; Cecilia, who has often been called "Philadelphia's First Nun," was the first to join Elizabeth Seton with the intention of forming a community.[82] Cecilia was twenty years old when Babade directed her steps to Baltimore, and she came in the company of her father on 7 December 1808, to meet Mrs. Seton. Although after Mrs. Seton's death Cecilia O'Conway went to Quebec City in Canada and joined the Ursulines there, she was the first Sister of Charity in North America and justly deserves the title of the first of Mother Seton's "daughters."[r] The second Philadelphia candidate, Anna Maria Murphy Burke, did not arrive until April 1809.

Meanwhile two very important steps had been taken. By the beginning of March the site in Emmitsburg had been decided upon for the prospective community, and on 25 March, Elizabeth Seton pronounced her vows privately before Archbishop Carroll. These vows, which were to have such far-reaching effects, made very little change in Elizabeth's interior life. Months before, she had written Philip Filicchi, "you well know it can be neither rest, repose, or exemption from poverty.[s] I have long since made the Vows which as a religious, I could only renew, and the thirst and longing of my soul is fixed on the cross alone."[83] But the effects on her exterior life began to appear at once, and Elizabeth told Cecilia Seton, "I can give you no just idea of the precious Souls who are daily uniting under

---

[q] The nuns who operated convent schools, usually imposed a severe set of rules on the young ladies who enrolled under their tutelage. These rules were designed to keep their pupils at a distance from young men. This may have been Cecilia Seton's frame of reference for using this term.

[r] Cecilia Maria O'Conway (1788-1865) arrived in Canada in July 1823. In a letter to her family she described herself as "a happy captive to Rules more congenial to my inclinations"; but she added, "Ever venerable will the Institution of St. Vincent de Paul be to my memory...Malicious tongues shall never say that I left the Society through a contempt for it." See *Records*, V, 453.

[s] Carroll had doubts that Mrs. Seton should take a vow of poverty considering her circumstances.

my banner which is the cross of Christ; the tender title of *Mother* salutes me everywhere, even from lips that have never said to me the common salutation among strangers."[84] She spoke of Louisa Caton, "one of the most elegant and highest girls in Baltimore," wanting to join the community, "she refuses the most splendid matches to unite herself to our Lord."[85]

Louisa Caton was one of the "Three American Graces" as she and her sisters Mary and Elizabeth were called. Her mother, Polly Carroll, was the daughter of Charles Carroll of Carrollton; her sister Mary was Mrs. Robert Patterson, the sister-in-law of Eliza Patterson Bonaparte. During the spring that Elizabeth Seton was contemplating going to Emmitsburg, Louisa Caton was seriously interested in joining her. John Carroll wrote of Louisa:

> She is resolved on renouncing the world altogether and joining the most virtuous Mrs. Seton in going with her to a place lately purchased by Mr. Cooper near Emmitsburg in Frederic[k] County, where a Sisterhood is to be begun to be established next month under the direction of this lady for the purpose of training piously disposed females...Louisa is not to join them, if she persists in her intentions, before August. [86]

The Caton family was, however, a worldly group and opposed Louisa's plan. After Elizabeth Seton left Baltimore, Louisa Caton was caught up in a whirl of social enjoyment in Washington. Elizabeth wrote to Archbishop Carroll in August, "Your account of Louisa cuts to the heart—I must say I had other hopes—but patience, she certainly cannot forget all her promises and resolutions."[87] But Louisa was lost to Mrs. Seton. Before August was over John Carroll admitted that his niece was referring "with rapture and gratitude of her entertainment at Washington, and particularly of the perfect freedom which reigns in our sister's family, and she might add, which she took without reserve."[88]

Although their paths diverged so widely after 1808, Louisa Caton and Elizabeth Seton remained friends. Louisa wrote to Mrs. Seton and visited her at Emmitsburg, when she was in the vicinity or relaxing at the Carrollton Manor estate located in Frederick County. The Catons and Scotts of Philadelphia exchanged visits and Elizabeth's letters to Julia carried frequent references to the high-spirited Louisa. After Mary Caton Patterson was presented to the court of St. James by the Duke of Wellington Louisa met and married Wellington's aide, Colonel Hervey, later Sir Felton Bathurst. The duke himself applied to Louisa's mother in Hervey's behalf, and Washington and Baltimore learned through Mr. Bagot[t] that Miss Caton was marrying a man of fortune and good looks. Robert Goodloe Harper sent the news to Emmitsburg and asked that Elizabeth Seton be informed, "since I know she will be pleased to learn that Louisa has such fair prospects of happiness."[89]

The loss of Louisa Caton was offset by the gain of other young women of greater constancy. A young woman of Emmitsburg, Eleanor Thompson, who had wanted to join Elizabeth as soon as she heard of the plan to come to the valley, wrote of her pleasure at receiving a letter from Mrs. Seton the very "day which sealed your consecration to God," and she added humbly,

> I am but a child, I only begin to crawl in the ways of God, and that interior spirit which detaches us from everything which is not God, and makes the true spouse of Christ, I have to acquire yet. I wish to do it, is all I can say yet.[90]

Rev. Jean Cheverus and Dr. Francis Matignon, to whom Mrs. Seton had written of her intention on 12 March, had prayed for her "every day some time before and ever since." Cheverus penned the prophetic paragraph:

> How admirable is Divine Providence! I see already numerous choirs of virgins following you to the altar, I see your holy order diffusing itself in the different parts of the United States, spreading everywhere the good odour of Jesus Christ, and teaching by their angelical lives and pious instructions how to serve God in purity and holiness. I have no doubt, my beloved and venerable Sister, that He who has begun this good work, will bring it to perfection.[91]

Susan Clossy[u] arrived 24 May from New York, and Mary Ann Butler came 1 June from Philadelphia, to join the little group who were to make their novitiate in the "beautiful country place in the mountains."[92] Mrs. Rose Landry White, a widow, and Catherine Mullen were added just before the journey to Emmitsburg began.[93]

The final decision to locate at Emmitsburg was also reached only by degrees. Nearly two decades after the foundations were made, Rev. Louis Dubourg, the first Sulpician superior of the group, and by then the Bishop of Montauban in France, wrote a letter to a fellow French priest in 1828, telling of his recollections of how the community came to be founded in Emmitsburg. This celebrated letter to the Abbé Henri Elèves has formed the

---

[t] Possibly the British Minister to Washington, the Honorable Charles Bagot.
[u] Also spelled Clossey.

basis of the previous accounts of the location and financing of Mrs. Seton's "mother house." Dubourg wrote:

> One morning in the year 1808, Mrs. Seton went to find her director, and told him ...she believed she should submit to him what our Saviour had just commanded in a clear, intelligible voice, after her Communion. "Go," He told her, "Address Mr. Cooper; he will give you all that is necessary to begin the establishment."[94]

The letter goes on to say that the very same day, but in the evening, Samuel Cooper called on this director, and in the course of a discussion over the education of Catholic girls, Cooper offered to furnish ten thousand dollars for such a purpose.[v] The director asked if Cooper had had any conversation with Mrs. Seton on the subject, to which Cooper replied, "Never." The letter concluded that Cooper announced:

> This establishment will be made at Emmitsburg, a village eighteen leagues from Baltimore, from whence it will spread over the United States. At the mention of Emmitsburg, the priest termed the plan folly. But Mr. Cooper, even while protesting that he did not wish to exert any influence on the choice of location, or the direction the work should take, repeated in an assured tone that it would be at Emmitsburg.[95]

To approximate more closely how the decisions were reached, it is both interesting and essential to consult the correspondence of Mrs. Seton herself at the time these matters were resolved. The question of financing a community of religious women was present in the young widow's mind almost from the day of her arrival in Baltimore. When writing to Antonio Filicchi on 8 July 1808 she had said:

> The gentlemen of the Seminary have offered to give me a lot of ground to build on. It is proposed (supposing such an object could be accomplished) to begin on a small plan admitting of enlargement...in the hope, and expectation that there will not be wanting ladies to join in forming a permanent institution...Mr. [John] Wilkes was willing to assist in forwarding the plan of erecting a small house on the ground proposed, but with such intimation of doubt in

[v] [In the first edition Melville gave the amount as "fifty million francs" but community documents state ten thousand dollars. The original manuscript copy reads: "J'ai cinquante mille francs à votre service pour cet objet!!!" ASJPH 1-3-3-2:102. Ed.]

respect of security from these dear Gentlemen, etc., etc...I dare to ask my Brother how far and to what sum I may look up to yourself and your honoured Brother in this position of things.[96]

Any hope of securing support from John Wilkes vanished with his letter written Christmas Day 1808 in which he explained "the various disappointments, crosses, and losses" he had experienced. He regretted that he could not help her as he wished, but he added that if she personally needed help he would make "any sacrifice in his power."[97] On receipt of this letter, Elizabeth wrote again to Antonio.

> Mr. Wilkes writes me from New York that Mr. Fisher[w] [sic, Vischer] tells him "the Filicchis have made a *mint* of money and he hopes they will not forsake me tho' the 'old proverb says out of mind'"—he himself laments that he cannot come forward to my assistance...I could not dream of applying to him for assistance in the promotion of a religious establishment—that establishment can never take place but by the special protection of Divine Providence...[98]

Mrs. Seton seems to have associated Divine Providence with the Filicchis, for the next week she wrote to Philip as well. Her letter to the elder brother, dated 21 January 1809 contained the following passage:

> Mr. Dubourg always says patience my child trust in Providence, but this morning at Communion, submitting all my desires and actions in entire abandonment to *His* will—the thought crossed my mind ask Filicchi to build for you—the property can always be his—to be sure thinking of it at such a moment shows how much it is the earnest desire—indeed it is as much wished as I can wish any thing which is not already evidenced to be the Will of our Lord. And if really the thought is practicable on your part the lot of ground stands always ready...[99]

Two weeks later Elizabeth Seton wrote a second letter to Philip Filicchi. This letter, because of its date and contents, and its relation to the statements made in the Dubourg letter, warrants reproduction in its entirety.

---

[w] The letter to which Mrs. Seton refers is dated 25 December 1808 and refers to W. Vischer not Fisher. Mr. Vischer had married Mrs. Mary Filicchi's sister, another Miss Cowper of Boston. John Wilkes had made the reference to the Filicchi good fortune at the close of his letter. The relevant portion reads as follows: "I was very happy to hear from W. Vischer who married Mrs. Filicchi's sister & who perhaps you may have seen as he was going to the Southward, that the Filicchi's have been extremely fortunate & made a <u>mint</u> of money." ASJPH 1-3-3-2:52.

Baltimore 8th February 1809

My dear Filicchi,

You will think I fear that the poor little woman's brain is turned who writes you so often on the same subject, but it is not a matter of choice on my part, as it is my indispensable duty to let you know every particular of a circumstance which has occurred since I wrote you last week relative to the suggestions so strongly indicated in the letters I have written both yourself and our Antonio [Filicchi] since my arrival in Baltimore. Some time ago I mentioned to you the conversion of a man of family and fortune in Philadelphia. This conversion is as solid as it was extraordinary, and as *the person* is soon to receive the tonsure[x] in our seminary, in making the disposition of his fortune he has consulted our Rev. Mr. Dubourg the President of the College on the plan of establishing an institution for the advancement of Catholic female children in habits of religion and giving them an education suited to that purpose. He also desires extremely to extend the plan to the reception of the aged and also uneducated persons who may be employed in spinning, knitting, etc., etc. so as to found a manufactory on a small scale which may be very beneficial to the poor. You see, I am bound to let you know this disposition of Providence that you may yourself judge how far you may concern [yourself] with it—Dr. [Francis] Matignon of Boston with Mr. [Jean] Cheverus the Bishop-elect [to whom] Antonio referred me on every occasion, had suggested this plan for me before the gentleman in question even thought of it. I have invariably kept in the back ground and avoided even reflecting voluntarily on anything of the kind knowing that Almighty God alone could effect it, if indeed it will be realized. My Father, Mr. Dubourg has always said the same, be quiet—God will in his own time discover his intentions, nor will I allow one word of entreaty from my pen—His blessed, blessed Will be done.

In my former letter I asked you if you could not secure your own property and build something for this purpose on the lot (which is an extensive one) given by Mr. Dubourg. If you should resolve to do so the gentleman interested will furnish

---

[x] Tonsure is one of the first steps a man takes when preparing for ordination to the priesthood. His hair is sheared and he is invested with the surplice.

the necessary expenditures for setting us off, and supporting those persons or children who at first will not be able to support themselves. Dr. Matignon will appoint a director for the establishment which, if you knew how many good and excellent souls are sighing for [this opportunity], would soon obtain an interest in your breast, so ardently desiring the glory of God. But all is in His Hands. If I had a choice and my will should decide in a moment, I would remain silent in His Hands. Oh how sweet it is there to rest in perfect confidence, yet in every daily Mass and at Communion I beg Him to prepare your heart and our dear Antonio's, to dispose of me and mine in any way which may please him. You are Our Father in him, thro' your hands we received that new and precious being which is indeed True Life. And may you in your turn be rewarded with the fullness of the Divine Benediction. Amen a thousand times.

MEA Seton[100]

Aside from the little inconsistency in the pledge "nor will I allow one word of entreaty from my pen," the letter shows quite clearly certain facts in regard to the original scheme for founding the community. First, the connection with Samuel Cooper began to have importance between 21 January and 8 February 1809. Second, the projected location was to be Baltimore. Finally, the Baltimore Sulpicians were not to be the superiors since Dr. Matignon would appoint a Director. As late as January 1810, Bishop Cheverus wrote of the possibility of Rev. J. S. Tisserant being associated with the sisterhood.[101] In any case, it is obvious that Mrs. Seton was quite compliant to whatever should appear to be the designs of Providence, but that she expected these designs to be manifested through the Filicchis in some way or another.

What part the Filicchi brothers might have played if they had received these letters early in 1809 can only be a subject for idle speculation. Months after Mrs. Seton had left Baltimore for Emmitsburg she wrote Antonio Filicchi that eighteen months had elapsed since she had received mail from Leghorn, and the letter that had just arrived was a year old.[102] This letter was the last she was to receive from the Filicchis until the end of 1815. The reason for the hiatus was the Continental System of Napoleon. This system, branded Napoleon's most grandiose conception, had first appeared, when in return for the cession of Hanover, Prussia had agreed to close her ports to the British. Later in 1806 the exclusion of British goods from the newly created Confederation of the Rhine, and the sealing of Naples together with virtually all of southern Italy, had extended the principle more widely. The Berlin Decree after the battle of Jena, proclaiming the British Isles to be in a state of blockade, and the Milan Decrees of 23 November and 17 December, denationalizing ships which entered British ports or submitted to British search, were replied to by British orders in council of 16 May 1806, and 7 January 1807. When Metternich prevailed upon the government of Vienna to co-operate with Napoleon by breaking off relations with England, after Tilsit, the continent of Europe was in fact closed against all British trade, and the "blockade became, officially at least, the law of Europe."[103] The Embargo Act which passed the United States House of Representatives in December 1807, only assisted Napoleon in closing the ports of Europe more effectively to trade.

Jean Cheverus wrote from Boston on 13 April 1809, that his last letter from Antonio bore the date of 26 March 1806, and he added that he hoped the rumor that Leghorn was to be a free port would prove true "so that we may have news from him and be able to write to him."[104] But Cheverus declined to act in Antonio's place, even though he had no doubt Filicchi would be eager to "lend a helping hand to your holy and useful establishment...What Mr. Dubourg proposed is not in my power. I am not authorized to do anything of the kind. I do not even know the name of Mr. Filicchi's correspondent in this country."[105] It seems evident that Dubourg had hoped Cheverus might secure funds for the new project in Antonio Filicchi's name.

Events did not wait for the Filicchi financial encouragement. Even before Cheverus took his pen in hand to reply to Dubourg's suggestion, Mrs. Seton's own pen had been busy. On 20 February 1809, she wrote to Rose Stubbs, a New York friend, that Mr. Cooper "has given a handsome property for the establishment of such females as may choose to lead a Religious life...We are going to begin our Novitiate in a beautiful country place in the mountains."[106] This letter hinted at the Emmitsburg site; one to Julia Scott the following month referred to that place, saying that Cooper was "about purchasing a place at Emmitsburg, some distance from Baltimore, not very considerable." The letter went on to sound out Julia's prospects as a possible investor in the new venture.

My Julia, when you write me, say if you have disposed of the funds which the embargo had embarrassed you with[y]... and if you would choose to lend three thousand or two thousand dollars on the best security in either Philadelphia or Baltimore to be refunded in a year. This question you will answer as to a stranger...It will be employed in the purchase of, or rather the arrangement of my future dwelling to be sure, but you are not to consider me in the case—[107]

Julia Scott replied immediately to her friend's inquiry, saying:

The funds you enquire about are already appropriated. Had your proposal been made at an earlier period, it might have prevented my engaging in a scheme of the eligibility of which I am by no means satisfied, but unable to invest my money to any advantage, the high rents and increased value of real property induced me to procure a lot of ground and commence building a house.[108]

Julia wrote at length of her objections to her friend's plan to leave Baltimore. How could Elizabeth think of exchanging such security for an uncertain new establishment which probably would not last? Mrs. Scott pointed out the difficulties to be faced in trying to combine rich and poor children in a single scheme, the arduous duties, the lack of experience. Further, Julia questioned, what of the Seton girls? Would they have the same advantages of education that Baltimore could offer? "My dearest friend," Julia lamented, "you will be overwhelmed—no peaceful hours, no peaceful moments will you know, anxiety and solicitude will cloud your days."[109]

Neither Mrs. Scott's apprehensions nor her inability to furnish financial aid deterred the completion of the plan. On 23 March 1809, Elizabeth replied "in unbounded confidence" that the difficulties were all gradually resolving themselves.[110] Samuel Cooper had purchased "a very valuable farm,[z] forty miles from this place, on which all the conveniences of life are abundant."[111] The necessary cash for the payment had been "immediately obtained from the brother of Mr. Cooper who was very glad to pay him the full value of his Philadelphia lots, as property of that kind is now so valuable."[112] The extent to which the vague plans of January had become clarified can be seen in the section of the letter which read:

---

[y] The Embargo Act had been passed in December and Baltimore received and enforced the law from 23 December 1807 to 16 March 1809. Citizens of Baltimore were all too familiar with the harmful effects of this law. The year Elizabeth Seton was in that city the exports of the state, largely those of Baltimore, dropped from over fourteen to less than three million dollars in value. In 1809, Baltimore had furnished five-sevenths of the state's export tonnage.

[z] The 269 acres of land included two tracts, one of 212 acres and the other, fifty-seven acres.

I shall be at the head of a community which will live under the strictest rules of order and regularity, but I shall not give those laws, nor have any care of compelling others to fulfill them if any person embraces them and afterward chooses to infringe them they will only find in me a friend to admonish, and it will be in the hands of Mr. Dubourg either to rectify or dismiss them. The order of Sulpicians...have a Seminary[aa] and a great part of their property at Emmitsburg on the Mountain where the farm in question is situated...I shall always be protected and taken care of as part of their family.[113]

Within two months time several changes had been made in the plan originally proposed to the Filicchis in January. Now Dubourg emerged clearly as the first superior of the nascent community; the Sulpicians were to be the ecclesiastical protectors of the group; Emmitsburg was the location of the motherhouse. In one respect the plan remained constant, that of encouraging both a "manufactory" and a boarding school for girls. Yet even the manufactory was to vanish in the problems of space, money, and necessity, after the relocation from Baltimore was accomplished.

If Mrs. Seton's disavowal of responsibility in her letter to Julia Scott was made to quiet Julia's fears, she admitted to Cecilia that Archbishop Carroll "at first hesitated on account of the children" whether she should take charge or not. Elizabeth wrote that she had assured the archbishop that Anna Maria was pleased to leave Baltimore and that even if they stayed in the world for her sake, she could be given none of the advantages society deemed necessary.[114] The fact of the matter was that Mrs. Seton was quite pleased to have an opportunity to remove her eldest daughter from Baltimore influences at this time. Although Anna Maria was only thirteen when the Setons went to Baltimore, Elizabeth told Julia that fall:

Since she is in Baltimore, the woman is so marked in her appearance and manner that indeed you would scarcely know her—her chest is very prominent and the shoulders quite in their right place—here she appears to advantage, as the girls associated with her dress in some style and she, of course, imperceptibly adopts their manner.[115]

The maturing beauty of the girl was noticeable to others as well as to her mother, and one of the young men of the college who saw Anna

---

[aa] This seminary of the Sulpicians was Mount Saint Mary's, Emmitsburg. This school for boys was founded in 1808 but the historians of the college disagree as to the exact details. By the spring of 1809, however, it was definitely underway, having been augmented by sixteen students from Pigeon Hill, Adams County, Pennsylvania.

Maria frequently at Mass at St. Mary's began to take an interest in the young lady. Before 1803 all the students, with few exceptions, came from the West Indies, foreign-born students continued to enroll during the early years.[116] Charles DuPavillon, the young man who became friendly with Miss Seton, was a resident of Guadeloupe who was completing his last year at the college during the winter of 1808-1809. Anna Maria was the recipient of bouquets and verses carried by her brothers, Richard and William, and before Mrs. Seton suspected the attachment it had become quite strong. From Father Babade, Mrs. Seton learned that DuPavillon seemed a sincere and solid young man of fortune, and that his only family was a charming mother who resided on the island; but Elizabeth's heart was filled with alarm by the sudden problem the girl's interest created. The acceptance of *billets-doux* or flowers without permission was in Elizabeth's world imprudence of real magnitude. It hurt the mother that, while Anna Maria was being secretive with her, the news had reached New York, and had given rise to gossip. Elizabeth wrote Dué:

> My Annina[bb]—so young, so lovely, so innocent, absorbed in all the romance of youthful passion—as I have told you, she has given her heart without my knowledge and afterwards what could a doating [sic] and unhappy Mother do but take the part of friend and confidant, dissembling my distress and resolving that if there was no remedy, to help her at least by my love and pity.[117]

Julia Scott, whose own daughter was far more mature, reproved Elizabeth for viewing poor Anna's conduct so severely. "I believe we expect too much from human nature if we hope *unlimited* confidence from our children, and Anna was too young and had been too little in society to be aware of the impropriety of receiving and answering a letter from a young man."[118] Julia feared much more the influence of the Caton girls, whose conduct was much less amenable to correction than Anna Maria Seton's.[cc] For her part, Anna Maria was very "sensible of the uneasiness and sorrow she had occasioned," and she became quite docile and eager to please her mother. Elizabeth, recalling her own impetuous youth, wrote to Julia, "Poor dear child, I do not know how she can be so patient; as I well remember at her age I should not have been."[119]

[bb] Anna Maria was affectionately called Annina during her visit to Italy and she went by that name for the rest of her life.

[cc] Mrs. Seton mentioned the unhappiness of the Catons over Emily's romantic tendencies. Emily, later Emily McTavish, is mentioned less frequently by historians than are Mary, Louisa, Elizabeth and Peggy Caton. Julia Scott's daughter, Maria, was friendly with the Caton family, visiting them in November 1808 and receiving Louisa in Philadelphia the following winter.

But until time could test the strength of the attachment, Mrs. Seton was relieved at the prospect Emmitsburg offered her eldest daughter, rather than otherwise. As for the boys, Richard and William could attend the Sulpician school at the Mountain as advantageously as in Baltimore, and thus remain near their mother. Rebecca and Catherine were still too young to be anything more than excited about living in the country. The move of Mrs. Seton's family to Emmitsburg in 1809 was not at all a foolhardy jaunt in that lady's eyes, and to many of her friends it sounded as logical as Mary Bayley Post seemed to find it, when she wrote on 6 May 1809:

> Since I cannot see you, Dear Sister, it must become my first pleasure to hear that you are well and happily situated. It has therefore been highly gratifying to hear an account of your new residence as you describe it, for its being so like what I have often heard you sigh for...It is of little consequence where that happiness is found, as I am convinced it will always be connected with piety and a desire to benefit others.[120]

By May the decision was firm for Emmitsburg. Elizabeth wrote Julia Scott that the middle of June was fixed as the time of departure, as the lease of the Paca Street house would be expiring at that time. She wrote firmly,

> Now, my dear friend, in His name I entreat you to be perfectly at ease on my account—every comfort and indulgence I could ever wish for will be mine—Mr. Dubourg has appointed a very amiable lady, who perfectly understands the management of things, steward of the family...And having almost as many assistants as there are new children going with us, and having an ample supply of all the good things a substantial country farm can produce, poultry, milk, etc., you can have no reason to be in the least anxious for us.[121]

By June the four candidates for the new community had appeared dressed alike in religious attire similar to that of Mrs. Seton's simple costume of mourning. It consisted of a black dress with a shoulder cape, set off by a simple white cap with black band which tied under the chin. On the feast of Corpus Christi 1809, the five women wore this habit for the first time at a public service, the Mass at St. Mary's Chapel. When Cecilia and Harriet Seton arrived in Baltimore on 12 June, they found their beloved "Sis" the leader of a small but very determined young community of religious women;

"estimable characters," Rachel Montgomery called them, "whose virtues and good example...will illuminate our darkened hemisphere, and disperse the clouds of prejudice which obscure the reasonable faculties of men."[dd]

On 21 June 1809, the feast of St. Aloysius Gonzaga, Elizabeth Seton set out for Emmitsburg. She took with her Anna Maria Seton, Anna Maria Murphy Burke, the invalid Cecilia Seton, and Harriet. Cecilia's health made her a logical choice for the first group to leave Baltimore, since it was believed the mountain air would prove beneficial. The younger Seton girls were to follow soon by carriage, while the boys would come in a wagon with the group left behind. By 30 July Cecilia O'Conway, Mary Ann Butler, Susan Clossy, Catherine Mullen, Rose Landry White, the Seton boys, and two students of the Paca Street School, Julia LeBreton, and Isabella Editha O'Conway, had arrived in the Valley.[122] The Paca Street house was closed and the Baltimore chapter of Elizabeth Seton's life was over.

[dd] Mrs. Montgomery was a Philadelphia convert of Rev. Michael Hurley, O.S.A., and a friend of Samuel Cooper. She had recently visited Baltimore and had promised to get material for the habits of the new community when she returned to Philadelphia. Her letter of 19 June reported her failure to secure "plain flannel" for the group she so intensely admired.

Notes

1 5.15, Elizabeth Seton to Eliza Sadler, Baltimore, 20 January 1809, *CW*, 2:50. In this chapter since most of Mrs. Seton's letters were written from Baltimore, place names will be omitted, except in those cases where Baltimore is not the place of origin.

2 Joseph Bayley to Elizabeth Seton, New York, 16 January 1809, ASJPH 1-3-3-2:98. Joseph Bayley had discussed the voyage with the captain of the *Grand Sachem* after his return from Baltimore.

3 5.15, Elizabeth Seton to Eliza Sadler, Baltimore, 20 January 1809, *CW*, 2:50.

4 5.1, Elizabeth Seton to Cecilia Seton, 9 June 1808, *CW*, 2:3.

5 Ibid., entry of 14 June 1808, *CW*, 2:3.

6 Ibid., *CW*, 2:4.

7 Thomas W. Griffith, *Annals of Baltimore* (Baltimore, 1824), p. 9. The census of 1810 gave the population as follows: white males, 19,045; females, 17,147; other free persons, 5,571; slaves, 4,672; total, 46,555. John O'Neill's *New and Easy System of Geography* (Baltimore, 1808), p. 119, gave the population of the city as 35,000.

8 "Diary of Jose Bernardo Gutierra de Lara," *American Historical Review,* XXXIV (January 1929), 281-282.

9 Ruthella Mary Bibbins, "City of Baltimore, 1797-1850," *Baltimore, Its History and Its People* (New York, 1912), 82-83.

10 William Dunlap, *Diary (1766–1839)* (New York, 1930), II, 375-6, entry for 1 February 1806. The manuscript of this portion of the *Diary* is owned by the Yale University Library.

11 Letitia Stock, *Baltimore, a Not Too Serious History* (Baltimore, 1936), 49-50.

12 John O'Neill, *New and Easy System of Geography and Popular Astronomy* (Baltimore, 1808), p. 119.

13 Ibid.

14 5.1, Elizabeth Seton to Cecilia Seton, 16 June 1808, *CW*, 2:6. See Rev. John M. Tessier's Journal, 9 June 1808, and 16 June 1808, ASMSU.

15 Ibid., *CW*, 2:7.

16 10.4, "Dear Remembrances," Corpus Christi, 1808, *CW*, 3a:520.

17 Frances Trollope, *Domestic Manners of Americans* (New York, 1904), p. 183.

18 5.1, Elizabeth Seton to Cecilia Seton, 17 June 1808, *CW*, 2:7.

19 5.22, Elizabeth Seton to Cecilia Seton, 3 April 1809, *CW*, 2:65.

20 Ibid., 64. The lower chapel was consecrated on 5 March 1809. Here Negroes were taught the Catechism.

21 5.6, Elizabeth Seton to Cecilia Seton, 12 August 1808, *CW*, 2:25. See Tessier's Journal, 18 July 1808, ASMS. The practice of ringing the Angelus three times a day on the chapel bell was begun at St. Mary's on 18 July 1808.

22 Pierre Babade, S.S., "Compliment d'Aglae Dubourg," Baltimore, June 1808,

ASJPH 1-3-3-4:1, 3. See Babade to Eccleston, 12 February 1833, AAB, AASMU, 24-A-8. Both French and English versions of this poetic greeting are preserved at Emmitsburg.

[23] 5.7, Elizabeth Seton to Antonio Filicchi, 20 August 1808, *CW*, 2:29; 5.5, Elizabeth Seton to Cecilia Seton, 8 August 1808, *CW*, 2:24; 5.10, Ibid., 6 October 1808, *CW*, 2:34.

[24] 5.15 Elizabeth Seton to Eliza Sadler, 20 January 1809, *CW,* 2:48.

[25] 5.2, Elizabeth Seton to Catherine Dupleix, 20 June 1808, *CW*, 2:9.

[26] James Silk Buckingham, *America, Historical, Statistic and Descriptive* (London, 1841), I, 457.

[27] 5.15, Elizabeth Seton to Eliza Sadler, 20 January 1809, *CW*, 2:48. See Tessier's Journal, 28 August 1805, ASMSU.

[28] John Carroll to James Barry, Baltimore, 29 December 1803, AAB, AASMU, 9-D-5. The ceremony took place on 24 December 1803.

[29] Jerome N. Bonaparte, Mount Saint Mary's Seminary, to Elizabeth Seton, 21 June [1816], ASJPH 1-3-3-4:100. On reverse are drafts of Elizabeth Seton, answer to above, and a comment of Simon Bruté. Young Jerome attended Mount Saint Mary's at Emmitsburg, and the archives of the college contain a letter from Eliza Patterson to John Dubois, Paris, 27 June 1816, expressing pleasure at the boy's progress and good conduct. The letter from the boy to Mrs. Seton was a request for an "Agnus Dei" to take home over a vacation and it referred to Jerome as "Your little child who always thinks of you with respect and love."

[30] 5.22, Elizabeth Seton to Cecilia Seton, 3 April 1809, *CW*, 2:65. For further reference to the Catons, see *Harpers,* LXI (September 1880), 489-495, for an article by Eugene L. Didier, "The American Graces."

[31] Robert Goodloe Harper to John Dubois, Emmitsburg, 30 September 1820, ASJPH 1-3-3-2:43; Josephine Seton to Juliana Sitgreaves Scott, 2 February 1821, ASJPH 1-3-3-11:B61.

[32] 5.1, Elizabeth Seton to Cecilia Seton, 17 June 1808, *CW*, 2:7.

[33] 5.3, Elizabeth Seton to Julia Scott, 4 July 1808, *CW*, 2:14.

[34] 4.56, Elizabeth Seton to Philip Filicchi, New York, 2 November 1807, *CW*, 1:481. See *Records of Catholic Historical Society,* XXIV (1913), 63; *Researches,* XIV (1897), 9.

[35] 5.8, Elizabeth Seton to Cecilia Seton, 26 August 1808, *CW*, 2:30.

[36] 5.21, Elizabeth Seton to Julia Scott, 23 March 1809, *CW*, 2:61.

[37] Theresa (Cecilia) Seton to Elizabeth Seton, 7 July 1808, ASJPH 1-3-3-4:202.

[38] 5.5, Elizabeth Seton to Cecilia Seton, 8 August 1808, *CW*, 2:24. John E. McGarity, C.S.P., "Reverend Samuel Sutherland Cooper, 1769-1843," states incorrectly that Cooper entered St. Mary's the fall of 1807. This biography of Cooper, published in *Records,* XXXVII (1926), 305-40, is unfortunately the only lengthy account available and perpetrates some other errors of this type. Cooper entered St. Mary's Seminary, Baltimore, 19 September 1808. See Tessier's Journal, 19 September 1808, ASMS;

39 Theresa (Cecilia) Seton to Elizabeth Seton, 4 August 1808, ASJPH 1-3-3-4:203. Louis Sibourd added several paragraphs in perfect English to this letter.

40 5.2, Elizabeth Seton to Catherine Dupleix, *CW,* 2:9. When Mrs. Seton said she was "two miles from the city," she probably meant the waterfront and business section. White gives the population of the city as approximately 46,000 in 1808. C. I. White, *Life of Mrs. Eliza A. Seton* (New York, 1853), 483.

41 5.3, Elizabeth Seton to Julia Scott, 4 July 1808, *CW*, 2:15.

42 5.4, Elizabeth Seton to Antonio Filicchi, 8 July 1808, *CW*, 2:19. See 5.2, Elizabeth Seton to Catherine Dupleix, (June 1808), *CW*, 2:9.

43 5.2, Elizabeth Seton to Catherine Dupleix, [June 1808], *CW*, 2:9.

44 5.3, Elizabeth Seton to Julia Scott, 4 July 1808, *CW*, 2:15.

45 5.2, Elizabeth Seton to Catherine Dupleix, [June 1808], *CW*, 2:10.

46 5.3, Elizabeth Seton to Julia Scott, 4 July 1808, *CW*, 2:15.

47 Cecilia Seton to Elizabeth Seton, 4 August 1808, ASJPH 1-3-3-4:204.

48 Louis Dubourg to Elizabeth Seton, Baltimore, 27 May 1808, AMSV.

49 5.9, Elizabeth Seton to Cecilia Seton, 5 September 1808, *CW*, 2:31.

50 5.11, Elizabeth Seton to Julia Scott, 3 October 1808, *CW*, 2:37.

51 5.13, Elizabeth Seton to Julia Scott, 6 December 1808, *CW*, 2:41.

52 5.14, Elizabeth Seton to Antonio Filicchi, 16 January 1809, *CW*, 2:46.

53 Ibid. Elizabeth Seton told Antonio Filicchi that if her school increased she would be "obliged to call" Cecil.

54 John Wilkes to Elizabeth Seton, New York, 29 August 1808, ASJPH 1-3-3-2:51.

55 George Dupleix to Elizabeth Seton, New York, 12 July 1808, ASJPH 1-3-3-11:33; Ibid., 24 August 1808, ASJPH 1-3-3-11:34.

56 Wright Post to Elizabeth Seton, 16 July 1808, ASJPH 1-3-3-11:2; Ibid., 29 September 1808, ASJPH 1-3-3-11:4.

57 Joseph Bayley to Elizabeth Seton, New York, 16 January 1809, ASJPH 1-3-3-2:98.

58 Harriet Seton to Elizabeth Seton, New York, 5 March 1809, ASJPH 1-3-3-8:75.

59 Harriet Seton to Elizabeth Seton, New York, 12 August 1808, ASJPH 1-3-3-8:72.

60 Harriet Seton to Elizabeth Seton, New York, 29 November 1808, ASJPH 1-3-3-8:74.

61 Harriet Seton to Elizabeth Seton, New York, 5 March 1809, ASJPH 1-3-3-8:75.

62 Cecilia Seton to Elizabeth Seton, New York, 8 July 1808, ASJPH 1-3-3-4:200.

63 Catherine Seton [of James] to Annina Seton, New York, 4 August 1808, ASJPH 1-3-3-4:107; Cecilia Seton to Elizabeth Seton, New York, 4 August 1808, ASJPH 1-3-3-4:204.

64 Cecilia Seton to Samuel Waddington Seton, New York, 22 December 1808, ASJPH 1-3-3-4:206.

65 Cecilia Seton to Elizabeth Seton, New York, 8 January 1809, ASJPH 1-3-3-4:208.

66 5.10, Elizabeth Seton to Cecilia Seton, 6 October 1808, *CW*, 2:33.

[67] Leo Ryan, *Old St. Peter's,* 97. Affairs in St. Peter's Church in 1808 worried Bishop Carroll who believed "the crisis is as important to Religion as can almost happen." With Sibourd's departure in August, John Byrne was left alone with a congregation estimated by some at "more than 52,000 souls." Carroll wrote to Kohlmann on 15 August, that he wished one of the Fenwicks and Kohlmann to go to New York if Sibourd should fail to return. See John Carroll to Anthony Kohlmann, 15 August 1808, Archives of Georgetown University, Washington, D.C., 65. Hereinafter cited as AGU.

[68] Cecilia Seton to Elizabeth Seton, New York, 8 January 1809, ASJPH 1-3-3-4:208.

[69] Cecilia Seton to Elizabeth Seton, New York, 5 March 1809, ASJPH 1-3-3-4:209.

[70] Ibid.

[71] 5.22, Elizabeth Seton to Cecilia Seton, 3 April 1809, *CW,* 2:64.

[72] Ibid.

[73] Cecilia Seton to Elizabeth Seton, New York, 20 March 1809, ASJPH 1-3-3-4:210.

[74] Samuel Waddington Seton to Cecilia Seton, New York, ASJPH 1-3-3-17:11.

[75] [Ethelinda] Agnes Seton to Annina Seton, New York, 31 May 1809, ASJPH 1-3-3-4:104.

[76] 5.28, Elizabeth Seton to Cecilia Seton, New York, n.d., *CW,* 2:72.

[77] Samuel Waddington Seton to Elizabeth Seton, New York, 25 May 1809, ASJPH 1-3-3-17:4. There seems to be a question as to whether Carlton Bayley, the young doctor, accompanied Cecilia Seton. This letter written just before the departure says he was unable to go. Mother Rose White's Journal at ASJPH, states that he did come; as do the Annals, I, 85.

[78] Cecilia Seton to Elizabeth Seton, New York, 20 March 1809, ASJPH 1-3-3-4:210.

[79] Ibid.

[80] Theresa (Cecilia) Seton to Elizabeth Seton, New York, 13 September 1808, ASJPH 1-3-3-4:205.

[81] 5.10, Elizabeth Seton to Cecilia Seton, 6 October 1808, *CW,* 2:34.

[82] *Records of the American Catholic Historical Society,* V (1894), 420-520, contains a brief biography of Cecilia O'Conway by Sara Trainer Smith entitled "Philadelphia's First Nun."

[83] 5.17, Elizabeth Seton to Philip Filicchi, 21 January 1809, *CW,* 2:53. See John Carroll to Elizabeth Seton, 24 March, no year, AMSV, I, 16.

[84] 5.22, Elizabeth Seton to Cecilia Seton, 3 April 1809, *CW,* 2:65.

[85] Ibid., 66.

[86] John Carroll to "My dear Sisters," 20 April 1809, Shea Transcripts, 31-3, AGU. See *The John Carroll Papers*, 3:84.

[87] 6.4, Elizabeth Seton to John Carroll, 6 August 1809, *CW,* 2:79.

[88] John Carroll to Elizabeth Carroll, Baltimore, 18 August 1809, Shea Transcripts, 31-3, AGU. See *The John Carroll Papers*, 3:92.

[89] Robert Goodloe Harper to John Dubois, 8 May 1817, AMSMU. For an interesting account of the Catons and their marriages into British nobility, see Annie Leakin Sioussat, *Old Baltimore* (New York, 1931), pp. 201-5. The wedding took place on 1 March 1817. Robert Goodloe Harper had married Emily Carroll, the second daughter of Charles Carroll, and was uncle to the Caton beauties.

[90] Eleanor Thompson to Elizabeth Seton, Emmitsburg, 2 May 1809, ASJPH 1-3-3-2:17.

[91] Jean Cheverus to Elizabeth Seton, Boston, 13 April 1809, ASJPH 1-3-3-1:10.

[92] A-5.10a, Sister Cecilia O'Conway, Memoir, 1805-1815, *CW*, 2:713. 5.19, Elizabeth Seton to Rose Stubbs, 20 February 1809, *CW*, 2:57.

[93] Ibid. Rose Landry White was the widow of Captain Joseph White.

[94] Louis Dubourg to Abbé Élèves, 15 June 1828, ASJPH 1-3-3-2:102. Cf. McGarity, 315. This copy of the Dubourg letter was made by Louis Regis Deluol, director of the Seminary of St. Sulpice at Paris, in 1858, for the Daughters of Charity at Emmitsburg. The original was then the property of Count Jules de Mensu who had received it from Abbé Élèves. It has sometimes been mistakenly assumed that the letter was written to Deluol.

[95] A-5.10a, Sister Cecilia O'Conway, Memoir, 1805-1815, 28 July 1809, *CW*, 2:713.

[96] 5.4, Elizabeth Seton to Antonio Filicchi, 8 July 1808, *CW*, 2:19.

[97] John Wilkes to Elizabeth Seton, Baltimore, 25 December 1808, ASJPH 1-3-3-2:52.

[98] 5.14, Elizabeth Seton to Antonio Filicchi, 16 January 1809, *CW*, 2:45.

[99] 5.17, Elizabeth Seton to Philip Filicchi, 21 January 1809, *CW*, 2:52.

[100] 5.18, Elizabeth Seton to Philip Filicchi, 8 February 1809, *CW*, 2:54. The M stood for Mary, Mrs. Seton's confirmation name.

[101] Jean Cheverus to Elizabeth Seton, Baltimore, 24 January 1810, ASJPH 1-3-3-1:11.

[102] 6.10, Elizabeth Seton to Antonio Filicchi, 8 November 1809, *CW*, 2:89. See Antonio Filicchi to Elizabeth Seton, 30 November 1808, ASJPH 1-3-3-10:39. The letter just received was written by Filicchi 10 November 1808.

[103] Louis Madelin, *The Consulate and Empire, 1789-1809* (New York, 1934), pp. 377-85; Geoffrey Bruun, *Europe and the French Imperium* (New York, 1938), 95-98.

[104] Jean Cheverus to Elizabeth Seton, Baltimore, 13 April 1809, ASJPH 1-3-3-1:10.

[105] Ibid.

[106] 5.19, Elizabeth Seton to Rose Stubbs, 20 February 1809, *CW*, 2:57.

[107] 5.20, Elizabeth Seton to Julia Scott, 2 March 1809, *CW*, 2:60. Cf. Thomas W. Griffith, *Annals of Baltimore* (Baltimore, 1824), pp. 187, 192.

[108] Julia Scott to Elizabeth Seton, Philadelphia, 15 March 1809, ASJPH 1-3-3-11: B24.

[109] Ibid.

[110] 5.21, Elizabeth Seton to Julia Scott, 23 March 1809, *CW*, 2:63.

[111] Ibid., 61.

[112] Ibid. A small note in Simon Bruté's writing in the archives of Mount Saint

Mary's University, Emmitsburg, reads, "14ʰ mars, 1809, resolve to buy the plantations of Emmitsburg to found Daughters of Charity..." The deed or indenture was drawn and recorded on 26 April 1809, at Frederick County Land Records. It stated that Robert Fleming for the sum of $6,961 deeded to Samuel Cooper, Louis Dubourg and John Dubois as "joint tenants forever" two tracts of land in "St. Mary's Valley," Frederick County. The deed was witnessed by William Emmit and Henry Williams. The original deed is in the possession of the Sisters of Charity, Emmitsburg, ASJPH 1-3-6-2f. The Frederick County Land Records Liber W. R. no. 35, folios 6, 7, 8, 9 record the deed.

[113] Ibid, 62. Cf. Charles G. Herbermann, *The Sulpicians in the United States* (New York, 1916), pp. 128-130; Joseph W. Ruane, *The Beginnings of St. Sulpice in the United States, 1791-1829* (Washington, 1935), pp. 158-186; Thomas F. O'Connor, "The Founding of Mount Saint Mary's College, 1805-1835," *The Maryland Historical Magazine,* XLIII (September, 1948), 197-210. See also Christopher J. Kauffman, *Tradition and Transformation in Catholic Culture. The Priests of Saint Sulpice in the United States from 1791 to the Present* (New York, 1988), 77-85.

[114] 5.22, Elizabeth Seton to Cecilia Seton, 3 April 1809, *CW,* 2:64.

[115] 5.11, Elizabeth Seton to Julia Scott, 3 October 1808, *CW,* 2:38.

[116] Charles F. Herbermann, *The Sulpicians in the United States* (New York, 1916), p. 96; James J. Kortendick, "History of St. Mary's College, Baltimore, 1799–1852," an unpublished master's thesis in the Mullen Library of the Catholic University of America (Washington, 1942), 8-13. See also Kauffman, *Tradition and Transformation*, 38-54.

[117] 6.45, Elizabeth Seton to Catherine Dupleix, Emmitsburg, 4 June 1810, *CW,* 2:138.

[118] Julia Scott to Elizabeth Seton, Philadelphia, 15 March 1809, ASJPH 1-3-3-11: B24.

[119] 5.20, Elizabeth Seton to Julia Scott, 2 March 1809, *CW,* 2:59.

[120] Mary Bayley Post to Elizabeth Seton, New York, 6 May 1809, ASJPH 1-3-3-11:7.

[121] 5.26, Elizabeth Seton to Julia Scott, 9 May 1809, *CW,* 2:69.

[122] A-5.10a, Sister Cecilia O'Conway, Memoir, 1805-1815, *CW,* 2:713. Cf. A-6.3a, Mother Rose White's Journal, *CW,* 2:717.

ᵩ∞ᵩ

CHAPTER 9

MOTHER SETON

The journey from Baltimore to Emmitsburg in 1809 could not be made in one day.[a] The route the women took that June passed through Westminster, and the road became rougher as their wagon drew farther away from Baltimore. As late as 1815 Rev. John Dubois was petitioning with the commissioners of Taneytown for "a turnpike road to be made between Westminster and Emmitsburg."[1] Northern Maryland, it is true, had developed rapidly in the early years of the nineteenth century, but the road to wealth lay through Frederick County. The Ellicott brothers had inaugurated a fine road to this wheat-growing area to supply the mills of Baltimore, and after 1805 demands were met for turnpikes to York, Reisterstown, and Frederick.[2] Carroll County developed more slowly, and Westminster did not become a county seat until 1837.[3] This village from which Mrs. Seton sent a note back to Baltimore, had been laid out in 1764 by William Winchester, and was named after him until confusion over the Virginia town of the same name led the Maryland General Assembly to adopt the name of Westminster. Elizabeth Seton used the earlier name when she reported to Louis Dubourg,[b] "We are so far safe tho' our progress is so much slower than you expected. Your turnpike is to be sure a very rough one and we were obliged to walk the horses all the way."[4] It may not have been until Saturday (24 June) that the tired women reached Emmitsburg and passed on to "Saint Mary's Mount" on the other side of the village.

The village of Emmitsburg was not yet twenty-five years old when Elizabeth Seton first saw it. Among the odd notes Rev. Simon Bruté left behind him was one which read, "Mrs. Hughes told me she thought it was about 1786 that she came on the spot of the present town then a complete wood."[5] According to local tradition the settlement was first called Poplar Fields and tradition has it that the first white man in the area was a Catholic,

[a] If the Seton party left on the feast of St. Aloysius Gonzaga, the trip took more than three days in 1809 since 21 June 1809, fell on Wednesday. [Dating the journey is baffling. See Rose Landry White recorded in her journal that "they left Baltimore on the 22nd." ASJPH 7-2-1, 2. Cecilia O'Conway also records 22nd June as the departure date, ASJPH 1-3-3-4:118, #1. Or did the travelers depart so early in the darkness that some scribes considered the pre-dawn darkness to still be 21 June although the women dated the trip in daylight as 22 June? It is also possible that the reference to departure on the feast of St. Aloysius was given to invoke blessing on the future mission of education of youth by the nascent sisterhood. 6.1, Elizabeth Seton to Louis Dubourg, *CW*, 1:74, was written from Winchester (sic, Westminster, Maryland) Friday afternoon, which in 1809 would have been 23rd June. Ed.].
[b] This would be 23 June 1809, if White, 256, is correct in regard to the date of departure. The date of 21 June given in *CW* is an error since Elizabeth Seton clearly writes "Friday afternoon," which would have been 23 June, unless Mrs. Seton was mistaken.

William Elder, who gave the Mountain its name in 1734.[6] There was already a Catholic church in the village, St. Joseph's founded in 1793,[c] when the Seton party went through.

The property on which the women intended to settle was not in readiness in June and so they rode by their valley farm and went on to the Sulpician settlement on the mountainside. Their first home was a

Log Cabin where the Setons stayed for six weeks at Mount St. Mary's College & Seminary.

log house situated half-way between the school buildings and the chapel on the hill.[7] It was originally designated as a retreat house for Baltimore Sulpicians, and later came to be called "Mr. Duhamel's House," but during the month of June 1809, it was the first home of the Sisters of Charity of St. Joseph's.[d]

Elizabeth Seton wrote happily to Matthias O'Conway, "We are half in the sky, the height of our situation is almost incredible—the chapel *elegant Simplicity*."[8] It was here that Elizabeth welcomed her daughters, Kit and Bec some days later, here that Sally Thompson joined the group whose arrival she had so impatiently awaited. Here, too, Harriet Seton began to go to Mass and evening adoration, and on one moonlight night in July made her decision to become a Catholic.[9] In later years Elizabeth was to recall that happy month with a grateful sigh, "Oh, oh, how sweet," and warm praise for the kind reception of Rev. John Dubois, (1764–1842), and Mrs. Thompson's assistance to the women her two daughters were joining.[e] By the end of July, however, the mountain interlude was over; for when the second group of women arrived from Baltimore the farmhouse in the valley

---

[c] Scharf, I, 590 states that Rev. Matthew Ryan was the first resident pastor. Bruté said Ryan came originally from Frederick. Ryan died on 5 January 1817, yet his name does not appear in any of the accounts after Mrs. Seton's arrival in Emmitsburg. On 15 August 1796, Father Francis Bodkin of Hagerstown wrote to Bishop Carroll, "I this day met a strange clergyman, a Mr. Ryan. He attends a congregation 34 or 35 miles from this, called Emmitstown." Apparently his active duties ceased before 1809 for John Dubois was in charge when Mrs. Seton arrived. Father Ryan may have been the priest of whom Dubois wrote in 1816, "When I used to live in Frederick town a scandalous priest was in charge of Emmitsburg, a character queer, violent, in fact insisting on money even to the extent of creating scenes at the altar ...the event had created a schism." See John Dubois to Antoine Gamier 18 April 1816, AMSM. Copies of letters in the Archives of St. Sulpice, Paris. In 1809 Charles Duhamel came from Hagerstown and was pastor until his death on 6 February 1818. Duhamel was succeeded in his turn by John Hickey, John Dubois, Simon Bruté, Samuel Cooper and Simon Bruté again. Bruté was in charge when Mrs. Seton died in 1821.

[d] The Sisters of Charity of St. Joseph's is the official name of the community founded by Mrs. Seton which appears in the 1817 *Act to Incorporate the Sisters of Charity of Saint Joseph's in Frederick County, Maryland*, ASJPH 3-1-3a.

[e] "Excellent Mrs. Thompson," the mother of Sally and Ellen Thompson, worked at the mountain college. 10.4, "Dear Remembrances," *CW*, 3a:522.

was ready to receive its occupants.[f] When Rev. Louis Dubourg returned to Baltimore on 31 July; his "family" members in Emmitsburg were happily united under their own roof.

The Stone House, as it has since been called, housed the young community through their first autumn and Christmas in the valley. It was far from offering all the comforts Elizabeth had so optimistically described for Julia Scott. Sixteen people, two-thirds of whom were adults, occupied four rooms, two upstairs and two down, with one of the small lower rooms used as a temporary chapel. The upstairs was in reality a garret where winter snow sometimes sifted over the women sleeping on the floor. At first only two cots were available, and these were continuously occupied by the sick members of the band. Elizabeth slept on her mattress side by side with Bec and Kit in the room adjoining the chapel. There was no pump inside the house, and drinking water came from a spring in a hollow west of the house; washing was carried further to Toms Creek and was scrubbed rigorously in tubs set up under the trees. Sister Sally Thompson was a godsend to the rest of the women during their first weeks of adjustment to these primitive conditions. Strong and cheerful, well-acquainted with the neighborhood, the Emmitsburg woman

The Stone House in Saint Joseph's Valley where the Sisters of Charity were founded 31 July 1809.

---

[f] The exact date of arrival at the farm house, or "Stone House" is subject to question. A long-standing tradition in St. Joseph's Valley has commemorated the arrival on 31 July 1809, but the fact is that 31 July is the foundation date of the Sisters of Charity of St. Joseph's. Evidence seems to point to an earlier date for the arrival of Mrs. Seton, her companions, daughters, and sisters-in-law. The entrance record at Mount St. Mary's College has the Seton boys listed on 28 July 1809. A chronology compiled by Bruté gives the date of removal to the farm house as 28 July 1809. Mother Rose White's journal says her party arrived before Sunday, and on Sunday heard Mass and talked with Louis Dubourg. Tessier's Journal reports Dubourg as being back in Baltimore on 31 July 1809, which was a Monday according to the calendar. It would seem clear that the women must have been in the farm house by 29 July 1809, which fell on a Saturday. The reason for not conclusively accepting 28 July is that Mother Rose's Journal describes the difficulty her party had in securing food on Friday night, a day of abstinence. It seems difficult to believe these women could have been mistaken about a Friday. Since Friday was 28 July it seems probable that the women moved from the mountain on 28 July, were joined on 29 July by Rose White's party, attended Mass together on Sunday, 30 July, and on 31 July 1809, they began their first new week as an integral unit. [31 July, feast of Saint Ignatius of Loyola, patron of the Jesuit missions in Maryland, marked the beginning of the sisterhood living a regular way of life in accord with *Provisional Regulations of St. Joseph's Sisters.* See A-6.4a, *CW,* 2: 737. Ed.]

willingly acted as business manager, making the purchases and directing the household concerns.[g]

The sisters were not always able to have Mass offered in their chapel since at this time Rev. John Dubois was the only priest stationed in the vicinity. He served Mount St. Mary's, St. Joseph's Church in the village of Emmitsburg, as well as the Stone House. But distance offered no barrier to these eager women. Often on Sunday they would tramp over to the mountain Mass after having already participated in an early one in town or at home. When the early Mass was offered at the farmhouse, the villagers attended. "It was a sight for angels to see," Sister Rose recorded, "the sick and the well, the young and the old, externs all crowded round the little altar and the sick beds."[10]

When the community was augmented by two new arrivals from New York, the Stone House literally overflowed, and it became necessary to send some of the sisters to sleep in the house which was being built for their permanent home. This house which is known today as the White House was the original "St. Joseph's House" of the community and served as the first motherhouse and ministry

St. Joseph's House, called the White House, where Mother Seton lived 1810-21.

center.[h] The basic log structure was completed but the plastering remained to be done. Six postulants impatiently awaited its completion so that they might be admitted,[11] but in December Elizabeth told Archbishop John Carroll, "There seems to be no intention of removing us to St. Joseph's[i] this winter. I have refused to give the least sentiment on the subject, there are so many difficulties in staying and dangers in going that unless obliged in

---

[g] The Journal of Mother Rose White contains a typical journal of events from June 1809 to August 1817, biographical details of sisters in the community, obituaries, letters and odd items. As second superior of the community Mother Rose was revered and her papers were preserved. A typed paginated copy of the original has been used for these citations. Both the original and the typed copy are preserved at the Daughters of Charity Archives, Emmitsburg, Maryland. There is a tradition that on the first Christmas the sisters had "some smoked herrings for their dinner and a spoonful of molasses for each." (White, 266.) But the ledger containing the account of the "Sisterhood of St. Joseph" in the archives of Mount St. Mary's University shows that in the month of December 1809, the women were charged with "5 dozen herrings, 19 lbs. beef, 13 lbs. lard, two turkeys, 1 goose, 128 ¾ lbs. beef, and 2 chickens." The last two items were secured on 29 December, but the turkeys and goose were listed under 24 December 1809. It would appear that the ladies could have eaten more than molasses and herring for their Christmas repast.

[h] The present "White House" is actually a restoration of the original and stands on a location twice-removed from the original site. Some of the timbers and floors are from the original, however, as are sections of the woodwork, the altar, and other cherished items.

[i] [Elizabeth Seton named the house under construction St. Joseph's House. Ed.]

Obedience, I cannot take it upon me."[12] By the middle of January, however, the crowded conditions at the farmhouse necessitated a trial of St. Joseph's House and Elizabeth told Carroll of their intention. If it proved too cold they could return. "Our moveables are not very weighty," she added drily.[13] Sisters Sally, Kitty, and Rose were named to go and for several weeks they slept in one of the new house's unfurnished rooms. When the weather proved stormy the three Spartans remained there all day, spinning at their wheels to keep busy, and the hardiest of the trio would cross the muddy, ploughed ground to bring them something to eat.[14]

Work on the log house progressed slowly and on 25 January Elizabeth noted in a letter to the archbishop that they were still waiting to settle in the new home.[15] Moving day finally arrived in February, and on the twentieth of that month the Blessed Sacrament was carried in procession from the Stone House to St. Joseph's by John Dubois, followed by the mother and her daughters. Cecilia Seton was so ill she had to be carried but she shared in the general rejoicing. The chapel was completed in March, and the first high Mass within its walls was sung on the feast of St. Joseph.

Elizabeth Seton later described the new house in the words, "We have an elegant little chapel, thirty cells holding a bed, chair and table each, a large infirmary, a very spacious refectory besides parlor, school room, my working room, etc."[16] But the first spring the community lived there it presented quite a different picture. The carpenters had not even finished and when the plastering was begun the women had to move from room to room to avoid the workmen. On occasion they lived in the hall, and as late as 23 July 1810, Mrs. Seton notified their superior that the masons had only completed the first coat on the cells.[17] Meanwhile the hair kept in the building for the plaster became infested with fleas and the women were plagued by bites while they dozed uneasily on the garret floor.[18] Gradually the shavings and chips were cleared from the yard and permanent steps replaced the blocks of wood at the front door. The house of St. Joseph was settled at last and the ardent community adapted itself to what was to be for most of them their last earthly home. Certainly for Elizabeth Seton it would witness many "miracles of grace," as Jean Cheverus termed them.[19] By the time Mary Magdalen Bayley Post visited her sister two springs later the affairs of the house were so well adjusted that Mary commented, on her return to New York:

> I left you, dear Sister, with sensations I cannot describe.
> It seemed to me as if I must have crossed the threshold of
> existence...It seemed to me I had actually seen an order of

beings who had nothing to do with the ordinary cares of this life and were so far admitted to the society of the blessed as to take pleasure in the same employments.[20]

The almost complete disregard for physical discomforts which amazed Mrs. Post was second nature to the women of the valley, and Elizabeth said rather impatiently to Julia Scott,

They tell me a hundred ridiculous stories are going about relative to our manner of living here, but I hope you will, not listen to them a moment, if they should reach you—and believe me again when I assure you that I have with my darlings true peace and comfort [in] every way.[21]

Housing problems produced only a momentary delay in the phenomenal growth of the household in the first years in Emmitsburg. Postulants came from many directions. New York contributed to the infant community not only the head, but many members as well. Rev. Anthony Kohlmann, S.J., after his passing reluctance to see Cecilia Seton join the group, became a constant sponsor of new entrants.[22] On 7 July 1809, he wrote of his pleasure that Susan Clossy was satisfactory to Mrs. Seton, and recommended another young woman, Jane Corbett,[j] who was a recent convert. By the time Elizabeth had sent her cordial reply to this communication, the Jesuit pastor of St. Peter's had another candidate, Martina Quinn,[k] to offer, with the remark:

The more, it seems, you are drawing nigh the time of the contemplated commencement of your religious institution,[l] the more the grace of God seems to work upon the hearts of those whom, from all Eternity, He has designed for the fulfilling of His holy will.[23]

Another New Yorker, Mrs. Eliza Grim,[24] was anxious to join Mrs. Seton at this time but she was discouraged by Elizabeth because of the difficulty of arranging for the Grim children.[m] Anthony Kohlmann frankly confessed that he hoped his own diocese[n] would eventually benefit from

---

[j] Jane Corbett was twenty-four at the time Kohlmann proposed her name. She came to Emmitsburg but did not remain long in the community. The community records give no details concerning her departure. She was back in New York City, however, when Jean Cheverus stopped there in December 1810. See Jean Cheverus to Elizabeth Seton, 4 January 1811, AMSV, Letters I, 2.

[k] Sister Martina Quinn died at St. Joseph's on 26 May 1816. She was sixteen when she came to Emmitsburg.

[l] At this time the sisters were living under a provisional rule at the stone farm house.

[m] Mrs. Seton finally arranged for one son, Charles Grim, at Mount St. Mary's on 19 April 1816. She used Filicchi funds provided for her own sons to pay for the Grim boy. Mrs. Grim had other children, however, to care for and there is no record that she ever entered St. Joseph's.

[n] Kohlmann left New York City in 1815, two years before the first Sisters of Charity of St. Joseph's arrived from Emmitsburg.

these contributions to Emmitsburg, and he anticipated the day when Mrs. Seton would return "a small colony of your great order to this city."[25] Again in 1811 he recommended three women to St. Joseph's, this time a mother and her two daughters. Mrs. Corish, the mother, he explained, "wishes to accompany her daughters° to your convent both to be edified by the example of your pious community and to render in the teaching line all the services in her power."[26]

The New York Jesuit was not alone in giving encouragement to the new group. Rev. John Francis Moranvillé, C.S.Sp., (1760-1824), the zealous pastor of St. Patrick's Church in Baltimore, had begun his efforts in Mrs. Seton's behalf while she was yet in Baltimore. It was there he introduced Elizabeth Boyle and Ann Gruber to their future mother. After the Emmitsburg establishment was started Moranvillé continued to foster vocations in these young women and he informed Elizabeth, "I communicated your affectionate remembrance to Betsy and Ann...they would not refrain their tears; oh, how they long to see themselves united to the dear family."[27] When the sisters moved from the farmhouse to St. Joseph's they were able to welcome Father Moranvillé's postulants, who arrived on 16 March 1810.[28]

Father Moranvillé sent boarders to Mrs. Seton's school, as well. Writing to Sister Elizabeth Boyle in 1811 he said:

> I am sorry to hear that our good Mother is in a poor state of health. I wish from my heart that God may long preserve her for the good of the community which she supports by her example and her activity. Present her with my best respects and ask her when it will be time to send the three young ladies as boarders from Fell's Point, and what they are to be provided with.[29]

When a group of women hoping to become the nucleus of a Trappist convent met with serious setbacks in 1812, Moranvillé suggested that they come to Emmitsburg to join Mrs. Seton. But this tentative plan failed to materialize immediately and the Baltimore priest wrote in October:

> You will not see our poor Trappist Sisters;[p] the Superior having promised them to receive them into the order they first chose, they thought it was their duty to wait still more...

° The daughters, Benedicta and Camilla Corish, remained at St. Joseph's but the mother, apparently desiring a more cloistered life, later became a Visitation nun.

[p] This probably was written in 1812 since a letter dated 12 April 1812, also deals with the proposed Trappist convent. The group planned to settle in Pennsylvania at that time. In January 1813, the women were still in Baltimore and Moranvillé said of Mrs. Seton, "Tell her candidly I have wished this long while to have here another like herself to be at the head of my poor Trapists [sic]. The Superior we had has been these six weeks absent from the convent for cause of a weak health."

I was ready to go with them to Emmitsburg...I hope that... their attachment to their first calling will not be unfavorably interpreted by your dear family.[30]

The Trappist experiment was doomed to failure nevertheless, and in 1814 when the group withdrew from the United States, the American subjects were given the privilege of remaining. Four of these nuns[q] came to St. Joseph's "at the earnest solicitation of Rev. Mr. Moranvillé," on 27 November 1814.[31]

Rev. John Baptiste David, (1761–1841), who became the second superior of the sisterhood, also added recruits. Arriving at St. Joseph's for a retreat on 1 August 1810, he was accompanied by Fanny Jordan, Angela Brady, and Julia Shirk, all of whom proved valuable additions to the household. Nor did Rev. Louis Dubourg, their first superior, forget the community when he went to Martinique in 1810, for his health. Soon after his return to Baltimore in early July 1811, he wrote exuberantly to Elizabeth:

Behold, I am just arrived, and what will please, if not surprise you, I sit down to write to your Reverence even before I have seen any of my friends in this part of the world. Pretend after this to be ignorant of the rank you hold in my affections. I bring you two novices and one rather advanced in age...who can patiently sit a whole day at the workbasket, a piece of furniture which you told me you stood in great need of...[32]

Dubourg's three protégées were Louise Rogers, Adele Salva, and the latter's sister, Madame Guérin. Mme. Guérin brought her only son [Eugène] and placed him at Mount St. Mary's College where the widows of the community educated their sons.[r] Mme. Guérin served as an added tie between Boston[s] and Emmitsburg since Bishop Cheverus was interested in her welfare.[33] Contrary to Dubourg's expectations, she became a sister in the community, and until her death in 1816 she was noted for her pious and industrious example.

---

[q] Two of these women, Scholastica Bean and Mary Joseph Llewellyn, remained and died happily as Sisters of Charity. [Lewellyn is also spelled Llewellyn.]

[r] These children later elicited from John Dubois the comment, "Experience has proved to me that although children of a mother who has come to St. Joseph's commands a double interest from us, they rivet our chains. If they turn out well they double our joy. If they prove worthless, we are hemmed up between the feelings of the mother and the dearest interests of our institutions," John Dubois to John Hickey, 5 November 1818, AMSMU. Francis Guérin entered on 23 July 1811. [ASJPH records give the son's name as Eugène Guérin. He continued at Mount Saint Mary's until his mother died. Sometime after 1816 he returned to Martinique. See Joseph Mannard, "Widows in Convents of the Early Republic: The Archdiocese of Baltimore, 1790-1860, *U.S. Catholic Historian*, 26, no. 2 (Spring 2008), 111-32. Ed.]

[s] Mme. Guérin was related to the Wallys of Boston; Thomas Wally was one of Cheverus' "fervent converts."

After Louis Dubourg was appointed administrator of the Diocese of Louisiana his affection for the Maryland community continued.[t] Writing from New Orleans on 1 September 1813, he told Simon Bruté at the Mount that although the time had not yet come to establish Sisters of Charity in New Orleans he wished Bruté to "beg of them and their dear Father Superior to keep us in their good will for God's own hour. Commend me to their prayers and assure them that I do not cease to bear them in my heart."[34] On a later occasion he told Bruté:[u]

> The good news of the valley and mountain covers me with joy. Be assured that my heart is there and will always be. Are they not my children? *Majorem non habeo gratiam quam ut audiam filios meos in charitate ambulare.* The day when I can have a swarm of bees from the hive of St. Joseph's will be a great day for me.[35]

Bishops Benedict Flaget and Jean Cheverus, as well, had the sisterhood's interests at heart, although their efforts were to prove less fruitful as far as the membership of the community was concerned. It was Cheverus who had first directed the Trappistine, Sister Mary Joseph Lewellyn,[v] southward with the remark, "The sister is a very sensible woman and would, I think, make an excellent instructress of youth. Should her expected companions not arrive, I think she would be a valuable acquisition to the Sisterhood at Emmitsburg."[36] But a later attempt to direct a postulant to St. Joseph's proved abortive. A young woman of "pretty good English education" and a "strong desire" to become a sister disappointed the Boston prelate.[37] On 20 January 1815, Cheverus confessed to Elizabeth, "The poor creature has dropt on the road vocation, letters, and even gratitude, for she has not favored me with a line...No more of her. Our intentions were pure, the event is in a higher control."[38]

Bishop-elect Benedict Flaget attempted to bring over French sisters but his effort was to prove equally barren. On his trip to France in 1810 Flaget had visited a "manufacture" carried on by little orphan children of Bordeaux under the direction of the Daughters of Charity.[39] Flaget suggested that some of these women might come to Emmitsburg, perhaps with the knowledge that one of the objectives of the original Cooper-Seton scheme was "to found a manufactory on a small scale which may [prove to] be very

[t] Chief among Archbishop Carroll's reasons for appointing Dubourg to New Orleans was among which was Dubourg's ability to speak three languages. Dubourg was about forty-five years old at the time of his appointment.

[u] In this letter Dubourg requested "four or five Sisters capable of teaching." The first Sisters of Charity from Emmitsburg did not leave for Louisiana, however, until 20 December 1829, at the request of Bishop Joseph Rosati, C.M.

[v] Sister Mary Joseph Llewellyn and two Trappist monks left Boston on 1 November 1811, and went to St. Inigoe's, Maryland, where Father Moranvillé became interested in their concerns.

beneficial to the poor."[40] In any case, French sisters would prove helpful in training the American women in the spirit and usages of the rule of St. Vincent de Paul and St. Louise de Marillac which Flaget intended carrying to St. Joseph's on his return. Three French sisters,[w] Sister Marie-Anne Bizeray (1778–1849), Sister Servant (local superior), Sister Augustine Chauvin (1765–1818), and Sister Marguerite Woirin (1762–1844), were selected to make the journey to the United States, and on 12 July 1810 the women wrote to "Our Sisters of Mount St. Mary's aspiring to be of the company of the Daughters of Charity," and they voiced their hope of joining the American community.[41] The French *Common Rules of the Daughters of Charity* were brought to Emmitsburg that August, but the French sisters never arrived.

It has always been assumed that the French women did not leave Europe because of obstacles thrown in the way by Bonaparte's government which denied them passports.[42] Undoubtedly these obstacles created some delay. But other considerations developing meanwhile in the United States may have played a larger part than has been hitherto suggested. The discussion of the French rules during the year 1810-1811 brought to the fore the difficult position Elizabeth Seton held as a mother of five dependent children while she simultaneously acted as the spiritual mother of an infant community. Writing to her close friend John Carroll on 5 September 1811, Elizabeth explained:

> The constitutions proposed have been discussed by our Rev. Director [Dubois] and I find he makes some observations on my situation[x] relative to them, but surely an individual is not to be considered where a public good is in question, and you know I would gladly make every sacrifice you think consistent with my first and inseparable obligations as a Mother.[43]

Carroll was always as concerned as Elizabeth herself over the welfare[y] of her five children[44] and he replied immediately, "Before anything is concluded you will hear from me or if possible, we shall see one another. My great anxiety is for the benefit, and consequently, the quiet, union, and perfect contentment of yourself and your interesting family."[45] But the archbishop's concern did not prevent the discussion over Elizabeth's position from waxing warmer in Baltimore and Emmitsburg.

---

[w] The full names of the sisters are: Sister Marie-Anne Bizeray, Sister Augustine (Ange Françoise) Chauvin, and Sister Marguerite (Marie) Woirin. Community records list Marguerite Woirin as Voisin although Woirin appears clearly in her signature.

[x] Mrs. Seton was a widow and mother with minor children who were dependent on her.

[y] Mrs. Seton wrote that Carroll "considers my welfare more than I do myself & the 5 dear ones as his own."

218

Elizabeth's own mind was very clear in regard to her obligations. Even before the French rules arrived she had told Julia Scott:

> The thought of living out of our Valley would seem impossible, if I belonged to myself, but the dear ones have their first claim which must ever remain inviolate. Consequently if at any period the duties I am engaged in should interfere with those I owe to them, I have solemnly engaged with our good Bishop Carroll, as well as my own conscience, to give the darlings their right, and to prefer their advantage in everything."[46]

As the discussion of the rules progressed, her conviction never wavered. In February 1811, she told Dué, "By the law of the church I so much love I could never take an obligation which interfered with my duties to them, except I had an independent provision and guardian for them, which the whole world could not supply to my judgment of a mother's duty."[47] To George Weis,[z] Elizabeth confessed wearily, "The only word I have to say to every question is, *I am a Mother.* Whatever providence awaits me consistent with that plea I say Amen to it."[48] [About six months before, a weary but faith-filled Mrs. Seton had written Weis: "Everything here is again suspended and I am casting about to prepare for beginning the world again with my poor Annina, Josephine and Rebecca, as we have reason to expect from many things passed lately that our situation *is more unsettled than ever* but, we will be ...[in any] case under the refuge of the most high."[49] Ed.]

The proposed addition of French Sisters at this juncture presented several difficulties. On 13 May 1811, Elizabeth begged Archbishop Carroll for advice and aid in clarifying her situation. Her questions suggested some of the points of discussion in regard to the rules and the French women. She asked:

> What authority would the Mother they [the French sisters] bring have over our Sisters (while I am present?)...How could it be known that they would consent to the different modifications of their rules which are dispensable if adopted by us? What support can we procure to this house but from our Boarders, and how can the reception of Boarders sufficient to maintain it accord [sic, be reconciled with] with their statutes? How can they allow me the uncontrolled privileges of a Mother to my five darlings?...My duty to [my Anna]

---

[z] George Weis was a Baltimore resident whose family befriended Mrs. Seton's group when they started for Emmitsburg in 1809. He remained a helpful friend to the community during his lifetime. His name was spelled "Wise," "Wyse," and "Weise" on different occasions. He used "Weis," himself.

alone would prevent my throwing her in her unprotected [sic, unmarried] state in the hands of a French Mother.[50]

The issue of the French sisters went beyond the question of Elizabeth Seton's personal position, however. It involved a disagreement over general policy between Sulpicians Flaget, David, and possibly Dubourg on one hand and Carroll, Dubois, and to a lesser extent, Cheverus on the other.[51] Both John David and Benedict Flaget advocated the immediate importation of French sisters accompanied by a strict application of the rule of St. Vincent de Paul and St. Louise de Marillac.[52] The more conservative party believed that some modifications in the rules would be necessary in Emmitsburg, and that the time was not ripe for a union with France. Archbishop Carroll, with his Anglo-Irish background, was more prone to stress the disparity between the French milieu which had nurtured the rules and the Maryland scene in which they were to operate. Recalling the controversy three years later he said:

> At the very institution of Emmitsburg, tho it was strongly contended for its being entirely conformable to & the same with the Institute of St. Vincent of Paul, yet this proposal was soon and wisely abandoned for causes, which arose out of distance, different manners, and habits of the two countries, France & the U.S.[53]

It is quite possible that John Carroll would have preferred an entirely American community under his own supervision. There seems to be a hint of such a preference in two remarks he addressed to Mrs. Seton. The first, made in 1809 before the French issue was posed, suggests that it had not been the archbishop's idea to have even the gentlemen of St. Sulpice direct the infant community. He said:

> You know, ever honoured and most esteemed Madame, that after the choice made by yourselves, your chief benefactor, of living under the protection of the priests of St. Sulpice, I surrendered, as much as a Bishop can surrender, your government into their hands.[54]

Whether or not this remark implied any chagrin at the choice the women made in 1809 to exchange Carroll's superintendence for that of the French Sulpicians, Carroll's comment in 1811, after the rules were finally adopted, cannot be misunderstood. He said bluntly:

> I am rejoiced...that the idea of any other connection than of charity is abandoned between the daughters of St. Joseph's

and the Society of St. Sulpice; I mean that their interests, administration and government are not to be the same, or at least under the same control. No one of that body but your immediate superior, residing near you, will have any share in the government or concerns of the sisters, except (on very rare and uncommon occasions) the superior of the seminary of Baltimore, but not his society [the Sulpicians]. This, however, is to be understood so as not to exclude the essential superintendence and control of the Archbishop over every community in his diocese.[55]

If the archbishop was jealous of his own authority, the Society of St. Sulpice in the United States had members who were equally anxious to prevent their control over the Emmitsburg community of women from passing into other hands. John Dubois was evidently opposed to a union with France at this time, for Cheverus had written to Elizabeth from Boston on 4 January 1811:

I concur in opinion with Mr. Dubois about the propriety of your establishment remaining independent from the Sisters [Daughters] of Charity & continuing to be merely a house of education for young females...However I have some reason to think as you do, that very likely things will speak for themselves & show the usefulness & necessity of leaving you in your present situation. Have another conversation with the Rev. Mr. Dubois on the subject & then do with simplicity what he will prescribe or even wish.[56]

It was after she received this letter that Elizabeth wrote to Carroll the detailed queries about her own position. It is possible that her letter was prompted by questions outlined by Dubois.

John Dubois was not opposed to union with France, except at this particular time and under these particular circumstances. In 1816, when he was overburdened with two parishes, a college and seminary, and the sisterhood, he reported to Paris:

I desire more than anything else in this world to be free of the care of the sisters but I see no other hope than that of uniting them to some other society to take care of them. If the reverend superior approves, I will try to enter into correspondence on this subject with the superior of the

Fathers of the Mission,[aa] formerly Lazarists, to see if it were not possible to form a union between the sisters here and those in France...[57]

Although this suggestion came to naught, it is obvious that Dubois was not categorically opposed to eventual union with France.

The Cheverus letter contained a reference to a third factor complicating the French issue: the different interpretations given the functions and purposes of Mrs. Seton's group. This last factor was probably more influential in preventing the arrival of French sisters in 1811–1812 than either of the other two. Although both the Rule of St. Vincent de Paul and the openly avowed purposes of the St. Joseph's community included educational and charitable work, the Daughters of Charity in France at this time were predominantly engaged in charitable activities while the Emmitsburg group was chiefly concerned with the school for girls which was their solitary means of support. There was no question of incompatibility. St. Vincent, as early as 1649, had discussed the work of Sisters employed in teaching schoolgirls. In another conference addressed to the French sisters in 1653 he had said clearly, "The spirit of the Company consists in giving yourselves to God to love Our Lord and to serve Him corporally and spiritually in the person of the poor in their homes or elsewhere; to instruct poor young women, children, and generally all those whom Divine Providence may send you."[58] Elizabeth Seton's community, from its very inception at Baltimore, had cherished the hope of being "very beneficial to the poor."[59] It was, rather, a question of emphasis which in the end operated against a union with France at that time. Although the archbishop was a poor prophet, Carroll believed in 1811 that:

> A century will pass before the exigencies and habits of the country will require and hardly admit of the charitable exercises toward the sick, sufficient to employ any number of sisters out of our largest cities. Therefore they must consider the business of education as a laborious, charitable, and permanent object of their religious duties.[60]

He was still convinced in 1814 that while in France "the soul and life of St. Vincent's institution" was attendance on hospitals and the sick, "yet here in America no more can be required of [the sisters] than a disposition of readiness to embrace that charitable duty, if imposed

---

[aa] [The Congregation of the Mission founded by St. Vincent de Paul in France in 1625, is commonly called the "Lazarists" after their first mother house in Paris, Saint Lazare. In most English-speaking countries they are called "Vincentians." Ed.]

on them."[61] Yet almost at that very moment sisters from Emmitsburg were planning to leave for Philadelphia to take over an orphanage!

Carroll was not alone in fearing this difference in emphasis in 1811. By October even Bishop Flaget, who originally favored the importation of French sisters, confessed to Simon Bruté:

> I dread the arrival of the religious women who are to come from Bordeaux. . .Their hopes will be frustrated; they will be unhappy, be it at Baltimore or at Emmitsburg. If there were yet time to turn them back, I would be of the opinion it should be done. I would wish at least that they be informed in detail of the spirit which reigns in the house at Emmitsburg, of the slight hope of serving in hospitals, and if they wish to come after that, we would not have to reproach ourselves.[62]

It is a matter of history that, when David and Flaget organized the Sisters of Charity of Nazareth in the Diocese of Bardstown not long afterward, they did not import French sisters, but made their first requests for women from Emmitsburg. The requirements of the American frontier community in the first decades of the nineteenth century were noticeably different from those of the older civilization of Europe. When Archbishop Ambrose Maréchal, (1764–1828), the successor to John Carroll, made a report to Cardinal Lorenzo Litta[bb] in 1818 he praised the Emmitsburg "Daughters of St. Vincent de Paul" as:

> Sisters who live holy lives according to the rules of their holy founder, with the exception of the modifications demanded by American customs and dispositions. They do not take care of hospitals nor could they since the administration of these hospitals is Protestant. Their principal work is the pious education of Catholic girls, those of the poor as well as those of the rich.[63]

Thirty years and more would elapse before the urbanization of the eastern seaboard and the expanding charitable activities of American Sisters of Charity would completely erase this difference in emphasis. It was not until 1850 that the union with France occurred but as a result of different circumstances of time and place. General Assemblies held in Paris by the Society of Saint-Sulpice during post-Revolution France issued mandates which obliged the

---

[bb] Cardinal Lorenzo Litta was Prefect of the Sacred Congregation for the Propagation of the Faith (1814-1818) at the Vatican.

Baltimore Sulpicians to take action which would enable them to solely focus on their founding charism of preparation of candidates for the priesthood.

It seems clear, then, that in addition to the barriers erected by the Napoleonic regime in France, the migration of the women from Bordeaux was further discouraged by conditions and sentiments prevailing on the other side of the Atlantic. There was a definite reluctance on the part of Elizabeth's friends, Carroll, Dubois, and Cheverus, to have her position complicated while her children were still dependent upon her. There was an absence of clearly defined agreement as to the general superintendence of religious orders and communities in the still young Archdiocese of Baltimore. But principally, there existed in 1811–1812 a very marked difference between the immediate needs of the Church on the American, Protestant frontier and the experience of the Daughters of Charity in the more stable, Catholic society of Europe. After 1812, the subject of the French sisters never loomed large again while Elizabeth Seton lived.

In spite of the final failure of Flaget's attempt to introduce French women, he deserves full credit for bringing to the community in Emmitsburg the rules which they were to adopt with minor modification. This rule guided all Setonian Sisters of Charity until the Vatican II renewal which gives contemporary expression to the Charity charism in the Vincentian tradition.[cc] Before receiving the French rules, St. Joseph's community had lived according to thirteen provisional rules.[64] The women had made their first retreat in August 1809, at the farmhouse under the direction of Louis Dubourg. That same month they had set up a council of three to assist Mrs. Seton and Rose Landry White, the first and second in charge. The council members were Catherine Mullen, Cecilia O'Conway, and Cecilia Seton.[65] No permanent pattern of religious life was adopted or confirmed until January 1812. It is scarcely surprising that some confusion and dissension arose to plague the infant community.

On 22 August 1810, Benedict Flaget left Baltimore for Emmitsburg, carrying with him a manuscript copy of the *Common Rules* of the Daughters of Charity which he had secured in France.[66] Several months elapsed while the rules were being put into English copies and not until December did Elizabeth write to Archbishop Carroll, "The Superior desires me to send the constitutions of the Sisters of Charity which Rev. Mr. Flaget brought, as you now have leisure to consider them."[67] More than a year passed before these rules were officially confirmed by Archbishop John Carroll and Rev. John M. Tessier, the superior of the Sulpician seminary in Baltimore. Much

---

[cc] The Vincentian tradition includes the spirit and teachings of Saints Vincent de Paul and Louise de Marillac.

of this delay was undoubtedly caused by the serious controversy over superiors, both within and without the house of St. Joseph's, which reached a climax in 1811. Another cause for delay was the series of discussions over the degree of modification necessary to adapt the rules to American conditions and Mrs. Seton's peculiar situation. A third cause for delay was the disagreement over the exact authority of the archbishop and the Society of St. Sulpice over the sisterhood.

After all the adjustments were made, the constitution and rules remained substantially the same as those Flaget had brought from France.[dd] Minor modifications allowed Elizabeth Seton to be head of the community in spite of the dependence of her five children, included education of the young as a specific purpose of the community, and allowed the taking of boarders. The enforcement of the rules and amendments to be made in the future would require the approval of the archbishop, the superior of the Sulpician seminary in Baltimore, and the superior of the community residing in Emmitsburg. When the amended copy was forwarded to Carroll Mrs. Seton said, "The rules proposed are nearly such as we had in the original manuscript of the Sisters of France. I never had a thought discordant with them as far as my poor power may go in fulfilling them."[68] The archbishop replied that it afforded him great pleasure "to learn that all material points on which a difference of opinion was thought to exist" had been cleared up. "I shall and do now give my approbation," he wrote, "to the Constitution exhibited to me by Mr. Dubois after they shall have received the alterations suggested by him."[69] The amended rules were adopted by the women themselves with only one dissenting vote.[70] The final confirmations by the archbishop and John Tessier[ee] were made on 17 January 1812.[71] In the words of John Carroll, the sisters were now freed "from a state in which it was difficult to walk straight;" they were able to live by a permanent and acceptable plan.

While the matter of uncertainty over rules was causing confusion, the question of superiors for the community produced outright resentment, and at one time it seemed to threaten the very existence of the sisterhood

---

[dd] At this time the Daughters of Charity in France were governed by documents promulgated by successors to St. Vincent de Paul in the office of superior general of the Congregation of the Mission and the Daughters of Charity: *Common Rules* (René Alméras, 1672) and *Statutes* (Jean Bonnet, 1718). The *Statutes* dealt with the juridical nature of the Company of the Daughters of Charity and may be considered like a Constitution. This is probably the document the Sulpicians and others referred to as constitutions. Sister Rose White in her Journal wrote: "Rev. Mr. Flaget returned from France and brought us the rules, constitutions, and conferences of Sisters of Charity founded by St. Vincent de Paul." A-6.3a, Sister Rose White's Journal, *CW,* 2:730. See also Ellin Kelly, Appendix A "The Rule of 1812," and Appendix B, "Constitutions of the Sisters of Charity in the United States of America," *Numerous Choirs,* 1:243-80.

[ee] Rev. John Mary Tessier had become superior of the Sulpician seminary in Baltimore after Rev. Charles-François Nagot resigned on 8 November 1810.

itself. At this point the historian must proceed with the greatest caution since the documentation is very scanty and, in some instances, incomplete. Personalities appear to serious disadvantage. The several complex issues of the first years of the community are all interwoven. In some respects final judgment must be withheld, but it must be suspected that the controversy was the most dangerous the infant establishment experienced.

At the very outset, when the women placed themselves under the protection of the Sulpicians in Baltimore, it was expected that Rev. Charles-François Nagot, S.S., would be their superior. Elizabeth had written to Julia Scott:

> The Superior of our Seminary here, who is graced with all the venerable qualities of seventy-five, which is his age, a mind still strong and alive to the interests of our little family as if we were all his own...is going to take charge of our community and reside in Emmitsburg.[72]

Nagot had gone with Dubourg and Cooper to supervise the final arrangements for the Emmitsburg property in April 1809.[73] But the old man's health was not robust, and after his serious illness that summer it became clear that he should not undertake the task. Carroll agreed that Nagot should resign as superior at Baltimore, if he insisted, but stipulated that the Sulpician remain at the seminary at least until May of the following year. In regard to Emmitsburg, the archbishop warned, "You cannot have the same assistance spiritual and temporal always at hand as in Baltimore. Mr. Dubois must often be obliged to be absent."[74]

Louis Dubourg thus came to act as the first superior of the Sisters of Charity of St. Joseph's at Emmitsburg. His reign was brief and not entirely happy. Almost as soon as the first sisters arrived in Emmitsburg dissatisfaction arose over Dubourg's policy in regard to correspondence. The women were forbidden to write to their former confessor in Baltimore, Pierre Babade. Elizabeth admitted to Archbishop Carroll that Father Babade was "the only one of nine different priests I have confessed to from necessity, to whom I ever yet had opened my heart or been able to draw the consolation and instruction so necessary to my situation."[75] Being a convert, she explained, and very much left to herself in spiritual devotions, how could she help being gratefully attached to the "one who has shown unceasing care for my soul, done everything to enlighten it and discover to it the full consolation of our holy faith."[76] Father Babade was beloved by most of the other women as well. In the short time Cecilia and Harriet Seton had known him, he had become their close friend. The zealous priest was consumed with a desire to see Harriet within the fold, addressing her as his "dear new child in Jesus Christ, and soon, I hope, in his holy church, our common mother."[77] After Harriet went to Emmitsburg a veritable torrent of supplication followed her, and Babade's joy knew no bounds when Harriet made her first Communion that September.[78] Mrs. Seton's daughters were equally fond of the white-haired Sulpician and they had begun an exchange of little notes even before they left Baltimore. Except for Rose White and Kitty Mullen, who had joined the group close to the eve of departure, all the women were "of one heart and voice with respect to Father B."[79]

The restriction on writing, then, came as a blow to these religious children of Pierre Babade. The five sisters, Cecilia Seton, Cecilia O'Conway, Mary Ann Butler, Susan Clossy, and Maria Murphy Burke, were "greatly chagrined" when Dubourg ordered that, as far as possible "confidence and attachment" to Babade was to be eradicated. Elizabeth told the archbishop, "I should have acquiesced quietly tho' my heart was torn to pieces but the others could not bear it in the same way." Dubourg clarified his position by giving the sisters "a copy of the rule relating to correspondence," which permitted writing to the director each preferred once in two months, on subjects of direction designated. This lessened the feeling of resentment but did not remove it.[80]

While Babade was away on missionary work in the area of Philadelphia, Germantown, and Burlington in August 1809, he received letters from both Dubourg and Carroll instructing him to go to Emmitsburg as soon as possible to receive Harriet Seton into the Church. Happily Babade notified Harriet that as soon as he could finish his work in Pennsylvania and New Jersey he would hasten to "the sacred place which encircles what is dearest to my heart."[81] He planned to go to Baltimore first, however, to consult the archbishop, who had requested that they discuss the regulations pertaining to the sisters. To Elizabeth Father Babade wrote, "I will explain to him [Carroll], according to my custom, that in order to make a just application of the laws it is necessary to examine the spirit, the purposes and the circumstances. Such has been my procedure in studies of canon law."[82]

When Elizabeth received word from Dubourg that Babade was coming to Emmitsburg she wrote pleadingly to Carroll, in the name of Cecilia and "the names of four other sisters who desire the comfort and feel the necessity as she does of unfolding their souls to him," that they be allowed the privilege of going to confession to Father Babade. She added earnestly:

For my part I assure you that if it is not granted to me, you will leave a Soul so dear to you in a cloud of uneasiness which can be dissipated in no other way. It would seem as if our Lord has inspired this confidence in my Soul and in those of many others round me for my severe and most painful trial, circumstanced as I am.[83]

Meanwhile, Louis Dubourg resigned. Dubourg in later years wrote Elizabeth Seton, "My disposition must be known to you: a sensibility perhaps too great for my own happiness, an openness of heart rather bordering on indiscretion than on reserve."[84] It was quite probably this sensitiveness which prompted his action in 1809. The Sulpicians in general felt that Babade was interfering in affairs which did not concern him, which "providence had addressed to another."[85] Babade, for his part, maintained that in the exterior affairs of the community he had never wished to interfere, but that in their spiritual concerns he had every right according to the principles of his vocation.[86] Dubourg's precipitate action brought matters to an unfortunate crisis. Nagot, too ill to act himself, chose Rev. John Baptist David to assume the duties refused by Dubourg.[87]

When Elizabeth learned that Dubourg had resigned she was overcome with remorse that any perverseness of hers should have prompted such an action, and she wrote entreatingly to her old friend:

My Father—the pleading of so weak a creature does not merit your attention I know—yet once more be patient with one you have born with so long—it seems but a dream that things are as they are—that you have given your children to a father-in-law while their real father still lives and loves them with a parent's tenderness—and why—the mother is worthless—pity them—pity her and if she ever even vexes you again, quit her and them forever.

The Rev. Mr. David may make an excellent Superior—his merits as a Father are undoubted, but our Lord did not give him that place with us—the charge was pointedly given to you [and] my perverseness has driven [you away].[88]

This abject apology quite appeased the capricious Dubourg, who wrote on 13 September, "I wish to be with you tho' absent, share in every distress, be edified in every good action, assist in every doubt."[89] But Elizabeth's desire to see Dubourg reinstated met with disappointment. Receiving no assurance that Dubourg would resume his former duties, she penned a letter to Nagot in Baltimore and sent it over to Dubois at Mount St. Mary's for his opinion. Dubois sent it back after underlining the parts he considered "rather too harsh coming from you." He told Mrs. Seton he had received a letter from Tessier, and one from Babade mentioning David's appointment. "Wait," he advised her, "for the answer of Mr. Dubourg or rather for the visit of the Bishop. Both, with what your own reflexions will suggest to you, will enable you to form a final opinion on a subject of too much consequence to be treated slightly."[90]

John Dubois, himself, sympathized with Mrs. Seton in her distress and tried to solve the tangle in another way. He wrote to Pierre Babade, offering to ask for him as an assistant at Mount St. Mary's. Dubois needed aid and he believed that Mr. Duhamel, who was expected to help at Emmitsburg, would be unable to leave Hagerstown for at least another two years. Dubois warned Babade that he might not be able to serve the sisters immediately, if Baltimore should withhold his faculties.[ff] Babade replied that he was very grateful for this mark of friendship, but that he felt he must remain absolutely passive in the affair.[91]

There is no record of what Archbishop Carroll advised when he visited the valley in October and confirmed, among others, Anna Maria and Harriet Seton.[92] Soon after Carroll's departure, Dubourg arrived and Elizabeth renewed her pleas. On 2 November she told Carroll, "I am not without hope that he will again resume his charge as superior—You know there are many reasons why I wish it."[93] If David should go to Kentucky with Flaget, as it was rumored, the community would have three changes in one year. Since it was her first superior whom she had offended, it was to him she should make reparation. "The truth is," she admitted, "I have been made a Mother before being initiated."[94] She saw now that she should have offered her disappointment over Father Babade as a sacrifice to God. She closed her letter with the humble words, "You will see how good a child I am going to be— quite a little child, and perhaps you will have often to give me the food of little children yet, but I will do my best as I have promised you in every case."[95] The archbishop replied, "If Mr. Nagot, or the council of the Seminary see fit to restore Mr. Dubourg to the place he filled, you may depend upon my concurrence, tho' I plainly see formidable objections. Your motives for desiring it are truly edifying and worthy of your humility..."[96]

[ff] Priestly faculties are the authorization given to a Roman Catholic ordained priest by his diocesan bishop or religious superior, legally permitting him to administer the sacraments. Usually, a priest's faculties are limited to a particular diocese or religious order.

But even before Carroll's letter was written, the matter was settled. Writing to a friend in Philadelphia on 8 November, John Dubois announced, "The resignation of the late Superior, Mr. Dubourg, and the appointment of the Rev. Mr. David in his place is finally concluded upon. The former could not continue without injuring the college which requires all his time and exertions."[97] A few days later Mrs. Seton received from Nagot a reprimanding letter in which the Sulpician superior refused categorically to reinstate Dubourg. "I am persuaded," he wrote bluntly, "it is God's holy will that Mr. David today be superior of your house." Nagot said he would have preferred that Carroll make the final decision, but since he must obey his archbishop the decision rested with Nagot. He concluded:

> Conform with all the simplicity of a humble servant of God, docile to His commands, like a child. Inspire the same sentiments in all your Sisters; it is the true way to have peace and to find that the yoke of the Lord is as sweet as self-will is disquieting and discontenting, so long as one does not know how to conceal it, and sacrifice it, and obey in silence.[98]

It is not known what Father Nagot said to Mrs. Seton when he went to Emmitsburg in person on 14 November 1809, but a month later Elizabeth wrote to John Carroll:

> I have had a great many very hard trials, my Father, since you were here, but you of course will congratulate me on them as this fire of tribulation is no doubt meant to consume the many imperfections and bad dispositions our Lord finds in me—indeed it has at times burnt so deep that the anguish could not be concealed, but by degrees custom reconciles pain itself...I determine dry and hard as my daily bread is, to take it with as good grace as possible. When I carry it before our Lord sometimes he makes me laugh at myself and asks me what other kind I would choose in the Valley of tears than that which himself and all his followers made use of.[99]

Although Louis Dubourg carried out his promise to Mrs. Seton to ask to resume his former position, when he "saw that Providence had fixed things contrary" to her wishes he wrote sympathetically:

> Have patience, be strictly & cheerfully & fairly obedient in action, in heart & judgment & depend upon it. All things will soon wear a different appearance. Our Saviour tries you very surely in your family & in your affections. Shall I pity?

Indeed I dare not, for I am dearly attached to you and I very much hope it is all for your perfection. Oh!! that we could cling to none but God, and equally love him in all things and in all persons![100]

Enduring the deprivation of both Babade's spiritual consolation and Dubourg's guidance was merely the beginning of Elizabeth Seton's trials in Emmitsburg. In October, her eldest son William was taken seriously ill, and he was brought from the Mountain to St. Joseph's. When he grew steadily worse his shroud was made and the last sacraments were administered. To his mother's intense relief, the lad then made an amazing recovery. But the shroud was used before the year was gone. Harriet Seton, Pierre Babade's "Magdalena, the child of my heart," was stricken in the last week of November. On 18 December, she received communion for the last time. For four days thereafter she remained delirious, singing hymns, calling for Babade. Three days before Christmas she died. The shock was overpowering, especially since it was Cecilia Seton who had been the invalid for so many years. No one was prepared for the death of the lovely older sister. Less than a month before, her brother Samuel Waddington Seton had written Harriet, begging her to return as soon as Cecilia's health permitted. Sam said that if her new religion barred her from the Farquhars, he would gladly take a cottage near town and Harriet could live with him.[101] When Elizabeth broke the news to Julia, she added painfully, "So it goes with your friend, tribulation is my element—if only it carries me Home at last, never mind the present."[102]

Elizabeth's friends realized what a loss she suffered in Harriet's death and consolation poured in from all sides. Dubourg reminded her, "How mercifully our good Lord has treated our Harriet, and what congratulations can be equal to her happiness!"[103] David, the new superior, admonished,

Let us adore the unsearchable, but always wise and merciful ways of Providence; and let us more than ever convince ourselves, that Jesus wishes to be the sole possessor of our hearts, to abandon themselves with perfect resignation into His Hands...having no other thought, in troublesome and painful encounters, than to submit lovingly to whatever God will be pleased to ordain.[104]

Anthony Kohlmann was glad to know that Mrs. Seton was taking her "many trials in the light the saints considered them," that instead of wavering at the repeated strokes, her courage increased, her confidence strengthened, her love of God grew more and more inflamed.[105] Both Cheverus and Carroll were more and more convinced that Elizabeth was marked for special graces, Cheverus wrote, "I look upon your trials, difficulties, etc., as the stamp of divine favour and protection upon your establishment. Remember St. Teresa [of Avila], St. [Jane] Frances Chantal, etc. Like them, I hope you will become saints and the mothers of many saints."[106] John Carroll, who was suffering a personal loss at the same time in the death of his friend, Rev. Francis Beeston, wrote of his dismay on Christmas morning, when the news of Harriet's death had arrived. He said:

> It seems to be the order of Divine Providence to lead you to perfection thro' the road of sufferings, interior & exterior; and may you always correspond with the graces bestowed on you and walk in the way of the cross with resignation and consequently with much spiritual profit.[107]

The death of Harriet was followed by a period of continuous illness and sorrow. Anna Maria Seton and Sisters Susan and Martina Quinn were sick with a pulmonary ailment, while Cecilia suffered increasingly from her consumption and was unable to rise without fainting. The house was in reality an infirmary as the new year came in, yet Elizabeth could write:

> You must not think our courage fails—Oh no, when the clock struck 12 last night and ended the old year, Annina laying in my arms in a violent ague,[gg] I felt happy, contented, embracing my lot with joy—but this is only the force of grace...[108]

Only Mary Bayley Post, Elizabeth's sister who knew her so well, feared the effects of these trials, and wrote, "Knowing that you possess an unusual degree of fortitude does not hide from me the conflicts of mind you endure when your feelings are excited by those who are dear to you."[109] Elizabeth's emotions were to be violently roused as winter waned. In March Cecilia Seton was definitely on the decline and Elizabeth told Eliza Sadler sorrowfully, "Oh Eliza, how many strings draw us up as well as downwards—yet my heart faints when I think of this separation—no one can conceive what she is to me."[110] On the advice of Archbishop Carroll and Dr. Chatard, Elizabeth resolved to take Cecilia to Baltimore.[hh] Accompanied by Anna Maria and Sister Susan, Cecilia and Elizabeth Seton went to Baltimore where they stayed at the home of George Weis near Paca Street, arriving 11 April.[111] It was a fruitless journey. The week after Easter Cecilia Seton, "innocence and peace itself," died in Baltimore. Elizabeth and Sister Susan

---

[gg] Ague is a condition marked by paroxysms of chills, fever, and sweating that recurred at regular intervals or a fit of shivering due to illness.

[hh] Dr. Pierre Chatard had studied at Paris, Montpellier, and Toulouse before settling in Baltimore. His wife, Marie-Françoise Adelee Buisson, became a firm friend of Mrs. Seton.

started back to Emmitsburg immediately with their sad burden. The death of Cecilia left them almost lightheaded with pain and fatigue, and the two women rode through the dismal rain "as cheerful and gay as two *folles*." They could "hardly look at Mr. Clorivière[ii] with proper gravity" when that young cleric appointed to escort them finally caught up with them at Westminster.[112]

It was under this succession of trials that Elizabeth Seton had to adjust herself to the policies of her new superior, John David. Whether David's attitude toward her was colored by his knowledge of her predilection for Babade and Dubourg, or whether his cold firm method of dealing with women or the new community was simply a matter of principle cannot be determined. But that David intended to rule, and that Mrs. Seton found her superior's attitude unpleasant cannot be denied. Before the women had even moved from the crowded farmhouse, David issued orders regarding the school to be established, with little concern for the women's experience and their views. When Elizabeth told Dubourg of her dissatisfaction with David's pronouncements, the former superior replied:

> I have communicated to the Rev. Superior your ideas concerning the school and many reflexions of mine concerning the latitude he should allow you to direct with your own council what is to be done in your house, consulting only when you feel at loss...All things must no doubt be done as gently as possible and if it happens that you are crossed in the best of views, doubt not that it is good for yourself.[113]

Dubourg's sanguine hope that David concurred with him was belied in the letter sent the same day from David to Mrs. Seton. He instructed her, "Take care, Dear Mother, to establish very strict regulations," and announced, "I have begun to write some regulations for the organization of the school at St. Joseph's. I will complete them as soon as I can, and after having proposed them to the approbation of my Brothers, I will send them... for your revision."[114]

Elizabeth found Father David's method of dealing with her community very distressing and by the end of January wrote to her archbishop at length.

> St. Joseph's House is almost ready...now the moment approaches when *order must be the foundation of all the good we can hope to do*, and as so much depends on the

---

[ii] Joseph-Pierre Picot de Limoëlan de Clorivière (1768-1826), was at St. Mary's Seminary, Baltimore, from 1808 to 1812. He was ordained in 1812 and served at Charleston and Georgetown Visitation.

Mother of the Community, I beg you to take her first in hand for I must candidly tell you she is all in the wrong—*not from discontent with the place* I am in since every corner of the world is the same to me if I may but serve our Lord, *nor with the intention of our institution* for I long to be in the fullest exercise of it—but circumstances have all combined as to create in my mind a confusion and want of confidence in my Superiors which is indescribable...Sincerely I promised you and really *I have endeavored to do everything in my power* to bend myself to meet the last appointed Superior [David] in every way but after continual reflection on the *necessity of absolute conformity with him,* and *constant prayer* to our Lord to help me, yet the *heart is closed*, and when the pen should freely give him the necessary detail and information he requires, it stops...*An unconquerable reluctance and diffidence takes the place of those dispositions* which ought to influence every action and with every desire to serve God and these excellent beings who surround me—I remain motionless and inactive. It is for you, my most revered Father, to decide if this is temptation or what it is.[115]

In reply Carroll admonished her:

Let it be your only concern to progress more and more towards the union of your soul with God, and an entire disengagement from the things of earth. It would be a triumph for heterodoxy and irreligion, and what is of much more consequence, the disappointment of pious and admiring Catholics should anything happen, to shake the stability of your holy establishment...I declare an opinion and belief that its ultimate success under God depends on your sacrificing yourself, notwithstanding all the uneasiness and disgust you may experience, and continuing in your place as Superior.[116]

The archbishop told her to make every effort to meet Father David who was coming to Emmitsburg soon. This letter contained the first hint of dissension within the sisterhood, a circumstance which could only add to Elizabeth's unhappiness. Carroll had said, "I will answer our dear Sister Rose [White] and she will receive mine with the more pleasure when handed by [David] whom she deservedly honours so much."[117] Sister Rose, the former Rose Landry White, was ten years younger than Elizabeth Seton, but like Elizabeth, was a widow. Born in Baltimore on 23 March 1784, Rosetta Landry had married at fourteen a Captain Joseph White, a friend of her father. John Carroll, who had known Rose from childhood, witnessed the marriage vows between herself and Captain White, whom she wed on Valentine's Day of 1799. When her husband was lost at sea, leaving the young widow with two young children,[jj] Mrs. White was given spiritual consolation by Father David, who was then serving in Baltimore. It was David who interested the bereaved woman in charitable work in the city, a work which soon directed her steps toward Emmitsburg.[118] Sister Rose had never joined in the general clamor for Babade, and when David was made superior she was sincerely pleased with the appointment. Her devotion to her former confessor and friend was no less than Elizabeth Seton's toward hers. In the light of the antipathy which developed between Father David and Mrs. Seton, it is easy to see how faction might arise within the household at St. Joseph's. It was not long before rumors began to circulate that Sister Rose would replace Mrs. Seton as head of the community.

While Elizabeth was in Baltimore attending the dying Cecilia, her situation was under discussion at the Sulpician seminary on Paca Street. It is quite apparent that this discussion considered replacing her because Elizabeth wrote to Baltimore after her departure, "I shall wait for further directions before announcing to the Sisters the change that is intended in my situation as in Rose's absence no one else would be willing to take the place of Mother without your immediate order."[119] Again, when writing to John Carroll, Elizabeth said of Rose, "She was proposed as Mother of this house in my place and everyone in it should prepare themselves for the change (which I was directed myself to inform them by a special letter immediately after my return from Baltimore.)"[120] Whether the archbishop hoped to separate the antagonistic factions or whether David first thought of a division is not clear, but in May Elizabeth wrote to Antonio Filicchi, "Our blessed Bishop intends removing a detachment of us to Baltimore to perform the same duties there. We have here a very good house tho' a [log] Building, and it will be the Mother House and retreat, in all cases a portion of the Sisterhood will remain in it..."[121] Anna Maria Seton, who had remained in Baltimore after Cecilia's death,[kk] told her mother in June:

> The Bishop told me the other day tho as in secrecy (and you
> will keep it such) that you would probably be down in the
> fall again, and still more probable not go back. At least he

[jj] Margaret Mary Ann, (1801-1804), did not long survive the captain, but Charles White (1803-1839), entered Mount St. Mary's College, 31 July 1810.

[kk] Anna Maria stayed with the Robert Barry family. Her friend, Charles DuPavillon, was soon to leave the country and Elizabeth Seton wanted her fifteen year old daughter to have a chance to see him before his departure.

said you would be down before October with a few [sisters], I hope he means Father [Babade's] children.[122]

When Elizabeth read her daughter's letter, she wrote at once to Carroll stating that "if it should please our Lord to suggest to you any plan of bringing us nearer to you,"[123] she had [available funds], $500.00 with John Dubois and $500.00 with Robert Barry, sums she would gladly place in his hands. "Why trouble you with this account—only because I wish you to know whatever concerns us...[so that] you may know how far my means may go. If you think proper to prevent Barry from investing it as he did a little sum of Anna Maria's which I have no power over, you will tell him to keep it in his own hands."[124]

Then in July Sister Rose went to Baltimore "on business."[ll] Immediately rumors began to travel to Emmitsburg that she would return as head of the sisterhood. Elizabeth wrote to Carroll to learn if this were true.[125] The prelate replied that probably Dubois knew more of the plans of Dubourg and David than he. Neither David nor any of "Mr. Nagot's council called Directeurs" had informed him of any change. Carroll's own preference was clearly stated:

> Their good sense must and will cause hesitation before they resolve finally to assign to Sister Rose the government of the monastery, and limit you to the school. I once thought that this might be attended with some relief of your present disquietude...but it would be in my opinion a fatal change to the prosperity of the Sisterhood...If therefore it should be again proposed to me, it is my determination to resist the proposal until Mr. David has finished his visitation and made his report.[126]

Events moved rapidly during the next few months. In July John David came to Emmitsburg with Sister Rose and three new recruits[mm] for the community.[127] The second week in August saw the arrival of Benedict Flaget from France, with rules and constitutions for consideration.[128] In October Jean Cheverus in Boston began his preparations for departure, hoping to reach Baltimore on "the 23, in time to make a retreat" before his consecration as Bishop.[129] On 8 November 1810, at a banquet given in honor of the new bishops, Flaget, Cheverus, and Michael Egan, Charles Nagot resigned as superior of the Sulpicians, to be succeeded by Tessier.[130] In September, John Carroll had informed Mrs. Seton that Bishop-elect Flaget planned to

---

[ll] This business probably concerned her son, Charles, whom she brought back with her to enter the mountain college for boys. A-6.3a, *Mother Rose White's Journal*, CW, 2:728.
[mm] Ibid. These three recruits were Fanny Jordan, Angela Brady, and Julia Shirk.

take David with him into Kentucky after his consecration, adding, "and of course some change must ensue in the government of St. Joseph's."[131] With the resignation of Nagot and the elevation of Flaget as first Bishop of Bardstown,[nn] it began to look as if affairs for Elizabeth might resolve themselves easily. It was with deep joy and newly discovered hope that she welcomed her first meeting with Jean Cheverus when he visited Emmitsburg.

When Elizabeth reported the happy event to Eliza Sadler she described the Bishop of Boston as perhaps less handsome than Mr. Tisserant but quite his equal in "spirit or mind." Cheverus himself delivered this letter to Mrs. Sadler, who wrote Mrs. Seton that she discovered in Cheverus "his uncommon amiable manners and his being the most *chère confrère* of our most valued Mr. [John] Tisserant who has the advantage of Bishop Cheverus exteriorly but not in the *Spirit of the mind*." [132] Cheverus stopped in New York to administer confirmation in the absence of a successor to Bishop Richard Luke Concanen, O.P. The two friends of over five years of letter writing must have enjoyed several conversations face to face, for two days later Cheverus and Egan came again from Mount St. Mary's with a note from John Dubois saying he felt sure Cheverus could be persuaded to stay over to officiate on Sunday if the Bishop of Philadelphia would consent to relinquish his claim to Boston's company. "Exert all your insinuating eloquence," Dubois humorously advised. "It will have a good effect if it has half the influence which it has on your devoted, etc."[133] But Cheverus sent his respects and thanks on Saturday, 24 November, and begged never to be forgotten in the prayers of his dear sisters. From the Jesuit mission station at Conewago, Pennsylvania, two days later the Boston prelate wrote his archbishop that he had "visited the holy mountain and have been very much edified."[134] Elizabeth told Carroll herself of the visit of the Bishops of Boston and Philadelphia, adding, "I need not tell you our consolation in receiving the blessed Bishops, nor how many benedictions they poured upon us—We have been very sensible of this special favor."[135]

The respite was brief, indeed. Flaget and David made plans not to leave for Kentucky until the following May and the latter showed no disposition to relinquish the reins at St. Joseph's. Elizabeth learned from a friend[oo] who sat next to Father David at a dinner in Baltimore that the Sulpician was openly discussing his plans for the women. He said he had no intention of sending any sisters yet to Kentucky, as he was unacquainted with the country, but that he hoped to establish a community in Baltimore.

[nn] The seat of the diocese of Bardstown, Kentucky, moved to Louisville in 1841.

[oo] The friend was Margaret Cecilia George (1787–1868), the widow of Lucas George (d.1808), who later entered the Sisters of Charity of St. Joseph's 2 February 1812.

"You know who would be *Superior,*" this friend wrote. "If such a thing does take place it will be merely for the sick alone."[136] When Sister Rose was summoned to Baltimore by David speculation became rife. Rose suffered from distemper that winter and David told Mrs. Seton, "I should have reproached myself had I not in this instance complied with the Doctor's & Archbishop's requests. Whatever be the success of our undertakings we must always rest contented when we have followed the advice of those who are to direct us."[137] When weather and lack of proper conveyance kept Rose in Emmitsburg, David became more impatient and sent repeated letters "for her coming at every risk," and Elizabeth reported to Archbishop Carroll that "from that time on there has been some reserve between us." She said:

> Rose's virtues are truly valued by me and by us all, but from the time she knew she was proposed as Mother of this house in my place and that everyone in it should prepare themselves for the change, (which I was directed myself to inform them by a special letter immediately after my return from Baltimore), her conduct has undergone an entire change and has been very unfavorable to her happiness and ours.[138]

Elizabeth was by then convinced that David intended starting a house in Baltimore, leaving the school in Emmitsburg to her, but establishing a charitable enterprise in the city. After Rose reached Baltimore, Elizabeth received a heartening letter from the archbishop in which he said that he had not heard recently "the slightest mention of a proposed change in the government of St. Joseph's nor of settling our dear Rose here with and at the head of a colony" from Emmitsburg. Rose had not mentioned anything of the kind to him when he saw her recently. Even though he had not directly questioned her on the subject, he had approached the matter obliquely, and felt sure she would have informed him, such was her candor. Carroll said again plainly that any thought of placing Rose at the head of a community would be governed by "good heart rather than the dictates of reason, deliberation, or experience."

> If you should ever be permitted to resign your maternal charge over your community, I would rejoice on your own individual account; but my hope for the continuance of the establishment would be very much weakened...

You have had heavy trials in pursuing the way to perfection, and heavier perhaps still remain; during these, you will never lose sight of the consoling words of Christ, take courage; for *I overcome the world.*[139]

Elizabeth said wearily to George Weis, "the Bishop has again committed himself for me. Everything is now in confusion. When and how it will end God only knows. I am always quiet on the subject...but I look to no one but God alone—in a few weeks all will be settled."[140]

In spite of the fact that David was to leave early in May for Kentucky with Bishop Flaget, he notified the sisters that he would conduct a retreat before he left. This seemed to Elizabeth Seton the last straw. Writing in protest to Carroll she said that this was scarcely the time for a retreat. When the retreat had first been proposed at the time of David's summer visitation the sisters had been "unhappy." Now that David was leaving and no new successor was appointed, it seemed futile to discuss the rules with David. She bluntly asked the archbishop to refuse his consent to the retreat at this time. The retreat was not held.[141] At the same time Mrs. Seton wrote David a very spirited letter in which she demanded:

> What object can a retreat have at this time except it is to be followed by an immediate application of those rules so long looked for, rules which are to be discussed and presented to the Bishop for his approbation and afterwards to serve as a guide to the Superior providence may assign us—of what use can it be to discuss those rules with any other than the one who is to take your place of Superior as he may on many points think differently from yourself and of course his opinion will subject us to new changes and uncertainty.[142]

Later, when time and spiritual growth had removed her from the exasperation of this period, Simon Bruté wrote on the back of her scratch copy of this letter: "Could you think your poor mother was guilty of such impertinence? O our Jesus, pity the ignorance of such a moment."[143] But the spring of 1811 found her courage at its lowest ebb, and when David and Flaget started for Kentucky on 12 May 1811, Elizabeth wrote Archbishop Carroll of her discouragement.

> Now after two years trial, experience has too well proved how illy [sic] I am qualified to meet the views of the Rev. gentlemen [Sulpicians] who have the government of this house—who require a pliancy of character, I would for some reasons wish to possess, and may eventually be the fruit of Divine Grace, but as yet is far from being attained.[144]

The precise moment of John Dubois' appointment as David's successor is not noted in the records of the sisterhood at Emmitsburg. Mrs.

Seton had favored Dubois for some time, writing to Baltimore that, "being on the spot he sees things in a different point of view from those who are distant." She told Carroll that "Rev. Mr. Dubois in one point has always had my preference as a Superior—he always and invariably has recommended me to refer constantly to you, which is not only in the order of Providence but the only safety I can find for the peace of my mind."[145] Toward the end of June Elizabeth told George Weis, "You know there has been a new appointment which will make a new *administration*—but I am so worn out now that it is almost a matter of indifference how it goes."[146] This remark scarcely conveys the satisfaction to be expected if Elizabeth knew John Dubois were the "new appointment." The explanation may be in the letters of John David to Simon Bruté written that summer.

On 18 July 1811, David wrote from Kentucky asking Bruté to tell his "good Philotheas"[pp] that their former father hoped they would pray for the work in Kentucky. He commented, "Ah well, the dear Philotheas are gathering more and more around you. How happy I am. Do not doubt that God wishes to use you to lead these brave souls in the ways of perfection."[147] Since David usually referred to the sisters as "philotheas," it seems that Bruté was serving them in some capacity. Mrs. Seton in a letter to Carroll some weeks later noted that "Mr. Bruté in the purity of his heart is doing his very best, and much more than it could possibly be supposed so young a man would venture on."[148] By the middle of September, however, David was lamenting:

> The news of the prohibition they have just made of your
> continuing to be the father of my dear children afflicted me as
> much as the contrary news had elated me. You might at least
> have told me the cause for so strange a change. I presume it
> is because Mr. Dubourg has returned and has consented to
> take charge. But if they have confidence in you how can they
> promise him confidence to the same degree?[149]

From this meager evidence it is difficult to do more than suggest that Simon Bruté could have been in charge for two months during the summer of 1811.

Louis Dubourg, who had returned from Martinique early in July, certainly never resumed control, although it is quite true that he maintained a lively interest in the community until his departure for Louisiana.[150] In

---

[pp] Philothea is a Greek term meaning "lover of God." St. Francis de Sales wrote the allegorical character Philothea" in his *Introduction to the Devout Life* which was used for spiritual reading by Mother Seton and the Sisters of Charity.

February 1812, he encouraged Margaret Cecilia George, another widow, and Teresa Conroy to enter the community. He recommended that the sisters use the stone farmhouse to quarantine consumptive members. "I may appear over meddlesome," he apologized, "but what would I appear if I were silent upon what I consider one of the greatest dangers for your institution?" Hoping that no disagreements in the past were remembered, no ill-will harbored against him, he told Elizabeth:

> You are too good to set some value upon my friendship. I wish you could know what wounds your apparent suspicion of its sincerity have inflicted on my heart. You have been mistaken, and God has permitted it to try us both. Let his holy will be done. I hope we shall meet in heaven, where no clouds will overshadow our union, no suspicions will distress and harrow our hearts.[151]

In April, Dubourg sent the struggling community "about 200 images which I thought would be very valuable encouragements for your pupils and some very acceptable to your Sisters." He wished to be repaid in prayers measured by his needs and not by the value of the gift. He congratulated the women on the approaching feast of St. Joseph's patronage and added, "I hope the dear Saint will do something for us for having procured him so many dutiful children."[152]

But John Dubois was the superior of the community after the fall of 1811. Archbishop Carroll's initial approval of the American modification of the *Common Rules* of the Daughters of Charity that September clearly refers to a superior residing near the community, and mentions Dubois by name.[153] The final approval of the *Regulations for the Society of Sisters of Charity in the United States of America* was given 17 January 1812. Mrs. Seton's letter to Mrs. Marie-Françoise Chatard in November mentions Dubois' "double charge at St. Joseph's."[154] The chronological table kept by the community shows that the third annual retreat opened 2 February 1812, "by the Superior, Mr. Dubois." The only thing lacking is the exact date of his accession.

One last word should be added to the subject of these hectic years. Mrs. Seton's stiffness toward Father David may be partially explained by the fact that during his incumbency she felt under no obligation to obey him. Early in February 1811, she told Catherine Dupleix, "That vow which was binding on my conscience but one year does not exist, as it was no longer necessary, and I am free, and even more free than dear Sad."[155] Three months later Elizabeth wrote to John Carroll:

It appears, my dear Father, by your letter by Mr. Kenny that you still consider me under religious vows, tho when in Baltimore you assured me that those which have been so inauspicious were no longer binding, and certainly I have made no renewal of them, and I entreat you (for my repose in case of my death before I see you) to relieve me from them if you think any obligation remains.[156]

The archbishop's reply was not available but Bruté at a later period wrote of Carroll, "He was extremely attached to her [Mrs. Seton]. He advised her not to take a perpetual vow to her confessor. I have his letter."[157] Elizabeth obviously was in good conscience in her dealings with Father David. Docility and submission were never easy for her ardent nature. Future occasions would find her hard pressed by the decisions of her superiors; but the one period of what might be misconstrued as flagrant resistance must be viewed in the light of the preceding evidence.

By the fall of 1811 the stormy period was past. The position of Mrs. Seton was firmly established. The coolness between Baltimore and Emmitsburg had vanished. Sister Rose, who left Baltimore for Emmitsburg on 24 May 1811 returned after Father David's departure for Kentucky, was once more Elizabeth's most valued assistant.[158] God's abundant grace provided that the rift was easily healed, for even at the height of the dissension, Elizabeth had said in Sister Rose's regard, "Our reserve is of the mind, not of the heart; her affectionate kindness to my children binds me by gratitude independent of our spiritual connections."[159] The community was ready to live by the French rule under the direction of Father John Dubois. From this point on Elizabeth Seton may be truly called "Mother Seton."

CHAPTER 9. MOTHER SETON
Notes

[1] John Dubois to Joseph Carrière, Emmitsburg, 16 February 1815, Archives Mount St. Mary's University, Emmitsburg, Maryland. Hereinafter cited as AMSMU.

[2] Ruthella M. Bibbins, *Baltimore, Its History and People* (New York, 1919), p. 82.

[3] Thomas Scharf, *History of Western Maryland* (Philadelphia, 1882), II, 929.

[4] 6.1, Elizabeth Seton to Louis Dubourg, Winchester [Westminster], Friday afternoon, *CW*, 2:74.

[5] Simon Bruté Papers, AMSMU.

[6] Scharf, I, 581. This name is given as "Saint Mary's Mount" as well as Mount St. Mary's.

[7] Simon Bruté sketch, AMSMU. This excellent pen drawing shows the location of the college, the log house, and the chapel.

[8] *Records of the American Catholic Historical Society*, V (1894), 433. 6.2, Elizabeth Seton to Matthias O'Conway, Emmitsburg, 25 June 1809, *CW*, 2:75. Since after Mrs. Seton's arrival in June 1809, all her correspondence originated in Emmitsburg, place names will be omitted for any of her letters written after that time.

[9] 10.4, "Dear Remembrances," *CW*, 3a:522.

[10] Ibid.; See A-6.3a, Mother Rose White's Journal, *CW*, 2:723.

[11] 6.10, Elizabeth Seton to Antonio Filicchi, 8 November 1809, *CW*, 2:89.

[12] 6.12, Elizabeth Seton to John Carroll, 14 December 1809, *CW*, 2:92.

[13] 6.20, Elizabeth Seton to John Carroll, 19 January 1809, *CW*, 2:102.

[14] A-6.3a, Mother Rose White's Journal, *CW*, 2:726.

[15] 6.23, Elizabeth Seton to John Carroll, 25 January 1810, *CW*, 2:106.

[16] 6.22, Elizabeth Seton to Rose Stubbs, n.d., *CW*, 2:105.

[17] 6.51, Elizabeth Seton to John David, 23 July 1810, *CW*, 2:148.

[18] A-6.3a, Mother Rose White's Journal, *CW*, 2:727.

[19] Jean Cheverus to Simon Bruté, Boston, 14 February 1812, UNDA.

[20] Mary Bayley Post to Elizabeth Seton, New York, 14 May 1812, ASJPH 1-3-3-11:16.

[21] 6.14, Elizabeth Seton to Julia Scott, 27 December 1809, *CW*, 2:95.

[22] Anthony Kohlmann to Elizabeth Seton, New York, 7 July 1809, ASJPH 1-3-3-2:24.

[23] Anthony Kohlmann to Elizabeth Seton, New York, 19 August 1809, ASJPH 1-3-3-2:25.

[24] Record of Students' Entrance, AMSMU.

[25] Anthony Kohlmann to Elizabeth Seton, New York, 27 September 1809,

ASJPH 1-3-3-2:26.

[26] Anthony Kohlmann to Elizabeth Seton, New York, 14 November 1811, ASJPH 1-3-3-2:29. See Rose White's Journal (1809-1841), entry on Sister Benedicta Corish, 14 January 1814, ASJPH 7-2-1, (32, 41, 58).

[27] John F. Moranvillé to Elizabeth Seton, Baltimore, 18 September 1809, ASJPH 1-3-3-2:34.

[28] Maria Dodge, S.C., *The Life of Elizabeth Boyle* (Staten Island, New York: Sisters of Charity of New York, 1893), 18.

[29] Moranvillé–Boyle Letters, 22 April 1811.

[30] Ibid., 18 October, no year. See Moranvillé-Boyle Letters, 12 January 1813, AMSV.

[31] Chronological Table of the Sisters of Charity of Saint Joseph's, 27 November 1814, ASJPH 7-13.

[32] Louis Dubourg to Elizabeth Seton, Baltimore, July 1811, ASJPH 1-3-3-2:3. See John M. Tessier's Journal, AAB, AASMSU.

[33] Jean Cheverus to Elizabeth Seton, Emmitsburg, 20 January 1815, ASJPH 1-3-3-1:14; Ibid., 24 June 1816, ASJPH 1-3-3-1:15.

[34] Louis Dubourg to Simon Bruté, New Orleans, 1 September 1813, UNDA. John M. Tessier's Journal states that Dubourg left for New Orleans on 18 October 1812. Carroll Letterbook I, John Carroll to Ambrose Maréchal, 12 February 1812, AAB, AASMSU, gives Archbishop Carroll's reasons for appointing Dubourg to New Orleans.

[35] Louis Dubourg to Simon Bruté, New Orleans, 22 July, no year, UNDA.

[36] Jean Cheverus to John Carroll, Boston, 16 October 1811, AAB, AASMSU, 2-0-5. See Jean Cheverus to Elizabeth Seton, 20 January 1812, AMSV.

[37] Jean Cheverus to Elizabeth Seton, Emmitsburg, 12 April 1814, ASJPH 1-3-3-1:13.

[38] Jean Cheverus to Elizabeth Seton, Emmitsburg, 20 January 1815, ASJPH 1-3-3-1:14.

[39] Benedict Flaget to Henry Clay, Bardstown, 21 September 1825. See Bernard Mayo, "Bishop Flaget and Henry Clay," *Catholic Historical Review*, XXVII (July 1941), 212. For a life of Benedict Flaget. see Martin J. Spalding, *Sketches of the Life, Times, and Character of the Rt. Rev. Benedict Joseph Flaget, First Bishop of Louisville* (Louisville, 1852).

[40] 5.18, Elizabeth Seton to Philip Filicchi, 8 February 1809, *CW*, 2:54.

[41] Soeur Marie Bizeray, Soeur Marguerite Woirin, et Soeur Augustine Chauvin, Bordeaux, 12 July 1810, ASJPH 1-3-3-2:13.

[42] Charles I. White, *Life of Mrs. Eliza Seton* (New York, 1853), 296; De Barberey-Code, *Elizabeth Seton* (New York, 1927), 295-298; A-6.3a, Mother Rose White's Journal, *CW*, 2:730.

[43] 6.83, Elizabeth Seton to John Carroll, 5 September 1811, *CW*, 2:195.

[44] 6.70, Elizabeth Seton to Catherine Dupleix, 4 February 1811, *CW*, 2:172.

[45] John Carroll to Elizabeth Seton, Baltimore, 11 September 1810, AMSV, I, 17.

[46] 6.50, Elizabeth Seton to Julia Scott, 20 July 1810, *CW*, 2:146.

[47] 6.70, Elizabeth Seton to Catherine Dupleix, 4 February 1811, *CW*, 2:172.

[48] 6.74, Elizabeth Seton to George Weis, [27 April 1811], *CW*, 2:181.

[49] 6.57, Elizabeth Seton to George Weis, [9 August 1810], *CW*, 2:155.

[50] 6.76, Elizabeth Seton to John Carroll, 13 May 1811, *CW*, 2:185.

[51] See Betty Ann McNeil, D.C., "Sulpicians and Sisters of Charity, Concentric Circles of Mission,"*Vincentian Heritage* 20, 1 (1999). For excellent historical studies of the nineteenth- century Vincentian context, see Edward Udovic, C.M., *Jean-Baptiste Etienne and the Vincentian Revival* (Vincentian Studies Institute, 2001). Louise Sullivan, D.C., *Sister Rosalie Rendu: A Daughter of Charity on Fire with Love for the Poor* (Vincentian Studies Institute, 2007).

[52] Charles Leon Souvay, C.M., "Mother Seton's Daughters," a lecture delivered on 31 July 1917. (Privately printed), 16. Souvay stated, "That the idea of the union [with France] came from Father David may be readily admitted." Mrs. Seton's letter to Carroll on 13 May 1811, bears out this contention. See also footnote 62.

[53] John Carroll to John David, AAB, AASMSU, 8-A-F. This summary is jotted on the bottom of the following letter, John David to John Carroll, 17 September 1814.

[54] John Carroll to Elizabeth Seton, Baltimore, 9 November 1809, AMSV, I, 15.

[55] John Carroll to Elizabeth Seton, Baltimore, 11 September 1811, AMSV, I, 16.

[56] Jean Cheverus to Elizabeth Seton, Boston, 4 January 1811, AMSV, I, 2.

[57] John Dubois to Antoine Garnier, Emmitsburg, 18 April 1816, AMSMU. Copies from Archives Society of Saint-Sulpice, Paris.

[58] Charles L. Souvay, 19. Citing Pierre Coste, C.M., *St. Vincent de Paul Correspondance, Entretiens, Documents* (Paris, 1923), 9:428-29; 529-532. ["If God is pleased to grant you the grace of being able some day to earn your living, dear Sisters, and to be able to serve villages that are unable to support you, I know of nothing more beautiful. *Quoi!* by working for others, Sisters will be in a place where they'll be serving poor persons and educating girls with no contributions whatever, able to do so thanks to the work they themselves have done during their free time! What a favor, Sisters, and what a blessing of God that you who are already in a village or in the parishes, serving

persons who are poor and teaching children, contribute by your work to help others do the same good in the future by bringing your surplus to the Community! If, as we've already seen, bees do this by gathering honey from flowers and taking it back to the hive to feed the others, why wouldn't you, who should be like heavenly bees, do likewise?" #42 "Love of Work," conference of Vincent de Paul to the Daughters of Charity, 28 November 1649, Marie Poole, D.C., trans., ed., *Saint Vincent de Paul Correspondence, Conferences, Documents*, 14 vols., (New City Press: New York, 1983-2008), 9:388. Hereafter cited as *CCD*. "Now, for you to understand this clearly, dear Sisters, you must know the difference between your Company and many others that profess to assist poor persons as you do, but not in the way you usually do. The spirit of the Company consists in giving yourselves to God to love Our Lord and to serve Him corporally and spiritually in the person of the poor in their homes or elsewhere; to instruct poor young women, children, and generally all those whom Divine Providence may send you." #51 "Spirit of the Company," Conference of Vincent de Paul to the Daughters of Charity, 9 February 1653, Ibid., 9:465.

[59] 5.18, Elizabeth Seton to Philip Filicchi, 8 February 1809, *CW*, 2:54.

[60] John Carroll to Elizabeth Seton, Baltimore, 11 September 1811, AMSV, I, 16.

[61] John David to John Carroll, Bardstown, 17 September 1814, AAB, AASMSU, 8-A-Fl.

[62] Benedict Flaget to Simon Bruté, Bardstown, 17 October 1811, UNDA.

[63] Copy of Archbishop Maréchal's report to Cardinal Litta, Prefect of Propaganda, 16 October 1818, ACUA. See *Catholic Historical Review*, I, January 1916, 439-53, for the Latin version of the report.

[64] The surviving manuscript of these rules is in the handwriting of Sister Cecilia O'Conway but their origin remains obscure. A-6.4a, "Provisional Regulations for St. Joseph's Sisters" (c. 1809-1810), *CW*, 2:737. Sister Cecilia was appointed the first secretary of the Sisters of Charity of St. Joseph's. See A-6.3a, Mother Rose White's Journal, *CW*, 2:720.

[65] 12.1, Minutes of the First Council Meeting, *CW*, 3b:115.

[66] John M. Tessier's Journal, 22 August 1810, AMSMU. These rules are preserved in excellent condition at ASJPH. See 149a, Common Rules of the Daughters of Charity, *CCD*, 13b:147. Cf. A-12.3, *Regulations for the Society of Sisters of Charity in the United States of America*, *CW*, 3b:499.

[67] 6.65, Elizabeth Seton to John Carroll, 5 December 1810, *CW*, 2:165.

[68] 6.83, Elizabeth Seton to John Carroll, 5 September 1811, *CW*, 2:195.

[69] John Carroll to Elizabeth Seton, Baltimore, 11 September 1811, ASJPH 1-3-3-1:45.

[70] A-6.3a, Mother Rose White's Journal, *CW*, 2:731. It is not known which sister dissented.

[71] White, 491-2, gives the text of the confirmation. AAB, AASMSU, 11A-G-1, has a copy of the rules of the "Confraternity" of the Sisters of Charity in what appears to be Nagot's handwriting.

[72] 5.26, Elizabeth Seton to Julia Scott, 9 May 1809, *CW*, 2:69.

[73] John M. Tessier's Journal, 26 April 1809, ASMS.

[74] John Carroll to Charles-François Nagot, Baltimore, 23 September 1809, ASMS. Nagot was very ill in Baltimore in August 1809, after his return from Pigeon Hill. Cf. Tessier's Journal, 14-16 August 1809.

[75] 6.4, Elizabeth Seton to John Carroll, 6 August 1809, *CW*, 2:77.

[76] 6.9, Elizabeth Seton to John Carroll, 2 November 1809, *CW*, 2:88.

[77] Pierre Babade to Harriet Seton, Baltimore, 17 June 1809, ASJPH 1-3-3-1:72.

[78] Poem composed by Pierre Babade to Harriet Seton, 24 September 1809, ASJPH 1-3-3-1:83.

[79] 6.4, Elizabeth Seton to John Carroll, 6 August 1809, *CW*, 2:77.

[80] Ibid.

[81] Pierre Babade to Elizabeth Seton, Emmitsburg, 20 August 1809, ASJPH 1-3-3-1:63.

[82] Pierre Babade to Harriet Seton, Emmitsburg, 30 August 1809, ASJPH 1-3-3-1:64. Tessier's Journal records that Babade returned to Baltimore on 6 September 1809.

[83] 6.6, Elizabeth Seton to John Carroll, 8 September 1809, *CW*, 2:81.

[84] Louis Dubourg to Elizabeth Seton, n.p., 29 October 1817, AMSV, I, 54.

[85] Tessier told Babade this. See Pierre Babade to Elizabeth Seton, Emmitsburg, 20 August 1809, ASJPH 1-3-3-1:63. French.

[86] Ibid.

[87] A letter of Charles-François Nagot to Mrs. Seton dated 9 November 1809, refers to a letter of August 1809, in which David's appointment was discussed, but this August letter has not been preserved. No explanation appears in any archival material for Babade's failure to be considered as a possible candidate for the role of superior. Nagot's confidence in David is attested by provisions of his will, drawn up on 29 April 1805, which made David his heir in case of John M. Tessier's death. See Nagot's will, ASMS. David was with Flaget in Emmitsburg the last week in August but it is impossible to say whether the subject of superiors was discussed at this time. Cf. Tessier's Journal, 22, 30 August 1809. For a life of David, see Sister Columba Fox, O.S.B., *The Life of the Right Reverend John Baptist Mary David, 1761-1841* (New York, 1925).

[88] 6.8, Elizabeth Seton to Louis Dubourg, *CW*, 2:86. This is only a fragment of a letter, but the implications suggest that it was written in late August or early September 1809.

[89] Louis Dubourg to Elizabeth Seton, Baltimore, 13 September 1809, AMSV, I, 8.

[90] John Dubois to Elizabeth Seton, Emmitsburg, 6 October 1809, ASJPH 1-3-3-5:16.

[91] Pierre Babade, Journal, 11 October 1809, ASJPH 1-3-3-1:65.

[92] The sacrament of confirmation was administered 20 October 1809.

[93] 6.9, Elizabeth Seton to John Carroll, 2 November 1809, *CW*, 2:87.

[94] Ibid., 88.

[95] Ibid.

[96] John Carroll to Elizabeth Seton, Baltimore, 9 November 1809, AMSV, I, 15.

[97] John Dubois to Mrs. Charlotte Melmoth, Emmitsburg, 28 November 1809, ASJPH 1-3-3-5:3.

[98] Charles F. Nagot to Elizabeth Seton, Baltimore, 9 November 1809, ASJPH 1-3-3-2:7.

[99] 6.12, Elizabeth Seton to John Carroll, 14 December 1809, *CW*, 2:92.

[100] Louis Dubourg to Elizabeth Seton, Baltimore, 15 December 1809, AMSV, I, 9.

[101] Samuel Waddington Seton to Harriet Seton, 28 November 1809, ASJPH 1-3-3-17:5.

[102] 6.14, Elizabeth Seton to Julia Scott, 27 December 1809, *CW*, 2:94.

[103] Louis Dubourg to Elizabeth Seton, Baltimore, 28 December 1809, AMSV, I, 10.

[104] John David to Elizabeth Seton, Baltimore, 28 December 1809, AMSV, I, 23.

[105] Anthony Kohlmann to Elizabeth Seton, New York, 17 January 1810, ASJPH 1-3-3-2:27.

[106] Jean Cheverus to Elizabeth Seton, Boston, 24 January 1810, ASJPH 1-3-3-1:11.

[107] John Carroll to Elizabeth Seton, Baltimore, 28 December 1809, AMSV, I, 16.

[108] 6.15, Elizabeth Seton to George Weis, 1 January 1810, *CW*, 2:96.

[109] Mary Bayley Post to Elizabeth Seton, New York, 16 March 1810, ASJPH 1-3-3-11:8.

[110] 6.26, Elizabeth Seton to Eliza Sadler, 8 March 1810, *CW*, 2:111.

[111] A-6.3a, Mother Rose White's Journal, *CW*, 2:726. See a letter written by Mrs. Seton to George Weis bears the notation, "Dear Cecil arrived in my house April 11," ASJPH 1-3-3-2:57(2).

[112] 6.34, Elizabeth Seton to John David, n.d., *CW*, 2:121.

[113] Louis Dubourg to Elizabeth Seton, Baltimore, 28 December 1809, AMSV, I, 10.

[114] John David to Elizabeth Seton, Baltimore, 28 December 1809, AMSV, I, 23.

[115] Elizabeth Seton to John Carroll, 25 January 1810, AAB, AASMU, 7-M-7. 6.23, *CW*, 2:106. The few letters extant of Mrs. Seton to Father David bear out her description. They are characterized by brevity and frigidity. See 6.36, Elizabeth Seton to John David, *CW*, 2:122; 6.51, Ibid., *CW*, 2:148; 6.60, Ibid., *CW*, 2:159.

[116] John Carroll to Elizabeth Seton, Emmitsburg, 11 March 1810, ASJPH 1-3-3-1:42. This letter refers to one written the preceding day to Mrs. Seton, but the letter of 10 March 1810 could not be found.

[117] Ibid.

[118] *Mother Rose White*, (Emmitsburg, Maryland: Daughters of Charity, 1936), ASJPH 7-2-1:2-6. This is one of a series of biographies of superiors of the Emmitsburg community, privately printed for community use. See Record of Students' Entrance, AMSMU.

[119] 6.34, Elizabeth Seton to John David, n.d., *CW*, 2:120. This letter is only a fragment beginning "Dear Sir" but internal evidence indicates that it was written immediately after the return from Baltimore, 28-29 April 1810. ASJPH formerly classified it under Nagot, but since Mrs. Seton's direct superior was John David, and because of the coldness of the salutation and contents, Melville believes it was addressed to David.

[120] 6.73, Elizabeth Seton to John Carroll, 16 March 1811, *CW*, 2:179.

[121] 6.39, Elizabeth Seton to Antonio Filicchi, 20 May 1810, *CW*, 2:127.

[122] Anna Maria Seton to Elizabeth Seton, 10 June 1810, ASJPH 1-3-3-9:37.

[123] 6.47, Elizabeth Seton to John Carroll, 15 June 1810, *CW*, 2:143. ASJPH has a draft dated June 14 which contains substantially the same material.

[124] Ibid.

[125] This letter is missing but Carroll's reply notes its arrival.

[126] John Carroll to Elizabeth Seton, 18 July 1810, ASJPH 1-3-3-1:44.

[127] A-6.3a, Mother Rose White's Journal, *CW*, 2:728.

[128] Ibid., 730. "Rev. Mr. Flaget returned from France and brought us the rules, constitutions and conferences of the Daughters of Charity founded by St. Vincent de Paul."

[129] Jean Cheverus to Louis Dubourg, Boston, 2 October 1810, ASMS.

[130] John M. Tessier's Journal, 8 November 1810, ASMS.

[131] John Carroll to Elizabeth Seton, Baltimore, 11 September 1810, AMSV, I, 17.

[132] 6.64, Elizabeth Seton to Eliza Sadler, 21 November 1810, *CW*, 2:163.

[133] John Dubois to Elizabeth Seton, Emmitsburg, 23 November 1810, ASJPH 1-3-3-5:17.

[134] Jean Cheverus to John Carroll, Conewago, 26 November 1810, AAB, AASMSU, 20-L.

[135] 6.65, Elizabeth Seton to John Carroll, 29 November 1810, *CW*, 2:165.

[136] Mrs. Margaret C. George to Elizabeth Seton, Baltimore, 25 December 1810, ASJPH 1-3-3-2:19.

[137] John David to Elizabeth Seton, Baltimore, 23 February 1811, AMSV, I, 24.

[138] 6.73, Elizabeth Seton to John Carroll, 16 March 1811, *CW*, 2:179.

[139] John Carroll to Elizabeth Seton, Baltimore, n.d., ASJPH 1-3-3-1:43.

[140] 6.52, Elizabeth Seton to George Weis, [July 1810], *CW,* 2:149.

[141] 6.59, Elizabeth Seton to John Carroll, n.d., *CW*, 2:157.

[142] 6.60, Elizabeth Seton to John David, n.d., *CW*, 2:159.

[143] Ibid., n.2.

[144] 6.76, Elizabeth Seton to John Carroll, 13 May 1811, *CW*, 2:184. John M. Tessier's Journal, 12 May 1811, ASMS.

[145] Ibid.

[146] 6.78, Elizabeth Seton to George Weis, 24 June 1811, *CW*, 2:186.

[147] John David to Simon Bruté, Bardstown, 18 July 1811, UNDA.

[148] 6.82, Elizabeth Seton to John Carroll, 9 August 1811, *CW*, 2:194.

[149] John David to Simon Bruté, Bardstown, 16 September 1811, UNDA. John M. Tessier's Journal states that Bruté returned to Baltimore on 23 August 1811.

[150] John M. Tessier's Journal, ASMS. Louis Dubourg returned to Baltimore on 6 July 1811; he departed for Louisiana on 18 October 1812.

[151] Louis Dubourg to Elizabeth Seton, n.d., ASJPH 1-3-3-2:2.

[152] Louis Dubourg to Elizabeth Seton, 7 April 1811, ASJPH 1-3-3-2:4.

[153] John Carroll to Elizabeth Seton, Emmitsburg, 11 September 1811, ASJPH 1-3-3-1:45. Copy; Carroll to Seton, Emmitsburg, n.d., Ibid, 43.

[154] 6.86, Elizabeth Seton to Julia Scott, 5 November 1811, *CW*, 2:198.

[155] 6.70, Elizabeth Seton to Catherine Dupleix, 4 February 1811, *CW*, 2:172.

[156] 6.76, Elizabeth Seton to John Carroll, 13 May 1811, *CW*, 2:184.

[157] Simon Gabriel Bruté, Notes, ASJPH 1-3-3-12:107.

[158] Joanna Barry [Mrs. James] to Elizabeth Seton, n.d., ASJPH 1-3-3-2:49.

[159] 6.73, Elizabeth Seton to John Carroll, 16 March 1811, *CW*, 2:180.

ৡৡৡ

WARS AND RUMORS OF WAR

While Mother Seton was earning her title of spiritual mother to the religious community, her resources as a physical mother to her five children were just beginning to be tried. Self-effacement and submission to others were the lessons of the controversy over superiors, while her resignation to the will of God would be most tried in the events which ensued.

Anna Maria Seton, the first-born of Elizabeth Seton's "darlings," had many claims to her mother's heart. It was Anna Maria who was most like her mother in the complexity of her personality. Anna Maria had shared the arduous voyage to Italy, and the desolate return; and it was she who most immediately shared the wonders of the new faith. Her very nickname recalled the generous Filicchis, who had called her "Annina." It was Annina's budding romance which recalled so poignantly Elizabeth's own youthful impatience to be with William Magee Seton. It was her maternal yearning to see her daughter happy that prompted Mother Seton to permit the girl to remain in Baltimore after Cecilia Seton's death, so that Anna Maria might have some last meetings with young DuPavillon before he left for Martinique.[a] After Anna Maria returned to Emmitsburg, her poise and serenity pleased her mother who wrote contentedly to Julia:

> We are all all well—Anna as quiet as puss in the corner, keeps her sensibilities all in order—has not [received] letters since I wrote you [but] takes the matter coolly. [She] gathers nuts, dries fruits, and shares in all the amusements of the boarders of the house, and seems to have resigned all to Him who knows best. Yet, her D [DuPavillon] may return when she least expects it.[1]

Charles DuPavillon did not return, however; and young Anna Maria had to bear the news that he had made an alliance on the island which was his home.[2] Although Elizabeth Seton was out of patience with the young man's conduct, she confessed to Julia, "I am very thankful she is left quietly with me as she seemed to dread the separation had it been ever so small and had long since felt the imprudence of connecting herself so soon, and with so little experience."[3]

---

[a] Charles Du Pavillon was enrolled at St. Mary's College from 1804 until 1810, according to the college records. Anna Maria met him sometime after her arrival in June of 1808.

After the disappointment of this first romance, Anna Maria Seton drew even closer to her mother. She began to take a great interest in the younger children of the school, helped them to prepare themselves for First Communion, and organized a special group, her "decury," with little rules and rewards all their own.[4] During the fall of 1811, when Annina was worn out from fever and coughing, when William Seton had intermittent fever, and their mother suffered from an old complaint, Elizabeth wrote to Mme. Chatard in Baltimore, "I never had more tranquility than during these exterior pains—exterior,[b] for my children [are] good, and if they are taken, will go but a little while before and no doubt smooth the way I must follow."[5] During the leisurely rides on horseback, taken to rebuild Anna's strength, the mother and daughter shared the pleasure of the view of the Mountain so "very black but the scene below bright and gay," with the "dear ones skipping" on the still-green meadows with the sheep.[6] But while Elizabeth chatted gaily with Annina, she could not help noticing the burning cheeks, the slender form, the racking cough. With inner dread she told Julia that, "Anna, my sweet and precious comfort and friend, is undergoing all the symptoms which were so fatal to our Celia and so many of the family."[7]

When Mary Bayley Post heard of her sister's suspicions in regard to Annina she was deeply disturbed, fearing that Elizabeth might sink under the repeated trials of all this sickness and death. She asked Elizabeth to send Annina to them for the summer, so that Dr. Post could supervise her recovery.[8] Dué wrote anxiously from New York, too, inquiring for news of the girl who had been so dear to her in days when Mrs. Dupleix was "Aunt Doux" to the little Setons.[9] Elizabeth Seton needed the comfort of these friends; for as winter progressed it was clear that Annina was not going to recover. Elizabeth frantically tried everything that might relieve her daughter's suffering. She had George Weis send up a stove and a carpet from Baltimore, so that the girl might be moved "down stairs in the room next to our Adored." When Anna Maria expressed a desire for oysters, the same good man dispatched them.[10]

As Anna Maria Seton's debility became more pronounced her piety seemed to flourish more noticeably. On 30 January 1812, she received the last sacraments, and the following day she was "consecrated" as a Sister of Charity of St. Joseph's.[11] It was the gratification of her most fervent wish, and she said happily, "Now it is done, that I may become a Sister and be numbered among the children of blessed St. Vincent."[12] Hour after hour, when the agonizing pain bathed the fragile body in cold sweat, Anna Maria

---

[b] Mrs. Seton was suffering at the time from boils under the arms. 6.87, Elizabeth Seton to Eliza Sadler, 25 November 1811, *CW,* 2:199.

gasped alternately, "My Mother, My Saviour." Elizabeth wrote Julia from the bedside in February:

> So quiet and so exhausted I know not how soon the moment will come. So, Julia dear, so it is—dear and lovely to be sure is my Darling but much rather would I see her go in her lovely innocence than wait to take my sin and sorrow. She will not allow any of us to shed a tear around her.[13]

It seemed to Elizabeth Seton that her child was, indeed a saint. "Her precious soul stretching out towards heaven—the singular purity of her life" made the mother regret her own overpowering grief at the impending separation. It was as if the child had become the mother, and in a few months had learned the hard lesson of the years.

> When the last change took place and cold sweat, gasping breathing and agonizing pain indicated immediate dissolution, the pain of her eyes [was] so great she could no longer fix them, she said "I can no longer look at you, my dear crucifix, but I enter my agony with my Saviour. I drink the cup with Him. Yes, adorable Lord, your will and yours alone be done—I will it too. I leave my dearest Mother because You will it, my dearest, dearest Mother"—[14]

It was the mother who in the secret places of her heart cried out:

> Eternity always at hand! Oh Annina—I look to the far, so far distant shore, the heaven of heavens—a few days more and Eternity—*now* then, all resignation, love abandon. Rest in him—*the heart in sweet bitterness Amour, anéantisement, abandon. A A A.*[15]

Try as she would, Elizabeth could not repress the tears toward the end as she rubbed those "cold, cold feet." Annina asked wonderingly, *"Can it be for Me, should you not rejoice—it will be but a moment and reunited for Eternity!"* Mrs. Seton said later, *"Eternity* was Anna's darling word."[16]

Mother Rose's journal recounts the death of Anna Maria Seton in this manner:

> She made her vows on her death bed and expired like an angel in the arms of one of the Sisters who was supporting her. Her last movement was to raise her eyes to Heaven and clasp her hands which remained clasped, that we may say she died in prayer. Our dear Mother who was kneeling by

the bed made her offering and retired before the Blessed Sacrament, giving directions that her hands should not be unclasped, which was attended to...so that we laid her out with her hands in the position she had placed them before her death...she died on the 12th of March 1812.[17]

Friday, at one o'clock, Mother Seton "left her Darling in the woods with Harriet and Cecilia," and entered a valley of shadows from which she feared, at times, she might never emerge. Jean Cheverus wrote from Boston, "I bless the God of infinite mercy who has granted her to die the death of the Saints and has endowed her dear Mother with the Faith and courage of the Mother of the Macabees."[18] But Elizabeth Seton and her spiritual director knew how severe was the drain upon that faith and courage. From the depths of her desolation she cried:

Our Jesus! Compassionate—Thou so merciful, best, only powerful—*Thee alone*—I can do nothing but earnestly pray—Jesus, beloved Master—my Jesus—have pity, give at least full grace *for the moment.* Pity a Mother, a poor Mother, that she may persevere with you in the garden, or nailed to the cross, given up perfectly resigned in her long agony.[19]

She turned to her old friends in her anguish, reliving in her letters to Julia, to Sad, to Dué, the last months of Anna's life. She pushed back the icy wave which threatened to engulf her by repeating the phrases of wonder and praise.

The remembrance of my lovely one now forces itself in every moment—her singular modesty and grace of action, the lifting her eyes from the ground to cast the rays of her very soul into mine, which was often her only expression of her desires or wishes. Now I am so happy to think I never contradicted any of them—her rational and pure sentiments set down in so many ways—the neatness and order of all her little affairs, and ingenious way of uniting economy and elegance in her plain and simple dress. This was always a delight to poor Mother but now an admiration and it appears to me I never saw, or shall see, anything to be compared to her—poor, poor, Mother let her talk to you, Eliza—[20]

To her sister, Mary, Elizabeth sent some of Annina's little exercises along with a flower from the grave, and she was comforted by Mary's words, "She is gone to a soil more suited to her celestial and aspiring qualities. She is gone to bloom in a world congenial to her pure and refined nature."[21] Eliza Sadler, in her customary pointed fashion, had replied to the news, "Are you not a favored instrument in the hands of the all wise to raise a family for heaven? I do not tell you my heart bleeds for you—I sometimes feel as if I should rather say rejoice with you."[22] But rejoicing was not to be easily achieved.

John Dubois, Mrs. Seton's director, had seen the possibilities for temptation in her adulation of her daughter, yet when he tried to suggest the danger to Elizabeth she withdrew, as if unable to cope with such distinctions. Dubois wrote to Bruté, who had been present in those last hours of Anna Maria Seton's life, asking him to continue to write to St. Joseph's.[c] "You do good," Dubois told him, and as for Mother Seton:

> I fear the terrible trial she has had in the death of Annina may have been to arrest or repress the too great pleasure she took in exalting her, too much fear that she would do or say something too human when there was someone in the room...A hundred times I have wished to probe this wound. It is only recently I have dared to touch it.[23]

Dubois, a very humble man, continued with the words:

> God grant that you may someday know this soul. What character! But like gold brocade, rich and heavy, how hard to handle. For many years she was flattered too much. As for my part, poor fellow, what can I do? I can say no more; the double role I play here imposes silence. Try to open a heart such as this one—one talks of the surface, the tinsel, one fears to reveal the essential. As a result, you can only judge by appearances and beat around the bush. I have been tempted a hundred times to give up this charge. What a soul it would take, it needs a saint of the first caliber—St. Francis de Sales—and I am only an ugly little wretch. Try to have her examine with you humility, obedience, detachment from everything, renouncing self-esteem, the love of order, uniformity, the rule, in a word, the religious life.[24]

The previous deaths which had deprived Mother Seton of loved ones had found her spirit ready and capable of sustaining the loss. She had

---

[c] Bruté himself later wrote of this period, "Mother then much tried, as if, she said, she had taken too much complacency and joy in the holy dispositions of that blessed child." *Mother Seton* (Emmitsburg, Maryland: Daughters of Charity, 1884), 105.

expressed it nicely to Julia in 1810 after Harriet Seton's death and just prior to the death of Cecilia Seton in April when she explained:

> We part—nature groans—for me it is an anguish that threatens dissolution, not in convulsive sighs but the soul is aghast, petrified, after ten minutes it returns to its usual motion and all goes on as if nothing had happened. This same effect has followed the death of all so dear. Why, Faith lifts the staggering soul on one side, Hope supports it on the other, experience says it must be—and love says let it be—[25]

But now this easy resignation did not come. Flesh of her flesh, bone of her bone, the first-born child lay in the grave. Mrs. Seton confessed to George Weis that "for three months after Nina was taken I was so often expecting to lose my senses and my head was so disordered that unless for the daily duties always before me I did not know much of what I did or what I left undone."[26] To Eliza Sadler, Elizabeth wrote six months after Annina's death, "in truth the separation from my Angel has left so new and deep an impression on my mind that if I was not obliged to live in these dear ones, I should unconsciously die in her." Resignation was growing, however, as the next words testified, "unconsciously, for never by a free act of the mind would I ever regret his Will."[27]

The struggle resumed in full force when autumn came. Mother Seton described her anguish at her daughter's grave in these words:

> Begging, crying to Mary to behold her Son and plead for us, and to Jesus to behold his Mother—to pity a mother—a poor, poor Mother—so uncertain of reunion—then the Soul quieted even by the desolation of the falling leaves around began to cry out from Eternity to Eternity thou art God—all shall perish and pass away—but Thou remainest forever. Then the thought of Our Dearest stretched on the cross and His last words coming powerfully, stood up with hands and eyes lifted to the pure heavens crying out "forgive they know not what they do." Did she? adored, did she know?—and all the death-bed scene appeared—at this moment in the silence of all around, a rattling sound rushing towards—along Annina's grave a snake stretched itself on the dried grass— so large and ugly, and the little gate tied—but Nature was able to drag to the place and strong enough to tie and untie, saying inwardly, my darling shall not be rooted by the hogs for you—then put up the bar and softly walked away—Oh,

my dear ones [are] companions of worms and reptiles!—and the beautiful Soul Where?[28]

The fall brought respite, nevertheless, in the form of several healing distractions. Rev. Simon Gabriel Bruté returned to Emmitsburg to become Dubois' assistant.[d] Bruté, whose relation to Mother Seton will be the subject of a subsequent chapter, was admirably suited to the task of spiritual direction of this complex soul. In September, too, Sister Maria Murphy Burke became mortally ill and called constantly upon Elizabeth for support. Fearing "the Enemy" would find her too weak, Sister Maria relied upon her spiritual mother's assistance, and Mother Seton found reserves of courage which she had feared destroyed by Anna's death. Her zeal for souls overpowered all else and for six weeks she proved a constant ally. "What delight," she recorded, "for poor Mother to have been and to be still her *Mother*–the natural one[e] was *present* but the spiritual one who had all her dear little Secrets of the Soul was the dearest and so more and more united in parting that it has been hardly possible to escape from her for the last six weeks."[29] Elizabeth found that her work was still far from complete and that Annina's "dear Eternity" must wait.

Physical as well as spiritual problems of the community demanded discriminating attention from Mother Seton and the superior, Father John Dubois. Chief among the former was the matter of expanding the work of the Sisters of Charity into other regions. Almost as soon as Bishop Flaget and his colleague, Rev. John David, reached Kentucky David wrote to Bruté:

> We are determined to form a society of virtuous women for the education of young people of their sex. I believed, when I was in Baltimore, that the Sisters of Charity would not be suitable to this work, rather the Ursulines. But since we are on the spot it is evident that cloistered Sisters would not suit as well as Sisters of Charity as regards small pupils.[30]

David went on to request Bruté, who was then at St. Mary's Seminary in Baltimore, to secure a copy of the rules of the Sisters of Charity from the copy in the possession of the archbishop. Father Bruté may have misunderstood David's request, for the latter wrote rather assertively in November:

---

[d] A note by Simon Bruté says "I was sent to assist Mr. Dubois 28 September 1812," ASJPH 1-3-3-12:108.

[e] Margaret Carey Murphy Burke, Sister Maria's natural mother, who worked at Mount St. Mary's, had originally opposed her daughter's entering the Sisters of Charity of St. Joseph's. Daniel Nusbaum, "This Venerable House, Part I: The Beginnings," *Analecta: Selected Studies in the History of Mount St. Mary's College and Seminary,* I, no. 3 (2000), 8.

You tell me, my dear brother, that I have asked for Daughters of Charity. I assure you I do not recall making this request, for I have never thought of it. I have asked you to make me a copy of the rules...from which I could trace those of our Sisters; that is all. I repeat this request. Perhaps Mr. Nagot who has recovered his facility in writing could render me this service...[31]

Whether Brute's failure to comply with David's demands was solely responsible or not, a year went by before the Kentucky community made any start. David told Bruté in September 1812, "We hope to begin our community of daughters this fall," and he added that Bishop Flaget would be able to explain more fully on his forthcoming visit to the east.[32] Eventually, busy Bruté copied the constitution of the American Sisters of Charity and sent it to Kentucky. David replied on 12 July 1813, that his own community was at last under way. He had "united six girls in a log house on our plantation a half-mile from the Seminary. Thank you very much for the trouble you took to copy the constitutions," he said graciously. "You could give me great pleasure by copying also the rules; they are very necessary to us."[33]

One can only guess what difficulties faced the frontier priest in his efforts to found a community, but by September 1813, he had changed his position in regard to sisters from Emmitsburg, and had asked Mother Seton's community for the assistant, Rose White. Writing to Bruté on 7 September, David complained:

I am very annoyed that they could not give me Rose [White]; she is perfectly suited to this important work. If Sister Kitty [Mullan] had enough health she would do very well for my purpose. Fanny [Jordan] is the one I need for instruction. But I see that after having given me a choice, they refuse the ones I ask for.[34]

The council records at Emmitsburg of this period are minimal so that only David's version of this request and refusal is available.[f] It is rather apparent, however, that Kentucky was still without the desired rules, for David's letter to Bruté continued petulantly, "We suffer also from a lack of rules. I have given them the provisional ones resembling those of St. Joseph's as far as memory serves me. If they would but send me the order of exercises—but they seem to take little interest in an establishment so far

---

[f] Council Minutes of the Sisters of Charity of Saint Joseph's are missing after August 1809 until August 14, 1812.

away."[35] Bishop Flaget added his voice to the demand, saying "Hasten to have sent us the rules requested for so long a time."[36]

The first record of relations with Kentucky to be found at Emmitsburg is an entry in the Council Book for 2 April 1814, which reads, "Rt. Rev. John David of Kentucky in accordance with Rt. Rev. Dr. Flaget proposed a union of an Establishment in their Diocese with ours and requiring some alterations."[37] The council record then set down three questions which such a union posed: was such a union compatible with the Emmitsburg rules; could the bishop of the diocese cause alterations in these rules; and would the novitiate necessarily be located at Emmitsburg. The council of St. Joseph's appears to have been very liberal in its attitude toward these first three proposals, agreeing that such an establishment was possible, but not at Emmitsburg's expense; that the bishop could make such alterations as the constitution allowed; and that the novitiate need not be required at Emmitsburg, but that the Kentucky sisters "should be disposed, in case the Council of the Motherhouse required it," to come to the motherhouse for the novitiate.[38]

John David was not content, however, with the three stipulations the council minutes record. Writing to Bruté that same April he said he had told both Mr. Dubois and Sister Kitty that although he would "consent to have my house depend on St. Joseph's," he could not consent to have the superior take the name of sister servant "in a country where the name is synonymous with slave." He continued in a somewhat dictatorial vein; "I demand also that we form all novices for Kentucky here, and finally that the Superior of the community be named by the bishop, as well as the confessors, ordinary and extraordinary."[39]

The complete lack of archival evidence that might indicate whether David ever consulted Mother Seton on these issues casts some reflection upon the tact of the Kentucky priest. His own letters, and those of Dubois, to Baltimore leave no doubt as to the arbitrary tone David chose to adopt. Even though St. Joseph's was quite willing to send one of their number to serve as superior to the Kentucky group, they insisted upon their right to pass upon the qualifications of candidates aspiring to become one of the Sisters of Charity. When this issue came before the council in August, that body voted unanimously "No" to any union with Kentucky on such terms, and the council records thereafter do not refer to Kentucky again. A possible clue to Mother Seton's attitude during the Kentucky affair is found in a letter to her from Pierre Babade, 19 October 1814, in which the priest said, "You are right, my dear daughter, to tell me, and repeat that you are more wicked than I can conceive. The foundation of this jealousy and antipathy for your Superior is truly the old Adam. What consoles me is that the new Adam prevails and that you do your duty." It is difficult to imagine that "Superior" refers to Dubois; it is easier to believe that Babade meant "former Superior" and referred to David. However, this is only a speculation and cannot be used to make a conclusive statement.[40]

But the proposals for union did not cease, and the debate continued in Baltimore. Dubois wrote to Archbishop Carroll on 10 October 1814, presenting the Emmitsburg version of the controversy. He commented that, respecting Sister Fanny's appointment for Kentucky, "it is a business which can be referred to the Council of Sisters when the time is come to decide upon it."[g] He approached the matter from a constitutional point of view. Probably no one in Mother Seton's lifetime better understood the spirit of this constitution than John Dubois, the man who had developed the American version for these Sisters of Charity modeled on the Paris-based community. He pointed out that changes in this constitution could be effected only with the consent of the archbishop, the superior of the seminary at Baltimore, and Dubois himself. He showed that St. Vincent's regulations allowed for only one motherhouse. In France, where the rules had originated, separate novitiates were not granted to Daughters of Charity even as far distant as Poland at that time. There, no sister could be admitted to her vows without special consent from the central council of the motherhouse, to which six months notice must be given pending an investigation of the candidate's qualifications. Dubois applied the analogy to St. Joseph's and Kentucky. "In case we should be informed from Europe, after free communications are established, that even in Poland they are obliged to send Sisters to the Motherhouse...then no more should Sisters be bred there [in Kentucky]."[41]

Dubois sent these same arguments to his fellow Sulpician in Kentucky, but Father David refused to accept the Paris-Poland analogy. He demanded, instead, an immediate final answer from Dubois. Dubois wrote again to Carroll on 27 October, repeating the necessity for a decision from both the archbishop and Tessier before the constitution could be amended. Dubois in this letter introduced another complicating factor involved in a union with Kentucky. The new community, he pointed out, was supported only by Bishop Flaget's financial contributions and David's zeal. If either should fail, St. Joseph's would be left financially responsible for sisters

---

[g] The three Sisters who seem to have been David's choice from St. Joseph's were Sisters Rose White, Catherine (Kitty) Mullen, and Fanny Jordan. Sister Rose was sent to Philadelphia in September 1814, to take over the orphanage there; Sister Kitty was ill and died on 25 December 1814. Thus by the fall of 1814, David's choice devolved upon Fanny Jordan.

whose qualifications they had not been allowed to judge. Surely, Dubois urged, "Our precautions cannot appear unreasonable."[42]

Meanwhile, David had presented his own case to Baltimore in phrases more courtly, but undeniably insistent that the title "sister servant" be abolished, and the Kentucky novitiate be allowed.[43] The archbishop replied that he was delayed by his consideration of Dubois's "lengthy reasons" on the other side, but found no cause to disapprove David's two stipulations. Carroll said he did feel that "it should be a matter of agreement between the house of St. Joseph and your establishment how far should extend the intercommunity of property."[44] When the archbishop's attitude became known Dubois dispatched Bruté to Baltimore to deliver a letter which contained Dubois' most masterly defense of the rule of St. Vincent de Paul as contained in the constitution of the Daughters of Charity. Seven full pages in length, this letter defined for the archbishop the spirit which inspired the constitution. It reviewed the entire case for St. Joseph's, and again pointed out why David's desire to remodel the rules according to his personal wishes was not compatible with the concept of the rules the original community maintained. Time and again he adverted to French custom and precedent in the application of the rule.[45] Before the month had passed, Dubois wrote the blunt, decisive pronouncement:

> The constitution of the Sisters cannot be modified according to the various opinions of each Bishop. Each of them is at liberty to approve or disapprove of our constitutions for his diocese. If he does not approve of them he can establish another community according to his own ideas. The Sisters of Charity owe them obedience only in what is not contrary to their constitutions once approved.[46]

The proposed union with Kentucky never materialized. The community at Nazareth was the work of Bishop Flaget and John David, and although its rules were based upon the Emmitsburg rule, a modification of those of St. Vincent de Paul and St. Louise de Marillac, it was never connected in any administrative way with the first Sisters of Charity of St. Joseph's in the United States.

While the scheme for expansion toward the southwest was proving abortive, Philadelphia to the north was eager to accept the sisters exactly as they were. As early as 1809, according to one source, Rev. Michael Hurley, O.S.A., the pastor of St. Augustine's Parish, is supposed to have requested Sisters of Charity for his city.[47] There is also a tradition that after Bishop Egan's visit to the Valley in 1810, with Jean Cheverus, the Philadelphia prelate favored the importation of Mother Seton's daughters. However that may be, on 1 August 1814, the managers of St. Joseph's orphanage in Philadelphia unanimously "agreed that Rev. Mr. Hurley apply to the Sisters of Charity at Emmitsburg for a matron and two assistant Sisters," offering $600.00 a year for their services.[48]

On 14 August 1814, it was decided to send Sisters Rose White, Susan Clossy, and Teresa Conroy in answer to this request.[49] On 29 September 1814, the first leaven from the motherhouse went forth to Philadelphia. The journey was made overland, and Father Dubois accompanied the three women as far as Taneytown, giving "lessons of economy all the way." In her journal Sister Rose explained why the travelers went by land instead of sea. "As it was not safe to go by the packets[h] as the English were still in the Bay, a private carriage was hired, and Sisters went by way of Little York and Lancaster, with directions to beg hospitality on the way..."[50]

Mother Seton wrote to Julia Scott in Philadelphia:

My Julia, there is one of the sweetest souls gone to Philadelphia from this house, who has lived [in] my very heart and been more than an own sister to me ever since I have been here. She even slept always behind my curtain and has nursed Cecil, Harriet, Anna, William and Rebecca through all her [sic, their] sufferings with inconceivable tenderness. She has the care of the poor orphans belonging to our church with our good Sister Rose White who has the little institution in her care. If you have ever a wish to find a piece of myself it will be in this dear Susan Clossy who is one of her assistants. If you ever see them, love them for me, for they love me most tenderly as I justly do them.[51]

The three sisters took formal charge of the Philadelphia orphanage on 6 October 1814. Their first endeavors were particularly encouraged by two admirers of Mother Seton from earlier years, Father Michael Hurley and the convert, Mrs. Rachel Montgomery. Sister Rose found the latter who was president of the newly-founded "Lady Managers" of the orphanage, a "kind benefactress and the true Mother of Charity." Rachel Montgomery worked tirelessly to assist these sisters whose foundation she had hailed so enthusiastically in 1809.[52] It was Mrs. Montgomery's society of ladies who paid the traveling expenses of the sisters to Philadelphia, paid their salaries, and furnished their shoes. Mother Seton was deeply pleased at the welcome

---

[h] Packets are passenger boats which also usually carry mail and cargo.

her daughters received and she reported happily to Archbishop Carroll in November:

> We have heard again of our excellent Rose [White] by Mrs. Carroll[i] who is much delighted with her and the little establishment. She is full of courage as usual but I believe her greatest difficulty is to resist the abundant kindness poured upon them.[53]

While Elizabeth Seton was preoccupied with grief and community affairs, the world outside the Valley was concerned with economic distress and war. The Philadelphia venture was begun in perilous times. The war in Europe had interested the Church in the United States as well as the government in Washington. In December 1809, Louis Dubourg had said to Mother Seton, "Above all pray for the church who never was in a more melancholy and frightful crisis than at the present time."[54] On 30 December, he reported that it was believed Pius VII had "died as a martyr to his confinement in the Island of St. Margaretta near the coast of Provence." He asked:

> What would you think of making a Novena to the Sacred Heart for the necessities of the Church, and associating to it as many pious souls of your neighbourhood as could be mustered? Propose the idea to your spiritual Father. The Pope in his hasty passage thro' France, where tho a prisoner he was as much honoured by the people and probably more fervently than if he had been on a throne, was heard to say: *Orate & Nolite timere*: Pray and fear not. Docile to his fatherly call, I wish all those who love the Church should unite to address to our Lord [with] a concert of fervent prayers.[55]

Elizabeth had relayed the news to a New York friend with the words, "It is said that Pope Pius VII has gained the palm of martyrdom & probably there is now no pope, or if there is it is a relation of Bonaparte."[56] A year later, however, John David wrote to Emmitsburg that the Pope was still alive, even though the Society of St. Sulpice was "still on foot" in France and "Mr. Emery[j] does not act as Superior."[57] Elizabeth was greatly impressed

---

[i] Possibly Henrietta (Harrietta) Chew Carroll (1775-1861), wife of Charles Carroll, Jr., the grandson of Charles Carroll of Carrolltown. Mrs. Carroll is listed as a benefactor of St. Joseph's Asylum, Philadelphia. See Sr. Rose White to Rev. Louis DeBarth, 8 October 1815, published in *Records of the American Catholic Historical Society* XI, No. 3 (September 1900), 352.

[j] Jacques André Emery was the eighth superior general of the Society of St. Sulpice in Paris. In May 1810, Napoleon ordered the Minister of Public Worship to dissolve the Society of St. Sulpice. Emery, at the age of seventy-eight, was compelled to leave the seminary and Sulpician motherhouse.

by the sufferings of Pius VII, and his prayer of submission to the will of God became her favorite prayer for the rest of her life.[k]

Meanwhile, the precarious balance which had existed between the governments of the United States and Great Britain when Mother Seton came to Emmitsburg was daily growing more delicate. When Bishop Cheverus congratulated Archbishop Carroll on having been invested with the pallium in 1811, he had found it "not a little remarkable that the British minister should have been the bearer of it."[58] Augustus John Foster, who had come as British minister plenipotentiary in August, was one of a succession of ministers who failed to produce a peaceful adjustment of British disputes with the United States.[l] He, like David M. Erskine and Francis J. Jackson before him, went home. By June the United States Congress was ready for a war message. Even before the declaration of war on 18 June 1812, President James Madison had asked for 10,000 troops and Governor Robert Bowie of Maryland had, in turn, asked his general assembly to make the appropriations necessary for Maryland's quota. In Baltimore the guns on Fort McHenry were mounted, and the city became a seething caldron of conflicting patriotism and pacifism. When the *Federal Republican* published an ill-advised editorial attacking the war efforts, a riotous mob drove the publishers from the city and, when the editors tried to re-establish themselves in Baltimore an actual massacre resulted, lasting for two days, 27-28 July 1812.[59] The city became notorious over the nation for its violence and disorder. Eliza Sadler, who was then in Wilmington, Delaware, returned to New York without daring to proceed to Emmitsburg.[60]

Baltimore very quickly became the chief port from which privateers went out to prey upon the enemy. These small craft, bearing such names as *Falcon, Globe, Rossie,* and *Nonsuch,* totaled as high as fifty-eight, the largest number listed from any port during the war. The British declared the ports and harbors of the Chesapeake and Delaware Bays blockaded on 26 December 1812, and from that time on the shores of Maryland were constantly harassed by expeditions from Admiral George Cockburn's fleet. When this fleet threatened Baltimore in April of the following year, the Niles' *Register*[m] gloomily predicted, "If the squadron remains six months as near Baltimore as it now is, many of the inhabitants, and particularly the poor, will have to seek refuge in the country."[61] By this time even the

---

[k] This prayer was: "May the most just, the most high and the most amiable will of God be in all things fulfilled, praised and exalted above all forever."

[l] Augustus John Foster had served previously as secretary to the British legation at Naples. Archbishop Carroll received the pallium on 18 August 1811.

[m] The *Niles' Register,* founded by Hezekiah Niles in 1811, was also known as *The Weekly Register* and *Niles' National Register.* The publication was noted for the reliability of its content about both the United States and the world.

"back country" was beginning to feel the press of war and when the state legislature asked for $16,000,000 that year, Frederick County was second only to Baltimore in her contribution.

The economic effects of the war were felt in many ways by those dear to Elizabeth. Archbishop Carroll's hope of holding a provincial council[n] was vetoed by Cheverus of Boston, who wrote that in the distracted state of the country a council was scarcely feasible. There had been no news from the Holy Father. Further, in his own diocese the poor had no employment and his purse was empty. The good man wrote, "I am more Parish priest than Bishop," and had concluded that he seriously doubted "the propriety of holding our assembly at this time and particularly of holding it in your city,"[62] Helen Bayley wrote from New York that her fiancé, Sam Craig, was already gone to South America to try his luck there, to earn enough to marry. Richard Bayley had left the city, too, despairing of ever making a living as a merchant. He had bought a place in the country, near his father-in-law. Richard and Helen Bayley were the half brother and half sister of Mother Seton. Richard Bayley married Catherine White on 26 October 1812.[63]

One friend of Mother Seton was not diverted from her plans by the war. Catherine Dupleix, Elizabeth's dear Dué, made the long trip to Emmitsburg in September 1813, to visit her friend in the Valley. Mrs. Dupleix had become a Catholic in the fall of 1812. It is not clear just when she became seriously interested in Catholicism, but she had told Mother Seton on 30 December 1811, "I am still what I was when I left you, between both ways, I know you will pray for me when I desire it, which I now do."[64] The following October, Mrs. Sadler wrote a letter which seems to indicate that Mrs. Dupleix was then a Catholic.[65] In January 1813, Rev. Anthony Kohlmann, the pastor of St. Peter's, informed Mother Seton that Captain Dupleix had just returned from Lisbon and he feared Mrs. Dupleix might suffer from her husband's objections. Kohlmann was confident, he said, that "Our Lord has prepared this great soul by imparting to her a confidence and intrepidity, at which she herself was amazed." He praised the convert as "a mother to a Widow and orphan, and her lively faith goeth a pace with her charity."[66] It is not improbable that Dué, like Elizabeth before her, did suffer for her change in faith, for Mary Post told Elizabeth that summer that Dué seemed "very unhappy at present" and was anxious to visit Emmitsburg.[67]

When Elizabeth Seton got word that Dué really planned to come she wrote excitedly to Sad:

[n] The Provincial Councils of Baltimore were councils of Roman Catholic bishops in the United States of America which contributed to the development of ecclesiastical legislation, organization, and administration of the Church in the new republic.

The very possibility of seeing Dué is like a foretaste of heaven to me. If she is only delayed by fear of not finding entrance in St. Joseph's House, tell her the front door, the back, the side door which will lead her to the chapel, and all the windows up and down, will open at her approach.[68]

And so Dué came to the Valley and visited her dearest friend in the fall of 1813. Mother Seton's joy at seeing once again this now doubly-dear friend was overwhelming. That very night she sent off a hasty note to Sad "to say Dué dear is behind my curtain with the children...Could you see my heart in the silence of this moment while she rests—no—you can guess a little and only a little...You shall know at least that this happy Tuesday night 28th she is safe and surrounded by love and tenderness..."[69]

Catherine Dupleix found Elizabeth living in a very lively household. Based on a report prepared by Simon Bruté for the Archbishop in 1813 there were eighteen sisters, thirty-two paying boarders, seven "pensioners," and two servants living in the White House.[o] During the summer months twenty day students also came from the surrounding countryside, although only two or three attended classes in the winter. The "pensioners"[p] were the daughters of Mother Seton, a protégé of Father Moranvillé, two young Burke children, and two "*grandes*"[q] who taught in the school.[70] Only the preceding July the sisters and Mother Seton had made their vows for the first time as Sisters of Charity of St. Joseph's[r] under the rule of St. Vincent de Paul and St. Louise de Marillac which had been modified for America.[71] Dué visited the community at a time when the most glowing reports could be carried back to New York. The following spring when Eliza Sadler was apologizing for not having written to Elizabeth, she said that since Dué's return, "I find so much satisfaction in her account of the many comforts of your situation that there seemed little left for me to ask or to wish, except the repeated assurance of health."[72] St. Joseph's seemed like an island of serenity in a national sea tossed by fear and war.

Events in Europe in 1814 were more cheering than those at home. Cheverus wrote on 18 March:

---

[o] The Bruté report takes no cognizance of the deaths of Anna Maria Seton and Maria Burke in 1812 and so lists the sisters as nineteen and the pensioners as eight.

[p] A pensioner was a non-paying boarder.

[q] "*Les grandes*" were Mme. Madeleine Guérin and Mrs. Bridget Farrell, both of whom became Sisters of Charity of St. Joseph's at a later date.

[r] This simple act, took place 19 July 1813, on the feast of St. Vincent de Paul in the little chapel of St. Joseph's House. The vows of the Daughters of Charity are private and made again annually on the Feast of the Annunciation of the Blessed Virgin Mary, which usually is celebrated 25 March.

We are in this town very gloomy and very poor. Our only comfort is to forget home and look abroad. We smile with hope and feel some joy in beholding the wonderful and happy events which have taken place in Europe.[73]

Father Pierre Babade in Baltimore voiced sanguine hopes that commerce would soon be resumed with Europe and that once more letters could be exchanged with the Filicchis.[74] And July saw the reappearance of Filicchi notices in the Boston *Gazette*.[75] The defeat of Napoleon in March, followed by his abdication on 7 April, was second only in Archbishop Carroll's mind to "the Intelligence received here yesterday of the delivery [of] our Holy Father the Pope from his imprisonment at Fontainebleau,[s] and departure for Rome. If this should be confirmed, our prayers for our captive Pontiff will be exchanged for a Te Deum."[76] So it was that Mother Seton's first letter in four years to Antonio Filicchi began with the words, "The glad and happy news of the Restoration of Our Holy Father..."[77]

The fall of Napoleon, however, left England temporarily free to enlarge her forces in America and new attacks were immediately envisaged against Canada, Louisiana, and Baltimore. Admiral John B. Warren was reported to have said in 1814, "Baltimore is a doomed town."[78] After the disasters of Bladensburg, Maryland, and Washington, D.C., in August, Baltimore prepared for the worst. In September it came. On 11 September, enemy vessels were seen off North Point twelve miles away. The following day, on Monday, a detachment under General Robert Ross was landed. In spite of the death of Ross in the combat, the advance on the city continued, and on 13 September the now celebrated firing upon Fort McHenry took place. The city resisted more valiantly than had the neighboring capital, and re-enforcements poured in from the country towns. Emmitsburg men and students from Mount St. Mary's co-operated, and one biographer of Father Bruté says he "addressed the volunteers in sentiments of true patriotism...He himself became so anxious that he walked to Baltimore to render ministerial services, if needed."[79] On 19 September 1814, Major General Samuel Smith was free to issue his general order of congratulation to the city for its heroic resistance.[80] But it was several weeks before a sense of security pervaded the city. Babade wrote on 19 October, "Today they are saying a very large English fleet has returned to the Bay and already is very near. God knows what will happen." Father Moranvillé was greatly overworked tending the wounded and wished for Sisters of Charity.[81] News of the peace negotiations

---

[s] Pope Pius VII had been made a prisoner by Napoleon at Grenoble, Savona, and Fontainebleau successively. When the Allies entered Paris in March the Pope was returned to Rome amid general rejoicing.

which had started as early as August did not cross the Atlantic for some time, and a feeling of suspense hung over the whole state.

Although the siege of Baltimore was miles away from St. Joseph's, the progress of the war in 1814 brought it close to Mother Seton in the person of her son, William. In March Elizabeth told Julia Scott:

> William seems rather inclined to follow the drum. Young Brent, one of his fellow students and some other of his companions, left the Seminary for a commission. If it was not for the boundless love for Mother and Rebecca and Kitty he would probably be off—poor child—he doesn't know for what endless regret perhaps—however, I must try soon to get him some employment as he is already in his 18th year.[82]

Writing to Eliza Sadler about the same time, Mother Seton made similar comments on "Young Carroll" who had "gone out in the suit of Mr. Clay"[t] and William's chagrin at his own situation.[83] She wondered if sending him to New York might be the solution.

> Sometimes I have thought of asking dear Craig[u] to take the four hundred dollars a year Filicchi allows for them [her sons] and fix him in some respectable counting house, but Craig has already had so much trouble with our family and William is not determined in his wish to be a merchant.[84]

When Eliza Sadler read this letter, and another one by Elizabeth addressed to Helen Bayley, she tried immediately to discourage any thought of reviving New York connections. "You have little in New York to make your thoughts rest there," she said plainly. "Of the name of Seton there is not one." As for Craig, he had done no business for three years; his brother Sam was still trying to make his fortune far from New York. The letter to Helen made Sad apprehensive, sincerely fearing her friend would reopen old wounds. In her direct fashion she wrote:

> Did you not try to bring back former times, to dwell on them and *for a time* lose the present in the past? I feel as if you had succeeded but too well. Can you forgive me this freedom—or conceive it possible for me to think so? Yet, honestly, I must

---

[t] Henry Clay was one of the best-known leaders of the "War Hawks." After the Battle of Leipzig, 16-19 October 1813, Robert Stewart, Viscount Castlereagh offered to enter upon direct peace negotiations with the United States at either London or Gottenburg. Clay was named, with John Q. Adams, James A. Bayard, Jonathan Russell and Albert Gallatin, to serve as a commissioner, and he sailed that fall for Sweden. Clay refused to negotiate at London and it was not until 8 August 1814, that the peace commission was ready to proceed at Ghent, where the treaty was finally drawn.

[u] William Craig had married Emma Bayley, Mother Seton's oldest half-sister. He had been kind to Mrs. Seton before her departure from New York.

confess that if my mind had not been previously satisfied that you possessed every real comfort this life affords the perusal of that letter would have made me see the banishment that circumstances and chances alone had forced you to live in. No one else would feel this perhaps. I look upon your situation as exalted. I like to look upon it as so.[85]

Sad suggested, as an alternative, turning to the Filicchis, and trying to interest them in William's plight. Once again Mother Seton's friends in religion would fill the breach New York could not. She wrote to Leghorn, and while waiting for a reply she confided in Archbishop Carroll as well. Borrowing a phrase from Father Matignon, Mother Seton said:

Your paternal heart has not forgotten William I am sure, but we cannot hasten the moments of Providence. He is 18 this very month and I do not know how he can be sheltered from being called out, which he wishes much to avoid—poor, poor child—he will never know his mother's heart.[86]

William Seton did not know his mother's heart; but Elizabeth Seton tried her best to read his. She suspected that her own hopes for a mercantile career for her son were not his. He seemed to lean toward a career in the Navy. Mother Seton was torn between a desire to keep him safe and her yearning to have his every wish gratified. One may imagine the misgivings with which she enlisted Carroll's intercession in behalf of an appointment for William, or the mingled emotions with which she relayed to her impatient son the prelate's words:

Truly since the misfortunes of the city of Washington and the deplorable condition to which the ignorance and perception of our leaders has brought our national affairs, I see little prospect of Wm. profitting by any appointment he may obtain—Yet, every attention will be paid.[87]

Meanwhile the good offices of Mr. Daniel Brent[v] of Washington had been sought, and Elizabeth wrote Julia in December that William's "berth in the Navy" had really been applied for, and that he was now at the Mountain "anxiously desiring to be off."[88] Before the naval commission could be secured, an alternative appeared, to Mother Seton's great joy. Her valued friend, Simon Bruté, was making plans to return to France and he offered to take William Seton with him and set him on his way to Italy. Mother Seton wrote at once to Antonio Filicchi, asking him to consider William as if he were a son. She spoke of her fears for William's faith if he were to join the

---

[v] Daniel Brent was Archbishop Carroll's nephew. He was a clerk in the Department of State.

army or navy. "No kind of business can be done here in the distracted state of the country," she explained. [89] Until affairs with the British took a turn for the better it was futile to try to place her son in a Catholic counting house in Baltimore. If Antonio would consent to receive her son, Father Bruté would escort him to France. [90] Mother Seton wrote to Carroll, telling him of her plan and said she hoped Anna's insurance money would be available to defray part of William's expenses. [91]

Unknown to the community at Emmitsburg, the terms of the peace treaty were drawn up by the commissioners at Ghent, but because this news had not reached the United States, and because spirits had sunk so low, the President set aside 12 January 1815, as a day of fasting, humiliation, and prayer. It was amid this gloom and uncertainty that Mother Seton saw her son set out from Emmitsburg for Baltimore, accompanied by the Sulpician priest. When Bruté and young Seton reached Baltimore, all was confusion and delay. William went to Dr. Pierre Chatard's home to stay until passage from the city could be secured. While he waited, William, who was not at all anxious to leave his native land, tried to secure a place with Luke Tiernan, one of Baltimore's leading business men. When Elizabeth got this news her hopes rose swiftly that William might not need to go so far from home, and she wrote earnestly:

> Let me see it as it is, not considering *me* but *yourself*—If you should be received by Mr. Tiernan, surely it would only be to try if you could engage your mind in the career pointed out to you, and you would conduct yourself there as you have always done, with attention and good will to everyone. However, as I know that in such houses, order and exactness are of the greatest necessity, I point them out to you as of first importance. [92]

She was trying so hard to see all sides, William's personal preferences, Tiernan's requirements, and the urgent necessity of her own heart. John Dubois preferred the trip to Leghorn; Richard Seton wished his brother would stay in America. Elizabeth concluded with the words, "You have my full consent and blessing for a decision either way. Nature would plead much for your stay, but our God knows best and that is the only wish I indulge." [93] The delay in Baltimore was most trying to them all. Up until 16 February 1815, Mother Seton was still addressing letters to Baltimore and sympathizing with her son over the painful detention. "How we long for the first letter which will tell us you are engaged in some business with our Filicchis, or which ever way the Patriarch provider will point out," she wrote. [94]

News of the peace treaty finally reached Emmitsburg, and when Mother Seton heard the rumor she was elated, but she warned her son against excesses of emotion.

> You have enjoyed the gazettes so much I know. I cast my eye on General [Andrew] Jackson's name and read it with pleasure knowing you had read the same more than for the events of the day, for my dear one, your poor mother looks only at souls. I see neither American nor English, but souls redeemed, and lost—but you must—your case is quite different—love your country—and yet also all countries, my William—see things as they are. Passions and excesses you will find everywhere.[95]

Two days later the peace treaty was ratified. The news of the treaty and the victory of Andrew Jackson at New Orleans were received with "every demonstration of joy" at Baltimore. Mary Post wrote of the celebration in New York:

> We have had illuminations, fireworks, and all demonstrations of joy at the return of peace ...Our new State House which is a very beautiful building and said by people of judgement to be the equal, if not superior, to any in Europe was superbly illuminated. The construction of the building is particularly favorable for lighting to advantage and putting up many and appropriate pictures as transparencies. The cupola was covered with variegated lamps and moving lights placed in different situations gave it the effect of enchantment.[96]

Mary said, now that peace had come, why did William not come to New York to live with them and try to get a place in Abraham Ogden's counting house? Mary's own son Lionel was there and she could have Dr. Post speak for William. But Mother Seton and William were now determined upon the European trip. The mother gave her son letters for friends in New York, for Eliza Sadler and John Wilkes.[97] To her son she gave her final advice. Simon Bruté was so impressed with these instructions that he made a copy and it is this copy which is preserved at Emmitsburg. Elizabeth Seton omitted nothing. She recommended gratitude to Mr. Bruté, "as our true friend," filial devotion to the Filicchis, caution with strangers, strict economy in everything. "I beg you so much," she wrote, "not to give way to national prejudices, but to allow for many customs and manners you will see. Why should not others have their peculiarities as well as we have ours?"[98]

Then she poured out her heart to him on the subject that worried her most.

My William—and be not, my dear one, so unhappy as to break willfully any command of our God, or to omit your prayers on any account—Unite them always to the only merits of our Jesus and the maternal prayers of our Mother and His. With them you will always find your own poor, poor mother. You cannot even guess the incessant cry of my soul to them for you. Don't say [that] Mother has the rest to comfort her. No, no, my William, from the first moment I received you in my arms and to my breast you have been consecrated to God by me and I have never ceased to beg Him to take you from this world rather than you should offend Him or dishonor your dear soul; and as you know my stroke of death would be to know that you have quitted that path of virtue which alone can reunite us forever. Separations, everything else I can bear—but that never—your mother's heart must break if that blow falls on it. Think much of your tender loving Josephine and Rebecca, of Richard's [wanting to] set out and the future consequences of your example to him.[99]

From that moment until she died, Mother Seton's greatest concern was this fear for William's soul. Her son seemed unable to give her the reassurance she craved. He had a certain stiffness and restraint that prevented him from impressing people as favorably as other Setons had done. When Eliza Sadler met him in New York that year before he sailed she commented, "William has an exterior so grave that one might be induced to think it not natural at his age and think him under some restraint."[100] Bruté, who had known the young man for three years at Mount Saint Mary's, wrote of William Seton:

A true English and American mien [sic, mind] and character. Good and estimable indeed in many excellencies, but too narrowed by the national [prejudices] and gentleman[ly] selfish[ness] to be raised to great exertions. Could succeed in any study but will have emulation for none and will have rather a life for the other common occupations of the town or country than any pursuit of the liberal arts and professions. I do not even suppose he will engage far in political concerns.[101]

Elizabeth Seton did not deceive herself as to her sons' talents. She readily admitted that they were "not brilliant."[102] But she expected and prayed that they might excel in honor and virtue. It was with gratitude and relief that she relinquished her older son to Bruté's care. Knowing that William would be welcomed in France by Father Bruté's family and friends, she told Eliza Sadler happily, "God is too too good to me. If you knew the friend who takes charge of him. Dué may tell you. I feel as secure as old good Tobias was."[103] Bishop Cheverus shared Mother Seton's sentiments, writing to Bruté, "Dear William is lucky to have a friend and protector such as you."[104]

On 27 March 1815, Simon Bruté and William Seton left Baltimore for New York. Robert Barry, who handled Mother Seton's private financial affairs, wrote that he had paid Bruté $700 for William's expenses before they left.[w] He was glad William was on his way to Leghorn. "Although *you* may have no relish for the world," he said approvingly, "it is no reason that you should deprive your children of the opportunity of availing themselves of the chances of its lottery."[105] Julia Scott's gift of $100 was used "to settle the unavoidable expense of his narrow little outfit," and William was all ready to leave by the 6th of April.[106] On the eve of his departure William wrote from New York, "Tomorrow we sail in the *Tontine* for Bordeaux." He spoke of his gratitude to the Posts who had provided him with "shirts, cravats, handkerchiefs and all kinds of underclothing." Uncle Post had even insisted that the young man have a coat and "pantaloons" from the tailor. The Sadlers, Craigs, and Murrays had entertained him royally, and William was leaving New York with warm recollections.[107]

Mother Seton followed the voyagers' progress with intense interest. She had scarcely received the news of their departure when one Sunday at the Mountain John Dubois came "running out of the little cell down the hill, without hat, calling "Mother, Mother" with news that Napoleon had escaped from Elba.[108] Mother Seton wrote to her son, "Many think the *Tontine* will return if you should meet the last accounts half way. For me I can but look up and dare not even *wish,* knowing so little what is best."[109] Before this letter was even mailed she had received news of their arrival in Bordeaux, and Elizabeth relayed the news to Julia that William "is now between Bordeaux which is besieged and Italy which is in a state of insurrection."[110] It was the 100 Days of Napoleon, and Elizabeth's great concern now became William's

---

[w] Four hundred of this money was the yearly allowance drawn upon John Murray in New York from the Filicchi account. The remainder may have been the insurance money Mother Seton mentioned in her letter to Carroll.

escape from death. But William went safely from Bordeaux to Marseilles[x] and the next report to Philadelphia notified Mrs. Scott that William

> Writes in the full expression of his heart's content; says he is quite safe through all the rough scenes around him under his American cockade and Eagle[y] which he is obliged to wear—the most dangerous voyage, both sides of the vessel staved in, cargo thrown over.[111]

While in Marseilles, young Seton had been befriended by a family named Preudhomme de Borre. Mr. Preudhomme de Borre was "a very respectable old gentleman" who, with his family, had crossed in the *Tontine* with William and Father Bruté. From Marseilles William wrote his mother, "I lodge with him at the house of his sister, Madame de St. Cesaire, who treats me as the son of her brother."[112] On 15 June, C. Preudhomme de Borre wrote to Father Bruté in Bordeaux that William was already on his way to Italy, not by vessel as had been planned, but by land. The American consul had advised against a Sardinian ship as unsafe, and so William had departed on 14 June, for Nice, from which place he would proceed to Genoa, and finally to Leghorn. Preudhomme told Bruté that a Mr. Parangue, who had known William Magee Seton in New York, had given himself as much trouble over the younger William as if he had been his own son.[113] By 17 July, Simon Bruté had it from William's own hand that he was safe at Leghorn.[114] By the end of that month Elizabeth, too, knew her son had arrived at his destination.[115]

Her worry now became a doubt as to William's reception by the Filicchis. No reply had yet been received to the letters she had written in 1814, and Elizabeth had expected that once he was in France, William would wait for word of assent from Antonio or Philip before proceeding to Italy. No one could have foreseen the conditions that made necessary the young man's hurrying out of France. Elizabeth wrote William, "Not that I doubt a moment of every Kindness yet your going might have been ill-timed and inconvenient."[116] To Antonio Filicchi she dispatched a hasty letter of pleading apology for William's precipitate arrival, saying that her only wish was that his kindness should not be abused. "Scold me if you are angry (but gently) and tell me if anything can be done in any way to alter what I could so little foresee."[117] Writing at the same time to Philip, Mother Seton explained that Carroll, Cheverus, and Dubois had all advised her sending

---

[x] Archbishop Carroll wrote Mother Seton that two letters from Bruté had arrived with news that on 23 May Bruté had "committed William, in perfect health, to the care of a most respectable family traveling to Marseilles, from which place he could easily reach Leghorn." John Carroll to Elizabeth Seton, 12 May 1815, AMSV, I,21.
[y] Symbols of the United States of America.

William to Leghorn, but "to abuse and take advantage of your goodness to us was far from my intention."[118] She explained to the elder Filicchi her fears for William's faith, and her strong wish to have him live for a time in a Catholic country where he might see Catholics and the Catholic religion "as they are instead of the shadows he sees here." To Philip, Elizabeth added honestly that her William was a cold, reserved personality. "If only he can master his bad pride I believe all the rest would be secure."[119]

When Jean Cheverus learned from Mother Seton her fears he reproached her for doubting the Filicchis for a moment; and soon a letter came from Philip bearing out the bishop's opinion. Philip wrote, gently chiding her for having "sent your son without previous leave," but explaining that if William were willing and capable, he should have an excellent chance to improve.[120] Young Seton was placed in the home of one of the Filicchi clerks to board and he seemed quite pleased with his situation. Antonio Filicchi was at the baths in Lucca when William arrived and her failure to hear from him continued to worry Elizabeth. She wrote a second letter of apology to the younger brother, begging him to send just a few lines. "I am so afraid now that William should forfeit your protection that I think it almost a temptation," she confessed. "Our God knows the struggles I have had about it."[121]

Gradually Mother Seton's qualms vanished. When Simon Bruté returned from France in November he reported direct word from the Filicchi brothers that William was showing a "favorable disposition to make progress."[122] Louis Dubourg, her first superior, was in Rome that September and he had informed Bruté at Bordeaux:

> I have seen William Seton in Leghorn. Mrs. Filicchi seemed very much attached to him, and well pleased with his behavior. He also appeared very well to me. We chatted just a moment (for I enjoyed him but half an hour) of his dear Mother, Sisters, Mr. Dubois and yourself.[123]

The final "treasure of consolation" came with the arrival of Antonio's long-awaited letter, written on 8 August 1814, but long in coming. Elizabeth sent her immediate and happy reply:

> I cannot hide from our God, though from everyone else I must conceal the perpetual tears and affections of boundless gratitude which overflow my heart when I think of him [William] secure in his *Faith* and your protection. Why I love him so much, I cannot account, but own to you, my

Antonio, all my weakness ...[I try to] purify it as much as I can, and our God knows it is their souls I look at.[124]

During the two years William Seton stayed in Leghorn Mother Seton felt secure in the bounty and good example of these excellent Filicchis. She and the sisters never ceased to pray for these "tenderest friends and benefactors." And to the Filicchis and their American friends it really seemed "a fine bill of exchange."[125]

CHAPTER 10. WARS AND RUMORS OF WAR
Notes

[1] 6.62, Elizabeth Seton to Julia Scott, 23 October 1810, *CW*, 2:162. See James J. Kortendick, "The History of St. Mary's College, Baltimore, 1799-1852" (Washington, 1942), an unpublished manuscript in the Mullen Library of the Catholic University of America, 200.

[2] 6.80, Elizabeth Seton to Julia Scott, *CW*, 2:191.

[3] Ibid.

[4] [Sister Loyola Law, D.C., ed.,] *Simon Bruté in His Connection with the Community* (privately printed, Daughters of Charity: Emmitsburg, 1886), 38. Original letter is Simon Bruté to Elizabeth Seton, 5 July 1812, ASJPH 1-3-3-12:15, (1-4).

[5] 6.86, Elizabeth Seton to Marie-Françoise Chatard, 5 November 1811, *CW*, 2:198.

[6] 6.14, Elizabeth Seton to Julia Scott, 27 December 1809, *CW*, 2:95.

[7] 6.89, Elizabeth Seton to Julia Scott, 2 December 1811, *CW*, 2:201.

[8] Mary Bayley Post to Elizabeth Seton, New York, 8 December 1811, ASJPH 1-3-3-11:12.

[9] Catherine Dupleix to Elizabeth Seton, New York, 30 December 1811, ASJPH 1-3-3-11:35.

[10] 6.91, Elizabeth Seton to George Weis, n.d., *CW*, 2:203; 6.94, Ibid., 11 January 1812, *CW*, 2:208.

[11] A-6.99a, Elizabeth Seton's Journal of Anna Maria Seton's Last Illness and Date, *CW*, 2:749. Printed in Robert Seton *Memoirs,* II, 123-134, with some omissions and minor changes.

[12] Ibid.

[13] 6.98, Elizabeth Seton to Julia Scott, 18 February 1812, *CW*, 2:211.

[14] 6.97, Elizabeth Seton to Eliza Sadler, 13 February 1812, *CW*, 2:210.

[15] 10.1 St. Mary Magdalen de Pazzi Notebook, *CW*, 3a:432.

[16] 6.104, Elizabeth Seton to Eliza Sadler, 3 May 1812, *CW*, 2:217.

[17] A-6.3a, Mother Rose White's Journal, *CW*, 2:732.

[18] Jean Cheverus to Elizabeth Seton, 26 February 1812, ASJPH 1-3-3-1:12.

[19] 10.1 St. Mary Magdalen de Pazzi Notebook, *CW*, 3a:433.

[20] 6.104, Elizabeth Seton to Eliza Sadler, 3 May 1812, *CW*, 2:216.

[21] Mary Bayley Post to Elizabeth Seton, New York, 4 June 1812, ASJPH 1-3-3-11:17.

[22] Eliza Sadler to Elizabeth Seton, New York, 17 April 1812, ASJPH 1-3-3-11:B13.

[23] John Dubois to Simon Bruté, Emmitsburg, 7 May 1812, AMSMU.

[24] Ibid.

[25] 6.30, Elizabeth Seton to Julia Scott, 26 March 1810, *CW*, 2:117.

[26] 6.114, *Mother* (Emmitsburg, 1884), Elizabeth Seton to George Weis, 30 July 1812, *CW*, 2:224.

[27] 6.116, Elizabeth Seton to Eliza Sadler, 14 September 1812, *CW*, 2:227.

[28] 6.118, Elizabeth Seton to Simon Bruté, 22 September 1812, *CW*, 2:228.

[29] 11.8, "Well Now Our Dearest," *CW*, 3b:7; 11.7, "Dearest Maria," *CW*, 3b:6.

[30] John David to Simon Bruté, St. Thomas Seminary, 6 July [1811], UNDA.

[31] John David to Simon Bruté, St. Thomas Seminary, 3 November 1811, UNDA.

[32] John David to Simon Bruté, St. Thomas Seminary, 8 September 1812, UNDA.

[33] John David to Simon Bruté, St. Thomas Seminary, 12 July 1813, UNDA.

[34] John David to Simon Bruté, St. Thomas Seminary, 7 September 1813, UNDA.

[35] Ibid.

[36] Benedict Flaget to Simon Bruté, Bardstown, 21 September 1813, UNDA.

[37] Council Minutes, Sisters of Charity of St. Joseph's, 2 April 1814, ASJPH 3-3-5.

[38] Ibid.

[39] John David to Simon Bruté, St. Thomas Seminary, 21 April 1814, UNDA.

[40] Council Minutes, Sisters of Charity of St. Joseph's, 18 August 1814, ASJPH 3-3-5. See Pierre Babade to Elizabeth Seton, Emmitsburg, 19 October 1814, ASJPH 1-3-3-1:70.

[41] John Dubois to John Carroll, Emmitsburg, 10 October 1814, AAB, AASMSU, 3-F-14.

[42] John Dubois to John Carroll, Emmitsburg, 27 October 1814, AAB, AASMSU, 3-F-15.

[43] John David to John Carroll, St. Thomas Seminary, 27 October 1814, AAB, AASMSU, 8AF-1.

[44] Ibid. A brief of Carroll's reply is jotted down on the letter he received from David. The full letter as sent to David has not come to light.

[45] John Dubois to John Carroll, Emmitsburg, 5 December 1814, AAB, AASMSU, U3-F-16.

[46] John Dubois to John Carroll, Emmitsburg, 27 December 1814, AAB, AASMSU, 3-F-17.

[47] *Centennial of St. Joseph's Orphan Asylum, 1814-1914,* p. II. This memorial pamphlet has no date or place of publication. ASJPH records give the date of 1 August 1814 for the agreement, when the Managers of the Roman Catholic Society of St. Joseph for Education and Maintaining Poor Orphan Children, Philadelphia, and the Sisters of Charity, through Rev. Mr. Hurley, that two Sisters be sent to run orphanage, ASJPH 7-10-2, #9.

[48] Application of managers of "Roman Catholic Society for Education and Maintaining Poor Orphan Children," 1 August 1814, ASJPH 7-10-2, #9.

[49] *Missions—Establishments Formed Prior to the Union with France,* ASJPH 11-0, 3. This is a handwritten record of early missions made by sisters from St. Joseph's Emmitsburg, in the first half of the nineteenth century.

[50] A-6.3a, Mother Rose White's Journal, *CW,* 2:732.

[51] 6.175, Elizabeth Seton to Julia Scott, 1 December 1814, *CW,* 2:287.

[52] Rachel M. Montgomery to Elizabeth Seton, Philadelphia, 19 June 1809, ASJPH 1-3-3-4:73. See A-6.3a, Mother Rose's Journal records the early days at Philadelphia, *CW,* 2:732-737.

[53] 6.172, Elizabeth Seton to John Carroll, 8 November 1814, *CW,* 2:283-284.

[54] Louis Dubourg to Elizabeth Seton, Baltimore, 28 December 1809, ASJPH 1-3-3-2:6. Copy. The original is in AMSV.

[55] Louis Dubourg to Elizabeth Seton, Baltimore, 30 December 1809, ASJPH 1-3-3-2:7. Copy. The original is in AMSV.

[56] 6.22, Elizabeth Seton to Rose Stubbs, 24 January 1810, *CW,* 2:105.

[57] John David to Elizabeth Seton, Baltimore, 23 February 1811. Cf. Charles G. Herbermann, *The Sulpicians in the United States* (New York, 1916), 5-13.

[58] Jean Cheverus to John Carroll, Boston, 3 October 1811, AAB, AASMSU, 2-0-4. See Peter Guilday, *Life and Times of John Carroll* (New York, 1922), II, 804.

[59] Thomas Scharf, *History of Maryland* (Baltimore, 1879) III, 1-5. *Maryland Historical Magazine,* V (June, 1910), 191.

[60] 6.115, Elizabeth Seton to Eliza Sadler, 2 August 1812, *CW,* 2:225.

[61] Niles *Register,* IV, 87, cited in Scharf, III, 37.

[62] Jean Cheverus to John Carroll, Boston, 31 August 1812, AAB, AASMSU, 2-0-8. Other letters opposing the council were written by Jean Cheverus 30 December 1812, and 5 January 1813. See AAB, AASMSU, 2-0-10.

[63] Helen Bayley to Elizabeth Seton, New York, 4 February 1814, ASJPH 1-3-3-11:38.

[64] Catherine Dupleix to Elizabeth Seton, New York, 30 December 1811, ASJPH 1-3-3-11:35.

[65] Eliza Sadler to Elizabeth Seton, New York, 29 October 1812, ASJPH 1-3-3-11:14.

[66] Anthony Kohlmann to Elizabeth Seton, New York, 17 January 1813, ASJPH 1-3-3-2:31.

[67] Mary Bayley Post to Elizabeth Seton, New York, 16 July [1813], ASJPH 1-3-3-11:18.

[68] 6.139, Elizabeth Seton to Eliza Sadler, 28 [September] [1813], *CW*, 2:252.

[69] 6.141, Elizabeth Seton to Eliza Sadler, 28 [September] [1813], *CW*, 2:254.

[70] Report prepared by Simon Bruté for Ambrose Maréchal, December 1813, Section XXIV, AMSMU.

[71] Chronological Table of the Sisters of Charity of Saint Joseph's, ASJPH 7-13.

[72] Eliza Sadler to Elizabeth Seton, New York, 6 April 1814, ASJPH 1-3-3-11:15.

[73] Jean Cheverus to John Carroll, Boston, 18 March 1814, AAB, AASMSU, 2-P-1.

[74] Pierre Babade to Elizabeth Seton, Baltimore, 28 March 1814, ASJPH 1-3-3-1:69.

[75] Jean Cheverus to Elizabeth Seton, Emmitsburg, 20 January 1815, ASJPH 1-3-3-1:14.

[76] John Carroll to Elizabeth Seton, 11 September 1811, ASJPH 1-3-3-1:45; Ibid., Baltimore, 29 March 1814, ASJPH 1-3-3-1:53b.

[77] 6.167, Elizabeth Seton to Antonio Filicchi, 1 July 1814, *CW*, 2:276.

[78] Scharf, III, 99.

[79] Sister Salesia Godecker, O.S.B., *Simon Bruté de Remur* (St. Meinrad's, 1931), 69.

[80] Scharf, III, 123.

[81] Pierre Babade to Elizabeth Seton, Baltimore, 19 October 1814, ASJPH 1-3-3-1:70.

[82] 6.152, Elizabeth Seton to Julia Scott, 14 March 1814, *CW*, 2:263. William M. Seton was born on 25 November 1796.

[83] 6.154, Elizabeth Seton to Eliza Sadler, 23 March 1814, *CW*, 2:266. See Samuel F. Bemis, *A Diplomatic History of the United States* (New York, 1942), 161-163.

[84] Ibid.

[85] Eliza Sadler to Elizabeth Seton, New York, 6 April 1814, ASJPH 1-3-3-11:B15.

[86] 6.172, Elizabeth Seton to John Carroll, 8 November 1814, *CW*, 2:283.

Francis Matignon had said, "We cannot hasten the moments of Providence" in his letter of 29 November 1806, when advising Mrs. Seton about her removal from New York. See Francis Matignon to Elizabeth Seton, New York, 25 November 1806, ASJPH 1-3-3-1:37.

[87] 6.173, Elizabeth Seton to William Seton, 28 November 1814, *CW*, 2:284. This letter contains the direct quotation from Carroll's letter, clearly marked. The original letter from Carroll has not been located.

[88] 6.175, Elizabeth Ann Seton to Julia Scott, 1 December 1814, *CW,* 2:286.

[89] 6.177, Elizabeth Seton to Antonio Filicchi, 20 December 1814, *CW*, 2:289.

[90] Ibid.

[91] 6.178, Elizabeth Seton to John Carroll, 28 December 1814, *CW*, 2:291.

[92] 6.186, Elizabeth Seton to William Seton, n.d., *CW*, 2:301.

[93] Ibid., 303.

[94] 6.189, Elizabeth Seton to William Seton, 16 February 1815, *CW*, 2:306.

[95] Ibid.

[96] Mary Bayley Post to Elizabeth Seton, New York, 7 March [1815], ASJPH 1-3-3-11:19.

[97] 6.183, Elizabeth Seton to Eliza Sadler, n.d., *CW*, 2:299; 6.184, Ibid., *CW*, 2:300.

[98] 6.182, Elizabeth Seton to William Seton, January 1815, *CW*, 2:297.

[99] Ibid., 298

[100] Eliza Sadler to Elizabeth Seton, New York, 16 April 1815, ASJPH 1-3-3-11:B16.

[101] Simon Bruté's estimates of character of his students. "William Seton," AMSMU.

[102] 6.121, Elizabeth Seton to Julia Scott, 29 October 1812, *CW*, 2:233.

[103] 6.183, Elizabeth Seton to Eliza Sadler, n.d., *CW*, 2:299.

[104] Jean Cheverus to Simon Bruté, Boston, 17 March 1815, UNDA.

[105] Robert Barry to Elizabeth Seton, Baltimore, 27 March 1815, ASJPH 1-3-3-4:52.

[106] 6.191, Elizabeth Seton to Julia Scott, 30 March 1815, *CW*, 2:308-309. De Barberey-Code's *Elizabeth Seton* gives the date of departure as 27 April 1815. White's biography gives 6 April 1815. The latter is undoubtedly correct since Eliza Sadler's letter of 16 April 1815, describes the departure as having taken place some days earlier. See Eliza Sadler to Elizabeth Seton, New York, 16 April 1815, ASJPH 1-3-3-11:B16. A letter of Mrs. Seton a year later seems to fix the date as being 7 April 1815. This letter says "a year ago Sunday" William left; and Sunday in this case was 7 April 1816. William's

letter dated 5 April 1815, states, "Tomorrow we sail in the *Tontine* for Bordeaux."

[107] William Seton to Elizabeth Seton, Boston, 5 April 1815, AMP #339-341.

[108] 6.195, Elizabeth Seton to Simon Bruté, 28 April 1815, *CW*, 2:315.

[109] 6.192, Elizabeth Seton to William Seton, 10 May 1815, *CW*, 2:310.

[110] 6.193, Elizabeth Seton to Julia Scott, 20 May 1815, *CW*, 2:312. See John Carroll to Elizabeth Seton, Baltimore, 12 July 1815, AMSV, I, 21.

[111] 6.201, Elizabeth Seton to Julia Scott, 14 August 1815, *CW*, 2:340.

[112] William Seton to Elizabeth Seton, Marseilles, 14 June 1815, ASJPH 26-0-1, (2). Copy. The original is in AMSJ.

[113] C. Preudhomme de Borre to Simon Bruté, Marseilles, 17 July 1815, UNDA II-1-a.

[114] Simon Bruté to Elizabeth Seton, Rennes, 17 July 1815, UNDA.

[115] 6.199, Elizabeth Seton to William Seton, 29 July 1815, *CW*, 2:336-337.

[116] Ibid., *CW*, 2:335.

[117] 6.197, Elizabeth Seton to Antonio Filicchi, 29 July 1815, *CW*, 2:333.

[118] 6.196, Elizabeth Seton to Antonio Filicchi, 29 July 1815, *CW*, 2:332.

[119] Ibid., 333.

[120] Philip Filicchi to Elizabeth Seton, Leghorn, 12 August 1815, ASJPH 1-3-3-10:44.

[121] 6.203, Elizabeth Seton to Antonio Filicchi, n.d., *CW*, 2:341.

[122] Philip and Anthony Filicchi to Simon Bruté, Leghorn, 6 September 1815, ASJPH 1-3-3-10:45.

[123] Louis Dubourg to Simon Bruté, Rome, 15 September 1815, UNDA. Dubourg was the newly-created Bishop of Louisiana and the Floridas.

[124] 6.214, Elizabeth Seton to Antonio Filicchi, 20 November 1815, *CW*, 2:356.

[125] Ibid., 357.

CHAPTER 11

ॐ‿❧

ANGELS IN THE VALLEY

During the difficult years of her family's personal necessities, Mother Seton's community and her own immeasurable contribution to its work went rapidly forward. This work was for several years primarily concerned with the education of young women and girls. There was no real break in continuity between the school on Paca Street in Baltimore and the school at St. Joseph's in Emmitsburg.[a] When the second group of women arrived from Baltimore in 1809, they had with them two pupils, Julia LeBreton and Isabella Editha O'Conway, a younger sister of Cecilia O'Conway.[1] That very summer Sister Cecilia was appointed "Secretary and School Sister," and took charge of her pupils, the three Seton girls and the two from Paca Street.[2] When the farmhouse became so crowded that fall, John David advised Mother Seton to send the children during the day to the new house being built, to make possible an expansion of the school.[3] It was not until the sisters themselves moved to St. Joseph's house in February, however, that any new pupils were received.[4] The initial plan was to provide free education to children of families living in poverty.[b] The three day scholars (externs) who came in February were augmented by five tuition-paying boarders from Frederick in May, and by the middle of June Mother Seton could tell Archbishop Carroll, "Our school is very respectable and has increased *to forty*, including Boarders."[5]

Although the exterior of the community was buffeted by the summer storms over superiors and sites, the inner life went serenely on from the very first. Mother Seton described her community to Dué as "united only with the views of schooling children, nursing the sick, and manufacturing for ourselves and the poor, which to my disposition you know is the sum of all earthly happiness."[6] The surrounding farm lands supplied eggs, milk, butter, and fresh vegetables. Meat and coffee were common items in the accounts

---

[a] [Although there may have been some continuity of instruction for the Seton girls and the two other pupils, the school on Paca Street in Baltimore was a tuition-based dame school for Catholic boarders. Mrs. Seton intended to teach "poor country children" at Emmitsburg but soon circumstances necessitated the admission of day scholars and boarders, Catholic or Protestant. 7.87, Elizabeth Seton to Antonio Filicchi, 1 June 1817, *CW*, 2:479. Ed.]

[b] [Mother Seton began Saint Joseph's Free School in Saint Joseph's House, now the White House, 22 February 1810, with day pupils from the immediate area. This was the first free Catholic school for girls staffed by religious women in the country. Two months later the first tuition-paying boarders arrived 14 May for the Academy. Governed, funded, and administered by the Sisters of Charity of Saint Joseph's, Saint Joseph's Academy and Free School was rooted in methods to foster faith-based education and character formation to educate girls to lead devout lives as Catholic women and mothers. Ed.]

for the sisterhood kept at Mount St. Mary's which sent them provisions during the early years, as was the flour used to make the bread. Mother Seton cheerfully denied any burden upon herself, saying, "I never do the least work of any kind [except] to walk around with knitting in hand and give the look of encouragement or reproof thro' the house...[the] school is my chief business."[7] The contentment she found in her work was a real and lasting joy throughout her life. With welling heart she wrote Dué:

> The solitude of our mountains...skipping children over the woods which in the spring are covered with wild flowers they would gather for you at every step—the regularity of our house which is very spacious and in an end wing contains our dear, dear chapel[c] so neat and quiet, where dwells (as we *believe*) night and day *you know Who*. This is no dream of fancy and only a small part of the reality of our blessing. You must be a witness to believe that from Monday to Saturday all is quiet, no violation of each other's tranquillity, each helping the other with a look of good will which must indeed be seen to be believed—all the world would not have persuaded me if I had not proved it so...[8]

She complained to Eliza Sadler of "her lazy sleepy soul" so at peace among her fifty children. The days passed in quiet and order, and the energetic little head-mistress went about with her "manner of looking upon twenty people in a room with a look of affection and interest, showing an interest for all and a concern in all their concerns."

> You know I am as a Mother encompassed by many children of different dispositions—not equally amiable or congenial, but bound to love, instruct and provide for the happiness of all, to give the example of cheerfulness, peace, resignation and consider the individual [rather] as proceeding from the same origin and tending to the same end than in the different shades of merit or demerit. I assure you the little woman [Elizabeth Seton] is quite a somebody—and perhaps you are the only one of all who ever knew her who could justly appreciate her means of happiness.[9]

The house was very quickly filled and John Dubois reported to Carroll in 1813 that the sisters could not take any more at that time. Three children in the neighborhood were waiting for the first vacancy, but Dubois feared to

---

[c] The chapel was located in a one-story annex which was attached to the western side of St. Joseph's House, today known as the White House.

increase the number, even for orphans. "Mrs. Seton," he explained ruefully, "would take the whole county if she could."[10] Fifty children and eighteen sisters in the summer and scarcely less in the winter, filled the White House to overflowing. The report Simon Bruté prepared for Ambrose Maréchal in 1813 indicated that this large household was financed by thirty-two paying boarders and the fees[d] paid by "externals" who varied in number from twenty in the summer to three or fewer in winter. At first the boarders paid $100 a year, "a half in advance every six months."[11] When Bruté prepared his report the amount had already been increased by ten dollars; by the end of the war the charge was $125.00 with extra charges for music and French lessons.[12] St. Joseph's favored the custom of the day of payment in advance but the girls from well-to-do families ran up bills for stationery, medicines, candy, and clothes, and sometimes these accounts dragged on long after Mother Seton's death. Some girls who were in school in 1813 were still on the books in 1829.[13] It is astonishing, therefore, to find that the community flourished financially. Writing to Tessier[e] in 1816, John Dubois admitted that one of his reasons for wishing to have sisters at the Mountain was their "admirable economy." They had so managed affairs at St. Joseph's that they were "up to the point of even liquidating all their debts, and even having an advance when their creditors are paid...a promise of what I may hope for," Dubois explained "while they are here."[14]

The community did not achieve this solvency without some severe trials. The first winter in Emmitsburg, before boarders had begun to become such an asset, was a period of hardship for everyone at St. Joseph's. Although Louis Dubourg was no longer their superior, he was very anxious about the brave women enduring the discomforts of the crowded farmhouse and he wrote to Mother Seton:

> The thought has struck me that you should write letters... to various ladies[f] exposing with candor the object of your institution, and asking assistance which you want in the beginning to complete it. Mrs. Caton, Mrs. Harper, Mrs. Patterson, Mrs. Montgomery, then thro' Louisa and Emilia the old gentleman [Charles Carroll] and also Mrs. Bonaparte,

---

[d] Bruté gives yearly tuition as $110, but all individual accounts show that the regular "six months advance" was $62.50. French tuition for six months was $5.00 extra, and music was $8.00 a quarter with an added charge for use of the piano.

[e] Rev. John Mary Tessier, S.S., was Superior, St. Mary's Seminary and second Superior of the Society of Saint Sulpice in America (1810–1829) and Protector of the Constitutions of the Sisters of Charity of Saint Joseph's.

[f] These ladies were for the most part friends Mrs. Seton had made in Baltimore during her stay there. Anne-Marguérite-Henriette Rouillé de Marigny was the wife of French minister to the United States. Jean-Guillaume Hyde de Neuville, was known to Bishop Cheverus of Boston, and later became a friend of Eliza Sadler in New York.

who being now an imperial princess might perhaps think it suitable to her new dignity to pay for the honor of protecting [sic, supporting] the Sisters of Charity. There is another lady in New York called Mme. de Neuville...who would, I believe, be gratified at the idea of being one of your foundresses, as she had been in France a great benefactress of your society...It may be the means by which He [God] intends to supply you, as indeed it is the one by which St. Vincent of Paul has made all his great foundations.[15]

There, is little evidence that the community ever wrote many such letters, but some[g] of these women did contribute to the foundation at Emmitsburg.[16] Another friend, Mrs. Joanna Barry, left $500.00 to Mrs. Seton in her will, and her grand piano and music to one of the Seton girls.[h] The community meanwhile was often on the verge of failure while war clouds threatened. During the fall and winter that Anna Maria Seton lived out her last months, conditions became so desperate that Mrs. Seton considered going on a "begging tour" to raise some support for her community and school. When Jean Cheverus heard of her proposal he tried to discourage it. He was deeply grieved to hear of her troubles, especially since he could offer no substantial hope that they would abate. He said:

To leave your house and travel and make collections, etc., does not appear to me an eligible plan, although it would procure me the happiness of seeing you in Boston. In the present situation of affairs very little, I am afraid, would be collected. An application by a circular letter would hardly produce anything...The words of our respected friend Mr. Filicchi are so positive that it seems to me you cannot draw upon him except for your personal wants and those of your dear children...Did I possess the means how happy I would be to come to your help.[17]

The sisters tried to augment their meager resources by sewing for the men and boys at Mount Saint Mary's. Coats and greatcoats, vests, pantaloons, roundabouts, and underwear were cut and sewn in a variety of sizes.[i] But,

[g] Louisa Caton, before she left for Canada, left a letter and bank note for Mrs. Seton. Mrs. Mary Ann Patterson, the former Mary Ann Caton, was also a benefactor.

[h] Joanna Barry was Mrs. James Barry whom the Setons had known in New York. She had died in Baltimore in October not long after her return from Europe, where she had been since the fruitless voyage to improve her daughter Ann's health. The piano and music were left to one of the Seton girls, whichever had been Ann Barry's favorite! Each of the Seton daughters enjoyed playing the piano.

[i] A schedule of prices in the archives at Mount St. Mary's shows that the sisters were paid for "1st size" coats and greatcoats $1.50; roundabout, 87 ½ cents; vests and pantaloons, 62 ½ cents; with lower prices for smaller sizes.

before the invention of the sewing machine this work was slow and tedious. It became clear that the school for girls would perforce become the principal source of revenue for the Sisters of Charity at Emmitsburg. So it was that St. Joseph's became a school for girls representing many of the better families of the day. It was with something akin to relief that the community learned in 1812 that the wife[j] of the English consul at Alexandria, Virginia, was anxious to have her daughter admitted to St. Joseph's "college."[k] John Grassi, the Jesuit, wrote Bruté that if Mary Patton were accepted there were five other Patton girls who would in time probably follow her to Emmitsburg.[18] Robert Goodloe Harper sent his daughters to St. Joseph's,[19] as did Maximilian Godefroy, the architect and artist of Baltimore.[20] It was Godefroy who made one of the earliest "views" of the sisterhood of St. Joseph's, which he sent them in 1813. But this picture seems to have disappeared with the years. Young members of the Carroll family attended St. Joseph's School. Nancy Carroll was on the account books early in the institution's history, and the archbishop himself wrote from Rock Creek in 1813 asking Mother Seton to accept one of his numerous great-nieces, Jane Brent of Washington.[21] Dr. Pierre Chatard of Baltimore sent his children to Emmitsburg, the boys going to the Mountain, and Emily to the Valley.[22] Mother Seton confessed to Antonio Filicchi that her hope of establishing "a nursery only, for our Saviour's poor country children" had been of necessity changed so that by 1817 she was "forming *city* girls to faith and piety as wives and mothers."[23] The school was never without some orphans and poor girls, but it was in large measure an institution where families of substance and reputation liked to send their daughters. That there was a great need for such a school is attested by its rapid growth. Toward the end of 1816, Elizabeth told Dué:

> Every moment I may say of life someone is looking to me to say or do Something—60 or more children boarders besides the country children, treble the Sisters we had when you were here...You must give me up as I do myself into His hands who has done so much for us both.[24]

The school deserved to grow, founded as it was on solid principles of religious values, piety and culture. John David, at the beginning of his career as superior of St. Joseph's, warned Mrs. Seton "to establish very strict regulations" to define education in her school. "The principal part," he said, "is to form the tender minds of the pupils to piety and sound morals."[25] Mother Seton quite agreed, but she may have wondered why Father David found it necessary to assume complete supervision over her pupils, whom

---

[j] Mrs. James Patton was a Catholic; her husband was not.

[k] St. Joseph's Academy was a boarding school for what is now elementary, middle, and secondary education.

she had been quite capable of handling at Baltimore. David's pronouncement carried an irritating connotation and for a brief period it seemed as if the tension between Father David and Mrs. Seton might be reflected in the affairs of the school, but distance diminished the acerbity. John Dubois was near St. Joseph's, while John David was not. Dubois had experience with organizing a school, as had Mrs. Seton. The two respective heads of these Emmitsburg schools very naturally came to be the real regulators of the girls' school in the Valley, and some of the school rules preserved at St. Joseph's are in the handwriting of Dubois. It was he who applied and interpreted them for the women across the valley, after David went to Kentucky. Other regulations, however, are in the handwriting of Mrs. Seton, including *The Regulations for the School of St. Joseph's.*[26]

One of the earliest schedules of the distribution of work at St. Joseph's, in Mother Seton's handwriting, shows how well-organized the school was from the very start. Mother Seton was at the head; Sister Kitty Mullen was in charge of discipline. The school mistresses were Sisters Cecilia O'Conway, Fanny Jordan, Margaret George, and Elizabeth Boyle. The sister in charge of discipline preserved "good order" during both class and recreation periods, and was responsible for decorum when the girls went "abroad in a body." Mother Seton was informed by weekly written reports of any "capital fault" in behavior, and she prescribed the suitable remedial measures. The prayers and other exercises of the school were, of course, her province, unless her absence made necessary the substitution of the assistant, Rose White or Sister Kitty Mullan. Mother Seton also "consented to take upon herself the Historical Class and the religious instruction."[27] This religious instruction was very simple and was limited chiefly to a study of the catechism in the early days of the school. When Mother Seton begged George Weis for some pictures of the stations of the cross[1] in 1811, she said, "I have preached the catechism and rosary so long I now want another subject."[28] The expense accounts for the school's first year, show that catechisms, spellers, and grammars were the three chief texts purchased.[29]

As the school grew, the organization became more intricate and the curriculum expanded. The principal subjects were reading, spelling, grammar, geography, arithmetic as a basis, and music, needlework, and languages as electives. Cecilia O'Conway was able to give instruction in French, Spanish, and Italian, having been reared in the household of a Spanish teacher.[30] When Madame Madeleine Guérin came from Martinique

---

[1] The medallions of the *Stations of Cross*, which now hang in the chapel of the White House are of the style which was very popular in the nineteenth century. Made from meerschaum, these may be the ones George Weis obtained for Mrs. Seton.

she, too, was employed as a French teacher, and Mother Seton herself was quite proficient in the language.[31] The latter may have taught music on occasion, as well, since music had always been a favorite pursuit in the old days, and her daughters were equally devoted to the piano. Catherine Josephine Seton taught music to the "scholars" in later years and earned "her full $200 a year."[32] Music was regularly taught by a widowed French woman, a Madame Séguin, who had two orphan children to support, and who was given very liberal terms at St. Joseph's School. The widow must have been accomplished in her field, for Mother Seton told Dué, "She gives us an advantage very precious to our house."[33] However, when Sister Augustine Decount (1786–1870) took over the music teaching after 1817, Madame Séguin's services were no longer required.

The routine of the school day varied very little from summer to winter, and because the pupils were for the most part boarders the schedule governed their entire day. They rose at a quarter to six, were allowed a half hour to dress, and were at prayers by 6:15 a.m. Breakfast was at 7:30 and the time before eating was divided between Mass and study. Travel conditions were so uncertain that full allowance was made for the priest's tardy arrival, and thus the study time might precede or follow the celebration of the Mass. Classes began at 8:00 a.m. and continued until 11:30 a.m., when "beads take place." From dinner time until mid-afternoon a recreation period was provided. At 3:00 p.m. classes were resumed after a brief period of "adoration in the school room." In two hours time a second recreation period followed and the girls could then study until the supper hour at 7:15 P.M. After supper one of the older girls read some spiritual selection which might be explained by Mother Seton or one of the other sisters. The younger children were often sent to bed immediately after supper, if Mother Seton felt they needed the longer rest. So the days went by with the semi-weekly variations for special catechism study on Wednesdays, and confessions and Benediction on Sundays. In the pleasant weather the girls who liked to go to the mountain chapel could attend a second Mass and catch a fleeting glimpse of the male population of Mount St. Mary's College. On these favored Sundays the visitors from the Valley often carried cold ham and cream pies to eat in the scenic grotto above the chapel where they went to say "the Divine office."[34]

The discipline was just as efficiently planned. Teachers at St. Joseph's were expected to keep daily notes on the degrees of achievement of their pupils. "Bad points" had to be remedied by "two good points" by the end of each month. Mother Seton tried to visit each class at least once a month to inspect the mode of teaching employed, to witness improvement or neglect, and to make suggestions. Medals and certificates were used as rewards for application, and the six girls who excelled received extra bonuses in the form of books. No talents were to be "esteemed without behavior," but the means of insuring good behavior did not exclude humiliation, for the educational theory of John Dubois held that "as there are tempers incapable of emulation and which cannot be drawn to virtue and study by any other motive than fear," a list of miscreants was made up every Tuesday to be read publicly in the refectory. "In no case will the child be suffered to have his own way," was Dubois' admonition to the teachers.[35]

The social life at St. Joseph's School in the second decade of the nineteenth century was a far cry from the frenzied activity of a twentieth-century progressive school. The sisters in charge of pupils in that day were called "Angels" and were guardians in a very literal sense. One role, for example, stated:

> The children shall be divided by Mother into several bands
> or societies which will be particularly recommended to the
> care of one of the School Sisters or Angels, who will pay
> a particular attention to their behaviour during recreation,
> keep their company when they can, and endeavor to be their
> guides and counsellors.[36]

Only the most prudent and discreet girls were allowed to congregate or "form parties" without such supervision. No girls were allowed to go to town except on recreation days or with Mother Seton's permission in the case of "some unavoidable or unforeseen necessity." Whenever the girls went out walking, they were attended by two "Angels," one walking ahead to prevent too fast a pace, the other following behind to round up the stragglers. Girls were expected to go on these expeditions unless excused. The only occasions which permitted a girl's going without her group were those when her parents or guardians came to take her to dine.[37]

The rigidity of the rules attracted parents with willful daughters to try the beneficial discipline of the school. But many a girl chose to return to St. Joseph's of her own volition because of the peace and happiness she experienced there. The contrast between the serenity of the Valley and the clamor of the worldly city was expressed by one former pupil in these words, which in spite of their nineteenth-century flavor, still carry a deep sincerity.

St. Joseph's the blest abode of innocence and virtue how I Long to see it. How vividly does it differ from this corrupt world...Bad example is so prevalent in the world that it discourages my endeavor to be pious and fervent. The truth of all, my dearest Mother [Seton], told me I learn by experience. How easy it is to be good where we have good examples before us and where every one is inciting us to piety.[38]

The warm encouragement followed the girls from St. Joseph's out beyond the White House walls. Mother Seton wrote innumerable letters to her former pupils, helping them adjust to the worldly scene. When one girl returned to Baltimore, Mother Seton wrote:

Try to keep all your intentions to our Lord. When you go to your dearest companions go in His Name and send up the little sign to beg Him to stay with you, even *most* in your liveliest moments. Dearest Ellen, it will soon become so easy and *so sweet,* and when death comes, O then the blessed practice will be your great consolation.[39]

Mother Seton tried to make the girls feel that because they were young and pleasures so dear to them the Lord delighted especially in them, and their sacrifices were particularly pleasing.[40] Her own ardent love was a shining example, and the devotion to the sacraments which girls learned at her side often recalled them in later years or in distant places. One girl wrote back to Mother Seton, "What ought I not to do after such an example but I am so weak and so easily diverted from my good resolutions. I have made a great many today, pray for me my own ever dear Mother that I may keep them."[41] Girls who had learned to love the seasons of the liturgical year felt grateful to their zealous instructor. One such girl, Juliana White, wrote on 22 December 1815:

Your Julian often, very often, has thoughts of you during this time of Advent, but more particularly now as it draws near the happy period of Christmas, which brings back to my mind many sweet remembrances. Could I but spend this happy time with you again it would be a happiness that your Julian has not experienced since I last spent it at St. Joseph's.[42]

Elizabeth Seton, with her "passion for babies" and her great love for the Blessed Virgin must have made Christmas a very special time for all who ever knew her.[43] She loved to contemplate Mary, the Mother of God.

How happy the Earth to possess her so long—a secret blessing to the rising Church—the Blessed Trinity could not part so soon with the perfect praise arising from the Earth as long as she remained. How darkened in the sight of angels when she was removed from it![44]

How sensitive and poignant was her cry, "Jesus on the Breast of Mary feeding on her milk—how long she must have delayed the weaning of such a Child!!!!"[45] Herself a mother five times over, Mother Seton possessed so vivid a sense of the humanity of the Holy Family that the girls under her care felt very close to the scenes Mother Seton described.

Mother Seton's maternal tenderness radiated beyond the meadows of the valley and encompassed the mountain regions as well. For many a homesick boy she filled the place of his absent mother. While her own sons were at Mount St. Mary's, it was natural for Elizabeth Seton to visit the school, as well as to make the Sunday trips to St. Mary's Church on the Mountain. Relatives of boys in the school came to consult Mother Seton in several cases. The Chatards of Baltimore recommended their sons to her attention, and Charles, Henry, and William Chatard became as much a part of her concern as were the girls at St. Joseph's. John Dubois and Simon Bruté wrote detailed reports to the parents, but women like Mme. Chatard preferred a woman's point of view and wrote frequently for advice about proper clothing and matters of health.[m] Mme. Chatard was very grateful for Mother Seton's "bontés pour nos enfants."[46]

Another child at Mount St. Mary's in whom Mother Seton was interested was Charles Grim. This boy's widowed mother was another New York convert and Elizabeth helped to get the child, who was about thirteen years old, established in the school at Mount St. Mary's on 19 April 1811. She contributed fifty dollars a year toward his expenses and clothed him; the school furnished his books.[47] Mother Seton eked the money out of the allowance Antonio Filicchi made for her own sons, and she told him, "Good Mrs. Grim with a whole sweep of children...all have shared his [God's] bounty from YOUR hands and your blessed Filippo's."[48] Many a boy on the Mountain had reason to write back in later years, "Give my respects to Mother Seton when you see her again; tell her to pray for her son as she kindly used to call me."[49] One of these was young Jerome Bonaparte whose

---

[m] Mrs. Seton performed similar services for Ellen Wiseman, whose brother Joseph was at the Mountain.

mother was far away in Paris, and whose father had put both mother and son aside. The lonely little boy and the tender-hearted mother of many became fast friends and just prior to a vacation period Jerome penned this note:

> My dear Mother, I am very anxious to get an Agnus Dei[n] before I go home to preserve me in the vacations from the dangers that will surround me. I will keep it as a memorial of kindness and love for your little child who always thinks of you with respect and love and who will think of you with gratitude also, especially if I shall have an Agnus Dei from you as a present.[50]

Mother Seton replied on the reverse of the request:

> Dear Jerome—It is a great pleasure to me to send you the *Agnus Dei*—I wish I had one handsomely covered—but you will mind only the virtue of the prayers our holy Father has said over it. I earnestly beg Our Lord to preserve in you the graces he has so tenderly bestowed on you. Take care yourself not to lose them. Pray for me and I will for you. Your true friend EAS[51]

The more tragic events at the boys' school interested the sisters as well. When John Delaney, a seminarian who died 27 October 1812, and was "the first of the Clergy who died at this place," was buried, the women went in solemn procession to the funeral. Simon Bruté composed a poem on the occasion of this death.[52] When young Picot de Clorivière [sic, Picot de Boisfeillet][o] was buried the next May, the challenging words of Bruté at the grave stirred Elizabeth Seton so deeply that she copied the exhortation in her notebook along with other "Dear Remembrances."[53] When Theophilus Cauffman fell on his knife in March 1814 and was mortally wounded, Mother Seton was as horror-stricken as Father Bruté who tended the dying boy. When death came 5 April, Mother Seton wrote a long letter to the bereaved parents, describing the fatherly care of Bruté, the ardor of the boy's faith, and his dying moments.[54] The mother who had suffered so keenly the loss of her own child knew well the words to bring solace to others.

---

[n] [*Agnus Dei* literally means "Lamb of God." Its usage here refers to a small piece of pure wax, bearing the impress of a lamb supporting the standard of the cross, which was worn devoutly about the neck or suspended in a glass frame from the wall. Ed.]

[o] [This is a case of mistaken identity. Rev. Mr. Joseph-Pierre Picot de Limoëlan de Clorivière (1768-1826) escorted the sisters back to Saint Joseph's from Baltimore when Cecilia Seton died in 1810. Melville based her conclusion on Bruté and Elizabeth Seton who erroneously had written Picot de Clorivière when referring to Joseph Picot de Boisfeillet, who was buried 23 May 1813 at Mount St. Mary's. Perhaps both men went by the name "Picot." Ed.]

Mother Seton also followed the spiritual events at Mount St. Mary's with eager appreciation. Young Michael de Burgo Egan[p] wrote to his uncle, the Bishop of Philadelphia, in 1813 that he was preparing to make his first communion. "The day appointed is the second of February," he explained.[55] The thoughts which that day inspired in Mother Seton are recorded in her notebook under the notation, "the 1st communion at St. Mary's Mount, 2 Feb. 1813."

> Piety must be habitual, not by *fits*. It must be persevering because temptations continue all our life...and *perseverance* alone obtains the crown...Its means are the presence of God, good reading, prayer, the Sacraments...good resolutions often renewed, [and] the remembrance of our last ends. Its advantages [are] habits which secure our predestination, making our life equal, peaceable and consoling, leading to the heavenly crown where our perseverance will be eternal!![56]

The young lad making his first communion and the older woman renewing her intentions that February morning became close friends in the days that followed. When Elizabeth Seton lay desperately ill in the days before her death, Michael de Burgo Egan was in her thoughts.[57] After her death, Egan wrote to her own son, "I often imagine I see...our Dearest Mother looking down on us here below and afflicted when we do wrong— rejoicing when we do well and praying hard for us to obtain a seat (in heaven)."[58] Five years after Elizabeth Seton was buried in the "little wood," Egan, as a young priest, was still dwelling thoughtfully on the inspiration she had furnished. Reminiscing with Catherine Josephine Seton, he said:

> I remember Dearest Mother's repeated expressions of Faith and *Love*. How well she possessed them. Faith enlightened her, love inflamed her and the more I reflect on it, the more I perceive how justly she insisted on those two great virtues... I cannot help thinking it is harder for a priest to get to heaven than anyone else—though indeed surrounded and loaded with graces—yet beset with dangers and overwhelmed with difficulties also...Would to our Lord I had some small share of that holy love which inflamed the heart of our Dear Mother—Love would sweeten everything. Love would triumph over everything.[59]

---

[p] His sister was Sister Mary Teresa Egan, who entered the Sisters of Charity of St. Joseph's 27 November 1816, always had delicate health and died the next year on 20 June.

The respect and love Elizabeth Seton felt for the priestly vocation were so pronounced that she often yearned to be a man, to serve her God the better. The failure of her two sons to find vocations in the priesthood was one of the great sorrows of her life. But many vocations were fostered by her burning love, and bishops valued her intercession above their own. One of her finest letters was addressed to a young man who was uncertain about his future. Its message is still clear.

My dear Smith

My Heart has gone home with you as a parent follows the child she loves when she sees it treading in uncertain steps, doubtful whether it will find the right way—To be engaged in the Service of our Adored Creator, to be set apart to that service, and thereby separated from all the contentions the doubts and temptations that surround the man whose lot is cast in the busy scene of the world, is in itself a sufficient plea on the side which I wish you to engage—but to be placed as a representative of God Himself—to plead for Him, to be allowed the exalted privilege of serving Him continually, to be His instrument in calling Home the wandering soul and sustaining, comforting, and blessing your fellow creatures are considerations which bear no comparison with any other and should lead you to consider the very possibility of your realizing the hope they present as the most precious and valued gift life can afford...

—A man may be a very good man in the pursuit of any other profession—but certainly that of a clergyman is the easiest, surest road to God, and the first, the highest, and the most blessed that can adorn a human being

The Peace of God is the full, the sure, and certain compensation for any discouragements or obstacles the world may throw in the way—and His Guidance and favor till death. In death and after death the reward and crown of Him who faithfully serves him.[60]

Being a mother of many children, both of the flesh and of the spirit, was not, however, all pleasure and satisfaction. The girls who attended St. Joseph's Free School and Academy were sometimes ungrateful, sometimes immune to the salutary spirit of the institution. Mother Seton once reported to Archbishop Carroll of two girls'[q] whom he had placed there:

> A[nn] finds school rules, on the minutia of which general order must depend, extremely hard since her return, and poor *Lotte* went away very much troubled about her situation with us, wishing openly [that neither] she nor Ann had never entered the house—so much in this world for the sad trials we have had from them—but such foolish words will not prevent our continual care to fulfill the Providence of God to them.[61]

On other occasions girls were sent home when they failed to comply with the spirit of the school. Mother Seton wrote to Ambrose Maréchal in 1817 that Mary Kelly, a child whom he had sent on trial, "being found after the expiration of three months candidateship not suited to the object of our institution," would be sent home to Baltimore.[62] In the case of Mary Diana Harper the school was more patient and tried for several years to "check the little proud heart which becomes really insupportable to her teachers." Mother Seton wrote to the father, Robert Goodloe Harper, that she was obliged to complain of Mary Diana's bad example and the necessity of excluding her if she did not mend her ways.[63] Mary Diana[r] stayed on at St. Joseph's until the following year when her parents took her abroad where the twelve-year old girl died at France in 1818.

If the girl who failed to respond to the efforts the teachers put forth was a relative of a friend, Mother Seton felt doubly sorrowful. Eleanor (Ellen) Hickey,[s] the younger sister of Rev. John Francis Hickey,[t] seemed to be one of those "who will not turn to God but through severe chastisement," and Mother Seton wrote the priest, "We must look up—His ways are all beautiful, he will hear our prayers by and by and in the meantime I trust she will get the good and purifying whippings which alone will awaken her."[64] When it became obvious that Eleanor was not suited to the life in the valley, Elizabeth confessed to Hickey that after writing the "hard word" to William Hickey, the girl's guardian in Washington, her heart could not send the letter. She begged

---

[q] Ann and Charlotte (Lotte) "Nelson," protégées of John Carroll, were in reality Ann and Charlotte Smith who had been sent by Bishop Egan of Philadelphia to Baltimore to compensate for unfortunate family circumstances.

[r] Mary Diana Harper was still at St. Joseph's on 16 February 1815. Her brother told John Dubois "She died as ought one that had been brought up at St. Joseph's."

[s] Eleanor Hickey (1801–1858) and her younger sister Johanna (?–1872) joined the Sisters of Charity at Emmitsburg in 1830 (Sister William Anna) and 1831 (Sister Mary) respectively. In 1846 both became founding members of the Sisters of Charity of New York.

[t] Rev. John Francis Hickey, (1789–1869) was the first seminarian ordained to the Catholic priesthood at Mount St. Mary's and the first American member of the Sulpicians of Baltimore. He became the fifth superior general (1830–1841), Sisters of Charity of St. Joseph's in Emmitsburg.

the priest to tell his brother that Eleanor was on her way home. "I never had a heavier heart for a child that left us than for Ellen," she said sadly, "but who knows how it may turn to the GREATER GLORY of our only beloved."[65]

Again, it was occasionally a parent or guardian who brought grief to Mother Seton. Sometimes a cruel letter charging her with "the wages of iniquity" caused Mother Seton's heart to sicken.[66] It was not unusual at one time for non-Catholic girls to be placed in St. Joseph's school. Mother Seton wrote Simon Bruté, in May 1815, "We have eleven Protestant girls entered since you are gone—one today from a heart-broken father who begged she might receive the strongest religious impressions."[67] But the difference in religious opinion sometimes led to criticism from the child's family. One older sister wrote Mother Seton of her distress that a younger girl attending St. Joseph's wished to become a Catholic. "I am fully aware," she wrote, "that any objection I may make to Caroline's[u] becoming a Catholic will naturally be attributed to usual illiberality and prejudice of Protestants but would it not be strange...with a person professing and venerating the creed of their own church to *advise* or even *permit* a child while under their influence to embrace any other."[68] Mother Seton understood the scruples of this sincere woman. She had asked permission for the younger girl's baptism, and she now felt impelled to answer with care. She began by pointing out that they were agreed in the beginning that religion was "our best hope for the reformation" of the young girl's character. Then she proceeded to explain what becoming a Catholic had meant in her own life, the loss of friends, the bitterness of separation, the financial insecurity for her children. "You will forgive me the tedious explanation," she pleaded. But the details were necessary to her defense of her position in regard to the Catholic religion, that she "could never teach or advise any other to one committed to my charge."[69] Eventually the difficulties caused by such cases led Dubois to advise Mother Seton:

> I think it is time for Dear Mother and her Council to determine upon the propriety of admitting Protestant children to St. Joseph's. Experience, I think, proves that their admission becomes very injurious to piety in general amongst the girls without providing any advantage to the Protestant.[70]

The Society of St. Sulpice in Baltimore had recently forbidden Dubois to admit Protestants to his school at Mount Saint Mary's, and Dubois felt the council of the community in the valley should take similar action.

---

[u] There is no evidence to show whether Caroline was baptized or not.

But the Sisters of Charity of St. Joseph's did not bar non-Catholics,[v] then or later.[71] Mother Seton became quite accustomed to parental discontent in one form or another. She explained philosophically to Father Bruté, when he took over his duties as president of St. Mary's College in Baltimore:

> I will tell you what I know American parents to be most difficult—In *hearing the faults of their children*—in twenty instances, when you see the faults are not to be immediately corrected by the parents but rather by good advice and education, it is best not to speak of them to Papa and Mamma, who feel as if you reflected on their very *self* and while to you it will be, "Yes Sir I know, I perceive"—in the heart they think it is not so much, and they will soften and excuse the child they condemn to us and our efforts afterwards avail very little—so that [is] a *big* point.[72]

Nothing altered her deep contentment in her work, and Mother Seton wrote happily to Antonio Filicchi in 1818, "All I know is about my little world in St. Joseph's House, of about 100 precious souls, which we cherish and prepare in silence and under a rather common look of no pretension, to go over our cities like a good leaven."[73] The reality confirmed Bishop Jean Cheverus's forecast to Mrs. Seton that "such an establishment would be a public benefit for Religion, and...a real advantage to yourself & amiable family."[74] Likewise true to Pierre Babade's prophecy, Elizabeth Seton had become, indeed, "the mother of many daughters."[75]

But before leaving the subject of Mother Seton's educational work, some cognizance must be taken of the claims of previous writers that Elizabeth Seton was the "foundress of the parochial school system"[w] in the United States.[76] It is not the writer's purpose to renew any controversy over definitions of the parochial system, or the extent to which schools in a period after Mother Seton's death reproduced her educational establishment. It is worthwhile, nevertheless, to have as clear a picture as archival research can depict of the exact nature of the so called "free school" of Mother

---

[v] Protestants could be admitted as boarders, if they conformed to all the duties of the institution except frequentation of the sacraments. The number was not limited to any specific figure, but the council reserved the right to see their admission did not become detrimental to the institution.

[w] [Parochial schools got their start later in the century, circa 1852, through John Neumann (1811–1860), fourth bishop of Philadelphia, who was a strong advocate of parochial schools. Neumann participated in the deliberations of the First Plenary Council of Baltimore (1852) and served on the Committee for the Education of Catholic Youth. The First Plenary Council of Baltimore urged the establishment of parish free schools and pledged to finance them with Church revenue. Bishop Neumann of Philadelphia served on the Committee for the Education of Catholic Youth during the Council. Building on the educational foundations in existence, the bishops adopted an expanded vision of Catholic education and decreed the creation of the parochial school system in the United States. Ed.]

Seton's own time. Although the sources are very scanty, certain facts can be established. It is with these facts alone that the biographer is concerned.

At the very outset there can be no question that a day school [for girls from poor families] was part of Mother Seton's intention very early in her stay at Emmitsburg. Even before the community left the stone farmhouse, Mrs. Seton had broached the subject to her superiors in Baltimore, for Louis Dubourg, in his letter of 28 December 1809, said plainly, "Far from objecting to your plan of opening a day school at St. Joseph's, Mr. David and myself beg it should be done without loss of time, if as we hear from Mr. Caff the house is dry enough."[77] The community records of the Sisters of Charity of St. Joseph's simply verify a sentence in Mother Rose's journal stating that on 22 February 1810, three pupils were received. If these children were from the surrounding country, then this was the official beginning of the day school. Since the five children from Frederick who came in May were designated as "boarders," it seems reasonable to assume that the first three were not. Mother Seton herself usually referred to her pupils in round numbers "including boarders," so that it is virtually impossible to determine how many day students there were at a given time.[78] It is clear, however, that country children, as Mother Seton called them, or externs, as Father Bruté termed them, were part of the establishment from 1810 until Elizabeth Seton died.[79]

The pupils were apparently all accorded the same treatment in the very beginning, but soon some distinction seems to have been deemed necessary, for Rev. Charles Ignatius White states that "when the orphans educated there were formed into a class separate from the boarders they were at first pained by the humiliation which this distinction seemed to imply."[80] This class is referred to in the council book of the community as "St. Joseph's class" as distinct from the boarders. For example, when the question arose as to which group should receive pupils who paid "limited sums," the boarders or St. Joseph's class, the council decided that students who paid less than full tuition should not be included among the boarders.[81] It is quite clear that "St. Joseph's class" was never entirely free to all comers. The Bruté report of 1813 shows that externs paid eleven dollars each. The council book which covers the years from 1813 to 1821 gives substantial proof that although orphans were received and were charged nothing, other girls making partial payments were also part of St. Joseph's class.[82] In one case a girl was refused admittance to St. Joseph's class because her relatives were quite able to pay for her.[83] No child admitted at the community's expense could be younger than ten years.[84] The students in St. Joseph's class, after 1816, were never to be allowed to enter the classes held for the boarders; but if they were talented, they were given opportunities for private instruction. After they reached the age of sixteen, if desirable, the poor children could be hired by the school and work for wages under the direction of the sisters. The policy of the Sisters of Charity of St. Joseph's at this time seems to emerge rather clearly as one based on a sliding scale or the ability-to-pay theory. Wealthier girls went among the boarders and were entitled to an education suited to their social and economic status. Those girls who could pay less went into St. Joseph's class to be taught simultaneously with the free students. Even the poorest were encouraged to be economically independent by the promise of work when they were able to engage in it. When times were bad and funds were low, non-paying pupils were refused.[85] When times were more prosperous the number "at our expense" increased.

By the summer of 1819, the number of the day students had grown so large that the council considered erecting a new building, but economic conditions argued against it.[86] The following spring, however, found the council agreed to build "two rooms below and one above for the convenience of day students and workmen."[87] That May contracts for the building were discussed, and 30 June 1820, the contract was given to Edward Yates for a one-story brick building without a cellar, and consisting of rooms twenty feet square. Later the contract was modified to include a second story. This building proved faulty and on 29 December 1820, it was agreed not to pay any more to the builder until these defects should be remedied. Since Mother Seton died within a week's time, it is quite probable that in her lifetime the day-school remained in the White House in which she lived.[88]

There is no question that both the boarders and St. Joseph's pupils received their education in a religious atmosphere and under teachers who were primarily sisters, or priests from Mount Saint Mary's.[x] The matter of religious auspices or the parochial nature of the school is not quite so easy to dispose of if arbitrary definitions are to be accepted. There is no doubt that John Dubois, the superior from 1811 to 1826, was a supervisory head of the school in Mother Seton's time, but the exact degree of responsibility for the school of Dubois to the bishop and to the parish scarcely parallel the modern situation. Dubois was a member of the Society of St. Sulpice during this period, and as such was directly responsible to his superior in Baltimore

---

[x] A few lay professors taught extra subjects, and several [alumnae] eventually became sisters in the community. [Louisa Daddisman (1797–1889), of Frederick County, Maryland, attended St. Joseph's Academy in 1810 and entered the Sisters of Charity two years later. At the time of her death she was the last surviving companion of Mother Seton. Ed.]

for his office as superior of the women at St. Joseph's. Archbishop Carroll, it may be recalled, had told Mrs. Seton quite plainly in November 1809:

> You know, ever honoured and most esteemed Madame, that after the choice made by yourselves, your chief benefactors, of living under the protection of the priests of St. Sulpice, I surrendered, as much as a Bishop can surrender, your government into their hands.[89]

While Carroll lived, he maintained a policy of general non-intervention in the relations between the Sulpicians and the Sisters of Charity of St. Joseph's. Archbishop Neale's reign was too brief to indicate any noticeable change from this policy. When Ambrose Maréchal, S.S., became third Archbishop of Baltimore in 1817, the bonds between Sulpicians in Baltimore and Dubois in Emmitsburg were strengthened, but the choice of superior for the women still remained in the hands of the society and not the episcopacy.

To further complicate this subject of the relation of bishop-to-pastor-to-school, the situation in Emmitsburg during these years was scarcely analogous to that of modern parish administration. The priests in that area in reality administered two parishes, a seminary and college, and the sisterhood simultaneously. The work was for the most part done by Sulpicians and most of the time there were two or three regular priests to handle the three congregations: "the Mountain Congregation," St. Joseph's Church in the village, and the sisters and students at St. Joseph's house. During Mother Seton's life these priests included John Dubois, Simon Bruté, Charles Duhamel, John Hickey, and Samuel Cooper.[90] The exact limitations of physical boundaries and spiritual responsibility were never clearly delineated in Mother Seton's time; and the difficulties of clarifying these boundaries formed the subject of many a letter from Dubois to his successive bishops.[y] Writing to Ambrose Maréchal in the summer of 1817, Dubois explained that under Carroll the two parishes of the Mountain and Emmitsburg were not divided because Carroll had feared the "inconveniences." Archbishop Leonard Neale, S.J., (1746–1817), successor to Carroll, had told Dubois he wished to continue things as Carroll had left them. Now Dubois wanted from Maréchal some hint of what to expect.[91] Maréchal, after due consideration, seems to have favored a separation of the two parishes with the sisters to be served by the priest of the Emmitsburg parish. Dubois, when replying to a letter from his archbishop in February the following year, pointed out that

---

[y] The premier See of Baltimore was led by the following ordinaries during the lifetime of Elizabeth Bayley Seton: John Carroll (bishop, 1789-1808; archbishop, 1808-1815); Leonard Neale (1815-1817); Ambrose Maréchal (1817-1828).

the sisters' confessors were usually appointed by the superior and that this priest should be one of the directors of Mount Saint Mary's. The alternative of having a separate priest for the sisters living on community property was not to be thought of. The sisters had no place to lodge him. Even if they found a willing one, he would be too old to undergo the strenuous life of the Emmitsburg mission. And finally, Dubois stated:

> Mrs. Seton knows so well the impossibility and the inconvenience, perhaps even scandals, which would result, from the admission of a priest there, that she has declared that she will never consent to such an arrangement, at least in the present situation of the community.[92]

Meanwhile the whole issue of suppressing the seminary of Mount St. Mary's rose to complicate the subject of jurisdiction. The priests on the Mountain became directly responsible to St. Sulpice in Paris in 1818, while remaining parish priests under the general superintendence of the Archdiocese of Baltimore.[93] John Hickey was recalled to Baltimore and the burden of the parishes fell upon Dubois and Bruté, who made the choice of remaining with the Mountain seminary.[z] In spite of their admiration for each other, the two priests found the joint responsibility onerous enough to produce mild bickering over their respective duties. Each wrote to Archbishop Maréchal in plaintive tones, discussing, the difficulties involved in reaching a just distribution of work and responsibility.[94] It would be very difficult to pronounce finally as to which parish or priest was directly responsible to the archbishop for Mother Seton's day school.

One last characteristic of the day school is worthy of note. In regard to the pupils there is no evidence anywhere to suggest that boys were ever members of St. Joseph's class or of the boarding school. Furthermore, the charter of incorporation stated clearly that the purposes of the sisters included "Education of young females."[95] None of the characteristics of Mother Seton's day school, however, are incompatible with the concept of a parochial school as it later emerged from the nineteenth-century conciliar legislation.[96] [In the post-Vatican II and post-millennium era sponsorship, governance, financial support, and Catholic Identity have emerged as significant issues. Ed.] Certainly the Emmitsburg school of today, *Mother*

---

[z] John Dubois protested the action taken by St. Sulpice in Baltimore and the recall of Father John Hickey. Bruté decided to stay on with Dubois. In 1826 Mount St. Mary's ceased to have any connection with the Sulpicians, either in America or France.

Seton School, is the direct descendant of "St. Joseph's class" through a line of continuous existence. Only the location of the building has changed.[aa]

In the last analysis, it is quite unimportant what slogans or appellations are associated with Mother Seton's name. All can agree that she made an invaluable contribution to nineteenth-century education, a contribution which was in accordance with American traditions of the highest rank. Her work was begun under unusual circumstances of disorganization, economic duress, and geographic handicaps. It was located in an area which represented the westward progress of seaboard culture to northwest Central Maryland. It faced the hazards of wartime economy and endured. It linked those "indispensable supports," religion and morality, to a respect for the inherent love for independence and self-sufficiency that characterized American life everywhere. It was Christian charity in the broadest sense applied to the American scene. Whatever she may have founded, Elizabeth Seton in her lifetime represented the peculiar American genius for adaptation within the bounds of dignity and discipline, but transcending distinctions of class and discrimination. In her modest, unassuming way this little gentlewoman who was born two years before the Republic, who had been nurtured in one of its early capitals, the cosmopolitan port of New York, had followed the seat of government southward, this Elizabeth Bayley Seton, American woman nineteenth-century style, personified the trend of her day. Not every pioneer woman was the muscular, sun-bonneted amazon that some later-day artists like to re-create. There were these others, some in widow's caps, clasping a catechism instead of a rifle, giving soft instruction in the Romance languages of the old world, counting out the delicate minuets at the piano, cherishing and preparing "under a common look of no pretension" these fine young American girls who would go out "over our cities like a good leaven."

Quietly living out her days in her valley in the Catoctin spur of the Blue Ridge Mountains, Elizabeth Seton described her days for her older friend, Eliza Sadler, in these words:

> Your _matron step_ and _quiet look_ and independent _intention_ are now precisely the rule of my life...Able to fulfill so many more duties in the little service of our little world contained in St. Joseph's, everything seems to wear a new color, and life has a charm for me which I often wondered [what] you found in it. So far from the world, surrounded by all the

---

[aa] Mother Seton School is sponsored by the Daughters of Charity and traces its roots to the foundation of St. Joseph's Free School and Academy (1810–1890) through St. Joseph College High School (1890–1945), St. Joseph High School (1945–1982), St. Euphemia's School (1878–1956), and St. Anthony's School (1903–1956). The latter two schools merged to form Mother Seton School in 1956.

sweets of the country and retirement, an old woman to whom the nearly 100 souls in our house look for their daily solace of a Mother's smile, incapacitated by my *want of capacity to manage and bustle* from taking any other part, but to try and keep off the evil spirits which always would steal in such a multitude, and turn everything to the account of peace and order—writing and translating, my ever darling pastime now as ever, with the knitting always on the same table with the pen, to show the visitors they are not unwelcome.[97]

Peace, order, and industry, how these ideals tempered life at St. Joseph's. Peace which comes with patience, that "salt of the prophet Elezius [sic, Elisha],[bb] which purifies the polluted waters of our passions, and sweetens all the bitterness of life." Order, "the thread of *Ariadne* which guides our actions in the great labyrinth of time."[98] Industry, the lesson of Mother Seton herself whom Simon Bruté liked to call "little woman of the fields," whose hands indoors and out were never idle. This was the educational formula of Mother Seton's school.

[bb] Cf. 2Kings 2:19-22.

Notes

[1] A-6.3a, Mother Rose White's Journal, *CW*, 2:718.

[2] Sister John Mary Crumlish, D.C., "The History of St. Joseph's Academy, Emmitsburg, Maryland, 1809-1902." An unpublished master's dissertation preserved in the Mullen Library of the Catholic University of America, Washington, D. C., 1.

[3] John David to Elizabeth Seton, Baltimore, 28 December 1809, AMSV, I, 23.

[4] A-6.3a, Mother Rose White's Journal, *CW*, 2:726. The sisters moved on 20 February, and the new pupils were received 22 February 1810.

[5] 6.47, Elizabeth Seton to John Carroll, 15 June 1810, *CW*, 2:142.

[6] 6.45, Elizabeth Seton to Catherine Dupleix, 4 June 1810, *CW*, 2:136.

[7] Ibid., 138.

[8] 6.70, Elizabeth Seton to Catherine Dupleix, 4 February 1811, *CW*, 2:172-173.

[9] 6.54, Elizabeth Seton to Eliza Sadler, 3 August [?1810], *CW*, 2:154.

[10] John Dubois to Carroll, Emmitsburg, 11 January 1813, AAB, AASMSU, 3-F-13.

[11] 6.46, Elizabeth Seton to Matthias O'Conway, 5 June [1811], *CW*, 2:140.

[12] Simon Bruté Report for Ambrose Maréchal, Section XXIV, "Sisterhood," AMSMU. See Bills of Mary Godefroy, Cecilia Thompson, etc., 20 October 1812. Record of Joanna Fennell, November 1814-1816, ASJPH RB #70, *Records of the Pupils of Saint Joseph's Academy and College, 1809-1936.*

[13] Ledger, 1813, ASJPH 3-3-7:1, 55. One of these pupils was Eliza Boarman.

[14] John Dubois to John M. Tessier, Emmitsburg, 18 January 1816, ASMS.

[15] Louis Dubourg to Elizabeth Seton, Baltimore, 30 December 1809, AMSV, I, 11.

[16] John Carroll to Elizabeth Seton, Baltimore, 12 July 1815, AMSV. See a letter asking for contributions to St. Joseph's, 6.93, Elizabeth Seton to Robert Goodloe Harper, 28 December 1811, *CW*, 2:206.

[17] Jean Cheverus to Elizabeth Seton, Boston, 20 January 1812, AMSV, I, 3.

[18] John Grassi to Simon Bruté, Georgetown, 27 October 1812, UNDA II-3-n.

[19] John Carroll to Elizabeth Seton, Baltimore, 11 September 1811, AMSV, I, 16. This letter speaks of Mr. Harper's desire to send Mary Diana Harper. In later years other Harper girls came. See 7.234, Elizabeth Seton to Robert Goodloe Harper, 1 January 1820, *CW*, 2:636.

[20] Maximilian Godefroy to John Dubois, Baltimore, 8 August 1813, AMSMUU. Godefroy was one of the great multitude impressed by Mother Seton's humility and he added a postscript to this letter

sending "un mot de respect et de remerciement puisque *deux* seraient trop pour elle." See Carolina V. Davison, "Maximilian and Eliza Godefroy," *Maryland Historical Magazine,* XXIX (March, 1934), 1-20.

[21] John Carroll to Elizabeth Seton, Rock Creek, 5 September 1813, UNDA.

[22] 7.29, Elizabeth Seton to Marie-Françoise Chatard, n.d., *CW*, 2:400; 7.149, Ibid., *CW*, 2:538. There is correspondence between Mrs. Chatard and Mother Seton preserved at ASJPH.

[23] 7.87, Elizabeth Seton to Antonio Filicchi, 1 June 1817, *CW*, 2:479.

[24] 7.65, Elizabeth Seton to Catherine Dupleix, n.d., *CW*, 2:452. Written after Rebecca's death in November 1816.

[25] John David to Elizabeth Seton, 28 December 1809, ASJPH 1-3-3-2, (S-1). Copy; the original is in AMSV.

[26] 12.8, Regulations for the School of St. Joseph's, *CW,* 3b:124.

[27] 12.9, "Distribution of the external employment at St. Joseph's," *CW*, 3b:127. This schedule is in the handwriting of John Dubois, with corrections added by Elizabeth Seton.

[28] 6.67, Elizabeth Seton to George Weis, 15 January 1811, *CW*, 2:167.

[29] 12.19, List of Expenses, 1810, *CW*, 3b:162. The account shows the purchase of six "practical reflections" and six *Following of Christ,* which were probably for community use, since the other books were purchased in amounts varying between two and three dozen. [See Appendix B-2, Book Chart, Catholic Period, 1805-1821), 616. *A Brief Method of Meditation* (Practical Reflections) appears on page 632. Ed.]

[30] 6.7, Elizabeth Seton to Julia Scott, 20 September 1809, *CW*, 2:83. Matthias O'Conway, was a Spanish interpreter from Philadelphia. See *Records of the American Catholic Historical Society,* X (1890), 292.

[31] A-6.3a, Mother Rose White's Journal, *CW*, 2:729.

[32] 7.4, Elizabeth Seton to William Seton, 1816, *CW*, 2:369.

[33] 6.70, Elizabeth Seton to Catherine Dupleix, n.d., *CW*, 2:172. For the terms See *Mother Augustine Decount* (Emmitsburg: Daughters of Charity, n.d.), 7.

[34] 6.41, Elizabeth Seton to Eliza Sadler, 27 May 1810, *CW*, 2:131-132. See also John Dubois to Sisters of Charity, "Regulations for the School at St. Joseph's," c.1811, ASJPH 1-3-3-5:10; "Rules for the School in the Winter," c.1811, ASJPH 1-3-3-5:11; "Sundays & Holydays [School]," c.1811, ASJPH 1-3-3-5:12.

[35] John Dubois to Sisters of Charity, "Schools at St. Joseph's," c.1811, ASJPH 1-3-3-5:9; "Sundays & Holydays [School]," c.1811, ASJPH 1-3-3-5:12; "School," c.1811, ASJPH 1-3-3-5:13. These items are rules given by John Dubois to the sisterhood.

[36] John Dubois to Sisters of Charity, "Schools," c.1811, ASJPH 1-3-3-5:13.

[37] John Dubois to Sisters of Charity, "Sundays & Holydays [School]," c.1811, ASJPH 1-3-3-5:12.

[38] "Cos" to Elizabeth Seton, Baltimore, 25 July 1814, ASJPH 1-3-3-2:88. It was not possible for the present writer [Melville] to identify this pupil, except to state that she came from Baltimore. See A-12.18, St. Joseph's Academy and Free School Roster (1809-1821), *CW*, 3b:565. Catherine and Eliza Coskery (Cosskery) are listed on page 567 but it is not known if their home was in Baltimore. Ed.]

[39] Ellen Wiseman to Elizabeth Seton, 14 October 1815, ASJPH 1-3-3-12: B5.

[40] Ellen Wiseman to Elizabeth Seton, 12 August 1813, ASJPH 1-3-3-12: B4.

[41] Charlotte Smith to Elizabeth Seton, Baltimore, 23 March 1812, ASJPH 1-3-3-3:73.

[42] Juliana White to Elizabeth Seton, Baltimore, 22 December 1815, ASJPH 1-3-3-3:77.

[43] 7.84, Elizabeth Seton to Julia Scott, 10 April 1817, *CW*, 2:476. This letter uses the phrase "passion for babies."

[44] 11.9, "Departed St. Teresa's Day," entry entitled ASSUMPTION 1813 Mt. St. Mary, *CW*, 3b:19.

[45] Ibid.

[46] Mme. Chatard [Marie-Francoise-A. Buisson] to Elizabeth Seton, ASJPH 1-3-3-4:76-85. These letters range from March 1811, through December 1816. Ellen Wiseman to Elizabeth Seton, 6 April 1817, ASJPH 1-3-3-12:9.

[47] John Dubois to person unknown, Emmitsburg, 23 November 1812, ASMSU. Mount St. Mary's record of entrance of students.

[48] 6.167, Elizabeth Seton to Antonio Filicchi, 1 July 1814, *CW*, 2:277.

[49] William Gillespie to John Hickey, Brownsville, 21 July 1817, ASMS.

[50] Jerome N. Bonaparte to Elizabeth Seton, Emmitsburg, 21 June [no year], ASJPH 1-3-3-4:100.

[51] 7.30, Elizabeth Seton to Jerome Bonaparte, [June 1816], *CW,* 2:401.

[52] Scrapbook, AMSMU. A printed account of the funeral of John Delaney taken from a letter written from Emmitsburg, 12 November 1812. See Bruté Papers, at AMSMU.

[53] 11.9, "Departed St. Teresa's day," *CW*, 3b:13. A copy of the sermon in Bruté's hand is at AMSMU, Bruté Papers, 23 May 1813. See also 10.4 "Dear Remembrances," *CW,* 3a:510-23. [These documents confuse Joseph Picot de Boisfeillet, who was buried 23 May 1813, with Rev. Mr. Joseph Joseph-Pierre Picot de Limoëlan de Clorivière. Ed]

[54] Bruté Papers, including an undated letter of Mrs. Seton to Mr. Cauffman, AMSMU.

[55] Michael de Burgo Egan to Michael Egan, Emmitsburg, 25 January 1813, UNDA.

[56] 11.9, "Departed St. Teresa's Day," *CW*, 3b:12.

[57] Michael de Burgo Egan to Catherine Josephine Seton, Emmitsburg, 3 January 1824, Robert Seton Collection, UNDA. Egan wrote, "Oh how much I feel myself bound to pray for her who told me that when she thought she was giving the last sigh, she had me on her heart. I cannot forget those words."

[58] Michael de Burgo Egan to William Seton, Emmitsburg, 19 June 1822, Robert Seton Collection, UNDA.

[59] Michael de Burgo Egan to Catherine Josephine Seton, Emmitsburg, 6 January 1826, Robert Seton Collection, UNDA.

[60] 7.304, Draft of Elizabeth Seton to Mr. (?) Smith, n.d., *CW*, 2:695.

[61] 6.209, Elizabeth Seton to John Carroll, 9 August 1811, *CW*, 2:349. See Michael de Burgo Egan to John Carroll, Philadelphia, 10 May 1810, AAB, AASMSU, 3-H-9.

[62] 7.115, Elizabeth Seton to Ambrose Maréchal, September 1817, *CW*, 2:505.

[63] 6.171, Elizabeth Seton to Robert Goodloe Harper, 15 October 1814, *CW*, 2:282. Robert Goodloe Harper to John Dubois, Paris, 28 June 1818, AMSMU.

[64] 7.204, Elizabeth Seton to John Hickey, 19 February 1819, *CW*, 2:603. The original is in AASUS, AASMSU, RG 1, Box 14. This was a postscript added by Mrs. Seton to a letter from Eleanor Hickey to John Hickey.

[65] 7.215, Elizabeth Seton to John Hickey, [June 1819], *CW,* 615.

[66] 6.209, Elizabeth Seton to John Carroll, 9 October 1815, *CW*, 2:348.

[67] 6.195, Elizabeth Seton to Simon Bruté, May 1815, *CW*, 2:329.

[68] Ann C. Tilghman to Elizabeth Seton, St. Michael's, Talbot County, MD, 1 January 1820, ASJPH 1-3-3-7:84.

[69] 7.236, Elizabeth Seton to Ann C. Tilghman, n.d., *CW*, 2:639.

[70] John Dubois to Elizabeth Seton, n.d., AMSV, I, 25.

[71] Council Minutes, Sisters of Charity of St. Joseph's, May 1816, ASJPH 3-3-5, 14.

[72] 7.1, Elizabeth Seton to Simon Bruté, n.d., *CW*, 2:366.

[73] 7.175, Elizabeth Seton to Antonio Filicchi, 8 August 1818, *CW*, 2:573. For other details of Mother Seton's educational work and influence, see AASMSU William J. Fletcher, "Mother Elizabeth Seton, Educator and Foundress of the American Catholic Parochial School," an unpublished dissertation, Baltimore, St. Mary's Seminary, 1940; C.

I. White, *Life of Mrs. Eliza A. Seton* (1853 ed)., 357-369. [For a modern study, see Betty Ann McNeil, D.C., "Historical Perspectives on Elizabeth Seton and Education: School Is My Chief Business," *Journal of Catholic Education* 9, 3 (2006), 284-306. See also Appendix D. Chronology of Elizabeth Ann Seton and Catholic Education]

[74] Jean Cheverus to Elizabeth Ann Seton, Boston, 12 May 1808, ASJPH 1-3-3-1:9.

[75] 5.10, Elizabeth Seton to Cecilia Seton, Baltimore, 6 October 1808, *CW*, 2:34.

[76] Mary Regis Hoare, *Virgin Soil* (Boston, 1942), 15; Agnes Sadlier, *Elizabeth Seton* (New York, 1905), 128; Peter Guilday to Mary Regis Hoare, 22 April 1932, cited in Hoare, 32; Mary Agnes McCann, S.C., *History of Mother Seton's Daughters* (New York,1917), I, 9. Code called Mother Seton "patroness of the parochial school system." See Joseph B. Code, *Great American Foundresses* (New York, 1929), 72. [Melville opines that Code's work often lacks historical accuracy. Ed.]

[77] Louis Dubourg to Elizabeth Seton, Baltimore, 28 December 1809, AMSV, I, 10.

[78] 6.47, Elizabeth Seton to John Carroll, 15 June 1810, *CW*, 2:142; 7.65, Elizabeth Seton to Catherine Dupleix, n.d., *CW*, 2:451.

[79] Since the Bruté report of December 1813, and Mother Seton's letter to Antonio Filicchi in 1817 are central points within the period (1809-1821) of Mother Seton's life in Emmitsburg, it seems valid to accept them as strong proof that the "poor country children" were a minority group. [See Council Minutes, Sisters of Charity of St. Joseph's, (1812-1829), February 1816, ASJPH 3-2-5, 9. See A-12.18, St. Joseph's Academy and Free School Roster (1809-1821), *CW,* 3b:565, n.1. See also Simon Bruté Report for Ambrose Maréchal, AMSMUU, and 7.87 Elizabeth Seton to Antonio Filicchi, 1 June 1817, *CW*, 2:479.]

[80] White, 376. White gives no archival references to support this statement but he is a reliable biographer in most other instances.

[81] Council Minutes, Sisters of Charity of St. Joseph's, 18 February 1816, ASJPH 3-3-5.

[82] Ibid., 14 August 1814; 24 April 1814; June 1818; 20 October 1819; 24 April 1820.

[83] Ibid., 24 April 1820.

[84] Ibid., 18 February 1816.

[85] Ibid., 20 October 1819. John Dubois to John Carroll, Emmitsburg, 11 January 1813, AAB, AASMSU, 3-F-13.

[86] Ibid., 1 June 1819.

[87] Ibid., 17 May 1820.

[88] Rev. John Dubois to Elizabeth Seton, 26 May 1820, ASJPH 1-3-3-5:33; Rev. John Dubois and Edward Yates, builder, articles of agreement for erection of the Free School building at St. Joseph's, 30 June 1820, ASJPH 1-3-3-5:34; Jacob Marshall and Sebastian Adelsperger, stop payment to Edward Yates for Free School building at St. Joseph's, 29 December 1820, ASJPH 1-3-3-5:35; Edward Yates, receipt in full, 7 November 1821, for work on Free School building at St. Joseph's ASJPH 1-3-3-5:36.

[89] John Carroll to Elizabeth Seton, Baltimore, 9 November 1809, AMSV, I, 15.

[90] Although Cooper was not a Sulpician, he had received some of his priestly formation at their seminary in Baltimore.

[91] John Dubois to Ambrose Maréchal, Emmitsburg, 8 July 1817, AAB, AASMSU, 15-T-21.

[92] John Dubois to Ambrose Maréchal, Emmitsburg, 25 February 1818, AAB, AASMSU, 15-T-8.

[93] John Dubois to Ambrose Maréchal, Emmitsburg, 21 June 1818, AAB, AASMSU, 15-T-9. See Charles G. Herbermann, *The Sulpicians in the United States* (New York, 1916), 136; Joseph W. Ruane, *The Beginnings of the Society of St. Sulpice in the United States (1791-1829),* (Washington, 1935), 178-185.

[94] Simon Bruté to Ambrose Maréchal, Emmitsburg, n.d., AMSMU; John Dubois to Ambrose Maréchal, Emmitsburg, 21 March 1820, AAB, AASMSU, 15-U-20.

[95] Charter of Incorporation, 18 January 1817, ASJPH 3-1-3. See A-7.73a, Act of Incorporation of the Sisters of Charity of St. Joseph's in Maryland, *CW,* 2:758.

[96] Francis P. Cassidy, "Catholic Education in the Third Plenary Council of Baltimore," *Catholic Historical Review,* XXXIV (October 1949), 292-8.

[97] 7.72, Elizabeth Seton to Eliza Sadler, n.d., *CW,* 2:463.

[98] 10.2, "Maxims," Red Leather Notebook, n.d., *CW,* 3a:488.

CHAPTER 12

꙳

THE ANGEL OF THE MOUNTAIN

In February 1818, Simon Gabriel Bruté returned to Mount St. Mary's to assist John Dubois and to fill the place made vacant by the death of Charles Duhamel.[1] Bruté's return to Emmitsburg brought Mother Seton the spiritual direction which was to guide her over her last years, and which in earlier days had so noticeably increased her fervor. Probably no other man knew the secret of her inner forces so well. Simon Bruté first saw Elizabeth Seton in the summer of 1811. She was one of the people who tried to help the young French émigré priest learn to pronounce English. Another woman, Mrs. Charlotte Melmoth,[a] also helped Simon Bruté with English pronunciation at Emmitsburg in 1811.[2] It was at this time that they first shared an enjoyment of *The Following of Christ,* "especially the Chapter Twenty-first, Third Book."[3] Although Bruté's stay in Emmitsburg was very brief, that summer marked the beginning of a lasting friendship.

Simon Gabriel Bruté de Rémur was born in France, at Rennes in Brittany, 20 March 1779, four and a half years after Elizabeth Ann Bayley was born in New York. He graduated from the Sorbonne as a physician prior to studying for the priesthood. He sailed from France in June 1810, as part of the group which brought the *Common Rules of the Daughters of Charity* crafted by St. Vincent de Paul and St. Louise de Marillac to Mother Seton's community, and Bruté later referred to them, the modification for America, as "the constitutions to which I had my original humble enough part,"[4] although there is no evidence that Bruté came to Emmitsburg in August of that year when the *Common Rules* of the Daughters of Charity were brought to St. Joseph's by Flaget.[b] The young priest was kept very busy

---

[a] Mrs. Melmoth was an actress from New York City. Matthew O'Brien mentioned her in a letter to Bishop Carroll as a convert, an actress from England and Ireland, who wanted to adopt a penitential life. Mrs. Melmoth was in Baltimore at the same time as Mrs. Seton, and impressed Pierre Babade and Matthias O'Conway as "noblehearted" and of laudable intentions. Mrs. Melmoth followed Mrs. Seton to Emmitsburg and made the first retreat with the sisters in August 1809. John Dubois in November of that year wrote her, "How much do I rejoice to see you persevering in the idea you had of settling amongst us." Mrs. Melmoth did settle in the village of Emmitsburg for awhile, for Mrs. Seton mentioned her in October 1810, as "an old lady in the village near us." Simon Bruté said "I saw her in his sanctuary in the Sisterhood and in Emmitsburg," in August 1811. Not long after this Mrs. Melmoth decided to return to New York, and was hurt in a stage coach accident en route. She was first reported dead, but later found to be only injured. She returned to the New York stage, where her last engagement began on 12 August 1812. Her age compelled her to retire and she conducted a "seminary" on Washington Street in New York until her death in September 1823.

[b] [Community records state that a young French cleric destined in the designs to be the future expounder of those Rules, Rev. Simon Gabriel Bruté, accompanied Flaget to the United States in 1810. Chronological Table (1766–1891), entry of 10 August 1810, ASJPH 7-13. Ed.]

in Baltimore that fall, especially after Louis Dubourg left for Martinique, and Father Bruté was called upon to assume his parochial work.[5] The first positive proof of Bruté's presence in northwestern Maryland is an entry in Tessier's journal for 18 July 1811, which says simply, "Bruté left for Emmitsburg," and Mother Seton's letter to Archbishop Carroll mentioning Mr. Bruté's zeal and "purity of heart."[6]

The brief sojourn near St. Joseph's community that first summer produced a lively friendship between the priest who spoke such broken English and the mother of the community who used rather fluent French; Father Bruté said to Mother Seton gratefully:

> You whom I like to call a mother here, as I call one in France...
> you have so well helped me better to know, yes better still, a
> priest of His as I was, to know my happiness and desire, but
> alas, [I] so vainly desire to impart the same to others to know
> and love and say Jesus...[7]

His advice to her from the very beginning was, "Make all happy, open-hearted supernaturally minded about you."[8] These two desires were the keynotes of their friendship: Bruté's desire to become a better priest, and Mother Seton's striving to share her ardor more fully with those about her. Each tried to temper the excesses of the other; each tried to bring new impetus to the other's zeal. Bruté supplied the exuberant mysticism that Elizabeth Seton and her children had loved in Pierre Babade in Baltimore. Mother Seton furnished the practical common sense which Simon Bruté was to emulate and to apply to his problems in later life as a college president and as the first Bishop of Vincennes, Indiana. (His diocese became the archdiocese of Indianapolis.)

From the moment of their meeting their dependence upon each other grew rapidly. Whether Simon Bruté was at the Mountain, in Baltimore, or in far-away France, Mother Seton could rely upon his interest in her concerns, feel comfort in his almost instantaneous grasp of her difficulties, and find fresh inspiration in his words, whether spoken or written. In spite of the busy life in Baltimore his first winter after meeting Elizabeth Seton, Bruté found time to keep informed of her sorrow as Anna Maria Seton lay dying. He was pleased to learn of the young woman's reception into the community.[9] He managed to be present the last day Anna Maria lived.

> He told her he would say Mass for her [and] suggested
> many things for the moment to which she replied with all
> her soul, tho' a little before he came she had appeared to

wander a little...when Mr. Bruté left her for the altar she called after him, earnestly repeated [that] she prays for all, all her dear Sisters, [the Mount] Seminary, and all as he had suggested.[10]

In the barren months that followed the death of Mother Seton's first-born child, Bruté exercised all his ingenuity to bring her out of this terrible trial possessed of complete resignation, but without any impairment of her joyous service. He skillfully used her yearning to dwell on Anna Maria's virtues, on her last moments, to lead the mother to a greater concept of eternity, while maintaining a strong emphasis on her duty to her living children. He asked for a copy of Anna's rules for her "decury children,"[c] her letter to her first communion class, and an account of Anna Maria's last words written after extreme unction.[11] He wrote for Mother Seton the answer to her morbid thoughts over the snake on Anna Maria's grave, creating an imaginary soliloquy by "Anna to her mother praying at her grave."[12] He drew delicate sketches showing Anna's angelic form hovering near the altar to share her mother's communion joys.[13] Writing on the anniversary of Anna's death he elaborated:

> This very Anniversary day I came to our dear dearest dying and heard her *be blessed!* I read ...an interpretation of St. Paul's that the women must veil their head in the holy temple for *Angel's* sake...It was the opinion of the first Christians as well as ours, that the *angels* of heaven fill the holy temple when we are there at prayer, but most particularly during the holy sacrifice. [14]

Bruté went on to quote St. John Chrysostom, St. Ambrose, St. Gregory, and other writers on the subject, concluding, "O mother that for our tears! What would be this earth if faith [were] everywhere in its splendor and charity in its fervour? What? Anticipated heaven. Thou truly blessed, Annina, Annina, thou, thou!!!! Eternity."[15]

Under Bruté's direction Mother Seton came to feel about her daughter as she had felt before about her other lost friends and relatives. She had been able to say of Harriet and Cecilia Seton, "I do not miss them half as much as you would think as according to my *mad notions* it seems as if they are always around me."[16] Now Bruté taught her again to see the graveyard as a "lovely little wood, happy little corner of earth."[17] He made her feel again the continuity of the present with eternity. He wrote:

---

[c] A decury was a small group of ten pupils at Saint Joseph's Academy, based on the Ursuline model of education.

Eternity—Eternity

Annina is there—what thinks she of this little nothing of our Earth? She remembers only the little valley, her mother, her sisters, her decury children, and cries with a voice to be everywhere understood in the room, the choir, the little wood.

Eternity, Eternity

To love and serve Him only

To be loved and eternally served and praised in heaven.

O mother, how much good [there is] to do in your blessed family; what a celestial commission entrusted to you, mother of Daughters of Charity to whom also so much is [given] to do for God and souls through this short life.[18]

Elizabeth Seton, whom Dubois had found it difficult to assist, exclaimed to Bruté:

Blessed G[d]— I am so in love now with rules that I see the bit of the bridle all gold, or the reins all of silk—you know my sincerity, since with the little attraction to your Brother's [Dubois] government, I ever eagerly seek the grace [to bear the] little cords He entangles me with.[19]

During this first summer after Anna Maria Seton died Simon Bruté was engaged in missionary work on the eastern shore of Maryland. He told Benedict Flaget:

I am trying to learn practically my English. I have said Mass and preached, bad preaching as it may be, in six different places. This must force this dreadful English into my backward head or I must renounce forever to know it ...On Monday I will be making English and blunders on my Eastern Shore.[20]

When Bruté wrote to a friend in August he explained, "I am occasionally in this congregation, St. Joseph, Talbot County, Maryland, at M. Monelly."[21] He also served at Queenstown in Queen Ann County on the eastern shore during his two months of missionary activity.[22] He felt discouraged at the lack of success he believed his efforts produced and wrote in French to Mother Seton:

---

[d] Elizabeth Seton frequently referred to Simon Bruté as simply "G" for Gabriel.

I spoke again to a congregation so rough, so sad, so boisterous that you would have suffered, Mother of charity, to have heard me. I no longer know in these too fleeting visits how to take a tone simple, sweet, tranquil, and instructive, which alone, I feel, will produce solid fruits.[23]

Simon Bruté was soon to receive cheering news. On 28 August 1812, Louis Dubourg wrote him from Conewago, Pennsylvania:

I have written to Mr. Tessier that after new reflections I agree that they send you to the Mountain ...You see now if I love you, assuredly nothing could afford you greater pleasure. I would advise you to come back as soon as possible and I am convinced that the thing in question would pass in the Council without much opposition.[24]

In September Bruté said happily, "My prospect is, as soon as returned to Baltimore, to go and live with Mr. Dubois at Mount St. Mary's. I have already received my mission for that purpose." On 28 September 1812, Father Bruté went to Emmitsburg.[25] One of his numerous chronological notes says, "I was sent to assist Mr. Dubois. Said Mass for the Sisters Monday, Tuesday, Wednesday, and Thursday."[26] He arrived in time to witness the last meeting between Archbishop Carroll and Mother Seton on the occasion of the confirmation at the sisterhood.[27] It was Bruté who gave the funeral sermon when Sister Maria Murphy Burke died on 15 October 1812. Linking her name with Anna Maria's he urged, "Let us rather from this amiable view of death, of Eternity, of thoughts of heaven; turn towards this life in which we are detained." Elizabeth Seton was deeply moved by his exhortation:

Let us be courageous and accept with love and Zeal the *Will* and *order* of Providence. Let us not refuse to live. The longest life is nothing to Eternity. The most generous Saints desired to remain.[28]

When Sister Ellen Thompson died the next month, Bruté exclaimed to Mother Seton:

O happy mother, already three of your dear daughters in heaven, not counting the two first, the tender sisters[e] whom your example has already led there. Give, oh give, thanks and redouble your zeal to follow these heavenly souls![29]

---

[e] The three "daughters" were Anna Maria Seton, Maria Murphy Burke, Ellen Thompson; the two "sisters" were Harriet and Cecilia Seton.

In the days that followed, Father Bruté applied again and again to Mother Seton for assistance in developing his lectures for his classes and his sermons in English. In the beginning he sent to the Valley the barest outlines of ideas, leaving spaces in between, asking his friend to "blot out and write down better, principally when this poor French-English will be quite unamendable."[30] He enlisted her aid for translations of the works of Jean-Jacques Olier, the founder of the Society of St. Sulpice. Again when some passage of a letter from a friend seemed to him particularly effective he would ask for several copies:

> I wish sent it to my dear Bishop Flaget who knows him well and Mr. David who can do so much good with it to his young men. One to Mr. Dubourg would surely be most acceptable.[31]

Mother Seton became one of his closest of collaborators. One retreat sermon of Bruté's, on the subject of the last judgment, shows how much the secretary contributed to the author. Bruté wrote the scattered phrases; Mother Seton wrote the completed meditation.[32] The close union and understanding between the two, priest and mother, is vividly emphasized when this sermon is studied. With what facility did Mother Seton take the cryptic half-sentences and develop a powerful, dramatic sermon. The thoughts of Bruté in the words of Mother Seton emerged in phrases like these:

> Cover yourself in prayers and communions with His Precious Blood, as the little birds when they see the rising storm and coming rain they dip into the ocean ...and as the saint who said strike, strike indeed, but where can you find a place, my Jesus, not covered with Your own blood.[33]

Mother Seton's help was soon in evidence. A young student at Mount St. Mary's College wrote to his friend in Baltimore, "Mr. Bruté preaches nearly every Sunday and likewise explains catechism at the time of vespers. I prefer his preaching to Mr. Dubois but not his catechism, he speaks English plainly in preaching."[34]

Elizabeth Seton not only served as a temporary amanuensis, but she was for the young priest a kind of depository for his troubles and woes. Bruté had mercurial emotions and a sensitive disposition. His fervor was often followed by severe discouragement, and like many young priests, he was sometimes impatient and irritated by his older, more deliberate *confreres*. Mother Seton once commented to Father Bruté:

All is a true mystery to me in your disposition—much greater mystery than any of *Faith*. A man of your particular principle *on paper,* who has evidently the most dear and special graces, not given drop by drop as to other souls, but poured over your head in a daily torrent—Yet, I seldom see you but in such wild enthusiasms of your own particular impression of the moment that you can see nothing, hear nothing, but that one object, or else quite *reserved hurt* and *anxious* because you have not been consulted in things *which spoke for themselves.*[35]

John Dubois, who really loved Simon Bruté and preferred him to any other assistant, was often driven to the limit of his patience. He once wrote dolefully to his bishop:

You know Mr. Bruté; his zeal knows no bounds. If he no longer has Emmitsburg [parish] he will pass all his Sundays at the Sisters, instead of coming to my aid the days I am overburdened...During the week he wants to help me—but in foolish ways—he will go ten times to visit my sick without necessity. He even goes to visit those who are not sick, with the best of intentions, but without doing any good by it— interrupting my simple but regular program, fatiguing the horses unnecessarily, mixing everything up.[36]

His sudden changes of mood Dubois labeled "coups de tête." Mother Seton was called upon to equalize the differences in these two temperaments, sometimes a delicate affair. On his morning visits to St. Joseph's, Bruté might burst out in a rapid recitation of his difficulties. Later, when he was back at the college he would regret his outpourings, and on one such occasion he implored:

My mother, what shall I do? If I pour [out] all that comes to my heart in regret of so often adding pains to your pains, afflictions to tribulations, I will appear to you in the other excess. Alas! How bad the bad excesses of this morning— the good ones would pour now I say—but all excess must displease a pious heart and soul of sense [such] as yours. Forgive, then, only and if this is tedious being so often requested, remember our Lord tells you to forgive by the seventy times over.[37]

Simon Bruté more than atoned for any burdens he added to Mother Seton's already heavy load. He became a real friend and brother to her children. He shared the happy preparations for Rebecca's first communion, "her happy Christmas." To her mother he exclaimed:

> Oh, for her, for innocent children bread of Angels! For us under the heat and weight of the day the food of travellers "cibus viatorum." But a moment I will, you will, receive it ...Glad expectation, morning bliss, hasten happy hour.[38]

Later, when Bruté was on the high seas, journeying to France, Rebecca Seton said longingly to her mother, "If he was but my *real* brother as well as my *spiritual* one!" And her mother, in relating the remark to the priest, added:

> Poor darling, she does not know that is the only *real*...Oh yes, the only *real*—our spiritual world how *real* and unchangeable its dear dependencies—no dividing oceans, variations of time and the painful etceteras.[39]

Bruté felt deeply his responsibility toward Mother Seton's spiritual progress. Calling her his "child of heaven, of Eternity" he said:

> Charged with your soul, at least, with all the Lord disposes in his Providence for it, in my quality of spiritual father, my mother, my dear mother, what am I doing to help you sanctify yourself with a purity, and fervor always increasing? But what can I do? What better than [recommend] simplicity, peace, abandon, daily fidelity, upright intentions, *all* and entirely each one of them directed to God alone.[40]

To Mother Seton he sent countless effusions from his "lonely corner" on the Mountain. His love for the woody valleys, the gardens, the river gave him a text: "None wd. please if enjoyed against that ever blessed Will" of God.[41] When the beauty of the scriptures seemed overpowering, he wrote to Mother Seton his reflections, apologizing for "these rhapsodies," yet wanting her to share his love for the "admirable old Latin."

> Sometimes I could almost weep all of a sudden with what only one of the most harmonious, tender, sorrowful words does to me—this Latin version, my old friend, these twenty years past. *Oh flumina Babylonis.* O Sion. O Eternity! Annina![42]

While he was at Mount St. Mary's these first two years, Bruté was in charge of the library.[43] His constant contact with books enabled him to recommend to Elizabeth reading which would extend her spiritual horizon. Once, recommending opuscula[f] of St. Francis of Assisi, he said, "I would it were rather in English for you—it is the very suavity and unction of St. Francis de Sales, with something of a higher heaven."[44] He pointed out particular letters of St. Teresa of Avila which applied to problems Mother Seton faced.[45] Another time, after reading Father Berthier,[g] Bruté sent the book to her saying, "Some lines in his reflections have so moved my heart that I desire you read over, and find the same places."[46] The gratitude Elizabeth Seton felt for Bruté's thoughtfulness was boundless, and after he had sailed for France she wrote:

> I read again the hundred *direction* papers[h] of the two years past with yet greater delight than the first reading and gather new courage and stronger Faith as when they were first applied—the grace as present as when they came fresh from the hot press of the burning heart—now cold perhaps—and *surely* far and far away—.[47]

Early in November 1814, Simon Bruté sought permission from his superiors to go abroad.[i] His reasons were varied, including a desire to see his mother, a wish to get his own library, and the intention "to produce good results for the Church in America."[48] When it was decided that William Seton should accompany Father Bruté, Elizabeth Seton wrote a letter to Antonio Filicchi introducing the priest as:

> a most distinguished Soul as you will know in a moment ...There is no possible recommendation I could give him which would not be ratified by our Revd. Abp. [Carroll] and the Blessed [Jean] Cheverus by whom he is most highly loved and esteemed, our Archbishop indeed values him as an inestimable treasure in the church and you will find if you have the happiness to know him yourself that his

---

[f] Opuscula are minor or short works of literature. Bruté may be referring to the opuscule by St. Francis of Assisi, "Letter to All the Faithful," which contains this sentence: "Those who will not taste how sweet the Lord is and who love darkness rather than the light, not wishing to fulfill the commandments of God are cursed: of them it is said by the prophet: 'They are cursed who decline from Thy commandments.'" See "Letter to All the Faithful," *The Writings of St. Francis of Assisi*, tr. By Paschal Robinson, [1905], at sacred-texts.com

[g] Guillaume François Berthier, the Jesuit author, wrote five volumes of "Réflexions Spirituelles" during his exile from France.

[h] Many of these "direction papers" could be read only with the proper scriptural passage at hand. Bruté often made only the chapter and verse reference with brief comments.

[i] Bruté may have wished to explain the challenges and opportunities at Mount St. Mary's to the Sulpician superiors in Paris and attempt to persuade them to reconsider their decision about withdrawal of Sulpician sponsorship.

uncommon PIETY, learning and excellent qualifications (and even his family since you Europeans take that in account), entitle him to the distinguished friendship and regard of M. Filippo [Filicchi] and yourself. He has adopted the *great* interests of my William so generously, that with yourselves, I consider him our truest friend in God—what more can your little Sister say to interest you—judge for yourself—[49]

While Simon Bruté was absent in 1815, Mother Seton kept a journal-letter of the life that went on without him around Emmitsburg; she referred once to her eye having fallen "on an old black stump in the corner, and a big inward sigh to the live coal far away which used to give it the blaze in a moment," the tone of these entries is joyous and humorous as often as it is serious. [50] She described for him the difficulties young Father Hickey experienced in trying to fill Bruté's place; she referred glowingly to the communion of "our thirty white caps;" she spoke of her grief that her sons were not priests; she wrote with elation of Mr. Tessier's pride in Bruté, adding, "*Tu es sacerdos in Eternum*—there the soul's grand triumph, all else but smoke."[51]

Rev. John Francis Hickey, who had been ordained in September 1814, was sent by Tessier to take "the various parts which were performed by Mr. Bruté." His superior had admonished the young priest to pattern himself after John Dubois. "You cannot have a better model for piety, assiduity, constant application, zeal, vigilance, charity, patience, and all the virtues," said Tessier. "I hope one day to see all these virtues shine in you."[52] But young Hickey had difficulty both in emulating Dubois and in replacing Bruté. He was embarrassed on his trips to the sisterhood, and when Mother Seton waited on him, standing by his table on the mornings after he offered Mass for the community, he acted as if it were "the plague of his life." Mother Seton tried to relieve his awkwardness, "to show him what he is in the eyes of my Faith," as she expressed it, and give him "all the little cares we could."

When Hickey gave a careless sermon one Sunday to a crowded church containing many strangers, Mother Seton did not hesitate to take him to task. When he explained that he had not taken much trouble with it, Mother Seton exclaimed, "O Sir, that awakens my anger! Do you remember a priest holds the honor of God on his lips. Do you not trouble you[rself] to spread his fire he wishes so much enkindled. If you will not study and prepare when young, what when you are old? There is a Mother's lesson!"[53]

But Hickey did not improve immediately. Not long after this occasion Mother Seton wrote to Simon Bruté:

No one would believe anyone so drole in hesitations and unconnected—trying to say how the *flesh* was our *enemy* he would detail the senses—O and coming to the smell, after hems and haws and stops, folding his arms—*the smell my brethren distracts us*!! I pray for him more than for your crazy English and scold him with all the authority of an *Ancient*.[54]

John Hickey was, indeed, a poor substitute, and although Dubois admitted him to be "pure as an angel" he found him without judgment or intelligence. He said sadly to Mother Seton, "Not one soul, Mother, on whom I can rely to see a class well kept much less to give a *spiritual* instruction."[55] Father Duhamel, the other priest who served the area, was in very poor health that year, and it made Elizabeth Seton's heart ache to see Dubois' predicament. Often the over-worked priest could not eat his meals because his head ached so from lack of sleep. Once he said laughingly to her, "You see my hair cut? I met a barber in the woods and I sat down on a stone and let him do it there as there is no time at home." Mother Seton told Father Bruté that remonstrating with Dubois was as futile as speaking to the moon. His affairs seemed all "comprised in his *cautious, equal, daily* grace almost, miraculous."

The simple fact was that Simon Bruté in his zeal had done more than one man could have been expected to do. Father Duhamel, in his droll way of speaking, told Mother Seton:

Poor [John] Hickey got a great compliment this morning— an Irishman told him the three priests at the Mountain all put together is not worth one Bruté...They tell me to my face, now [that] Bruté's gone, all is gone. Some say they will not go to confession till he comes again—poor, dear good Bruté, did you see his letter, ma'm, *to everybody, to save souls?* ...He could tend six congregations at least. He can do what would kill ten men, if you only give him bread, and 2 or 3 horses to ride to death, one after the other.[56]

Simon Bruté left a void which only his return could fill.

Although Elizabeth Seton began expecting Father Bruté's return in August, a letter from Tessier dated 6 August 1815, told Dubois and Hickey that Bruté could not hope to leave for Lyons and Bordeaux for several weeks.[57] Tessier added that there was very little hope that Bruté would find any priests to bring to America, even though he was doing all he could "to bring succour for the church of the United States." By the middle of October Bruté was ready to leave France,[58] and by 28 November 1815 he had arrived in Baltimore bringing one young Irish student to enter the Baltimore seminary.[59] When Mother Seton learned of his return she wrote:

> You would never believe, dear G., the good *Your return* does to this soul of your little Mother—to see you *again* tearing yourself from all that is dearest—giving up *again* the full liberty you lawfully and justly possessed—exchanging for a truly heavy chain, and the endless labyrinth of discussions and wearisome details to give the softest expressions—in proportion as my PRIDE in you increases, my own littleness and empty sacrifice to our Beloved is more evident, and I am ambitious (indeed G. often with many tears) to get up with you a little by a generous will, and more faithful service in the little I can do—and really take it as my most serious affair to pray *well* for you, and get prayers from *All* ...Yes, our dear President, you will, you shall have prayers...Look up confidently. He will not leave you who have left all for him.[60]

Before his installation as president of St. Mary's in Baltimore, Simon Bruté went to Emmitsburg and "received excellent advice from mother to do good there."[61] Mother Seton laughingly told her "monsieur le President" that she saw him plunged deep in the labyrinths of science, growing "fat as a Doctor." Then she added seriously:

> Well, at least he will have abundant sacrifice of dearest, choicest consolations. He will act in full opposition to his own choice. His daily bread will be dry and hard. He will be a bond of union and peace to his confreres, a spirit of purest ardent piety to worldlings and an example of cheerful and tender forbearances to his pupils—poor dear G. After a little while of subjection and patience to his wild heart, it *shall* be set free from the yoke, improved and experienced, to return with new ardor to its more simple and heavenly delights.[62]

But while she offered this sound advice to the young college president, Mother Seton did not try to conceal how heavily the pain of parting from him so soon again bore down upon her heart. She confessed sadly:

A volume would not have been enough to say [about] half the heart that fastens to yours more and more if possible—but with such freedom of the local circumstances or position of the moment, that I shall see you go again, to fulfill your big *Presidentship* (O bad omen, *G*, I did not know that tear [in the paper] was there)—Well, I will see you go to do *His Will of the present moment* with no other signs or desires but for its most full and complete *accomplishment.*

Your silly little woman in the fields (most happy name and place for her G.) Your little woman, silly of our dear sillyness [and] of prayers and tears, will now hold closer and closer to *Him* who will do *all in you,* as He does in my poor little daily part and try always to bring you the...support [of] a Mother's prayers, her cry to him for *your* full fidelity.[63]

So Simon Gabriel Bruté was installed "in the office left vacant by Father Jean-Baptiste Paquiet" on 18 December 1815.[64] For a second time he had left his beloved France and his loving mother. For a second time, too, he had left Emmitsburg and the missionary work he preferred. For two years he was to be separated from Mother Seton, but the bond never weakened. Bruté in Baltimore was as devoted to Elizabeth Seton's interests as he had ever been. He interceded for young Richard Seton so that he might secure "a good situation in Baltimore,"[65] and he continued his correspondence with William Seton in Leghorn.[66] He tried to draw Mary Bayley Post into the Catholic Church, and wrote with the same intention to Eliza Craig Sadler.[67] Although Mother Seton's concern for Father Bruté's welfare could take a less demonstrable course, her intercession for his success in spiritual affairs never ceased. When Bruté welcomed a band of thirteen missionaries of the Congregation of the Mission,[j] led by Felix de Andreis, C.M., during the summer of 1816, Mother Seton's joy rivaled that of Bruté and she directed her community to offer their communions and thanksgivings for "the blessed missionaries sent to enlighten our savage land."[68]

Earlier that same summer Simon Bruté came to Emmitsburg for a few days.[69] He was on one of his typical walking trips and went on into Pennsylvania, writing Mother Seton from Hanover. Mother and the sisters

---

[j] This group of missionaries bound for the Missouri Territory was the nucleus of the Congregation of the Mission (Vincentians) which furnished the priests who served as directors for the Daughters of Charity at Emmitsburg after the Sulpicians concluded arrangements for the union with France of the Sisters of Charity based at Emmitsburg in1850. [The Sulpicians of Baltimore served as ecclesiastical superiors for the Sisters of Charity of St. Joseph's from the foundation in 1809 until 1849. For a number of years the Sulpicians had been negotiating with the Congregation of the Mission to assume this responsibility. The Emmitsburg-based community of the Sisters of Charity of St. Joseph's officially united with the Daughters of Charity of St. Vincent de Paul, based in Paris, on 25 March 1850. Ed.]

"laughed gladly at the thought that like some Ignatius of Loyola or Anthony of Padua" Bruté, too, made "walking journeys with an anticipated agility to be perfected in the high eternal regions."[70] But the visit from Father Bruté made Elizabeth Seton realize how much he was missed at St. Joseph's and she wrote wistfully:

> If you should...travel *back* [here] leaving the President's chair and suite of Apartments it would be most beautiful... that childish—You did not leave *All* the whole delight of your France and family but to do His only Will...My son—be most careful to find *the will,* not by the dear coaxing your Mother charged you with, but by a prayer of *full* confidence such as Your Silly Sinner dares to use.... From the last look out of the gate, I hastened to the dear bench in the choir (where the clay of the so "beautiful feet"[k]—yet remained and left their full blessing of Peace) to begin this FULL PRAYER...to take Him by storm G.—I will be faithful to it, you know how many times a day and the nights so near him until we know the FINAL word.
>
> ...But you know the only Security and heavenly Peace in that point so dear rests all on this essential abandon—so at least you taught me —so understand and *honor* his grace in your little woman of the fields—but you do so fully—[71]

It was while Bruté was president of St. Mary's College in Baltimore that Elizabeth received the sad news of Philip Filicchi's death.[l] William Seton had written in August that the elder Filicchi brother was in his death agony, that "the hundreds of poor fed at his hands, the orphans depending on his support, the prisoners relieved by his charity" were already mourning their lost benefactor.[72] When Bruté forwarded this news to Mother Seton in October she replied:

> So it must be—Filicchi gone. You will not forget him. If you knew how much *I had counted* on his life you would laugh at me—But God alone—I am too happy to be forced to have no other refuge.[73]

None of the events of 1816 could compare in tragic quality, however, with the rapid decline in young Bec Seton's hold on life. Four years earlier, when her sister Annina was dying, Rebecca Seton, while

---

[k] The footprint of Bruté on the floor of the chapel.
[l] Philip Filicchi died 22 August 1816.

playing, had slipped and fallen on some ice. In order not to distress others while Anna Maria Seton required so much attention, the child had tried to keep to herself the pain that did not leave her after the mishap. When a definite limp made concealment of the girl's injury impossible, Mother Seton was relieved to be able to consult her brother-in-law, Dr. Wright Post, who with Mary Bayley Post, was visiting Elizabeth that spring. But Post could give her no encouragement at all, saying that he knew of no remedy for Bec's condition.[74] It seemed incredible to Elizabeth that Bec could not be aided, and so, when the Catons and Harpers offered to take the little girl to Baltimore that summer, the frantic mother sent the child to Dr. Chatard's home for observation and consultation.[75] Mrs. Chatard wrote immediately upon the completion of the doctor's examination that nothing seemed to be broken and that warm baths and "friction" might prove beneficial.[76] So Bec came back to St. Joseph's to try the baths and rubbing under the direction of "an eminent Physician[m] at the mountain seminary."[77]

Not long after this Rebecca Seton began to prepare for her first communion. When she could not be with her, her mother sent Bec little notes of love and encouragement such as the following:

> With the little pen I answer my dear, every day, dearer little darling. How much I desire she should go and unite still closer to our only Beloved...Make your careful preparation of the purest heart you can bring Him that it may appear to Him like a bright little star at the bottom of a fountain. O My Rebecca! Child of Eternity! Let Peace and love stay with you in your pains and they will lighten and sweeten them all—Be blessed forever, my darling.[78]

On Christmas day, at 6 o'clock in the morning, the child received her first communion. The added grace of the sacrament was sorely needed, for Elizabeth Seton told Julia Scott a month later that "lovely gay little Beck" was entirely lame and never left her mother's room even with crutches.

> All this we take in the course of things from the hand of our dear compassionate Master who no doubt intends to take more care of this darling and bless her more than the rest...she is often in great pain, but goes on at her perpetual delight, the piano, or says very gaily, "Oh this leg will carry me to heaven."[79]

---

[m] This may have been Dr. Daniel Moore, who attended St. Joseph's community until 1820, when his brother Robert succeeded him.

Although Mary Post urged Bec's coming to New York, neither the child nor her mother wished to be separated. "Death is nothing to this kind of separation," Mother Seton told Julia.[80] The best way to bear suffering was to share it, and Bec had many friends who were eager to share hers. Mrs. Chatard in Baltimore loved Rebecca Seton as one of her own children and sent letters of encouragement and cheer.[81] Father Babade wrote admiringly that Bec was truly "a child of the Cross."[82] He corresponded regularly with Bec and talked to her as if she were a mature martyr. He told her to thank God for her fear of death and judgment. "The more we fear here, the less we have to fear there," he told her.[83] Julia Scott's financial support was always at hand and she wrote chidingly to Elizabeth, "Hesitate not my friend to receive what God enables me to send you...It is also a debt strictly your due for when I was in distress, were you not my friend and the friend of my little ones?"[84]

The year 1814 passed and Bec showed no improvement. In the warm weather she was sometimes taken to Mount St. Mary's in a little cart pulled by a faithful Negro, Joe.[n] The year Simon Bruté was abroad it was decided that Bec should go to Philadelphia to consult Dr. Philip Syng Physick.[o] Julia Scott came herself to Emmitsburg to get her, but Mother Seton had planned to have her daughter stay with the Sisters of Charity in Philadelphia and Julia arrived just too late.[85] It was the first and last hour these two old friends would spend together in all the years Mother Seton had lived away from New York; the joy it gave can only be imagined. When Julia got back to Philadelphia, Bec was comfortably settled at the orphan asylum on Spruce and Sixth Streets where Sister Rose White would do "all a nurse can do." Elizabeth wrote Eliza Sadler that if an operation proved necessary she would go herself to Philadelphia.[86] Meanwhile the mother advised her daughter to "be affectionate and grateful to Aunt [Julia] Scott, but try to go as little as possible." All Bec's affairs were to be referred to Sister Rose.[87] But in spite of Mother Seton's desire not to impose on Julia's generosity more than was necessary,[p] that warm-hearted woman came to take Rebecca riding to see the museum, the Bank of Pennsylvania, the water works, and

---

[n] Simon Bruté to Elizabeth Seton, Emmitsburg, n.d., ASJPH 1-3-3-13:20, 19, When Joe died, Simon Bruté wrote of him, "Simple, honest, faithful, zealous, humble, affectionate friend of God and Man...May my death be as holy, my judgment as easy." Joe was the man who also dug the graves at St. Joseph's and Mount Saint Mary's. Bruté, who loved to commemorate the dead, asked Mother Seton to "write some notes for Joe—a few little anecdotes of his waggoning, carrying Bec, his Christmas, Epiphanies, little books, so great affection and respect to the Sisterhood, digging graves, etc."

[o] Philip Syng Physick (1768–1837) had studied with Edward Jenner at William Hunter's school in London. He specialized in new methods of treating hip-joint diseases, being the first to prefer manipulation to traction. Rebecca Seton could not have been sent to a better qualified specialist. Physick may be considered the father of American surgery. He later became interested in Roman Catholicism but there is no evidence to show that he ever converted.

[p] Julia Scott also paid the medical bills for Rebecca Seton.

other institutions of which Philadelphia was so proud. Bec met Julia's son, John, who was running for the state assembly, and the young Seton girl was delighted when John Scott was elected. Yet, being her mother's daughter, it was the trip to the poorhouse with Sister Rose that she liked best.[88]

In spite of the care and attention she received on all sides, Bec's hopes for relief from her pain were doomed to disappointment.[89] The doctors who consulted with Dr. Physick could offer no solution and Bec told her mother, "My tumor is getting very soft and my hip is nearly even with my other."[90] By the beginning of November 1815 the girl was home again and Elizabeth wrote to Julia:

> Little wild crazy darling, it would take me a month to hear half her perpetual conversation—imagine our meeting *after all dangers past* as she says, for the overset of the stage [coach] between New Castle and Frenchtown had given such a shake to her nerves that she thought everything dangerous afterwards, though she was so happy to meet with a most easy private carriage from Baltimore home and had every possible attention—her fatigue from the journey makes it impossible to judge of the effect of what has been done for her by Doctor Physick.[91]

Rebecca was in reality much weaker after the Philadelphia trip, and it was in the midst of her own discouragement that Mother Seton learned of Archbishop Carroll's last illness. She confessed to Ellen Wiseman that "Our blessed Archbishop's situation, tho! we must give and resign him, presses hard on me as well as on thousands—harder on me than you would imagine."[92] John Carroll's death on 3 December 1815, deprived Elizabeth Seton of a friend who had been a constant if unobtrusive support during the hardest decade of her life, and she was very grateful to a former pupil who wrote:

> I suppose you have heard all about it by Mr. Bruté who could tell you more about him than I could...I [had] seen him [Carroll] a few days before he died and received his last Benediction. He spoke for about five minutes to me. What I understood was beautiful. He was laid out in the church for two days...We had prayers every evening for the space of nine days. It was the most solemn scene I ever witnessed. The church is still in mourning and looks lost without him and for two weeks it was distressing to go near the church.[93]

And so it was that Mother Seton and Bec faced 1816 with Father Bruté gone from Emmitsburg and Archbishop Carroll gone from the world. Some small relief came when Bec's tumor broke in March, but it was only a temporary respite. Jean Cheverus told Bruté that his thoughts were constantly with "the venerable Mother and her dear little martyr."[94] Father Moranvillé consoled Mother Seton with the words, "The glory above must be proportioned to our sufferings here."[95] On Pentecost Sunday, Mother Seton and Rebecca received communion together, and the mother wrote in her prayerbook a supplication for them both:

> O my Lord Jesus Christ who was born for me in a stable, lived for me a life of pain and sorrow, and died for me upon a cross, say for me in the hour of my death, *"Father, Forgive,"* and to Thy Mother, *"behold thy Child."* Say to me thyself *"this day thou shalt be with me in Paradise."* O my Saviour, leave me not, *forsake* me not. I *thirst* for Thee and long for the Fountain of Living Water—my days pass quickly along, Soon all will be CONSUMMATED for me. "Into thy *hands I commend my spirit now* and forever." Amen.[96]

Mother Seton sent her other daughter, Catherine Josephine (Kit), off to Baltimore to visit,[q] promising to send word if Bec grew worse. "Do not take the example of my weakness," she admonished. "Keep your dear heart quiet and trust all to our Lord."[97] Bec was now able to get relief only by sitting up all night in a chair and even this became unbearable before long. Mother Seton held the girl in her arms, or across her knees for long hours, and she confessed to Kit in Baltimore, "We wet each other pretty often with tears."[98] When she wrote to William Seton in September that Bec was much worse, she said, "There are moments of life when resignation and courage are scarcely to be thought an exertion and this is one with us."[99] It seemed quite obvious that Mother Seton was "going to send another saint to heaven," as Cheverus put it.[100]

Simon Bruté never decreased his love and spiritual solace to both mother and daughter during this ordeal. He wrote consoling letters to the suffering Bec, comparing her sleepless nights to the "standing or sitting watch as the knights of old on the eve they were to be knighted."

> Let the storms roar round the walls and grates of this transitory, hard lazaretto of life; let suffering cruel and unrelenting bid you stand and watch when the smallest bird enjoys his rest; let, let let! The soul still knows how to cheer up, seeing and

---

[q] Catherine Josephine Seton visited at the home of Luke Tiernan whose daughter Ann was her school friend.

feeling her God, her Father, and Almighty Lover in all. Ah Yes! If I know your faith, and your love, my Bec, they will be as unrelenting and pressing as the sufferings can be, and more.[101]

He asked her to pray for his retreat, feeling the exquisite efficacy of her sighs, her tears.[102] All her suffering was his because Mother Seton kept him constantly informed of Bec's decline, writing from their "sea of sorrows." To Father Bruté the mother reported humbly:

Poor darling...she told me as I knelt by her "ah, dearest Mother, I now hardly dare tell God I love Him, I prove it so badly—sometimes not even that I *desire* to love Him for you know very well that what I desire very much, I can soon enough show it and it seems like a bold falsehood to say, and not do anything to prove it. Indeed I think Our Lord sent me this sickness for my neglect of my little practices of piety since the retreat"...dear, simple heart these her exact words with such pure looks of sincere meaning—Oh My God how piercing to my cold, dead heart so truly without proof or effect.[103]

Bec's love for Father Bruté was equal to his and she insisted on having his picture "no where but opposite my eyes at the foot of my bed."[104] Her joy in seeing him in October, when he brought Dr. Chatard from Baltimore, was not even slightly dimmed by the doctor's pronouncement which confirmed Elizabeth's fear that "sweet Bec must go."[105] Simon Bruté was scarcely back in Baltimore when he received the fated letter from John Dubois and the message, "Our angel died this morning a little before four o'clock." Dubois said Rebecca had preserved a very lively faith in her last moments, and when he asked Bruté to have the Sulpicians offer Mass for the dear child of Elizabeth Seton, he wrote:

The Mother is a miracle of divine favor. Night and day by the child, her health has not appeared to suffer. She held the child in her arms without dropping a tear all the time of her agony and even eight minutes after she had died. *Mulierem fortem.*[106]

Mother Seton had learned the bitter-sweet act of resignation well. Breaking the news to her son William, she said:

It would be too selfish in us to have wished her inexpressible sufferings prolonged, and her secure bliss deferred for our longer possession...though in her I have lost the little friend of my heart who read every pain or joy of it.[107]

This time when "the rattling earth fell" on her darling, "laid so low aside Annina almost touching her coffin which could plainly be seen," Elizabeth Seton "could think of nothing but *Te Deum*...her heart high above—a hymn to the holy Spirit returning."[108] This time she remained willingly behind in the "snug little nest with a window looking direct on the little woods where my darlings sleep," telling Julia "it keeps up my heart to look over twenty times a day, first thing in the morning and last at night and think no more pain now—and up, up, up the beautiful joyous Souls."[109] Bec was in her heart as much as Annina had ever been. As before, Mother Seton had kept a lengthy journal of Bec's last days; as before she shared these thoughts with her close friends.[110] But this time Elizabeth was sharing in pleasure, not in pain. She wrote in her prayerbook:

> *My God and my all—m*y Soul, oh if you can make the purchase of so infinite a good so immense an inheritance for the smallest trifle—and what but a trifle is your best services to God—our Saviour calls them merits—that is he covers them with his own merits—you think them Sacrifices—look at the Sacrifice of Calvary and compare yours with it— you think life long and tedious—look at the Eternity of bliss to repay it. Your sufferings press hard—but look at your sins. My God and my all—Save—Save, that I may return you an eternity of gratitude and praise...Afflictions are the steps to heaven.[111]

Without loss of time, and in spite of her lameness contracted during the nine weeks of supporting Bec,[r] Mother Seton plunged into the work of the school and community.[112] To Father Bruté she said gratefully:

> Well, at least my blessed Father *you* are acquitted, and all that the kindest best invention of the most compassionate heart could do has been done by you to carry me thro' this hard moment which is past and gone as easily as if our *High Comforter* had spread his soft wings over every fiber—I have not done as much community work of hearing, seeing,

---

[r] Mother Seton often ate her meals with one hand behind Bec's pillow or supporting her on her knees. She seems to have developed a "contraction of the sinew" or inflamed tendons. This lameness persisted into the summer of 1817.

and speaking, in the last 6 months as this day with a heart "still as a calm at sea."[113]

Elizabeth Seton's letter to Boston announcing the death of her youngest daughter just missed Bishop Cheverus,[s] who had started southward to confer the pallium on Archbishop Neale at Georgetown.[114] Jean Cheverus arrived in Baltimore from Philadelphia on 13 November 1816 and he made a retreat there before proceeding to Georgetown, where on Sunday, the Feast of John of the Cross, he invested the archbishop with the insignia of his office. It was not until he returned to Baltimore that Cheverus learned of Rebecca Seton's death. By this time he was busy conferring major and minor orders at St. Mary's Seminary, and making plans to officiate at the solemn anniversary service for the "lamented and venerable" John Carroll.[115] Busy as he was, the Bishop of Boston wrote Mother Seton his congratulations that "angelical Rebecca has fled into the bosom of her heavenly parent." He recalled with pleasure his visit of six years ago, and said he hoped, in spite of his full schedule, to get to Emmitsburg on this trip. He confided to Mother Seton Archbishop Neale's suggestion that he accept the position as his coadjutor for the Archdiocese of Baltimore. "Pray to our Lord," he begged her, "to look down on this Diocese and to preserve it and myself from what is intended. The very idea is more than I can bear."[116]

Bruté wrote to Mother Seton describing his impressions of the sermon Bishop Cheverus had given that 2 December in Baltimore in these words:

> All hearts still moved by the good de Cheverus. Nothing, my Mother, could express to you what he said. You have had the pleasure of hearing him, you know his manner, so mild, so sensible, and the subject! The worthy archbishop would have been charmed himself, and I could see him stretched out at the bottom of his tomb, listening with pleasure and smiling at his second successor,[t] for it appears that it shall be so. He will surely be coadjutor and surely one cannot hear it without desiring it.[117]

Although Father Bruté was disappointed in his desire to see Jean Cheverus come to Baltimore permanently, Mother Seton was gratified to have Cheverus visit once more in the Valley. Father Moranvillé wrote

[s] Father Matignon relayed the news to Cheverus at Baltimore. His own letter to Mother Seton contained the interesting news that Mrs. John Curzon Seton, the second wife of Elizabeth Seton's brother-in-law, had been baptized and confirmed on All Saints' Day in Boston. John Curzon was married twice See Appendix A. Bayley-Seton Genealogy.

[t] Archbishop Neale, urged the appointment of Cheverus as assistant to himself but Cheverus refused and remained in Boston until he returned to France in 1823.

her as Cheverus left Baltimore, "The amiable and universally beloved Bishop of Boston goes to visit you and your family.... an angel in your holy retirement."[118] Bruté notified Mother Seton and John Dubois simultaneously of the prospective visit:

> Bishop Cheverus is going Friday afternoon [in order] to be Saturday afternoon at the Mountain and Valley—Sunday to give confirmation at the Sisterhood....Spare his fatigues for he has almost as bad a cold as our venerable archbishop, when he was there. Sunday evening he comes back to Uniontown [Pennsylvania], being obliged to leave Baltimore Tuesday, every moment being strictly calculated, Philadelphia, New York, till Boston before Christmas.[119]

And so Jean Cheverus came in Advent to see again his valiant friend. He found her thin and haggard, "an old worn out thing whose first quality and strength could scarcely be believed," as Mother Seton liked to express it; but the courage the bishop saw shining in her still beautiful, dark eyes was immeasurably greater than ever before. It was the last time he ever saw her, but he came away with a renewed admiration for the "excellent Sisters, their happy and edifying pupils, the Mother with her children in heaven and on earth." He told Mother Seton that the seventh and eighth of December would always be "treasured up in the memory and affections" of his heart.[120] He remarked to Bruté later how much he had wished he could have Mother Seton and her Sisters of Charity for Boston.[121] The thought of Elizabeth was never absent in the years that followed. Cheverus told Bruté, "I can never think of the Mountain nor the Valley without a thrilling heart."[122] And the last letter Mother Seton ever received from her old friend contained the warm words, "You are every day with me before the Lord and you know how much I love you in the bowels of Jesus Christ."[123]

Not long after the Bishop of Boston left Emmitsburg Mother Seton lost one of her most patient and humble sisters. Mme. Guérin, called Sister Madeleine, died on 20 December 1816, "a death as sweet as that of Rebecca." John Dubois, who described the scene for Bruté, said that when the crucifix was presented to her,

> She appeared to savor it as if her mouth was filled with an exquisite food—such is the comparison of the Mother who was there. Then she turned toward Mother "O, my Good Mother, my dear friend!" and she cast her dying arms around her neck. Then she turned and kissed again the crucifix...

The Mother lives amongst the angels....she has heard her name intermingled with that of our Jesus.[124]

The death of Rebecca had brought its blessing in this increased humility to Elizabeth Seton. Now she felt abased in the presence of death and hesitated to distract her departing sisters by her presence, overwhelmed at hearing her name whispered in the same breath that called upon her Lord. Father Bruté in Baltimore fostered this new gentleness, writing:

Yes, infinite, immense, eternal delights and thanksgivings at such graces as have been granted; and return now more fervor, and holiness of misery than ever to so good a God. You understand, my Mother, only with such an increase of peace and amiableness to all around you—trying so gently to gain every heart to so good a God—[can you succeed]. But, indeed, if I preach [to] you it is to preach [to] me the [one who is] most distant from that happy point of duty, "to render piety amiable and desirable."[125]

Mother Seton's humility extended to her teaching duties as well and the day after Christmas she wrote to Father Bruté of her scruples when the matter of religious instruction was involved. "How dangerous for me," she said, "should I only darken [their minds] by the heterogenous mixture of words and feelings *you* so well *know* in your poor Mother," Dubois would not admit her inability, she complained, but Bruté understood her anxiety. "Alas," she added, "You would say more to her in two hours than I in years." Her only consolation was to rely on Divine inspiration, turning to "the Father most tender, Father of *all,* my immense God, I *his* alone."[126]

This feeling of being lost in the immensity of God was increasingly part of Mother Seton's love. When New York asked for sisters the following year she complied joyfully, obeying His will, "the only will for his atoms who builds upon nothing."[127] On Trinity Sunday, 1817, she exclaimed, "Magnificent day for the soul—mine swells, the poor Atom."[128] When she was near death in 1818 she wrote, "Not even little acts for obtaining fear and anxiety about this *Death* can move that strong hold of peace, thanksgiving and abandon of every atom of life and its belonging to him—even William I can see but in the great Whole."[129] Again she cried out, "INFINITE LOVE, INFINITE GOODNESS, multiplied and applied by OMNIPOTENCE is enough FOR his little worm to make it smile and rejoice even on his calvary where it nailed him to show such wonders!"[130] As time passed the wonder grew, of how great was the grace that had brought her this far. She said to Father Bruté:

Oh if all goes well with me, what will I not do for you—you will see— But alas—Yet, if I am not one of His Elect, it is I only to be blamed and when *going down* I must still lift the hands to the very last look in praise and gratitude for what He has done to save me. What more could He have done? —That thought stops all.[131]

Ardor grew with humility and Mother Seton wrote gratefully to Bruté:

My Father, *blessed*, as you find it hard to put words for your heart, so I, an impossibility to own enough what mine enjoys ever by your *words*. What then when the *seeing* and *praise* shall be added to the *love*—Now I think for every spark of desire I have ever had to love our God and to *show* I love, I have a towering flame—but—but—*proof* you say poor little soul. Well, blessed, I will try for that too, and I do beg you in the name of OUR ETERNITY to tell me everything I may do to prove it better. Conscience reproaches aloud, how little charity and delicacy of love I practice—in that vile habit of speaking of the faults of others, of the *short, cold, repulsive* conduct to my betters; as all certainly are, and for much of my behavior to you my VISIBLE SAVIOUR. . .I would put them and it out with my blood.[132]

Bruté replied:

Pray always for the worthy father of your first years. Pray for all the others to whom the Lord has confided—your soul successively, that is, pray for your proper grace. You have the consolation of observing now, in your most holy vocation all that you first offered Him who wish one day be the only Spouse of that soul. Be faithful, humble, fervent, peaceful, patient. A time of trial; a moment and eternity follows. What heart would not feel drawn and encouraged by this word of love.[133]

As 1817 was ushered in and Elizabeth was wishing Bruté a "happy Eternity to you, blessed President of St. Mary's. May she take good care of you this 1817 coming," physical changes were approaching to affect the community.[134] Through the kind offices of Robert Goodloe Harper, the Sisters of Charity of St. Joseph's had received a charter of incorporation from the State of Maryland.[135] After being named Bishop of Louisiana and the Two Floridas, Louis Dubourg relinquished his claim to the property on 25 March 1815, when he deeded it to Samuel Cooper and John Dubois. Samuel Sutherland Cooper, who had furnished the money for the original farm, had come to Emmitsburg the November Rebecca Seton died, to discuss the matter of incorporation with John Dubois and Mother Seton.[136] The terms of the charter stated the purposes of the community to be: the care of the sick, service of aged, infirm and meritorious persons, and the education of young girls. The size of the establishment was limited to 800 acres of land and a capitalization of $50,000. The name of the corporation was "The Sisters of Charity of St. Joseph's," and the list of members names twenty-two sisters.[u] The women were now ready to assume full control of their business negotiations.

With the temporal affairs of the community so well determined, it would need only the return of Father Bruté to Emmitsburg to fill Mother Seton's cup to overflowing. Father Duhamel was never in very good health, and toward the end of 1817 he became much weaker. Early in November John Dubois wrote to Tessier asking that something be done immediately about an assistant. From the contents of this letter it is plain Dubois had wanted another assistant for some time. He told Tessier he did not want "Mr. Babade," and he complained that John Hickey, who was "a good child and a good priest," was inadequate and "has no method of conducting a class."[137] By January it was clear that Duhamel was dying and Simon Bruté went, temporarily, to assist Dubois over the busy season.[138] Tessier noted in his journal:

> Father Bruté was sent to Emmitsburg to help Father Dubois
> who was fatigued because Father Duhamel was dying and
> he had nursed him for several nights. After Father Duhamel
> died, Father Bruté remained there.[139]

When Charles Duhamel died on 6 February 1818, Dubois hastened to plead with Archbishop Maréchal that Bruté be allowed to remain, citing "his piety, his pure virtue, his capable zeal, his purely spiritual direction," as reasons why he should be left at a mission which involved the direction of the sisters. Tessier had offered him others, but Bruté was "le seul qui veuille bien venir partager mon esclavage."[140] And so it came about that Simon Gabriel Bruté was once more at his beloved Mountain. Tessier confided to his "Epoques:"

---

[u] Sister Madeleine (Magdalene) Guérin's name appears on the list, although had died 20 December 1816, ASJPH 3-1-3.

On the 3rd of June, Father Damphoux was installed president of the College [St. Mary's in Baltimore] to replace Father Bruté who had for a long time been asking to be relieved of this office not because be was not quite capable of fulfilling the functions of president, but because he did not like it, he discharged this duty very imperfectly. He was sighing for the Mountain, where as a matter of fact I appointed him to help Father Dubois, who had absolute need of help.[141]

Simon Bruté wrote to Mother Seton:

In this new beginning it seems as [if] we all together [should] want to renew our best confidence in Our Lord Himself, for how can I hope to be his blessed instrument but through His adorable will, and most tender mercies to souls so entirely offered to Him in the ways of His most prefect service on earth. Indeed, let all be confidence, all pure faith and love and we may be sure his grace will be confirmed in every heart, even by the most unworthy and unfit instrument. Humility, Simplicity, and Charity. How well these blessed names of the three virtues marked out by St. Vincent [and St. Louise de Marillac] will carry us through. Indeed, it is but my most sacred duty to try to assist your dear family and yourself Mother. My heart and my eyes, I might say at this very moment fill at the thought of it.[142]

CHAPTER 12. THE ANGEL OF THE MOUNTAIN

Notes

[1] John Dubois to Ambrose Maréchal, Emmitsburg, 9 February 1818, AAB, AASMSU, 15-7-17.

[2] Simon Bruté wrote, "I first saw Mother [Seton] in 1811. She read with me the *Following of Christ* to form my English pronunciation." Simon Bruté to Melmoth, 1 August 1812, ASJPH 7-3-1-3, #B273. Regarding Charlotte Melmoth, see Matthew O'Brien to John Carroll, 6 May 1802, AAB, AASMSU, 11-A-5. See also *Researches,* XXVIII (1912), 425; John Dubois to Charlotte Melmoth, 28 November 1809, ASJPH 1-3-3-5:3; 6.62, Elizabeth Seton to Julia Scott, 23 October 1810, *CW*, 2:160; Bruté to Melmoth, 1 August 1812, ASJPH 7-3-1-3, #B273; *Historical Records and Studies,* II (1901), 434.

[3] [Sister Loyola Law, D.C., ed.], *Mother Seton, Notes by Rev. Simon Gabriel Bruté* (Emmitsburg, Maryland: Daughters of Charity, 1884), 52. Hereafter cited as *Mother Seton Notes.*

[4] Simon Bruté to James Whitfield, Emmitsburg, 5 March 1830, UNDA.

[5] Louis Dubourg to Simon Bruté, Martinique, 5 December 1810, UNDA.

[6] John M. Tessier's Journal, 18 July 1811, AASMSU; 6.82, Elizabeth Seton to John Carroll, 9 August 1811, *CW*, 2:193.

[7] Simon Bruté to Elizabeth Seton, Emmitsburg, n.d., ASJPH 7-3-1-3, #B164. The majority of the Simon Bruté notes bear no addresses or dates, but the degree to which he uses French and bad English gives some indication, however slight, of the chronological progress of his friendship with Mrs. Seton. Simon Bruté's style, always difficult, under the stress of deep emotion became at times incoherent.

[8] Ibid.

[9] A-6.99a, Elizabeth Seton's Journal of Annina's Last Illness and Death, *CW*, 2:749.

[10] Ibid., *CW*, 2:757.

[11] Simon Bruté to Elizabeth Seton, Emmitsburg, 25 June 1812, ASJPH 7-3-1-2, #A 12. French.

[12] Simon Bruté to Elizabeth Seton, n.p., n.d., ASJPH 7-3-1-2, #B61.

[13] Simon Bruté sketch, ASJPH 1-3-3-13:150.

[14] Simon Bruté to Elizabeth Seton, n.p., n.d., ASJPH 1-3-3-13:83.

[15] Ibid.

[16] 6.45, Elizabeth Seton to Catherine Dupleix, 4 June 1810, *CW*, 2:138.

[17] Simon Bruté to Elizabeth Seton, n.p., n.d., ASJPH 7-3-1-2, #B59. French.

[18] Simon Bruté to Elizabeth Seton, n.p., n.d., ASJPH 7-3-1-2, #B61.

[19] 6.146, Elizabeth Seton to Simon Bruté, n.d., *CW*, 2:259.

[20] James Roosevelt Bayley, *Memoirs of the Right Reverend Simon Wm. Gabriel Bruté*, D.D. (New York, 1876), 49.

[21] Simon Bruté to Charlotte Melmoth, St. Joseph's, Talbot County, [Maryland], 1 August 1812, ASJPH 7-3-1-3, #B273.

[22] Simon Bruté to Charlotte Melmoth, Queenstown, [Maryland], 15 September 1812, ASJPH 7-3-1-3, #B208.

[23] Simon Bruté to Elizabeth Seton, n.p., n.d., except "Sunday 2 o'clock." ASJPH 7-3-1-2, #A41. French.

[24] Louis Dubourg to Simon Bruté, Conewago, 28 August 1812, UNDA.

[25] Simon Bruté to Charlotte Melmoth, Queenstown, [Maryland], 15 September 1812, ASJPH 7-3-1-3, #B208.

[26] Simon Bruté, 28 September 1812, ASJPH 1-3-3-12:107. A list of presidents and vice-presidents of Mount St. Mary's College gives Simon Bruté's term as vice-president as extending from 12 July 1812 to December 1815, but this would seem to be belied by Simon Bruté's own correspondence.

[27] Ibid.

[28] Simon Bruté's eulogy on Sister Maria Murphy Burke, ASJPH 7-3-1-3, #193. See 11.8, "Well now our dearest...," *CW*, 3b:7. See 11.7, "dearest Maria...," *CW*, 3b:6; 11.9, "departed St. Teresa's day," *CW*, 3b:8; ASJPH 7-3-1-2, #B59. French.

[29] Simon Bruté to Elizabeth Seton, Emmitsburg, n.d., ASJPH 7-3-1-2, #B59. French.

[30] Simon Bruté to Elizabeth Seton, Emmitsburg, 20 November [1812], ASJPH 1-3-3-13:10.

[31] Simon Bruté to Elizabeth Seton, Emmitsburg, n.d., ASJPH 7-3-1-3, # B186.

[32] 9.16, "Last Judgment Meditation," 1814, *CW*, 3a:332.

[33] Ibid.

[34] William Byrne to John Hickey, Emmitsburg, 22 and 24 June 1813, ASMSU.

[35] 7.191, Elizabeth Seton to Simon Bruté, n.d., *CW*, 2:591.

[36] John Dubois to Ambrose Maréchal, Emmitsburg, 21 March 1820, AAB, AASMSU, 15-U-20.

[37] Simon Bruté to Elizabeth Seton, Emmitsburg, n.d., ASJPH 7-3-1-2, #B52.

[38] Simon Bruté to Elizabeth Seton, Emmitsburg, n.d., ASJPH 1-3-3-13:1B.

[39] 6.195, Elizabeth Seton to Simon Bruté, n.d., *CW*, 2:330.

[40] Simon Bruté to Elizabeth Seton, Emmitsburg, n.d., excerpt 10 November, ASJPH 7-3-1-2, A47.

[41] Simon Bruté to Elizabeth Seton, Emmitsburg, n.d., ASJPH 7-3-1-2, #A44.

[42] Simon Bruté to Elizabeth Seton, Emmitsburg, n.d., ASJPH 7-3-1-2, #B62. In this quotation the original contained so many inversions that editing was used for purposes of clarity. The original read, "I would weep almost sometimes on a sudden with one only of the most harmonious, tender, sorrowful words that does to me this my old friend Latin version these twenty years past. Oh flumina Babylonis. O Sion. O Eternity! Annina!"

[43] Journal for 1811-1812, inserted list of library rules, AMSMU.

[44] Simon Bruté to Elizabeth Seton, Emmitsburg, n.d., ASJPH 7-3-1-2, #B52.

[45] Simon Bruté to Elizabeth Seton, n.d., ASJPH 7-3-1-2, #A51. French. This particular note recommends the "Thirty-Sixth letter of St. Teresa [of Avila]" which Simon Bruté used in discussing Anna Maria Seton's death.

[46] Simon Bruté to Elizabeth Seton, Emmitsburg, n.d., ASJPH 7-3-1-2, #B62. See John Corbett, "Guillaume François Berthier," *The Catholic Encyclopedia* (New York, 1907), II, 519.

[47] 6.195, Elizabeth Seton to Simon Bruté, n.d., *CW*, 2:330.

[48] Godecker, 69-70. Theodore Maynard, in his life of Simon Bruté, says "he was

commissioned to explain conditions at Mount St. Mary's to the Sulpician superiors in France. They perhaps could be persuaded to back the college against the seminary in Baltimore." See Theodore Maynard, *The Reed and the Rock* (New York, 1942), 106. This seems difficult to reconcile with Simon Bruté's own words: "In 1814 I was appointed president of St. Mary's College of Baltimore and for it early in 1815 I went to France." Simon Bruté chronology, Archives of Georgetown University, 92:6.

[49] 6.185, Elizabeth Seton to Antonio Filicchi, n.d., *CW*, 2:300.

[50] 6.195, Elizabeth Seton to Simon Bruté, 25 May 1815, *CW*, 2:316.

[51] Ibid., 327.

[52] John M. Tessier to John Hickey, Baltimore, 15 December 1814, ASMSU.

[53] 6.195, Elizabeth Seton to Simon Bruté, St. Michael [May 8], *CW*, 2:323.

[54] Ibid., 331.

[55] Ibid., 330.

[56] Ibid., 320.

[57] John M. Tessier to John Hickey, Baltimore, 8 October 1815, ASMSU.

[58] Simon Bruté to Elizabeth Seton, Bordeaux, 17 October 1815, UNDA.

[59] John M. Tessier's Journal, entry for 28 November 1815, ASMSU.

[60] 7.1, Elizabeth Seton to Simon Bruté, n.d., *CW*, 2:365-6.

[61] Simon Bruté, December 1815, ASJPH 1-3-3-12:107.

[62] 7.3, Elizabeth Seton to Simon Bruté, n.d., *CW*, 2:368.

[63] 7.31, Elizabeth Seton to Simon Bruté, n.d., *CW*, 2:401.

[64] John M. Tessier's Journal, 18 December 1815, ASMSU.

[65] 7.7, Elizabeth Seton to William Seton, 23 February 1816, *CW*, 2:374.

[66] Simon Bruté to William Seton, Baltimore, 17 October 1816, UNDA.

[67] Simon Bruté to Mary Bayley Post, Baltimore, 6 August 1816, ASJPH 7-3-1-3, B#173; Eliza Sadler to Rev. Simon Bruté, New York, 30 November 1816, ASJPH 1-3-3-11:B19. Neither woman ever became a Catholic.

[68] 7.47, Elizabeth Seton to Simon Bruté, 2 September 1816, *CW*, 2:420. For a brief account of their arrival in Baltimore in 1816, Godecker, pp. 87-89. [For a discussion of the role of the Vincentians with the community at Emmitsburg after 1850, see Betty Ann McNeil, D.C., "Sulpicians and Sisters of Charity, Concentric Circles of Mission,"*Vincentian Heritage* 20, 1 (1999). Ed.]

[69] 7.43, Elizabeth Seton to William Seton, 22 July 1816, *CW*, 2:416.

[70] 7.47, Elizabeth Seton to Simon Bruté, n.d., *CW*, 2:419.

[71] Ibid., 420.

[72] William Seton to Simon Bruté, Leghorn, 22 August 1816, ASJPH 7-3-1-3, B#204.

[73] Simon Bruté to Elizabeth Seton, Baltimore, 23 October 1816, ASJPH 1-3-3-12:81; 7.60, Elizabeth Seton to Simon Bruté, n.d., *CW*, 2:445.

[74] 6.121, Elizabeth Seton to Julia Scott, 29 October 1812, *CW*, 2:232.

[75] Ibid.

[76] Mme. B. [Marie-Francoise-A. Buisson] Chatard to Elizabeth Seton, Baltimore, 27 June 1812, ASJPH 1-3-3-4:77. Rebecca Seton arrived in Baltimore on 26 June 1812.

[77] 6.121, Elizabeth Seton to Julia Scott, 29 October 1812, *CW*, 2.232.

[78] 6.109, Elizabeth Seton to Rebecca Seton, n.d., *CW*, 2:221.

[79] 6.126, Elizabeth Seton to Julia Scott, 25 January 1813, *CW*, 2:238.

[80] Ibid.

[81] Mme. B. [Marie-Francoise-Adelaide Buisson] Chatard to Elizabeth Seton, Baltimore, 29 January 1813, ASJPH 1-3-3-4:82.

[82] Pierre Babade to Elizabeth Seton, Baltimore, 21 July 1813, ASJPH 1-3-3-1:68.

[83] Pierre Babade to Rebecca Seton, Baltimore, 26 September 1813, UNDA.

[84] Julia Scott to Elizabeth Seton, Philadelphia, 23 November 1813, ASJPH 1-3-3-11:B28.

[85] 6.206, Elizabeth Seton to Rebecca Seton, 5 September 1815, *CW*, 2:343.

[86] 6.207, Elizabeth Seton to Eliza Sadler, 8 October 1815, *CW*, 2:346.

[87] 6.206, Elizabeth Seton to Rebecca Seton, n.d., *CW*, 2:345.

[88] Rebecca Seton to Elizabeth Seton, Philadelphia, ASJPH 1-3-3-9:46.

[89] Many former St. Joseph's girls visited Bec in Philadelphia and brought her books, paints, etc. One even managed to have a piano brought for the daughter of Mother Seton.

[90] Rebecca Seton to Elizabeth Seton, Philadelphia, ASJPH 1-3-3-9:46. See Thomas McCrae, "Philip Syng Physick," *Dictionary of American Biography,* XIV, 554-555. John Hughes to John Purcell, Philadelphia, 8 June 1831, UNDA.

[91] 6.213, Elizabeth Seton to Julia Scott, 10 November 1815, *CW*, 2:354.

[92] 6.217, Elizabeth Seton to Ellen Wiseman, 27 November 1815, *CW*, 2:361.

[93] Julianna White to Elizabeth Seton, Baltimore, 22 December 1815, ASJPH 1-3-3-3:77.

[94] Jean Cheverus to Simon Bruté, Boston, 23 March 1816, UNDA.

[95] John F. Moranvillé to Elizabeth Seton, Baltimore, 28 May 1816, ASJPH 1-3-3-2:36.

[96] 11.51, Elizabeth Seton's Prayerbook, *CW*, 3b:75.

[97] 7.39, Elizabeth Seton to Catherine Seton, n.d., *CW*, 2:412.

[98] 7.45, Elizabeth Seton to Catherine Seton, n.d., *CW*, 2:418.

[99] 7.48, Elizabeth Seton to William Seton, 4 September 1816, *CW*, 2:422.

[100] Jean Cheverus to Simon Bruté, Boston, 7 October 1816, UNDA.

[101] Robert Seton's Scrapbook, Simon Bruté to Elizabeth Seton, Baltimore, n.d., ASJPH 3-3-9, #8. This scrapbook, consisting of mementoes, Simon Bruté's notes and drawings, etc., was presented "to the Sisters of St. Joseph's" on 28 August 1872. [When Melville was doing research for this biography, she noted that the scrapbook was kept in the Museum of St. Joseph's Central House, rather than in the archives. It is now in ASJPH. Ed.]

[102] Simon Bruté to Rebecca Seton, Baltimore, n.d., ASJPH 7-3-1-2, #A7.

[103] 7.26, Elizabeth Seton to Simon Bruté, 20 May 1816, *CW*, 2:397.

[104] 7.53, Elizabeth Seton to Simon Bruté, n.d., *CW*, 2:428.

[105] 7.54, Elizabeth Seton to William Seton, 14 October 1816, *CW*, 2:429.

[106] John Dubois to Simon Bruté, Emmitsburg, 4 November 1816, ASJPH 1-3-3-5:25.

[107] 7.61, Elizabeth Seton to William Seton, 11 November 1816, *CW*, 2:447.

[108] 7.56, Elizabeth Seton to Simon Brute, n.d., *CW*, 2:431.

[109] 7.63, Elizabeth Seton to Julia Scott, 14 November 1816, *CW*, 2:449-450.

[110] Among these friends were Mary Post, Mme. Chatard and Louis Sibourd. Sibourd

found the last thoughts of Bec very edifying and kept the journal until February 1817 at Philadelphia where he was awaiting an operation. Louis Sibourd to Elizabeth Seton, 3 February 1817, ASJPH 1-3-3-2:56; Mme. B. [Marie-Francoise-A. Buisson] Chatard to Elizabeth Seton, 2 December 1816, ASJPH 1-3-3-4:84; Mary Bayley Post to Elizabeth Seton, 16 January 1817, ASJPH 1-3-3-11:20.

[111] 11.51, Elizabeth Seton's Prayerbook, *CW*, 3b:76.

[112] 7.84, Elizabeth Seton to Julia Scott, *CW*, 2:476.

[113] 7.62, Elizabeth Seton to Simon Bruté, n.d., *CW*, 2:448.

[114] Francis Matignon to Elizabeth Seton, Boston, 10 November 1816, ASJPH 1-3-3-1:36. Robert Seton, *Old Family* (New York, 1899), p. 26, states that Mrs. Seton later married a Mr. Gorham of Boston. This is not correct. Bishop Cheverus states clearly that Mrs. Seton had three children "by a former marriage with a Mr. Gorham." See Rev. Jean Cheverus to Elizabeth Seton, 22 August 1820, ASJPH 1-3-3-1:17. Monsignor Seton apparently did not know that John Curzon had two wives. The first, Miss Mary Wise of Alexandria, Virginia, was killed in an accident in 1809. AMSV, I, 15. The second wife was this widow, Mrs. Charlotte Gorham of Boston.

[115] John M. Tessier's Journal, entries from 13 November, and 3 December 1816, ASMSUU.

[116] Jean Cheverus to Elizabeth Seton, 28 November 1816, ASJPH 1-3-3-1:16.

[117] Simon Bruté to Elizabeth Seton, Baltimore, n.d., ASJPH 1-3-3-13:146.

[118] John F. Moranvillé to Elizabeth Seton, Emmitsburg, 4 December 1816, ASJPH 1-3-3-2:37.

[119] Simon Bruté to Elizabeth Seton, Baltimore, 3 December 1816, ASJPH 7-3-1-2, #B28. See ASJPH 1-3-3-12:107; Tessier's journal, 11 December 1816. Cheverus was back in Baltimore on Wednesday, 11 December 1816.

[120] Jean Cheverus to Elizabeth Seton, Boston, 30 December 1816, AMSV, I, 5.

[121] Jean Cheverus to Simon Bruté, Boston, 5 January 1820, UNDA. When referring to his establishment for the Ursulines, Bishop Cheverus said, "Just between us, I would have preferred your Sisters, and above all the Mother, but the testament was positive."

[122] Jean Cheverus to Simon Bruté, Boston, 17 December 1820, UNDA.

[123] Jean Cheverus to Elizabeth Seton, Boston, 17 December 1820, ASJPH 1-3-3-1:18.

[124] John Dubois to Simon Bruté, Emmitsburg, 20 December 1816, ASJPH 1-3-3-5:26.

[125] Simon Bruté to Elizabeth Seton, Baltimore, n.d., ASJPH 7-3-1-3, B#276.

[126] 7.66, Elizabeth Seton to Simon Bruté, 26 December 1816, *CW*, 2:453.

[127] 7.103, Elizabeth Seton to Simon Bruté, 1 August 1817, *CW*, 2:494.

[128] 7.88, Elizabeth Seton to Simon Bruté, 4 June 1817, *CW*, 2:480.

[129] 7.156, Elizabeth Seton to Simon Bruté, April 1818, *CW*, 2:549.

[130] 7.257, Elizabeth Seton to Simon Bruté, n.d., *CW*, 2:664.

[131] 7.208, Elizabeth Seton to Simon Bruté, n.d., *CW*, 2:606.

[132] 7.257, Elizabeth Seton to Simon Bruté, n.d., *CW*, 2:663.

[133] Robert Seton's Scrapbook, Simon Bruté to Seton, Emmitsburg, n.d., ASJPH 3-3-9:8. Simon Bruté may have referred to Father Dubourg in the first sentence since Dubourg was the first superior of the community. The expression "father of your first years" is too general to allow any conclusion.

[134] 7.66, Elizabeth Seton to Simon Bruté, 31 December 1816, *CW*, 2:454.

[135] 12.2, Charter of Incorporation, 18 January 1817, *CW*, 3b:116.

[136] Simon Bruté to Elizabeth Seton, Baltimore, 7 November 1816, ASJPH 7-3-1-3, #276. See Land Records of Frederick County, Liber J.S. No. 5-82. Cooper and Dubois deeded the property in turn to the Sisters of Charity of St. Joseph's on 11 June 1819. See also Land Records, Liber J.S. 9-98.

[137] John Dubois to John M. Tessier, Emmitsburg, 4 November 1817, ASMSU.

[138] John Dubois to Elizabeth Seton, 7 January 1818, ASJPH 1-3-3-5:28. Simon Bruté was in Emmitsburg as early as 7 January 1818, according this letter.

[139] John M. Tessier's Journal, 10 February 1818, ASMSU.

[140] John Dubois to Ambrose Maréchal, Emmitsburg, 9 February 1818, AAB, ASMSU, 15-T-I7.

[141] John M. Tessier's Journal, 3 June 1818, ASMSU.

[142] Simon Bruté to Elizabeth Seton, Emmitsburg, n.d., ASJPH 7-3-1-3, #B191.

స్

CHAPTER 13

҂∞ल

THE CHILDREN

After Father Bruté's return to Emmitsburg in 1818 Mother Seton worked with ever-increasing intensity to put her affairs in order. Although she was never again in good health her courage did not falter, and when Archbishop Maréchal[a] and Rev. James Whitfield, (1770-1834) made their visit in September of that year they found "a very precious institution."[1] After visiting Mount St. Mary's and administering communion to ninety-four persons in a service at which the sisters "sang and very well—all decent and truly edifying," the archbishop and his assistant went to the Valley the following day. After the celebration of the Mass at St. Joseph's the prelates "graced dinner, visited the houses, garden, and graveyard." Maréchal noted the ravages consumption had made in Mother Seton and was impressed that she was "still animated with pious cheerfulness."[2] Coming back from the little wood he commented to Bruté on "how bewitching her conversation" always was. "Elle a une manière unique," he said, "de peindre et d'exprimer ce qu'elle veut dire."[3]

In the afternoon after Benediction, Archbishop Maréchal granted a holiday to "the Academy" in the traditional gesture of generosity on the part of visiting dignitaries. There were fifty-seven boarders to share the fruits of Maréchal's beneficence, not to mention the sixteen sisters and two postulants, as well as the orphans who swelled the White House's inhabitants to over eighty. Elizabeth reported happily to Antonio Filicchi:

> All goes pretty well my, dear Antonio, for religion—the Archbishop says he could never have believed the increase of the true Faith [to] be half what it is if he had not verified it on his tour—and I assure you if I had another house as large as the one we are in we could fill it with Sisters and children. We are obliged to refuse continually for want of room.[4]

The Sisters of Charity of St. Joseph's in 1818 were already in three other places besides the mother house at St. Joseph's. After the Philadelphia establishment in 1814 the next mission was made at Mount St.

---

[a] Ambrose Maréchal was consecrated Archbishop of Baltimore on 14 December 1817, by Jean Cheverus of Boston, assisted by John Connolly of New York, and Louis de Barth, the administrator of Philadelphia. Anthony Kohlmann, the Jesuit superior, and Michael Hurley, O.S.A., of Philadelphia were also there, and Hurley preached the sermon. Cheverus had hoped Mother Seton could attend the ceremonies which involved so many of her close friends, but she was content to write her congratulations to Maréchal. The new archbishop was consoled by her letter.

Mary's College. John Dubois had been having difficulty with the domestic assistants for some time prior to 1815.[b] He reported to the superior general of the Society of St. Sulpice in France, "I discovered some abuses which arose from the circumstances and customs of a country where everyone wants to be master and no one wants to obey." Dubois needed either women of a more cooperative spirit or someone capable of governing the women already at the Mountain. When Elizabeth saw the predicament of her loyal friend and superior she offered him three sisters, "one in charge of linen and clothing, the other of expenses, and the third who would be superior at the head of the entire economy, particularly put in charge of the infirmary."[5] Dubois received the proposition with gratitude, the sisters' council adopted the plan, and on 12 August 1815, Sisters Ann Gruber, Bridget Farrell and a novice, Anastasia Nabbs,[c] went to Dubois' assistance. In December Sister Angela Brady joined the others at the mountain college as sister servant [local superior] for the little group.[6] Although Dubois' superior in Baltimore, Tessier, did not approve of this arrangement, the Mountain establishment was most grateful to the women. Tessier told Dubois, "We must avoid calumnies and preserve intact the reputation of our holy company, and the admission of secular servants, being the universal among the ecclesiastics of this country does not present the same opportunity for accusation. The only reason you might have for asking to keep the Sisters with you is the impossibility of finding other domestiques[d] to replace them. As long as the impossibility lasts, it is necessary that you keep them, but it is my intention that you do all in your power to replace them."[7] Writing to Rev. Antoine Garnier, S.S., in 1820, Dubois commented, "In general, order, piety, and contentment reign throughout the house. I am indebted for all these consolations to the zeal, to the virtue of the good Sisters of Charity whose order, cleanliness, economy and especially whose piety, supervision of the domestic help and good example are above all praise."[8]

Mother Seton had no fears of her spiritual daughters' ability to cope with new problems once they left the mother house. She explained to Julia Scott that "6 years experience of our daily duties and way of life has made many of our good Sisters as much old women as I am, tho' only two of them are as old in years." She added:

---

[b] Among the lay assistants to Dubois was a widow, Margaret Carey Murphy Burke, whose sons attended Mount St. Mary's and daughters St. Joseph's Academy. Mrs. Burke was the sister of the famous Philadelphia publisher, Matthew Carey. Her daughter, Anna Maria Murphy Burke (c.1787–1812) was one of the earliest companions of Mrs. Seton. See Rev. Daniel C. Nusbaum, "This Venerable House," *Analecta Selected Studies in the History of Mount St. Mary's College and Seminary* 1, #3(2003), 8.

[c] Anastasia Nabbs was the domestic servant who had worked for Mother Seton in Baltimore and later joined the community at Emmitsburg in 1813.

[d] Dubois found it very difficult to employ and retain lay staff in service roles.

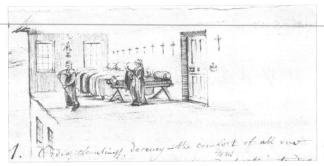

Dormitory, St. Joseph's House,
Rev. Simon Bruté, S.S., 1819.

Perhaps you have no idea of the order and quiet which takes place in a regular way of life—everything meets its place and time in such a manner that a thing once done, is understood by the simplest person as well as by the most intelligent.[9]

This admirable training which the women received at Mother Seton's side made them quite sufficient to the "new tasks to be undertaken. John Dubois found the sisters "a precious treasure" and Simon Bruté never ceased to marvel at the neatness and efficiency of the Mountain sisters. Once, when he viewed their handiwork in arranging Father Duhamel's effects, he was moved to tears, "seeing with what perfect order all the ornaments, the linens, the folds, all arranged," and he said to Mother Seton:

> You know I do not always appear sufficiently sensible of this work of love. I recognize it, nevertheless, thanks to God, and I bless Him, seeing Him thus loved, adored, revered in the smallest things...O my Mother, let us bless, love, serve in the little things with great joy and expansion of heart.[10]

On another occasion the "order, cleanliness, and decency" of a dormitory so impressed Bruté that he made a pen and ink sketch of sisters at work, making beds, and sweeping the floor. Then he wrote a meditation in which he included the words:

> Let us bless here our Sisters who do the same in other places for poor little ones to whom orphan infancy and youth, Himself the Divine Father gives them through His Providence for their true Mothers. O bless them, bless their happy work, O sweet Saviour! As we remember them amidst our own.[11]

The work of the Sisters of Charity in Philadelphia meanwhile was progressing rapidly and in 1816 the orphanage already contained twenty-two orphans.[12] Bishop John Connolly of New York began to consider the possibility of securing sisters for his diocese to undertake a similar work. In a letter to Mother Seton of 14 July 1817, he asked for three sisters to occupy a house which Francis Cooper and Robert Fox would vouch for as suitable to receive them. He said that two gentlemen would come to Emmitsburg to accompany the women to New York if his invitation were accepted. Mother Seton already knew Fox as the father of some of her St. Joseph's pupils and she told him she would be very happy if the plan should materialize. His daughters would be delighted if he should come for the sisters.[13] Although New York had voiced a preference for Sister Margaret George, the first beginnings seemed to Mother Seton to demand the best experience, and she preferred Sister Rose White, who had already done so well at Philadelphia.[14] Elizabeth told Father Bruté of her preference for Rose, saying:

> I write her earnestly about New York—the desire of my heart and soul for her going to New York has been long pressing for so much must depend, as says the good gentlemen who write about it, on *who* is sent to *my "native city"* they say, not knowing that I am a citizen of the world—the bishop [John Connolly] also writes about it, asking 3 Sisters for such an *orphan* asylum as in Philadelphia to begin on a small plan— *excellent*—the little mustard seed—Oh if my Rose [White] can go I shall be proud. She will keep so well the dignity of rules and pure intentions.[15]

Meanwhile, John Dubois replied for the community to Bishop Connolly's request. Writing as the superior of the sisters, Dubois enumerated the terms upon which they would be pleased to come: that the management of the money be left in the hands of the trustees of the asylum, that an association of ladies be formed "with whom the Sisters will keep a freer intercourse than with the gentlemen," that the trustees allow thirty-six dollars a year for each sister's clothes and other expenses, that traveling expenses to New York be paid, and that the head sister should be consulted when orphans were removed or admitted. Referring to the request for Sister Margaret, Dubois said:

> As she has not the honour to be personally known to your reverence or to your trustees, it is evident that it proceeds from the recommendation of some children who have been educated here or of their parents who are not sufficiently acquainted with her, to know whether she is a suitable person for the office. Was your institution a high-styled grammar school, Sister Margaret would suit better than any, and great

as the loss of her would be to this house, we would freely part with her but for such an asylum as that of Philadelphia, the main object is to have a zealous, prudent, economical Mother to govern it...We contemplate to send, at least for a time, the excellent Sister Rose who is now in Philadelphia—having acquired experience in Philadelphia, she will be better calculated to guide the beginners of New York.[16]

It was Sister Rose therefore who on 13 August 1817, set out with Cecilia O'Conway, and Felicitas[e] Brady for New York City to begin the first establishment of Mother Seton's daughters in their foundress's birthplace. Only after the institution was well under way was Sister Margaret George made its sister servant.[17] Robert Fox, one of the men who came to escort the ladies, wrote to Mother Seton of their safe arrival on 20 August 1817, and in spite of Sister Cecilia's indisposition on the journey, the institution soon got under way.[18] Elizabeth Seton wrote at once to Eliza Sadler so that Sad and Dué might know that the sisters were in New York, and call on the newcomers.[19]

Both orphanages, in Philadelphia and in New York, were soon to take on additional work. St. Joseph's in Philadelphia was asked to take over the free school for German Catholics,[f] and on 10 October 1818, Sister Fanny Jordan was named to augment the group of sisters already stationed in that city.[20] Soon the New York asylum expanded in a similar manner. Sister Margaret wrote, in January 1820, that the trustees of the asylum would like additional sisters to operate a "pay school" to accommodate children who could not afford to go to Emmitsburg. John Dubois was authorized to negotiate with the trustees if it was understood that "a plain English education" would be offered.[21] This school was eventually opened on the property of Cornelius Heeny, who had furnished the orphanage building.[22] In May, the sisters received another request, this time from Bishop Connolly, asking that they keep a free school. This third New York project is least easy to define. It seems to have been termed "the Lancastrian school"[g] and Dubois first appeared to believe another sister servant should be appointed for this school but no action was taken by the community

---

[e] Sometimes the name Sister Felicitas appears as Felicita or Felicity.

[f] This school was managed by the Sisters of Charity of St. Joseph's until 7 August 1825. The request for a school sister came from the vicar-general, Louis de Barth.

[g] Joseph Lancaster, (1778–1838), an English educator and the founder of the "Lancastrian method" of instruction, came to New York in 1818. By 1820, he had instituted a school in Baltimore applying his principles. It is quite possible that the New York school referred to here was also a result of his visit to the United States. [Lancaster taught in a free school of a thousand boys and organized corps of elder boys as monitors and peer instructors of those in lower classes. The Lancastrian system of education was adopted widely by Nonconformists in competition with Andrew Bell's system supported by the Church of England. Ed.]

council.[23] In August, Mother Seton wrote to Madame Chatard in Baltimore that Dubois had given up the idea of the Lancastrian school in New York, "so uncertain as to the purposed good, and So great a distance in so distracted a place, while we see so good a prospect of schools among our best friends and much nearer to us."[24] The first positive proof of connection between the sisters and a New York free school came in April 1822, when Sisters Fanny Jordan and Agnes O'Connor were named by the council, "to take charge of the free school."[25] But this was after Mother Seton's death.

In 1820, Mother Seton and John Dubois were much more interested in proposals relating to an establishment in Baltimore. After his episcopal visit to St. Joseph's in 1818, Archbishop Maréchal had reported to Lorenzo Cardinal Litta, the Prefect of Propaganda:

> This pious institute has produced most abundant fruits of religion. If at some future time, with God's favor, I may be able to collect a large enough sum of money, I intend to erect another house, besides that at Emmitsburg and this house for girls I intend to erect at Baltimore.[26]

In June, Dubois wrote a detailed plan to Archbishop Maréchal discussing the terms under which sisters would work in schools in Baltimore. The plan envisaged both a free school and a "pay school" operated separately. Financial arrangements[h] similar to those reached in Philadelphia and New York were proposed.[27] Mother Seton told Antonio Filicchi in October, "Our archbishop is going to take a company of us to Baltimore in the house where our Bishop Carroll of happy memory lived."[28] But Elizabeth Seton did not live to see the event. The first Sisters of Charity missioned in Baltimore, Sisters Benedicta Parsons and Mary Benedicta Doyle, left St. Joseph's for Baltimore on 4 July 1821, six months after Mother Seton died.[i]

Elizabeth Seton's physical resources were heavily taxed during the last three years of her life. Her health had declined very rapidly after Bec's death in 1816, and Elizabeth's thoughts turned with deeper yearning toward her heavenly home. When Sister Ellen Brady died in April 1818, Mother Seton commented:

---

[h] The customary $36 for clothes and shoes, $100 for board, traveling expenses, etc., were stipulated. If the pay school made a profit, the sisters were to receive some of it to buy clothes for poor pupils, furnish prizes, etc. The business acumen which Dubois displayed in his negotiations for the sisters would belie the reputation he has been given for mismanagement of the affairs of Mount Saint Mary's. Melville indicated that a definitive biography of John Dubois remains to be written but Richard Shaw has since authored *John Dubois: Founding Father* (Yonkers, New York: US Catholic Historical Society, 1983).

[i] The Baltimore school was sponsored by "The Lady Managers of St. Mary's Poor School." On 5 October 1820, the school was merged into an "Asylum and School." The officers of the group were Ann Tiernan, Sarah White, and Elizabeth Gross. It is interesting to note that they, too, requested Sister Margaret George. Establishments, ASJPH 11-0-1. See Letter to John Dubois, 8 May 1821, ASMSU.

What a life indeed! A greyheaded carpenter whistling over the plank he measures for Ellen's coffin—just beyond the ground plowing to plant *potatoes*, just beyond again good *Joe* (I believe) making the pit to plant Ellen for her glorious Resurrection—beautiful life, the whole delight *in God,* Oh what relish in *that word* [29]

And to Julia she wrote, "Here I jog on [to] the grave, patting my own back, and hushing up poor pride and sorrow, till both will go off with me bye and bye."[30] In June it seemed as if she were to take her pride and sorrow off without delay. Early that month the abscess in her breast produced such inflammation that she was bled in both arms. Catherine Josephine Seton informed Julia Scott that her mother was very sick, and young Leo Post, Elizabeth's nephew, reported to Mary Bayley Post, on his return from a visit to St. Joseph's, that Elizabeth's condition was alarming.[31] Pierre Babade wrote her in July and suggested that her life story should be written and published, but Mother Seton begged him to promise that she be allowed to die in obscurity.[j] Babade gave his word, approving fully her desire, although he felt that such a biography would be "for the edification of a great many." He added that he hoped she might be relieved of some of her cares as superior, commenting:

Ten years are passed; your work is consolidated. I desire nothing more for you but a holy death...I would like very much to see you before you die but I foresee that the superior will not allow me to go to Emmitsburg in the present state of things...Nevertheless, you know I will never cease praying for you, to have you prayed for and blessed as the priests of Bethulia blessed Judith.[k] As soon as I hear of your death I will say Mass for the repose of your dear soul, as I have prayed during your sickness that you may have a happy death. If you find mercy as I hope you will, do not forget above this one who has thought so much of you here below.[32]

Jean Cheverus wrote from Boston:

I do not pity you...I envy your situation, running now to the embraces of Him Who is love...I beg a few lines when your situation permits it. They will be received and preserved as a treasure to the heart of him who in Our Dear Lord is truly devoted to you...You are most fervently remembered

[j] [L'Abbé J. Babade, a nephew of Rev. Pierre Babade, published *Vie de Madame E.A.Seton* (Paris and Baltimore, 1857), which was a French translation of the prototype Seton biography by Charles I. White (New York, 1853). Ed.]

[k] [Cf. Judith 15:8.]

at the Altar and will be as long as I shall celebrate the Holy Mysteries. Pray for me here and in heaven.[33]

Elizabeth Seton, herself, would have welcomed death that summer. She exclaimed, "Sisters of Charity, Visible angels by the bed of Death—the angels of departing souls rejoice at their approach—for us we will live in habitual preparation for Death...instead of avoiding Death to look continually for its approach, rather be ready to go forward and meet him—as our door of entrance in[to] eternity. We stand always by this door, it may open in a moment."[34] To Bruté and Antonio Filicchi she wrote, "Death grins broader in the pot every morning and I grin at him."[35]

But death was not to be lured by an ingratiating smile and Bruté admonished her:

> From that first summit of desires you thought you were to plunge in the blessed abyss. No, another station still receives you — resign — offer — watch — prepare — do good — be thankful for all—bless his Will—humble yourself as not prepared—though indeed never to trust his tender and infinite mercies—*happily!* Thanks *be to God!* O life O Eternity![36]

When Elizabeth expressed her disappointment and sorrow at being delayed in her glad rush to her "Adored," Bruté consoled her gently, telling her death was afraid to come.

> She wants to surprise as a robber—oh watch then first you not then be surprised, second she will be long postponing, waiting how to catch you and meanwhile leaving you *with us*. No harm to you. You will serve a little more Whom you love and gather a little more of the flowerets of our low valleys for your crown.[37]

So Mother Seton became reconciled to her stay and wrote to Ellen Wiseman, "Our God knows, and we will and do delight that it is all in *his dear hands.*"[38] To Bruté she said with sweet humility, "I see nothing in this world but the blue sky and *our* altars, all the rest is so plainly not to be looked at, but all left to him, with tears only for Sin."[39] The "hoarseness in the breast" did not leave her that fall, and she acquiesced to the admonition that she give up receiving the visitors who came to St. Joseph's. Elizabeth Seton had once said humorously to Father Bruté. "I might not love my Vocation had I tried it—I don't know, but for this part of *sitting at the pen, smiling at people*, young and old—it is too dangerously pleasing—his dear will is *All* though."[40] But now she found it a loss she was quite willing to bear. She refused the importunings of Julia Scott and Mary Post that she come to Philadelphia or New York.[41] She joked about "such an old ruined carcass...bundled up in old shawls and flannels," and went steadfastly about her work as her strength returned.[42] Elizabeth Seton survived the year that saw the deaths[l] of Rev. Francis A. Matignon in Boston, William Augustus Bayley, her half-brother, John Wilkes, her loyal New York friend, and even old Tillary whom her father had loved.[43] But it was only a reprieve, and everyone but her children seemed to know it.

If anything made Elizabeth Seton wish to live on in 1818, it was the thought that she might still serve her children's interests. Although each of the three remaining Setons seemed established in a state of life suited to his tastes and talents: William in the U.S. Navy, Richard with the Filicchi firm, Kit spoken for by the Harpers; Mother Seton never ceased to worry over their spiritual affairs. None of the last three showed signs of a religious vocation, and Elizabeth was particularly fearful of the boys' devotion to their faith. Catherine Josephine gave her less cause for anxiety.[m]

Catherine Josephine Seton[n], called "Kit," "Kate," or "Jos," at different times, was Elizabeth's second daughter, the child she had offered as a sacrifice in exchange for Dr. Bayley's well-being in 1801. Elizabeth referred to the girl in 1819 as "my only dear companion left of all [God] once gave with bounteous hand—the little relic of all my worldly bliss."[44] Kit was the only one of the children present at Mother Seton's death. Elizabeth never tried to force her daughters toward the religious life, however ardently she desired it; and when she saw Kit's interest in a more worldly life, the wise mother arranged for experience and travels as best she could. Kit was allowed to go to Baltimore in Madame Chatard's carriage to visit her friend, Ann Tiernan, whom Mother Seton knew as a student at St. Joseph's. While Elizabeth in her valley put little white violets in a tumbler on her work table, or fed the cat with many thoughts of her absent child, Kit was getting a taste of town life and learning something of her mother's own girlhood. It was in Baltimore that Catherine Josephine Seton first saw, in 1817, the published version of her mother's Leghorn journal. This journal had been published in Elizabeth, New Jersey, that year as *The Memoirs of Mrs. S*...There was no indication given in the book of how the publisher, Isaac Kollock, had obtained the journal, but Simon Bruté was always convinced that Bishop

---

[l] Francis A. Matignon died 19 September 1818; Dr. James Tillary died 25 May 1818; William Augustus Bayley died in Batavia in 1817; the date of John Wilkes' death is also uncertain.

[m] Catherine Josephine Seton died in her ninety-first year in New York City, at St. Catherine's Convent of Mercy, 3 April 1891. She was one of the first received into the Sisters of Mercy established in New York by Archbishop John Hughes. See Robert Seton, *An Old Family*, 325-6.

[n] Baptized Catherine Charlton Seton, she seems to have taken the name Josephine sometime after 1809, perhaps at confirmation or in honor of St. Joseph to whom her mother had great devotion.

Hobart had "treacherously" had the papers printed.[45] Whether John Henry Hobart was guilty of such an unwarranted liberty or not, Mother Seton was very distressed at the baring of convictions she had held while still a non-Catholic.[46] Catherine Seton wrote reassuringly from Baltimore that there was probably only one copy in the whole city and there was no reason to be ashamed of the journal, since there was "not one single protestant expression in it." She said, "Dearest, I believe any other woman but you would be proud of it. Don't be uneasy. I don't think it will ever be printed here in Baltimore."[47]

Kit's travels seemed destined to reopen many doors to Elizabeth's past. When she returned from visits to New York and Philadelphia, the old ties of love and friendship between Mother Seton and the friends of her youth were renewed. In January 1818, she asked Julia Scott if Kit might visit her in Philadelphia that spring.

> The reason of Kit's breaking her resolution not to go out of my reach is that every month of April and May the poor darling has been sick since the critical moment of life, and we think it may be owing to her want of exercise here, as the roads of a country place like this are almost impassable in the spring, you know. She will have no brother in Baltimore to draw her there, and so we concluded that she would go to you if it is perfectly convenient for you to receive her, and if not, to our amiable Cauffmans° who have been always begging for her since we knew them.[48]

In February, Kit set out for Philadelphia, with fifty dollars Julia had sent to Elizabeth. But far more valuable was the little red book Kit took with her, a book which she treasured all the rest of her life.[49] For her daughter, at her "first set out," Elizabeth Seton had written in it advice covering the full range of worldly problems as she knew them. She warned Kit against gossip saying, "You can never be bound, my love, to speak on any occasion, or on any subject, unless you are sure of doing good by speaking." She told Kit to avoid all conversations about marriage. "Remember, darling, the uncertainty of life and how much *you*, in the motives I have told you before, should guard the purity of your heart."[50] She pleaded:

> Oh, do try to be quite independent in Virtue—take its true dignity, and never let impious custom, or the shame of being laughed at, or even the contempt of unreasonable minds,

---

° The Cauffman girls had been in school at St. Joseph's and had been kind to Rebecca Seton when she visited Philadelphia in 1815.

tempt you to treat anyone with the least slight. I beg you so, earnestly because I know how difficult it is to behave to some persons (who in certain circumstances of life or by coarseness of manners would take our proper reserve for pride and insult) with that sweet dignity of charity which acts to everyone as their temper requires, and yet keeps itself free from the least familiarity.[51]

In regard to her dress, Mother Seton told her to avoid extremes of fashion. "Be sure that simplicity should be your only rule. It makes a lovely woman more lovely, and even an ugly one pleasing." [52] And then Elizabeth Seton spoke of amusements:

The best and wisest men who ever lived have thought the theatre a place of danger for young and old. Why should you or I put our conduct and opinion in opposition to theirs. Not *I* indeed, who turn with abhorrence only at a remembrance of the effect the frequentation of the theatre had on my passions, and the extravagant ideas I imbibed in it. . .Poor, poor Betsy B.[p] had no mother, nor even principles to keep her from folly. How different will your Judgment be.[53]

On the subject of dancing, Elizabeth was less severe, saying:

I don't know much of the style of the present day...but cannot remember the least of indecency or pride in dress, or the smallest familiarity or impropriety in dancing, which in truth, if you consider it as a good exercise and if you must be in company preferable to private chit chat...Look at St. Francis de Sales chapter about it. [54]

Mother Seton had no fears for Kit's behavior. The mother and daughter were too closely associated in their habits and beliefs for these ventures of Kit's into society to cause any serious estrangements. Kit valued her mother's judgment too highly to violate her instructions. Once, in Baltimore, she had written home that she could wait to go to confession until she came home because she wanted to examine her conscience with her mother's help. "You don't know what a difference," she wrote, "no mother to consult, and I have things I ought to talk first to you about. Oh how I love you, my Mother!"[55] While she was in Philadelphia and New York, Catherine Josephine wrote freely of all her actions and problems to her mother. Elizabeth, in return, gave the young woman full confidence, allowing her to make important decisions, saying, "You know how unwilling

[p] Referring to herself as Betsy Bayley. Dr. Bayley called his daughter Betty.

353

I am to judge of things when not on the spot (even at home) and how much more at such a distance where you and I cannot *pro* and *con* it over."[56] Kit never abused that confidence, and wrote her mother of the military ball whose temptation she resisted, because it was Lent, and she promised, "I shall lay a penance on myself to read no novels except one which [Aunt Scott] says has so many good morals in it."[57]

From Philadelphia, Catherine Josephine went on to New York, and there she visited all her mother's relatives and friends. Aunt Mary Post wanted her to stay the whole summer and Aunt Helen Bayley Craig, Sam Craig, Mrs. Sadler, and Dué could scarcely express their delight at seeing her.[58] She saw Mrs. John Wilkes, the former Mary Seton, a cousin to William Magee Seton, in deep mourning for her husband, and received a call from the young John. She met Bishop Hobart, who seemed very glad to see her, and she went to the wedding of Ann Hoffman to Anthony Livingston. She saw old Mrs. Sarah Startin, Elizabeth's godmother, and the Maitland cousins the old lady had adopted. Catherine even called on old "Aunt Charlton," and spent several days with Mary Hoffman, her Seton aunt.[59] Everyone seemed to find Catherine Josephine very much like her mother, and they welcomed the young woman cordially. Sad wrote to Elizabeth that she would like Kate to stay with her awhile. Dué took her to visit the Sisters of Charity at the orphanage, and even though Kit was surprised at the wickedness of the world, she was greatly excited to be such a center of attraction, and to find she had so many relatives and connections. It was with something of reluctance that she complied with her mother's wish[q] that she should not overstay her welcome.[60]

Mother Seton had planned to have her daughter come home in June with Sister Rose White or Robert Fox, who would be coming for his children, but Kit's cousin Lionel (Leo) Post, decided to accompany her to Baltimore and Emmitsburg the last part of May.[61] Leo, as his aunt liked to call him, was forced to extend his visit longer than he had planned.[r] On his arrival the community horse, Old Sultan, had jumped at the stranger from the city and Father Bruté had to be summoned from Mount Saint Mary's, to come and get the injured young man. In spite of his mishap, Lionel Post was pleased to see his aunt and the "good Mr. Bruté" who had called on his mother in New York in 1815. He was "soon cured" and enjoyed his stay so

---

[q] Mother Seton believed that Catherine Josephine would be more welcome after her mother died if she did not overstay her welcome now.

[r] Lionel Post was one of several New York visitors to St. Joseph's. Edward Augustus Seton had come in 1810, Dr. Wright Post and Mary Post after Anna Maria's death in 1812; Mrs. Catherine Dupleix in 1813. Wright and Mary Post visited St. Joseph's again the spring following Bec's death, and brought Mary Fitch Bayley, Elizabeth's half sister, with them, as well as the Post's daughter, Catherine. Soon afterwards Mary Fitch Bayley married, Robert Henry Bunch, an Englishman and went to live in the Bahamas at Nassau.

much he planned to return to the valley again soon.[62] But the condition of Elizabeth Seton, that summer of 1818 was enough to alarm both Kit and her cousin. Kit wrote Aunt Julia Scott that she was glad she had arrived home when she did.[63]

Elizabeth was more than glad to see her daughter at home and hear the ecstatic reports of Aunt Scott's kindness, the delights of New York, and the fascination of the Setons. But more than her pleasure in Kit's return was the great peace of mind that came when she considered the girl's future. For even should the kindness in New York diminish, Catherine Josephine would be provided for. When John Dubois was in Baltimore that May, he had had a conversation with Robert Goodloe Harper about Mother Seton's affairs. Harper, a friend of many years, had proposed that in the event of Mrs. Seton's death the girl should come to the Harpers to fill the place left by the death of their daughter Mary Diana.[64] Although the Harpers had gone to Europe that same month,[65] Elizabeth Seton's heart was at ease, knowing that if death came the Harpers would protect her child. She told William, her son, "I wish her much to be with them as they propose."[66]

After the Harpers returned from Europe, Catherine Josephine visited them and their relatives. Early in May 1820, she went to Baltimore and after a visit with the Tiernans, Kit went on to Carroll Manor with Mrs. Harper. Meanwhile, at Annapolis, she had seen "old Mr. Carroll," the younger Charles Carroll, Emily McTavish, and Mrs. Caton. Most of July and August were spent with the Harpers at "the Manor."[67] The family was more than satisfied with Miss Seton's demeanor and Mr. Harper wrote again assuring Elizabeth Seton that while the Harpers lived, Catherine would be protected.[68] This explains why Catherine Josephine, the sole beneficiary of her mother's last will and testament,[s] refused the kind invitations of Julia Scott, Mary Post, Mme. Chatard, and the rest went to live with the Harpers of Baltimore.[69]

In 1818 Mother Seton was also at ease about her son, William, although his career had taken a turn she had once hoped could be avoided. William had never been satisfied with his situation in Leghorn. He had written his mother early in 1817 that he felt quite useless to the Filicchi business and that he did not have the requisite qualifications for a merchant. Elizabeth Seton wrote at once to Antonio for his opinion of William and his future. She felt distressed that her son had not been able to take some of the

---

[s] Catherine Josephine Seton, after visiting Julia Scott and Mary Post, briefly went to the Harpers in April after her mother died. Elizabeth Seton's will, made 14 November 1820, and probated 16 June 1821, left all that she had, or that was due her, to Catherine Josephine Seton. She undoubtedly had in mind the legacy due from her maternal uncle John Charlton's estate which she believed to be $1000. A lawyer, Fred Schley, wrote Dubois that the daughter was entitled to a legacy of $1000 and some articles of personal property.

burden off Filicchi's shoulders, now that Antonio was without Philip. She confessed to William's patron that she dreaded the attraction the Navy still seemed to hold for her son.[70] Then she wrote to William. She told him she was consulting Antonio Filicchi in his regard, and said:

> I have gained my main object in parting with you, my beloved son, which was not so much to fix you with affluent friends, or in a tide of fortune, as to give you time to know yourself a little, to know the world a little, and to overcome your *first* ardent propensity for the Navy; which *I* know is even now the passion of your heart.[71]

And then, in the complete generosity of her maternal love, Elizabeth Seton promised:

> All I can say is *that you will never want every nerve of my heart to exert itself for you in whatever path you enter*— what more can your own Mother say. I would write, or even go to anyone on earth I could reach, if I might help you, my William. If a Mother's love could be a fortune to you, you *would be rich indeed,* alas it is poor coin in this world.[72]

Antonio Filicchi wrote a letter to Mother Seton on 4 June 1817, which William Seton carried back to America with him. In it Filicchi broke a silence of two years, saying he hated to write to her since he knew his report on William would grieve her. He said that after watching her son closely he could only conclude William had "a moral indifference, if not aversion, to trade in general." The young man had a mild disposition but his "great reservedness" made it impossible for Antonio to really know him. William preferred associating with his own countrymen [Americans] in Italy to adjusting to Italian life, and Antonio feared he did not "much improve his Catholicism though in a Catholic country." On the practical side, Filicchi stated that William was not suited to commercial work because of his poor handwriting.[1]

William Seton did not arrive with this letter until two months later, and Antonio Filicchi waited anxiously to hear Elizabeth's reaction to William's return.[73] On 14 July 1817, he forwarded four letters for William and asked her to write, telling her he cherished her letters as "holy relics from my heavenly American sister." He concluded, in the vein of the old charming Tonino, with an apology for his own poor letters, "I often play the indifferent and rough, for fear of making myself too *lovely.*"[74] Antonio

---

[1] It was typical of Elizabeth Seton that she blamed herself for William's failure to become a good writer. She told Eliza Sadler his fingers were weak because she had allowed him to suck them as a baby.

Filicchi was still quite willing to aid his "American sister" and offered to take Richard Seton in William's place. All he required was "a good handwriting and a good will," he said.[75]

When William Seton arrived home in August that year his mother began at once to negotiate for a place in the Navy for him.[u] Robert Fox of New York was asked to help, and he wrote early in September that he had already spoken for William to Captain Stewart's brother-in-law.[v] Mr. McCawly had advised a letter from the vice-president of the United States, Daniel D. Tompkins, to the Navy department, and Fox said he would try to see him at Staten Island as soon as the vice-president had recovered from his indisposition. Fox included a letter from Francis Cooper to Captain Charles Stewart on William's behalf, and he said, "I am also in hope that if Mr. [John Q.] Adams returns here I shall be able to procure one from him. On my part nothing will be omitted."[76] William meanwhile, without waiting for Fox to act, had gone directly to Washington where Daniel Brent had presented him to the acting Secretary of the Navy who received Seton "with much politeness."[77] When Mother Seton wrote of William to Antonio in September she said hopefully, "The President of the Navy department has promised him an appointment before Christmas."[78] But while uncertainty over the appointment existed, William went back to Mount St. Mary's to study mathematics and navigation, and Elizabeth had the happiness of knowing her son was near.[79]

The letter of Francis Cooper to Captain Stewart, which Seton delivered in person in Philadelphia, together with one from the vice-president to Benjamin Crowninshield had its effect, and by 4 November 1817, William Seton had his appointment.[80] The appointment was followed by several months of waiting before Seton received a designation and Julia wrote inquiringly on 20 January 1818, saying she had been looking for William to pass through Philadelphia for some time.[81] Finally in February the orders came for William to report to Commander William Bainbridge in Boston.[82] Simon Bruté, who had seen the young man off on his first venture in 1815, wrote him a beautiful letter of exhortation, pleading with William to love God above all things and to serve Him and obey His laws.[83] His mother wrote her parting words:

> My soul's darling—You go—so *adieu* once more—with
> how much more courage I say it now than in 1815. You must

---

[u] At this time Benjamin W. Crowninshield was Secretary of the Navy; Daniel D. Tompkins of New York was vice-president; John Quincy Adams was Secretary of State.

[v] For his heroic services during the War of 1812, as commander of the *Constitution* and other ships, Charles Stewart had received a sword of honor from the Pennsylvania legislature and a gold medal from Congress. From 1817 to 1820 he was in command of a Mediterranean squadron.

fill a station and take a part in our life of trial and all your own Mother can beg is that you keep well with your good pilot, and as says old Burns,[w] this correspondence fixed with heaven will be your noble anchor. Go when you can to the sacraments as a child to his Father will be a main point for that and the next best is to look to your Mother's old rule of *intentions* the comfort of my life...O *my* William—You know all I would say. Dearest, dearest child of my Soul. Mind we *must* be one day where we will part no more.[84]

William Seton was thus the escort of his sister, Catherine when she went to visit Julia Scott that spring of 1818. He carried a package for Sister Rose of the New York asylum, and his mother promised Robert Fox that even if William had only one hour in New York he should call upon Fox and Francis Cooper.[85] William had more than an hour in New York, and Sister Rose reported to Mother Seton what she knew would give her the greatest joy that William had come to Mass with Dué on Sunday.[86] Young Seton soon reached Boston and went aboard the *Independence* in the harbor on 24 February to begin a career which was to last for several years.[87]

His mother started writing to him immediately. Scarcely a week after he had started off with Kit for Philadelphia Elizabeth began, "Your little Ship left behind has had cloudy weather and dragged scarcely three knots an hour."[88] As March progressed and the pain in her chest became greater, Mother Seton found she could not sleep. After Sister Anastasia, her "night company," was safely asleep, Elizabeth would draw up a basket of chips, make a little blaze to warm her stiff hands, and pour out her heart to this son. Sometimes it seemed her heart must break before his return. As she wrote on one occasion, "Reasoning is in vain or even religion. I look up a hundred times at the dear Crucifix and *resign* but too often with such Agony of heart that nothing stops it." His night watch was on her mind and she often lay awake invoking blessings on him.[89] It was her custom to keep a map of Boston harbor on her little table where she wrote so that she could feel closer to him.

William Seton, meanwhile, seeing no prospect of getting to sea except in one of the frigates was corresponding with Washington to ask for a transfer to another ship.[90] Elizabeth Seton was disturbed by this news asking, "Will it not be a disadvantage if you quit Commodore Bainbridge since he expressed himself as particularly interested for you?"[91] Bainbridge had been a friend of William's father, and Robert Harper told Mother Seton

---

[w] [Mrs. Seton is alluding to the poem "Epistle to a Young Friend" (1786) by Robert Burns (1759–1796), who many considered the national poet of Scotland, the ancestral country of the Setons. Ed.]

he felt William was unwise to leave his command.[92] But young Seton, who could not leave Leghorn fast enough the summer before, was now eager to transfer, with Charles Wilkes, to the *La Guerrière* which was scheduled to make a Mediterranean cruise. As if this were not enough to cause uneasiness to his mother, William wrote the first of May to say he had narrowly escaped death in an accident in which he lost all his money.[x] He asked his mother to send some at once. Elizabeth replied immediately, ill as she was:

> I hasten to ease your dear heart, mine is far from troubled at the loss of our pennies, but so grateful to our God for your escape of instant and (alas perhaps) unprovided death. Oh, my love, not a word must I say on that point—that only point to my Soul. I write Mr. [Robert] Barry pressingly to send you speedily as possible the $100...I pray and trust he will advance it, there is not now as high as a $5 bill in the house, and Mr. Grover[y] is pressing for the debt it owes him for spring goods, so I have no resource for the moment in either, but cannot think Mr. Barry will hesitate, if *he* does, I will surely get it somewhere. Mr. Dubois is sick in Baltimore and they are over run with demands so I cannot apply there.[93]

Although Mother Seton tried to secure the money for her son as fast as she could, he gave her no indication of receiving any and his letter of 3 June 1818, instead of putting her mind at rest in this regard, made a further request that she get Mr. Brent to write a letter to speed his transfer to either the *La Guerrière* or *Macedonian.*[94] When she wrote back, Elizabeth apologized for mentioning the money so often, but said

> You are tired of hearing about it but that cannot be helped until you can tell me the welcome news that you have it. We must not mind these things, dear one, but well I remember when I was young how I hated them—Your letter of 3rd June was immediately attended to—I had been bled in both arms for a slight inflammatory attack of the breast and I got Mr. Dubois to write the very hour I received your letter...

> Sweet Kit came just in good time to save us both a deal of anxiety, but I am much recovered now eating green peas, strawberries, and cherries in great abundance with the regular tears in the eyes at the thought of my sailor who gets neither, nor smells our sweet roses, nor roves our green fields.[95]

---

[x] It is not clear what the accident was, but it seems to implicate young Seton since his mother hesitated to ask Bishop Cheverus to come to William's rescue.

[y] George Grover was the local grocer who supplied St. Joseph's House.

Mother Seton could never see the selfishness of her eldest son, who was now in his twenty-second year. The only real reproof she could bring herself to utter was in connection with his religious practices. When she failed to hear from him that July she wrote:

Dearest dear dear dear William—

I could fill all my paper with that so unavailing repetition— good and dear son, and child of my heart, be comforted. You never gave pain to that heart but the pain of parting and separation. Now indeed some fears that you are giving up all too human views, etc. Yet all I judge from is the entire silence of Bishop Cheverus who has never written me once since you are at Boston, and I have had so many full proofs of the kindness of his heart that I am sure if he could have said a word of your approach to our God he would have taken time from sleep to tell me.[96]

William Seton did not write for a month because he had been busy transferring to the *Macedonian,* and the letter Mother Seton received on 1 August 1818, announced that he was to make a two-year cruise on that vessel in southern and Pacific waters. He would need clothes and some money before starting off, but since they might not leave before October or November William had written:

The ship will go round Cape Horn into the Pacific as high up as Columbia River, and higher if the captain chooses, but so far she is ordered. She will cruise in the Pacific two years, visiting all the important cities on the western coast of North and South America...It will be, in fact, one of the most interesting voyages ever made from this country...I long to hear that you have perfectly recovered from your late illness, if not do, dearest mother, let me know it and I will use every endeavor to come to you. It would be a great satisfaction indeed to pass a little time with you before so long a voyage.[97]

William's suggestion that he might come home for a visit was a bittersweet temptation; but, Elizabeth Seton, thinking only of her son, and knowing how sick she really was, wrote to Bishop Cheverus asking him to help her conceal her condition from William. Cheverus agreed, and promised her, "I shall carefully conceal from William your real situation. You justly remark it would only add to his anxieties and hardships." Cheverus had

had the young man to dinner and exacted from him a promise to fulfill his religious duties before he sailed. He said to the mother:

> Dear child! He is then to see you no more in this world. But I have confidence that he will one day be with you in heaven. "The child of so many tears and prayers cannot perish."[98]

To her son, Elizabeth wrote that he must not think of coming home. "*One* only thing I cannot stand in this world," she said, "That is *taking leave of you.*" She told him that he must not be uneasy about her health; inflammation of the lungs always left a long weakness. She might live to welcome his joyful return from many a cruise. As for his clothes and money, perhaps Mrs. John Seton in Boston could help him with his clothes, "as none but a woman can do it."[z] She would see that he received fifty dollars, although she could cry to think that was all he would have for his voyage.[99]

But Providence decreed that Elizabeth Seton should see her son once more before her death. William had proudly described the *Macedonian* as "a most beautiful frigate, pierced for fifty (carrying forty-eight) guns, more completely and handsomely fitted out than any other ship that ever sailed."[100] She was commanded by Captain John Downs, and manned by thirty midshipmen and eight lieutenants. On 18 September 1818, before a stiff breeze, the *Macedonian* left Boston for the south, destination Valparaiso, Chile.[101] But off the coast of Virginia she ran into storms. Midshipman Seton was dreaming of his mother. She stood by him, asking sorrowfully the oft-repeated question, "Are you prepared?" When he sprang from his hammock the water reached his knees.[102] The damage to the frigate was so serious that she put into Norfolk, Virginia, for repairs, and William hastened to Emmitsburg to see his mother. Elizabeth Seton had her "happy moment with my soul's William" after all.[103] His visit was well worth the pain of another parting. The peace of soul Mother Seton retained is reflected in the cheerful little "holy Book of the Shady Retreat" which she kept of the days following his departure.[104] The contentment of October was in sharp contrast to the words of anguish she had penned in September. When Elizabeth believed that her son was starting off without her seeing him again she had, written:

> Oh, my William, now indeed is my true courage called for to see things as they are...Yet I protest to you that I could give you up to *duty* with a free heart, if the way was but clear for our dear *futurity*, but oh, who but our God can know

---

[z] Charlotte Gorham Seton, wife of John Curzon Seton, was not well, and Jean Cheverus offered to give William money enough to care for his linen.

my anguish at the thought of resigning you *there* also...My soul's William! How strange to be a *man* and *God* but a secondary consideration, or no thought at all; to be a few years beating through this world after shadows, then enter an eternity of existence quite unprepared, though to prepare for it is the only end of our being here below. You know, beloved, I seldom say much of these things; but it would be concealing the sharp arrow in your mother's own soul from yours, into which I would pour every thought of my heart... Everything else in this world has its place in my affections in measure but my love for you has no bound or measure, and can never be satisfied but in our eternity. Oh! Hear, then the cry of a mother's soul, my beloved, and take care of what is dearer to her a thousand thousand times than herself.[105]

After William left, Elizabeth wrote happily to Julia Scott thanking her for the hundred dollars which had just arrived and telling her of William's eight-day visit. If ever the Seton boys were a credit to their country,[aa] Mother Seton said, Julia Scott would be responsible. As for herself, Elizabeth remarked:

Do not think of me dearest but—under the line of my beautiful Providence which has done so well for us so many years. You keep me *out of debt* and that is the greatest trouble I could ever have and as to comforts, pity knows, I have them abundantly.[106]

Nothing mattered now that she had seen her son, heard his promises of fidelity to his faith, and made sure his physical needs were attended. She stored up every memory of his visit against the long months of his absence. A year after his departure she wrote him, "Let no one say that deep affliction can kill since I grow strong in my absence from you for it is like a daily Death to me in which every minute carries the pain of separation."[107]

The third Seton requiring his mother's intercession and causing her deep concern was Richard, the younger son. Bruté's estimate of Richard Bayley Seton had described him as "very like his brother" though with many characteristics distinctively his own. He had "a good heart yet turned to pride and selfishness."[108] The expense accounts of Mount St. Mary's show him to have been less thrifty than his brother.[109] The pride Bruté noted took forms prevalent among certain strata of Maryland society: race, prejudice,

---

[aa] William Seton served in the United States Navy from February 1818 to July 1834. His commission as a midshipman was issued 4 July 1817; he became a lieutenant in February 1826, and he resigned on 5 July 1834.

and extravagance. Once when Richard sent John Hickey some crosses and medals from Baltimore he stipulated that they were "for your people, I mean blacks, for they are too ugly for any white man."[110] With all his faults, his quickness of temper, Richard Seton was a lovable boy, possessing much of the charm of his uncle, Sam Seton. His mistakes stemmed more from impulsiveness than from bad intentions. He knew how much his mother wished her sons to be priests and he regretted his own lack of a vocation. He once told Father Hickey:

> I have not such a calling, and very unhappily, too. Many a time do I wish I had tried and (you may almost say) forced myself to it. I would not have experienced so many unhappy hours as I have been prey to; and what is more, am daily experiencing. I can tell you this, such a favour was never destined from above.[111]

After William Seton went off to Leghorn in 1815, Richard became restless and took less and less interest in his studies at the Mount. His mother remarked, "Richard, like all young people, drags his chain. He wants to be busy and getting on," and she begged William to write to his brother about the importance of using his time at school to advantage.[112] Although this was the year that Bec was so much worse, Elizabeth Seton never slighted the concerns of any of her children, and she racked her brain to find some solution for her second son's problem.[bb]

Mary Post had suggested the year before that one of the Seton boys might come to live with the Posts, and, like their son Leo, go into Abraham Ogden's counting house.[113] Abraham Ogden[cc] was an old friend of the Setons, but only bitter memories were roused by the recollection of the younger Ogdens.[114] The thought of applying to them for Richard was quite abhorrent.[dd] Mother Seton explained to William, "I doubt much their receiving a child of mine. You know it was they who wrote the threatening letter that the house would be burned over my head, calling me Siren, etc, etc."[115] She much preferred to interest Baltimore people in Richard's case. She first approached Luke Tiernan but when he gave her little hope for any immediate opportunity for her son, she turned "to attach [to] poor Mr. Barry's continued kindness."[116] When she wrote to Julia in March she told her she was saving the latest Scott remittance for "Richard's setting out," adding:

[bb] Richard Seton was seventeen years old the summer of 1815 and it was not long after this that Simon Bruté began his efforts to secure the younger Seton a position in Baltimore.

[cc] At the time Seton & Maitland Company failed in New York, Abraham Ogden had been William Magee Seton's dearest friend.

[dd] Charlotte Seton Ogden and Gouverneur Ogden, her husband, had been particularly bitter over Cecilia Seton's conversion in 1806.

He is bent on a counting house in order to meet his brother's plans. I have written Mr. [Robert] Barry to try and procure him a place. He is an enormous young man, very well disposed, but like his brother before he left us, shows no remarkable talents...[117]

As spring wore on affairs assumed a darker aspect. Baltimore was suffering from commercial doldrums in 1816. For nearly twenty-five years before the Congress of Vienna, Europe had been at war, and the eastern coastal cities of the United States had all but monopolized the carrying trade. But now, not only were European ships resuming their competition, but the American steamboat was rapidly directing the coastwise shipping, which Baltimore had formerly enjoyed, to the Mississippi River and New Orleans. Crews hung idle about the water fronts. The tobacco trade was declining because of changing European tastes; planters were abandoning its cultivation.[118] The flour trade, which had been "the backbone of the port's commerce" was slowing because the British were once more carrying to the West Indies. The experimental cotton mills were threatened by annihilation by British "dumping" in the post-war markets.[119] Richard Seton wrote to his brother in May 1816, "The merchants are all idle it seems—many ships are lying in port and none of them know what to do."[120]

In April, Richard turned in desperation to the chance offered him by a wholesale grocer to work for him. Mother Seton was determined to prevent it if she could.[121] She had heard the Tiernan firm in Baltimore was doing "a great deal of business" and she applied once more, this time offering to meet whatever financial terms he might propose. John Dubois told her that St. Joseph's house would "come forward if necessary."[122]

May came in with cold and frosts. A "black spot in the sun" gave rise to many gloomy conjectures. And then a forest fire broke out on the mountain and the young men of the college, Richard Seton among them, all ran out to "give their mighty aid" as Kit laughingly described it.[123] In the middle of these signs and portents came the summons to Baltimore; Luke Tiernan would accept Richard at last. Mother Seton told the glad news to Mme. Chatard with the joyous words, "Our God is too, too good."[124] On 14 May 1816, Richard Seton started for Baltimore where he would live in the Tiernan household, which made Elizabeth Seton feel secure about the religious influences surrounding her son.

Richard was at first a very satisfactory correspondent. His mother boasted that in one day they had received six letters from him.[125] When Kit went to Baltimore on her birthday in June she reported that Dick was very happy, that he took her calling upon the Cursons[ee] who were very kind.[126] When the news of Bec grew worse, Dick escorted his sister back to St. Joseph's in the public stage, and Mother Seton could see her "giant" for herself.[127]

But the rumors that came up from Baltimore during the winter months caused uneasiness to Mother Seton, at a time when Bec's death was most keenly felt. Not only was there uncertainty as to whether Tiernan would remain in business,[128] but Richard Seton was not showing signs of responsibility. When he first arrived in Baltimore, Richard went almost every evening to the Cursons' or Chatards' homes. But as June progressed the families who had country seats left town, and Seton complained to his mother, "there is nothing doing now; times are remarkably dull."[129] For a while it seemed that the restless Dick would settle down, and his mother drew comfort from his report that he went every Sunday to the seminary where he sang at Vespers. "You know how I always liked to sing," he reminded her.[130] In July Kit wrote from Baltimore that Dick was very busy in the store all day, and was very happy.[131]

But when Richard appeared in Emmitsburg in August, Elizabeth was worried to see him in an indifferent mood. His belated apology after his return to Baltimore did little to ease the pain of his cold leave-taking.[132] Nevertheless, his repeated requests for winter stockings set Elizabeth knitting busily for her tall son after Bec's death.[133] Although Richard took little interest in young women,[134] his mother told William:

> You could not guess half the trials we have had with him in Baltimore through his childish, thoughtless disposition...Mr. Williamson, Mr. Tiernan's son-in-law who lives in the house with him, says "he is a fine young man but will be lost for want of employment, and by company." Not that he keeps any out of the house that I ever heard, but there is so much *in it*...Mr. Tiernan (has) that easy way [so] that everyone does as they please.[135]

In February it became clear that Richard Seton's days in Baltimore were numbered. Elizabeth told Antonio Filicchi that he probably would not be with Tiernan after May or June, since Tiernan's son was returning from Europe and Tiernan was forming a partnership which would use this son. She begged Filicchi to ask some Italian merchant to take Richard.[136] Although Dick was still in Baltimore in April his prospects looked even gloomier.[137] It was under this strain that Elizabeth received the news that

---

[ee] The Cursons were the family into which the Seton children's paternal grandfather had married twice. The name is also spelled Curzon.

William was dissatisfied at Leghorn and wanted to return.[138] The same June, when Richard was writing to his friends at the Mount that he was through in Baltimore, William Seton embarked at Leghorn for his return to the United States. Dick wrote Hickey that he hoped he would not find him "the wild rattle brained fellow I was,"[139] and to Father Dubois he confessed that Baltimore was not all he had expected. He deplored the wickedness of the city, but he concluded cheerfully, "Farewell, may I return to you as I went, I fear not such a good fellow, but one who will know how to act and do better in the future."[140] Mother Seton wrote William of Richard's return, saying, "His mind is bent on a country life,[ff] but I believe it is only to preserve himself from the distraction of bad company and the dangers he has past in Baltimore."[141]

Richard went to Mount St. Mary's on his return from Baltimore and spent the summer hunting and fishing with the seminarians Hickey, Mullen, Doyle, and Elder.[142] He wanted to learn of William's plans before taking any further step.[143] When his brother arrived in August with Antonio Filicchi's offer to take Richard, Elizabeth Seton lost no time in getting Richard off for Italy. Again Robert Barry was importuned to secure money, this time for Dick's passage. Barry drew on Robert Fox of New York, and Richard Seton sailed in September "on the Brig Strong, Captain Gerry."[144] He left his mother with "a thorn in the heart," as she explained to Julia:

> Poor fellow, which now, no doubt he feels more than ever though his tears and sobs in his acknowledgments to me were enough to move a stronger mother than I am. For we find when too late that the good and most respectable Mr. [Luke] Tiernan with whose family he made his home, took no account of his expenses, and poor Dick not having fortitude or good sense to keep himself in the character of *Son of a poor widow*, spent not only the $200 M. Filicchi allowed for his regular wants, but all that poor Kit had saved by her piano lessons and your constant remittances—indeed her loving heart wanted it only for her brothers but we are hurt and mortified enough that he should have been playing the fool in that way—yet on tracing it we find he has been imposed on just like the poor countryman in the fable, for a more innocent simple young man can scarcely be met with and we must hope he will do well in the event with a little more experience and Judgment.[145]

[ff] Just before leaving Baltimore Richard Bayley Seton had received an offer from a Quaker, Mr. Cook, to run a country store and farm about thirty miles from Gettysburg.

To Antonio she wrote, "Here is Richard" and introduced her second son as quite different from William. His quick temper and want of experience, she said, were his chief faults.[146] Although her great love could never let her condemn her sons for their selfishness, it must have been a deep sorrow to Mother Seton that she could not present more responsible young men to her generous patron after his years of kindness to her sons. Antonio Filicchi more than proved his devotion to Mother Seton by continuing his support. The house of John Murray & Son in New York, in which the Filicchis had much of their American funds, went bankrupt in 1817 and cost Antonio $30,000. In addition, the death of Philip Filicchi had removed the $200 he furnished toward the Seton boys. Antonio's share was more than absorbed by the expenses of Richard and William Seton, yet he ordered Cheriot, Wilkes, and Company of New York to pay money to Elizabeth Seton whenever she needed it.[147]

Richard Seton arrived in Leghorn on 4 December 1817, "all good resolves to succeed and be good,"[148] and for more than two and a half years stayed in the Filicchi counting house. While he was in Leghorn, Dick sent home urns for the churches at St. Joseph's, Mount Saint Mary's, and the village. He relayed gossip of duels, weddings, and visits to Pisa. He remarked on the political flavor of Sunday sermons in Leghorn, his efforts to teach the little Filicchi girls to speak English, his meeting with Samuel Cooper, and the rumors of war between Spain and the United States.[149] His frequent letters the first year always contained "the same expression of his most happy condition," yet Elizabeth wrote to Mme. Chatard of the true hardship of separation.

> What a business, my dearest friend...to live thousands and thousands of miles from a part of one's own self, I have to reason and reason, and conclude at last— well, if we are to be together in this [life], and if we are to be together in the next world, it is little matter to be separated in this [world]— unless we could help their salvation, but boys give a mother so little share in that comfort after early years are past.[150]

The second year of Richard's absence brought a sharp decrease in the number of letters from Leghorn. His mother, in a letter dated 8 May 1820, told him they had been six or eight months without a line from him.[151] The next letters she received were full of schemes about settling on the Black River. Elizabeth said sorrowfully to Ellen Wiseman, "Black indeed will it be to him if he carries it through. He says commerce is dead loss of time at present. Poor fellow I fear his Faith is dead by the whole tenor of his letters, yet he puts change aside till another year. So we will see."[152]

Although his mother feared he would procrastinate, Richard Seton did not wait even a year to change his plans. On 8 August 1820, the month before Mother Seton entered upon her last illness, Antonio Filicchi wrote from Italy, "Your son sailed a fortnight ago on board the American frigate *La Guerrière* having been furnished by me of the requisite money for his intended passage home."[153] He said Richard had proved neither willing nor able to assist in the counting house, and his moral conduct had not given full satisfaction either. Antonio thought that perhaps Richard, too, would profit by entering "your growing Navy's service." His own loyalty to Mother Seton was as strong as it had always been, and he concluded with the comforting assurance, "Consider me, beloved Sister, firm at all times as a Rock in my brotherly sentiments for you."[154]

Before this letter could inform Elizabeth Seton of the return of her son, she had already been stunned by receiving from Alexandria, Virginia, a letter from Richard himself, dated 1 October 1820. "He wrote he was in Norfolk, [Virginia] in some difficulty with a protested bill."[155] The frantic mother, not knowing whether he might be arrested or not, wrote to General Robert Goodloe Harper, "Who can I venture to address but you at this moment of real distress?" She asked him to see what could be done for her son.[156] The letter must have wrenched the good man's heart, for Elizabeth Seton was dying. As a matter of fact, two weeks earlier she had received the last sacraments. Yet the frightful worry over Richard helped to keep her alive until he was safe once more. The handwriting of her October letters to Harper and Filicchi is pitiful in its weakness, yet magnificent in the fierce maternal protectiveness it attests. These letters are in terrible contrast to the one Richard Seton wrote to Robert Harper a month and a half later. Seton explained that he had arrived in October from Gibraltar on "the Ship America Captn. Barrett."

> To pretend, Sir, to give an account of my reasons for leaving Leghorn, to you would be useless—suffice it to say, that religious matters were the principal causes of it: that I have been in the wrong and acted imprudently I candidly confess—and to pretend glazing my faults with excuses, would be but to destroy the merit of confessing them.
>
> Mr. Filicchi gave me $180 when I left: but having ½ a year's expenses to pay, I had a surplus of $80——a mess bill of 3 Doubloons to Gibraltar left me $30. With $30 I got stores to come to America—and on arrival I went to a miserable place to live, where my expenses have been $22 for two months.

I am now trying to get on board some vessel. I have not written Mama for money as I know her situation. I would live half my life to see her—but fear I never shall again. For 3 weeks I was very sick or I should have walked there.[157]

It was for this wretched young man's return that Mother Seton maintained her feeble hold on life. Whether Harper furnished money, or how it was managed, no one can say, but Richard Seton did see his mother once more. He was in Emmitsburg in December 1820 but he did not stay. Two weeks after "her poor heart had keenly felt the pain of last separation," Richard Seton's mother died.[158] But if her prayers counted for him, Richard was not long away. He, himself, died on 26 June 1823, on board the brig *Oswego,* on its passage from Cape Mesurado to St. Jago.[gg] The Boston paper which published his obituary described him as "Richard B. Seton, Esq. of Baltimore, late U. S. assistant agent at Monrovia."[159]

Seton Children, Rev. Salvator Burgio, C.M., (c.1950).
(Top Left): William M. Seton; (Top Middle): Anna Maria Seton; (Top Right): Richard Bayley Seton
(Bottom Left): Catherine Charlton Seton; (Bottom Right): Rebecca Mary Seton.

[gg] Richard Seton was never a commissioned officer, but did serve with the Navy as civil servant in the role of captain's clerk on the U.S.S. *Cyane,* June 1822 to April 1823. This ship was on duty off the African coast, and it was in this way that Seton made his connection with the capital of Liberia. The director of the colony there, recommended that Richard Seton be appointed assistant agent at Cape Mesurado. He contracted a fatal fever from the U.S. minister, Jehudi Ashmun, whom he had nursed back to health and was buried at sea off the coast of Liberia.

[1] Account book of episcopal visits of Archbishop Ambrose Maréchal and Archbishop James Whitfield, 23 September 1818, UNDA. Maréchal told her, "Since my consecration I have received many hundred letters. Very few, perhaps none, have given me so much consolation as yours." AMSV, Letters, Ambrose Maréchal to Elizabeth Seton, 18 December 1818; Jean Cheverus to Ambrose Maréchal, 18 November 1817, ABA, AASMSU, 14-1-17; John M. Tessier's Journal, 14 December 1817, AASMSU.

[2] Ibid. Mother Seton wrote to Antonio Filicchi, 27 September 1818, "Your friend Mr. Whitefield [sic] has just been here with our blessed Archbishop whom he accompanies on his rounds." 7.181, Elizabeth Seton to Antonio Filicchi, CW, 2:580.

[3] Simon Bruté, 19 May 1821, ASJPH 1-3-3-12:13.

[4] 7.181, Elizabeth Seton to Antonio Filicchi, 27 September 1818, CW, 2:580.

[5] John Dubois to Antoine de Pouget Duclaux, Emmitsburg, n.d., AASMSU. Copies of Paris Archives. These copies of letters of John Dubois in the archives of the Society of St. Sulpice in Paris were made by the Archivist of Mount St. Mary's College, Hugh J. Phillips, from the originals while they were in Baltimore during the war of 1939-1945.

[6] ASJPH 7-2-1, 3. See also Rev. Daniel C. Nusbaum, "This Venerable House," Analecta Selected Studies in the History of Mount St. Mary's College and Seminary 1, #3(2003), ASJPH 25-4-6.

[7] John M. Tessier to John Dubois, 27 January 1816, ASMSU. Dubois, for his part, found that lay servants were most difficult to secure. Americans, he said, did not like to lower themselves; "they prefer to eat bread and water and even beg to putting themselves in service."

[8] John Dubois to Antoine Garnier, Emmitsburg, 14 April 1820, ASMSU. Copies of Paris Archives. Garnier became superior general of the Society of St. Sulpice after Antoine Duclaux.

[9] 7.9, Elizabeth Seton to Julia Sitgreaves Scott, 23 March 1816, CW, 2:378.

[10] Simon Bruté to Elizabeth Seton, Emmitsburg, n.d., ASJPH 7-3-1-2, #A14.

[11] Meditation, "The Dormitory," ASJPH 1-3-3-13:154.

[12] 7.16, Elizabeth Seton to William Seton, 9 April 1816, CW, 2:386.

[13] John Connolly to Elizabeth Seton, New York, 14 July 1817, ASJPH 1-3-3-4:61.

[14] 7.102, Elizabeth Seton to Robert Fox, 25 July 1817, CW, 2:493.

[15] 7.103, Elizabeth Seton to Simon Bruté, 1 August 1817, CW, 2:494.

[16] John Dubois to John Connolly, Mount St. Mary's Seminary, 24 July 1817, ASJPH 7-10-2, #6.

[17] *Missions—Establishments Founded Prior to Union with France*, 13 August 1817, ASJPH 11-0-1. Margaret George became sister-servant on 26 May 1819, and Rose White returned to Philadelphia. Mother Seton wrote to John Hickey, "Good Sister Margaret is gone to take care of the dear Orphans in New York to let Sister Rose return to Philadelphia in place of Sister Fanny [Jordan] who has been at death's door & perhaps so still." See 7.214, Elizabeth Seton to John Hickey, n.d., *CW*, 2:613.

[18] Robert Fox to Elizabeth Seton, New York, 7 September 1817, ASJPH 1-3-3-4:72.

[19] 7.112, Elizabeth Seton to Eliza Sadler, 24 August 1817, *CW*, 2:503.

[20] Missions 1809-1850, ASJPH 11-0-5. See Council Minutes, Sisters of Charity of St. Joseph's, 1813-1829, 4 September 1818, ASJPH 3-3-5:24, 23.

[21] Council Minutes, Sisters of Charity of St. Joseph's, 1813-1829, 26 January 1820, ASJPH 3-3-5:31.

[22] John Dubois to Cornelius Heeny, 20 October 1821, and 21 November 1821, ASJPH 7-10-2, #1; articles of agreement between Dubois and Heeny. The pay school was suppressed on 7 August 1825.

[23] Council Minutes, Sisters of Charity of St. Joseph's, 1813-1829, 13 May 1820, and 12 July 1820, ASJPH 3-3-5:59, 61. See Joseph Lancaster to Burwell Bassett, Baltimore, 29 February 1820, in *Letters on National Subjects* (Washington, 1820), 45-60.

[24] 7.259, Elizabeth Seton to Marie-Françoise Chatard, 24 August 1820, *CW*, 2:665. Mrs. Seton may have had in mind Baltimore and neighboring Conewago, Pennsylvania, where, as she told Antonio Filicchi, "they now prepare us an extensive establishment." See 7.265, Elizabeth Seton to Antonio Filicchi, 19 October 1820, *CW*, 2:670. The Sisters of Charity of St. Joseph's did not settle in Conewago, however, until 19 June 1834.

[25] Missions 1809–1850, 4 April 1822, ASJPH 11-0-1:10.

[26] The American Catholic History Research Center and University Archives. The Catholic University of America, copy of Report to Propaganda, Ambrose Maréchal to Cardinal Litta, Baltimore, 16 October 1818. Hereinafter cited as ACUA.

[27] John Dubois to Ambrose Maréchal, 10 June 1820, ABA, AASMSU, 15-U-21.

[28] 7.265, Elizabeth Seton to Antonio Filicchi, 19 October 1820, *CW*, 2:670.

[29] 7.156, Elizabeth Seton to Simon Bruté, 21 April 1818, *CW*, 2:549.

[30] 7.159, Elizabeth Seton to Julia Scott, 5 May 1818, *CW*, 2:552.

[31] Catherine Josephine Seton to Julia Scott, 12 July 1818, ASJPH 1-3-3-11: B54; Mary Bayley Post to Elizabeth Seton, New York, 4 August 1818, ASJPH 1-3-3-11:27.

[32] Pierre Babade to Elizabeth Seton, Baltimore, 12 July 1818, ASJPH 1-3-3-1:71. It is possible Babade got to Emmitsburg after all, for a letter to Dubois written by a Mount St. Mary's student in August sent regards to both Bruté and Babade. See Dionire to John Dubois, 27 August 1818, ASMSU.

[33] Jean Cheverus to Elizabeth Seton, Boston, 11 August 1818, AMSV.

[34] 10.1, "Death—3ʳᵈ Instruction," St. Mary Magdalen de Pazzi Notebook, *CW*, 3a:454.

[35] 7.170, Elizabeth Seton to Simon Bruté, n.d., *CW*, 2:566; 7.192, Elizabeth Seton to Antonio Filicchi, 11 November 1818, *CW*, 2:593.

[36] Simon Bruté to Elizabeth Seton, Emmitsburg, n.d., ASJPH 7-3-1-3, #B171.

[37] Simon Bruté to Elizabeth Seton, Emmitsburg, n.d., ASJPH 7-3-1-2, #B27.

[38] 7.187, Elizabeth Seton to Ellen Wiseman, n.d., *CW*, 2:586.

[39] 7.170, Elizabeth Seton to Simon Bruté, n.d., *CW*, 2:567.

[40] 7.283, Elizabeth Seton to Simon Bruté, n.d., *CW*, 2:683.

[41] 7.183, Elizabeth Seton to Julia Scott, 2 October, 25 October 1818, *CW*, 2:581; 7.186, Ibid., *CW*, 2:585. This last letter of 25 October is not published in Joseph Code's collection of *Letters of Mother Seton to Mrs. Juliana Scott.*

[42] 7.201, Elizabeth Seton to Juliana Sitgreaves Scott, 12 January 1819, *CW*, 2:599.

[43] Jean Cheverus to Ambrose Maréchal, Boston, 7 October 1818, AAB, AASMSU, 14-J-25; Mary Bayley Post to Elizabeth Seton, New York, 25 May 1818, ASJPH 1-3-3-11:26; Catherine Josephine Seton to Elizabeth Seton, Philadelphia, 6 March 1818, ASJPH 1-3-3-9:54; Mrs. Eliza Sadler to Elizabeth Seton, New York, 16 April 1818, ASJPH 1-3-3-11:B20. Cheverus said of Matignon, "He died as he lived, a saint." See 7.150, in a letter to William Seton, 24 March 1818, *CW*, 2:539. Mother Seton relays the news of William Bayley's death which she just received from Mary Post. Mary Bayley Post to Elizabeth Seton, New York, 12 February 1816, ASJPH 1-3-3-11:13.

[44] 7.219, Elizabeth Seton to Catherine Josephine Seton, [28 June1819], *CW*, 2:619.

[45] Bruté notation, n.d., ASJPH 1-3-3-20B. The journal was published by Isaac Kallock of Elizabeth, New Jersey, in 1817 under the title, *Memoirs of Mrs. S—.*Bruté stated, "I am sure it is Bishop Hobart

who printed the journal of Mother Seton. She had trusted it to him. He took a copy and he probably makes a private use of it for his devotees."

[46] Mary Bayley Post to Elizabeth Seton, New York, 5 April 1817, ASJPH 1-3-3-11:14. It is interesting to note that Hobart, who had become diocesan bishop and rector of Trinity Episcopal Church in 1816, had a renewed interest in Mrs. Seton in 1817. "In a late visit from your old friends Bishop and Mrs. Hobart, after many inquiries after you, I showed them your last letter to me. I felt the conviction that the sensible, candid, and amiable exposition of your feelings and motives in regard to religious impressions particularly must gratify every good heart—therefore, particularly one that I believed knew how to appreciate them. I was not mistaken. The high encomium he bestowed on you convinced me you have his former friendship with increased approbation, admiration I think more appropriate." When Hobart returned Mrs. Seton's letter to Mrs. Post, he wrote, "Dr. Hobart feels himself very much indebted to Mrs. Post for the opportunity of perusing a letter so interesting as a picture of the most amiable, frank, and affectionate heart of the writer...No person has seen the letter but Mrs. Hobart." Cf. About Dr. Hobart, 31 March 1817, ASJPH 1-3-3-11:B71. From the tone of these two letters of March and April 1817, it seems difficult to believe a book already in circulation in Baltimore in May 1817, could have been sponsored by the bishop. Melville believes, in the face of so little conclusive proof, that a reasonable doubt may be entertained regarding Bruté's conviction that Hobart was responsible for the *Memoirs of Mrs. S...*

[47] Catherine Josephine Seton to Elizabeth Seton, Baltimore, 26 May 1817, ASJPH 1-3-3-9:52.

[48] 7.130, Elizabeth Seton to Julia Scott, 19 January 1818, *CW*, 2:520.

[49] 10.3, Catherine Josephine Seton's Little Red Book, *CW*, 3a:489. This little book is in the archives of the Daughters of Charity at Emmitsburg. At her death the little volume became the property of her niece who in 1896 presented it to the Daughters of Charity at Emmitsburg. All of the advice in the ensuing paragraphs is taken from this book of "advices."

[50] Ibid., 490.

[51] Ibid.

[52] Ibid., 491.

[53] Ibid.

[54] Ibid., 492.

[55] Catherine Josephine Seton to Elizabeth Seton, Baltimore, 26 May 1817, ASJPH 1-3-3-9:52.

[56] 7.151, Elizabeth Seton to Julia Scott and Catherine Josephine Seton, 4 April 1818, *CW*, 2:543.

[57] Catherine Josephine Seton to Elizabeth Seton, Philadelphia, 24 February 1818, ASJPH 1-3-3-9:53.

[58] Ibid., 55.

[59] Ibid., 56.

[60] 7.160, Elizabeth Seton to Seton, 5 May 1818, *CW*, 2:553.

[61] Ibid. See Mary Bayley Post to Elizabeth Seton, New York, 25 May 1818, ASJPH 1-3-3-11:26. 7.100, Elizabeth Seton to William Seton, 24 July 1817, *CW*, 2:490. See Mary Bayley Post to Elizabeth Seton, New York, 25 May 1818, ASJPH 1-3-3-11:26. In 1818 Mary Post wrote that Mr. Bunch had seen in an English paper the death of a Mr. Savage dying without heirs. The title of Lord Rivers and a large income would probably revert to his majesty. Mr. Bunch considered himself a distant branch of the family and was going to England to try for the title. Mary Post concluded, "Should Mary become Lady Rivers and a resident of England I think she will be apt to change her democratic opinions." Mary Bayley Post to Elizabeth Seton, New York, 4 August 1818, ASJPH 1-3-3-11:27. Mary Bunch, her husband and his mother went to England in August 1818. On 17 November 1818, Helen Bayley Craig wrote, concerning the rumor of the Earldom of Rivers, "as we have heard nothing of it from Mary we conclude it one of those idle stories. . .His (Bunch's) letters to Brother are entirely those of a man of business. His last is full of a commercial establishment at Havana." Helen Bayley Craig to Elizabeth Seton, New York, 17 November 1818, ASJPH 1-3-3-11:B41. In March 1819, Mary Post wrote that it was expected that Mary Fitch Bayley Bunch would leave Liverpool in April to spend the summer in New York where "Mr. Bunch" would meet her. Mary Bayley Post to Elizabeth Seton, New York, 12 March 1819, ASJPH 1-3-3-11:24. Since none of the later references to the Bunches indicate that Bunch succeeded in substantiating his claim to the title and legacy, one wonders if Robert Seton was quite correct in referring to Bunch as "Sir Robert Henry." See Seton, "Record of the Bayley Family in America," UNDA. See also Appendix A. Bayley-Seton Genealogy.

[62] 7.166, Elizabeth Seton to William Seton, 7 June 1818, *CW*, 2:561-562.

[63] Catherine Josephine Seton to Julia Scott, Emmitsburg, 12 July 1818,

ASJPH 1-3-3-11:B54.

[64] John Dubois to Elizabeth Seton, Baltimore, 5 May 1818, ASJPH 1-3-3-5:29. Robert Harper had written to Mother Seton, 15 April 1818, announcing the death of his daughter. Robert Goodloe Harper to Elizabeth Seton, Baltimore, 15 April 1818, ASJPH 1-3-3-2:42.

[65] Robert Goodloe Harper to Elizabeth Seton, Baltimore, 5 May 1818, ASJPH 1-3-3-2:44.

[66] 7.173, Elizabeth Seton to William Seton, 21 July 1818, *CW*, 2:569.

[67] Catherine Josephine Seton to Elizabeth Seton, 12 May 1829, ASJPH 1-3-3-9:59; Ibid., n.d., ASJPH 1-3-3-9:60; Ibid., 10 July 1820, ASJPH 1-3-3-9:61; 7.261, Elizabeth Seton to Ellen Wiseman, 28 August 1820, *CW*, 2:667.

[68] Robert Goodloe Harper to John Dubois, Baltimore, 30 September 1820, ASJPH 1-3-3-2:43. Carroll Manor on the Monocacy River in Frederick County was the nucleus of St. Joseph's Parish, below Frederick, near Buckeystown. Old Charles Carroll, the Pattersons, Catons, Harpers, McTavishes, and many others contributed to the parish. The Manor was a favorite vacation spot for members of the Carroll family. For a full description of the Harper-Seton friendship, see 7.238, Elizabeth Seton to Julia Scott, *CW*, 2:641-2.

[69] Catherine Josephine Seton to Julia Scott, Emmitsburg, 15 January 1821, ASJPH 1-3-3-11:B59; Robert Goodloe Harper to John Dubois, Baltimore, 1 April 1821, ASMSU. Schley to John Dubois, 22 January 1821, ASMSU. Mrs. Seton once said, "My mother's own brother who loved me more than anything in the world made his will of an immense fortune and left me (the lawful heir) only $1000 I believe for I have never heard of it since." 6.180, Elizabeth Seton to Simon Bruté, *CW*, 2:293. After Catherine Josephine Seton's visit to New York in 1818, the hope of receiving the legacy from Dr. Charlton's widow, Mary de Peyster Charlton, seems to have revived, for Mrs. Seton wrote her son, "Kit says now if Aunt Charlton pays us our little fortune how gladly will I give up my share to Will." Arthur Burns' investigation of the Seton-Jevons collection shows that Dr. John Charlton's will actually provided that both Mary Bayley Post and Elizabeth Bayley Seton should receive $2,500 each. See Arthur Burns, "New Light on Mother Seton," *Historical Records and Studies,* XXII (1932), 86.

[70] 7.81, Elizabeth Seton to Antonio Filicchi, 1 April 1817, *CW*, 2:471. In a letter of 18 May 1817, William Seton referred to many previous letters voicing his dissatisfaction. See William Seton to Elizabeth Seton, Leghorn,

18 May 1817, ASJPH 26-0-2, (6). Copy. The original is in ASCSE.

[71] 7.82, Elizabeth Seton to William Seton, n.d., *CW*, 2:472.

[72] Ibid., 473.

[73] 7.105, Elizabeth Seton to William Seton, *CW*, 2:496. Mother Seton was still writing to William on 9 August 1817.

[74] Antonio Filicchi to Elizabeth Seton, Leghorn, 14 July 1817, ASJPH 1-3-3-10:47.

[75] Ibid., 46.

[76] Robert Fox to Elizabeth Seton, New York, 8 September 1817, ASJPH 1-3-3-4:72. See Ray W. Irwin, "Charles Stewart," *Dictionary of American Biography* (New York, 1936), XVIII, 7.

[77] William Seton to Elizabeth Seton, The Manor, 9 September 1817, ASJPH 26-0-2, (12). Copy. The original is in ASCSE.

[78] 7.117, Elizabeth Seton to Antonio Filicchi, 16 September 1817, *CW*, 2:508.

[79] 7.120, Elizabeth Seton to Robert Fox, 10 October 1817, *CW*, 2:511.

[80] 7.124, Elizabeth Seton to Robert Fox, 4 November 1817, and 28 October 1817, *CW*, 2:514; 7.118, Ibid., *CW*, 2:509. The University of Notre Dame Archives preserve a fragment of William Seton's acceptance of a midshipman's warrant from the Navy Department dated 4 November 1817. Mother Seton had written Julia Scott, 5 October 1817, "William was not twenty-four hours in your city where his good angel had delayed Captain Steward to the very moment, or he would have missed him." 7.119, Elizabeth Seton to Julia Scott, *CW*, 2:510.

[81] Julia Scott to Elizabeth Seton, Philadelphia, 20 January 1818, ASJPH 1-3-3-11:B31.

[82] 7.142, Elizabeth Seton to Ellen Wiseman, 20 February 1818, *CW*, 2:530.

[83] Simon Bruté to William Seton, Emmitsburg, 15 February 1818, ASJPH 7-3-1-3:A65.

[84] 7.137, Elizabeth Seton to William Seton, 6 February 1818, *CW*, 2:524.

[85] Elizabeth Seton to Robert Fox, 16 February 1818, AMSV; 7.138, Elizabeth Seton to Robert Fox, *CW*, 2:525. William and Catherine Josephine Seton left for Philadelphia 19 February 1818.

[86] 7.146, Elizabeth Seton to William Seton, 10 March 1818, *CW*, 2:535.

[87] William Seton to Elizabeth Seton, 27 February 1818, ASJPH 1-3-3-18:58.

[88] 7.144, Elizabeth Seton to William Seton, 25 February 1818, *CW*, 2:532.

[89] 7.150, Elizabeth Seton to William Seton, 24 March 1818, *CW*, 2:539.

[90] 7.160 Elizabeth Seton to Catherine Josephine Seton, Boston, 5 May 1818,

CW, 2:553.

[91] 7.153, Elizabeth Seton to William Seton, 6 April 1818, *CW*, 2:546.

[92] 7.168, Elizabeth Seton to William Seton, 15 June 1818, *CW*, 2:564; 7.148, Elizabeth Seton to Ellen Wiseman, [22 March 1818], *CW*, 2:537.

[93] 7.163, Elizabeth Seton to William Seton, 10 May 1818, *CW*, 2:557. She said, "You know I cannot write him (Cheverus) myself about it without letting out the accident which might pain you." See 7.164, Elizabeth Seton to William Seton, Ibid., 558.

[94] William Seton to Elizabeth Seton, 3 June 1818, ASJPH 26-0-1, (2). Copy. The original is in AMSJ.

[95] 7.168, Elizabeth Seton to William Seton, 15 June 1818, *CW*, 2:563.

[96] 7.173, Elizabeth Seton to William Seton, 21 July 1818, *CW*, 2:569. In fairness to young Seton it must be added that he wrote to his mother in June, but the letter was delayed. The letter would scarcely have consoled her on the point of religious practice, however, devoted as it was to financial matters and Seton's anxiety to transfer to the *Macedonian. See* William Seton to Elizabeth Seton, Boston, 19 June 1818, ASJPH 1-3-3-18:57. Bishop Cheverus had written Simon Bruté in April, "William Seton is in good health but has very rarely the liberty to come on land, and his duties prevented him from assisting at our solemnities which have been consoling and were beautiful." See Jean Cheverus to Simon Bruté, Boston, 9 April 1818, UNDA.

[97] Ibid.

[98] Jean Cheverus to William or Elizabeth Seton, 11 August 1818, AMSV115Bx1 #17.

[99] 7.174, Elizabeth Seton to William Seton, 1 August 1818, *CW*, 2:571. See Jean Cheverus to Seton, 11 August 1818, AMSV.

[100] William Seton to Elizabeth Seton, Boston, 29 August 1818, ASJPH 1-3-3-18:59.

[101] William Seton to Elizabeth Seton, U.S. Ship *Macedonian*, Boston, 18 September 1818, Robert Seton, *Memoir, Letters and Journal of Elizabeth Seton,* 2 vols. (New York: 1869), 278. The original of this document is no longer available.

[102] 7.188, Elizabeth Seton to Ellen Wiseman, [October 1818], *CW*, 2:587.

[103] Catherine Josephine Seton to William Seton, 20 October 1818, ASJPH 26-0-1, (20). Copy. The original is in AMSV. See 7.185, Elizabeth Seton and Catherine Josephine Seton to William Seton, 21 October 1818, *CW*, 2:583. William Seton made this last visit to his mother just prior to this date.

[104] 7.185, Elizabeth Seton to William Seton, 21 October 1818, *CW*, 2:584.

[105] A-7.179, Elizabeth Seton to William Seton, 8 September 1818, *CW*, 2:761.

[106] 7.186, Elizabeth Seton to Julia Scott, 25 October 1818, *CW*, 2:586.

[107] 7.226, Elizabeth Seton to William Seton, 7 November 1819, *CW*, 2:627.

[108] Simon Brute's notebook on character, Richard Seton, ASMSU.

[109] Ledger 1813-1816, Richard Seton, ASMSU.

[110] Richard Seton to John Hickey, 12 September 1816, AASMSU.

[111] Richard Seton to John Hickey, 11 June 1817, AASMSU.

[112] 6.199, Elizabeth Seton to William Seton, 4 August 1815, 18 March 1816, *CW*, 2:337; 7.8, Elizabeth Seton to Seton, *CW*, 2:375.

[113] Mary Bayley Post to Elizabeth Seton, New York, 7 March 1815, ASJPH 1-3-3-11:19. Mrs. Post had been thinking of William Seton when she made the suggestion.

[114] 7.37, Elizabeth Seton to William Seton, 2 July 1816, *CW*, 2:409.

[115] 7.11, Elizabeth Seton to William Seton, 3 April 1816, *CW*, 2:382.

[116] 7.8, Elizabeth Seton to William Seton, 18 March 1816, *CW*, 2:375.

[117] 7.9, Elizabeth Seton to Julia Scott, 23 March 1816, *CW*, 2:379.

[118] Sister Mary Anthonita Hess, C.Pp.S.*, American Tobacco and Central European Policy: Early Nineteenth Century* (Washington, 1948), 59, 92.

[119] Hamilton Owens, *Baltimore on the Chesapeake* (Garden City, 1941), 203-205.

[120] Richard Seton to William Seton, 9 May 1816, UNDA.

[121] 7.11, Elizabeth Seton to William Seton, 3 April 1816, *CW*, 2:381.

[122] 7.20, Elizabeth Seton to William Seton, 25 April 1816, *CW*, 2:392.

[123] Catherine Josephine Seton to Julia Scott, 14 September 1816, ASJPH 1-3-3-11:B51. See 7.36 Elizabeth Seton to Catherine Dupleix, [July 1816], *CW,* 2:407; 7.54, Elizabeth Seton to William Seton, Ibid, 439.

[124] 7.23, Elizabeth Seton to Marie-Françoise Chatard, n.d., *CW*, 2:395.

[125] 7.37, Elizabeth Seton to William Seton, 2 July 1816, *CW*, 2:410.

[126] Catherine Josephine to Elizabeth Seton, 16 July 1816, ASJPH 1-3-3-9:50.

[127] Catherine Josephine Seton to Julia Scott, 14 September 1816, ASJPH 1-3-3-11:B51.

[128] 7.48, Elizabeth Seton to William Seton, 4 September 1816, *CW*, 2:423.

[129] Richard Bayley Seton to Elizabeth Seton, Baltimore, 9 June 1816, ASJPH 26-0-2, (13). Copy. The original is in AMSV.

[130] Richard Seton to Elizabeth Seton, Baltimore, 14 June 1816, ASJPH 1-3-3-18:51.

[131] Catherine Josephine Seton to Elizabeth Seton, Baltimore, 16 July 1816, ASJPH 1-3-3-9:50.

[132] William Seton to Elizabeth Seton, Baltimore, 3 September 1816, ASJPH 26-0-1, (2). Copy. The original is in AMSJ.

[133] Richard Bayley Seton to Elizabeth Seton, Baltimore, 12 October, and 13 December 1816, ASJPH 26-0-2, (12). Copy. The original in ASCSE.

[134] Ibid., 12 October 1816.

[135] 7.69, Elizabeth Seton to William Seton, n.d., *CW*, 2:459.

[136] 7.78, Elizabeth Seton to Antonio Filicchi, 24 February 1817, *CW*, 2:468.

[137] 7.84, Elizabeth Seton to Julia Scott, 10 April 1817, *CW*, 2:476.

[138] 7.85, Elizabeth Seton to William Seton, 25 April 1817, *CW*, 2:477.

[139] Richard Seton to John Hickey, Baltimore, 11 June 1817, ASMSU.

[140] Richard Seton to John Dubois, Baltimore, 20 June 1817, ASMSU.

[141] 7.100, Elizabeth Seton to William Seton, 24 July 1817, *CW*, 2:490. Richard wrote to his mother, Elizabeth Seton, "I have no contract or bargain but I leave it all to you and dear Mr. Dubois. If you two like it, Amen." See Richard Bayley Seton to Elizabeth Seton, 19 June 1817, ASJPH 26-0-2, (12). There is no evidence as to what answer either Mother Seton or John Dubois made, but the offer was not accepted. Copy. The original is in ASCSE.

[142] 7.105, Elizabeth Seton to William Seton, 9 August 1817, *CW*, 2:496.

[143] 7.101, Elizabeth Seton to Julia Scott, 24 July 1817, *CW*, 2:491.

[144] 7.118, Elizabeth Seton to Robert Fox, 28 September 1817, *CW*, 2:509; William Seton to Elizabeth Seton, Baltimore, 19 September 1817, ASJPH 1-3-3-18:52.

[145] 7.119, Elizabeth Seton to Julia Scott, 5 October 1817, *CW*, 2:510.

[146] 7.117, Elizabeth Seton to Antonio Filicchi, 16 September 1817, *CW*, 2:507.

[147] Antonio Filicchi to Elizabeth Seton, Leghorn, 5 January 1818, ASJPH 26-0-2, (10). Copy. Original is in AMSJ.

[148] 7.250 Elizabeth Seton to Ellen Wiseman, [29 June 1820], *CW*, 2:657.

[149] Richard Bayley Seton to Elizabeth Seton, Leghorn, 27 January, 30 April, 1 May, 10 June, 1 July; ASJPH 26-0-2, (6). Copy; original in ASCSH; 21 August 1818, ASJPH 26-0-1, (2). Copy; original in AMSJ.

[150] 7.228, Elizabeth Seton to Marie-Françoise Chatard, 11 November 1819, *CW*, 2:629.

[151] 7.246, Elizabeth Seton to Richard Seton, 8 May 1820, *CW*, 2:650.

[152] 7.250, Elizabeth Seton to Ellen Wiseman, n.d., *CW*, 2:657. Internal evidence indicates this letter was written on 1 May 1820.

[153] Antonio Filicchi to Elizabeth Seton, Leghorn, 8 August 1820, ASJPH 26-0-2, (10). Copy. Original is in AMSJ.

[154] Ibid.

[155] 7.265, Elizabeth Seton to Antonio Filicchi, 19 October 1820, *CW*, 2:670.

[156] 7.263, Elizabeth Seton to Robert Goodloe Harper, 15 October 1820, *CW*, 2:668.

[157] Richard Bayley Seton to Robert Goodloe Harper, Alexandria, VA, 23 November 1820, ASJPH 26-0-2, (7). Copy. The original is in AAB, AASMSU.

[158] Cecilia O'Conway to Simon Bruté, account of Mother Seton's last days, ASJPH 1-3-3-12:6. See A-7.268, Account by Rev. Simon Bruté of Mother Seton's Last Days, *CW*, 2:764-70.

[159] For an inquiry into the public careers of both Richard Seton and William Seton, see *Mother Seton Guild Bulletin,* IV (September 1942), 1-2. A copy of Richard's obituary is found in Seton, *Memoir and Letters,* II, 304.

৵৹৶

CHAPTER 14

ৡৢৢ৵

ETERNITY

Mother Seton wrote to Ellen Wiseman in August 1818, "why [be] uneasy at the fulfillment of the merciful designs of so dear a Providence who left me to take care of my Bec, to bring Jos to an age to take care of herself, and our dearest Boys to enter the way of life they were to choose... St. Joseph's House [is] well established [and] wants not even my Nominal care—what would you have, darling, why be anxious if your poor tired

The Mortuary Chapel and Saint Joseph's Cemetery, original graveyard of the Sisters of Charity, Emmitsburg.

friend goes to rest."[1] Her words were reminiscent of Mary Post's letter the year before in which Mary had remarked to her sister, "I still think you are blessed beyond the usual lot of mortals. I believe in a presiding providence, and that you have always been in its peculiar care is to me most certain."[2] But if either woman expected Elizabeth Seton's last days to be serene and free from care, events were to belie their hopes. The recurring problems posed by her children, during 1817 and after, were only part of a host of events which enlisted the attention of Elizabeth Seton, aroused her sympathies, or required her energy.

One of the crises of 1818 involved not St. Joseph's house, but their friends on the Mountain, Mount St. Mary's Seminary and College. The Society of Saint Sulpice had for some time been dissatisfied with affairs at the Mountain seminary. This dissatisfaction arose from a variety of sources, including the admission of Protestant boys, the nature of the seminary (that is, whether it was to be merely a preparatory seminary, or whether it should compete with the Baltimore major seminary), the shortage of Sulpician priests capable of maintaining such work, and, very important, the financial difficulties of Dubois' establishment.[3] Early in 1818 John Dubois wrote a masterly defense of his institution to Archbishop Maréchal, hoping to prevent drastic action against the Emmitsburg establishment.[4] But this letter did nothing to deter the Sulpicians in Baltimore from continuing their consideration of suppressing Mount Saint Mary's. Rev. John M. Tessier wrote to Rev. John F. Hickey 1 April 1818 in a letter marked "Private," instructing him to "take a very attentive view of current expenses." The Sulpician superior in Baltimore had found Dubois very touchy on the subject, he said, and he preferred Hickey's unprejudiced views. Tessier stated pointedly:

> The Sisters are more fortunate on their spot. I hear that they are going to build a large addition to their house and that they have the funds ready for the purpose. Whence comes it that they have been able to pay their debts and raise such a sum for building, whilst you with the same means in the Seminary, you have rather increased your debt?[5]

Although Tessier had an exaggerated confidence in the prosperity of the Sisters of Charity of St. Joseph's in 1818, his letter indicated that the financial burden at Mount St. Mary's was a considerable factor in Baltimore's eventual decision. Both Bruté and Dubois, loving the Mountain school as they did, found the prospect of suppression unbearable, and Tessier told Hickey in May:

> Mr. Bruté has been here half a day and gave us to understand that in case we would pronounce against the continuation of your college, he and Mr. Dubois might resolve to go on in opposition to the will of the majority. This disposition is in direct contradiction with the spirit of the Society [of St. Sulpice].[6]

Archbishop Maréchal had been present at the meeting on 22 May in Baltimore when the Sulpicians had discussed the issues involved.[7] He was not wholeheartedly in favor of radical action at that time, and when Dubois later learned of the Society's decision to discontinue Mount St. Mary's he wrote to Maréchal bitterly:

> If it is true...that you have given your sanction to the precipitous decision made without the least examination by our gentlemen [the Sulpicians] of Baltimore to destroy this establishment here—over which these gentlemen have only a right of limited surveillance, it seems useless to call on you to suspend the proceedings.[8]

When Dubourg heard the strange accounts about "our dear foster-child of the mountain," he wrote sympathetically to Bruté, "I partake in all your feelings on the occasion. I still hope that Divine mercy will direct everything for his greater glory."[9]

Tessier meanwhile had sent his ultimatum and John Hickey was recalled to Baltimore, as Dubois put it, "without time to put his affairs in order."[10] At this juncture the people of Emmitsburg became interested, and Mother Seton told her son, William:

> A most interesting scene took place here last week,[a] the Sulpicians of Baltimore (except poor Mr. [Simon] Bruté) solicited Mr. Dubois' suppression of the Seminary, thinking he was rather getting in debt, and that the Masters he employed would be more useful in Baltimore and lo our good Emmitsburgers came forward [and] offered Mr. Dubois 8 or 10,000 [dollars] in hand and to buy the Seminary for him if he chose, if only he would not leave them—the Archbishop [Maréchal] seeing how hard it would go, has directed all to be left as it was before—so much for the good "country peeps" as Mr. [Charles] Duhamel called them.[11]

Mother Seton was not quite accurate, however, in saying all was to be left as it was before. Mount Saint Mary's, it is true, continued as a Sulpician seminary, and Dubois and Bruté remained: but the title of the property passed from Tessier to Dubois, and "the Mountain became dependent on Paris alone."[12] In July Dubois requested that in fairness to his institution an advertisement should be put in the papers, signed J.D. and S.B., and announcing that the Mount St. Mary's school would not be suppressed.[13] September found him informing Tessier that a bond of conveyance would be shorter than a deed in detail, and would suffice for a transfer of the property.[14] The archbishop visited Emmitsburg on 21-26 September and gave official approval to the new arrangement since Dubois had passed the property to his Sulpician confrere, Bruté.[15] On 3 November 1819, John Tessier noted in his journal:

> I sent to Father Dubois the act of transfer of the property at Emmitsburg which I transferred to him with the consent of my confreres, that he might possess it, as I did, in the name of the Society of Saint Sulpice.[16]

The confusion which the controversy over the Mountain illustrated was another evidence of the difficulties the Church faced as it adjusted to the American environment. Just as in the case of the adoption of the rules of St. Vincent by the sisters earlier, the exact delimitations of authority were not easily achieved. John Dubois said to Antoine Garnier with perspicacity:

---

[a] John Dubois reported this incident to Paris explaining that some neighbors offered an interest-free loan.

It must appear evident to you that Saint Sulpice has not yet any government in America, that, indeed, we need a constitution adopted to our local situation and to our distance from the central government; that we need leaders who by their talent for government, their inspiration and experience, their great virtues, can be the trustees of the authority of our Superior General, the faithful interpreters of his will, who can govern without a constitution, and what is more, without a council; for as a matter of fact, we haven't any and we won't be able to have any for a long time.[17]

Dubois on his mountain, like Mother Seton in the valley, was coping not only with a geographic frontier, but also with the subtleties of organization which adaptation to that frontier called into question and the impact of the ripple-effect of European politics on this side of the Atlantic.

The arrangement which separated the seminary in Baltimore from the one in Emmitsburg left a small legacy of rivalry between the two schools. One loyal "Mountain man" who later attended the seminary in Baltimore wrote to Dubois:

They call the Mount the little seminary. No doubt they allude to the house for we are now but 8 seminarians, all studying divinity and I expect in a short time we will be but seven so that the large sanctuary here is to look at, and this is the *big seminary* with only 8 *students* and yours is the *little one* with 20. However, I hope one day things will get their true names.[18]

For the most part, however, the crisis passed without serious consequences. Archbishop Maréchal continued to allow seminarians to assist with teaching at Mount Saint Mary's.[19] After Samuel Cooper was ordained he was sent to Emmitsburg to assist Dubois and Simon Bruté in their varied labors.[b] Following Cooper's departure in 1819, Maréchal considered sending a French priest[c] to relieve some of Dubois' burden,[20] but when Hickey, who had been quite ill, recovered and showed a strong desire to return to Dubois, he was permitted to do so.[21]

Mother Seton and her daughters were greatly relieved to have matters settled in this way. Elizabeth Seton had said when she planned to go to Emmitsburg that the protection of the Sulpicians was a great factor

---

[b] Samuel Sutherland Cooper arrived 20 August 1818.

[c] John B. Randanne served briefly as pastor of the Emmitsburg congregation in 1818, but his effectiveness was impeded by his lack of proficiency in English.

in her decision to locate there.[22] The possibility of a complete suppression of Mount St. Mary's in 1818 offered many causes for apprehension to the women in the valley. The presence of a superior in the immediate vicinity had been desirable in the early years of the sisterhood, and custom had increased this desire during subsequent years. Dubois and Bruté, in their own right, had proved invaluable friends to the community; their loss in 1818 would have "pressed hard." The mountain school had provided a haven for sons of widows wishing to live at St. Joseph's. The accounts at Mount Saint Mary's[d] also included St. Joseph's business in many cases.[23] Much of the manual work of St. Joseph's farm was directed from the Mountain. Building projects were the province of the men as well. It was Dubois who made the contracts, met the obligations, and handled other negotiations. The removal of the Sulpician establishment from Emmitsburg at this time would have appeared calamitous to the Sisters of Charity of St. Joseph's. The women rejoiced that their friends on the Mountain remained. Indeed, affairs at Mount St. Mary's seemed to prosper by the change,[e] for Mother Seton wrote to Richard in 1820:

> Mr. Dubois, like a prince on his Mountain. Full school, debts paid, improvements in all directions, Egan, Mullen, Jamison, Wiseman still there. They are cutting the mountain in terraces to bring the garden up to Mr. Duhamel's house.[24]

The continued existence of Mount St. Mary's indirectly led to the re-entry of Samuel S. Cooper into Mother Seton's concerns. Although Mr.

---

[d] The account books at Mount St. Mary's University include pages listed "St. Joseph's Sisterhood." It is impossible to determine to what extent the transfer of property from John M. Tessier to John Dubois involved St. Joseph's but Mother Seton's letter to the Sulpician Louis-Regis Deluol of 30 December 1819, implies some community of interest. Referring to John Dubois' direction that she write to Deluol she said, "I offered him indeed to obtain any compensation to the house of St. Joseph he might think proper rather than call back the affairs of former times, but he has no intention as I understand but to drop all in peace... With respect to what is further necessary than the notes already given, he will arrange all, he says, to the satisfaction of Mr. [John] Tessier." (2.32, *CW*, 2:633) Louis-Regis Deluol was the business manager of Baltimore's Society of Saint Sulpice. Deluol later became successively superior of the Sisters of Charity of St. Joseph's and the Sulpicians in the United States. In these roles he negotiated the union of the Sisters of Charity at Emmitsburg with the Daughters of Charity of Paris under the superior general of the Congregation of the Mission and the Daughters of Charity. Mother Seton also had an account with St. Mary's College in Baltimore from 18 June 1808, to 1 November 1819. This account shows a deposit of $1028.50 in June 1808, and $400.00 in July 1809, and deductions for chairs, rent for Paca Street house, wood, bread, etc. Some of the items, however, go beyond the period of her Baltimore residence and deal with boarders at St. Joseph's. All together, Mrs. Seton had entrusted to Louis W. Dubourg's management a total of $2350, according to Deluol's "remarks on Mrs. Seton's expenses." This sum included money from the Filicchis, Mrs. Julia Scott, Wright Post, and boarders at Paca Street. It was the residue of this money, perhaps, that Mother Seton intended in her phrase about compensation proper to the House of St. Joseph.

[e] Melville believed that a revised history of Mount St. Mary's University seemed warranted, as well as a definitive biography of John Dubois. [The biography by Shaw had not yet been written. See ch.12, footnote g.] It has always been assumed that John Dubois was a poor business man, but there seems to be sufficient doubt appearing to justify a re-examination of the facts.

Cooper had entered the seminary the year Mrs. Seton arrived in Baltimore, he was not ordained until the summer of 1818, a decade later. During the interval, he had suffered from poor health, had traveled in Europe and had returned; but his path crossed that of his friend's at several points. In 1810 he had supplied the community during their economic hardships with dried fruits and cloth, and Elizabeth told Julia Scott, "He will never let us want what he can give—We never see him—or even thank him for his pure Benevolence. Many strange beings are in this world."[25] Cooper was a strange being in many ways, but his generosity to St. Joseph's was never in question. Although he very soon became tired of the three-way ownership of the property, and would have preferred to vest it in Mother Seton alone,[26] he co-operated quite willingly in the plan for incorporation proposed in 1816 and went on foot to Emmitsburg that November to discuss it with Dubois.[27] He wrote to Mother Seton on 23 January 1817 when the legislature had finally passed the act, that it had long been his wish. "The property of St. Joseph's can now be held in your own names," he said simply "and I will make the conveyance[f] when everything is prepared."[28]

> Early that summer Samuel Cooper prepared to sail for Europe. His plans for leaving coincided with those of John Grassi, the Jesuit,[29] and Mother Seton prepared letters for the Filicchis and William Seton to be carried by either Cooper or Grassi.[30] Cooper returned from Rome in 1818 but Grassi was compelled to stay on because of Jesuit affairs relating to England.[31] In August of that year, Cooper was ordained to the priesthood by Archbishop Maréchal and on 18 August 1818 Father Moranvillé wrote to Emmitsburg, "I heard that the Revd. Mr. Cooper who was ordained priest last Saturday will take the pastoral charge of Emmitsburg. If this be the case, our good friends will have one great care off their hands." He added: I have some time ago asked that little place for myself, but the archbishop would not hear of it."[32]
> On 30 August, Samuel Cooper arrived to assume the pastoral duties of the village congregation in Emmitsburg, and went to live at the home of Thomas Radford, a parishioner.

The newly-ordained priest attacked his new duties with energy and fervor. Bruté described Cooper's first sermon in Emmitsburg for John Hickey with the words:

---

[f] The conveyance was made 11 June 1819.

I wish I could have sent you the beautiful picture Mr. Cooper has drawn of the pulpit. He speaks indeed extremely well, such forcible, dignified simplicity, good sense, piety and elegance and delivered with the imposing countenance the good man has.[33]

His enthusiasm drew larger numbers to the little church and the Easter confessions and communions[g] in 1819 jumped from the 190 of Duhamel and Hickey to 225.[34] Elizabeth Seton, who was always roused by a zealous priest, found Cooper's example very edifying, and she commented to Father Bruté:

I glance a fearful look at you and Mr. [Samuel] Cooper and say secretly if I was one or the other, then adore and think I know nothing about it, only it seems to me that those who have light and grace already might be trusted to keep it and I would not stop night or day till I reached the dry and dark wilderness where neither can be found where such horrid crimes go on for want of them and where there is such a glorious death to be gained by carrying them. Oh, G., if I was light and life as you are I would shout like a madman alone to my God and roar and groan and sigh and be silent all together till I had baptized a 1000 and snatched these poor Victims from Hell—

—and pray Madame Bête, say you, why does not your zeal make its flame through your own little Hemisphere? True, but rules, prudence, subjections, opinions etc., dreadful walls to a burning SOUL wild as mine and somebody's—for me I am like a fiery horse I had when a girl, whom they tried to break by making him drag a heavy cart, and the poor beast was so humbled that he could never more be inspired by whips or caresses, and wasted to a skeleton till he died ...but you and Mr. Cooper might waste to skeletons to some purpose, and after wasting be sent still living to the glories of the Kingdom.

In the meantime that Kingdom come. Every day I ask my bête soul what I do for it in my little part assigned, and can see nothing but to smile, caress, be patient, write, pray and WAIT before Him—[35]

---

[g] Charles Duhamel had 190 in 1817; John F. Hickey, 191 in 1818; Samuel Cooper, 225 in 1819.

The reports of Cooper's good work reached Baltimore, and Archbishop Maréchal wrote approvingly:

> I heard the other day with great pleasure that you are going very well indeed in your congregation. God be praised for it!! But be careful of your health. People express a fear that you lead a too mortified life.[36]

Samuel Cooper, as his superior suspected, was prone to overdo things, and only too soon his zeal went beyond the confines of prudence. The Emmitsburg community in the early nineteenth century was, like most towns of the day, liberally supplied with alcoholic beverages. Brute's description of the town says:

> The town numbers about seven hundred inhabitants. There are four principal taverns and perhaps seven or eight tippling-shops under the sign: "Liquors and fruits." But besides these, the principal groceries and dry goods stores, of which there are six, quite considerable, sell drams and whiskey to anyone coming, particularly to their *customers*.[37]

It was quite natural that drunkenness was to be encountered in the village congregation. Father Cooper wished to take severe measures to cope with the problem, and he finally resolved upon public penance as the best solution. Writing to the archbishop on 15 March 1819, Father Cooper decried the scandal drunkenness created, "the mischief it produces among the Protestants is bringing disgrace on the Catholic Church." He said:

> Now, reflecting on the means the most probable to affect a change, it appears to me that if all those who give public scandal were obliged to kneel or stand, or sit in some particular place in the Church, and that their names should be mentioned from the pulpit, it would soon produce a most salutary effect.
>
> As I did not wish to act upon this principle from my own private authority, it occurred to me that I should write to your Reverence for permission, in case it should not meet with your approbation.[38]

When Maréchal was first faced with the matter he wrote moderately of the difficulties involved.

> If public penance be exacted, the law must embrace not one congregation only, but all those which exist in the diocese...

and if drunkards be subjected to it, why should it not be required from sinners addicted to any other vices equally scandalous? Not being sufficiently acquainted with the mind of the Christian people of Emmitsburg, I beg you to confer upon the subject with Rev. Mr. Dubois.[39]

When John Dubois spoke of the matter to Maréchal he said that Cooper's desire to make public examples of four or five people[h] seemed unwise.[40] To Cooper himself, Dubois said he feared the resistance to public penance would make Cooper's plan dangerous.[41] Cooper, however, not having been positively forbidden to use public penance, went ahead. On Palm Sunday he announced from the pulpit that public injury required a public satisfaction. Reporting his action to Maréchal, Cooper described the scene:

> The Church was full, and the impression this communication produced was truly affecting. The young and old, men and women were in tears. One man only got up and went out of the Church and the Congregation showed strong marks of indignation at his conduct, so as to leave the pleasing conviction on my mind that his holy regulation for public penance meets with the unqualified approbation of the people. My joy and satisfaction has been increased since, in observing with what avidity, zeal and sincerity they approach the holy confessional. It looks a little like the primitive times.[42]

He excluded the one recalcitrant offender, Radford, from the village church, and asked Dubois to refuse him entrance at the Mountain and St. Joseph's.[43] The storm of protest which followed belied Cooper's sanguine predictions and caused the archbishop to forbid public penance. The pastor then found himself in a difficult position. Samuel Cooper was never a calm, judicious man, and this predicament was one he found hard to bear. After several trips to Baltimore, he concluded that he could not remain in Emmitsburg with his discipline thus repudiated.

John Dubois, Simon Bruté, and Mother Seton each hated to see Cooper go. Dubois wrote Maréchal that it was with pain he witnessed "Mr. Cooper's resolution to withdraw from this congregation." He suggested that, perhaps, public penance might be given a fair trial. Public scandals

---

[h] One of the chief offenders seems to have been Thomas Radford, a cobbler and the man at whose house Samuel Cooper first lived. Samuel Cooper later removed to a Mr. Govern's house. Radford, along with Robert Moore, later witnessed Elizabeth's last will and testament. See A-7.269, *CW,* 2:771.

were prevalent. Perhaps public penance was the solution after all.[44] Bruté told Mother Seton:

> I think calumny the most easy thing to bear with and think I would not get angry at it—nor sad—as I do unwillingly at *defeated good—Mr.* Cooper goes—past interfering! Nay, after seeing him I too *dropped* all interference. Maybe Providence and better!—excellent man— let him go. What a soul of fire— but what evidence *more* of the beautiful St. Paul's "sober in good."...Alas, alas, alas, Mother, my Mother, is not good impeded, embarrassed, prostrated worse than Calumny![45]

On 15 June 1819, Cooper left Emmitsburg and returned to Baltimore. Not long afterward he went to Augusta, Georgia. It was there he received the news of Mother Seton's death in 1821.[46] Bruté and Dubois[i] were once more faced with the Emmitsburg congregation and the unruly Mr. Radford.[47] Mother Seton was saddened by the loss of her friend, and particularly, by what seemed like a defeat for the forces of good. Her own zeal redoubled and she tried more earnestly to overcome by prayer the obstacles to grace which persisted around her.

The blindness of the good non-Catholics, particularly, made a "deep, sad impression" on her soul. She exclaimed on one occasion:

> Our God—they think they know him and love him, but have not the least glimpse of what Spirit He is of or their direct contradiction to it—Oh, the deep, sad impression to my soul—but we must pray this lady declares the Catholic faith is the true faith—but I see plainly she has obstacles to grace which our God alone can remove—Oh, then, to pray, pray is all I see. She kept my heart so well under the press showing all her oppositions to the reign of our Jesus (herself obstinately bent to support them) that I spent truly a day of tears and interior cry to him, to see how they bind His blessed hands, pervert His Word, and yet hold up the head in boast that they are true Christians—let my heart then bleed with yours.[48]

Again, when the uncertainty of another young woman caused her pain, she cried to Bruté, "Oh then pity and pray for such poor blind ones incessantly—can you lift the blessed chalice without thinking of them? I would say nothing to him but Thy Kingdom come all life long—Our God—

---

[i] Radford visited Dubois and gave an energetic account of what Maréchal had told him after the Archbishop discussed the matter with Cooper.

our all—and we enjoying his fullness with what dreadful account if not improved."[49]

Many became interested in Roman Catholicism as a result of their acquaintance with Mother Seton and the Sisters of Charity. Some converts were among the girls who came to St. Joseph's to be educated.[50] Others were among women whom she met through benefactors and friends of the school, or through visits to homes in the neighborhood.[51] The ones Elizabeth would have been happiest to see in Church, Julia, Sad, Mary Post, however, never came in. She accepted their attitudes but continued to pray. As she said to Julia the last time she brought up the subject of religion, "Well, dearest one, I carry you constantly in my heart before Him who loved us, and so much more than any friend can love friend—may He bless you, strengthen you, and make you truly pleasing to him, own dear friend of my heart."[52] The closer she got to death, the more it seemed to Mother Seton that the best she could do was pray. She explained to Father Bruté, "For at last, how much more good can we do by staying within with God, than by most zealous speculations. Plenty of people in this world to mind planning and opinions, but how few to build in God and be silent, like our JESUS."[53] As she contemplated the unity she so fervently implored, she conceived it as a chain, and elaborated:

> Link by link the blessed chain:
>
> One Body in Christ—He the head we the members
>
> One Spirit diffused thro' the Holy Ghost in us all
>
> One Hope—Him in heaven and eternity
>
> One Faith—by his Word and his Church
>
> One Baptism and participation of His sacraments
>
> One God, our dear Lord
>
> One Father, We His children—He above all, through all and *in all.*
>
> Who can resist, all self must be killed and destroyed by this artillery of love one one one one. Who could escape this bond of unity peace and love? O my soul be fastened link by link, strong as *death, iron,* and Hell as says the sacred Word.[54]

The longer she thought about the consolations of her faith, the more grateful she became. Catherine Josephine Seton said of her mother, after Elizabeth's death,

My mother was asked upon her dying bed by Revd. Bishop Dubois or Bruté[j] what she considered the greatest blessing bestowed upon her by God during her life—she replied "that of being brought into the Catholic Church."[55]

It was with inexpressible gratitude that Mother Seton wrote:

O, Our Lord Jesus how great is the merit of that Blood which abundantly redeems the whole world—and would redeem a million more—and would redeem the DEMONS themselves if they were capable of penitence and salvation as I am—Yes, Lord, though your thunder should crush me, and a deluge overwhelm me, I will yet hope while you destroy my Body you will save my Soul.[56]

While Mother Seton was increasing her zeal for souls, numberless minor concerns ebbed and flowed around her. Father Bruté, her friends in Baltimore and New York, her children, all clamored for her attention. When Simon Bruté returned to Emmitsburg in 1818, John Dubois had given him the care of "the college and young men and the congregation with Mr. Hickey, keeping to himself Emmitsburg, the Sisters and the general administration."[57] Bruté chafed at the arrangement and voiced his impatience to Mother Seton, whose reply, though sympathetic, contained a note of reproof. She said:

I see a quiet moderate experienced man put in the center of a Congregation who is not "SAVED" for want of an active zealous driving man, because they must have "fire" cried in their ears—and I see a zealous driving man without experience, put in a Seminary where he will "SAVE" none because he cannot wait to gain a heart, or unfold a temper... His zeal instead of bedewing the plant in the thirsty ground crushes it under foot—alas, well if he does not root it out forever.[58]

Bruté talked restlessly that spring of leaving America to do missionary work abroad. Cheverus wrote disapprovingly. "I cannot help desiring your stay among us,"[59] and Elizabeth Seton exclaimed:

Again your restless thoughts strike me to the Soul—you made the lesson of *"the grace of the moment"* so very plain to me, I owe you perhaps my very salvation by the faults and sins it has saved me from, yet physician you will not heal yourself—you surely would not leave your brother [John

---

[j] [John Dubois was third bishop of New York in 1826–1842. Simon Bruté was the first bishop of Vincennes, Indiana, 1834–1839. Ed.]

Dubois] now, and if our God does indeed graciously destine you for China, will he not seeing the overflowings of your boiling heart for it, open an evident door—the "infidelities" blessed which may keep his designs suspended—at that another thing—that the point of reparation! And WE WILL DO OUR BEST![60]

Mother Seton jotted down, for herself, the warning:

Our misery is not to conform ourselves to the intentions of God [but] as to the manner in which He will be glorious… what pleases Him does not please us—He wills us to enter in the way of suffering, and we desire to enter in action—we desire to give rather than receive—and do not purely seek *His Will.*[61]

It may have been at this point that Simon Bruté sent her the lovely lines:

O, then, that I had true humility, and humility is so gentle! That I might come to think only of my own misery, and easily "give up" every dear Brother's and Sister's little trial [which] I myself give them in life as little as possible.

A stillness of expectation of that grand, grand eternity I hear [about] me seems, drawing near, with its only praise, only love only peace; and no more offense; a silence and forgetfulness of our puny troubles in sight of that grand, beautiful, magnificent eternity filled with God alone. His Majesty, Sweetness and Goodness. O Eternity! O my God alone! Still now to *act,* and now in peace. Help, O help, my Lord![62]

In the end Bruté stayed, and supported John Dubois through the painful crisis involving Mount Saint Mary's.

Changes came to Mother Seton's friends in New York. William Craig was bed-ridden with rheumatism. After suggesting [that] he ask Sister Rose what she used for relief, Elizabeth exclaimed, "Oh bless you all. I wish I had all your pains, if God would give them to me."[63] Young Leo Post was growing more feeble and toward the end of 1819 he started for Havana with Mary Bayley Bunch. Eliza Sadler,[k] Mother Seton's dearest friend in New York sailed for France on 25 October 1819, and Elizabeth knew now that she would never see her Sad again.[64] Dué still went her rounds helping the poor

<hr>

[k] Eliza Sadler sailed with her friends, the de Neuvilles, the French Minister, and his wife. After his return to France, Baron Hyde de Neuville served as intermediary between Archbishop Ambrose Maréchal and Louis XVII.

and Cecilia O'Conway in her letters to Emmitsburg called her "the refuge of the miserable." It was to Dué that Elizabeth Seton wrote, "When I think of what *I deserve,* and what I *have*, I can never be too grateful."[65] But when Mother Seton's thoughts wandered to New York they were more concerned with work still undone, and she wrote, beseeching Robert Fox about his daughters:

> I cannot resist the desire of my heart this morning which has so often pushed me to entreat you to let your dear one come who has not made her first Communion...Jane and Eliza will be a great comfort to their dear Mother and yourself I trust... do hear my prayer for their dear sister who has not had their good opportunity...When we poor parents meet our beloved children in the great day of account and judgment, how happy if we can present them to Him from whom we received them without reproach at least on our part. I tremble often for my omissions and excessive indulgence to mine. Don't say I take too great a liberty saying all this to you. You will never know in this world how tenderly I love your family. [66]

In November 1819, Dr. Chatard became very ill in Baltimore, and Elizabeth Seton heard the news with sorrow. She directed the community to pray for him.[67] No one rejoiced more than Mother Seton when good news arrived a few days later. She wrote to Mme. Chatard, "I have two communions this week to thank and praise for you and with you—I would say so much to you, but can say nothing—you know my heart, your pains or comforts can never be more felt or shared by any as by yours EAS."[68] It was to Marie Françoise Chatard[1] she addressed her last letter of the year, telling her happily:

> We had 15 first communions in a peace and simplicity of delight never enjoyed with the children before. It happened there was no doubtful or difficult one in the number. The instructions had been anticipated for several weeks by our fervent friend and Father [Bruté], and his daily letters he addressed with his rapid pen and burning heart to the children—the beautiful meditations written also by him for the blessed occasion [of First Communion] made all alive and happy in their fervor...Oh, the goodness of our God to us, dearest friend, how well indeed is my heart turned with yours to thank Him.[69]

---

[1] [Mrs. Seton addressed this letter to "Mrs. Chatard" and its text indicates that she was writing to the mother of Emily although Melville cited it differently in the first edition of this work. Ed.]

Spring, the last Mother Seton was ever to see, came in 1820 with its perennial wonders. Kit Seton went off to visit Ann Tiernan in Baltimore in April, and Elizabeth wrote to her:

> Lilacs, little blossoms of many kinds and tiny branches from our dear graves are all around me. Our room looks so pinky from morning till night. You would laugh for I keep close by the cabinet and pick up my books so carefully that Sister Susy[m] twirls in and out ten times a day and finds nothing to do.[70]

In the evenings Sister Agnes or Sister Martha read Chateaubriand and Elizabeth's renewed "delight in him" made her copy some phrases out for the absent Kit. News came second-hand from Boston that all on board the *Macedonian* were well when the ship was in Havana.[71] In May, the contracts were discussed for the new brick school building, in spite of the gloomy economic conditions. The year before Mother Seton had commented that Dubois feared "to go on with the building since every one rich and poor it is thought are failing and our house may be empty enough next year."[72] It was a time of "trouble of Banks and General distress" owing to the war clouds which threatened.[73] Writing to William Seton that fall of 1819,[n] his mother had complained, "We hear of nothing but war war on all sides ...everything stands just as you left it. Losses plenty in the money way by our crazy merchants—but we push along—no new building in such hard times."[74] But by spring John Dubois felt more optimistic and contracts were the subject of exchanges between Dubois and Elizabeth. Although Mother Seton had written to Richard on 8 May 1820, that there was no building at St. Joseph's,[75] by the end of June the contract for the one story was given to Edward Yates.[76]

June turned to July and Mother Seton's thoughts rushed ahead toward January and the prospect of William's return.[77] To Ellen Wiseman she wrote, *"January* will come, my Ellen, but what it will bring he only knows who does all well."[78] William Seton, cruising off the coast of Panama that summer, wrote that his ship was heading south toward Valparaiso. "I shall come like the prodigal son," he warned. "I shall be ready for the newest fashions."[79] But his mother's thoughts were busy with her old concern, and she wrote sorrowfully:

> William, William, William, is it possible the cries of my heart don't reach yours? I carry your beloved name before

---

[m] Sister Susan Clossy

[n] The panic of 1819 had complex causes, chief of which were the inability of manufacturing to reach a stable footing after the abnormal growth during the war was checked, and the speculation which accompanied the post-war expansion. Economic distress was very severe.

the tabernacle and repeat it there as my prayer, in torrents of tears which our God alone understands.

Childish weakness, fond partiality, you would say, half pained if you could see from your present scene, the agonized heart of your Mother, but its agony is not for our present separation my beloved one, it is our long eternal years which press on it beyond all expression. To lose you here a few years of so embittered a life is but the common lot, but to love as I love you and lose you forever, oh unutterable anguish—

A whole eternity miserable, a whole eternity the enemy of God, and such a God as He is to us—dreading so much your faith is quite lost having everything to extinguish, and nothing to nourish it. My William, William, William if I did not see your doting Bec and Nina above [in heaven] what would save my heart from breaking?[80]

Yet her heart was not too full to remember her other friends, and it was touched by the sight of Cheverus' letter in which he explained that frequent trembling in the hand prevented him from writing to her more often.[81] She was distressed to learn of the illness of "The Revd. Dr. Carr"° and Michael Hurley in Philadelphia.[82] She learned with a pang that her dear "Père," Father Babade, was returning to France, "breaking all the ties which bound him to many people in this country."[83] She was disturbed by John Hickey's discontent in Baltimore and his wish to return to Dubois and Bruté at Mount Saint Mary's. She wrote to him these words:

My heart and soul this week past has been under the press of the Beatitude, "Blessed are the Pure of heart; they SHALL SEE GOD!" O, my Brother, take the words on yours, and [at] my Sunday dear Communion I will beg our God to write them on it. Happy, happy are you to love all for Him, every bent of your heart's affections, every power of your soul turned wholly to Him, without even the mixture of the innocent sojourning awhile with your old Father and dear Brother. How much purer is your service where you are above the midst of earthly attraction. One thing I hope you are convinced of (I as a wretched sinner know it well) that wherever we meet a little prop of human comfort, there is always some subtraction of Divine Comfort. And for my part, I am so afraid to cause any such subtraction that I feel

---

° Rev. Matthew Carr, O.S.A., died 29 September 1820, but Michael Hurley survived Mother Seton by sixteen years.

a reserve and fear in every human consolation that makes them more my pains than my pleasures, yet the liberty of children of God—I hope in all, I only mean to say we should be too happy when the Providence of our God keep[s] us wholly to Himself.

Your Father and Brother here are doing what would seem far beyond human possibility, but God will support and in his own time give them help, no doubt. You are remembered and loved here too much to make it a safe place for you unless you were sent by God Himself without the least agency of your own.[84]

Mother Seton's spiritual life was incalculably refined during her last years. After 1818 her resignation was complete. She had written then to Sad, "Oh Eliza, I am to stay—Very well."[85] From then on she practised her own precept, "the Lamb which keeps nearest to its shepherd is the most loved—if he sleeps it does not quit him till he wakes or till it wakens him—then he redoubles his caresses.[86] She explained to John Hickey:

All the illusioning and spider web of *earthly weaving* is broken, and nothing now more bright and steady than the *divine lamp* He feeds and trims himself *because as I suppose I stayed in obedience.* Oh, this Master and *Father* we serve. You in Your Glorious Embassy, I in my little errand! How can we be happy enough in his service—[87]

As her health seemed to improve in 1819, she wrote cheerfully to Father Hickey:

I am so much better—cannot die one way it seems, so I try to die the other, and keep the straight path to *GOD ALONE,* the little daily lesson [is] to keep soberly and quietly in His Presence, trying to turn every little action on His Will, and to praise and love through cloud or sunshine, is all my care and study—*Sam* [the devil] offers his battle from time to time, but Our Beloved stands behind the wall and keeps the wretch at his distance.[88]

She lived in the very sanctuary of the divine Presence, she told Antonio, since "we have but a partition between my little room and our chapel." [89] She added, "I try to make my very breathing a thanksgiving."[90]

In July 1820, when Sister Jane Frances Gartland[p] became mortally ill, Elizabeth's yearning for heaven redoubled its force and she wrote longingly to Hickey:

> Oh, my Father, friend, could I hear my last stage of cough and feel my last stage of pain in the tearing away my prison walls, how would I bear my joy—thought of going home called and by His Will—what a transport, but they say, don't you fear to die? Such a sinner must fear but I fear much more to live and know, as I do, that every evening examen finds my account but lengthened and enlarged. I don't fear death half as much as my hateful vile self.[91]

And to her daughter Kit she said in a wry humor, "I am so well I despair of dying even when you won't want me." Then she added gently alluding to wheels, "[all] goes round. Peace and Love, My Soul's Darling, look up at the blue heavens and love Him, He is so good to us."[92]

That last summer Mother Seton and Father Bruté were closer in spirit than ever before, although they seldom saw each other now. Bruté was very busy and Mother Seton told Hickey, "We have broken our old bonds; I seldom speak to him but in the tribunal. What a lofty Grace for this low earth, but it is to be nearer in heaven I hope. *PEACE*."[93] The love they had for each other could not be measured in sentences. Elizabeth had said to him once, "O my Brother for the day of language without measure!! How much I shall say to you—when it will be by a look of the Soul."[94] Simon Bruté directed the last retreat Elizabeth Seton ever made, and the instructions he gave are still preserved at St. Joseph's.[95] September ushered in the last problems they would face together.

The summer of 1820 saw the beginning of the school building for the day students. As the season waned, and the valley winds grew colder, Mother Seton grew weaker. One day, the enthusiastic Dubois summoned her to survey the progress the carpenters were making. He insisted that she climb a pile of boards, and when the sharp wind struck her, Elizabeth Seton felt the first real clutch of death's icy hand. A strong fever developed rapidly and a few days later Dubois was summoned hurriedly to anoint her. The next Sunday Mr. Bruté began "Depart Christian Soul"[96] it was the recommendation for the dying.

This illness apparently set in toward the end of August for Bruté noted at the top of a meditation on St. Augustine, "News of the Extreme Unction of Rev. M. Hickey. Mother Seton very sick too."[97] On 16 September, on

[p] Sister Jane Frances Gartland died a few weeks later on the 20th of August.

one "of his hurried trips back to Mount Saint Mary's, Bruté left a scribbled message for Dubois, "I was coming to inform how is Mother, (the same truly badly)."[98] On Sunday, 30 September, Bruté was hastily summoned from Emmitsburg with the words, "Mother is dying." He borrowed the "first horse at hand" and rode to St. Joseph's, passing the sisters who had brought the message. The calmness of the house, as Bruté entered, struck his heart. But when he saw Mother Seton his hope returned. He had to hurry back to town for a high Mass and so he had her make a general confession and "announced her the last indulgence." Mother Seton was "so calm, so present, so recollected and wholly trusted to her blessed Lord; her eyes so expressive—the look that pierces heaven and the soul visible in it" as she renewed her vows in the presence of Josephine and some of the sisters. It was on this Sunday, 24 September 1820 that he said "Depart Christian Soul!"[99]

When Bruté returned to St. Joseph's that evening he heard the sisters singing a hymn, *Praise God*, at the close of Benediction. They told him Mother Seton had requested it. But she apologized to Father Bruté later, saying, "I only pronounced the words, 'Praise God,' they thought I asked for it." Bruté suggested that he might write to some of her former friends thanking them for their affection and attention, and she named some. Bruté named others. The list included Cheverus, Maréchal, Sibourd, Dubourg, Flaget, Hickey, Filicchi. When she came to John David her emotion increased and she said brokenly, "Mr. David—to ask him pardon for all pains I gave him." When one of the sisters suggested sitting with her during the night, Elizabeth demurred but she expressed a wish that Bruté remain in the sacristy. Bruté wrote afterward:

> I knew her faith for the presence of the priest and indeed the
> wish of the rituals that he might remain by the dying souls,
> but on my observing, "Better not, besides I trust you do not
> die this night," she did not insist one word.[100]

So Bruté spent the night in Emmitsburg at the house of a parishioner, James Hughes.

The week which followed was filled with alternating hope and fear. On Tuesday Mother Seton seemed much better and on Wednesday, out of danger. But on Thursday the doctor said he failed to see why Bruté and the sisters were optimistic. In October the sisters brought in a feather bed to ease the aching emaciated frame and when Bruté called, Elizabeth burst into tears. She had not asked for it, she said, but it felt so much better she feared the luxury of such comfort. Father Bruté told her she must submit to the charity of her sisters, and she humbly complied.

On 6 October, Bruté penned the following note for Mother Seton and also recorded her appearance in a sketch:

Your poor Spiritual Physician sees you seldom, but it is in order not to spare you fatigue. He maintains himself in tranquility knowing that the celestial Physician, the Well-Beloved, the only Spouse of your soul is present.

Present in love, confidence, abandon—all the most tender, the most simple, the most entire abandon.

Present in repeated avowals of penitence of contrition, of humility, of dependence, and resignation to suffer all united to Him, to His cross.

Present with His peace, His calm joy, His profound detachment, His grace for each moment, pain, or consolation.

"For all flesh is grass." All the glory thereof, O Mother! O Josephine! as the flowers of the grass!—but, the Word of our God— His grace, His love liveth and remaineth forever! O joy! O sweet abandon to Him!

For the mother in glory 1820[101]

Bruté was amazed to find that Mother Seton kept fasting all night in order to receive Holy Communion, in spite of being desperately thirsty from the persistent fever. Though he disapproved of her fast, Bruté did not withhold communion. He described one scene in these words:

Her joy was so uncommon that when I approached, and as I placed the ciborium upon the little table, she burst into tears, and sobbing aloud covered her face with her two hands.[q] I thought first it was some fear of sin, and approaching her, I asked, "Be still Mother! Peace, peace be to you! Here is the Lord of Peace! Have you any pain? Do you wish to confess?" "No, no only give Him to me" as she said with an ardor, a kind of exclamation and her whole pale face so inflamed that I was much affected and repeating, "Peace, dear Mother, receive with great peace your God of Peace." I have proceeded to give her communion and she has received it with great feeling and aspiration.[102]

---

[q] [Although Melville stated that Simon Bruté drew a sketch of Mother Seton with her hands covering her face, at the bottom of this description. The sketch and written document are detached. Mother Seton's face is clearly visible. See ASJPH 1-3-3-12:2. Ed.]

For a little while after this she seemed to regain her lost strength. Bruté recorded years later that among her greatest spiritual gifts was

> Her unabating desire of the holy communion, missing none—since September but one that I can remember because I came too late, and then she had it the morning after, as she had not joined [in attending Mass] that day with the community—so this morning, I remember, I said [when] leaving her, "Think not of yourself, think but of your Jesus whom you have tried to love and received so often in communion," to which she gave her usual expressive assent of the yes [sic, eyes] lifted up, which I wish ever to remember[103]

Julia Scott heard with relief, by a letter from Catherine Josephine Seton, that Elizabeth was "happily recovering."[104] Bruté wrote to John Hickey, who was also recovering from illness in Baltimore:

> My good friend, had we the eminent perfection to say: Neither life nor death but thy will and thy love! I hope you tried to keep so in the critical juncture and, so Mother Seton did, having almost no other answer for all how are you but "quiet," or "His Will." She thanks you for your kind remembrance and weak as yourself seems now however obliged to remain.[105]

Elizabeth Seton, herself, wrote, "Now I am again better, he spares me a little while to see if any fruit will grow on his barren tree—and perhaps to make amends for the bad example I have often given."[106] From this time on her favorite prayer was always said for her or with her by the community. She would often begin the prayer herself. It was the beautiful prayer of Pius VII:

> May the most just, the most high and the most amiable will of God be in all things fulfilled, praised and exalted above all forever.[107]

The brief respite in October seemed designed so that Elizabeth Seton might bear the unhappy return of her son Richard from Leghorn. She rallied enough strength to pen the letters to Antonio Filicchi and Robert Harper. In October, too, she wrote a detailed letter about community concerns to Sister Elizabeth Boyle at Philadelphia. But after that, Kit again handled the letters for her mother. Mother Seton learned well the lesson that, "The virtues of the infirm are *meekness, humility, patience, resignation,* and *gratitude* for help received."[108] Kit wrote to Julia in November that her mother was far from recovered from the "abscess on the breast,"[r] and that she found her chief substantial support in a little port wine.[109] Mother Seton rested uneasily, taking comfort from her own admonition, "Let broken rest be filled with good aspirations—anciently the just were called *Crickets of the night.*"[110]

Simon Bruté, again busy with his other responsibilities,[s] came seldom that November, but he wrote to Elizabeth:

> My good Mother, your poor spiritual physician sees you seldom, but it is in order to spare you fatigue. He maintains himself in tranquillity knowing the celestial Physician—the Well-Beloved, the only Spouse of your soul is continually present. Present in love, confidence, abandon, the most tender, the most simple the most entire abandon.[111]

Mother Seton's condition naturally became the concern of many. Some like Cheverus[t] knew her well and wrote to Bruté, "I hope that our saintly Mother will be preserved for her children again. Our Ursulines unite with me to beg this favor of God."[112] Others, who knew her less well, wrote, "I heard with sorrow of the indisposition of...that best of women Mrs. Seton. With gratitude to Heaven have I returned my thanks for...such valuable lives."[113] But all these good wishes and prayers could not prevent the steady decline which was obvious by Christmas. The abscess discharged so slowly that Elizabeth was reduced to almost a skeleton.[114] The first day of the new year, a time which Mother Seton always welcomed as a new beginning of hope and high resolve, this time would be her last New Year's Day. When Father Bruté, after Benediction, said the words of absolution she requested, and added "My peace I leave you," she simply nodded in assent.

On 2 January 1821, John Dubois came at one o'clock and administered extreme unction. Then he called the community together and said to them:

> Mother being too weak, gives me charge to recommend you at this sacred moment in her place—first to be united together as true Sisters of Charity— secondly to stand most faithfully by your rules—thirdly she requests that I ask your pardon for all the scandals she may have given you—I obey her desire. You know she gave none by the indulgences she means particularly in what she had to eat or other allowances for her situation in which she did but follow my express prescriptions and of the physician.[115]

---

[r] It is generally believed Mother Seton died of tuberculosis, but not of the bone. The cause for this abscess is not certain. It seems clear, however, that it hastened her death.

[s] Probably Bruté may have been shouldering more pastoral duties since John Dubois was sick this fall, also.

[t] The same day Bishop Cheverus wrote to Mother Seton assuring her of his daily prayers.

On 3 January 1821, Father Bruté opened a retreat for the children who were to make their first Communion on the feast of the Epiphany. Knowing how Elizabeth Seton loved the feast he said to her, perhaps the Lord would spare her one Communion more on that day. "Ask Heaven," he said, "to praise and love Him." They were the last words he ever spoke to her, "indeed the last words of any priest on earth." Mother Seton died that night,[u] not long after midnight.[116] Sister Anastasia Nabbs, the loyal woman who had been Mother Seton's housekeeper in Baltimore, was watching over her friend when the hour came. She ran for the sister-assistant, Mary Xavier Clark, who rushed to the room. In a short time, Cecilia O'Conway, Susan Clossy, Josephine Seton, and several others came too. Josephine sobbed convulsively while her mother began, "May the most just, the most high..." Sister Mary Xavier, who knew how much Mother loved the French prayers, softly repeated in that language the *Gloria in Excelsis* and portions of the *Magnificat*. After an hour of agony, Elizabeth Seton became tranquil, and without any sound or movement, went to her beloved Eternity. A quarter of an hour later Simon Bruté arrived.[117]

Bruté, as pastor of St. Joseph's Parish, Emmitsburg, included a notation[v] in the parish register for the 5th of January 1821.[118] It was also Bruté who wrote her greatest eulogy. Writing to Josephine Seton some time later, after talking to Bishop Flaget, Simon Bruté said, in the confused phrases high emotion always produced in him:

> Oh Mother, Mother, we said, could she ever have known what in the secret of our dear Lord was prepared to meet her simple offering of herself to His only glory and love as He would Himself see last,—only so purely, but the consequences so perfectly unforeseen to herself; nay equally so to those who at first could have feared to suggest too much sacrifice if, as she used to tell me, anything could be called sacrifice for God, for our Eternity!...*All* sacrifices were made with a heart that God Himself, whose grace accomplished them, through it, did know; although those who saw nearest that heart, so duly felt...Dwell also a moment, as I was doing with that good Bishop, on the present consequences, far and wide—far from these parts. Could I not add that it prompted

---

[u] Simon Bruté's says the time was "two after midnight"; Cecilia O'Conway says "½ past one o'clock"; John Dubois says "2 ¾ de la nuit."

[v] [Buried at Saint Joseph's [Valley] Anna Elizabeth Seton, the first mother of the Daughters of Charity come to be established in this parish in 1809. Let her rest in peace. She lived and died in the utmost peace and good will of this congregation–and I thought but proper and according to the feelings of all to enter this memorandum of it here—S. Bruté. Ed.]

and encouraged his own wilds in Kentucky thus to bud and prosper? Mr. David went, would have Sisters—had them. All, also, so beautifully blessed there...Look from your vale [sic, valley] to New York and every side. Not the 100s but now far above the 1000s of children blessed from heaven... by your Mother.[119]

A New York paper carried, on 9 January 1821, the simple announcement:

Died: at Emmitsburg on the 3rd inst. Mrs. Elizabeth Seton, wife of the late Wm. M. Seton and daughter of the late Dr. Richard Bayley of this city.[120]

Even the date[w] was wrong in this brief salute to the passing of one of the city's most noteworthy daughters. But the day would come when the little woman from Manhattan would be famous around the world.

---

[w] Elizabeth Seton died 4 January 1821, but the error of the 3rd was made several times and is understandable, since she died at night.

CHAPTER 14. ETERNITY

Notes

[1] 7.176, Elizabeth Seton to Ellen Wiseman, 20 August 1818, *CW*, 2:574.

[2] Mary Bayley Post to Elizabeth Seton, New York, 5 April [1817], ASJPH 1-3-3-11:14.

[3] Charles G. Herbermann, *The Sulpicians in the United States* (Encyclopedia Press: New York, 1916), 131; Mary M. Meline and Edward F. X. McSweeney, *The Story of the Mountain* (Emmitsburg, 1911), I, 71-72.

[4] John Dubois to Ambrose Maréchal, Emmitsburg, February 1818, AAB, AASMSU, 15-T-18.

[5] John M. Tessier to John F. Hickey, Baltimore, 1 April 1818, ASMSU.

[6] John M. Tessier to John F. Hickey, Baltimore, 27 May 1818, ASMSU.

[7] Herbermann, 131.

[8] John Dubois to Ambrose Maréchal, Emmitsburg, 21 June 1818, AAB, AASMSU, 15-T-9.

[9] Louis Dubourg to Simon Bruté, New Orleans, 4 July 1818, UNDA.

[10] John Dubois to Ambrose Maréchal, Emmitsburg, 21 June 1818, AAB, AASMSU, 15-T-9.

[11] 7.169, Elizabeth Seton to William Seton, Emmitsburg, 1 July 1818, *CW*, 2:566. John Dubois reported this incident to Paris with the words, "A certain number of our good neighbors banded together to offer to loan me $8000 without interest. I thanked them for their good will and observed to them that not having need of it I could not accept their offer but that if the occasion arose I would avail myself of their good will." John Dubois to Antoine Garnier, 17 February 1819, AMSMU. Copies of Paris Archives.

[12] Meline and McSweeny, I, 77.

[13] John Dubois to Ambrose Maréchal, Emmitsburg, 28 July 1818, AAB, AASMSU, 15-T-11.

[14] John Dubois to John M. Tessier, Emmitsburg, 4 September 1818, ASMSU.

[15] Bruté chronology, AMSMU. Simon Bruté says, "September 26, Mr. John Dubois passed him the property as to a Sulpician."

[16] John M. Tessier's journal, 3 November 1819, ASMSU.

[17] John Dubois to Antoine Garnier, Emmitsburg, 17 February 1819, AMSMU. Copies of Paris Archives.

[18] John F. McGerry to John Dubois, Baltimore, 7 September 1820, AMSMU.

[19] Herbermann, 132.

[20] John Dubois to Ambrose Maréchal, Emmitsburg, 5 October 1820, AAB, AASMSU, 15-U-22. John B. Randanne proved "quite incapable

of rendering any service for want of a knowledge of English." Simon Bruté Papers, list of Emmitsburg pastors, 17 February 1819, AMSMU. Copies of Paris Archives.

[21] Herbermann was in error in regard to the date of John F. Hickey's return to Mount Saint Mary's. John F. Hickey had been very ill the fall of 1820 and in November John Dubois invited him to come to the Mount to repair his shattered health and offered to send a gig, a light two-wheeled one-horse carriage, to get him. See 19 November 1820, AMSMU. John M. Tessier wrote to John F. Hickey the following June giving him permission to remain, saying he felt it was the Will of God that John F. Hickey remain with John Dubois. See also John M. Tessier to John F. Hickey, 19 June 1821, AMSMU.

[22] 5.21, Elizabeth Seton to Julia Scott, 23 March 1809, *CW*, 2:61-63.

[23] 7.232 Elizabeth Seton to Louis-Regis Deluol, Emmitsburg, 30 December 1819, *CW*, 2:633. See Betty Ann McNeil, D.C., "Sulpicians and Sisters of Charity, Concentric Circles of Mission," *Vincentian Heritage* 20, 1 (1999). See also "Account of Mrs. Seton and the St. Mary's College, Baltimore," ASMSU.

[24] 7.246, Elizabeth Seton to Richard Seton, 8 May 1820, *CW*, 2:651.

[25] 6.30, Elizabeth Seton to Julia Scott, 26 March 1810, *CW*, 2:118.

[26] 6.128, Elizabeth Seton to Julia Scott, 12 March 1813, *CW*, 2:241.

[27] Simon Bruté to Elizabeth Seton, Baltimore, 7 November 1816, ASJPH 7-3-1-3, #276.

[28] Samuel S. Cooper to Elizabeth Seton, Baltimore, 23 January 1817, ASJPH 1-3-3-1:92.

[29] John A. Grassi, S.J., to Simon Bruté, Georgetown, 20 May 1817, UNDA.

[30] 7.88, Elizabeth Seton to Simon Bruté, 4 June 1817, *CW*, 2:480.

[31] John A. Grassi to Simon Bruté, Rome, 30 March 1818, UNDA. Cooper left Leghorn in May, carrying a letter from Richard Seton to his mother. See Richard Seton to Elizabeth Seton, Leghorn, 10 June 1818, 26-0-1, (2). Copy; original is in AMSJ.

[32] John Moranvillé, C.S.Sp., to Elizabeth Boyle, Baltimore, 18 August 1818, AMSV.

[33] Simon Bruté to John F. Hickey, Emmitsburg, 8 September 1818, ASMSU.

[34] Simon Bruté Papers, "Easter Confessions and Communions," AMSMU.

[35] 7.193, Elizabeth Seton to Simon Bruté, n.d., *CW*, 2:593-594.

[36] Ambrose Maréchal to Samuel Cooper, Baltimore, 22 March 1819, UNDA.

[37] Handwritten copies of Bruté's "description of Emmitsburg in 1823" are to be found in the archives of both the Daughters of Charity and

Mount St. Mary's University at Emmitsburg, Maryland. ASJPH 7-3-1-1, #14.

[38] Samuel Cooper to Ambrose Maréchal, Emmitsburg, 15 March 1819, AAB, AASMSU, 15-D-7.

[39] Ambrose Maréchal to Samuel Cooper, Baltimore, 22 March 1819, UNDA.

[40] John Dubois to Ambrose Maréchal, Emmitsburg, 23 April 1819, AAB, AASMSU, 15-U-13. Rev. Simon Bruté, "Emmitsburg in 1823," ASJPH 7-3-1-1, #14.

[41] Samuel Cooper seems to have misunderstood John Dubois for he told Ambrose Maréchal "he was of the opinion with me that it might be tried." Samuel Cooper to Ambrose Maréchal, 13 April 1819, AAB, AASMSU, 25-D-8.

[42] Samuel Cooper to Ambrose Maréchal, Emmitsburg, 13 April 1819, AAB, AASMSU, 15-D-8.

[43] Simon Bruté Papers, 15 June 1819, AMSMU. This is a mere scrap of paper with one of Simon Bruté's innumerable jottings.

[44] John Dubois to Ambrose Maréchal, Emmitsburg, 11 June 1819, AAB, AASMSU, 15-U-16.

[45] Simon Bruté to Elizabeth Seton, Emmitsburg, n.d., ASJPH 7-3-1-3, #B169.

[46] Samuel Cooper to John F. Hickey, Augusta, 26 February 1821, ASJPH 7-3-7, #1.

[47] Simon Bruté to John F. Hickey, Emmitsburg, 20 June 1819, ASMSU. Simon Bruté wrote "Mr. Radford comes to visit Mr. John Dubois and gives *viva voce* an account of what he says the Archbishop told him after having spoken to Mr. Samuel Cooper. I wish if Mr. Samuel Cooper is still with you might know what has been settled as penance in that case."

[48] 7.109, Elizabeth Seton to Simon Bruté, 18 August 1817, *CW*, 2:500.

[49] 7.86, Elizabeth Seton to Simon Bruté, n.d., *CW*, 2:479.

[50] Ibid. See 7.236, Elizabeth Seton draft to Ann C. Tilghman, 1 January 1820, *CW*, 2:637-638.

[51] Simon Bruté Papers, 4 May 1819, AMSMU. Simon Bruté wrote, "Mother announced to me a Protestant convert—a mother with child." Another Protestant with whom Mrs. Seton discussed religion was introduced by Mrs. Montgomery. See 7.108 Elizabeth Seton to Simon Bruté, [August 1817], *CW*, 2:499. Mrs. Nat Elder was the means of bringing Mother Seton to another "poor eighty-odd years sinner from over the Mountain." 6.195, Elizabeth Seton to Simon Bruté, *CW*, 2:330.

[52] 7.101, Elizabeth Seton to Julia Scott, 24 July 1817, *CW*, 2:492.

53 7.291, Elizabeth Seton to Simon Bruté, n.d., *CW*, 2:687.

54 11.57, Prayerbook Inscription, *CW,* 3b:108.

55 Provincial Annals, copy of Catherine Seton's Recollections, ASJPH 7-8-1, (2), 48. The original is in AGU.

56 10.1, St. Mary Magdalen de Pazzi Notebook, *CW*, 3a:478.

57 Simon Bruté Papers, chronological list, 4 April 1818, AMSMU.

58 7.121, Elizabeth Seton to Simon Bruté, n.d., *CW*, 2:512.

59 Jean Cheverus to Simon Bruté, Boston, 9 April 1818, UNDA.

60 7.208, Elizabeth Seton to Simon Bruté, n.d., *CW*, 2:607.

61 11.28 "Servant of Jesus...," *CW*, 3b:42.

62 Simon Bruté, "Humility," n.d., ASJPH 7-3-1-2, #B30.

63 7.158, Elizabeth Seton to Eliza Sadler, 5 May 1818, *CW*, 2:551.

64 Mary Bayley Bunch to Elizabeth Ann Seton, New York, 25 October 1819, ASJPH 1-3-3-11:B40. See *Maryland Historical Magazine,* XXXIV, (December 1939), 344-5; Ambrose Maréchal to de Neuville, 4 October 1819.

65 7.221, Elizabeth Seton to Catherine Dupleix, 21 August 1819, *CW*, 2:623.

66 7.162, Elizabeth Seton to Robert Fox, 9 May 1818, *CW*, 2:555.

67 7.229, Elizabeth Seton to Marie-Françoise Chatard, 30 November 1819, *CW*, 2:630.

68 Ibid., 1 December 1819, *CW*, 2:631.

69 7.233, Elizabeth Seton to Marie-Françoise Chatard, 31 December 1819, *CW*, 2:634. See "Our Glorious Faith in the Holy Eucharist," *Meditations by Father Bruté*, ASJPH 7-3-1-4, C 44; Reflections by Father Bruté, Ibid., 7-3-1-4, B.

70 7.242, Elizabeth Seton to Catherine Josephine Seton, n.d., *CW*, 2:646.

71 Jean Cheverus to Simon Bruté, Boston, 4 April 1820, UNDA.

72 7.219, Elizabeth Seton to Catherine Josephine, [28 June 1819], *CW*, 2:620.

73 7.220, Elizabeth Seton to Julia Scott, 19 August 1819, *CW*, 2:621.

74 7.226, Elizabeth Seton to William Seton, 7 November 1819, *CW*, 2:628. See David R. Dewey, *Financial History of the United States* (New York, 1939), 166.

75 7.246, Elizabeth Seton to Richard Seton, 8 May 1820, *CW*, 2:651.

76 John Dubois and Edward Yates, builder, articles of agreement for erection of the Free School building at St. Joseph's, 30 June 1820, ASJPH 1-3-3-5:34.

77 7.254, Elizabeth Seton to Julia Scott, 19 July 1820, *CW*, 2:661.

78 7.256, Elizabeth Seton to Ellen Wiseman, 25 July 1820, *CW*, 2:663.

79 William Seton to Elizabeth Seton, on board the *Macedonian,* 10 June

1820, ASJPH 26-0-2, (14). Copy; original is in AMSV. William Seton did arrive home, a "prodigal son." He wrote to Robert G. Harper of his plight and tried to borrow some money from him. See Seton to Harper, 21 June 1821, AAB, AASMSU, 20-N-21.

[80] 7.255, Elizabeth Seton to William Seton, 23 July 1820, *CW*, 2:662. Copy. The original is in UNDA.

[81] Jean Cheverus to Elizabeth Seton, Boston, 22 August 1820, ASJPH 1-3-3-1:17.

[82] Williamson to John Dubois, 2 October 1820, AMSMU.

[83] John M. Tessier's journal, 27 August 1820, AASMSU.

[84] 7.237, Elizabeth Seton to John F. Hickey, n.d., *CW*, 2:640.

[85] 7.177, Elizabeth Seton to Eliza Sadler, n.d., *CW*, 2:575.

[86] 10.1, *St. Mary Magdalen de Pazzi Notebook*, *CW*, 3a:424.

[87] 7.147, Elizabeth Seton to John F. Hickey, n.d., *CW*, 2:536.

[88] 7.214, Elizabeth Seton to John F. Hickey, 10 June 1819, *CW*, 2:614.

[89] 7.240, Elizabeth Seton to Antonio Filicchi, 18 April 1820, *CW*, 2:644.

[90] Ibid., 643.

[91] 7.252, Elizabeth Seton to John F. Hickey, 2 July 1820, *CW*, 2:658-9. Mother Seton was "her Visible General." See also 7.259, Elizabeth Seton to Marie-Françoise Chatard, 24 August 1820, *CW*, 2:666.

[92] 7.253, Elizabeth Seton to Catherine Josephine Seton, 10 July 1820, *CW*, 2:660.

[93] 7.252, Elizabeth Seton to John F. Hickey, 2 July 1820, *CW*, 2:659.

[94] 7.294, Elizabeth Seton to Simon Bruté, n.d., *CW*, 2:689.

[95] "Retreat of the Sisters, 1820." ASJPH 7-3-1-2, # B115.

[96] 7.266, Elizabeth Seton to Elizabeth Boyle, 25 October 1820, *CW*, 2:671.

[97] Simon Bruté, "Meditation on St. Augustine's Penitent & Humble Death Model for Our Own," 3 September 1820, ASJPH 7-3-1-2, #B53.

[98] Simon Bruté to [John Dubois], Emmitsburg, 16 September 1820, AMSMU.

[99] See A-7.268, Account by Rev. Simon Bruté, S.S., of Elizabeth Seton's Last Days, *CW*, 2:765-70. Unless otherwise noted, all the facts of Mother Seton's illness and death are taken from this account.

[100] Ibid.

[101] Simon Bruté, 6 October 1820, ASJPH 1-3-3-12:2. French. White includes additional text which is not with the document in ASJPH. See White, 515, n.43.

[102] Cf. White, 440. Melville included this quotation attributed incorrectly to ASJPH 1-3-3-12:2. Ellin Kelly cites this quote as ASJPH 1-3-3-12:1, however, an exhaustive search of the Bruté and Seton collections

resulted in the conclusion that the page with this quote has inexplicably become separated from the rest of the document and is now missing. The passage does not appear in the published account of A-7.268, Bruté's Account of Elizabeth Seton's Last Days, *CW*, 2:764-70.

[103] 7.268, Bruté's Account of Elizabeth Seton's Last Days, *CW,* 2:766.

[104] Catherine Josephine Seton to Julia Scott, Emmitsburg, 4 October 1820, ASJPH 1-3-3-11:B56.

[105] Simon Bruté to John F. Hickey, Emmitsburg, 10 October 1820, ASMSU.

[106] 10.1, St. Mary Magdalen de Pazzi Notebook, *CW*, 3a:436.

[107] Simon Bruté to William Seton, 29 June [1821], UNDA. Printed copies of this prayer used by Mother Seton are preserved in Robert Seton's scrapbook at Emmitsburg. Simon Bruté wrote to William Seton, "Herself began it [so] that they should say it for her, and with her, all her last days or rather [for] three or four months."

[108] 11.51, Elizabeth Seton's Prayerbook, *CW,* 3b:74.

[109] Catherine Josephine Seton to Julia Scott, Emmitsburg, 18 November 1820, ASJPH 1-3-3-11:B57. Catherine Josephine Seton wrote to Julia Scott after Mother Seton's death. "The abscess which we supposed was on or near her lungs having (as I told you) again gathered, to all appearances broke and she had not the strength to discharge it." Catherine Josephine Seton to Julia Scott, Emmitsburg, 15 January 1821, ASJPH 1-3-3-11:B59. See Exhumation of St. Elizabeth Ann Seton, 26 October 1962, "If Mother Seton died of tuberculosis, there is one thing certain: she did not have tuberculosis of the bone," ASJPH 1-3-5-3a, (2),16.

[110] 10.2, Red Leather Notebook, n.d., *CW*, 3a:489.

[111] Simon Bruté, 6 October 1820, ASJPH 1-3-3-12:2.

[112] Jean Cheverus to Simon Bruté, Boston, 17 December 1820, UNDA. Cheverus wrote to Mother Seton, "You are every day with me before the Lord & you know how much I love you in the bowels of J.C." Jean Cheverus to Elizabeth Ann Seton, 17 December 1820, ASJPH 1-3-3-1:18.

[113] John Gibney to John Dubois, Baltimore, 15 December 1820, AMSMU. (There is no identification of Gibney.)

[114] Catherine Josephine Seton to Julia Scott, Emmitsburg, 26 December 1820, ASJPH 1-3-3-11:B58.

[115] A-7.268, Account by Rev. Simon Bruté of Elizabeth Seton's Last Days, *CW*, 2:767.

[116] Ibid., *CW*, 2:768.

[117] Ibid., *CW*, 2:769. Mother Mary Xavier Clark to Rev. Simon Bruté, ASJPH 1-3-3-12:5; Sister Cecilia O'Conway to Rev. Simon Bruté, ASJPH 1-3-3-12:6. See A-7.268, Account by Rev. Simon Bruté of Elizabeth Seton's Last Days, *CW*, 2:767.

[118] AAB, AASMSU, St. Joseph's Parish Register, Combination Record (1812-1843), Emmitsburg, Maryland, entry dated 5 January 1821.

[119] Simon Bruté to Catherine Josephine Seton, Emmitsburg, n.d., UNDA.

[120] New York *Evening Post,* 19 January 1821.

EPILOGUE

ھوہو

The Seton Legacy of Charity
Betty Ann McNeil, D.C.

In writing the biography of an American woman of the early Republic, Annabelle Melville presented Elizabeth Bayley Seton as a woman of the young United States of America. In her own day her vision was broader than North America. Elizabeth considered herself a "citizen of the world"[1] although not anticipating that she would have international recognition as the first native-born canonized saint of the United States. Elizabeth Bayley Seton, the widow of William Magee Seton, was canonized as St. Elizabeth Ann Seton 14 September 1975.

Born in time but not bound by time, Elizabeth Seton defined herself by faith not by circumstances. Her experiences span the boundaries of time and space enabling others to identify with her and resonate with her steadfast courage and faith-filled hope in the face of life's challenges. St. Elizabeth Ann Seton is a role model for people of all ages and walks of life as saint, mother, and foundress.

Saint

Thousands of visitors come to Seton sites in Baltimore, Emmitsburg, New York City, and also in Italy. The holy grounds at Emmitsburg, where Elizabeth Bayley Seton lived from 1809 until her death in 1821, invite persons to walk where she trod, to experience the peace of her valley, to capture her spirit, and to pray for her intercession at the National Shrine of St. Elizabeth Ann Seton. The age of miracles is not over. Stories of blessings received are reported regularly at the Seton Shrine where her remains rest.

Decree of Canonization of Saint Elizabeth Ann Seton.

Elizabeth inspired her pupils, companions, friends, and associates to become their best selves and to serve God in others. The way she lived her belief in God inspired others to serve their neighbor with kindness and compassion. In so doing the little woman living in the midst of a field in a valley became a model of holiness.

Although a woman of yesteryear, Elizabeth Bayley Seton is today as a saint and friend for all time, continuing to teach and inspire us to discover our deepest vocation and develop our fullest potential. Her way of life was rooted in Sacred Scripture and her steadfast belief in God on whom she depended in the best of times and also when poverty and sorrow encircled her. Come what may, Elizabeth responded:

> Faith lifts the staggering soul on one side,
> Hope supports it on the other,
> experience says it must be—
> and love says let it be![2]

Mother

Elizabeth was a woman of her time whose legacy is for all times. She was an ordinary woman whose extraordinary ways as wife, mother, and widow, enabled her to parent five children alone, take initiatives, and

make life-changing choices because of her convictions. The earthly weaving of the tapestry of Elizabeth's life was strengthened by the warp and woof of both adversity and tranquility. She—

- As a child who barely knew her own mother[3] and as a grief-stricken pre-schooler who also lost her infant-sister by death—[4]

- As a rejected step-child in a blended family of preferred half-siblings—[5]

- As one who knew the terror of impending violence in lower Manhattan during childhood—[6]

Saint Elizabeth Ann Seton.

- As a pre-teen only too familiar with loneliness, family conflict, and separation—[7]

- As an idealistic and troubled adolescent who said "No" to a drug overdose of laudanum—[8]

She was a woman who enjoyed life, loved nature, relied on her friends, and trusted in Divine Providence at all times. Elizabeth Seton was not just any woman but she may be considered every woman who—

- Has enticed suitors to visit her during courtship—[9]

- Has known the joy of being a happy bride and the thrilling prospect of a bright future and new home—[10]

• Has pined for an absent spouse during business trips—[11]

• Has loved her husband and children with all her heart—[12]

Yet Elizabeth embraced her crosses when they came her way. The themes of her life are classic and have been lived by many a woman in all cultures who have—

• Experienced a complicated pregnancy and delivery—[13]

• Worried about sick children—[14]

• Nursed sick family members and friends at home all the while knowing so well the symptoms—[15]

• Worked long hours as a temporary secretary or bookkeeper for a family firm late into the night—[16]

• Encountered financial crises and faced bankruptcy while praying for relief—[17]

Elizabeth could exclaim over the beauty of a sunset and feel the consolation of her Creator in the midst of acute sorrow:

• As a foreigner detained in quarantine by immigration authorities—[18]

• As a brave wife caring for a terminally ill husband—[19]

• As a grieving widow in a foreign country—[20]

Strengthened by her beliefs and friends, Elizabeth is like anyone who enjoys the leisure of hobbies, pursues careers, and chooses ways to contribute to society. For Elizabeth the privilege of motherhood drew her into new ways of being which shaped who she became. Her varied experiences are among the ways we may identify or connect with Elizabeth and remember her—

• As a pianist, a needle woman, and parent of resiliency and poetry—[21]

• As a dear friend, benevolent worker, and woman of charity—[22]

• As a teacher, catechist, educator[23] and a risk-taker—[24]

• As one who desired to worship her God in Truth—[25]

When clouds and storms gathered round and swept across the road of her life, Elizabeth Seton walked with confident trust born of faith in her God. From childhood she read, reflected, and prayed with Sacred Scripture. She treasured her Bible and kept it near her. When sailing from New York on the Seton's futile journey of hope to restore her husband's health in 1803, Elizabeth quietly hugged her "hidden Treasure without looking behind or before—only upwards" toward God.[26]

Her favorite passage throughout life was Psalm 23: "The Lord is my shepherd; there is nothing I lack...you restore my strength. You guide me along the right path for the sake of your name...Even when I walk through a dark valley, I fear no harm for you are at my side." Elizabeth Seton was

• A woman who feared for the health of loved ones in the midst of epidemics—[27]

• One living in the midst of preparation for war and uncertainty about the future—[28]

• A caregiver who closed so many dear eyes in death, including her daughters, sisters-in-law, Sisters of Charity, relatives, neighbors, and friends —[29]

• A person of frail health who became terminally ill and serenely anticipated Eternity with God in faith—[30]

At her deathbed when Father Dubois began the prayers for the dying, Mother Seton

Lifted up her faint voice to say, 'I am thankful, Sisters, for your kindness to be present at this trial—be children of the church—be children of the church.' She repeated with a heaving breast as if under a great sense of the consolation and grace of the Blessed Sacrament which she was receiving [Holy Communion]— and the word 'O thankful!' with eyes and expression that however faint seemed...to absolutely speak that sense and feeling of faith and consolation. [31]

Foundress

Whether feminine intuition or simply passing on the news to family and friends, Elizabeth wrote a prophetic description of her future: "it is expected I shall be the Mother of many daughters."[32] Her primary vocation as mother to five children expanded after her conversion and relocation to Emmitsburg. There she became Mother Seton and founded the Sisters of Charity of St. Joseph's in 1809. From this "little mustard seed"[33] which developed and grew into several branches including the Daughters of Charity in North America and several congregations of Sisters of Charity. The spiritual daughters of St. Elizabeth Ann Seton share the common root of the Emmitsburg foundation and the apostolic tradition of St. Louise de Marillac and St. Vincent de Paul which Mother Seton adapted for America. These related congregations now constitute the Sisters of Charity Federation whose members collaborate in effectively responding to the cries of persons who are marginalized and living in poverty.

Christ's love impels the Sisters of Charity Federation to be in solidarity with impoverished persons at the fringes of society and to use their collective available resources to advocate for the creation of systemic change, locally and globally, for the common good of all.

The Seton legacy in North America includes an array of diverse human services in education, healthcare and social services. Mother Seton herself sent Sisters of Charity to Philadelphia to staff the first Catholic orphanage in the United States, to Mount St. Mary's College and Seminary to staff the infirmary and manage domestic services for the students and seminarians, and to New York to begin the first Catholic orphanage in that city. Wherever orphans were served the sisters also began educational programs, training for job-skills, and schools to address local needs. It was with justifiable pride that Mother Seton recorded that her "poor little mustard seed spreads its branches well."[34]

Free Catholic education in the United States may be traced to the pioneer work of Elizabeth Seton and the Sisters of Charity who began St. Joseph's Free School and Academy at Emmitsburg in 1810. Today St. Elizabeth Ann Seton is popularly considered a patron of Catholic schools in the United States although Bishop John Neumann may be credited with creating the first unified system of Catholic schools under a diocesan board in Philadelphia.

Elizabeth Seton crafted a mission which reflected "the joy" of her soul "at the prospect of being able to assist the Poor, visit the sick, comfort the sorrowful, clothe little innocents, and teach them to love God!"[35] Her vision of mission and charity on behalf of others has become a lasting legacy of charity.[36] Through words and deeds, she planted seeds of new life and nurtured growth.[37] In educating her students, Mother Seton consistently and conscientiously sought to prepare her pupils for the world in which they were destined to live.[38]

Basilica and Visitor Center of the National Shrine of Saint Elizabeth Ann Seton, Emmitsburg, Maryland.

Elizabeth was a woman of relationships woven through the mutuality of sharing joys and concerns within the context of friendship. She befriended and mentored others into maturity and even for Eternity.[39] As a person filled with hope in the midst of suffering, death, and transformation, Elizabeth Bayley Seton left an enduring legacy of charity. We remember her as saint, mother, foundress and so much more.

Indeed the little mustard seed which she planted and nurtured in St. Joseph's Valley has blossomed and borne fruit through the persevering efforts of a diminutive woman who acted out of faith and conviction, believing that "hope travels on" throughout life. On this earth Elizabeth Bayley Seton demonstrated that her life choices were value-based and faith-driven. She firmly believed and taught that "every good work, good word we do, [and deed] is a grain of seed for eternal life."[40]

EPILOGUE
Notes

[1] 7.103, To Rev. Simon Bruté, 1 August 1817, *CW*, 2:494.

[2] 6.30, Elizabeth Seton to Julia Scott, 26 March 1810, *CW*, 2:117.

[3] 10.3, "Catherine Seton's Little Red Book," *CW*, 3a:491.

[4] 10.4, Dear Remembrances," *CW*, 3a:510.

[5] 10.4, *CW*, 3a:512.

[6] Ibid.

[7] Ibid., 511.

[8] Ibid., 510.

[9] 1.2, Elizabeth Seton to William Magee Seton, *CW*, 1:2.

[10] 10.4, "Dear Remembrances," *CW*, 3a: 513.

[11] 1.7, Elizabeth Seton to William Magee Seton, *CW*, 1:7.

[12] 1.30, Elizabeth Seton to Julia Scott, *CW*, 1:49; 4.55, Spiritual Journal to Cecilia Seton, *CW,* 1:471.

[13] 1.24, Elizabeth Seton to Julia Scott, *CW*, 1:40; 1.25, Seton to Scott, Ibid., 41.

[14] 1.30, Elizabeth Seton to Julia Scott, *CW*, 1:50.

[15] 6.68, Elizabeth Ann Seton to Julia Scott, *CW*, 2:169.

[16] 1.78, Elizabeth Seton to Dr. Richard Bayley, *CW*, 1:114.

[17] 1.99, Elizabeth Seton to Julia Scott, *CW*, 1:140.

[18] 2.6, Journal to Rebecca Seton, 19 November 1803, *CW*, 1:249.

[19] 2.7, Journal to Rebecca Seton, 30 November 1803, *CW*, 1:261.

[20] 2.6, Journal to Rebecca Seton, 19 November 1803, *CW*, 1:275.

[21] 1.60, Elizabeth Seton to Eliza Sadler, *CW*, 1:90; 1.32, Elizabeth Seton to Julia Scott, *CW*, 1:52; 2.7, Journal to Rebecca Seton, Ibid., 269; 11.46, "When we by faith," *CW*, 3b:61.

[22] 5.2, Elizabeth Seton to Catherine Dupleix, 20 June [1808], *CW*, 2:11; 1.149, Elizabeth Seton to Julia Scott, Ibid., 1:196.

[23] 1.33, Elizabeth Seton to Julia Scott, *CW*, 1:54; 6.67 Elizabeth Seton to George Weis, 15 January 1811, *CW*, 2:167; 6.22, Seton to Rose Stubbs, *CW,* 2:104.

[24] 5.4, Elizabeth Seton to Antonio Filicchi, *CW*, 2:19.

[25] 3.31, Journal for Amabilia Filicchi, *CW*, 1:371.

[26] 2.2, Elizabeth Seton to Eliza Sadler, 3 October 1803, *CW,* 1:244.

[27] 1.27, Elizabeth Seton to Julia Scott, *CW*, 1:45; 1.25, Seton to Scott, Ibid., 42.

[28] 1.23, Elizabeth Seton to Lady Isabella Cayley, *CW*, 1:39.

[29] 6.68, Elizabeth Ann Seton to Julia Scott, *CW*, 2:169; 9.20, Exercise in *The*

Presence of God, Ibid., 417.

[30] 5.26, Elizabeth Seton to Julia Scott, 9 May 1809, *CW*, 2:69; A-7.268, Account by Rev. Simon Bruté, of Elizabeth Seton's Last Days, Ibid., 2:766.

[31] A-7.268, Ibid.:767.

[32] 5.10, Elizabeth Seton to Cecilia Seton, 6 October 1808, *CW*, 2:34.

[33] 7.103, Elizabeth Seton to Rev. Simon Bruté, 1 August 1817, *CW*, 2:494.

[34] 7.240, Elizabeth Seton to Antonio Filicchi, 18 April 1820, *CW*, 2:644.

[35] 5.21, Elizabeth Seton to Julia Scott, 23 March 1809, *CW*, 2:62.

[36] Ibid.

[37] 10.2, Red Leather Notebook, Maxims, *CW*, 3a:488.

[38] White, Charles I., *Life of Mrs. Eliza A. Seton, Foundress and First Superior of the Sisters of Charity in the United States of America.* (Baltimore, 1853), 362.

[39] 5.13, Elizabeth Ann Seton to Julia Scott, 6 December 1808, *CW*, 2:41-3.

[40] 1.7, Elizabeth Seton to William Magee Seton, *CW*, 1:7; 1.99, Elizabeth Seton to Julia Scott, *CW*, 1:140; 10.2, Maxims, *CW*, 3a:488.

ঙ৵৵

APPENDIX A

❦

BAYLEY-SETON GENEALOGY

The Bayley Line

William Bayley (1708?-1758?) of Hertfordshire, England, later of Fairfield, Connecticut, m. (1742/3) Susannah Le Conte (Le Compte) (b.1727?), daughter of William LeConte (LeCompte) and Marianne Mercier of New Rochelle, New York.
  Children:
  Richard Bayley, Sr. (1744-1801)
      [1] Married (9 January 1767) Catherine Charlton (d.1777), daughter of
          Mary Bayeux and Rev. Richard Charlton (1706?-1777).
          Children:
          Mary Magdalen Bayley (1768-1856)
              m. (1790) Dr. Wright Post (1766-1828)
                  Children:
                  Catherine Charlton Post (1798-1828)
                      m. (1824) James Van Cortlandt Morris (1796-1843)
                  Richard Bayley Post
                      m. Harriet Wadsworth Terry (b.1804)
                  Eugene Post (1810-1884) m.
                      [1] (1835) Pricella Ridgely Howard (1814-1837)
                      [2] (1838) Margaret Elizabeth Howard (1816-1901)
                  Lionel (Leo) Post (d.1819?)
                  Edward Post (1791-1816)
                  Mary Elizabeth Post
                      m. (1832) Robert Harwood Hawthorne
                  Emily Post (b.1802) m.
                      [1] (1824) Frederick Gore King (d.1829)
                      [2] (?) William Meredith Hawthorne
          Elizabeth Ann Bayley (1774-1821)
              m. (1794) William Magee Seton (1768-1803)
                  Children: (See pg. 423)
          Catherine Bayley (1777-1778)

[2] Married (16 June 1778) Charlotte Amelia Barclay (1759-1805), daughter of Helena Roosevelt (1719-1772) and Andrew Barclay (1719-1775) of New York

Children:

Charlotte Amelia (Emma) Bayley (1779-1805)
    m. (1799) William Craig (1775?-1826)
Richard Bayley, Jr., (1781-1815)
    m. (1812) Catherine White (1786-1878)
Andrew Barclay Bayley (1783-1811)
Guy Carleton Bayley (1786-1859)
    m. (1813) Grace Walton Roosevelt (1792-1828)
William Augustus Bayley (1788-1817)
Helen Bayley (1790-1849)
    m. (1814) Samuel Craig (1782-1830)
Mary Fitch Bayley (1796-1830)
    m. (1817) Sir Robert Henry Bunch (1789-1830)

William Le Conte Bayley (1745-1811)
m. (1771) Sarah Pell, daughter of Phoebe and Joseph Pell.

Children:

William Le Conte Bayley, Jr. (b.1772)
Susannah Bayley (b.1774) m. (1795) Jeremiah Schureman II
Joseph Bayley (b.1777) m. Susan (?)
Richard Bayley (b.1779)
Ann (Nancy) Bayley (b.1782) m. Captain James Hague
John Bayley (b.1784)

The Charlton Line

Rev. Richard Charlton (1706?-1777) of Ireland, later of Staten Island, New York, m. Mary Bayeux, daughter of Thomas Bayeux and Madeleine Boudinot, French Huguenot settlers of New Rochelle, New York

Children:

Catherine Charlton (d.1777)
    m. (1767) Dr. Richard Bayley (1744-1801)

        Children:

        Mary Magdalen Bayley (1768-1856)
            m. (1790) Dr. Wright Post (1766-1828)
        Elizabeth Ann Bayley (1774-1821)
            m. (1794) William Magee Seton (1768-1803)
        Catherine Bayley (1777-1778)

Mary Magdalen Charlton m. Thomas Dongan (1717-1765)

    Child:

    John Charlton Dongan (1763)

Dr. John Charlton (1736-1806) m. (1765) Mary de Peyster (1819?)

    Child:

    Mary Magdalen Charlton

William Seton, Sr., (1746-1798) of London, later of New York City, son of John and Elizabeth Seton (1718/19-1797), clan of Parbroath, Scotland, and of London

[1] Married (2 March 1767) Rebecca Curson (Curzon) (1746?-1775?), daughter of Richard Curson, Sr., (b.1726) and Elizabeth-Rebekah Beker of Baltimore, Maryland

Children:

William Magee Seton (1768-1803)
  m. (January 25, 1794) Elizabeth Ann Bayley (1774-1821)
James Seton (b.1770)
  m. (1792) Mary Gillon Hoffman (d.1807)
John Curson Seton (1771?-1815) m.
  [1] (1799) Mary Wise (d.1809)
  [2] (?) Mrs. Charlotte Gorham (1820)
Henry Seton (b.1774)
Anna Maria Seton (b.1775?)
  m. (1790) John Middleton Vining (1758-1802)

[2] Married (29 November 1776) Anna Maria Curson (Curzon) (d.1792), daughter of Richard Curson, Sr., (b.1726) and Elizabeth-Rebekah Beker of Baltimore, Maryland

Children:

Elizabeth Seton (1779-1807) m. (1797) James Maitland (d.1808)
Rebecca Mary Seton (1780-1804)
Mary Seton m. Josiah Ogden Hoffman
Charlotte Seton (1786-1853)
  m. (1806) Gouverneur Ogden (1778-1851)
Henrietta (Harriet) Madeleine Seton (1787-1809)
Samuel Waddington Seton (1789-1869)
Edward Augustus Seton (b.1790) m. Bazilide Belome Spence
Cecilia Barbara Seton (1791-1810)

Elizabeth Ann Bayley and William Magee Seton

Elizabeth Ann Bayley (1774-1821) m. (25 January 1794) William Magee Seton (1768-1803)

Children:

Anna Maria (Annina) Seton (1795-1812)

William M. Seton II (1796-1868) m. (1832) Emily Prime (1804-1854)

    Children:

    William Seton III (1835-1905)

        m. (1884) Sarah Redwood Parrish (1844-1895)

            Child:

            William Seton V (1886-1886)

    Henry Seton (1838-1904) m. (1870) Ann Foster

        Children:

        John Gray Foster Seton (1871-1897)

        William Seton IV (b.1873)

    George Seton (d. infancy)

    Robert Seton (1839-1927), ordained priest (1865); archbishop (1905)

    Elizabeth Seton (1840-1906)

    Helen Seton (1844-1906) entered Sisters of Mercy of New York (1879), known as Mother Mary Catherine, R.S.M.

    Emily Seton (1845-1868)

    Isabella Seton (1842-1929

        m. (1870) Thomas Edwin Jevons (1841-1919)

        Children:

        Marguerite Jevons (1871-1954)

        Reginald Seton Jevons (1872-1907)

        Thomas Seton Jevons (1874-1963)

        Ferdinand Talbot Roscoe Jevons (1876-1967)

        Infant Seton (d. infancy)

Richard Bayley Seton (1798-1823)

Catherine Charlton (Josephine) Seton (1800-1891) entered Sisters of Mercy of New York (1846), known as Mother Mary Catherine, R.S.M.

Rebecca Mary Seton (1802-1816)

APPENDIX B

৵৵

First Communion of Elizabeth Bayley Seton

When Elizabeth Seton wrote to her soul-sister Rebecca Seton in mid-August 1802, raving that the previous "night was surely a *foretaste* of the next" life, she added the following postscript after her signature: Yesterday shall, while I have any birth days to keep, always be considered the *Birth day* of the *Soul* never mind the 28th [August]." [1]

Robert Seton concludes from this that Elizabeth Seton made her first protestant communion August 15, 1802, at age 28.[2] Such a conclusion seems, to this writer [Melville], invalid in view of the following facts:

First, Elizabeth Ann Seton frequently applied such glowing descriptions to days when her soul was elevated with consolation. One example appears below:

> This Blessed day—Sunday 23d May 1802— my Soul was
> first sensibly convinced of the blessing and practicability
> of an entire surrender of itself and all its faculties to
> God—It has been the *Lord's day* indeed to me—tho' many
> many temptations to forget my heavenly possession in his
> constant presence has pressed upon me— but blessed be
> my precious shepherd in this last hour of *his day* I am at
> rest within his fold sweetly refreshed with the waters of
> comfort which have flowed thro the Soul of his Ministering
> Servant, our Blessed Teacher and faithful Friend. Glory to
> my God for this unspeakable blessing— Glory to my God
> for the means of grace and the hopes of glory which He so
> mercifully bestows on His unworthy Servant—[3]

Another example is an undated note describing the day William Magee joined her in worship:

> Mr. Hobart this morning—language cannot express the
> comfort the Peace the Hope—but Willy did not understand,
> that happy hour is yet to come...*Peace to you*[4]

Secondly, in an earlier letter Elizabeth sharply reprimanded Rebecca and said, "You should never violate a Strict rule not to leave home for any persuasion on Sacrament Sunday...I have often asked myself the question why should anyone be more earnest in prevailing with me for a trifle or thing of no consequence in itself than I in maintaining a thing I know to be right and that touches the interest of my soul's peace."[5]

Later writings of Mrs. Seton suggest that Mrs. Seton was accustomed, herself, to a strict observance of "Sacrament Sunday."[6]

APPENDIX C

§◦◦

CITIZENSHIP OF WILLIAM MAGEE SETON

The issues presented by William Magee Seton's claim to British citizenship are not easily resolved. The first aspect of the dilemma is concerned with William Seton's own citizenship. Clearly, before the American Revolution he was a British subject, born of English parents on board an English ship, the *Edward,* April 20, 1768.[7] After the United States became independent, the subjects of the crown therein became generally citizens of the United States. Authorities disagree as to the date, some citing 1778, others preferring 1783. "At any rate, a person who continued to reside in the United States after both of these dates was a citizen of the United States."[8] The courts of both the United States and England seem to have accepted this view.[9] Applying the principle in *Downes v. Bidwell*, the Supreme Court of the United States proclaimed in 1901, "The inhabitants residing upon the territory transferred have the right of election. They may remove from the territory...If they elect to remain their allegiance is due at once to the government to which the cession is made."[10] Although many Tories fled New York after 1783, the Setons and Bayleys remained, thus becoming American citizens. Elizabeth Bayley and William Magee Seton were such citizens at the time of their marriage. Although young Seton was not continually in the United States after 1783, he was a minor whose status was determined by his parents residing in New York. In 1786 he was employed by the Bank of New York, in 1794 he was married in New York where he continued his residence until 1803. It seems safe to assert that William Magee Seton was an American citizen for the twenty years, 1783–1803, preceding the voyage to Italy.

Could William Seton divest himself of American citizenship by the mere reception of a certificate from the British consul in 1803? As late as 1893 the courts held that "in the absence of any law of Congress as to the method of expatriation it could not be said to take place unless it was manifested by removal from this country and residence elsewhere.[11] Earlier, in 1830, Justice Joseph Story (1779-1845) pronounced in regard to expatriation, "The general doctrine is that no persons can by any act of their own, without the consent of the government, put off their allegiance and become aliens."[12] Seton went to Italy for his health. There was never any intent of permanent removal from the United States of America, nor is there any evidence that he sought the consent of the United States government to become a British subject.

Even presuming a termination of William Magee Seton's citizenship at the time of issuance of the certificate in 1803, there is still no enduring alteration in the status of Elizabeth Seton, his wife, necessarily implied. Although marriage to an alien was generally presumed to affect the citizenship of women before the passage of the Cable Act of 1922, the death of the alien spouse was held to alter the case. Prior to 1907 the cases were not in agreement. In *Shanks v. Dupont* (1830), the court ruled that a woman did not lose her national character by marrying an alien, either friend or enemy. In *Comitis v. Parkerson* (1893), the court held that after the death of an alien husband, a woman continuing to reside in the United States was not an alien. Previously, in New York, in *Beck v. Gillis,*[13] it had been argued in 1850 that neither the marriage of a female with an alien, nor her residence in a foreign country would constitute her an alien.[14] Finally in 1907 Congress enacted the law of 2 March which stipulated that "any American woman who shall marry a foreigner shall take the nationality of her husband, and that on the termination of the marital relation she may resume her American citizenship, if residing in the United States at that time by continuing to reside therein."[15] Considering the development of opinion in regard to post-marital status chronologically, it appears evident that the closer to 1803 these opinions were held, the stronger was their support of the theory that American citizenship was regained at the alien husband's demise.

Mrs. Seton's residence was New York City. The couple's four younger children were there, as was her personal property, at the time of William Magee Seton's death at Pisa. Immediately following her husband's death, Mrs. Seton made plans to return to New York and only unavoidable circumstances delayed this return until June of 1804. Upon her return she never again left the United States. No law of Congress existing in 1803 invalidated her American citizenship, and in the absence of a court decision respecting her particular case, the opinions of a majority of analogous cases support the contention for reversion to American citizenship after her husband's death. It may thus be concluded that after 1783 Mrs. Seton was probably never a British subject but if she were, this alien status lasted only briefly from 28 September 28 1803, to 27 December 1803, when Seton died.[16]

APPENDIX D

ৎঌ৵৵

ROLE OF ELIZABETH SETON IN CATHOLIC EDUCATION

CHRONOLOGY

1727   The Ursulines, under the leadership of Mother Marie Tranchepain, arrived in New Orleans from France "taught young women [The Ursuline Academy], cared for orphans, and made the first permanent establishment of women religious in the *present-day* United States."[17] This was an American foundation of an existing European congregation.

1790   The Carmelites established their monastery at Port Tobacco in Maryland. Although this was a foundation of an existing order in Europe, it was the *first* new foundation of religious women in the American Republic. After the deaths of key leaders of the founding generation and because of economic factors, the community closed the monastery at Port Tobacco and moved to Baltimore in 1831. To support themselves, they began "The Carmelite Sisters Academy for the Education of Young Ladies".[18]

1789   German Catholics in Holy Trinity Parish in Philadelphia established a school to meet the needs of their children in an immigrant community.[19]

1799   The Visitation nuns taught the neighborhood's poor children at Georgetown in 1799 and established The Georgetown Visitation Academy in 1816.[20]

1800   The first Roman Catholic Free School was established in New York City (Saint Peter's Parish) and operated at two sites. By 1806 it had become the second largest denominational school in the city.[21]

1804   Rev. Gabriel Richard, a Sulpician priest working in the Northwest Territory, founded a seminary and a school for girls in 1804 (later Detroit). Richard also published the first English language American Catholic Textbook, the *Child's Spelling Book*, in 1809.[22]

1808   In conjunction with the Sulpician priests in Baltimore, Elizabeth Bayley Seton established a small Catholic school for girls near St. Mary's Seminary on Paca Street. It was here that Saint Elizabeth Ann envisioned free education for girls from families living in poverty and unable to afford tuition. The school closed in June of 1809 when the Setons moved to Frederick County, Maryland.

1809   Elizabeth Bayley Seton, known as Mother Seton, and her companions established the Sisters of Charity of Saint Joseph's, 31 July 1809. This community of religious women is the first *indigenous* sisterhood established in the United States and later developed several branches. The Sisters and Daughters of Charity have been noted for excellence in education.

1810   Mother Seton and her Sisters of Charity of Saint Joseph's began St. Joseph's Free School (22 February) at Emmitsburg, Maryland in 1810. This was the first free Catholic school *for girls staffed by religious women* in the country.

1810   Mother Seton and her Sisters of Charity of Saint Joseph's established Saint Joseph's Academy (14 May) at Emmitsburg, Maryland in 1810. The school was governed, funded, and administered by the Sisters of Charity who admitted girls from the environs as well as boarders living at a great distance, even as far away as New York and Philadelphia. From the onset it was *not* a parish school.[23] Mother Seton and her Sisters of Charity were pioneers in Catholic education but *not* founders of the parochial school system, although their work may have had a formative influence on some of the bishops who later decreed its establishment. The first two orphanages established by the Sisters of Charity at Philadelphia (1814) and New York City (1817) had educational programs attached which also served day students.

1852   John Neumann (1811-1860), 4th bishop of Philadelphia, was a strong advocate of parochial schools and he brought additional communities of religious women into the diocese. At the time of his death, the *Metropolitan Catholic Almanac and Laity's Directory* listed thirty-seven parochial schools in his diocese. Neumann participated in the deliberations of the First Plenary Council of Baltimore (1852) and served on the Committee for the Education of Catholic Youth.[24]

1852   The First Plenary Council of Baltimore urged the establishment of free parish schools and pledged to finance them with Church revenue. Bishop Neumann of Philadelphia served on the Committee for the Education of Catholic Youth during the Council.[25]   Building on the educational foundations in existence the bishops adopted an expanded vision of Catholic education and decreed the creation of the parochial school system in the United States.

APPENDIX E

ৎ৵৵

RESOURCES FOR SETON STUDIES
Saint Elizabeth Ann Seton (1774-1821)
Mother—Foundress—Saint
<u>Chronology</u>

28 August 1774
Born in or near New York City as Elizabeth Ann Bayley.

25 January 1794
Married William Magee Seton (1768-1803).

3 May 1795
Gave birth to a daughter, Anna Maria Seton, who died 12 March 1812 and is buried in St. Joseph's Cemetery, Emmitsburg.

25 November 1796
Gave birth to a son, William M. Seton, who died 13 January 1868 and is buried in Mount St. Mary's Cemetery, Emmitsburg.

January 1798
Business failure and financial problems loomed on the horizon, culminating with the death on 9 June of her father-in-law, William Seton, senior, and the deterioration of her husband's health from tuberculosis.

20 July 1798
Gave birth to a son, Richard Bayley Seton, who died 26 June 1823, and is buried on board the *Oswego* and is buried at sea off the coast of Liberia.

28 June 1800
Gave birth to a daughter, Catherine Charlton Seton, who died 3 April 1891 and is buried in Sisters of Mercy plot (Sec 4-2-D), Calvary Cemetery, Woodside, New York.

7 December 1800
Officials made inventory of family assets in conjunction with bankruptcy proceedings.

20 August 1802
Gave birth to a daughter, Rebecca Seton, who died 3 November 1816 and is buried in St. Joseph's Cemetery, Emmitsburg.

2 October 1803
Departed New York with William Magee Seton and daughter Anna Maria to sail for Italy on the *Shepherdess*.

18 November 1803
Arrived at the port of Livorno and the Setons are immediately quarantined in the San Jacopo lazaretto because officials feared yellow fever (then spreading in New York).

19 December 1803
Released from quarantine and moved into a rented apartment in Pisa.

27 December 1803
William Magee Seton died in Pisa and was buried the next day in the English cemetery at Livorno.

8 April 1804
The Widow Seton and Annina sailed for New York in the company of Antonio Filicchi on the *Pyomingo*.

4 June 1804
The Setons and Antonio Filicchi arrive at the port of New York.

14 March 1805
Made profession of faith in the Roman Catholic Church at St. Peter's, Barclay Street, New York.

25 March 1805
Received first Holy Communion as a Roman Catholic at St. Peter's, Barclay Street, New York.

25 May 1806
Received the sacrament of Confirmation from Bishop John Carroll at St. Peter's, Barclay Street, New York.

9 June 1808
Mrs. Seton and her daughters sailed from New York for Baltimore on the *Grand Sachem*.

15 June 1808
The *Grand Sachem* arrived in the port of Baltimore at Fell's Point but the Setons did not disembark until the next morning.

16 June 1808
The Setons arrived at Saint Mary's Seminary as the new Chapel of the Presentation was being dedicated. Soon Mrs. Seton began a school for girls on Paca Street in Baltimore, Maryland.

29 June 1808
Traveled to Washington in the company of Rev. Michael Hurley, O.S.A., and seminarian, Samuel Sutherland Cooper, in order to bring her sons, William and Richard, for enrollment at Saint Mary's College, Baltimore.

7 December 1808
Cecilia Maria O'Conway arrived from Philadelphia and became the first candidate for the Sisters of Charity.

25 March 1809

Mrs. Seton pronounced private vows of chastity and obedience for one year before Bishop Carroll who bestowed the title of Mother Seton.

9 June 1809

Mother Seton and companion dressed alike in the black dress, cape, and cap as Sisters of Charity on the Feast of Corpus Christi.

21 June 1809

Mother Seton and the first group left Baltimore for Emmitsburg.

22 June 1809

The first group of travelers arrived at Mount St. Mary's but had to take up temporary residence there on the Mountain because their stone farm house in the Valley was not yet repaired. John Dubois gave them hospitality in cabin called "Mr. Duhamel's house."

29 July 1809

Elizabeth Seton welcomed the second group, Sister Rose White and her companions, to Saint Joseph's Valley. The travelers included two boarders, Isabella O'Conway and Julia LeBreton, along with Sisters Cecilia O'Conway, Mary Ann Butler, Susan Clossy, and Kitty Mullan.

30 July 1809

Mother Seton and companions attended Sunday mass at Saint Joseph's Church in the village of Emmitsburg.

31 July 1809

Founded the Sisters of Charity of Saint Joseph's and began community in the Stone House at St. Joseph's Valley life according to a provisional rule.

23 December 1809

Death of Henrietta (Harriet) Seton, sister-in-law of Elizabeth, the first to die in Saint Joseph's Valley and to be buried in the original graveyard, St. Joseph's Cemetery.

22 February 1810

The Sisters of Charity opened St. Joseph's Free School, the first free Catholic school for girls staffed by religious women in the United States.

17 April 1810

Death of Cecilia Seton, sister-in-law of Elizabeth.

18 May 1810

Establishment of St. Joseph's Academy, a tuition-based school for girls staffed by religious women in the United States.

22 August 1810

Rev. Benedict Flaget, S.S., left Baltimore for Emmitsburg with a French copy of the Common Rules of the Daughters of Charity for the Sulpicians to translate and adapt for use by the Sisters of Charity of Saint Joseph's.

17 January 1812
Official confirmation of the Rules and Constitutions of the Sisters of Charity in the United States based on the Common Rules of the Daughters of Charity by Vincent de Paul and Louise de Marillac, founded in 1633.

12 March 1812
Death of Annina, first vowed member of the Sisters of Charity of Saint Joseph's, and eldest child of Elizabeth Seton.

19 July 1813
First vow group of eighteen sisters pronounced vows for the first time under the American version of the Daughters of Charity rule in the chapel of the White House.

29 September 1814
Led by Sister Rose Landry White, Elizabeth Seton sent Sister Susan Clossy and Sister Teresa Conroy to Philadelphia to staff St. Joseph's Asylum, the community's first mission beyond Emmitsburg and the first Catholic orphanage in the United States.

12 July 1815
Mother Seton established a mission of Sisters of Charity at Mount St. Mary's in order to staff the infirmary, support liturgical ministries, and direct domestic services.

3 November 1816
Death of Rebecca, youngest child of Elizabeth Seton.

27 January 1817
The Maryland State Senate gave final approval for the legal incorporation of the Sisters of Charity of Saint Joseph's in the state of Maryland.

28 August 1817
Mother Seton sent Sisters Rose White, Cecilia O'Conway, and Felicitas Brady who arrived in New York to begin the New York Roman Catholic Orphan Asylum.

4 January 1821
Mother Seton died in the White House, Emmitsburg.

22 August 1882
After celebrating mass at Elizabeth Seton's tomb, James Cardinal Gibbons proposed the possibility of her canonization.

30 October 1907
Informative Cause of Process began which concluded in 1925 by forwarding Elizabeth Seton's writings to Rome.

5 January 1935
Cure of Sister Gertrude Korzendorfer, D.C., (1872-1942) in New Orleans, from cancer of the pancreas.

15 January 1936
Decree by the Sacred Congregation of Rites that "no obstacle exists against taking further steps relative to the Cause."

28 February 1940

Pope Pius XII signed the Decree of Introduction of the Cause for Beatification and Canonization of the Servant of God Elizabeth Ann Bayley, the Widow Seton.

28-29 October 1947

Establishment of the Conference of Mother Seton's Daughters which developed into the collaborative association, Sisters of Charity Federation.

13 April 1952

Cure of Ann Theresa O'Neill (b. 1948) from leukemia in Baltimore.

18 December 1959

Blessed John XXIII proclaimed the Heroicity of Virtues of Elizabeth Bayley Seton and declared her Venerable Mother Seton.

9 October 1963

Cure of Carl Kalin (1902-1976) of New York from fulminating meningo enchepalitis complicated by primary rubeola.

17 March 1963

The beatification of Blessed Elizabeth Ann Seton occurred during the pontificate of Blessed John XXIII.

18 April 1963

The relics of Blessed Elizabeth Ann Seton were enshrined over the main altar of Saint Joseph College, Emmitsburg.

4 January 1968

The relics of Blessed Elizabeth Ann Seton were transferred to the new chapel of St. Joseph's Provincial House now designated as the Shrine of St. Elizabeth Ann Seton. The Seton reliquary was enshrined beneath the altar of St. Elizabeth Ann Seton in the chapel dedicated to her memory.

14 September 1975

Pope Paul VI canonized St. Elizabeth Ann Seton who became the first native-born of the United States to be declared a saint in the Roman Catholic Church.

13 February 1991

Designation of the Chapel of St. Elizabeth Ann Seton as a minor basilica. The public celebration for the bestowal of this honor on the Basilica of the National Shrine of Saint Elizabeth Ann Seton was August 4.

4 January

Feast day of Saint Elizabeth Ann Seton, who was a pioneer in free Catholic education and popularly considered a patron of Catholic schools in the United States. Officially St. Elizabeth Ann Seton is patron of United States Sea Services and also of the state of Maryland.

SISTERS OF CHARITY FEDERATION[a]
MEMBERS 1947 TO PRESENT

"It is expected I shall be the Mother of many daughters."[b]

Daughters of Charity, North American Provinces
Les Religieuses de Nôtre-Dame-du-Sacré-Coeur
Sisters of Charity of Cincinnati
Sisters of Charity of Leavenworth
Sisters of Charity of Nazareth
Sisters of Charity of Our Lady of Mercy
Sisters of Charity of the Immaculate Conception
Sisters of Charity of Seton Hill
Sisters of Charity of St. Elizabeth
Sisters of Charity of St. Vincent de Paul of Halifax
Sisters of Charity of St. Vincent de Paul of New York
Sisters of Saint Martha of Antigonish
Vincentian Sisters of Charity of Bedford
Vincentian Sisters of Charity of Pittsburgh

[a] Betty Ann McNeil, D.C., "The Sisters of Charity Federation in the Vincentian and Setonian Tradition, Berard L. Marthaler, OFMConv., ed., *New Catholic Encyclopedia* (Catholic University of America Press and The Gale Group: Washington, D.C., 2002), 13: 172.
[b] 5.10, Elizabeth Seton to Cecilia Seton, 6 October 1808, *CW,* 2:34.

RECOMMENDED REFERENCES

Bechtle, Regina, S.C., and Judith Metz, S.C., *Elizabeth Bayley Seton Collected Writings.* eds., Ellin M. Kelly, mss. ed., 3 vols., New City Press: New York, 2000-2006.

Alderman, Margaret and Josephine Burns, D.C., *Praying with Elizabeth Seton,* Saint Mary's Press: Winona, WI, 1992.

Dirvin, Joseph I., C.M, *The Soul of Elizabeth Seton. A Spiritual Portrait.* Ignatius Press: San Francisco, 1990.

Kelly, Ellin M., Editor. *Elizabeth Seton's Two Bibles: Her Notes and Markings.* Our Sunday Visitor: Huntington, Indiana, 1977.

Kelly, Ellin M., *Numerous Choirs. A Chronicle of Elizabeth Bayley Seton and Her Spiritual Daughters. Volume I: The Seton Years, 1774-1821.* Evansville, Indiana, 1981.

Kelly, Ellin M. and Annabelle Melville, Editors. *Elizabeth Seton: Selected Writings.* Our Sunday Visitor: New York, 1987.

Laverty, Rose Marie, S.C. *Loom of Many Threads.* New York Paulist Press: 1958.

McNeil, Betty Ann, D.C., *15 Days of Prayer with Elizabeth Seton.* Liguori Publications: 2003.

McNeil, Betty Ann, D.C., Seton, Elizabeth Ann Bayley (1774-1821), *The New Catholic Encyclopedia*, 2nd (The Gale Group, 2002).

McNeil, Betty Ann, D.C., Sisters of Charity Federation in the Vincentian and Setonian Tradition *The New Catholic Encyclopedia*, 2nd ed., 15 vols., The Gale Group, 2002.

Melville, Annabelle, *John Carroll of Baltimore. Founder of the American Catholic Hierarchy.* New York: Charles Scribner's Sons, 1955.

Melville, Annabelle, *Louis William Dubourg: Bishop of Louisiana and the Floridas, Bishop of Montauban, and Archbishop of Besançon, 1766-1833.* 2 vols., Chicago: Loyola University Press, 1986.

Melville, Annabelle, *Jean Lefebvre de Cheverus 1768-1836.* Milwaukee: The Bruce Publishing Company, 1958.

Metz, Judith, S.C., *A Retreat with Elizabeth Seton. Meeting our Grace.* Saint Anthony Messenger Press: Cincinnati, 1999.

United States of America

Maryland

The Mother Seton House at St. Mary's Spiritual Center and Historic Site on Paca Street,
600 N. Paca Street, Baltimore, Maryland 21201.

The National Shrine of St. Elizabeth Ann Seton,
333 S. Seton Avenue, Emmitsburg, Maryland, 21727.

New York

Shrine of St. Elizabeth Ann Seton,
Church of Our Lady of the Rosary,
7 State Street, New York, NY 10004.

Italy

Livorno (Leghorn)

Parrocchia Sta. Elisabetta Anna Seton (Parrochia Madre Seton), P.zza G. M. Lavagna, 16, Livorno, Italy, 57125. Current burial site of remains of William Magee Seton and Antonio Filicchi in Seton parish garden since 2004.

APPENDIX
Notes

[1] 1.162, Elizabeth Seton to Rebecca Seton, New York, 16 August 1802, *CW*, 1:209.

[2] Robert Seton, *Memoirs, Letters and Journal,* I, 88.

[3] 8.10, "My peace I leave with you..." *CW*, 3a:23.

[4] 1.102, Elizabeth Ann Seton to Rebecca Seton, n.d., *CW,* 1:144.

[5] 1.135, Elizabeth Ann Seton to Rebecca Seton, 24, July 1801, *CW*, 1:178.

[6] 10.4, "Dear Remembrances," *CW*, 3a:514.

[7] Robert Seton, *An Old Family,* 273.

[8] *Corpus Juris* (New York, 1917), XI, 781.

[9] Sir William Blackstone, *Commentaries on the Laws of England* (New York, 1850), I, 284.

[10] *Downes v. Bidwell* (1901), 182 U.S. 244.

[11] *Comitis v. Parkerson* (1893), 22L. R.A. 148.

[12] *Shanks v. Dupont* (1830), 3 Pet. 24.6.

[13] (9 Barb. 35).

[14] *Century Edition of the American Digest.* (St. Paul, 1899), X, 15.

[15] (34 Stat, at L. 1228, Chap. 2534).

[16] For a summary of cited judicial opinions consult Judge Shaw's history of the issue in *McKenzie v. Hare, 5* August 1913, published in the *Lawyers Reports Annotated,* 1916 D. (Rochester, 1916), 129-31.

[17] George C. Stewart, "Ursulines (O.S.U.)," Michael Glazier and Thomas Shelley, eds., *The Encyclopedia of American Catholic History* (Collegeville, Minnesota: Liturgical Press, 1997), 1412.

[18] Constance Fitzgerald, O.C.D. "Carmelite Nuns, Discalced (O.C.D.)," Ibid, 216.

[19] F. Michael Perko, S.J., "Catholic Education, Parochial," Ibid., 255.

[20] Mary Virginia Brennan, V.H.M., "Visitation Nuns (V.H.M.)," Ibid., 1448.

[21] F. Michael Perko, S.J., "Catholic Education, Parochial," Ibid., 255.

[22] Ibid., 259.

[23] Ann Miriam Gallagher, R.S.M., "Seton, Elizabeth Ann Bayley," Ibid., 1279.

[24] Thomas J. Shelley, "Neumann, St. John," Ibid., 1029.

[25] Lawrence McAndrews, "Catholic Education and Government Aid," Ibid., 247; Michael J. Roach, "Provincial and Plenary Councils of Baltimore," Ibid., 1176.

෨ၡ

Pisa

- Home of Madame Tot on the Arno River where William Magee Seton died
- Site of Filippo Filicchi residence on opposite side of the Arno
- Chiesa della Spina (Crown of Thorns), constructed 1323 in Gothic style
- University of Pisa distinguished in botany, natural sciences, and medicine

Livorno (Leghorn)

- San Jacopo Church and adjacent site of former San Jacopo lazaretto
- Filicchi residence where the Setons stayed, via della Madonna
- Church of Sta. Caterina, via Forte S. Pietro
- Shrine of Our Lady of Montenero
- Anglican Church of St. George and English cemetery, via degli Elisi

Firenze (Florence)

- Church of SS. Annunziata (where Elizabeth attended mass)
- Church of Sta Maria de Novella (painting of the *Descent from the Cross*)
- Church of Sta Maria del Fiore (The Duomo or Cathedral), baptistery and bell tower
- Church of San Firenze on Piazza San Firenze
- Palazzo Medici Riccardi facing San Lorenzo, via Cavour
- Church of San Lorenzo and adjacent Capelle Medici
- The Opera House
- The Uffizi Art Gallery
- Natural History Museum, via Romana
- The Palazzo Pitti, Queen's Country Palace, and Boboli Gardens
- Academy of Sculptors, Galleria dell'Accademia, Piano Terreno (Michelangelo's *David*)
- Giardini dei Simplici (Botanical Garden of San Marco)

৵৹৵

[c] The Italian Journal of Elizabeth Bayley Seton is published in Regina Bechtle, S.C., and Judith Metz, S.C., *Elizabeth Bayley Seton Collected Writings*, eds., Ellin M. Kelly, mss. ed., 3 vols., (New City Press: New York, 2000), 1:243-305.

BIBLIOGRAPHY

I.   ARCHIVAL REPOSITORY

Archives of The Catholic University of America, Washington, D. C.

Archives of Georgetown University, Washington, D. C.
    Hickey Papers
    Seton Papers
    College Ledgers and Journals

Archives of Mount Saint Mary's University, Emmitsburg, Maryland.
    College Records
    Bruté Papers
    Dubois Papers
    Financial Ledgers
    Seton Notes

Archives of Saint Mary's Seminary & University, Roland Park, Baltimore, Maryland.
    Tessier's Journal
    Cooper Letters
    Hickey Letters
    Dubois Letters
    Harper Letters

Archives of Daughters of Charity, Emmitsburg, Maryland.
    Seton Papers
    Bruté Papers
    Carroll Letters
    Mother Seton Guild Records
    Provincial Annals
    Council Book
    Minutes of the Corporation
    Mother Rose White's Journal
    Recollections of Contemporaries of Mother Seton

Archives of the Sisters of Charity, Mount Saint Vincent, New York.
    Seton Diary
    Seton Notebooks
    Seton Letters

Cheverus Letters
Carroll Letters
Dubourg Letters
David Letters
Moranvillé Letters
Study of Mrs. Seton's Residences in New York

The Mother Seton Guild Collection, Daughters of Charity Archives,
    Emmitsburg, Maryland,.
    Rebecca Seton
    William Seton, Sr.
    William Magee Seton
    William M. Seton (son)
    Richard Seton
    Elizabeth Seton I
    Elizabeth Bayley Seton
    Catherine Charlton (Josephine) Seton
    Simon Bruté
    John Dubois

Archives of the University of Notre Dame, Notre Dame, Indiana.
    Mother Seton's Prayerbook
    Seton Letters
    David Letters
    Bruté Papers
    Dubourg Letters
    Flaget Letters
    Cheverus Letters
    Carroll Letters
    Cooper Letters

Archives Archdiocese of Baltimore, Associated Archives at St. Mary's
    Seminary & University, Baltimore, Maryland.
    Dubois Papers
    Seton Letters
    Dubourg Letters
    David Letters
    Cheverus Letters
    Sibourd Letters
    Barry Letters

Hurley Letters
O'Brien Letters
Carroll Letterbook
Filicchi Letters
New-York Historical Society, New York City, New York.

II. PRINTED SOURCES

Archives of the General Convention of the Protestant Episcopal Church in the United States. New York, 1911. Volumes I-III cover the correspondence of John Henry Hobart from 1757–1804.

Bayley, Richard. *An Account of the Epidemic Fever Which Prevailed in the City of New York During Part of the Summer and Fall of 1795.* New York, 1796.

_____, *Letters from the Health Officer to the Common Council of the City of New York.* New York, 1799.

Bayley, James Roosevelt. *Memoirs of the Right Reverend Simon Wm. Gabriel Bruté, D.D., First Bishop of Vincennes.* New York, 1876. *Rev. Simon Gabriel Bruté in His Connection with the Community.* Emmitsburg, 1886. This collection of Bruté papers was privately printed for the use of the community of the Daughters of Charity. The majority of these originals of these documents are in 1-3-3-13 of the Archives of the Daughters of Charity, St. Joseph's Provincial House, Emmitsburg, MD.

Bechtle, Regina, S.C., and Judith Metz, S.C., eds., Ellin M. Kelly, mss. ed., *Elizabeth Bayley Seton Collected Writings*, 3 vols. New York, 2000–2006.

Code, Joseph B. *A Daily Thought from the Writings of Mother Seton.* Emmitsburg, 1929.

_____, *Letters of Mother Seton to Mrs. Julianna Scott.* Emmitsburg, 1935.

Crèvecoeur, Hector St. John. *Letters from an American Farmer.* New York, 1925.

_____, *Sketches of Eighteenth Century America.* New Haven, 1925. Edited by Henry L. Boudini, Ralph H. Gabriel, and Stanley Williams. "Diary of Jose Bernardo Gutierrey de Lara, 1811–1812," *American Historical Review,* XXXIV, January, 1929, 281-2.

Directories of the City of New York, 1786–1808. The first directory was published in 1786. In 1791 the name became Duncan's *Directory and Register.* After 1797 the directory included an almanac and register, and was published by Longworth. Its title became Longworth's *American Almanac, New York Register and City Directory.*

Dunlap, William, *Diary, 1766-1839,* Volume II. New York, 1930.
Dwelle, Mary Myers, *A Sketch of the Life of Queen Charlotte 1744-1818*. Charlotte, 1968.

Kauffman, Christopher J., *Tradition and Transformation in Catholic Culture. The Priests of Saint Sulpice in the United States from 1791 to the Present*. New York, 1988.

Kelly, Ellin M., *Numerous Choirs. A Chronicle of Elizabeth Bayley Seton and Her Spiritual Daughters. Volume I: The Seton Years, 1774-1821*. Evansville, Indiana, 1981.

Kollock, Isaac A. *Memoirs of Mrs. S*. Elizabeth, New Jersey, 1817. "Letters of Mother Seton to Rev. John Hickey, St. Mary's College, Baltimore," *Researches of the Catholic Historical Society*, XI, 1894, 138-42.

Mannard, Joseph, "Widows in Convents of the Early Republic: The Archdiocese of Baltimore, 1790-1860, *U.S. Catholic Historian*, XXVI, no. 2 (Spring 2008), 111-32.

Names of Persons for Whom Marriage Licenses Were Issued by the Secretary of the Province of New York Previous to 1784. Albany, 1860.

Naval Documents Related to the United States Wars with the Barbary Pirates. Volume III. Washington, D. C., 1941.

Nelson, Robert. *A Companion for the Festivals and Fasts of the Church of England with Collects and Prayers for Each Solemnity.* London, 1736.

Nusbaum, Daniel, "This Venerable House, Part I: The Beginnings," *Analecta: Selected Studies in the History of Mount St. Mary's College and Seminary,* I, no. 3 (2000).

O'Callaghan, E. B. *Calendar of Historical Manuscripts in the Office of the Secretary of State.* Albany, 1866.

O'Neill, John. *New Easy System of Geography and Popular Astronomy.* Baltimore, 1808.

Pasko, W. W. *Old New York.* Volumes I-II. New York, 1889.

Mother Seton, Notes by Rev. Simon Gabriel Bruté. Emmitsburg, 1884. This volume was privately printed for use by the community at Emmitsburg. It contains letters of Mrs. Seton found in of the 1-3-3-12 Archives of the Daughters of Charity, St. Joseph's Provincial House, Emmitsburg, MD.

Seton, Robert. *Memoir, Letters and Journal of Elizabeth Seton.* 2 vols. New York, 1869.

Shaw, Richard, *John Dubois: Founding Father.* Yonkers, New York: US Catholic Historical Society, 1983.

Spalding, Thomas W., C.F.X., *The Premier See.* Baltimore, 1989.

Stevens, John A. *Colonial Records of the New York Chamber of Commerce, 1768-1784.* New York, 1867.

Warville, J. P. Brissot de. *New Travels in the United States of America.* Dublin, 1792.

III. NEWSPAPERS

American Register. 1807.
Greenleaf's New Daily Advertiser. 1798.
National Advocate. 1821.
New York *Commercial Advertiser.* 1797, 1798.
New York *Evening Post.* 1792, 1821.
New York *Packet.* 1790.
New York *Spectator.* 1798.
New York *Weekly Museum.* 1794, 1798.

IV. GENERAL WORKS

Abbott, William C. *New York in the American Revolution.* New York, 1929.

Albion, Robert Greenhalgh. *The Rise of New York Port 1815–1860.* New York, 1939.

Allen, Gardner W. *Our Naval War with France.* Boston, 1919.

Anstice, Henry. *History of St. George's Church.* New York, 1911.

Appleton's Cyclopoedia of American Biography. Volume V. New York, 1888.

Barberey, Helen Bailly de. *Elizabeth Seton et les commencements de l'eglise catholique aux Etats-Unis.* Paris, 1868.

Barck, Oscar T. *New York City During the War for Independence.* New York, 1931.

Blackstone, Sir William. *Commentaries on the Laws of England.* Volume I. New York, 1850.

Brown, Henry Collins. *Glimpses of Old New York.* New York, 1917.

Bruun, Geoffrey. *Europe and the French Imperium.* New York, 1938.

Buckingham, James Silk. *America, Historical, Statistic, and Descriptive.* Volume I. London, 1841.

Burns, James A., and Kohlbrenner, Bernard, C.S.C. *The Growth and*

Development of the Catholic School System in the United States. New York, 1912.

Burt, A. L. *The United States, Great Britain, and North America, 1783–1815.* New Haven, 1940.

Carthy, Mother Mary Peter, O.S.U. *Old St. Patrick's, New York's First Cathedral.* New York, 1947.

Channing, Edward. *The Jeffersonian System.* New York, 1906.

Cox, John J. *Quakerism in the City of New York, 1657-1930.* New York, 1930.

Curti, Merle. *The Growth of American Thought.* New York, 1943.

Davis, Joseph Stancliffe. *Essays in Earlier History of American Corporations.* Cambridge, 1917.

Mother Augustine Decount. Emmitsburg, 1938. A privately printed biography in a series of anonymous sketches of the superiors of the Sisters of Charity of St. Joseph's and Daughters of Charity at Emmitsburg, Maryland.

Dodge, Maria, S.C., *Mother Elizabeth Boyle, First Superioress of the Sisters of Charity, Mount St. Vincent, New York.* Staten Island, 1893.

Domett, Henry W. *A History of the Bank of New York, 1784-1884.* Cambridge, 1884.

East, Robert A. *Business Enterprise in the American Revolutionary Era.* New York, 1939.

Easterly, Frederick J., C.M. *The Life of Rt. Rev. Joseph Rosati, C.M., First Bishop of St. Louis, 1789–1843.* Washington, 1942.

Edwards, George William. *New York as an Eighteenth Century Municipality, 1731–1776.* New York, 1917.

Flick, A. C., ed. 10 vols. *A History of the State of New York.* New York, 1933.
_____, *Loyalism in New York.* New York, 1902.

Fox, Sister Columba, S.C.N. *Life of the Right Reverend John Baptist Mary David, 1761-1841.* New York, 1925.

Fuller, Mary Margaret, S.C. *Mother Seton's Favorite Devotions.* New York, 1940.

The General History of the Christian Church. New York, 1807.

Gibson, Sister Laurita, S.C.N. *Some Early Converts to Catholicism.* Washington, 1943.

Gilder, Rodman. *The Battery.* Boston, 1936.

Godecker, Sister Salesia, O.S.B. *Simon Bruté de Remur.* St. Meinrad's, Indiana, 1931.

Greene, Evarts Boutell. *The Revolutionary Generation, 1763–1790.* New York, 1943.

Griffith, Thomas W. *Annals of Baltimore.* Baltimore, 1824.

Guilday, Peter. *The Life and Times of John Carroll.* Volume II. New York, 1922.

Hall, Clayton Colman, ed. *Baltimore, Its History and Its People.* Volume I. New York, 1912.

Hardie, James. *The City of New York.* New York, 1827.

Headley, Joel T. *Great Riots of New York.* New York, 1873.

Hemstreet, Charles. *Nooks and Corners of Old New York.* New York, 1899.

Herbermann, Charles G. *The Sulpicians in the United States.* New York, 1916.

Herbert, Mary Elizabeth, ed. *The Life of the Rt. Rev. Gabriel Bruté, D.D., First Bishop of Vincennes.* London, 1870.

Hoare, Mary Regis. *Virgin Soil.* Boston, 1942.

Kelly, Howard A., and Burrage, Walter L. *Dictionary of American Medical Biography.* New York, 1920.

Lamb, Martha J. *History of the City of New York.* Volume II. New York, 1877.

Lord, Robert H., John E. Sexton and Edward T. Harrington. *History of the Archdiocese of Boston.* Volume I. New York, 1944.

McCann, Sister Mary Agnes, S.C. *The History of Mother Seton's Daughters, the Sisters of Charity of Cincinnati, Ohio, 1809-1917.* 2 vols. New York, 1917.

McKay, Richard Cornelius. *South Street, a Maritime History of New York.* New York, 1934.

McVickar, John. *The Early Years and Professional Life of Bishop Hobart.* Oxford, 1838.

Madelin, Louis. *The Consulate and the Empire.* Translated by E. F. Buckley. New York, 1934.

Malloy, Louise. *The Life Story of Mother Seton.* Baltimore, 1924.

Malone, Dumas, ed. 20 vols. *Dictionary of American Biography.* New York, 1928–1937.

Maynard, Theodore. *The Reed and the Rock.* New York, 1942.

Meline, Mary M. and McSweeny, Edward F. X. *The Story of the Mountain.* Volume I. Emmitsburg, 1911.

Morais, Herbert M. *Deism in Eighteenth Century America.* New York, 1934.

National Cyclopedia of American Biography. New York, 1921.

New York, a Metropolitan City of America. New York, 1853.

Owens, Hamilton. *Baltimore on the Chesapeake.* Garden City, 1941.

Packard, Francis R. *History of Medicine in the United States.* 2 vols. New York, 1931.

Pomerantz, Irving. *New York, An American City, 1783–1803.* New York, 1938.

Ponet, Marthe Bordeaux. *Une fille americaine de Monsieur Vincent: Elizabeth Anne Seton.* Paris, 1938.

Ray, Sister Mary Augustina, B.V.M., *American Opinion of Roman Catholicism in the Eighteenth Century.* New York, 1936.

Report on American Manuscripts in the Royal Institution of Great Britain. Volumes III-IV. Hereford, 1907.

Ruane, Joseph William. *The Beginnings of the Society of St. Sulpice in the United States, 1791–1829.* Washington, 1935.

Ruskowski, Leo F. *French Emigré Priests in the United States, 1791–1815.* Washington, 1940.

Ryan, Leo R. *Old St. Peter's.* New York, 1935.

Sabine, Lorenzo. *The American Loyalists.* Boston, 1847.

Sadlier, Agnes. *Elizabeth Seton: Foundress of the American Sisters of Charity.* New York, 1905.

Scharf, Thomas J. *Chronicles of Baltimore.* Baltimore, 1874.

_____, *History of Maryland.* Volume II-III. Baltimore, 1879.

_____, *History of Western Maryland.* 2 vols. Philadelphia, 1882.

Seton, Robert. *An Old Family or The Setons of Scotland and America.* New York, 1899.

Shea, John Gilmary. *The Life and Times of John Carroll.* New York, 1888.

Singleton, Esther. *Social New York Under the Georges, 1714–1776.* New York, 1902.

Sioussat, Annie Leakin. *Old Baltimore.* New York, 1931.

Smith, T. E. V. *The City of New York in the Year of Washington's Inauguration, 1789.* New York, 1889.

The Soul of Elizabeth Seton. New York, 1936.

Spaulding, E. Wilder. *New York in the Critical Period, 1 783-1789.* New York, 1932.

Stockett, Letitia. *Baltimore, a Not Too Serious History.* Baltimore, 1936.

Thacher, James. *American Medical Biography.* Volume II. Boston, 1828.

Tourscher, Francis E., O.S.A. *Old St. Augustine's in Philadelphia.* Philadelphia, 1937.

Trollope, Frances. *Domestic Manners of Americans.* New York, 1904. A reprint of the 1836 edition.

Walsh, William. *Spiritual Maxims of St. Vincent of Paul and Biographical Notice of Mrs. Seton.* New York, 1851.

Walsh, James J. *History of Medicine in New York.* 2 vols. New York, 1919.

Wertenbaker, Thomas J. *Father Knickerbocker Rebels.* New York, 1948.

Wheeler, W. O. *The Ogden Family in America.* New Haven, 1907.

White, Charles I. *Life of Mrs. Eliza A. Seton, Foundress and First Superior of the Sisters of Charity in the United States of America.* Baltimore, 1853.

Wilson, James Grant. *A Memorial History of the City of New York.* Volumes III-IV. New York, 1893.

Yeager, Sister M. Hildegarde, C.S.C. *The Life of James Roosevelt Bayley, First Bishop of Newark and Eighth Archbishop of Baltimore, 1814– 1877.* Washington, 1947.

V. PERIODICALS

"Biographical Notice of Mrs. Seton, Foundress and First Superior of the Sisters of Charity in the United States," *Catholic Almanac, 1842,* pp. 42-60.

"Biographical Sketch of Most Rev. John Carroll," *United States Catholic Magazine,* II, June, 1843, 341-50.

"Bishop Hobart's Views of the Catholic Church," *United States Catholic Magazine,* VII, December, 1848, 661.

Brownson, Orestes A., "Life of Mrs. Eliza A. Seton," *Brownson's Quarterly Review,* X, April-July, 1853, 165-84; 315-31.

Burns, Arthur J., "New Light on Mother Seton," *Historical Records and Studies* of the United States Catholic Historical Society, XXII, 1932, 85-98.

Campbell, Bernard U., "Memoir of Rev. John Francis Moranvillé, late Pastor of St. Patrick's Church, Baltimore," *Religious Cabinet,* I, August, 1842, 434-43.

Corrigan, Michael A., "Register of the Clergy Laboring in the Archdiocese of New York From Early Missionary Times to 1885," *Historical Records and Studies* of the United States Catholic Historical Society, I, January, 1899, 191-217.

Flick, Lawrence F., "Matthias O'Conway, Philologist, Lexicographer and Interpreter of Language, 1766, 1842," *Records* of the American Catholic Historical Society of Philadelphia, X, 1899, 257, 299; 385-422.

Griffin, Martin I. J., "History of Rt. Rev. Michael Egan, D.D., First Bishop of Philadelphia," *Researches* of the American Catholic Historical Society of Philadelphia, IX, 1892, 113-28.

_____, "Rev. Michael De Burgo Egan, President of Mount St. Mary's College, 1826–1829," *Researches,* VII, 1890, 146-153.

_____, "St. Joseph's Orphan Asylum, Philadelphia," *Researches,* XIV, 1897, 9-12.

Jameson, J. Franklin, "St. Eustatius and the American Revolution," *American Historical Review,* VIII, July, 1903, 683-708.

Jenkins, M. C., "Most Reverend Leonard Neale, Second Metropolitan of the Catholic Church in the United States." *United States Catholic Magazine,* III, January, 1844, 505-12.

———, "Notice of Most Rev. Ambrose Maréchal," *United States Catholic Magazine,* IV, 1945, 32-7.

McAvoy, Thomas T., C.S.C., "The Formation of the Catholic Minority in the United States," *Review of Politics,* X, January, 1948, 13-34.

McGarrity, John E., "Reverend Samuel Sutherland Cooper, 1769–1843," *Records* of the American Catholic Historical Society of Philadelphia, XXXVII, 1926, 305-40.

Medical Repository and Review of American Publications on Medicine, Surgery, and the Auxiliary Branches of Philosophy. Edited by Samuel L. Mitchell and Edward Miller. I, 1800, 121-131; II, 285-290.

Meehan, Thomas F., "Tales of Old New York," *Historical Records and Studies* of the United States Catholic Historical Society, XVIII, March, 1928, 121-69.

Middleton, Thomas Cooke, "An Old Time Philadelphia Matron and Convert from Presbyterianism," *Records* of the American Catholic Historical Society of Philadelphia, XIV, 1913, 55-63.

"Notice of Cardinal Cheverus, First Bishop of Boston." *United States Catholic Magazine,* IV, April, 1845, 261-267.

Parsons, Wilfrid J., S.J., "Father Anthony Kohlmann, S.J., 1771–1824," *Catholic Historical Review,* IV, April, 1918, 38-51.

"St. Joseph's Sisterhood," *United States Catholic Magazine,* V, 1846, 221-23.

Smith, Sarah Trainer, "Philadelphia's First Nun." *Records* of the American Catholic Historical Society of Philadelphia, V, 1894, 417-522.

Souvay, Charles L., C.M., "Queries Anent Mother Seton's Conversion." *Catholic Historical Review,* V, July-October, 1919, 223-38.

Westcott, Thompson, "A Memoir of the Very Rev. Michael Hurley, D.D., O.S.A.," *Records* of the American Catholic Historical Society of Philadelphia, I, 1884–1886, 165-212.

VI.   UNPUBLISHED MATERIAL

Crumlish, Sister John Mary, D.C., "The History of St. Joseph's Academy, Emmitsburg, Maryland, 1809–1902." Unpublished Master's thesis, the Catholic University of America, 1945.

Fletcher, William J., "Mother Elizabeth Ann Seton, Educator and

Foundress of the American Catholic Parochial School." Unpublished Bachelor's essay, St. Mary's University and Seminary, Baltimore, 1940.

Kortendick, James Joseph, S.S.,"History of St. Mary's College, Baltimore, 1799–1852." Unpublished Master's thesis, The Catholic University of America, 1942.

charge of health Establishment, 79; rejoices in Mrs. Seton's good fortune, 186.

Bayley, Mary Fitch, Elizabeth Bayley Seton's half sister, goes to Havana, 394; marriage, 354, note, r.

Bayley, Dr. Richard, ancestry, 2; early career, 2-4; the "Doctors' Riot," 9; on the faculty of Columbia College, 12; yellow fever report, 12; advice to daughter, 17; rift from second wife, 61; article in the *Monitor,* 62; journeys to Albany, 62; plans for Staten Island, 63; over-worked, 68-69; illness, 69; death, 70; burial, 71; will, 71, note, m.

Bayley, Richard, half brother of Elizabeth Bayley Seton, visits New York, 123; marriage to Catherine White, 265; biographic details, 62, note, c.

Bayley, William, of Hoddeston, grandfather of Elizabeth Bayley Seton, 2.

Bayley, William, brother of Dr. Richard Bayley, birth, 2; at New Rochelle, 10.

Bayley, William Augustus, half brother of Elizabeth Bayley Seton, death, 351, note l.

Beeston, Rev. Francis, death of, 232.

Berlin Decree, 197.

Bizeray, Soeur Marie, D.C., hopes to go to United States, 218.

Bloomingdale, 39, note l.

Boboli Gardens, 95.

Boisfeillet, Joseph Picot de, dies at Mount St. Mary's (May 1813), 293.

Bonaparte, Jerome, marriage, 182.

Bonaparte, Jerome, Jr., friend of Mother Seton, 292-293; attends Mount St. Mary's College, 204, note, 29.

Bonaparte, Napoleon, Northern Italian system, 94; Continental System, 196; delays departure of French sisters, 218; defeat and abdication, 267; escape from Elba, 273; naval plans, 104, note, q; dissolves Sulpicians, 263, note, j; Pius VII prisoner of, 267, note, s.

Bordeaux, Flaget's visit, 217; William Seton

and Bruté arrive in, 273.

Boston, delegates to Continental Congress, 1; candidates for priesthood, 158, note, 43; Antonio Filicchi goes to, 116-117; Filicchi lawsuit in, 122; clergy of, 122, 123, note f; Dubourg in, 169; and the Seton Baltimore project, 172; cut off from Leghorn, 197; poverty of diocese, 265; William Seton in, 358-360; Richard Seton's obituary, 369; desire for Sisters of Charity, 341, note, 121.

Bowie, Governor Robert, appropriation for troops, 264.

Boyle, Elizabeth, introduced to Mrs. Seton, 215; Mother Seton's last letter to, 402.

Brady, Angela, enters St. Joseph's, 216; goes to the Mountain, 344 .

Brady, Ellen, death, 348.

Brady, Felicitas, goes to New York, 347.

Brent, Daniel, clerk in Department of State, 269; presents William Seton to Crowninshield, 357; and Seton's transfer, 359.

Bruté, Simon Gabriel, S.S., on early history of Emmitsburg, 209; in Emmitsburg in 1811, 239-240; consoles Mother Seton after loss of her daughter, 257; 313-314; copies constitution for David, 258-259; addresses volunteers during war, 267; offers to accompany William Seton to Europe, 269-270; copies Mrs. Seton's instructions to son William, 271-272; estimate of William Seton, 272; goes to New York, 273; learns of William Seton's safe arrival in Leghorn, 274; return from France, 275; report to Maréchal, 1813, 284-285; fatherly care for Mountain boys, 293; president of St. Mary's College, 298, 322-324; and St. Joseph's Church, 301; biographic details, 311-312; first summer in Emmitsburg, 311-312; at Anna Maria Seton's death, 312-313; at Emmitsburg, 1812-1815, 315-320; European journey, 319-321; con-

perior of Seton community, 241; on the effects of Mrs. Seton's loss of Anna Maria, 255; opposes changes in rules, 260-261; accompanies sisters to Taneytown, 262; favors Leghorn for William Seton, 270; news of Napoleon's escape, 273; Dubourg chats of him at Leghorn, 275; report to Carroll on St. Joseph's school, 284-285; desires sisters at the Mountain, 285; experienced organizer, 288; educational theories, 290; supervisory head of St. Joseph's school, 300; opposes resident priest at St. Joseph's, 301-302; love for Bruté, 317; over-worked, 322; at Rebecca Seton's death, 329; at Mme Guérin's death, 332; asks for Bruté as assistant, 335; has sisters at the Mountain, 344; and New York school sisters, 347; and Baltimore sisters, 348; discusses Setons with Robert Goodloe Harper, 355; ill at Baltimore, 359; ready to aid Richard Seton, 364; defends Mount St. Mary's, 381; opposes suppression, 381-382; property transferred by Tessier, 383; letter to Garnier, 383-384; aid to St. Joseph's, 385; on public penance, 388-389; new building at St. Joseph, 398; anoints Mother Seton, 399; on children of widows at St. Joseph's, 216 note, r; offer of money from citizens, 405 note, 11.

Dubourg, Rev. Louis William Valentine, S.S., educates Protestants, 147; meets Mrs. Seton, 169; accompanies Seton boys to New York, 170; advice against Cecilia's coming to Baltimore, 172; shows Mrs. Seton St. Mary's "Calvary," 180; welcomes Setons, 181; nieces, 184; theories of education, 185; Bishop of Montauban, 192; account of the founding of Mother Seton's community, 192-193; appoints stewardess for community, 201; note from West-

minster, 209; returns to Baltimore, 211; return from Martinique, 216; administrator of Louisiana, 217; directs first retreat at St. Joseph's, 224; supervises final arrangements for Emmitsburg property, 226; dissatisfaction over his policies, 225-228; orders Babade to Emmitsburg, 226; resigns, 228; Nagot refuses to reinstate, 230; consoles Mrs. Seton, 230-231; learns of Mrs. Seton's dissatisfaction with David, 233; lively interest in Seton community continues, 240-241; suggests Novena to the Sacred Heart, 263; in Rome, 275; anxiety about Stone House, 285; on day school, 298; leaves for Martinique, 312; approves Bruté's going to the Mountain, 315; Mother Seton's last message, 399; in New York, 169 note, n; goes to New Orleans, 244, note, 34.

Duer, William, 6.

Duhamel, Rev. Charles, "Mr. Duhamel's House," 210; unable to leave Hagerstown, 229; serves St. Joseph's Church, 301; death of, 311, 335; poor health, 321; describes Bruté, 320-321; comes from Hagerstown, 210 note, c.

Dundas, Captain Ralph, 19.

Dunlap, William, description of Baltimore, 178.

DuPavillon, Charles, friendly with Anna Maria Seton, 200; ends romance with Anna Maria Seton, 251.

Dupleix, Catherine, and society for widows, 43; arrival from Ireland, 66; reaction to Elizabeth Seton's conversion, 141; defends White-Seton project, 143; alienated by Cecilia's conversion, 162; in Ireland, 170; learns of Elizabeth Seton's release from vow, 240; anxiety over Anna Maria, 252; becomes Catholic, 265; visits Mother Seton, 265; and New York sisters, 347; visit of Catherine Seton, 347; attends Mass with William Seton, 358; aids poor, 393.

456

cepts William Seton, 274-275; dies, 324; career, 87, note, f.

Flaget, Bishop Benedict, S.S., attempt to introduce French sisters, 217-218; advocates strict interpretation of rules, 220; organizes sisters in Bardstown, 223; dreads arrival of French sisters, 223; failure to introduce French sisters, 224; brings rules to Emmitsburg, 224, 311; bishop-elect of Kentucky, 236; plans for leave for Kentucky, 237; starts for Kentucky, 239; desires sisters for Kentucky, 257; proposes union with Emmitsburg, 259; foundation of Nazareth community, 261; and Bruté's efforts on the Eastern Shore, 314.

Florence, Mrs. Seton's tour, 94-97.

The Following of Christ, or *The Imitation of Christ*, by Thomas à Kempis, Mrs. Seton and Anna Maria read, 94; Mrs. Seton re-reads, 121; Mrs. Seton gives to Antonio Filicchi, 126; Bruté shares with Mother Seton, 311; purchase by community, 305, note, 29.

Fort George, 5.

Foster, Augustus J., brings pallium to Carroll, 264; secretary to British legation at Naples, 264, note, l.

Fournier, Victoire, sister of William Dubourg, welcomes the Setons, 181.

Fox, Robert, and house for sisters, 346; escorts sisters to New York, 347; aids William Seton, 357; William Seton's call, 358; and Richard Seton's passage money, 366; Mother Seton's concern for daughters, 394.

Free school, Mother Seton's day school, 298; contract for building, 299.

Gartland, Jane Francis, 398.

Genealogy, Bayley-Seton, 420-423.

George III, Dr. Charlton at court of, 2; letters patent for New York Hospital, 8.

George, Margaret, enters community, 241; New York requests, 346; sister-servant at New York, 347; New York

pay school, 346; requested for Baltimore, 348, note, i.

Godefroy, Maximilian, designs St. Mary's Chapel, 181; sends daughter to St. Joseph's, 287; on Mother Seton, 305, note, 20.

Graham, Isabella Marshall, foundress of society for widows, 43; meditations, 58, note, 44.

Grand Sachem, Mrs. Seton boards, 172; leaves New York, 177; arrives in Baltimore, 177.

Grassi, Rev. John, S.J., suggests Patton girls as pupils, 287; goes to Europe, 386.

Grim, Charles, at Mount St. Mary's, 292.

Grim, Mrs. Eliza, wish to join Mrs. Seton, 214; New York convert, 292.

Gruber, Ann, introduced to Mrs. Seton, 215; goes to the Mountain, 344.

Guérin, Madame, Dubourg protégée, 216; enters community, 216; taught French, 288; death, 332.

Guerrière, Charles Wilkes on, 359; Richard Seton returns on, 368.

Hall, Thomas, visits William Seton, 90; conducts burial of William Seton, 92; issues death certificate, 92.

Hamilton, Alexander, and the Bank of New York, 21; Secretary of the Treasury, 22; and the S.U.M., 22; at Albany, 62; duel with Burr, 112; funeral, 113.

Harbough, Leonard, 179.

Harper, Catherine Carroll, wife of Robert Goodloe Harper, as possible benefactor, 285; takes Catherine Seton to Carroll Manor, 355.

Harper, Mary Diana, daughter of Robert Goodloe Harper, sent to Mrs. Seton, 287; at St. Joseph's school, 296; death, 296, note, r.

Harper, Robert Goodloe, offers Catherine Seton a home, 182; news of Louisa Caton's marriage, 192; sends daughters to St. Joseph's, 287; receives complaint of daughter's conduct, 296; aids incorporation of sisters, 334; in Europe, 355; disap-

Sisters of Charity, 201; assists sisters in Philadelphia, 262; as possible benefactor, 285; conversion, 183, note, h.

Montreal, Antonio Filicchi visits, 144; college and seminary, 147; Filicchi's preference for, 147-148; appeals to Mrs. Seton, 168; bishop Carroll's views on, 169-170; College of Montreal, 146, note, o.

Moore, Benjamin, sermons at Trinity Church, 53; rector of Trinity Church, 7; succeeds provost, 28, note, 35.

Moore, Dr. Richard Channing, request for Dr. Bayley's views on yellow fever, 12-13; burial service for Dr. Bayley, 70.

Moranvillé, Rev. John Francis, sponsors entrants to Seton community, 215; and Trappists, 215; protégé at St. Joseph's, 266; tends Baltimore wounded, 267; consoles Mother Seton during Bec's illness, 328; on Mother Seton, 215, note, p; requests Emmitsburg, 406, note, 32.

Morris, Andrew, first Catholic office-holder in New York, 139; Highbinders' riot, 140-141; on Hurley, 165, note, i; entertains Dubourg, 175, note, 55.

Mother Seton Guild, *x, xx, xxiii.*

Mount St. Mary's, Emmitsburg (the Mountain), visited by Cheverus and Egan, 236; served by Dubois, 212; Babade invited to, 229; William Seton brought from, 231; and War of 1812, 266; sisters' accounts at, 284; sisters sew for, 286; and St. Joseph's girls, 290; Mother Seton's interest in, 292-295; Protestants forbidden at, 297; responsible to Paris, 300-301; Bruté returns in 1812, 315; Bruté's preaching at, 316; library, 319; visit of Maréchal and Whitfield, 343; sisters established there, 344; William Seton visits, 356-357; Richard Seton at, 362; Richard Seton visits, 362; returns from Italy, 367; Sulpicians dissatisfied with, 381-382; suppres-sion discussed, 382-385; property transferred to Dubois, 383; Hickey returns to, 384; affairs prosper, 385; origins of, 199, note, aa.

Mullen, Catherine, joins Mrs. Seton, 192; in unfinished White House, 212; on first council, 224; in Babade controversy, 226; David requests her for Kentucky, 260; in charge of discipline, 288.

Murphy, Maria (Sister Maria Burke), comes to Baltimore, 190; goes to Emmitsburg, 202; attachment to Babade, 227; illness, 257; Bruté gives funeral sermon, 315.

Murray, John, Filicchi account with 367; bankruptcy, 163.

Nabbs, Anastasia, goes to the Mountain, 344; Mother Seton's night company, 358; at Mother Seton's death, 403.

Nagot, Rev. Charles Francis, S.S., selects site of *One-Mile Tavern*, 184; considered as superior for Seton community, 226; names David superior of sisters, 228; reprimands Mrs. Seton, 230; resigns as Sulpician superior, 234; confidence in David, 247, note, 87.

Naturalization oath, 140, note, b.

Neale, Archbishop Leonard, demands for Seton boys, 148; Filicchi commends, 148; overcharges Seton boys, 154; brief reign as archbishop, 301; continues Carroll policies, 301-302; wants Cheverus for coadjutor, 331.

Nelson, Horatio, 104.

Nelson, Robert, 77, note, u.

Neuville, Baron Hyde de, wife, 285; aids Flaget, 285, note, f.

Newport, Rhode Island, 3.

New Rochelle, Bayleys of, 2; Dr. Bayley's daughters sent to, 5; Elizabeth Bayley visits uncle, 10; Mary Bayley revisits, 14; Elizabeth Bayley's life in, 14; Elizabeth Bayley's return from, 23.

Newtown, Long Island, 3.

New York City, in 1774, 1; British occupation, 3-5, 18-19; evacuated, 5; post-war problems, 5-8, 19-20; hospital founded, 8; "Doctors' Riot," 9; epidemics, 11-14; society in eighteenth century, 15-16; Chamber of Commerce revived, 21; bank established, 21; in 1790's, 36; deism in, 44; Setons sail from, 78, 86; Mrs. Seton's return, 111; Hamilton's funeral, 113; Catholicism, 123; Highbinders' riot, 140; Carroll's visit, 154; Dubourg's visit, 170; Mrs. Seton quits, 172; contributes sisters, 214; sisters established, 346; Elizabeth Seton's obituary, 404.

Niles' *Register,* 264.

O'Brien, Rev. Matthew, in New York, 123; letter to Bishop Carroll, 125; acting pastor in 1805, 128-129; received Mrs. Seton into the Church, 127; need for additional chapel, 140; advice on White-Seton project, 144; spiritual guidance for Mrs. Seton, 149; on fasting, 151.

O'Brien, Rev. William, O.P., pastor at New York, 123; appointed by Carroll, 129; commended by Dr. Bayley, 128; recommends John Byrne, 129.

O'Conway, Cecilia, comes to Baltimore, 190; arrival in Emmitsburg, 202; on first council, 224; in Babade controversy, 227; appointed school sister, 283; language instructor, 288; goes to New York, 347; indisposition, 348; praises Due, 393-394; at Mother Seton's death, 403; goes to Canada, 190, note, r.

O'Conway, Isabella 202.

O'Conway, Matthias, learns of Setons' arrival in Emmitsburg, 210; Spanish interpreter, 306, note, 30.

Ogden, Abraham, voyage to London, 47; his counting house, 271; Leo Post in counting house, 363.

Ogden, Gouverneur, marriage to Charlotte Seton, 47; worry over Catherine Seton, 162.

Olier, Jean Jacques, S.S., Bruté translates works of, 316.

O'Neill, Ann Theresa, *xvii*, 434.

Paca Street, Baltimore, house of Mrs. Seton, 184; Seton school, 185; Cecilia and Harriet Seton arrive, 201; lease on Seton house expires, 201; house closed, 202.

Paine, Thomas, *Age of Reason, 44*; death, 46.

Paul VI, Pope, *xvi, xvii, xxvii*, 434.

Parsons, Benedicta, 348.

Patterson, Elizabeth, marriage to Jerome Bonaparte, 182; imperial princess, 285.

Pattison, General James, commandant of New York City, 4.

Pearce, William, 22.

Pecci, Joseph, 108, note, 60.

Philadelphia, evacuation, 3-4; Bank of North America, 21; federal capital, 22; William and Elizabeth Seton visit, 33; William Magee Seton visits, 38; Julia Scott moves to, 51; Antonio Filicchi in, 131; Seton boys in, 148; Hurley recalled to, 165; Mrs. Seton considers, 170; conversions, 182; Babade's recruits, 190; Catons visit, 191; sisters' orphanage, 262; Rebecca Seton visits, 326; Catherine Seton visits, 352; Elizabeth Boyle, 401.

Physick, Dr. Philip Syng, Rebecca Seton consults, 326; treats Rebecca, 327; specialist, 326, note, o.

Pitti Palace, 95.

Pius IV, confession of faith, 114.

Pius VII, reported dead, 263; advice to his people, 264; sufferings impress Mrs. Seton, 264; freed from Fontainebleau, 267; prisoner of Napoleon, 267, note, s.

Plunket, Rev. Peter, influence on Elizabeth Seton, 93; daily exercise book, 124.

Poland, 260.

Post, Lionel (Leo), son of Wright and Mary Bayley Post, in Ogden counting house, 271; visits St. Joseph's, 349;

accompanies Catherine Seton to Emmitsburg, 354; illness, 349.

Post, Mary Magdalen Bayley, sister of Elizabeth Bayley Seton, childhood, 3, note, f; marriage to Wright Post, 6, note, j; education, 10; summer home with Elizabeth Seton, 37; at Long Island, 52; at father's death, 70; rescues Elizabeth Seton, 144; Elizabeth Seton lives with, 149; approves Emmitsburg plan, 201; visits Emmitsburg, 213; consoles Elizabeth Seton at Harriet's death, 232; anxiety over Anna Maria's illness, 252; consoles Elizabeth Seton, 254-255; mentions Dué's unhappiness, 265; recommends Ogden counting house for William Seton, 271; Bruté tries to convert, 323; tries to aid Rebecca Seton, 325; learns of Elizabeth Seton's alarming condition, 349; wants Elizabeth Seton in New York, 351-352; Catherine Seton visits, 354; believes sister blessed, 381; visits to Emmitsburg, 354, note, r.

Post, Dr. Wright, dueling, 6; marriage, 6; studies, 8; lecturer at Columbia College, 12; on child-discipline, 38; fever attack, 39; at Staten Island, 66; attends Mrs. Hobart, 74; takes Rebecca Seton, 78; assists Elizabeth Seton, 113; critic of Catholicism, 118; consents to White-Seton project, 143; takes Setons to Greenwich, 142; favors Baltimore plan, 172; secures passage for Setons, 177; forwards Hurley's picture, 186; outfits William Seton, 273; visits Emmitsburg, 354, note, r.

Preudhomme, C. de Borre, befriends William Seton, 274.

Protestants, at St. Mary's College, Baltimore, 147; at St. Joseph's school, 297; at Mount St. Mary's, 297, 301; Mother Seton's converts, 391.

Provoost, Bishop Samuel, made bishop, 7; marriage of Elizabeth Bayley Seton, 25.

Pyomingo, embarkation, 100-101; becalmed, 104; arrival in New York, 104; spellings of ship's name, 100, note, n.

Quinn, Martina, sponsored by Kohlmann, 214; death, 214, note, k.

Randanne, Rev. J. B., pastor of St. Joseph's Church, 384, note, c.

Redmond, James, assistant in New York, 188; calls on Cecilia Seton, 189.

Resources and References, Seton Studies, 430-4334.

Rogers, Louise, Dubourg protégée, 216.

Roosevelt, Isaac, bank director, 21.

Ross, General Robert, 267.

Rousseau, Jean Jacques, influence on Elizabeth Seton, 44.

Royal Gazette, Bayley advertisement, 3; Seton advertisement, 20.

Rules, French rules brought to Emmitsburg, 218; Mrs. Seton's reaction, 219; provisional rules, 223; modifications of French rules, 224; David requests copy for Kentucky, 259; David proposes changes in, 259-261; Dubois opposes changes, 260-261.

Ryan, Rev. Matthew, 210, note, c.

Sadler, Eliza, cancels tea party, 24; in Paris, 35; and society for widows, 43; enthusiasm for Rousseau, 45; return to New York, 61; visit to Staten Island, 64; family illness, 71; consulted about voyage, 78; distress for Elizabeth Seton, 122; reaction to Elizabeth Seton's conversion, 141; defends White-Seton project, 143; reproves Elizabeth Seton, 150; friend of Tisserant, 150-151; in Ireland in 1807, 170; learns of Harriet Seton's death, 232; meets Cheverus, 236-237; shares Mother Seton's anguish at Anna Maria's death, 254; learns of Elizabeth Seton's grief after death of Anna Maria, 257; in Wilmington, 264; pleased with Dué's report, 266; reproves

from Philip Filicchi, 119; Wilkes' plan for boarders, 122-123; impatience at her confusion, 122; Bible stories for her children, 123; reads Epiphany sermon, 123; seeks help from Cheverus, 125-126; becomes a Catholic, 126; question of baptism, 129; confession, 130; first communion, 130; spiritual debt to the Filicchis, 130-131; reaction to St. Peter's, 139-140; end of Hobart friendship, 141; support of friends after conversion, 141-142; White-Seton school, 143; plans for sons' education, 145-147; confirmed by Bishop Carroll, 154; blamed for Cecilia's conversion, 162-164; saddened by Hurley's departure, 165; journal of summer, 1807, 167; yearns for retreat from the world, 168; decline in boarders, 168-169; meets Dubourg, 169; decision to go to Baltimore, 171-172; leaves New York, 177; arrives in Baltimore, 178; welcomed to Baltimore, 181; goes to Washington, 182; attraction to Samuel Cooper, 183; school in Baltimore, 184; prepares first communion children, 185; reproves Cecilia, 187; desires life of a religious, 189-190; takes vows, 190; Louisa Caton wishes to join, 191; learns of Louisa Caton's marriage, 191; solicits aid from Filicchis, 193-195; distress over daughter's attachment for DuPavillon, 200; departure for Emmitsburg, 200-202; journey to Emmitsburg, 209; first winter in Emmitsburg, 211-212; and French rules, 218-220; adoption of French rules, 224; favors Babade as confessor, 226-227; opposes Dubourg's resignation, 228-229; opposes David's appointment, 229-230; confesses trials to Carroll, 230; death of Harriet, 231; dreads loss of Cecilia, 232; dissatisfaction with David, 233; trials with David, 233-238; release from vows, 242; reconcilia-

tion with Rose White, 242; relations with Anna Maria, 251; illness of Anna Maria, 252; death of daughter, 252-254; anguish at daughter's death, 254; Bruté's consolation, 257; at Maria Burke's deathbed, 256; sends sisters to Philadelphia, 261-262; impressed by sufferings of Pius VII, 263; joy at release of Pius VII, 267; concern for son, 268; asks Carroll's aid for William Seton, 268; advice to William on setting out for Europe, 271-272; confidence in Bruté, 273; learns of Napoleon's escape, 273; fears for son's reception by Filicchis, 274; Antonio Filicchi's letter of consolation, 275; as school mistress at St. Joseph's, 283-284; considers begging tour, 286; teaches history, religion, French, and music, 288-289; influence on girls, 290-291; influence on boys, 292-295; as "foundress of parochial school system," 298-302; as educator, 303; friendship with Bruté, 311, 328-335; last meeting with Carroll, 315; letter of introduction for Bruté, 319; reprimands John Hickey, 320-321; at death of Philip Filicchi, 324; sees Julia Scott for last time, 326; grief at Carroll's illness and death, 327; fortitude at Rebecca Seton's death, 328-329; second visit of Cheverus, 331-332; at death of Mme Guérin, 332; humility, 333-334; Maréchal's visit, 343; asked for sisters for New York, 345; Baltimore establishment, 348; death of Ellen Brady, 348; bled for abscess, 349; opposes biography, 349; near death in 1818, 350; uneasy over *Memoirs,* 351; advice to Catherine Seton, 352-353; assured of harpers' protection, 355; dreads William's interest in Navy, 355-356; gets William in Navy, 357; concern for William, 358-362; gratitude to Julia Scott, 362; intercedes for Richard, 363; begs Anto-

Ursulines, pray for Mother Seton, 402; Cheverus and, 438, note, 17.

Vallejo, Jose Maria, 128, note k.
Vanderbilt, John, loyalist, 19; bank director, 21.
Van Rensselaer, Steven, 14.

Waddington, Joshua, 21.
Wall Street, stone sewers, 10; Dr. Bayley at, 12; in 1790's, 36; Elizabeth Bayley Seton's home, 35; Elizabeth Bayley Seton leaves, 53; James Seton's offices, 78; Gouverneur Ogden's home, 162.
Warren, Admiral John B, 267.
Warville, J. P. Brissot de, on the New York Hospital, 8; on Dr. Richard Bayley, 16; on the Bank of New York, 21.
Watervliet, 14, 62.
Weis, George, learns of Mrs. Seton's confusion, 239, 256; Cecilia Seton dies at home of, 232-233; learns of new appointment, 240; provides comforts for Anna Maria Seton, 252; told of Mrs. Seton's grief, 256; furnishes religious pictures, 288.
Westminster, Maryland, 209.
White, Juliana, happy days at St. Joseph's, 291; describes Carroll's death, 327.
White, Patrick, plans school, 143; brings family from Albany, 144; failure of White School, 144.
White, Mrs. Rose, joins Mrs. Seton, 192; arrival in Emmitsburg, 202; in unfinished White house, 213; assistant to Mrs. Seton, 224; in Babade controversy, 227; biographic details, 234; in Baltimore, 236; David's plans for, 236; Mrs. Seton's remarks on, 238; Carroll's opposition to, 238; return to Emmitsburg, 242; describes death of Anna Maria Seton, 253-254; David asks for her for Kentucky, 258; sent to Philadel-

phia, 262; cares for Bec Seton, 326; goes to New York, 347; William Seton visits, 358.
White House, or St. Joseph's House, progress slow, 212; finished, 213; lively household in 1813, 266.
Wilkes, Charles, brother of John Wilkes, sponsored by William Seton, 19; teller of Bank of New York, 22; cashier of Bank of New York, 22; at Hamilton's funeral, 113; wishes Mrs. Seton to board sons, 145.
Wilkes, Charles, son of John Wilkes, 145.
Wilkes, John, sponsored by William Seton, 19; death of first wife, 51; learns of Rebecca Seton's death, 112; assistance to Elizabeth Seton, 113; plan for boarders, 121; delay in plan, 123; befriends Elizabeth Seton after conversion, 141-142; and White-Seton project, 143; revives boardinghouse plan, 144; remarried, 167; favors Baltimore plan, 172; learns of Mrs. Seton's safe arrival, 185; business losses, 194; unable to aid Mrs. Seton, 194; William Seton carries letter to, 271; death, 351; widow mourns him, 354.
Willetts, Isaac, 6.
Wills, absence of William Seton's, 40, note, n; Dr. Richard Bayley's, 71, note, m; Amelia Barclay Bayley's, 143, note, f; John Charlton's, 355, note, s.
Winchester, William, 209.
Wiseman, Ellen, Mother Seton's letters to, 149, 327, 350; aided by Mother Seton, 292, note, m.

Yellow fever, epidemics of 1791, 1793, 11; epidemic of 1795, 12; of 1798, 35, 39; Dr. Bayley dies of, 69-70; epidemic of July, 1805, 144; detention of *Shepherdess* at Leghorn, 87; fear of in Pisa, 91.